The Palgrave Handbook of Family Sociology in Europe

"Skillfully crafted around a diversity of concepts, theories, and methods, this handbook represents a wealth of knowledge on family change in twenty-first century Europe. It is a tribute to years of research, debate, and cross-country networking at the European Sociological Association and beyond. In thought-provoking and comprehensive contributions, European family sociologists invite us to explore the changing terrain of family and intimate lives in terms of relationships, proximity, gender, care, parenting, fertility, inequalities, migration, life course and family policy."
—Karin Wall, *Research Professor, ICS Institute of Social Sciences, University of Lisbon, Portugal*

"The handbook provides an excellent blend of reassessment and reflection on what we know and how we know about families and intimate lives in Europe. Critical overviews and new insights are offered across a carefully chosen range of starting points."
—Lynn Jamieson, *Professor of Sociology, University of Edinburgh, UK, and series editor for Palgrave Macmillan Studies in Family and Intimate Life*

"This handbook is an excellent compendium of recent scholarship on the sociology of the family by European scholars. It will be a valuable resource for American scholars who wish to keep up with the best research in Europe."
—Andrew Cherlin, *Professor of Sociology and Public Policy, Johns Hopkins University, USA*

Anna-Maija Castrén · Vida Česnuitytė ·
Isabella Crespi · Jacques-Antoine Gauthier ·
Rita Gouveia · Claude Martin ·
Almudena Moreno Mínguez · Katarzyna Suwada
Editors

The Palgrave Handbook of Family Sociology in Europe

Editors
Anna-Maija Castrén
Department of Social Sciences
University of Eastern Finland
Kuopio, Finland

Isabella Crespi
Department of Education
Cultural Heritage and Tourism
University of Macerata, Macerata, Italy

Rita Gouveia
Institute of Social Sciences
University of Lisbon
Lisbon, Portugal

Almudena Moreno Mínguez
Campus María Zambrano
University of Valladolid
Segovia, Spain

Vida Česnuitytė
Faculty of Human and Social Studies
Mykolas Romeris University
Vilnius, Lithuania

Jacques-Antoine Gauthier
University of Lausanne
Lausanne, Switzerland

Claude Martin
EHESP
CNRS (National Centre of Scientific Research)
Rennes, France

Katarzyna Suwada
Institute of Sociology
Nicolaus Copernicus University
Toruń, Poland

ISBN 978-3-030-73305-6   ISBN 978-3-030-73306-3   (eBook)
https://doi.org/10.1007/978-3-030-73306-3

© The Editor(s) (if applicable) and The Author(s), under exclusive license to Springer Nature Switzerland AG 2021, corrected publication 2021
This work is subject to copyright. All rights are solely and exclusively licensed by the Publisher, whether the whole or part of the material is concerned, specifically the rights of translation, reprinting, reuse of illustrations, recitation, broadcasting, reproduction on microfilms or in any other physical way, and transmission or information storage and retrieval, electronic adaptation, computer software, or by similar or dissimilar methodology now known or hereafter developed. The use of general descriptive names, registered names, trademarks, service marks, etc. in this publication does not imply, even in the absence of a specific statement, that such names are exempt from the relevant protective laws and regulations and therefore free for general use.
The publisher, the authors and the editors are safe to assume that the advice and information in this book are believed to be true and accurate at the date of publication. Neither the publisher nor the authors or the editors give a warranty, expressed or implied, with respect to the material contained herein or for any errors or omissions that may have been made. The publisher remains neutral with regard to jurisdictional claims in published maps and institutional affiliations.

Cover illustration: © Charles Harker/Moment/gettyimages

This Palgrave Macmillan imprint is published by the registered company Springer Nature Switzerland AG
The registered company address is: Gewerbestrasse 11, 6330 Cham, Switzerland

Preface

The edited collection *The Palgrave Handbook of Family Sociology in Europe* is a result of a joint effort of members of the European Sociological Association's Research Network 'Sociology of Families and Intimate Lives' (ESA RN13). As researchers and university teachers, we have frequently experienced the lack of high-quality English volumes on family phenomena that comprehensively presented the theoretical and methodological approaches used by contemporary sociologists from different parts of Europe. In order to rectify this, we invited scholars from various European countries (Belgium, the Czech Republic, Denmark, Estonia, Finland, France, Germany, Ireland, Italy, Lithuania, The Netherlands, Norway, Poland, Portugal, Romania, Spain, Sweden, Switzerland, the UK) to contribute to this volume. The main idea was that increased awareness about the research being conducted in different parts of the continent would be invaluable to the development of the European sociological community.

Original manuscripts from over 60 prominent scholars were selected using a double-blind review process. Consequently, the handbook provides an extensive overview of a variety of family forms, trajectories, policies, and values in different societal contexts. Not only does the handbook consider topical themes in family sociology as an academic discipline, it presents the empirical realities of European societies in order to familiarise various audiences—researchers, students, politicians, and family practitioners—with recent findings in the field. Because of its extensive contents, we hope that this handbook will become an integral part of European family sociology and that it will also stimulate international academic debates on family and intimate lives in the future.

National restrictions and lockdowns, which have heavily impacted academic research and teaching since spring 2020, have interrupted the completion of the handbook as the authors, reviewers, and editors had to adjust to the 'new normal' brought about by the COVID-19 pandemic. We want to express our sincere gratitude to everyone who has contributed to this handbook during these extraordinary times, particularly the following people: Susana Atalaïa, Jonathan Bradshaw, Benedicte Brahic, Julia Brannen, Valentina Cuzzocrea, Katherine Davies, Anna Escobedo, Charlotte Faircloth, Asuncion Fresnoza-Flot, Myriam Girardin, Marzia Grassi, Loveday Hodson, Jana Javornik, Majella Kilkey, Łukasz Krzyżowski, Francesca Lagomarsino, Mafalda Leitão, Åsa Lundqvist, Dawn Mannay, Sofia Marinho, Rense Nieuwenhuis, Rebecca O'Connell, Jolanta Perek-Białas, Vasco Ramos, Eveline Reisenuer, Clémentine Rossier, Lisa Smyth, Olivier Thevenon, Gil Viry, Karin Wall, and Minna Zechner.

Kuopio, Finland	Anna-Maija Castrén
Vilnius, Lithuania	Vida Česnuitytė
Macerata, Italy	Isabella Crespi
Lausanne, Switzerland	Jacques-Antoine Gauthier
Lisbon, Portugal	Rita Gouveia
Rennes, France	Claude Martin
Segovia, Spain	Almudena Moreno Mínguez
Toruń, Poland	Katarzyna Suwada

Contents

1 **Introduction**   1
   Isabella Crespi, Vida Česnuitytė, Katarzyna Suwada,
   Anna-Maija Castrén, Claude Martin,
   Jacques-Antoine Gauthier, Rita Gouveia,
   and Almudena Moreno Mínguez

Part I Researching Families and Intimate Lives in Europe: Theoretical and Methodological Trends
   Edited by Rita Gouveia and Vida Česnuitytė

2 **The Family of Individuals: An Overview of the Sociology of the Family in Europe, 130 Years After Durkheim's First University Course**   15
   François de Singly

3 **Gender, Social Class, and Family Relations in Different Life Stages in Europe**   45
   Bernardo Coelho, Diana Maciel, and Anália Torres

4 **What Law Has Joined: Family Relations and Categories of Kinship in the European Court of Human Rights**   69
   Linda Hart

5 **Family Demography and Values in Europe: Continuity and Change**   85
   Detlev Lück, Kerstin Ruckdeschel, Anna Dechant,
   and Norbert F. Schneider

6 **The Configurational Approach to Families: Methodological Suggestions**   107
   Eric D. Widmer

7	**Visual Family Research Methods** Irena Emilija Juozeliūnienė	133

Part II Welfare State and Family Policy Regimes in Europe
Edited by Katarzyna Suwada

8	**Family Transformations and Sub-replacement Fertility in Europe** Irena E. Kotowska, Monika Mynarska, and Anne H. Gauthier	159
9	**Reexamining Degenderisation: Changes in Family Policies in Europe** Steven Saxonberg and Dorota Szelewa	179
10	**Familialisation of Care in European Societies: Between Family and the State** Agnieszka Furmańska-Maruszak and Katarzyna Suwada	205
11	**Who Benefits from Parental Leave Policies? A Comparison Between Nordic and Southern European Countries** Ann-Zofie Duvander and Elisabetta Ruspini	223
12	**Family, Poverty, and Social Policy Interventions** Ryszard Szarfenberg	239

Part III Families as Relationships
Edited by Anna-Maija Castrén

13	**Redefining the Boundaries of Family and Personal Relationships** Rita Gouveia and Anna-Maija Castrén	259
14	**Money in Couples: The Organisation of Finances and the Symbolic Use of Money** Lars Evertsson and Charlott Nyman	279
15	**Sibling Relationships: Being Connected and Related** Eva Gulløv and Ida Wentzel Winther	301
16	**"It's a Balance on a Knife-Edge": Expectations of Parents and Adult Children** Bella Marckmann	321

Part IV Parental Arrangements, Parenting and Child
         Well-Being
         Edited by Claude Martin and
         Almudena Moreno Mínguez

17 Non-Parental Childcare in France, Norway, and Spain   345
    Gerardo Meil, Vicente Diaz-Gandasegui, Jesús Rogero-García,
    and Pedro Romero-Balsas

18 Sharing the Caring Responsibility Between the Private
    and the Public: Childcare, Parental Choice, and Inequality   361
    Michel Vandenbroeck, Wim Van Lancker, and Jeroen Janssen

19 Shared Parenting After Separation and Divorce in Europe
    in the Context of the Second Demographic Transition   377
    Lluís Flaquer

20 Subjective Well-Being of Children in the Context of Family
    Change in Estonia, Poland, and Romania   399
    Dagmar Kutsar and Oliver Nahkur

21 Assessment of Parental Potential: Socio-Economic Risk
    Factors and Children's Well-Being   415
    Judith Lind

22 Towards a 'Parenting Regime': Globalising Tendencies
    and Localised Variation   435
    Jan Macvarish and Claude Martin

Part V Family Lives in Migration: Intergenerational and
        Transnational Relationships
        Edited by Isabella Crespi

23 Migration and Families in European Society   455
    Laura Zanfrini

24 The Multidimensional Nature of Family Migration:
    Transnational and Mixed Families in Europe   475
    Dafina Kurti Sinatra and Inga Sabanova

25 Intergenerational Relations in the Context of Migration:
    Gender Roles in Family Relationships   495
    Mihaela Hărăguș, Viorela Ducu, and Ionuț Földes

26 Despite the Distance? Intergenerational Contact in Times
    of Migration   513
    Ronny König, Bettina Isengard, and Marc Szydlik

27 Parenting and Caring Across Borders in Refugee Contexts   537
    Lena Näre

Part VI Family Trajectories: (Un)Linking Lives Over Time and Place
Edited by Jacques-Antoine Gauthier and Rita Gouveia

28 The Contribution of the Life-Course Perspective to the Study of Family Relationships: Advances, Challenges, and Limitations 557
Gaëlle Aeby and Jacques-Antoine Gauthier

29 Varieties of Youth Transitions? A Review of the Comparative Literature on the Entry to Adulthood 575
Tom Chevalier

30 Transitions in Later Life and the Re-configuration of Family Relationships in the Third Age: The Case of the Baby Boomers 591
Catherine Bonvalet, Rémi Gallou, and Jim Ogg

31 From *Taken for Granted* to *Taken Seriously*: The *Linked Lives* Life Course Principle Under Literature Analysis 611
Magda Nico, Diana Carvalho, Helena Carvalho, and Maria Silva

32 Afterthoughts on an "Earthquake of Change" 639
Rita Gouveia, Jacques-Antoine Gauthier, Almudena Moreno Mínguez, Anna-Maija Castrén, Claude Martin, Vida Česnuitytė, Isabella Crespi, and Katarzyna Suwada

Correction to: Migration and Families in European Society C1
Laura Zanfrini

Index 645

Notes on Contributors

Gaëlle Aeby is Research Associate at the University of Geneva and member of the LIVES centre, Switzerland. She has a Ph.D. in Social sciences from the University of Lausanne (2015) and did her post-doctoral research at the University of Manchester (2016–2017). Her fields of specialisation include sociology of family and personal life, socio-anthropology of youth, child protection, life-course perspective.

Catherine Bonvalet is Emeritus Research Director at the French Institute for Demographic Studies (INED) and an Associate Researcher at the Research Unit on Ageing, French National Pension Fund (CNAV), France. She is a specialist in family and housing issues as well as family solidarity and is the author of several books and numerous journal papers.

Diana Carvalho is Research Assistant at ISCTE–University Institute of Lisbon, Centre for Research and Studies in Sociology, Lisbon, Portugal. She is a Ph.D. student in Sociology and has been working in the areas of Sociology of Family, Childhood and Youth Studies. Her current research interests are longitudinal and life-course analysis and youth trajectories and transitions.

Helena Carvalho has a Ph.D. in Sociology, in Theory and Method. Full Professor in the Department of Social Research Methods at ISCTE–University Institute of Lisbon, Portugal. She is Director of the School of Sociology and Public Policy. She coordinates the Postgraduate in Data Analysis in Social Sciences. Senior researcher at CIES-IUL, and expert in methodological issues and quantitative methods for categorical and quantitative variables.

Anna-Maija Castrén is Associate Professor of Sociology at the University of Eastern Finland, in Kuopio, Finland. She has published on adults and children's family understandings, marriage and weddings, post-separation families, and configurational approach. Currently, she is a member of the Executive Board of ESA RN13 Sociology of Families and Intimate Lives.

Vida Česnuitytė is Associate Professor at the Mykolas Romeris University, in Vilnius, Lithuania. Since 2017 is co-coordinator of the ESA RN13 Sociology of Families and Intimate Lives. Research interests include family conceptualisation, formation, and practices, and social research methods. Co-edited books published at Macmillan Palgrave *Families and Personal Networks. An International Comparative Perspective* (2018; with K. Wall, E. D. Widmer, J.-A. Gauthier, and R. Gouveia), and *Family Continuity and Change. Contemporary European Perspectives* (2017; with D. Lück, and E. D. Widmer).

Tom Chevalier is CNRS Researcher at Arènes, Rennes, France. He has a Ph.D. in Political Science (Sciences Po, Paris). He works on public policies targeted at young people in Europe (social policies, education, active labour market policies), and on youth poverty.

Bernardo Coelho is a Sociologist, invited Assistant Professor at the ISCSP-University of Lisbon, Portugal, Researcher and Founding member of Interdisciplinary Center for Gender Studies—CIEG-ISCSP at the University of Lisbon. He teaches sociology of gender, contemporary sociological theory, and methodology. He is co-coordinator of the Portuguese Sociological Association's gender and sexuality research network. He has published several books, articles, and book chapters.

Isabella Crespi is Associate Professor in Family sociology and Cultural sociology at the Department of Education, Cultural Heritage and Tourism, University of Macerata, Italy. She has a Ph.D. in Sociology and she works on family, gender equality, migration. She has been coordinator of the ESA RN13 Sociology of Families and Intimate Lives (2013–2017) and now she is a member of the Advisory Board.

François de Singly is Professor Emeritus at the Université de Paris-La Sorbonne's Faculty of Social Sciences, France. He has two doctoral degrees in sociology (University of Paris VIII; Université de Paris V). He has published more than thirty books and numerous scientific articles and is an editorial advisor. He is a member of the French Prime Minister's High Council of the Family, Childhood and Age.

Anna Dechant is Senior Researcher at the Federal Institute for Population Research (BiB) in Wiesbaden, Germany. Her recent research focuses on family sociology, in particular the division of paid work and care work within couples as well as cultural perspectives in family research.

Vicente Diaz-Gandasegui is Lecturer at the Department of Social Analysis of the Universidad Carlos III de Madrid, Spain. His current research lines are based on family studies, the social change produced by technological development and applied mathematical sociology.

Viorela Ducu is Associate Researcher at the Babeș-Bolyai University, Romania. She has a Ph.D. in Sociology, with an interest in mixed and transnational families, children's rights and qualitative research methods. Her main publications include *Romanian Transnational Families—Gender, Family Practices and Difference*, 2018, (author) at Palgrave Macmillan and Displaying grandparenting within Romanian transnational families, in Global Networks, 2020.

Ann-Zofie Duvander is Professor of Demography and Sociology at the Stockholm University, and Mid University in Östersund, Sweden. She has worked at the Swedish Social Insurance Agency and the Inspectorate for the Social Insurance. She is one of the coordinators of the International Network for Leave Policies and Research (leavenetwork.org).

Lars Evertsson is Professor in Social Work at the Department of Psychology and Social Work, Mid University, Sweden. He has a Ph.D. in sociology from the Department of Sociology, Umeå University, Sweden. His research interests include family sociology and sociology of the professions.

Lluís Flaquer is Emeritus Professor of Sociology at the Universitat Autònoma de Barcelona, Spain. In 1969, he took a degree in SciencesPo at the IEP in Paris. His main current research specializations are father involvement and shared parenting after separation. In 2018, he was awarded a prize by the Catalan Academy for his contribution to the sociology of the family.

Ionuț Földes is Research Fellow at the Interdisciplinary Centre for Data Science and lecturer at the Faculty of Sociology and Social Work, Babeș-Bolyai University, Cluj-Napoca, Romania. His doctoral research explored the change in intergenerational family ties in the context of mass emigration from Romania towards the West, focusing on the involvement of elderly parents in maintaining family solidarity across borders.

Agnieszka Furmańska-Maruszak is Assistant Professor at the Institute of Sociology, Nicolaus Copernicus University in Toruń, Poland. Her scientific interests are located in the areas of eldercare, labour market, and human resources management. She has worked as a national expert in Eurofound projects. Her research focuses on international comparisons of long-term care regimes and labour market participation of informal carers.

Rémi Gallou socio-demographer, is Researcher at the Research Unit on Ageing, French National Pension Fund (CNAV), France, and Associate Researcher at the French Institute for Demographic Studies (INED). Having researched the ageing of immigrants in France for several years, his current research focuses on questions relating to residential mobility and social inequalities during retirement.

Jacques-Antoine Gauthier holds a Ph.D. in Sociology, and is Senior Lecturer at the University of Lausanne's Life-course and inequality research centre and member of the LIVES centre, Switzerland. His current research concerns the time-related construction of individual life trajectories and their interdependencies. Currently, he is the coordinator of the ESA RN13 Sociology of Families and Intimate Lives (2019–2021).

Anne H. Gauthier is Director of the Generations and Gender Programme at the Netherlands Interdisciplinary Demographic Institute and Professor of Comparative Family Studies at the University of Groningen, the Netherlands. She holds a Ph.D. in sociology (University of Oxford). Her expertise lies in cross-national research on families including fertility decisions, family policies, parenting, and transition to adulthood.

Rita Gouveia is Post-doc Researcher in Sociology of family and personal life at the Institute of Social Sciences of the University of Lisbon, Portugal. She has a degree in Psychology and a Ph.D. in Sociology of Family, Gender and Youth. She is a member of the Executive Board of the ESA RN13 Sociology of Families and Intimate Lives.

Eva Gulløv is Professor of Educational Anthropology at the Department of Education, University of Aarhus, Denmark, and Professor at the Department of Education, University of Agder, Norway. She has a Ph.D. in social anthropology and has written extensively within the field of childhood studies.

Mihaela Hărăguş is Researcher at the Centre for Population Studies, Babeş-Bolyai University, Cluj-Napoca, Romania. She has Ph.D. in Sociology and she has conducted research on topics such as transition to parenthood, non-standard life-courses, and intergenerational relationships within the family. Her recent research focuses on transnational families and how intergenerational solidarity is reconfigured in migration context.

Linda Hart obtained a Doctorate in sociology (D.Soc.Sc) from the University of Helsinki (Finland) in 2016 with a dissertation combining legal sociology, family sociology, and gender studies. She has worked as a lecturer in social sciences and as a researcher in military sociology. Her ongoing research interests include socio-legal gender studies and sociology of preparedness.

Bettina Isengard is Senior Research Associate at the Department of Sociology at the University of Zurich, Switzerland, and a member of the research group 'LAbour, Generation, Stratification' (AGES). She has a Ph.D. in Sociology (University of Mannheim). Her current research activities include studies about generations, social structure, and inequality.

Jeroen Janssen is Ph.D. student at the Department of Social work and Social pedagogy of Ghent University, Belgium. His research is on the relations between families and childcare provision in contexts of diversity. He studies inequalities in search processes and the concept of choice.

Irena Emilija Juozeliūnienė is Professor of Sociology at the Vilnius University, Lithuania. She has research interests in visual family research methods, transnational family practices and identities. Her publications include the books *Mapping Methods in Image-Based Research* (2014), *Family Change in Times of the De-Bordering of Europe and Global Mobility* (2015; co-editing with J. Seymour), *Making Lithuanian Families Across Borders: Conceptual Frames and Empirical Evidence* (2020; co-editing with J. Seymour).

Ronny König is Senior Research Assistant at the Department of Sociology at the University of Zurich, Switzerland, and a member of the research group 'LAbour, Generation, Stratification' (AGES). He has Ph.D. in Sociology (University of Zurich). His main research interests are social inequality, stratification, and intergenerational relationships. Currently, he is a member of the Executive Board of ESA RN13 Sociology of Families and Intimate Lives.

Irena E. Kotowska Professor Emerita of Demography at the Institute of Statistics and Demography, the Warsaw School of Economics, Poland, and the country-level coordinator of the Generations and Gender Programme (GGP). Main fields of research interest include: fertility, family, gender, and the labour market; population ageing; population and economy; population-related policy, family policy.

Dafina Kurti Sinatra is doing a Ph.D. at the University of Cologne, Germany. She has been researcher at the GESIS—Leibniz Institute for the Social Sciences working for diverse EU-data infrastructure projects. Her research fields combine migration studies, social inequality, and sibling research.

Dagmar Kutsar is Associate Professor in social policy at the Institute of Social Studies, University of Tartu, Estonia. She has been an Executive Board member of ESA (2003–2007) and the Chair of the National Organisations (2007–2009).

Judith Lind is Senior Lecturer in Child Studies at the Department of Thematic Studies, Linköping University, Sweden. She is one of the editors of the book *Doing Good Parenthood: Ideals and Practices of Parental Involvement* (Palgrave) and is involved in several research projects on adoption, assisted reproduction and foster care.

Detlev Lück is Senior Researcher at the Federal Institute for Population Research in Wiesbaden, Germany, and project coordinator of the panel study FReDA. He is a former Coordinator of the ESA RN13 Sociology of Families and Intimate Lives (2017–2019) and currently is a member of the Advisory Board. His recent research focuses on cultural perspectives in family research.

Diana Maciel is Assistant Professor at ISCSP of the University of Lisbon, Portugal, and is on the scientific board of Interdisciplinary Centre for Gender Studies—CIEG. She is finishing her Ph.D. on gender at the individual level: agency, resources, opportunities, and constraints. She has co-authored 7 books, 7 book chapters, and 1 peer-reviewed paper and presented 71 papers in international and national conferences.

Jan Macvarish Sociologist, Visiting Research Fellow at the Centre for Parenting Culture Studies—CPCS, University of Kent, Canterbury UK. She is co-author of *Parenting Culture Studies* (Palgrave Macmillan, 2014) and author of *Neuroparenting: The Expert Invasion of Family Life* (Palgrave Macmillan, 2016).

Bella Marckmann is Senior Adviser at the Danish Evaluation Institute. She has a Ph.D. in Sociology from the University of Copenhagen and did the research in this book as part of a post-doc project entitled 'The Moral Economy of Families' funded by the Danish Council for Independent Research. Member of the editorial board of the journal Dansk Sociologi.

Claude Martin Sociologist, Research Professor at the CNRS (National centre for scientific research), University of Rennes (Arènes-UMR 6051), France; chair CNAF 'Childhood, well-being and parenting' at EHESP school of public health. He published extensively on family, parenting, childhood, childcare, and long-term care policies and more broadly on social policies and welfare states transformations. Currently, he is a member of the French Prime Minister's High Council of the Family, Childhood and Age and member of the Advisory Board of the ESA RN13 Sociology of Families and Intimate Lives.

Gerardo Meil is Full Professor in Sociology at the Universidad Autónoma de Madrid, Spain. His research fields focus on Family Sociology and Social Policies. Former President of the European Society on Family Relations, member of the International Network on Leave Policies and Research, and of the Advisory Board of the ESA RN13 Sociology of Families and Intimate Lives.

Almudena Moreno Mínguez has a Ph.D. in Sociology from the Universidad Autónoma de Barcelona in 2004. She is a professor in Sociology at the University of Valladolid, Spain. She is a specialist in family issues, welfare state, public policy and comparative research on gender. She has over a hundred publications in the form of articles, books, and book chapters. Currently, she is a member of the Advisory Board of the ESA RN13 Sociology of Families and Intimate Lives.

Monika Mynarska is Associate Professor at the Institute of Psychology, Cardinal Stefan Wyszyński University in Warsaw, Poland. She has a Ph.D. in social demography (University of Rostock, Germany). Her research interests cover family and fertility choices in life-course perspective.

Oliver Nahkur is Research Fellow in social well-being studies at the Institute of Social Studies, University of Tartu, Estonia.

Lena Näre (D.Phil., Ph.D., Docent) is tenure-track Associate Professor of Sociology at the University of Helsinki, Finland. Her research interests include the study of migration and asylum, work and employment, care and transnationalism, intersectionality and ethnographic methods. She served as the Vice-President of European Sociological Association in 2017–2019. She is the editor-in-chief of the *Nordic Journal of Migration Research*.

Magda Nico is a Sociologist. She is a Researcher at the Centre for Research and Studies in Sociology (CIES-ISCTE) and Assistant Professor at the Department of Social Research Methods at ISCTE-University Institute of Lisbon, Portugal. She is interested in life-course theory and methods, sociology of family, the linked and inter-personal relationships, and in the social mobility and trajectories of (young) people.

Charlott Nyman is Associate Professor in Sociology at the Department of Sociology, Umeå University, Sweden. Her research interests include family and couple relationships, with a special focus on money and finances in couples.

Jim Ogg is a Sociologist who specialises in the field of ageing. He is Associate Researcher at the Research Unit on Ageing, French National Pension Fund, and Honorary Visiting Research Fellow, Swansea University. He is editor-in-chief of the journal *Retraite et Société* since 2015.

Jesús Rogero-García is Lecturer in Sociology at the Faculty of Economics, Universidad Autónoma of Madrid, Spain. His research fields focus on Sociology of education and Sociology of the family.

Pedro Romero-Balsas holds a Ph.D. in Sociology, and is Lecturer at the Department of Sociology, Universidad Autónoma de Madrid, Spain. His research interests include work and family balance, gender, public policies, parenthood, and job mobility. He has been visiting researcher fellow at University College London, at the Federal Institute for Population Research (Germany) and at NTNU (Norway). He is a member of the Executive Board of ESA RN13 Sociology of Families and Intimate Lives.

Kerstin Ruckdeschel is a Senior Researcher at the Federal Institute for Population Research (BiB) in Wiesbaden, Germany. Her research focuses on family sociology, particular concepts of family and fertility intentions, and family demography.

Elisabetta Ruspini is Associate Professor of Sociology at the University of Milano-Bicocca, Italy. She is the Director of ABCD-Interdepartmental Center for Gender Studies, University of Milano-Bicocca, and the co-coordinator of the ESA RN33 Women's and Gender Studies. Between 2012 and 2018 she was the coordinator of the Research Committee Gender Studies, part of AIS-Associazione Italiana di Sociologia (Italian Sociological Association).

Inga Sabanova has a Ph.D. in Sociology (Trinity College Dublin, Ireland). Her research explores migrant parenting with a specific focus on ethnicity, gender, and social class.

Steven Saxonberg is Professor at the Institute of European Studies and International Relations at the Faculty of Social and Economic Sciences at the Comenius University in Slovakia, and at the Department of Social Policy and Social Work at the Masaryk University in the Czech Republic. The research was co-funded by the Erasmus+ Programme of the European Union, project number 611572-EPP-1-201 9-1-SK-EPPJ MO-CHAIR.

Norbert F. Schneider is Professor of Sociology and Director of the Federal Institute for Population Research in Wiesbaden, Germany. He teaches as an Honorary Professor at the Universities of Frankfurt/Main and Vienna. Currently, he is the Vice-President of the German Society for Demography (DGD). His research focuses on social demography, family sociology, and migration studies.

Maria Silva is an integrated Researcher at the ISCTE–University Institute of Lisbon, Centre for Research and Studies in Sociology, Lisbon, Portugal. She has a Ph.D. in Sociology of Education (University of São Paulo/Brasil) and has been working in the areas of Sociology of Family, Sociology of Education and Political Socialization. Her current research interests are families, life-course, and political socialisation.

Katarzyna Suwada is Assistant Professor at the Institute of Sociology, Nicolaus Copernicus University in Toruń, Poland. Her research interests include fatherhood, motherhood, gender inequalities in family life, family policy. She is an author of *Parenting and Work in Poland. A Gender Studies Perspective* (Springer 2021). She is a member of the Executive Board of the ESA RN13 Sociology of Families and Intimate Lives.

Ryszard Szarfenberg is Associate Professor in political sciences at the Faculty of Political Sciences and International Studies, University of Warsaw, Poland. He has a Ph.D. in political sciences and specialises in social policy and poverty. He is a member of the EU Inclusion Strategies Group, European Anti-Poverty Network, and an expert of the European Social Policy Network.

Dorota Szelewa is Assistant Professor at the School of Social Policy, Social Work and Social Justice, University College Dublin in Ireland, and an Editor in Chief of Journal of Family Studies. Her research interests are interdisciplinary and include the issues of social policy transformation in post-communist countries, gender studies, reproductive rights, migration, theories of institutional evolution, public administration and public management, and the problems of Europeanisation.

Marc Szydlik has been a Full Professor of Sociology at the University of Zurich since 2004, Switzerland. He previously worked at the German Institute for Economic Research, the Max-Planck-Institute for Human Development, the Free University of Berlin and the University of Erfurt. Currently, Szydlik directs the research group 'LAbour, Generation, Stratification'.

Anália Torres holds a Ph.D. in Sociology and is currently a Full Professor at the Institute of Social and Political Sciences, University of Lisbon, Portugal, where she coordinates the Sociology Department. She is the founder and coordinator of the Interdisciplinary Centre for Gender Studies. She is former President of the ESA, and President of the Portuguese Association of Sociology. She has published 29 books, 50 book chapters, and 31 articles.

Wim Van Lancker is Assistant Professor in Social Work and Social Policy affiliated with the Centre for Sociological Research (CESO) at the University of Leuven, Belgium. His research is focused on family policy (childcare, parental leave, and child benefits) and its social distribution, poverty and social inequality, the design and effectiveness of social policy measures, and the effectiveness of social work interventions. He co-edited the *Palgrave Handbook of Family Policy*.

Michel Vandenbroeck is Associate Professor and Head of the Department of Social work and Social pedagogy of Ghent University, Belgium. His main research is in early childhood care and education with a special interest in processes of in- and exclusion in the context of diversity. He is coordinating editor (with Liselott Olsson) of the Routledge book series 'Contesting early Childhood'.

Eric D. Widmer holds a Ph.D. in Sociology (1995, University of Geneva), and is Professor at the Department of Sociology of the University of Geneva, and a member of the board of directors of NCCR LIVES, Switzerland. His long-term interests include intimate ties, family and other inter-personal relations, life-course research and social networks. Eric D. Widmer has developed an approach to families as configurations of interdependencies, always on the move in the life-course (the book *Family Configurations. A Structural Approach to Family Diversity*, 2016). Professor has been conducting over the years a series of empirical research on couples, siblings, blended families, mobile families, etc. He is a member of the Advisory Board of ESA RN13 Sociology of Families and Intimate Lives.

Ida Wentzel Winther is Associate Professor of Educational Anthropology at the Department of Education, University of Aarhus, Denmark. She has a Ph.D. in educational anthropology. Winther has written extensively within the field of everyday life, family and home studies. She works both theoretically, practically and methodologically within the field of visual anthropology and cultural phenomenology.

Laura Zanfrini holds a Ph.D. in Sociology, and is Full Professor at the Fondazione ISMU, Milan, Italy, where she teaches 'Sociology of Migrations and Interethnic Relations', and 'Organizations, Environment and Social Innovation'. She is the Director of the research center WWELL (Work, Welfare, Enterprise, Lifelong-Learning). She is a member of several editorial boards, scientific networks, and consultative bodies and author of about 400 publications.

List of Figures

Fig. 3.1	Correlation between average hourly wage in PPP and average age of leaving parents' home (women aged 15–29), 2015	50
Fig. 3.2	Average hours spent on family care, by sex, age and country, 2012	51
Fig. 3.3	Average hourly wage, in PPP, by country and sex (Euros), 2014	52
Fig. 3.4	Employment rate of adults with children aged under six years, from 25 to 49 years, by country and sex, 2015 (%)	53
Fig. 3.5	Distribution of living in couple workers by type of household, aged 30 to 49, by country (%), 2015	55
Fig. 3.6	Average hours spent on family care, from 15 to 29 years and from 30 to 49 years, by country and sex (hours), 2012	56
Fig. 3.7	Monthly pay, by occupation type, in PPP, by sex, individuals aged 30–49, in Portugal and EU-27, 2014	56
Fig. 3.8	Average hours spent on family care, by sex, age and country, 2012	58
Fig. 3.9	Social class in the selected countries, aged 15–65, by sex, 2015 (%)	62
Fig. 6.1	Support relationships in the respondent's family configuration	118
Fig. 6.2	Conflict relationships in the respondent's family configuration	119
Fig. 7.1	Rūta (aged 15) family map	143
Fig. 7.2	Catherine (aged 10) emotion map	145
Fig. 8.1	Period total fertility rates by regions in Europe, 1960–2020	161
Fig. 15.1	Sibling group 'short and narrow'	308
Fig. 15.2	Sibling group 'long and wide'	309
Fig. 19.1	Scatter diagram of symmetrical JPC prevalence by gender equality index in the EU countries. CIRCA, 2010	387
Fig. 23.1	First permits by reason in the EU28	457
Fig. 26.1	Intergenerational Contact and Countries (Proportion)	519
Fig. 26.2	Intergenerational Contact in Native and Migrated Families (Proportion)	520
Fig. 26.3	Intergenerational Distance in Native and Migrated Families (Proportion)	521

Fig. 26.4	Intergenerational Contact and Distance for Native and Migrated Families (Proportion)	522
Fig. 28.1	Examples of two types of family trajectories	562
Fig. 31.1	Uses of the life course principles in ALCR articles (2000–2019)	621
Fig. 31.2	Uses of the life course principles in SLLS abstracts (2010–2018)	621
Fig. 31.3	Words in titles before the coming of age (2000–2009) in the Advances in Life Course Research Journal	623
Fig. 31.4	Words in titles after the coming of age (2010–2019) in the Advances in Life Course Research Journal	623
Fig. 31.5	Topological configuration of "family linked lives" profiles in the life course publications	627

List of Tables

Table 3.1	Main activity in past 7 days in Portugal, aged 50–65, by sex, 2014 (%)	58
Table 3.2	Gender pay gap (in euros) by life stage in Portugal and UE27 (2015)	60
Table 3.3	Determinants of monthly income of individuals by country and age group, 2015	61
Table 6.1	Matrix representation of interdependencies in one family configuration	117
Table 9.1	Parental leave schemes in 2019 with changes since 2013	191
Table 9.2	Daycare policies	198
Table 12.1	Four types of social policy instruments for reducing family poverty	244
Table 16.1	Interview participants	326
Table 17.1	Characteristics of family policies for 0 to 3 year-olds	350
Table 17.2	Percentage of children receiving non-parental care during at least 1 hour in a typical week and mean number of hours by agent, child's age and country	353
Table 17.3	Percentage of 0- to 3-year-old children receiving non-parental care by agent, household income, parental employment status and country	356
Table 19.1	Table of different indicators of JPC. Selection of European countries for which information is available	388
Table 20.1	Correlations between family relational aspects and overall life satisfaction	408
Table 26.1	Determinants of Intergenerational Contact in Europe	524
Table 26.2	Migration and Intergenerational Contact in Europe	526
Table 26.3	Internet Use, Residential Distance, and Migration	528
Table 31.1	Methodological Strategy: datasets and data analysis	616
Table 31.2	Discrimination measures and contribution of the variables	627
Table 31.3	Coding variables	633

CHAPTER 1

Introduction

Isabella Crespi, Vida Česnuitytė, Katarzyna Suwada, Anna-Maija Castrén, Claude Martin, Jacques-Antoine Gauthier, Rita Gouveia, and Almudena Moreno Mínguez

In the first decades of the twenty-first century, family life in Europe has faced multiple challenges prompted by economic, political, cultural, and technological developments. The changes are continuous. As a field of research, family sociology identifies and analyses family phenomena in order to better understand the social realities that people live in and seeks to propose effective solutions to problems encountered in societies. New questions and research topics are constantly emerging and novel approaches and methodologies are

I. Crespi (✉)
Department of Education, Cultural Heritage and Tourism, University of Macerata, Macerata, Italy
e-mail: isabella.crespi@unimc.it

V. Česnuitytė
Mykolas Romeris University, Vilnius, Lithuania
e-mail: v.cesnuityte@mruni.eu

K. Suwada
Institute of Sociology, Nicolaus Copernicus University, Toruń, Poland
e-mail: k.suwada@umk.pl

A.-M. Castrén
Department of Social Sciences, University of Eastern Finland, Kuopio, Finland
e-mail: anna-maija.castren@uef.fi

C. Martin
EHESP, CNRS (National Centre of Scientific Rese), Rennes Cedex, France
e-mail: claude.martin@ehesp.fr; claude.martin@cnrs.fr

© The Author(s), under exclusive license to Springer Nature Switzerland AG 2021
A.-M. Castrén et al. (eds.), *The Palgrave Handbook of Family Sociology in Europe*, https://doi.org/10.1007/978-3-030-73306-3_1

needed to address these topics. In this respect, family sociology is a dynamic sector of research that encourages the continuous revision of its theories and research instruments, in particular by establishing connections with other fields of research in social sciences (such as work and employment, inequalities and poverty, welfare state analysis, housing and education).

However, the majority of European family scholars are still predominantly experts on their own societies and may only have a vague perception of the state of the art and debates in other societies. The reason for this limitation is not language barriers per se; rather, it is specifically the lack of European publications in English (monographs, handbooks, journals, etc.) on contemporary research that would offer an overview and access to the variety of theoretical and methodological approaches being used, as well as to the cutting-edge research being conducted across the continent. Instead, European scholars are compelled to draw from and refer to American works, meaning that the research trends, theoretical and methodological approaches outside Europe tend to dominate, particularly in studies published in English.

The aim of *The Palgrave Handbook of Family Sociology in Europe* is to provide an overview of topical themes and current developments in family sociology in order to better understand family life in contemporary European societies. The handbook covers several 'hot topics' and introduces readers to the empirical realities of family life in Western, Southern, Northern, and Eastern Europe. The contributors were encouraged to provide cutting-edge research findings and to contextualise the national, political, and cultural trends in family and intimate lives in the wider European and sociological frame of reference. The analyses included in the handbook mostly move beyond a single society and offer a comprehensive understanding of the state of the art of the topic discussed. However, and perhaps unconventionally, original empirical case analyses are also included in order to offer an in-depth understanding of some of the micro-level dynamics of contemporary family life.

The handbook comprises six parts, each of them containing four to six chapters: Researching families and intimate lives in Europe: theoretical and methodological trends; Welfare state and family policy regimes in Europe; Families as relationships; Parental arrangements, parenting and child

---

J.-A. Gauthier
University of Lausanne, Lausanne, Switzerland
e-mail: Jacques-Antoine.Gauthier@unil.ch

R. Gouveia
Institute of Social Sciences, University of Lisbon, Lisbon, Portugal
e-mail: rita.gouveia@ics.ul.pt

A. Moreno Mínguez
Campus María Zambrano, University of Valladolid, Segovia, Spain
e-mail: almudena@soc.uva.esu

well-being; Family lives in migration: intergenerational and transnational relationships; and Family trajectories: (un)linking lives over time and place.

TRENDS IN RESEARCHING FAMILIES AND INTIMATE LIVES IN EUROPE

Throughout Europe, we have witnessed changes in the ways that individuals think, live, and build their families and intimate relationships, while some other aspects remain quite stable. Although European societies have followed quite converging pathways of change, family lives and practices are shaped by the socio-historical backgrounds, economical contexts and legal frameworks, as well as the gender norms, social inequalities, and life course dynamics characteristic of each society. In such a multi-layered context, the evolution of theories and methodologies of family sociology is deeply intertwined with the social, cultural, and demographic trends that affect individuals and families. The first part of the handbook 'Researching families and intimate lives in Europe: theoretical and methodological trends' offers insights into how theories and methodologies have developed to encompass family changes and diversity. Part I starts with François de Singly's critical reconstruction of the history of family sociology in Europe (Chapter 2) taking Durkheim's first university course in the field from 1888–1889 as its point of departure. Drawing on Elias' notion of a 'society of individuals' (2001), the author argues that families have been transitioning from a focus on the 'we-identity' to greater emphasis being placed on the 'I-identity', whereby individuals continuously struggle to balance cohesion and autonomy. Moreover, this 'we-I' balance is strongly shaped by gender and social structures.

Gender, social inequality, and life course are the three cornerstones of the next chapter (Chapter 3), authored by Bernardo Coelho, Diana Maciel, and Anália Torres. From a cross-national perspective, this chapter focuses on how family and gender relations develop over the life course and in accordance with an individual's unequal structural positions and participation in the labour market. This comparative analysis draws on the various statistical indicators associated with the timing of leaving the parental home, working hours, models of conjugal division of paid and unpaid work, as well as income.

Another key domain in understanding continuity and change in family relations is the law. By providing empirical examples of the European Court of Human Rights, Linda Hart shows (in Chapter 4) how political and legal changes in different national contexts contribute to the recognition of family, gender, and sexual diversity, but also how they legitimate certain kinship categories and principles that do not always overlap with affinity-based relationships and the lived experience. The intersection between family relations and law may be studied in many different contexts and new legislation may engender new forms of family relations.

Detlev Lück, Kerstin Ruckdeschel, Anna Dechant, and Norbert F. Schneider (in Chapter 5) provide a general landscape of the main family demographic trends in Europe before and after 1965, the periods referred to as *the First* and *the Second Demographic Transition*. The authors highlight common pathways of change, as well as features that have remained quite stable over the last century, by discussing structural and cultural factors such as the value change from materialism to post-materialism that was responsible for engendering both stability and transformation.

Finally, two innovative methodological chapters in Part I illustrate how family diversity and complexity demand the development of creative and sophisticated methodologies and instruments, allowing for more inclusive definitions of family that are closer to the individuals' subjective meanings. Eric D. Widmer (Chapter 6) introduces the configurational approach as a methodological perspective that conceptualises families and intimate ties as configurations of mutually dependent people rather than prescribed groups based on blood, marriage, and co-residency criteria. The author shows the heuristic potential of adopting social network techniques and the study of social dilemmas. Meanwhile, Irena E. Juozeliūnienė (in Chapter 7) discusses the pros and cons of using visual methods to research families and intimate lives. The author highlights the power of images; working with images has become a standard practice for many family researchers and involves the extensive use of photographs, video recordings, drawings, family albums, egocentric maps, etc., as well as the adoption of mixed methods.

Welfare State and Family Policy Regimes in Europe

European family life is heavily impacted by the institutional context, in particular, the family policy system. As Emanuel Ferragina and Martin Seeleib-Kaiser argue, family policy can 'have a multiplicity of functions: horizontal redistribution, the enhancement of individual choices, increasing fertility, supporting economic growth and productivity, as well as reducing gender inequalities' (Ferragina and Seeleib-Kaiser 2015, 2). Thus, Part II, 'Welfare State and Family Policy Regimes in Europe', describes the relationships between the welfare state and family in different European contexts.

Irena Kotowska, Monika Mynarska, and Anne Gauthier (in Chapter 8) discuss the issue of the persistent below-replacement fertility in European countries and potential future developments in family policies that need to consider the new diversity of family structures and gender roles. Changing gender roles are actually a key issue for policymakers today. Thus, Steven Saxonberg and Dorota Szelewa (Chapter 9) propose to examine family policies in different European countries using the conceptual axis of genderisation-degenderisation. They argue that even though there is a general trend in Europe towards increased degenderisation, most countries are still characterised by policies that reproduce traditional gender roles.

The reproduction of traditional gender roles in family is closely connected to the organisation of care for children and the elderly, as well as the way in which people reconcile their care obligations with paid work. This issue is discussed by Agnieszka Furmańska-Maruszak and Katarzyna Suwada (in Chapter 10), who analyse the support of family policy systems in The Netherlands, Poland, Portugal, and Sweden by using the concept of familialisation. They argue that despite there being different instruments that aim to support the family in providing care to its members, the family is still perceived as being the main provider of care. Elisabetta Ruspini and Ann-Zofie Duvander (Chapter 11) focus on parental leave as a policy instrument in two clusters of countries—the Nordic and the Southern European countries. They seek to identify which groups of parents benefit from parental leave systems in these two clusters of countries. Chapters 10 and 11 both discuss the role of family policy in supporting economic growth and productivity, as they focus on the issue of combining paid work with other family obligations. They also show the kind of role that family policy can play in enhancing or/and reducing individual choices in family life and paid work.

Finally, Chapter 12 addresses the issue of families living in poverty. Ryszard Szarfenberg shows how different social policy interventions can reduce poverty in European families.

Families as Relationships

Research that draws on the individuals' personal meaning-making, practices and interactions, as well as the inherent materiality and spatial aspects, is a vast field in present-day Europe. Much of this research is qualitative and small scale, making generalisations difficult. However, as highlighted by Carol Smart (2007), the incorporation of the meanings that people themselves ascribe to their relationships allows researchers to include the complex, contradictory, and changing reasons why people behave like they do in family life. The chapters in Part III 'Families as relationships' explore families as constellations of 'lived relations' and highlight aspects that are central to building and maintaining familial relationships. The authors discuss European families as comprising relationships in which there may be many different kinds of 'glue' that bind people and which may incorporate various dynamics that draw on emotions, feelings of intimacy and love, biogenetic relatedness and descent, cultural ideals and social norms, as well as on the social structures and hierarchies that are prevalent in our societies.

First, Rita Gouveia and Anna-Maija Castrén (Chapter 13) identify some of the key debates that have influenced contemporary understandings of families as relationships since the 1980s. The debates have highlighted everyday relatedness, feelings, and practices of closeness that may or may not overlap with the normative expectations of family and kinship. In Chapter 14, Lars Evertsson and Charlott Nyman offer a comprehensive review of couple relationships from the perspective of money and finances. Their focus is on how couples organise and share money, finances and consumption, and the consequences of the different ways of handling money. For couples, money is 'Janus-faced': on the one hand, it elicits gendered expectations and power imbalances, but, on the other hand, the ways in which money is shared, merged, or held separate inform us of the role it plays as an expression of commitment and love. The study of money gives insight into what being in a couple relationship means, and how partners balance between being separate individuals and forming a familial unit. Next, Eva Gulløv and Ida Wentzel Winther (Chapter 15) adopt a children's perspective in studying sibling relationships. The authors focus on everyday situations, such as sharing objects, commuting between households, carrying out chores, and spending leisure time together. The everyday doings of siblingship evoke feelings of togetherness, relatedness and longing, as well as obligation, doubt and frustration, all of which reflect the tensions between the ideals and the realities of family life. The chapter highlights the processual nature of relationships, drawing on the particularities of contemporary family life.

The final chapter, Chapter 16, discusses the relationships between parents and their adult children. While parenting small children is a widely researched and fervently debated topic, social expectations towards the parents of adult children have thus far been studied much less. This is surprising when taking into account, for example, the negative effects of the economic crises of recent decades on the attempts by young adults to transition to the work market and become financially independent. Author Bella Marckmann draws on an in-depth empirical study into parent-adult children relationships characterised by a continuous search for a balance between closeness and distance, between too much and too little.

Parental Arrangements, Parenting, and Child Well-Being

Part IV, 'Parental arrangements, parenting and child well-being', covers some of the main research developments related to parents and children in recent decades. These developments concern parenting roles, the division of labour in childcare arrangements between parents themselves and between parents and the complex network of non-parental services, along with the impact of these developments on child well-being. Although it is parents who are still primarily responsible for providing childcare, the development of the Early Childhood Education and Care (ECEC) sector has led to a great amount of research, often comparative research, being conducted. New childcare arrangements raise questions about quality and equal access to non-parental childcare, while also inspiring theoretical and empirical developments concerning specific parental (maternal and paternal) practices, or the ways in which parents assume their role, highlighted by the recent concept of parenting.

The first two chapters concern non-parental childcare. Gerardo Meil, Vicente Díaz Gandasegui, Jesús Rogero-García, and Pedro Romero-Balsas

(Chapter 17) propose a comparison between three quite typical national configurations that exist in Norway, France, and Spain. These countries represent different kinds of non-parental care strategies. As the analysis reveals, there is a relative convergence towards 'de-familialisation', while a significant impact of household income on the types of non-parental care can be observed in France and Spain. Michel Vandenbroeck, Wim Van Lancker, and Jeroen Janssen (Chapter 18) move beyond the usual observation that participating in ECEC services is very beneficial to children's cognitive and non-cognitive outcomes. They argue that poor families tend to have less access to ECEC services than higher-income families. Moreover, even if children from disadvantaged families do have access to ECEC services, such services are often of poorer quality. The authors document inequalities in childhood and examine how these inequalities affect the nature of parenthood and parenting.

Lluis Flaquer (Chapter 19) focuses on a major issue concerning the shared parenting arrangements after separation and divorce, which have generated many new regulations and experiments throughout Europe. The main thesis presented by the author is based on an idea that joint parental custody (JPC) should be considered in relation to the progress of gender equality. The chapter explores the availability of comparable quantitative data on the prevalence of JPC and gender equality with the aim of presenting the main differences between countries in the context of the Second Demographic Transition.

Much of the development in parental and parenting issues has a common objective, i.e. guaranteeing child well-being. This reference to child well-being is at the core of much of the research that has been undertaken in recent decades. Dagmar Kutsar and Oliver Nahkur (Chapter 20) present a comparative analysis of subjective child well-being in the context of family change in Estonia, Poland, and Romania using data from the second wave of the International Study of Children's Well-Being, 'Children's Worlds' (ISCWeB). The overall findings confirm that children's satisfaction with family life increases their subjective well-being regardless of the type of home or form of family in which they live. This innovative study employs the perspective and voice of children in order to enhance knowledge of the factors that contribute to improving the lives of children and their families. In order to guarantee the well-being of the child, many policies address the assessment of parental potential and capacities. Examining aspiring parents (through adoption, foster care, or assisted reproduction using donor gametes), Judith Lind (Chapter 21) analyses the evaluation criteria used for assessing parenting capacity to determine whether aspiring parents are capable of caring for a child. The author analyses how the consideration of socio-economic factors is justified in the assessment guidelines.

The neologisms 'parenting' or 'parentalité' are a success story in the fields of both research and family policy. Jan Macvarish and Claude Martin (in Chapter 22) outline the ways in which 'parenting' is primarily discussed as a problem of public and private disorder, and then consider how 'parenting' reconceptualises the role and status of parents. The authors argue that the emergence of these neologisms to describe family relations and the raising of children, as well as the adoption of these terms by policymakers, suggest the development of a new nexus through which families are understood.

FAMILY LIVES IN MASS MIGRATION CONTEXT

Part V 'Family lives in migration: intergenerational and transnational relationships' documents another crucial challenge for research on family: migration and its impacts. Migration is a globally growing phenomenon and international research confirms the centrality of the family in the migration plans and strategies of individuals (Attias-Donfut and Cook 2017; Crespi et al. 2018), for example, in decisions to emigrate and which family members will emigrate. The migrant family finds itself in a social system in which roles and relationships may be partially or completely different to what it has been used to and in which family relationships can act as bridges between migrants, their country of origin and their new context, as well as create a network of closed relationships in self-referential and poorly integrated communities (Kraler et al. 2010). In this process, the migrant family plays a key role in terms of time and space (Mazzuccato 2013; Zontini and Reynolds 2018; Baldassar and Merla 2013) and transnational and mixed families (Bryceson and Vuorela 2002) can be framed in the perspective of migrating families. Finally, the extent to which migrants and their families are integrated into society, welfare systems, and their political participation reveals the level of openness of society to change and innovation, challenging the ideal of equality and inclusion that has formed part of the creation of modern Western states.

In Chapter 23, Laura Zanfrini considers the presence of migrant families and of people from migrant backgrounds. According to the author, migrant families are a key issue in contemporary Europe and a crucial question as far as the sustainability of the European social model and the future of the European way of life are concerned. Beyond their demographic importance, migrant families are radically challenging European education systems, labour markets, and welfare regimes, since they are largely concentrated in the lower ranks of social stratification and are overrepresented in all categories at risk of exclusion.

Dafina Kurti Sinatra and Inga Sabanova (Chapter 24) provide an overview of recent research in the field of family and migration in Europe, particularly focusing on multicultural and transnational families and their role in migration processes. Greater emphasis is placed on the role of the transmission of family values and traditions to younger generations facing specific economic circumstances and challenges, as well as to the role of national migration and integration policies and regulation in the dynamics of transnational families.

Families whose members have experienced migration face challenges in intergenerational relations, as explained by Mihaela Hărăguș, Viorela Ducu, and Ionuț Földes (Chapter 25). Using various theoretical perspectives and different family configurations, particular emphasis is given to the imbalance of power in gender roles and the way in which gender relations have been reconfigured in families impacted by migration.

Chapters 26 and 27 focus on intergenerational transmission and care. Ronny König, Bettina Isengard, and Marc Szydlik (Chapter 26) emphasise that support and lifelong exchange among generations, along with the intergenerational transmission of education and concomitant unequal opportunities and insecurities, are important characteristics of family relationships in contemporary societies. Migration and distance are important matters, and the research highlights specific patterns in a group of migrants according to household composition, duration of stay, and country of origin.

In Chapter 27, Lena Näre focuses on different care practices across borders in migrant families. The author discusses childcare and elder care practices, negotiations of intergenerational care responsibilities and concepts such as transnational care, care circulation, and care loops in order to analyse how distance and borders shape care practices in migrant families. In addition, the chapter highlights the inequalities and hierarchies that emerge in relation to mobility and the opportunity for migrant families to provide hands-on care that stems from their migrant status, as well as from social class divisions.

FAMILY AND THE LIFE COURSE TRAJECTORIES

Standing at the intersection between life stories, longitudinal studies, historical demography, and the sociology of ageing (Giele and Elder 1998), the life course perspective has prompted the development of an interdisciplinary approach. The use of common terminology to formally describe life courses as a combination of events, phases, transitions, and trajectories (Levy et al. 2005) was a stepping stone to fruitful theoretical connections between neighbouring disciplines and for bringing social, biographical, and subjective dimensions more closely together. The life course may be conceptualised as multidimensional (as it involves different life domains such as occupation, family, health, and residence), multilevel (as it considers the joint influence of micro-, meso-, and macroscopical levels), and multidirectional (as some changes are associated with the passage of time) (Spini et al. 2017; Bernardi et al. 2019). However, it is often taken for granted that this interdependency of personal relationships and life domains is actually measured in this way.

Part VI 'Family trajectories: (un)linking lives over time and place' sheds some light on the connections between life transitions and the structures and dynamics of family relationships from a life course perspective. First, Gaëlle Aeby and Jacques-Antoine Gauthier (Chapter 28) explore the phase of 'activity' and discuss the diversity of family forms, of gender role structures and of family configurations over the life course and over historical time. They provide evidence of the added value of using measures of personal networks and the life history data of individuals to identify empirical typologies of family and occupational life trajectories and locate them in their social contexts.

Taking a long-term historical perspective, Kohli (2007) identified a process of standardisation that culminated in the 1960s. This process is characterised by life transitions such as marriage and parenthood on the one hand, and school completion and retirement on the other, being largely generalised and synchronous among individuals. This contributed to the 'tripartition' of the life course into three systemically integrated phases of preparation, activity, and retirement. Economic crises from the 1970s onwards and a significant decline in conforming to central traditional institutions (e.g. marriage, army, religion) contributed to both a de-standardisation and an individualisation of the life course. Levy (2013) highlighted the heuristic potential of considering together the sociology of the family and that of work, for example, through the notion of a gendered master status which assumes that a gendered standardisation of the life course has taken place. However, these structuring trends are not mutually exclusive but co-exist in various constellations in the social space.

The transition to adulthood marks the end of the phase of 'preparation' and is key to understanding the social integration of individuals. Tom Chevalier (Chapter 29) presents this complex and sensitive period of life under the lens of historical change and international comparisons. He shows how individualisation and structure are interdependent and delineate a network of constraints and opportunities.

The generation of baby boomers born just after World War II represents an ideal-typical case to study as this generation was raised in a standardised environment and lived its adulthood and 'retirement' years in an individualised context. Catherine Bonvalet, Rémi Gallou, and Jim Ogg (Chapter 30) examine in nuanced ways how the members of this generation managed to combine intergenerational solidarity with their aspirations for autonomy and personal development.

Finally, Magda Nico, Diana Carvalho, Helena Carvalho, and Maria Silva (Chapter 31) address *linked lives* as a priori assumption using a bibliometric analysis to show the variety of dimensions attributed to this generic term.

The chapter that concludes the handbook, which was authored by the editors, discusses the extraordinary times since the start of the COVID-19 pandemic that have characterised 2020 throughout the world and affected the lives of families everywhere. The chapter offers a short reflection on the theoretical and empirical contributions of the handbook in relation to the impact of the pandemic on family life, personal relationships, and interaction.

References

Attias-Donfut, Claudine, and Joanne Cook. 2017. "Intergenerational Relationships in Migrant Families. Theoretical and Methodological Issues." In *Situating Children of Migrants across Borders and Origins: A Methodological Overview*, edited by Claudio Bolzman, Laura Bernardi, and Jean-Marie Le Goff, 115–133. Dordrecht: Springer Netherlands. https://doi.org/10.1007/978-94-024-1141-6_6.

Baldassar, Loretta, and Laura Merla. 2013. *Transnational Families, Migration and the Circulation of Care: Understanding Mobility and Absence in Family Life*. Routledge. https://doi.org/10.4324/9780203077535.

Bernardi, Laura, Johannes Huinink, and Richard A. Settersten Jr. 2019. "The Life Course Cube: A Tool for Studying Lives." *Advances in Life Course Research* 41: 100258. https://doi.org/10.1016/j.alcr.2018.11.004.

Bryceson, Deborah Fahy, and Ulla Vuorela. 2002. *The Transnational Family: New European Frontiers and Global Networks*. Oxford: Berg Publishers.

Crespi, Isabella, Stefania Giada Meda, and Laura Merla. 2018. *Making Multicultural Families in Europe: Gender and Intergenerational Relations*. London: Palgrave Macmillan.

Elias, Norbert. 2001. *Society of Individuals*. Bloomsbury Publishing USA.

Ferragina, Emanuele, and Martin Seeleib-Kaiser. 2015. "Determinants of a Silent (R)evolution: Understanding the Expansion of Family Policy in Rich OECD Countries." *Social Politics: International Studies in Gender, State & Society* 22 (1): 1–37. https://doi.org/10.1093/sp/jxu027.

Giele, Janet Z., and Glen H. Elder Jr (eds.). 1998. *Methods of Life Course Research: Qualitative and Quantitative Approaches*. Thousand Oaks: Sage Publications.

Kohli, Martin. 2007. "The Institutionalization of the Life Course: Looking Back to Look Ahead." *Research in Human Development* 4 (3–4): 253–271. https://doi.org/10.1080/15427600701663122.

Kraler, Albert, Eleonore Kofman, Martin Kohli, and Camille Schmoll (eds.). 2010. Gender, Generations and the Family in International Migration. *IMISCOE Research*. Amsterdam: Amsterdam University Press.

Levy, René. 2013. "Analysis of life courses—A theoretical sketch." In *Gendered life courses between standardization and individualization: A European approach applied to Switzerland*, edited by René Levy and Eric D. Widmer, 13–36. Wien: Lit Verlag.

Levy, René, Paolo Ghisletta, Jean-Marie Le Goff, Dario Spini, and Eric D Widmer. (eds.) 2005. "Towards an interdisciplinary perspective on the life course." In *Advances in Life Course Research*, vol. 10. Amsterdam: Elsevier JAI Press.

Mazzucato, Valentina. 2013. "Transnational Families, Research and Scholarship". In *The Encyclopedia of Global Human Migration*. American Cancer Society. https://doi.org/10.1002/9781444351071.wbeghm541.

Smart, Carol. 2007. *Personal Life*. Cambridge: Polity.

Spini, Dario, Laura Bernardi, and Michel Oris. 2017. "Toward a Life Course Framework for Studying Vulnerability". *Research in Human Development* 14 (1): 5–25.

Zontini, Elisabetta, and Thomas Reynold. 2018. "Mapping the Role of Transnational Family Habitus in the Lives of Young People and Children". *Global Networks* 18 (3): 418–436.

PART I

Researching Families and Intimate Lives in Europe: Theoretical and Methodological Trends

Edited by Rita Gouveia and Vida Česnuitytė

CHAPTER 2

The Family of Individuals: An Overview of the Sociology of the Family in Europe, 130 Years After Durkheim's First University Course

François de Singly

Introduction

The ideal starting point for reconstructing the history of the sociology of the family in Europe is Emile Durkheim's course on the topic at the Université de Bordeaux in the 1888–1889 academic year.[1] Not only was it the first academic course devoted to the field, but it highlighted a significant dimension of the modern family in Europe—the importance of personal attachment to family members. This proposition gradually became established in sociology with the spread of a new social imperative for personal development and changes in the statuses of women and children. If the family has indeed been transformed, it was to adapt to "the society of individuals" (Elias [1987] 1991). It became what I term a "family of individuals," thus making the sociology of the family into the sociology of the family of individuals. As Norbert Elias argued in "Changes in the We-I Balance" ([1987] 1991), the weight of the *I* in modern European families gradually gained ground on the conjugal and familial *We*, marking a change from the preceding period, in the nineteenth century. This perspective has theoretical limitations, however, because it underestimates the impact of gender and the effects of masculine domination on the *I* and the *We*, and tends to downplay the contribution of the family in reproducing social inequality. The following five proposals address these lacunae in their socio-historical contexts, highlighting what I see as the primary characteristics of

F. de Singly (✉)
University of Paris, Centre de Recherches Sur Les Liens Sociaux (CNRS), Université de Paris, Paris, France
e-mail: francois@singly.org

© The Author(s), under exclusive license to Springer Nature Switzerland AG 2021
A.-M. Castrén et al. (eds.), *The Palgrave Handbook of Family Sociology in Europe*, https://doi.org/10.1007/978-3-030-73306-3_2

sociology of the family today. I conclude with considering if there is any point in keeping the "sociology of the family" as a subfield if the family is indeed a "zombie concept."

Proposal 1: A Balance Where the I Outweighs the Family We

I will start this exploration of the litany of changes to the family—more unmarried cohabitation, blended families, single-parent households, same-sex households, separation and divorce, and fewer marriages and families with many children—with Norbert Elias's formulation in "Changes in the We-I balance": "If we consider the relation of I-identity and We-identity, we might say that in all countries, both more and less developed, both are present, but in the former the accent on I-identity is stronger and in the latter the accent is on the pre-state we-identity, whether the family, the native village, or the tribe" ([1987] 1991, 178). Elias also states that "it is characteristic of the structure of the more developed societies of our day that the differences between people, their I-identity, are valued more highly than what they have in common, their We-identity" (156). This individualisation process pursuing differentiation is associated with the appearance of new forms of family life. Elias does not renounce the existence of society or socialisation, instead asserting that "there is no I-identity without we-identity" (184). However, the demands of the family *We* are not felt as strongly as they once were by each family member: "Only the weighing of the I-We balance, the pattern of the I-We relation, are variable" (184). I believe a third change should be added: the *I* is transformed as much as the family *We* is. The balance between *I* and *We* goes hand in hand with new definitions of the content of individual identities and family relations.

One statement from Durkheim's last lecture in the course on the family (given in 1892, still in Bordeaux, published posthumously[2]) makes particular sense alongside Elias' hypothesis: "We are attached to our family only because we are attached to the person of our father, our mother, our wife or our children" (Durkheim [1921] 1978b, 234). Edward Shorter reformulated this pronouncement in these terms: "Spouses and children came to be prized for what they were, rather than for what they represented or could do. That is the essence of 'sentiment'" (1975, 6). There would be two attachments, then: one to the place within the family, to the status within the family *We*, and another to the personal identity of each individual, how each asserts him or herself. According to Durkheim's statement, we can claim that we are attached to our father (as a status) and the person of our father (as a unique person), to our daughter (as a status) and the person of our daughter (as a unique person). Durkheim's writings insist on the historical reversal associated with Western modernity as status-based identity became secondary. This shift of balance may be understood by re-situating it in the history of Western individualism (Taylor 1989).

Elias and Durkheim each emphasize one aspect of the individualisation process that destabilises the family. Durkheim highlights the desire for personal recognition. Everyone expects the other members of their family to see them not just for their status, but also as a unique person. This is at the root of love and the personalisation and psychologisation of intra-familial relations. Family members—spouses and domestic partners in particular—must be *significant others* (Berger and Kellner 1964; Singly 2005b). Elias formulates individualisation differently, believing that the *I* now outweighs the *We*. Subsequent sociological writings call this change in balance a "pure relationship" (Giddens 1992) or "conjugal individualisation" (Widmer et al. 2004).

These two dimensions do not take us far enough in understanding the individualisation process completely, however, so a third dimension, one studied extensively in the sociology of the family since the 1960s, has to be added to the mix. Although Enlightenment philosophers asserted that every individual is autonomous (Kant [1784] 1996), women have long been excluded from that ideal. The women's movement has and still fights for the right for women to control their own lives and bodies through access to contraception and abortion and the ability to denounce rape that occurs within a conjugal relationship. The sociology of the family is now strongly influenced by feminist perspectives and critique of masculine domination.

Proposal 2: The Is' Need for Recognition, or "The Triumph of Love"[3]

In his course, Durkheim asserts that "the conjugal family is the result of a contraction of the paternal family. The latter consists of the father, the mother, and all generations descended from them except for daughters and their descendants. The conjugal family includes only the husband, the wife, and unmarried children who are not of age" ([1921] 1978b, 229). He associates the focus on individual people with this contracted form of the family.

This hypothesis is his most remarked upon and critiqued, especially by historical demographers, Peter Laslett and the Cambridge School chief among them. In his research on rural parishes in seventeenth-century Northamptonshire, Laslett (1972, 1988) demonstrates that the nuclear family is not novel to modern-period Western societies. Taking the liberty of reformulating Durkheim, the conjugal family can be understood as one of many possible forms of the nuclear family. In demography, the nuclear family is defined by the members composing it (father, mother, children), while the "modern family" is further defined by the kind of ties that connect them. To understand the difference between the nuclear and conjugal family, the form taken by personal attachment to family members also has to be considered.

Family and Kinship in East London (1957) by Michael Young and Peter Willmott helps us to understand the conjugalisation process as it played out in the working classes, where it probably occurred later than in other social milieus. In post-World War II Bethnal Green, families were nuclear but intergenerational relations were strong as, for instance, married women saw their mothers almost daily. Then Greenleigh, a new neighbourhood with comfortable modern housing, was built and young Bethnal Green couples moved there, away from their parents. They focused on family life, children, and the television, which was at the centre of the domestic circle (Spigel 1992). Some sociologists, notably Christopher Lasch (1977, 1997), saw this development as uprooting younger generations from the old collective culture to the benefit of consumption and mass culture, which weakened and discredited long-lasting ties.[4] Others saw this closing in on the home mainly as the success of an affective logic. Regardless, it resulted from parallel transformations in ties between spouses and between parents and children (Ariès 1960; Zelizer 1985).

Durkheim's pronouncements on personal attachment have remained more relevant than those on contraction. He rightly asserts that "each individual increasingly assumed his own character, his personal manner of feeling and thinking," and that individual variations "continually became more numerous and more important" ([1921] 1978b, 234). But he denies the effects of this individualisation, understood as the promotion of personal identity to the detriment of status-based identity, not wanting to acknowledge that this movement leads to centrifugal forces and thus the possibility of broken ties. This rejection is evident in Durkheim's fight against the proposed law to allow divorce by mutual consent ([1906] 1978c). Durkheim asserted that the only positive form of individualism is that of reason, rejecting "the glorification of the self" ([1898] 1973), and forgetting his analysis from his lecture on the conjugal family. Durkheim does not acknowledge the legitimacy of an *I*, sensitive to feelings and not exclusively obeying reason, contrary to Simmel, who asserted the existence of an "exclusively personal" individualism ([1921] 1978b).

A century later, Ulrich Beck associates love with singularity. Love can be considered a "secular religion" because it promises all singular individuals that they will find a dimension of community, based not on "outdated status symbols or money or legal considerations, but solely on true and immediate feelings, on faith in their validity and on the person they are directed towards" (Beck [1990] 1995, 181). Beck has a different form of community in mind than the traditional community described by Ferdinand Tönnies ([1887] 2001), assembling individuals defined by status and group affiliation. For Beck, the dream of a modern community unites individuals who are recognised as unique. This is why love is still appealing, despite its cost and drawbacks (especially weighty for women), because it is "the best ideology to counteract the perils of individualization" (Beck [1990] 1995, 181). Individualisation is not based on isolation or solitude—indeed, the singularity of a person demands a specific form of recognition that Axel Honneth calls "love" or "emotional support" ([1992] 1995, 95 and 129). Such recognition is necessary because the individual is vulnerable in a world dominated by the market and competition with everyone else (Beck [1990] 1995; Illouz 2012).

If intimacy is so valued, it is because the predominant form of individualism in societies in second (or advanced) modernity requires the confirmation of the unique character of each person.

This demand for personal recognition has gone through several phases (on calendars differing according to European country) since Durkheim first identified it in the late nineteenth century. From 1920 through the 1960s, the constraints of the familial institution and the expression of conjugal or parental love found ways to coexist. Peter Wagner (1993) refers to this period of state intervention to limit the effects of individualisation as "restricted liberal modernity," notably seen in the rarity of divorce by mutual consent, denial of control over reproduction through contraception and abortion (Guerrand and Ronsin 1990) despite women's demands (Stopes 1918), and an emphasis on discipline rather than autonomy in family childrearing (Alwin 1988). In the following period, a growing number of women rejected being confined to family roles. When such self-negation came to be felt in the couple, separation and divorce rose, leading to the proliferation of single-parent and blended families alongside a rise in cohabitation and a relative decline in marriage. In parallel, children's rights started to be acknowledged, with the Convention on the Rights of the Child (UN 1989), especially Article 12: "States Parties shall assure to the child who is capable of forming his or her own views the right to express those views freely in all matters affecting the child." Children are no longer defined solely by their status of "daughter/son of" and are granted recognition of their personal identities.

The logic of personal recognition destabilises the "conventional family" (Budgeon and Roseneil 2004), along with the legal recognition of same-sex families and the inclusion of non-heterosexual affiliations in reckonings of kinship. Conjugal and parental love are not limited to heterosexual families. Demand for recognition as an individual in the couple increase rates of separation. The model of an associative couple—a couple that is less inseparable than some, with less gendered roles (Widmer et al. 2004)—becomes more widespread. The *We* of couples in love is transformed. So, before they move in with each other, young adults who have already gone through several breakups and experienced disillusionment in love invent a new form of "serious and light" relationship combining sexual and sentimental exclusivity with the absence of long-term commitment (Giraud 2017). The imaginary of love, the foundation for establishing a conjugal relationship, is transformed with the greater complexity of amorous careers and the supply offered by dating websites (Marquet 2010a; Bergström 2019), but we do not know the precise nature of these changes since love has several models of reference, from passionate to tender (Luhmann [1982] 1987).

Which is not to say that that it is "the end of love" (Illouz 2019). Love is more than just a sentiment; it has an important function in the relational development of the *I*. A spouse or partner, a parent: these are "significant" others who validate the *I*'s world and thus make her or him less vulnerable (Berger and Kellner 1964). Between the *I* and the *We*, there is also the *You*, which serves to reveal and stabilise personal identities in reciprocal exchange; "There is no I as such but only the I of the basic word I-You" (Buber [1923] 1970, 53). Conjugal conversation is the medium of this exchange. Considered this way, communication is the means through which the "conjugal *We*" may evolve apace with each member of the couple. The couple seems stable from the outside, while it is being modified through constant exchange. If the *I*s change, as they do in the contemporary world, the conjugal *We* also has to change (Benjamin and Sullivan 1996). Conjugal conversation and "relational resources" also create the conditions for an explicit negotiation of the division of labour, both professional and domestic (Benjamin and Sullivan 1999), when leaving the issues implicit too often favours a conjugal routine following gender stereotypes (Coltrane 1989). Conjugal conversation engenders two shifts: one in personal differentiation and singularity, and another in the continual evolution of the couple (which can be under tension). If there is not enough of it in everyday life, divorce or separation becomes necessary, most often for women, who are unhappy due to inequality in the couple and insufficient recognition from her husband or partner (Singly 2011; Kalmijn and Poortman 2006).

Proposal 3: Gendered Inequalities Between Is

Durkheim tried to demonstrate the protection that the family provides to individuals, even in his book *On Suicide* ([1897] 2007). His belief in the necessity of maintaining the individual in a system of constraints for his own happiness rendered him largely blind to certain intellectual and cultural expressions of his time. He was interested in the enduring couple, and less in analysis of the couple itself or differences between partners. This is why, when studying suicide, he sets aside those attributed to "family troubles," resulting from male abuse, and fails to explain how so few widows "finally freed from their conjugal chains" (Stoczkowski 2019, 205) are tempted by suicide.

This blind spot is not due to the backwardness of his era. Indeed, twenty years earlier, in 1869, John Stuart Mill published *The Subjection of Women* and it was immediately translated into French. Inspired by her reading of the book, Suzannah Ibsen had her husband Henrik read it, and it inspired him to write *Et Dukkehjem* (*The Doll's House*) ([1879] 2008), which first ran in Copenhagen in 1879 and was staged at the Odeon in Paris in 1894. In act III, Nora announces to her husband Helmer that she is leaving him and their children. He protests in the name of her "most sacred duties". When Nora then asks him, "What do you consider my most sacred duties?", he responds, as if it is obvious: "Do I need to tell you that? Are they not your duties to your husband and your children?". Nora disagrees: "I have other duties, just as sacred [...] Duties to myself". Helmer replies with a status-based definition of his wife, asserting "Before all else, you are a wife and mother", but Nora goes on to insist that she is "before all else [...] a reasonable human being, a person" (Ibsen [1879] 2008, 164–165). So, at the very moment that marriage for love took root in the late nineteenth and early twentieth centuries, the unequal conjugal *We*, dominated by the husband, was challenged by feminist thought, which argued that marriage and family life often stifle the personal identity of the woman. Durkheim, along with most sociologists at the time (and later), forgot that the situations of women and men in a couple or family are incomparable.

Although Durkheim took the variable "sex" into account in *On Suicide* ([1897] 2007), he still did not understand gender inequalities in the couple, although some of his contemporaries were beginning to. His more lucid contemporary Georg Simmel described the "relationship between the sexes quite grossly as one of master and slave," proceeding to stress that "it is one of the privileges of the master that he never need think about the nature of that relationship. On the other hand, the position of the slave ensures that inferior status is not forgotten" (Simmel [1911] 1984, 103). Durkheim could not go that far, however; despite having observed the rising need for personal recognition, he could not see that this need is incompatible with the social superiority of the husband, as Ibsen drove home in his play.

The sociology of the family would generally hold this position until the 1960s, due largely to the prominence of Talcott Parsons in the discipline. Parsons and Robert Bales (1955) thought that the couple was comparable to a small group focused on one task, thus justifying the complementarity of the instrumental role falling to the man and the expressive role falling to the woman. This orientation expands on Durkheim's hypothesis that, in more modern societies, the division of labour between spouses is functional, leading to greater solidarity. Spouses are mutually dependent, and their differences are a factor of "mutual attraction" creating a feeling of sympathy (Durkheim, [1893] 1984). Feminism would critique functionalism for how it legitimates inequalities between members of a couple, since it attributes paid professional work to men and "domestic labor" to women (Johnson 1993). The notion of "sex roles" was abandoned precisely because it obscured masculine domination, for reasons similar to why sociologists did not speak in terms of "class roles" or "race roles" (Stacey and Thorne 1985, 307). In addition to examining roles or the distribution of work by sex, analysis also has to include the resulting asymmetry and inequalities, or, in a word, gender. In the 1960s and 1970s, feminism established the sex/gender distinction to highlight the social construction of genders and to designate the existence of a hierarchical relationship between them. This was the most major development in the sociology of the family since its inception.

Gender theory is not monolithic and has several modalities. One of the more theoretical was formulated by Christine Delphy (1974; Delphy and Leonard 1992), who thinks that the "domestic labour" assigned to women is central to analysis of masculine domination: the class of men extorts this labour, consisting of housework, elder care, and the raising and education of children, from the class of women without pay. The free provision of household labour is central to this theory. Kristin Natalier found evidence of this association between housework and wives in her research on male roommates: one justified his laxity in cleaning by saying "I'm not his wife" (2003). Delphy believes that this mode of domestic production (distinct from the mode of capitalist production) cannot be altered through individual actions.

Some studies take another perspective, suggesting that the division of labour between domestic partners could be transformed. For one thing, the development of paid employment for women with children in Europe in the 1970s raised hopes of a challenge to inflexible labour distribution between heterosexual spouses (Michel 1973) and the emergence of a more egalitarian "two-career family" (Rapoport and Rapoport 1971). In fact, it only led to the emergence of a nearly double workday for the vast majority of women and fewer hours devoted to domestic labour, instead of the egalitarian sharing of domestic and professional labour. This led researchers to wonder how women manage to reconcile these two lives, especially exploring the place of part-time employment (the "Mrs. Works-for-Peanuts" [*madame Gagne-miettes*] model [Périvier 2013]), to examine state and business interventions in these tensions (Le Bihan-Youinou and Martin 2008), and to rethink theories of the welfare state that focus on the male worker and breadwinner (Esping-Andersen 1990) or do not take adequate account of gender (Lewis 1992, 1997). Too often, this reconciliation is ambiguous, since it still mainly fobs the challenges of time management off on women.

This is why a more recent body of research has focused on couples that try to even out inequalities and men who do considerably more domestic work. Arlie Hoschschild (1989) has shown that some two-career couples search for equality in power, as well as sharing domestic labour (Vannoy-Hiller and Philliber 1989). This means that some men (albeit a minority) reject this conjugal asymmetry embedded in the daily routine (including the "mental load"), the things that are "our" responsibility (our laundry, our vacation...) that fall to the female *I* (Kaufmann 1992) and make the "our" a sort of illusion. The most egalitarian men not only commit to implementing this norm of equality, they change their priorities and put family ahead of their job (Deutsch and Gaunt 2020). They learn to do tasks by themselves and may even try to test their new domestic skills (Wall and Leitão 2016). They differ from men who became "house husbands" because their job pays less than their partner's (Trellu 2007), with lower relative resources (in Blood and Wolfe's [1960]) sense); one wonders how much the inversion of roles actually leads to a strong destabilisation of gender in such cases. To favour a greater implication of men, a number of countries in Europe have instated gender equality policies offering open parental leave, and some men take advantage of them.

The gender perspective necessitated methodological change in the sociology of the family. In fact, sociologists used to ask one member of a couple to respond to a questionnaire (usually the wife) and wrote up the results without noting the sex of the respondent, as if they had acquired the couple's account (Safilios-Rothschild 1969). This is no longer an option since marriage or cohabitation are no guarantee of the unity or creation of a common conjugal interest. Jessie Bernard was probably the first to formulate this way of considering the heterosexual couple in *The Future of Marriage*: "There are two marriages, then, in every marital union, his and hers," dryly adding, "His … is better than hers" (Bernard 1972; Cantor 1988). We can use the couple of Emile Durkheim and Louise Dreyfus as an ideal-type case of the production of inequalities between spouses. Louise came from a much wealthier family than Emile, and upon marriage she put herself at his service (Charle 1984). Durkheim's nephew Marcel Mauss described this devotion in detail:

> She always knew how to provide her husband with the most favorable working conditions. She was very well educated, and eventually able to collaborate on his work. For many years she copied some of his manuscripts, corrected all his proofs; without her, *Année Sociologique* would have been an overwhelming burden on Durkheim. She not only participated in all material chores of management, administration, correspondence, correction and distribution of proofs, but also manuscript preparation and even, often, discretely but surely, correction. (Mauss 1969, 523–524, our translation)

She even attended all his courses. For Bernard, the rise of individualism is not to be blamed for the distinction between "his marriage" and "her marriage" because it exists in all couples, as a result of the dissymmetry between men and women in the couple and the family. It's just that the distinction is more appreciable with women who resist gender inequalities, which could lead to separation if there is no change.

Despite these changes, conjugal and familial life still costs more for women than for men. Differences in careers vary according to gender and conjugal and family status: they are greater between men and women with two or three children than between those with no children (Singly 1987a). Sociologists may still interview only one member of a couple, but it should be made clear that it is only one partner's version in publications. When both are questioned, the versions can be compared to find their differences. Research on sleep provides a fine example of how versions can differ. Women are disturbed at night by crying children and snoring men (Hislop 2007; Meadows and Arber 2012; Venn et al. 2008; Kaufmann 2015), while men's sleep is disrupted by worries over unemployment and household finances (Maume et al. 2018). Having both men's and women's accounts of domestic labour (as defined by Delphy) demonstrates that women and men do not count contributions in the same way (Lennon and Rosenfield 1994) and thus have different conceptions of equality. Interviews can also be conducted with both members of the couple together, and the interaction itself can be used for insight into power issues through their speech interactions (Clair 2007) or how they act (in the theatrical sense, Janet Finch's "family display" [2007]) in front of the sociologist, who is a sort of audience (Bjornholt and Farstad 2012).

The inclusion of gender issues also unsettles certain classic notions of the sociology of the family. One notion deserving re-examination is homogamy as explanation for the "choice of a partner". The prefix "homo" emphasises the social and cultural resemblance between potential partners, and beyond that, the balance of their respective interests. Masculine domination disrupts this harmony of male and female interests (Rosa 2018) because (as we saw in work on the cost of marriage or cohabitation) men's capitals and resources are more valued than women's capitals and resources. This inequality rises as the life course advances and ends up turning early homogamy into heterogamy (Singly 1987a, 1987b). Gradually the woman's access to the wealth accumulated by her partner over the course of their life together becomes mediated. If she does not become dependent on her partner, she at least becomes dependent on the marriage (Delphy 1974). If she does not enter into another conjugal relationship, her lifestyle loses much more than her ex-partner's. The cost of marriage paradoxically becomes more evident upon separation, and is converted into a "cost of separation" (Holden and Smock 1991). Despite all that, women initiate divorce or separation more frequently than men (Kalmijn and Poortman 2006).

It has become difficult to challenge gender stereotypes for a reason that is rarely evoked where parenthood is concerned. At the very moment when sharing between parents is the most socially valued, new psychological norms impose greater expectations for investment in childhood development (Elias [1980] 1998; Martin 2014). Particular attention is required for the *I* of the child to blossom, and fathers are involved always less, but it is mothers who have ensured the response to these expanded childrearing demands. Sharon Hays (1996) argues that this increase subjects mothers to "cultural contradictions" when they are also engaged in a professional activity. Working women with children devote less time to parenting than mothers have in the past, but psychological norms have made this time more intensive and restrictive since they are supposed to be more attentive to their child's development.

Since the 1960s, the individualisation process affects women more than men. Men have actually benefited from even greater autonomy than women, and so women have collectively and individually demanded the same rights, rejecting the double standard of masculine and feminine norms and wanting to free themselves from a relationship of dependence and devotion to the family (Beck and Beck-Gernsheim 2002b). Inroads have indisputably been made, but are still limited. Women still have more responsibility in managing the *We*, partly to the detriment of their *I*. The path of individualisation stretches far ahead, and women have philosophical (Beauvoir [1949] 2012) and literary benchmarks signposting the way. Take, for instance, late nineteenth-century novelist Kate Chopin's "The Story of an Hour" ([1894] 2002). A woman has just learned of her husband's death, and, now sitting in front of her bedroom window, feels something arise from within: "free, free, free! [...] What could love, the unsolved mystery, count for in the face of this possession of self-assertion which she suddenly recognised as the strongest impulse of her being! 'Free! Body and soul free!'". Both dimensions of individualisation—finding oneself with the help of a loving companion and asserting oneself as a free and autonomous individual—are partially contradictory (just like competitive individualism and humanitarian individualism [Singly 2005a]). Having been transformed by the sociology of gender, the sociology of the family allows us to account for this tension between attachment to conjugal and familial relations and self-affirmation, between individualism and conjugal unity (Björnberg and Kollind 2005).

Proposal 4: The Resistance of We

Due to the persistence of the effects of gender, the *We* resists the rising strength of the *I*. One indicator that the *We* endures under the influence of the gender dissymmetry in heterosexual unions is that, in France at least, many women still change their family name after marriage, and children are usually given their father's family name. The equality of the sexes is forgotten in the name of the tradition of the father's name serving to unite the group. Although there is now a law in France allowing parents to choose which family name their child will take, only a small minority chose a hyphenated name (and even then, with the father's name first) (Rault 2017). In Finland, "the patriarchal mindset continues to have a hold over the formation of a family," and especially over its representation in a name (Castrén 2018). This is also an issue in lesbian couples, who may put the family name of the partner who did not bear the child first so she will not be left out (Courduriès 2017).

The construction of the conjugal *We* is also approached through the management of money in the couple. In "Mine, Yours or Ours?", Charlotte Nyman (2002; cf. Pahl 1997) describes how the *We* often obscures gendered spending patterns in heterosexual men and women. Everyday and unexpected expenses, a sort of grey zone, are more often paid by women, from their own account. So without making a decision or negotiating, out of the routine of everyday life reflecting the gendered division of labour, the female financial *I* contributes more than the masculine *I* to the family *We* (Nyman and Evertsson 2005). Individualisation (in the sense of domestic partners being independent) may also contribute to inequalities between men and women, especially when the *We* includes a child (Pahl 2005). The arrival of a child creates conditions for the production of the *We*, but a *We* with heavily gendered contributions. Laundry is the proof: before parenthood, each washes his or her own laundry, but after the child's birth the woman is usually the one that washes "their" laundry, including that of the man (Kaufmann 1992).

The *We* can also harbour class inequalities, in addition to gender inequalities. The cost of *We* is no longer measured according to the contribution of partners' personal identities; it reflects a struggle between families. Durkheim designates the "family *We*" with the term "communism" in his course ([1921] 1978b, 233), and this *We* diminishes under Western modernity to become merely conjugal. "It was quite different formerly, when the links which derived from things took precedence over those which derived from persons, when the whole familial organisation has as its primary object to keep the domestic property within the family, and when all personal considerations appeared secondary to these considerations" (234). The family group, symbolised by property and heritable wealth, dominated each of its members, defined by their position within the family. As Pierre Bourdieu also stressed ([1972] 1990, Book 2, Chapter 1), if the eldest—meaning the eldest boy—was so important, it is because he incarnated inheritance, not because he had qualities superior to his siblings.

From this perspective, the "family *We*" refers first of all to heritable capital, that which is passed from one generation to the next, and reproduces social differences. Since Durkheim hoped that individualism would end inequalities of inheritance so that the position of the individual could be based on her or his merit instead of her or his inheritance, he failed to see that intergenerational transmission was not vanishing, only taking a new form. He could even have realised it based on his own life, since he attentively and joyfully nurtured the studies of his son André, who followed his path to the exclusive École Normale Supérieure. The lesser importance of economic inheritance does mean neither the death of transmission nor the end of the family's contribution to order between the generations.

The concept of cultural inheritance would not exist until the 1960s, with the publication of Pierre Bourdieu and Jean-Claude Passeron's *The Inheritors* ([1964] 1979). They demonstrate that the diploma gradually became one of the most significant forms of capital to come from family worth under Western modernity. Even if these diplomas have to be validated by the academic institution, the certification is primarily an acknowledgement of something that the children of highly educated parents acquired from their family. Building on the work of Basil Bernstein (1961), Bourdieu and Passeron ([1970] 1977) explain how a family resource is transformed into educational capital by looking at two things: language differentiation according to social background and the investment in scholastic culture by the families of white-collar workers in positions of responsibility. Although the culture of these white-collar families does not always tally with scholastic culture or the culture of legitimate practices, research converges in demonstrating a strong transmission of parental cultural capital to their children. The school is charged with legitimising scholastic differences between children, thus allowing justification of the social differences between them. It has taken the power to designate heirs from the father (Bourdieu and Saint Martin 1978).

The epistemological consequence of this should be to include the sociologies of education, school, and social mobility in the sociology of the family. Failing to do so leads the sociology of the family to underestimate the family's function of social reproduction and overestimate the *I* of the child and his or her personal fulfilment when he or she has partly integrated the parental *We*. Inversely, the sociology of the trans-generational reproduction of inequalities asserts that there are few changes to the family, since nothing (or little) changes the mechanisms of social reproduction. But changes in how families function exists alongside continuity of reproduction; it is clear, since cultural transmission is simultaneously compatible with less authoritarian family relations and the rise in divorce and separations[5] and new, non-conventional forms of the family.

Just because family social worth is still passed on to the next generation does not mean that attachment to family members is an illusion or that no progress is being made towards equality of the sexes. Ultimately, family upbringing leads to tremendous scholastic and social success among children raised in well-endowed families at one end of the social spectrum, and shorter schooling for poor children at the other end. For lack of satisfactory results reducing inequalities through educational policy, social policy has focused on the welfare of the latter (Bradshaw 2016; Axford 2012).

Proposal 5: Looking for a New Balance Between I and We

As described earlier, Norbert Elias sums up the transformation of European society since the late nineteenth century with a change in the balance between *I* and *We* in the family. Even if the balance unquestionably leans towards the *I*, the calibration varies according to the country in Europe, the religion individuals may practice, their social milieu, gender, sexual orientation, and numerous other factors, some yet to be identified. Although they do not make specific reference to this hypothesis, many publications provide elements allowing us to describe variations in this balance, but this is not enough and it could even lead to a dead end. Indeed, sticking to this formulation focused on a sort of competition between the most *I* and the most *We* might lead us to think that individualisation is in opposition to the *We*. It ends up creating a theoretical rivalry between the assertions of theorists who think that community is being destroyed by increasingly independent individuals, and researchers who demonstrate that the familial and conjugal *We* carries on. Understood this way, the hypothesis of individualisation appears to be an oversimplified view of the social world, or, to borrow Carol Smart and Beccy Shipman's expression, a "vision in monochrome" (2004). The individualisation process does not necessarily lead to the end of collective existence and "liquid life" (Bauman 2003), because it could go hand in hand with new modalities of family life.

This is where the thesis of the "family of individuals" comes in. Individualism not only engenders a new balance between the *I* and the *We*; it also produces new *I*s and new *We*s. The parent/child relationship is thus significantly altered, because a new imperative has been added to the standard objective of family childrearing (transmission): the autonomy and personal development of the child. Therefore, compared to mothers of the preceding generation, today's mothers respond more readily to what they interpret as signals from their children, even at the youngest age, and play with them more often, but provide less physical and expressive warmth (Keller and Lamm 2005). Marianne Gullestad's comparison of the life histories of Norwegians of two age cohorts, fifty years apart, reveals this change in childrearing practices, with lowered emphasis on obedience and a greater value placed on "being oneself" (1995, 1996). The relationship between two new *I*s raises problems and could be contradictory. Breastfeeding on demand is a perfect illustration of these tensions. In order to develop without having to obey an imposed schedule from birth, the baby may express her needs without them being seen as whims, as they were by earlier generations. In breastfeeding this means that the mother has to subject herself to the baby's demands and be at her disposal. By mediating time, the infantile *I* hinders the mother's *I* (Andersson 2009). Women are encouraged to stop being "housewives" and become financially independent through paid employment, but also to breastfeed their child in order to foster her development. They are subjected to a paradoxical injunction: get out of the home, but you should stay home. Resolving this dual constraint bears a cost that Rippeyoung and Noonan (2012) measured using longitudinal data from first-time mothers who were questioned annually. Those who breastfed, and especially those who did it for a long time, had a loss in income that persisted years later. Here again, child development norms are nearly impossible to reconcile with the norm of professional equality for mothers.

In the family (as in the rest of society), it is difficult for someone to reconcile the care of their unique and autonomous self with the care of loved ones. Everyone is seeking a solution, usually without direct negotiation between partners (Nyman and Evertsson 2005) and with negotiation between parents and children. Some might seem paradoxical, such as "re-traditionalisation" as a way to reconcile the assertion of individualisation with enrolment in the tradition of the ritual of marriage (Duncan and Carter 2017; Carter and Duncan 2018). This is why so many brides still want to wear a white wedding gown, even when the couple has lived together for several years (Duncan 2011).

The model of the pure relationship offered by Anthony Giddens (1992) has been widely used in the sociology of the family because it offers an ideal-type of a union of two individualised *I*s: "a situation where a social relation is entered into for its own sake, for what can be derived for each person from a sustained association with another" (p. 58). He is also aware that this model engenders "a structural contradiction in the pure relationship, centering upon commitment" (p. 137). A sense of uncertainty may come from such unreliable longevity. The two partners are thus caught between either having to open up completely to create a relationship of reciprocal dependency with each other, or preserving the independence of their *I*s by keeping some parts of themselves to themselves, without letting the other in. Giddens argues that most men and women reject the dependence created by the engagement in order to reduce the tension.[6] This analysis has been criticised for the absence of sociological studies, which he made up for by analysing "therapeutic works and self-help manuals" (64), and his omission of persistent gender inequalities. Lynn Jamieson (1999) sees these critiques as connected: the pure relationship ties back to therapeutic discourse and the psychologisation of the conjugal relationship, and overlooks the social structuration of gender relations. Indeed, even if the equality of the sexes is asserted, the persistence of domestic and social inequalities makes the pure relationship unattainable.

Another model could be added alongside that of the pure relationship, that which François de Singly (2003) has called "the two-part life." The individualisation process leads partly to a kind of split identity as individuals fluctuate between times when they are primarily themselves and times when they are primarily members of a group (conjugal, familial), and partly to practices that are neither in the register of fusion ("joint") nor in the register of separation. Jan Pahl has observed that the most common way of managing household finances mixes the two, with a joint account and two personal accounts (2005). Concerning leisure-time pursuits, some are done as a couple and others separately, sometimes with friends. Time together is appreciated on one condition: the activity mustn't be chosen by only one member of the family, or it will be seen as a manifestation of arbitrary power. Accordingly, teenagers enjoy spending time with their parents provided that they do not play the role of teacher or authority figure (Singly and Ramos 2010). They like it when their family is "cool," applying a teen cultural category to their parents (Pountain and Robins 2001). The verticality of the relationship limits its appeal, since the family ideal is for each member to be considered as a person, which presupposes a degree of equality, but this is not often the case.

I can at least agree with the place that Giddens accords to sexuality in his pure relationship model, a topic that the sociology of the conjugal couple usually overlooks, leaving it to the sociology of sexuality. Giddens thinks that sexuality is "plastic" and acquires a degree of autonomy from the conjugal relationship; it becomes "one among other forms of self-exploration and moral construction" (1992, 144). Sexual exclusivity saps it of meaning, leading to the routinisation of the practice (Bozon 2001); moreover, for Giddens, exclusivity is not the only way to express engagement, since "it is not at all clear that episodic sexuality is inherently incompatible with emergent norms of the pure relationship" (1992, 147). Georg Simmel offers another way of understanding sexual fidelity. In "On Love (A Fragment)" he asserts that love is absolutely unitary, because "it is not one or the other of my 'aspects' or energies that loves, but rather the entire person." He likens this to the expression of love for God, appreciated not for any given quality but "exclusively because He exists" ([1921] 1984, 161). So sexuality can thus have several meanings: very impersonal in prostitution mediated by money, and very personal in some amorous relationships where partners' identities are fully engaged. Between the two are all the nuanced variations that women and men have created according to their desires, recently caught up in "connected individualism" (Demonceaux 2014) and the abundant supply on dating sites that leads them to develop procedures for evaluating themselves and others (Illouz 2019).

Researchers like Carol Smart (2007, 32–52) and David Morgan (1996, 2011) are right to emphasise the study of family practices, since the family of today is defined more by what its members do together than by institutional logics. In his lecture on the conjugal family, Durkheim speculated about what remained of familial "communism" ([1921] 1978b), and indeed one of the objectives of sociology of the family is to study all activities—such as those pertaining to food and eating (Kemmer et al. 2002; Kaufman [2005] 2010)—that are shared between domestic partners and parents and children.

Focusing on the things that change the most should not lead us to neglect the statutory dimension, often based in laws[7] but also in demands for rights such as legal recognition of the status of "intended parents." For instance, some countries, including France and Belgium, have created a formal distinction between the "conjugal couple" that may separate and the "parental couple" that must keep working together, maintaining joint parental authority after separation (Marquet 2010b). It is impossible to separate oneself from one's children when the state serves as guarantor of the child's interests. Both of these dimensions of attachment—statutory and personal, already identified by Durkheim—should thus be the object of specific enquiry in every instance. The personal *I*s do not exist without a statutory definition; they are caught up in gender relations, intergenerational relations, relations between social milieus, relations between so-called ethnic groups, but also in legal constraints.

Under the pressure of individualism, people dream of a life where it is possible to be "free together" (Burkart and Kohli 1992; Singly 2000) instead of "alone together" (Amato et al. 2007; Turkle 2012). It could take the form of "living apart together" (Levin 2004; Stoilova et al. 2017), while others choose to create a "family *We*" without going through the "conjugal *We*," most notably in the case of single mothers by choice (Murray and Golombok 2005; Ajandi 2011). Some prefer to experience family without children so that transmission and inheritance do not take up too much place in their plans (Gotman 2017), while others extol the virtues of a more complex model of "co-parenthood" (McHale et al. 2004). There are also couples—usually same-sex—that expand the definition of family by including their exes and friend networks (Donovan et al. 2001). To what extent can the affirmation of the self allow people to freely shape the outlines of their private lives and their families? According to Robert Goss, everyone "has the right to create family forms that fit his or her needs to realise the human potential for love in non-oppressive relationships" (1997, 19). However, this invention always occurs according to the socialisation of individuals, their experience, institutions, social and family policy… this is why it seems to be a *bricolage* (Duncan 2011). Family forms are not reproduced, but they do not have a clean slate either.

Conclusion: The Sociology of the Family is Not a "Zombie"

In the mid-nineteenth century, Honoré de Balzac wrote in the introduction to *The Human Comedy*: "I regard the family and not the individual as the true social unit. In this respect, at the risk of being thought retrograde, I side with

Bossuet and Bonald instead of going with modern innovators" ([1842] 2019). Balzac's view of a vanished family was borrowed from conservative politicians such as Louis de Bonald (who was behind the 1816 law repealing divorce by mutual consent, which had been imposed by the French Revolution) and a social scientist like Fréderic Le Play, who thought that the "revolutionary poison" (Bonald's words) of 1789 had contaminated the family as a stable group. By imposing equality among children for inheritance, the revolutionaries had destabilised the father. Yet the figure of the father (of the family, but also of the nation [the King] and moreover of all Creation [God the Father]) is what holds every individual and each group together. Balzac echoes this idea in one of his novels, *Letters of Two Brides* ([1842] 2011), asserting that the King's death on the guillotine had symbolically destroyed the true family: "In Louis XVI, the Revolution has decapitated every head of a family. The family has ceased to exist; we have only individuals".

A century and a half later, a comparable diagnosis is made: despite appearances, the family is dead due to the rise of individualism. The weight of the *I* is said to have become so great that the *We* has nearly disappeared. From the establishment of individualism, Ulrich Beck draws the conclusion that "The family is a good example of a zombie category" (2002, 204), and institutions had been made into the "living dead". To Beck's thinking, everyone, even most sociologists, carries on as if "the family" still exists, when the extent of its existence may mainly be due to institutional effects, such as the existence of family policies or a sociological subfield called "sociology of the family." Sociology could thus contribute to hysteresis, as Bourdieu called it[8]—a gap between a situation in the present (the inexistence of the family, in this case) and the conceptual persistence of a vanished entity ("the family").

But it is surprising that Ulrich Beck would come to this kind of conclusion: "After the industrial world order made of classes, social strata, and nuclear families there only flutters a loose aggregate of flying leaves composed of individuals" (1998, 18). Indeed, from a sociological perspective, there is no justification for asserting that the family as it was observed under the pre-Revolutionary *Ancien Régime* was the only possible form of the family. Conservatives are the ones to proclaim such a belief, dreaming of turning back time or stopping the course of history. I agree more with Durkheim's view as it was presented in the first lecture of his course on the sociology of the family, taught in the 1888–1889 academic year at the Université de Bordeaux. Durkheim distinguished himself from Le Play ([1871] 1982), refusing to look to "the families of previous ages as models." To the contrary, he asserted that "Today's family is neither more nor less perfect than that of yesterday; it is different because circumstances are different" ([1888] 1978a, 219).

Beck is not the only one to challenge the concept of the family. Carol Smart suggests replacing the problematic term with that of "personal life" (2007), which she considers to be broader. And it is, in that the *I* would have more spaces than the family in the strict sense of the term, especially in friendships. But in another sense, the family is broader than personal life because it partly structures (in Giddens' sense [1984]) individuals through laws, policies, and norms. The most interesting approach is to associate both concepts in order to study the shape of personal life within and without the family. Putting too much emphasis on personal life runs the risk of exaggerating the weight of personal identities by masking what these individuals desirous of being autonomous and independent are trying to forget—that they are the "heirs" of their family lines (regardless of the resources in question). The individualisation process has only partially unstructured the family, but it has not managed to entirely upend the "gender order", referring to both masculine hegemony and the obligation to make one's gender align with one's biological sex (Connell 1995). It has made even less progress in imposing equality of opportunity, since inter-generational inequalities have barely been reduced. Every *I* is still first of all a "son/daughter of," so his or her liberation is only limited.

Although it has changed considerably, the family is not a zombie category and still exists in a form that emphasises family relationships over structures. The sense of this shift was summed up by Ernest W. Burgess and Harvey J. Locke in the subtitle of their book on the family, "from institution to companionship": "its unity inheres less and less in community pressures and more and more in such interpersonal relations [as] mutual affection" (1960, vii). Even Ulrich Beck and Elisabeth Beck-Gernsheim keep this conception of the family and rehabilitate it by adding an adjective, "the *post-family* family" (2002a, emphasis ours), subtitling their text "From a community of need to elective affinities".[9]

This confusion between critique of the family as it is at a given moment in time and the ideal of a life in common still designated by the term "family" is evident in the work of David Cooper. This psychiatrist wrote *The Death of the Family* (1971) in a post-1968 spirit, against psychiatry of his time, and in it called for the demise of the repressive family that prevented people from becoming themselves. But in its pages he also thanks his brother, sister-in-law, and their two young daughters for having cared for him with "immense kindliness and concern" when he was unwell, "Just as true family should" (157). What emerges is a sketch of the family as a place where each member, adult or child, can enjoy the solicitude and care of the others, the family as a space of mutual respect and reciprocal support. As long as public policies use the term "family" (by, for example, designating "parental responsibility" [Lind and Keating 2008]), the sociology of the family is useful provided that it analyses all forms of practices inside families jointly with the policies that try to regulate them (Edwards et al. 2012). If sociology were to abandon the term it would be left entirely to other disciplines like economics and psychology, which would be tantamount to dissolving the social (Gilding 2010).

Unless one were to postulate that individuals are entirely alienated, one might ask them to indicate what they think family is, defined both by who they consider family members and what the underlying values of family to be. According to the first criteria, individuals' conceptions of the boundaries of the family do not necessarily correspond to what demography and statistics accept as such. There is no objective definition of individuals thought to belong to blended families, for example, since their inclusion or exclusion is variable (Castrén and Widmer 2015). In the same vein, many household pets are also considered as full-fledged members of the family (Power 2008; Charles 2014; Morand and Singly 2019). The family of individuals thus requires a "figurational approach" (Castrén and Ketovici 2015) to uncover each person's list, composed according to a dual logic combining loved ones of "fate" and "choice" (Pahl and Spencer 2004). Turning to the second criteria, according to Jane Ribbens McCarthy (2012) the family is still a reference as a space to which each person feels belonging, where each feels acknowledged regardless of his or her social value on the markets, where he or she is cared for, and where he or she feels safe (an under-studied aspect in the sociology of the family).[10] The "wings" dreamt of by so many autonomous and independent individuals do not rule out a need for "roots," as Pablo Neruda captures in his *Cuadernos de Temuco* (1997): "Be a tree. A tree with wings. Bare its roots in the powerful earth and deliver them to the ground and when everything around us is much more vast, spread our wings wide and start to fly". Charles Taylor quotes popular self-help manual from the 1970s, in which Gail Sheehy wishes readers "portable roots," in his argument that the *I*s do and will identify with "a world of changing affiliations and relationships" with weakened ties (1989, 508).

Another argument against the concept of the family is its function of "ideological veil" (Smart 2007). Using this concept in the 1970s was a demonstration of "familialism", or in other words, wanting to defend the family as natural and ignoring its contributions to the production of social inequalities. Pierre Bourdieu and Jean-Claude Passeron avoided the word "family" in *The Inheritors* ([1964] 1979), preferring to speak in terms of social class. For Smart, using the concept today would be an invocation of the "white, heterosexual, middle-class family" and everything this model imposes. I do not see why people living in other ways wouldn't have access to the term. Who decides the ownership of words? Why shouldn't a couple of lesbian mothers who talk about brushing their teeth together with their child not have the right to declare, seeing themselves in the mirror, "we're a real family" (Descoutures 2010)? Gay and lesbian requests to marry and have formalised kinship ties (Descoutures et al. 2008) are not merely expressions of submission to heterosexual norms, but can also be claims to equal access to the form of private life designated by the word "family". Why not admit that the "the family" is a malleable concept prone to redefinition—as the last few decades have shown— under pressure of social movements for women's and LGBT + rights? Why say "goodbye to the family" (Edwards and Gillies 2012) and consequently the sociology of the family? Should the family really be "abolished" (Munoz-Dardé 1999)? Rather than that, why not analyse how people "make a family," as blended families must do (Ribbens et al. 2003)? We have yet to learn the relative weight of the family for each individual: nothing says that the family is (still) a space superior to other kinds of relationships in their lives (Morgan 2011). How can the sociology of the family be a zombie if there is so much left to learn?

Acknowledgements Thanks to Juliette Rogers for the translation.

Notes

1. Only the first and last lecture were published (Durkheim [1888] 1978a, [1921] 1978b).
2. See also Lamanna (2002); Singly (1993).
3. This is the title of a play by Marivaux (1732), who used a farce of disguises to stage a reconciliation of disinterested Love and the utility of marriage.
4. Although he does not cite Lasch, Zygmunt Bauman holds a similar position, believing that modernity has destroyed the bridges between generations, leading to greater uprootedness and a more liquid form of life (2003).
5. Intergenerational transmission of separated fathers not living with their child is lower than that of non-separated fathers, however (Leeuw et al. 2018).
6. For more on how some women consider the conjugal relationship long-term, see Carter (2012).
7. The establishment of an uncrossable line in the fight against pedophilia illustrates the importance of the status socially accorded to the child as a specific age group (Déchaux 2014).
8. People may be destabilised because their habitus is poorly adapted to their present situation (Bourdieu 1962).
9. Beck and Beck-Gernsheim's subtitle follows the same model as Burgess and Locke's (1960), probably to emphasise the dawning of a new era. At the same time, Elisabeth Beck-Gernsheim makes this objective even more clear in *Reinventing the Family* (2002).
10. Giddens is not very clear on how the pure relationship is compatible with ontological security (1984, 1991).

References

Ajandi, Jennifer. 2011. "Single Mothers by Choice: Disrupting Dominant Discourses of the Family through Justice Alternatives." *International Journal of Child, Youth and Family Studies* 3/4: 410–431.

Alwin, Duane F. 1988. "From Obedience to Autonomy: Changes in Traits Desired in Children, 1924–1978." *Public Opinion Quarterly* 52 (1): 33–52.

Amato, Paul R., Alan Booth, David R. Johnson, and Stacy J. Rogers. 2007. *Alone Together: How Marriage in America is Changing*. Cambridge MA: Harvard University Press.

Andersson, Réka. 2009. "Breastfeeding on Demand: Negotiating Between Contradictory Ideals." PhD diss., Linköping University, Linköping, 2008. http://liu.diva-portal.org/smash/get/diva2:234135/FULLTEXT01.pdf.

Ariès, Philippe. 1960. *L'enfant et la vie familiale sous l'Ancien Régime*. Paris: Plon.

Axford, Nick. 2012. *Exploring Concepts of Child Well-Being: Implications for Children's Services*. Bristol: Policy Press.

Balzac, Honoré de. (1842) 2011. *Letters of Two Brides*. Translated by R. S. Scott. Floating Press.
Balzac, Honoré de. (1842) 2019. *The Human Comedy: Introductions and Appendix*. The Good Press.
Bauman, Zygmunt. (2000) 2003. *Liquid Love: On the Frailty of Human Bonds*. Cambridge, UK: Polity Press.
Beauvoir, Simone de. (1949) 2012. *The Second Sex*. Translated by Constance Borde and Sheila Malovany-Chevallier. New York: Doubleday.
Beck, Ulrich. (1990) 1995. "Love, Our Secular Religion." In *The Normal Chaos of Love*, edited by Ulrich Beck and Elisabeth Beck-Gernsheim, 168–201. Translated by Mark Ritter and Jane Wiebel. Cambridge UK: Polity Press.
Beck, Ulrich. 1998. "Le conflit des deux modernités et la question de la disparition des solidarités." *Lien social et politiques* 39: 15–26.
Beck, Ulrich. 2002. "Zombie Categories: Interview with Ulrich Beck." In *Individualization* edited by Ulrich Beck and Elisabeth Beck-Gernsheim, 202–213. Translated by Patrick Camiller. London: Sage Publications.
Beck, Ulrich, and Elisabeth Beck-Gernsheim. 2002a. "On the Way to Post-Family Modernity." In *Individualization*, edited by Ulrich Beck and Elisabeth Beck-Gernsheim, 85–100. Translated by Patrick Camiller. London: Sage Publications.
Beck, Ulrich, and Elisabeth Beck-Gernsheim. 2002b. "From 'Living for Others' to 'A Life of One's Own': Individualization and Women." In *Individualization*, edited by Ulrich Beck and Elisabeth Beck-Gernsheim, 54–84. Translated by Patrick Camiller. London: Sage Publications.
Beck-Gernsheim, Elisabeth. 2002. *Reinventing the Family: In Search of New Lifestyles*. Cambridge, UK: Polity Press.
Benjamin, Orly, and Oriel Sullivan. 1996. "The Importance of Difference: Conceptualising Increased Flexibility in Gender Relations at Home." *Sociological Review* 44 (2): 225–251.
Benjamin, Orly, and Oriel Sullivan. 1999. "Relational Resources, Gender Consciousness and Possibilities of Change in Marital Relationships." *Sociological Review* 47 (4): 794–820.
Berger, Peter, and Hansfried Kellner. 1964. "Marriage and the Construction of Reality: An Exercise in the Microsociology of Knowledge." *Diogenes* 12 (46): 1–24.
Bergström, Marie. 2019. *Les nouvelles lois de l'amour. Sexualité, couple et rencontres au temps du numérique*. Paris: La Découverte.
Bernard, Jessie. 1972. *The Future of Marriage*. New York: World Publishing Times Mirror.
Bernstein, Basil. 1961. "Social Class and Linguistic Development: A Theory of Social Learning." In *Education, Economy, and Society*, edited by A. H. Halsey, Jean Floud, and C. Arnold Anderson, 288–314. Glencoe: The Free Press.
Bjornholt, Margunn, and Gunhild R. Farstad. 2012. "'Am I rambling?' On the Advantages of Interviewing Couples Together." *Qualitative Research* 14 (1): 3–19. https://doi.org/10.1177/1468794112459671.
Björnberg, Ulla, and Anna-Karin Kollind. 2005. *Individualism and Families: Equality, Autonomy and Togetherness*. London: Routledge. https://doi.org/10.4324/9780203639535.
Blood, Robert O., and Donald M. Wolfe. 1960. *Husbands and Wives*. Glencoe: The Free Press.
Bourdieu, Pierre. 1962. "Célibat et condition paysanne." *Etudes rurales* 5/6: 32–135.

Bourdieu, Pierre, and Jean-Claude Passeron. (1970) 1977. *Reproduction in Education, Society, and Culture*. Translated by Richard Nice. London: Sage Publications.

Bourdieu, Pierre, and Jean-Claude Passeron. (1964) 1979. *The Inheritors: French Students and their Relation to Culture*. Translated by Richard Nice. Chicago: University of Chicago Press.

Bourdieu, Pierre, and Monique de Saint Martin. 1978. "Le patronat." *Actes de la recherche en sciences sociales* 20/21: 3–82.

Bourdieu, Pierre. (1972) 1990. *The Logic of Practice*. Cambridge, UK: Polity Press.

Bozon, Michel. 2001. "Sexualité et conjugalité." In *La dialectique des rapports hommes-femmes*, edited by Thierry Blöss, 239–259. Paris: PUF.

Bradshaw, Jonathan, ed. 2016. *The Well-being of Children in the UK*. Bristol, UK: Policy Press.

Buber, Martin. (1923) 1970. *I and Thou*. Translated by Walter Kaufmann. New York: Scribner and Sons.

Budgeon, Shelley, and Sasha Roseneil. 2004. "Beyond the Conventional Family." *Current Sociology* 52 (2): 127–134.

Burgess, Ernest, and Harvey Locke. 1960. *The Family: From Institution to Companionship*. New York: The American Book Company.

Burkart, Günter, and Martin Kohli. 1992. *Liebe, Ehe, Elternschaft. Die Zukunft der Familie*. Munich: R. Piper GmbH & Co.

Cantor, Muriel G. 1988. "Jessie Bernard, An Appreciation." *Gender and Society* 2 (3): 264–270.

Carter, Julia. 2012. "What is Commitment? Women's Accounts of Intimate Attachment." *Families, Relationships and Societies* 1 (2): 137–153. https://doi.org/10.1332/204674312X645484.

Carter, Julia, and Simon Duncan. 2018. *Reinventing Couples: Tradition, Agency and Bricolage*. London: Palgrave MacMillan.

Castrén, Anna-Maija, and Kaisa Ketovici. 2015. "Studying the Complex Dynamics of Family Relationships: A Figurational Approach." *Sociological Research Online* 20 (1): 108–121.

Castrén, Anna-Maija, and Eric Widmer. (2015). "Insiders and Outsiders in Stepfamilies: Adults' and Children's Views on Family Boundaries." *Current Sociology* 63 (1): 35–56.

Castrén, Anna-Maija. 2018. "Becoming 'Us': Marital Name, Gender, and Agentic Work in Transition to Marriage." *Journal of Marriage and the Family* 81 (1): 248–263. https://doi.org/10.1111/jomf.12519.

Charle, Christophe. 1984. "Le beau mariage d'Emile Durkheim." *Actes de la Recherche en sciences sociales* 55: 45–49.

Charles, Nickie. 2014. "'Animals Just Ove You as You Are': Experiencing Kinship Across the Species Barrier." *Sociology* 48 (4): 715–730.

Chopin, Kate. (1894) 2002. "The Story of an Hour." In *Complete Novels and Stories*, edited by Kate Chopin. New York: Library of America Press.

Clair, Isabelle. 2007. "Dire à deux le ménage." In *L'inégalité ménagère*, edited by François de Singly, 179–223. Paris: Armand Colin.

Coltrane, Scott. 1989. "Household Labor and the Routine Production of Gender." *Social Problems* 36 (5): 473–490.

Connell, Raewyn. 1995. *Masculinities*. Cambridge UK: Polity Press.

Cooper, David. 1971. *The Death of the Family*. New York: Penguin Books.

Courduriès, Jérôme. 2017. "Nommer son enfant lorsqu'on est deux parents du même sexe." *Clio. Femmes, Genre, Histoire* 45 (1): 151–169. https://doi.org/10.4000/clio.13533.
Déchaux, Jean-Hughes. 2014. "Consecrating the Child: Perspectives on a Contemporary Passion." *Revue Française de Sociologie* 55 (3): 537–561.
Delphy, Christine. 1974. "Mariage et divorce: l'impasse à double face." *Les Temps Modernes* 333–334: 128–146.
Delphy, Christine, and Diana Leonard. 1992. *Familiar Exploitation: A New Analysis of Marriage in Contemporary Western Societies*. Cambridge, UK: Polity Press.
Demonceaux, Sophie. 2014. "S'aimer à l'heure du numérique : la relation conjugale à l'heure de l'hyperconnectivité." *Sociologie et Sociétés* XLVI (1): 125–144.
Descoutures, Virginie, Marie Digoix, Eric Fassin, and Wilfried Rault. 2008. *Mariages et homosexualités dans le monde: L'arrangement des normes familiales*. Paris: Autrement.
Descoutures, Virginie. 2010. *Les mères lesbiennes*. Paris: PUF.
Deutsch, Francine M., and Ruth A. Gaunt. 2020. *Creating Equality at Home: How 25 Couples around the World Share Housework and Childcare*. Cambridge, UK: Cambridge University Press.
Donovan, Catherine, Brian Heaphy, and Jeffrey Weeks. 2001. *Same Sex Intimacies: Families of Choice and Other Life Experiments*. London: Routledge. https://doi.org/10.4324/9780203167168.
Duncan, Simon. 2011. "Personal Life, Pragmatism and Bricolage." *Sociological Review Online* 16 (4): 129–140. https://doi.org/10.5153/sro.2537.
Duncan, Simon, and Julia Carter. 2017. "Wedding Paradoxes: Individualized Conformity and the 'Perfect Day'." *The Sociological Review* 65 (1): 3–20.
Durkheim, Emile. (1898) 1973. "Individualism and the Intellectuals." In *Morality and Society, Selected Writings*, edited by Robert Bellah, 43–57. Translated by Mark Traugott. Chicago: University of Chicago Press.
Durkheim, Emile. (1888) 1978a. "Introduction to the Sociology of the Family." In *Emile Durkheim on Institutional Analyses*, edited and translated by M. Traugott, 205–228. Chicago: University of Chicago Press.
Durkheim, Emile. (1921) 1978b. "The Conjugal Family." In *Emile Durkheim on Institutional Analyses*, edited and translated by M. Traugott, 229–239. Chicago: University of Chicago Press.
Durkheim, Emile. (1906) 1978c. Divorce by Mutual Consent. In *Emile Durkheim on Institutional Analyses*, edited and translated by M. Traugott, 240–252. Chicago: University of Chicago Press.
Durkheim, Emile. (1893) 1984. *The Division of Labor in Society*. Translated by W.D. Halls. Glencoe: The Free Press.
Durkheim, Emile. (1897) 2007. *On Suicide*. Translated by Robin Buss. London: Penguin Classics.
Edwards, Rosalind, and Val Gillies. 2012. "Farewell to Family? Notes on an Argument for Retaining the Concept." *Families, Relationships and Societies* 1 (1): 63–69. https://doi.org/10.1332/204674312x633162.
Edwards, Rosalind, Jane Ribbens McCarthy, and Val Gillies. 2012. "The Politics of Concepts: Family and its (Putative) Replacements." *The British Journal of Sociology* 63 (4): 730–746. https://doi.org/10.1111/j.1468-4446.2012.01434.x.
Elias, Norbert. (1987) 1991. *The Society of Individuals*. Translated by Edmund Jephcott. Oxford: Basil Blackwell.

Elias, Norbert. (1980) 1998. "The Civilizing of Parents." In *The Norbert Elias Reader: A Biographical Selection*, edited by Johan Goudsblom and Stephen Mennell, 189–211. Translated by Robert van Krieken. Malden, MA: Blackwell.
Esping-Andersen, Gost. 1990. *The Three Worlds of Welfare Capitalism*. Cambridge, UK: Polity Press.
Finch, Janet. 2007. "Displaying Families." *Sociology* 41 (1): 65–81. https://doi.org/10.1177/0038038507072284.
Giddens, Anthony. 1984. *The Constitution of Society*. Cambridge, UK: Polity Press.
Giddens, Anthony. 1991. *Modernity and Self-Identity: Self and Society in the Late Modern Age*. Redwood City: Stanford University Press.
Giddens, Anthony. 1992. *The Transformation of Intimacy: Sexuality, Love and Eroticism in Modern Societies*. Cambridge, UK: Polity Press.
Gilding, Michael. 2010. "Reflexivity Over and Above Convention: The New Orthodoxy in the Sociology of Personal Life, Formerly Sociology of the Family." *The British Journal of Sociology* 61 (4): 757–777. https://doi.org/10.1111/j.1468-4446.2010.01340.x.
Giraud, Christophe. 2017. *L'amour réaliste. La nouvelle expérience amoureuse des jeunes femmes*. Paris: A. Colin.
Goss, Robert. 1997. *Our Families, Our Values: Snapshots of Queer Kinship*. Binghampton: Harrington Park Press.
Gotman, Anne. 2017. *Pas d'enfant. La volonté de ne pas engendrer*. Paris: Éditions de la Maison des sciences de l'homme.
Guerrand, Roger-Henri, and Francis Ronsin. 1990. *Le sexe apprivoisé. Jeanne Humbert et la lutte pour le contrôle des naissances*. Paris: La Découverte.
Gullestad, Marianne. 1995. "En Norvège, 'être utile' ou 'se trouver.'" In *La famille en Europe. Parenté et perpétuation familiale*, edited by Marianne Gullestad and Martine Segalen, 221–236. Paris: La Découverte.
Gullestad, Marianne. 1996. *Everyday Life Philosophers: Modernity, Morality, and Autobiography in Norway*. Oslo: Scandinavian University Press.
Hays, Sharon. 1996. *The Cultural Contradictions of Motherhood*. New Haven: Yale University Press.
Holden, Karen C., and Pamela J. Smock. 1991. "The Economic Cost of Marital Dissolution: Why do Women Bear a Disproportionate Cost?" *Annual Review of Sociology* 17: 51–78. https://doi.org/10.1146/annurev.so.17.080191.000411.
Honneth, Axel. (1992) 1995. *The Struggle for Recognition: The Moral Grammar of Social Conflicts*. Translated by Joel Anderson. Cambridge, MA: MIT Press.
Hislop, Jenny. 2007. "A Bed of Roses or a Bed of Thorns? Negotiating the Couple Relationship through Sleep." *Sociological Research Online* 12 (5): 146–158.http://www.socresonline.org.uk/12/5/2.html.
Hoschschild, Arlie, with Anne Machung. 1989. *The Second Shift: Working Parents and the Revolution at Home*. New York: Viking Penguin.
Ibsen, Henrick. (1879) 2008. *A Doll's House*. The Floating Press.
Illouz, Eva. 2012. *Why Love Hurts: A Sociological Explanation*. Cambridge, UK: Polity Press.
Illouz, Eva. 2019. *The End of Love: A Sociology of Negative Relations*. Oxford: Oxford University Press.
Jamieson, Lynn. 1999. I"ntimacy Transformed? A Critical Look at the 'Pure Relationship'." *Sociology* 33 (3): 477–494.

Johnson, Miriam M. 1993. "Functionalism and Feminism: Is Estrangement Necessary?" In *Theory on Gender, Feminism on Theory*, edited by Paula England, 115–130. New York: Aldine de Gruyter.
Kalmijn, Matthijs, and Anne-Rigt Poortman. 2006. "His or Her divorce? The Gendered Nature of Divorce and its Determinants." *European Sociological Review* 22 (2): 201–214.
Kant, Emmanuel. (1784) 1996. "An Answer to the Question: What is Enlightenment?" In *Practical Philosophy*, translated and edited by Mary J. Gregor, 11–22. Cambridge, UK: Cambridge University Press.
Kaufmann, Jean-Claude. 1992. *La trame conjugale. Analyse du couple par son linge*. Paris: Nathan.
Kaufmann, Jean-Claude. 2015. *Un lit pour deux. La tendre guerre*. Paris: JC Lattès.
Kaufmann, Jean-Claude. (2005) 2010. *The Meaning of Cooking*. Translated by David Macey. Cambridge, UK: Polity Press.
Keller, Heidi, and Bettina Lamm. 2005. "Parenting as the Expression of Sociological Time: The Case of German Individualization." *International Journal of Behavorial Development* 29 (3): 238–246.
Kemmer, Debbie, A. S. Anderson, and David W. Marshall. 2002. "Living Together and Eating Together: Changes in Food Choice and Eating Habits during the Transition from Single to Married/Cohabiting." *The Sociological Review* 46 (1): 48–72. https://doi.org/10.1111/1467-954X.00089.
Lamanna, Mary Ann. 2002. *Emile Durkheim on the Family*. Thousand Oaks: Sage Publications.
Lasch, Christopher. 1977. *Haven in a Heartless World: The Family Besieged*. New York: Basic Books.
Lasch, Christopher. 1997. *Women and the Common Life: Love, Marriage and Feminism*. New York: W.W. Norton.
Laslett, Peter. 1972. *Household and Family in Past Time*. Cambridge, UK: Cambridge University Press.
Laslett, Peter. 1988. "Family, Kinship and Collectivity as Systems of Support in Preindustrial Europe: A Consideration of the 'Nuclear-Hardship' Hypothesis." *Continuity and Change* 3 (2): 153–175.
Le Bihan-Youinou, Blandine, and Claude Martin, eds. 2008. *Concilier vie familiale et vie professionnelle en Europe*. Rennes: Presses de l'Ecole des Hautes Etudes en Santé Publique.
Leeuw, Suzanne de, Matthjis Kalmijn, and Ruben Gaalen. 2018. "The Intergenerational Transmission of Educational Attainment among Non-Residential Fathers and their Children." *Research in Social Stratification and Mobility* 55, 40–50.
Lennon, Mary, and Sarah Rosenfield. 1994. "Relative Fairness and the Division of Housework: The Importance of Options." *American Journal of Sociology* 100 (2): 506–531.
Le Play, Frédéric. (1871) 1982. *Frédéric Le Play on Family, Work, and Social Change*. Edited and Translated by Caroline B. Silver. Chicago: University of Chicago Press.
Levin, Irene. 2004. "Living Apart Together: A New Family Form." *Current Sociology* 52 (2): 223–240.
Lewis, Jane. 1992. "Gender and the Development of Welfare Regimes." *Journal of European Social Policy* 2 (3): 159–73.
Lewis, Jane. 1997. "Gender and Welfare Regimes: Further Thoughts." *Social Politics* 4 (2): 160–77.

Lind, Craig, and Heather Keating, eds. 2008. "Introduction: Responsible Parents and Responsible State." *Journal of Law and Society* 35 (1): 1–187. https://doi.org/10.1111/j.1467-6478.2008.00411.x.

Luhmann, Niklas. (1982) 1987. *Love as Passion: The Codification of Intimacy*. Translated by Jeremy Gaines and Doris Jones. Cambridge, MA: Harvard University Press.

Martin, Claude. 2014. *"Etre un bon parent". Une injonction contemporaine*. Rennes: Presses de l'Ecole des Hautes Etudes en Santé Publique.

Marivaux. (1732) 1998. *Le triomphe de l'amour*. Paris: Gallimard.

Marquet, Jacques. 2010a. "Des.clics@amoureux.com, ou les chats et les souris font-ils bon ménage ?" In *@mours virtuelles. Conjugalité et internet*, edited by Jacques Marquet and Christophe Janssen, 77–100. Louvain-la-Neuve: Academia Bruylant.

Marquet, Jacques. 2010b. "Couple parental—couple conjugal—multiparenté—multiparentalité. Réflexions sur la nomination des transformations de la famille contemporaine." *Recherches sociologiques et anthropologiques* XLI (2): 51–74.

Maume, David, Belinda Hewitt, and Leah Ruppanner. 2018. "Gender Equality and Restless Sleep Among Partnered Europeans." *Journal of Marriage and the Family* 80 (4): 1040–1058. https://doi.org/10.1111/jomf.12488.

Mauss, Marcel. 1969. *Oeuvres, Tome 3*. Paris: Editions de Minuit.

McHale, James, Regina Kuersten-Hogan, and Nirmala Rao. 2004. "Growing Points for Coparenting Theory and Research." *Journal of Adult Development* 11: 221–234.

Meadows, Robert, and Sara Arber. 2012. "Understanding Sleep among Couples: Gender and the Social Patterning of Sleep Maintenance among Young and Older Couples." *Longitudinal and Life Courses Studies* 3 (1): 66–79.

Michel, Andrée. 1973. *Activité professionnelle de la femme et vie conjugale*. Paris: Editions du CNRS.

Mill, John Stuart. 1869. *The Subjection of Women*. London: Longmans, Green, Reader and Dyer.

Morand, Emilie, and François de Singly. 2019. "Sociologie d'une forte proximité au chat, au chien." *Enfances Familles Générations* 32 (online). http://journals.openedition.org/efg/6445.

Morgan, David. 1996. *Family Connections*. Cambridge, UK: Polity.

Morgan, David. 2011. *Rethinking Family Practices*. London: Palgrave Macmillan.

Munoz-Dardé, Véronique. 1999. Is the Family to be Abolished Then? *Proceedings of the Aristotelian Society* (New Series) 99: 37–56.

Murray, Clare, and Susan Golombok. 2005. "Going it Alone: Solo Mothers and their Infants Conceived by Donor Insemination." *American Journal of Orthopsychiatry* 75 (2): 242–253.

Natalier, Kristin. 2003. "'I'm Not his Wife': Doing Gender and Doing Housework in the Absence of Women." *Journal of Sociology* 399 (3): 253–269.

Neruda, Pablo. 1997. *Cuadernos de Temuco 1919–20*. Barcelona: Editorial Seix Barral.

Nyman, Charlotte. 2002. "Mine, Yours or Ours? Sharing in Swedish Couples." PhD diss., Umeå University.

Nyman, Charlotte, and Lars Evertsson. 2005. "Difficultés liées à la négociation dans la recherche sur la famille: Un regard sur l'organisation financière des couples suédois." *Enfances, Familles, Générations* 2 (online). http://www.erudit.org/revue/efg/2005/v/n2/010913ar.html.

Pahl, Jan. 1997. "Our Money and My Money: What do Financial Arrangements Tell us about Relationships." Seventh Jackie Burgoyne Memorial Lecture, University of Kent at Canterbury.
Pahl, Jan. 2005. "Individualisation et modèles de gestion des finances au sein des familles." *Enfances, Familles, Générations* 2 (online). http://www.erudit.org/revue/efg/2005/v/n2/010912ar.html.
Pahl, Ray, and Liz Spencer. 2004. "Personal Communities: Not Simply Families of 'Fate' or 'Choice.'" *Current Sociology* 52 (2): 199–221.
Parsons, Talcott, and Robert Bales. 1955. *Family, Socialization and Interaction Process*. Glencoe: The Free Press.
Périvier, Hélène. 2013. "De madame Au-Foyer à madame Gagne-Miettes. État social en mutation dans une perspective franco-états-unienne." In *Travail et genre dans le monde*, edited by Margaret Maruani, 309–317. Paris: La Découverte.
Pountain, Dick, and David Robins. 2001. *Cool Rules: Anatomy of an Attitude*. London: Reaktion Books.
Power, Emma. 2008. "Furry Families: Making a Human-Dog Family through Home." *Social and Cultural Geography* 9 (5): 535–555. http://dx.doi.org/10.1080/14649360802217790.
Rapoport, Rhona, and Robert Rapoport. 1971. *Dual-Career Families*. New York: Penguin Books.
Rault, Wilfried. 2017. "Garder l'usage de son nom et le transmettre. Pratiques de la loi française de 2002 sur le double nom." *Clio. Femmes, genre, histoire* 45 (1), 129–149. https://doi.org/10.4000/clio.13526.
Ribbens McCarthy, Jane. 2012. "The Powerfull Relational Language of 'Family': Togetherness, Belonging and Personhood." *Sociological Review* 60 (1): 68–90.
Ribbens McCarthy, Jane, Rosalind Edwards, and Val Gillies. 2003. *Making Families: Moral Tales of Parenting and Step-Parenting*. London: Sociology Press.
Rippeyoung, Phyllis, and Mary Noonan. 2012. "Is Breastfeeding Truly Cost Free? Income Consequences of Breastfeeding for Women." *American Sociological Review* 77: 244–267.
Rosa, Rodrigo. 2018. "The Consequences of Gender in Homogamic Couples." *Sociology* 52 (1): 39–54. https://doi.org/10.1177/0038038516645752.
Safilios-Rothschild, Constantina. 1969. "Family Sociology or Wives' Family Sociology? A Cross-Cultural Examination of Decision-Making." *Journal of Marriage and the Family* 31 (2): 290–301.
Shorter, Edward. 1975. *The Making of the Modern Family*. New York: Basic Books.
Simmel, Georg. (1911) 1984. "The Relative and the Absolute in the Problem of the Sexes." In *On Women, Sexuality, and Love*, translated and edited by Guy Oakes, 102–132. New Haven: Yale University Press.
Simmel, Georg. (1921–1922) 1984. "On love (a fragment)." In *On Women, sexuality, and love*, translated and edited by Guy Oakes, 153–191. New Haven: Yale University Press.
Singly, François de. 1987a. "Théorie critique de l'homogamie." *L'Année sociologique* (troisième série) 37: 181–205.
Singly, François de. 1987b. *Fortune et infortune de la femme mariée*. Paris: PUF.
Singly, François de. 1993. *Sociologie de la famille contemporaine*. Paris: Nathan.
Singly, François de. 2000. *Libres ensemble. L'individualisme dans la vie commune*. Paris: Nathan.

Singly, François de. 2003. "Intimité conjugale et intimité personnelle : à la recherche d'un équilibre entre deux exigences dans les sociétés modernes avancées." *Sociologie et Sociétés* 35 (2): 79–96.
Singly, François de. 2005a. *L'individualisme est un humanisme*. La Tour d'Aigues: Editions de l'Aube.
Singly, François de. 2005b. *Le Soi, le couple et la famille*. Paris: Armand Colin.
Singly, François de. 2011. *Séparée. Vivre l'expérience de la rupture*. Paris: Armand Colin.
Singly, François de, and Elsa Ramos. 2010. "Moments communs en famille." *Ethnologie Française* 40 (1): 11–17.
Smart, Carol. 2007. *Personal Life: New Directions in Sociological Thinking*. Cambridge, UK: Polity Press.
Smart, Carol, and Beccy Shipman. 2004. "Visions in Monochrome: Families, Marriage and the Individualization Thesis." *The British Journal of Sociology* 55 (4): 491–509.
Spigel, Lynn. 1992. *Make Room for TV: Television and the Family Ideal in Postwar America*. Chicago: University of Chicago Press.
Stacey, Judith, and Barrie Thorne. 1985. "The Missing Feminist Revolution in Sociology." *Social Problems* 32 (4): 301–316.
Stoczkowski, Wictor. 2019. *La science sociale comme vision du monde. Emile Durkheim et le mirage du salut*. Paris: Gallimard.
Stoilova, Mariya, Sasha Roseneil, Julia Carter, Simon Duncan, and Miranda Philipps. 2017. "Constructions, Reconstructions and Deconstructions of 'Family' amongst People who Live Apart Together (LATs)." *The British Journal of Sociology* 68 (1): 78–96.
Stopes, Marie. 1918. *Married Love: A New Contribution to the Solution of Sex Difficulties*. London: A. C. Fifield.
Taylor, Charles. 1989. *The Sources of the Self: The Making of the Modern Identity*. Cambridge, MA: Harvard University Press.
Tönnies, Ferdinand. (1887) 2001. *Community and Civil Society*. Translated by Jose Harris and Margaret Hollis. Cambridge, UK: Cambridge University Press.
Trellu, Hélène. 2007. "Recompositions et résistances de la masculinité et de la féminité. De la paternité et de la maternité à l'épreuve du congé parental pris par les hommes en France." *Recherches sociologiques et anthropologiques* XXXVIII (2): 123–141.
Turkle, Sherry. 2012. *Alone Together*. New York: Basic Books.
UN (United Nations). 1989. *Convention on the Rights of the Child*. https://www.ohchr.org/en/professionalinterest/pages/crc.aspx.
Vannoy-Hiller, Dana, and William Philliber. 1989. *Equal Partners: Successful Women in Marriage*. Newbury Park: Sage Publications.
Venn, Susan, Sara Arber, Robert Meadows, and Jenny Hislop. 2008. "The Fourth Shift: Exploring the Gendered Nature of Sleep Disruption among Couples with Children." *The British Journal of Sociology* 59 (1): 79–98.
Wagner, Peter. 1993. *A Sociology of Modernity: Liberty and Discipline*. London: Routledge.
Wall, Karin, and Mafalda Leitão. 2016. "Fathers on Leave Alone in Portugal: Lived Experiences and Impact of Forerunner Fathers." In *Comparative Perspectives on Work-Life Balance and Gender Equality: Fathers on Leave Alone*, edited by Margaret O'Brien and Karin Wall, 45–67. Cham: Springer.

Widmer, Éric, Jean Kellerhals, and René Lévy. 2004. "Quelle pluralisation des relations familiales ?" *Revue Française de Sociologie* 45 (1): 37–67.
Young, Michael, and Peter Willmott. 1957. *Family and Kinship in East London.* London: Routledge and Kegan Paul.
Zelizer, Viviana, 1985. *Pricing the Priceless Child: The Changing Social Value of Children.* Princeton: Princeton University Press.

CHAPTER 3

Gender, Social Class, and Family Relations in Different Life Stages in Europe

Bernardo Coelho, Diana Maciel, and Anália Torres

INTRODUCTION

This chapter sets out to characterise family and gender relations at different life stages and in different geographical contexts.[1,2] We argue that, for a better understanding of family relations, it is fundamental not only to address social and cultural contexts but also to have a gender lens. This analytical strategy is developed in two steps. Firstly, mapping and characterising the differences and similarities between women and men in different life stages and European countries, concerning several dimensions: family, structural living conditions, and unpaid and paid work. Secondly, identifying income determinants, and clarifying how inequalities between men and women are also translated into social classes.

Our theoretical framework conceptualises inequalities as "inequalities in distribution and access to all kinds of socially valued resources: economic resources (...) but also power, education, culture, prestige"[3] (Almeida 2013,

---

B. Coelho (✉) · D. Maciel · A. Torres
Institute of Social and Political Sciences, University of Lisbon (ISCSP-ULisboa), Interdisciplinary Center for Gender Studies (CIEG-ULisboa), Campus Universitário Do Alto Da Ajuda, Lisbon, Portugal
e-mail: bmcoelho@iscsp.ulisboa.pt

D. Maciel
e-mail: dmaciel@iscsp.ulisboa.pt

A. Torres
e-mail: atorres@iscsp.ulisboa.pt

© The Author(s), under exclusive license to Springer Nature Switzerland AG 2021
A.-M. Castrén et al. (eds.), *The Palgrave Handbook of Family Sociology in Europe*, https://doi.org/10.1007/978-3-030-73306-3_3

25). Gender equality would therefore be reflected in the symmetry between individuals on the basis of their gender identity or sexual orientation, and in their access to resources, power, and rights.

Moreover, gender inequality refers to the material and symbolic disadvantages that women experience in relation to men (Connell 1987). These are more frequent and more significant although gender inequalities can also sometimes create disadvantages for men. That is the case of men who have occupations that tend to be more hazardous, or when they are incited to adopt deviant and violent behaviours; or even when institutional and cultural barriers do not recognise them as caregivers and homemakers. In addition, gender inequalities also refer to gender identities that depart from the traditional binary vision of male and female.

Gender must also be considered not as a property of individuals but something that is "done to us" and assigned since birth, and that we gradually construct and negotiate over the life course, in different social interactions (Holmes 2007). This performative vision of gender underlines the possibility of agency, i.e. the ability to act on a reality that can be felt as constrictive, and to combat deterministic logic—what is done can also be undone (Richardson and Robison 2008, 9–17). In order to understand how gender relations are characterised and developed, four analytical dimensions are taken into account: the **structural** dimension, from which it is assessed how being a woman or a man has differentiated effects in contexts that are more or less privileged or more or less deprived in terms of economic or cultural resources; the **institutional** dimension, which refers—on the one hand—to the effects that the welfare state may have on the life courses of women and men, through policies of redistribution, education systems, and gender equality policies; and on the other hand, it also considers the public and private institutions and organisation's specific norms, and the way those norms contribute for the reproduction of gender regimes; the **economic and social** dimension, which integrates economic and social dynamics, such as the more recent effects of globalisation, de-industrialisation, the shift towards the service sector, and specific situations such as the economic and financial crisis, that have an impact on how gender equality is experienced; and the **symbolic and cultural** dimension that sets out to assess the effect of gender values and stereotypes, and how generational contexts also influence individual life courses and the construction of gender identities.

To understand how gender relations, family, and work are currently interconnected, we must also take into account changes occurring in the second half of the twentieth century. In fact, in this period, female participation in the labour market increased significantly leading to a clear XXI century trend of dual-earner couples in most Western European countries. This dynamic—towards women's economic empowerment and less economic dependency on men—was even promoted by the European Union promulgating that the female employment rate should reach 60% by the year 2010 (Smith and Villa 2010).

These changes were accompanied with a European Commission policy agenda addressing work-life balance issues. Initially, these policies had a primarily social character, with actions that sought equal opportunities for men and women. In the late 1990s, the focus shifted to increasing female activity, with the promotion of part-time employment, or parental leave. These options did not correspond to a genuine policy promoting gender equality, a concern that only appears on the agenda more systematically in Scandinavian countries (Lewis 2009).

The objective of increasing female activity rates stems from the fact that more women in the labour market results both in a greater gross domestic product, and in an additional guarantee for social security sustainability. These occur, not only because of women's integration in the labour market, but also through the introduction of new activities and the formalisation of care, a work traditionally done by women that became professionalised, paid and taxed. In addition, work-life balance policies are also considered as a potential solution to other problems. In particular, they are a means of dealing with an ageing population and combating falling birth rates, supporting greater female involvement in the labour market (Lewis 2009).

However, the increase of female activity rate also had contradictory and even penalising effects in many countries (Anxo et al. 2007; Crompton 2006). On the one hand, the main responsibility for unpaid work remains with women and working mothers. Men did not increase their participation in the domestic sphere and in family care to the same extent that women became part of the labour market. On the other hand, the labour market has undergone profound changes, becoming flexible and competitive, with precarious jobs and short-term contracts. As a result, leaving the labour market or even reducing participation therein, for example, to have children, may have irreversible negative consequences for women in terms of financial and career advancement (Lewis 2009). These consequences, once anticipated by women, partially explain the falling of birth rates and an ageing population (Gregory and Milner 2009).

Moreover, the policies defined in the European framework, on the other hand, have problems of application in different countries. They are dependent not only on the cultural contexts in which they are implemented—more or less conservative with regard to gender equality (Cunha and Atalaia 2019), whether parenting is viewed as a private problem or not—and they are subject to changes in government that can translate into changes in ideological and political guidelines.

But it seems clear that, in the vast majority of EU countries, it can be concluded that there is a fundamental tension between policies that aim to promote the participation of women in the labour market, and the expectation that they generally remain responsible for domestic tasks and family care. This tension is certainly one of the factors that contribute to the persistent inequalities between women and men.

Policies to promote work-life balance do not fully meet their objectives when they do not take gender inequalities into account. This type of policies has been developed more as a way of easing the burden of women's double shifts, and less as a way of increasing men's participation in family care and household chores. Therefore, there is a tension in policies that aim to promote the participation of women in the labour market, and the expectation that they will remain primarily responsible for unpaid work.

The underlying problem in the work-life balance policies in the majority of countries is that gender equality has been a secondary objective or has not even been mentioned. Hence the importance of a gender lens when analysing family relations and the articulation between paid and unpaid work.

Gender affects both women and men according to their life stages, shaping social interactions, power relations, and material living conditions, educational and occupational opportunities, the working conditions or even life after work (Arber et al. 2003; Torres et al. 2007; Venn et al. 2011). Therefore, it becomes fundamental to analyse and assess how gender is experienced in different stages of life: youth (from 15 to 29 years), covering the end of the school trajectory and entry into the labour market; "rush hour of life" (from 30 to 49 years), main phase of family, parental, and professional investment, which includes the management of tensions between family and work demands, investment in lifelong learning, care for descendants, but also with other dependents, such as elderly (ascending) parents; and late working life stage (from 50 to 65 years), although work remains central to the lives of most people, there is already a significant fall in employability, both for men and women.[4]

To incorporate a cross-country comparison analysis, we opted for an approach that identifies, at each life stage and in each major domain analysed, the most relevant indicators for European Union countries, and for the EU 27 countries average. For a more systematic and precise focus, we selected eight countries (Portugal, Czech Republic, Poland, Germany, France, Sweden, Spain, UK). The country selection reflects the typology of welfare models initially developed by Esping-Andersen (1990), and deepened, reformulated and criticised by other authors (e.g. Ferrera 1996; Torres et al. 1999; Lewis 2009): Germany and France representing the continental model, the UK as an example of the liberal model, Norway and Sweden as examples of the Nordic model, Spain and Portugal as representatives of the southern European model, and the Czech Republic and Poland as previous countries of socialist regimes and more recently integrated into the European Union.

This analytical strategy considers the implications of social policies for structuring the living conditions of men and women, and gender (inequalities), allowing to identify potential institutional factors and context that may contribute to explain the inequalities found.

The following analysis is based on cross-national data from several databases: *European Social Survey* (ESS), and *International Social Survey Programme* (ISSP), *European Working Conditions Survey* (EWCS), *Structure of Earnings Survey* (SES), and the *Labour Force Survey*.

Youth, Gender, Structural Living Conditions and Family

Leaving parents' homes is an important indicator for youth autonomy, and a fundamental step towards adulthood (Nico 2014). Thus, it is imperative to look at potential differences in the European context between young women and men in their process towards independence, and the creation of their own families.

In several countries in Europe, young women and men between 15 and 29 still live in their parents' homes and only a small percentage already live in a conjugal relationship, but there are important gender and country differences to be stressed (Torres et al. 2018). Countries in southern and eastern Europe have the highest values for young people still living in their parents' homes, in contrast with northern European countries. In Portugal, for example, more than half of all men (66.8%) and women (53.3%), aged 15–29, still live in their parents' homes. Taking into account Portuguese and Swedish cases, this difference becomes clearer; Portuguese women leave home 8.6 years later than Swedish women, and Portuguese men 10 years later than Swedish men (Torres et al. 2018).

A series of factors are clearly at play here. Some authors point to what they call "familyism" or other cultural issues: gender cultures, norms and regimes, as well as a policy and institutional settings, assigning women to unpaid work (even when they are in the labour market). However, this is not only a Southern European issue. On the contrary, data shows (Fig. 3.1) a divisive line among European countries that seems to be of financial nature. In fact, there is a strong correlation between average hourly wages and the age of leaving the parental home: the lower the average hourly wage earned by young people, the later men and women leave their parents' homes (Slovakia or Bulgaria). Conversely, countries where young men and women earn higher wages are also those where they take steps to assert their independence at an earlier age (Denmark or Finland).

Structural constraints, determined either by economic resources or the conditions for labour market integration, are also crucial factors in the process of gaining independence, insofar as the transition to adulthood and leaving the parental home entails a certain degree of financial autonomy and stability. Therefore, unstable forms of labour market integration, flexible and precarious employment arrangements, low pay, and unemployment are factors that constrain the possibilities available to women and men for planning and "choosing" their life projects (Torres et al. 2018).

Institutional contexts also play an important role. Northern European countries, especially in Scandinavia, have widely accessible study grant systems and affordable halls of residence for young people who are studying, as well as other types of measures and public incentive policies that have for many years helped young people attain autonomy regarding where they live (Karamessini 2014; Rubery 2014; Ferreira 2014; Nico 2014).

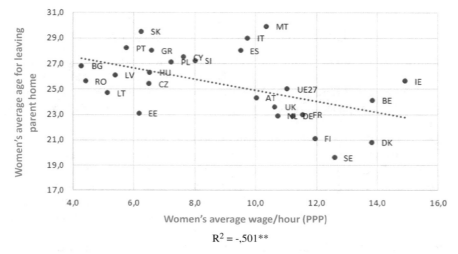

Fig. 3.1 Correlation between average hourly wage in PPP and average age of leaving parents' home (women aged 15–29), 2015 (*Source* Eurostat, Structure of Earnings Survey (SES), 2015; European Union Labour Force Survey, 2015)
Note PPP, Purchasing Power Parity, is an artificial monetary unit used to assess the amount of goods and services that wages can buy in each country

Therefore, any explanation of the inequality within Europe as to the age at which young people leave home entails identifying a different set of factors related more closely to issues that are economic, structural, or institutional in character, rather than exclusively cultural.

In the EU27 member states, girls leave parents' homes earlier than boys, more young women than men live in a conjugal relationship (Torres et al. 2018), and women tend traditionally to be socialised to conform to the idea that they are natural carers, acquiring skills and abilities needed to care for themselves and for their family and home. So, we may ask, what happens within the realm of unpaid work among young women and men?

Based on an analysis of ISSP (International Social Survey Programme—Family and Changing Gender Roles, Round 4, 2012) data,[5] on average weekly hours of unpaid work, it is found that women in employment and living with their spouse spend more hours than men in the same circumstances on caring for their home and family (Torres et al. 2018).

Poland is the country where, on average, young women spend more time per week on housework (21 hours). The gap between women and men (aged 15–29) in hours spent on housework is widest in Spain and Portugal. In both countries, women spend 7 hours more than men on this form of unpaid work. In contrast, there is no disparity at all in Finland, while France shows the second smallest disparity: 1 hours a week (Torres et al. 2018).

Among those considered in the analysis, Spain is the country where women spend the most time on family care and is also the country with the widest disparity between women and men: women spend 27 hours a week more than men. In Portugal, women aged 15–29, living in a conjugal relationship, spend almost twice as long as men on housework and looking after the family. On the one hand, women spend 16 hours on housework and men only 9 hours. On the other hand, women invest another 16 hours in looking after their families, and men only 8 hours. In total, women spend 32 hours a week on unpaid work, and men only 17 hours (Fig. 3.2).

So as early as this stage in life, women start to accumulate inequalities by being overburdened with caring responsibilities, encouraged, undoubtedly, by the persisting idea that women are natural carers, as well as the belief that caregiving is within the female domain. In all the countries analysed for looking after family members, the gender gap is greater than for housework, except in Sweden, where the average time spent looking after the family is identical to that spent on housework; and in the Czech Republic, where both young women and young men spend less time caring for the family than on housework.

In the overwhelming majority of countries, young women consistently earn less than young men, as may be seen in Fig. 3.3. In Europe, the average hourly wage for women at this life stage is lower than for men. The exceptions are Netherlands and Malta, where the average hourly wage for women is higher, and also Belgium, Greece, and Romania, where the same income indicator is equal to that for men. Moreover, in general, in the European context, the average hourly wage for younger women and men is lower than for the rest of the working population (Torres et al. 2018).

At this stage of life, Portuguese men and women, such as people from Latvia, Lithuania and Bulgaria, are among the lowest paid in Europe as average wages in purchasing power parity (PPP) are around half the EU27 average.

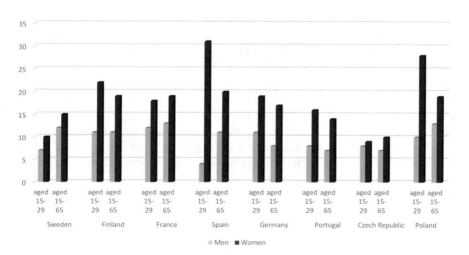

Fig. 3.2 Average hours spent on family care, by sex, age and country, 2012

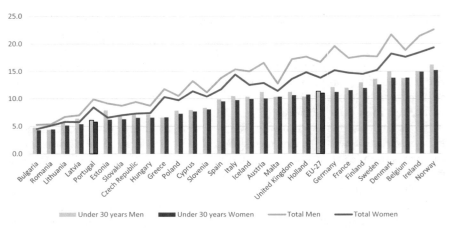

Fig. 3.3 Average hourly wage, in PPP, by country and sex (Euros), 2014 (*Source* Eurostat, Structure of Earnings Survey, 2014)
Note The average hourly wage is defined as gross earnings in the reference month, divided by the number of hours paid in the same period. The average hourly wage includes all employees of companies with more than ten employees

In Portugal, men under thirty earn per hour 6.1€ and in Bulgaria 5.3€, and women earn 5.8€ and 4.5€, respectively; while the average hourly wage (PPP) in the EU27 is 11.4€ for men, and 11.1€ for women.

Moreover, we found that women tend to have higher qualifications than men, but are consistently paid less. In the EU27, there are more women than men aged 29 or less with higher education credentials, and this difference is particularly significant in Portugal (22.8% of women compared to 13.4% of men) (Torres et al. 2018).

This mismatch between qualifications and wages—penalising women—may be explained by the combination of four main powerful obstacles constituting a specific gender order (Connell 2002) in the labour market.

First, symbolic and material undervaluation of what women do, especially in production and in the public domain, cutting across all occupations; second, the continued existence of "glass ceilings" a term illustrating a vertical segregation, limiting women's access to positions of power and leadership; third, horizontal segregation, i.e. the fact that women are represented in larger numbers in areas that are generally poorly paid at a level equivalent to the minimum wage; and fourth, conservatism and persisting stereotypes in the labour market, that continue to see women as natural carers, and regard them as less available for professional work.

Rush Hour of Life: Between Work and Family

The issue of work-life balance is particularly relevant at the rush hour of life, when men and women invest heavily and simultaneously in their family and professional lives, generating conflicting pressures which are hard to resolve. So, in this context, we need to understand what forms of work-family balance are most frequent in Europe at this life stage: the male breadwinner model, the dual part-time employment model, or the dual full-time employment model? And how are maternity and paternity reconciled with professional life? What impact do the different models have on gender equality?

In order to answer these questions, we analyse the employment rate of adults with and without children under the age of six, and the distribution of male and female workers by type of household. We take the Portuguese case as an example to compare with EU27 as it can be considered an extreme example. Lastly, we will observe, from a gender perspective, in a selected group of EU countries, how men and women use their time.

There is a high employment rate for mothers with children under six, throughout Europe. In most EU27 countries, the employment rate is high for women aged 25–49 with children under six, at over 60% (Fig. 3.4). In this European scenario, Portugal has the highest adult employment rate for women with children under six, followed by Scandinavian countries such as Denmark and Sweden, eastern countries such as Slovenia and Lithuania, and continental countries such as Netherlands and Austria. But it should be stressed that the labour market situations are not similar in all cases because countries, such as Netherlands and Austria, have considerable proportions of women working part-time (71.5 and 49.8%), which is not comparable with the situations in Portugal (9.6%), Slovenia (10.5%) or Lithuania (7.5%).

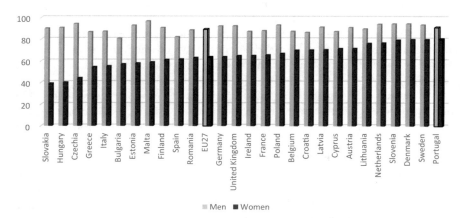

Fig. 3.4 Employment rate of adults with children aged under six years, from 25 to 49 years, by country and sex, 2015 (%) (*Source* Eurostat, European Union Labour Force Survey; *Note* Data unavailable for Norway and Iceland)

However, we should note that mothers often find themselves in a double bind. In countries where female part-time work predominates as a solution for reconciling work and family, disadvantages may result for women. Firstly, part-time contracts often result on long hours—sometimes thirty per week—and low-paid wages; secondly, male contribution in unpaid work also tends to be very small. In countries where mothers work full-time, but where caring and chores are not equally shared and policies are insufficient to encourage equality in unpaid work, mothers also tend to accumulate disadvantages (Torres et al. 2012). In these contexts, women are penalised both by the pay gap and the overburden; in other words, women's professional abilities and caring responsibilities are both devalued.

In most countries, the households of female and male workers aged 30–49, living in a conjugal relationship, are predominantly made up of both members of the couple working full-time. The countries where this situation is most frequent are Slovakia (92.3%), Hungary (91.1%), and Portugal (87.8%) (Fig. 3.5). In the EU27, the average figure for this type of household is 63.3%. The male breadwinner model is limited to 9.6% of European households and is less frequent than the situation where the man works full-time and the woman part-time (21.1%). In Netherlands and Austria, there are more households where men work full-time and women part-time (53.8 and 50.8%) than households where both members of the couple work full-time (26.7 and 37.3%, respectively).

With women's increased participation in the employment market, dual-earner couples have become the norm in most European countries, as we have already seen. However, men have not increased their participation in the domestic and family sphere as much as women have increased theirs in the labour market. The result is that the balance of occupational and family duties is not the same for both sexes, and is, instead, an added burden on women (Perista et al. 2016; Wall et al. 2016).

Women aged 30–49 continue to spend more time each week looking after their families. The greatest difference between men and women in this regard is observable in Spain (10 hours) and the smallest in Sweden (2 hours) (Fig. 3.6).

Moreover, it is also women who spend more time on housework. The biggest difference between men and women is found in the Czech Republic and Portugal (10 hours in each), and the smallest in Poland (3 hours) (Torres et al. 2018).

The rush hour of life is the life stage at which hourly wages are the highest. This life stage is one in which women and men invest heavily in their professional lives, and it can be seen that this investment results, in European countries, in an average hourly wage which is higher in this age group than in the total employed population (irrespective of life stage) (Torres et al. 2018).

The low level of wages in Portugal—even when compared with other southern European countries—deserves a closer look. First, it is important

3 GENDER, SOCIAL CLASS, AND FAMILY RELATIONS … 55

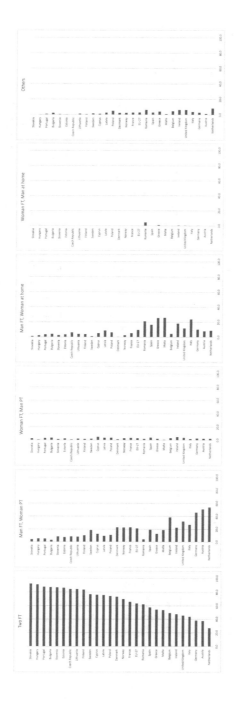

Fig. 3.5 Distribution of living in couple workers by type of household, aged 30 to 49, by country (%), 2015

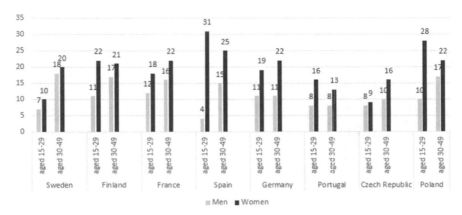

Fig. 3.6 Average hours spent on family care, from 15 to 29 years and from 30 to 49 years, by country and sex (hours), 2012

to underline low level of salaries in Portugal when compared to other European countries, as the average hourly wage, in purchasing power parity (PPP), in Portugal is 9.9€ for men and 8.6€ for women but rises to 17.2€ for men and 14.2 for women in the EU27. Moreover, and still considering the Portuguese case and the EU27 average, we may say that in both cases, male pay is always higher than that of women in all types of occupation, as we can see in Fig. 3.7. In general, the gap is wider in the EU27 than in Portugal,

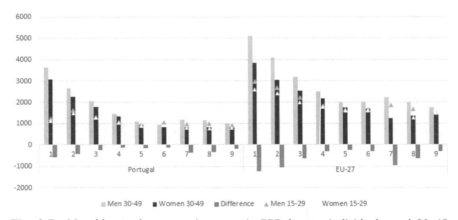

Fig. 3.7 Monthly pay, by occupation type, in PPP, by sex, individuals aged 30–49, in Portugal and EU-27, 2014 (*Source* Eurostat, Structure of Earnings Survey [2014]; *Note* 1—Managers; 2—Professionals; 3—Technicians and associate professionals; 4—Clerical support workers; 5—Service and sales workers; 6—Skilled agricultural, forestry and fishery workers; 7—Craft and related trades workers; 8—Plant and machine operators and assemblers; 9—Elementary occupations. Category 10 [Armed Forces Occupations] was excluded because there is no available data for Portugal)

above all, in senior management categories, in that of specialists in intellectual and scientific activities, and that of skilled industrial workers. In Portugal, the pay gap is smaller among clerical support workers (where women typically outnumber men) than, for example, among managers (where men typically outnumber women). In the EU27, the narrowest gap is in service and sales workers (Torres et al. 2018).

Furthermore, the low level of wages in Portugal results in creating generational inequality, insofar as women and men in the rush hour of life earn considerably more on average that younger workers (aged 15–29): from 6.1€/hour to 9.9€/hour for men (which is 3.8€/hour more); and from 5.8€/hour to 8.6€/hour in women (representing 2.8€/hour more) (Torres et al. 2018). At the rush hour of life, the pay gap in Portugal (12.9%) is narrower than the EU27 average (17.4%). If we go on to compare different life stages, we may observe that, despite heavy investment by women and men in their professional lives, in European countries, the pay gap between women and men is wider in the rush hour of life than in their youth (when they move into the labour market). Considering that Portuguese women have average hours of work very similar to those of men (Torres et al. 2018), the pay gap observed might, above all, be the consequence of horizontal gender segregation, with women tending to occupy positions in traditionally more poorly paid sectors, as well as being subject to insecure forms of employment (European Commission 2017).

Late Phase of Working Life: Women Taking Care of the Family

Despite the increase in female labour market participation and the massification of dual-earner couples, in most European countries, men aged 50–64 have not increased their participation in the domestic and family sphere to the extent that women have increased their participation in the labour market. This explains why women come off worst in reconciling their professional life with family responsibilities (Perista et al. 2016; Wall et al. 2016). Women in this age group continue to spend more time each week looking after their family. The greatest difference between men and women is observable in Spain (10 hours), and the smallest in Sweden (3 hours). Portugal has a difference between men and women of 7 hours each week, with women devoting 14 hours to looking after the family and men only 7 hours (Fig. 3.8).

Being aware that in Portugal female activity rate is for decades very high—at the same level of Nordic countries—and that there is still a very unbalanced division of care, it became significant to look closer to the Portuguese case as an example of the persistent women's overburden, particularly among older women's housework. In fact, in Europe women tend to spend more time during the week on housework than men. The largest difference between men and women occurs in Portugal (16 hours) and the smallest in France (4 hours) (Torres et al. 2018). This increase in the imbalance in unpaid work in late stage

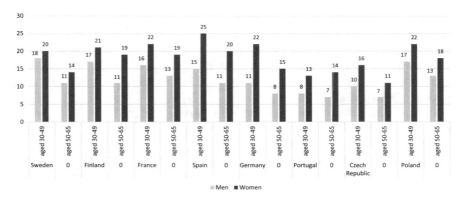

Fig. 3.8 Average hours spent on family care, by sex, age and country, 2012

working life to the detriment of women may be explained by the main activity of persons aged 50–64 in Portugal. As can be seen in Table 3.1, 20.8% of Portuguese women left the labour market to look after the home or family members, in contrast only 2.2% of men did the same move. Analysing the late stage working life, we witness a never-ending reproduction of gender roles and stereotypes, as women feel pressured to drop out of the labour force due to the demands of family, and on the opposite, most men remain in the labour force (57%).

The gendered character of housework and care is supported by other research, including the study coordinated by Wall et al. (2016), showing that women aged 45–64 spend more time on domestic tasks and care than younger women; and the study coordinated by Perista et al. (2016), stressing the widening gender gap in the 45–64 years age group (almost 3 hours a day).

When we compare the pay gap in the rush hour of life and in late stage of working life, not only does the phenomenon persist, but it also worsens. In all the countries analysed, men have higher average monthly wages than women, except in Slovenia, where women over 60 earn more than men. On

Table 3.1 Main activity in past 7 days in Portugal, aged 50–65, by sex, 2014 (%)

	Men	Women
Paid work	57.0	39.3
Education	1.5	1.2
Unemployment	9.6	10.7
Illness or permanent incapacity	8.1	8.3
Retirement	20.7	16.7
Looking after home or family members	2.2	20.8
Other	0.7	3.0
Total	100	100

Source European Social Survey (ESS), round 7

average in the EU27, it is found that the pay gap to the detriment of women stands at around 23% for people aged 50–59, and around 19% for people aged over 60. Going back, once more, to the Portuguese example because of its low waged reality, it becomes clear that besides the lower income the pay gap between men and women is wider than the EU27 average among people over 60 (30.7% compared to 18.9%), and narrower in the group aged from 50 to 59 (19.2% compared to 23.3%).

Men are better paid than women in the EU27 in all types of occupations, except personal protection and security services, and sales, where women over 60 earn more on average than men. In the EU27, the gap is generally wider for managers (where it actually increases with age). In Portugal, in both age groups, the gap is narrower among professionals and clerical support workers.

In short, in the late stage of working life, dual-earner couples continue to predominate in Europe, meaning it is essential to analyse the work-family balance from a gender perspective, clarifying and explaining that women's presence in paid work is not matched by an active male presence in unpaid work.

GENDER INEQUALITIES, INCOME DETERMINANTS, AND SOCIAL CLASSES

We have witnessed that the gender pay gap is a common feature in all life stages (Table 3.2). Therefore, the question is: What are the reasons for this gap? One of the ways to answer this question is to identify factors that may influence income determinants. Simple and multiple linear regressions identified the factors that influence monthly income, in a set of countries, for men and women over the course of life (Table 3.3).

At all stages of life, it emerges clearly that, in many of the countries analysed by two linear regressions (sex and ISCED—highest level of education), being a woman has a negative impact on monthly income as being a woman is associated with lower monthly income (Table 3.3). The exceptions are: in Poland, Sweden, Czech Republic, and the UK, in the youth group; in Sweden in the rush hour of life; and in Poland and the UK in late stage working life. The findings also show that, for all the countries considered, the higher the level of educational attainment, the higher the income of men and women—except for Spain in the youth group; and for Sweden and the UK in late stage working life.

Besides important transformations concerning family, namely the trend towards the dual-earner model, and the economic empowerment of women (both in family relations and in larger social contexts), we have been witnessing the accumulation of inequalities penalising women: from labour market integration, income and material living conditions, to the responsibility for the bulk of unpaid work. Therefore, we may ask in what way those disadvantages accumulated by women in different stages of life can suggest unequal positions in the social structure?

Table 3.2 Gender pay gap (in euros) by life stage in Portugal and UE27 (2015)

	Portugal				UE27			
	15-29 years old	30-49 years old	50-59 years old	More than 60 years old	15-29 years old	30-49 years old	50-59 years old	More than 60 years old
Managers	−82	−586	−1.406	−1.993	−372	−1.233	−2.200	−1.832
Professionals	−142	−417	−215	−167	−264	−1.058	−1.510	−1.112
Technicians and associate professionals	−3	−255	−456	−317	−214	−647	−880	−769
Clerical support workers	−20	−124	−217	−59	−71	−315	−467	−344
Service and sales workers	−38	−168	−318	−144	−36	−243	−215	68
Skilled agricultural, forestry and fishery workers	:	−118	:	:	−66	−323	−494	−366
Craft and related trades workers	−164	−364	−399	−349	−526	−955	−957	−753
Plant and machine operators and assemblers	−217	−353	−363	−204	−407	−636	−632	−299
Elementary occupations	−111	−203	−248	−119	−7	−313	−372	−178

Note Category 10 (Armed Forces Occupations) was excluded because there is no available data for Portugal
Source Eurostat, Structure of Earnings Survey (2014)

Table 3.3 Determinants of monthly income of individuals by country and age group, 2015 (Series of linear regressions, one by country)

		Portugal r	Poland r	Sweden r	Finland r	Germany r	France r	Spain r	Czech Rep. r	United Kingdom r
Youth	Sex (reference category: female)	0.013	n.s.	n.s. 0.006	0.16	0.01	0.066	0.023	n.s.	n.s.
	ISCED	0.287	0.007	0.182	0.055	0.139	0.055	n.s. 0,001	−0.004	−0.003
Rush hour	Sex (female)	0.013	0.088	n.s.	0.053	0.142	0.019	0.053	0.319	0.018
	ISCED	0.287	0.091	0.182	0.067	0.172	0.116	0.123	0.11	0.006
Late stage	Sex (female)	0.057	0.078	0.026	0.049	0.093	0.079	0.029	0.142	0.005
	ISCED	0.488	n.s.	n.s.	0.054	0.129	0.206	0.047	0.232	n.s.
			0.058						0.213	n.s.

$p \leq 0.05$
Source European Working Conditions Survey (EWCS), 2015; *Note* n.s.—relationship between variables is not statistically significant. The findings may not be statistically significant because of the small number of responses, because of invalid responses for a given variable or because there is no statistical difference; *Note 2* ISCED—highest educational level obtained

On the basis of data from the European Working Conditions Survey (EWCS), a European survey gathering information on the working population in different countries, it has been possible to identify a number of central tendencies in the distribution by social class[6] of men and women in the working population (Fig. 3.9).

In the first place, looking at the categories with greater economic and academic capital, we may conclude that, in nearly all countries, women are more highly represented than men in the group of technical and management professionals (TMP), except for France where this group accounts for 34.1% of men and 31.7% of women, and Portugal, where there is no gender difference, with both sexes at 15.2%. In the category of Entrepreneurs, senior management and liberal professionals (ESL), the proportion of men is greater than that of women in all the countries analysed. This difference points to the well-established phenomenon of vertical segregation, and unequal access by women to positions of power and management. Portugal is the country with the least men in this group (11.1%), closely followed by Germany (11.2%). However, of all the countries analysed, Portugal has the lowest number of women in the ESL category, at just 5.8%.

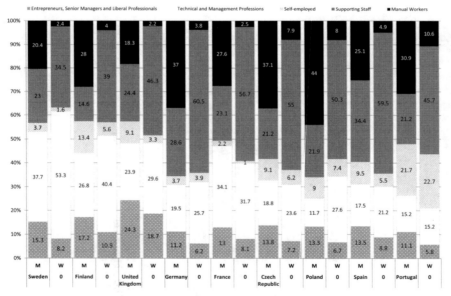

Fig. 3.9 Social class in the selected countries, aged 15–65, by sex, 2015 (%) (*Source* European Working Conditions Survey (EWCS))
(*Note* ESL—Entrepreneurs, senior management and liberal professionals; TMP—Technical and Management Professionals; SE—Self-employed; SS—Supporting Staff; and MW—Manual Workers)

A comparison of women and men in the categories with less resources leads to the conclusion that, in all the countries analysed, the former are better represented in Supporting staff (SS) and the latter in manual workers (MW). The category of Supporting staff corresponds to the service sector where the labour force is predominantly female, both in more operational positions, such as cleaning services, and in positions requiring basic technical qualifications, such as office services. In Portugal—a country where occurred profound transformation from rural to a service-based economy in the last four decades—this category accounts for 45.7% of women and 21.2% of men. Looking now at manual workers (MW), which encompasses workers in industrial production or civil construction, Portugal presents only 30.9%, but, nevertheless, has the largest number of women of all countries in this category—10.6%. Poland has the highest proportion of men (44%) in the MW category.

In the European context, Portugal stands out as the country with the highest proportion of men and women in the Self-Employed (SE) category, at 21.7 and 22.7%, respectively. These numbers may include atypical employment situations, such as freelance workers, in a range of technical and scientific professions, who, despite their high level of academic qualifications, are compelled by current conditions in the labour market to work on a self-employed basis.

Final Remarks

Findings disclose that gender inequality persists, in different domains of life, in Europe on a cross-country perspective. In general, this structural inequality penalises women over the life course, worsening the disadvantages on the rush hour of life, when work-life balance becomes more relevant, and on the late stage, when more traditional gender roles and stereotypes incorporated by men and women may be at play. This can be better understood as an accumulation of inequalities penalising women: from labour market integration, to wages and material living conditions, and to the responsibility for the bulk of unpaid work.

On the structural dimension, we concluded that being a woman or a man has differentiated effects on the access to more or less privileged or more or less deprived positions in terms of economic or cultural resources.

Findings show that being a woman in Europe still implies to have less privileged access to economic resources, even if they are better qualified than men (Torres et al. 2018). For instance, their access to the labour market is done through more precarious and less-paid jobs than men. In all professional groups, even in those more qualified, the pay gap always penalises women. Moreover, the pay gap penalising women tends to worsen on later life stages, even when women's professional careers should be on top.

Using a linear regression analysis to consider income determinants, it was concluded that there are two fundamental determinants. Firstly, in general, for all the European countries analysed and for all ages of life, being a woman is negatively associated with monthly income. Secondly, educational attainment has a positive effect. In other words, for all the ages analysed, the higher the level of educational attainment, the higher the income of both women and men.

The breakdown into social classes points to continued vertical segregation, with men predominating in the classes of entrepreneurs, senior managers, and liberal professionals, and women better represented in the category of technical and management professions. On the economic and social dimension, both the recent effects of financial crisis, and the continued growth of the services sector may be important additional factors explaining the persistence of fundamental inequalities between women and men across Europe.

Concerning the institutional dimension, findings show that besides the persistence of inequalities, in some countries public policies enable a more egalitarian trend on work-life balance, or at least, allow a more consistent participation of women in paid work. But, on the one hand, these policies generally lack a gender perspective and their effect mostly perceived in the rush hour of life, and lacking in younger or older ages.

We could also conclude that in the field of family and living conditions, young women attain autonomy earlier, leaving parental home earlier than men, in most cases on entering into a conjugal relationship. But in southern and eastern countries, young women and men leave home later, what is explained by some researchers has a cultural effect, considering specially the southern countries. However, a statistical analysis showed a strong correlation between low wages and young people staying in parental home.

Summarising gender equality issues in relation to the labour market for young women and men, we may conclude that it is more likely that both will be employed on a non-permanent basis, but this situation is faced more frequently by women.

Findings also showed that in the rush hour of life, the predominant model in the EU is a dual-earner household of full-time workers, only three countries have part-time/full-time model of division of labour (Netherlands, Austria, and Germany). We also found out that in Europe, the proportion of working women with children under six has increased. Among other factors, we need to consider the role of public policies to help reconcile family and professional life, in particular, the existence of child support services. In some countries, the coverage rate of this type of service grew significantly from 2005 to 2015.

In Europe, family and care have been gradually perceived as an equal responsibility for men and women (Torres et al. 2013), and some authors point out the increasing participation of men in housework and childcare, underlying the shortage of the gap of hours spent by men and women on housework and care (Aboim 2010; Cunha and Atalaia 2019). Despite this trend, our findings show that in most of the countries there is still a wide gendered division of unpaid work. Persists the gap in the distribution of housework and caring duties, which penalises women and has significant impacts on their income.

Considering unpaid work our findings reveal that from youth onwards, in Europe, there is a strong asymmetry. Women aged 15–29 spend almost twice as long as men on both housework and looking after the family. In the rush hour of life, this tendency is maintained, and women remain overburdened with regard to unpaid work. Women aged 30–49 also spend almost twice as long as men on both housework and looking after the family. In late stage working life, the pressure to drop out of the labour force due to the demands of family does not appear to be felt by all women in the same way. This is because the employment rate at this stage is higher for women with higher education, characterised by socio-professional situations that may entail higher wages and hence better opportunities to outsource domestic care.

Taking into account our findings, some features of the COVID-19 pandemic, lockdowns and its social and economic effects (economic downturn, unemployment rise, etc.), may increase the inequalities portraited.

Notes

1. Based on "Gender Equality over the life course: Portugal in the European context" (Author et al. 2018).
2. The revision of this chapter was funded by national funds through Fundação para a Ciência e Tecnologia (FCT), I. P., under project UIDP/ 04304/2020.
3. Translation by the author.
4. Retirement/old age (as a methodological option, we limited our study to working life, without addressing the life stage after 65 years of age).
5. Survey conducted in 2012 in 41 countries with a sample of 61,754 individuals. Results obtained from the question: Q16b *On average, how many hours a week do you spend looking after family members (e.g. children, elderly, ill or disabled family members)*? for individuals in employment living with their spouse. The data for Portugal is from 2014. https://www.gesis.org/en/issp/modules/issp-modules-by-topic/family-and-changing-gender-roles.
6. Social class was operationalized using the ACM typology of class locations (Costa et al. 2009). This typology uses occupation (ISCO) and employment status as primary variables, combining them in a matrix of class locations. Therefore, it takes into account a set of basic dimensions of contemporary social inequalities, such as employment status, types of occupations, qualification levels, and organisational hierarchies (Mauritti et al. 2016). Indicators available at the EWCS.

References

Aboim, S. 2010. "Gender Cultures and the Division of Labour in Contemporary Europe: A Cross-National Perspective." *The Sociological Review* 58 (2): 171–196.
Almeida, J.F. 2013. *Desigualdades e Perspetivas dos Cidadãos: Portugal e a Europa*. Lisboa: Editora Mundos Sociais.
Anxo, D., C. Fagan, I. Cebrian, and G. Moreno. 2007. "Patterns of Labour Market Integration in Europe—A Life Course Perspective on Time Policies." *Socio-Economic Review* (5): 233–260.

Arber, S., K. Davidson, and J. Ginn. 2003. "Changing Approaches to Gender and Later Life." In *Gender and Ageing: Changing Roles and Relationships*, edited by S. Arber, K. Davidson and J. Ginn, 1–14. Philadelphia, PA: Open University Press.

Connell, R. 1987. *Gender and Power: Society, The Person and Sexual Politics*. Stanford, CA: Stanford University Press.

Connell, R. 2002. *Gender*. Cambridge: Polity Press.

Costa, A. F., F. L. Machado, and J. F. Almeida. 2009. "Social Classes and Educational Assets: A Transnational Analysis." In *Knowledge and Society (Portugal in the European Context, vol. II)*, edited by A. F. Costa, F. L. Machado and P. Ávila, 5–20. Oeiras: Celta Editora.

Crompton, R. 2006. *Employment and the Family: The Reconfiguration of the Work and Family Life in Contemporary Societies*. Cambridge: Cambridge University Press.

Cunha, V., and S. Atalaia. 2019. "The Gender(ed) Division of Labour in Europe: Patterns of Practices in 18 EU Countries." *Sociologia, Problemas e Práticas* 90: 113–137.

Esping-Andersen, G. 1990. *Welfare States in Transition National Adaptations in Global Economies*. London and Thousand Oaks, CA: SAGE.

European Commission. 2017. *Report on Equality Between Women and Men in the EU*. Brussels: European Commission.

Ferreira, V. 2014. "Employment and Austerity: Changing Welfare and Gender Regimes in Portugal." In *Women and Austerity: The Economic Crisis and the Future for Gender Equality*, edited by M. Karamessini and J. Rubery, 207–227. London: Routledge.

Ferrera, M. 1996. "The Southern Model of Welfare in Social Europe." *Journal of European Social Policy* 6 (1): 17–37.

Gregory, A. and S. Milner. 2009. "Editorial: Work-Life Balance: A Matter of Choice?" *Gender, Work & Organization* 16: 1–13.

Holmes, M. 2007. *What is Gender? Sociological Approaches*. Los Angeles: SAGE.

Karamessini, M. 2014. "Introduction—Women's Vulnerability to Recession and Austerity: A Different Crisis, a Different Context." In *Women and Austerity: The Economic Crisis and the Future for Gender Equality*, edited by M. Karamessini and J. Rubery, 3–16. London: Routledge.

Lewis, J. 2009. *Work-Family Balance, Gender and Policy*. Cheltenham, UK and Northampton, MA, USA: Edward Elgar Publishing.

Mauritti, R., S. C. Martins, N. Nunes, A. L. Romão, A. F. Costa. 2016. "The Social Structure of European Inequality: A Multidimensional Perspective." *Sociologia, Problemas e Práticas* 81: 75–93.

Nico, M. 2014. "Padrões de mudança de casa e eventos de vida: Uma análise das carreiras habitacionais." *Sociologia* (28): 103–126.

Perista, H., A. Cardoso, A. Brázia, M. Abrantes and P. Perista. 2016. *Os usos do tempo de homens e mulheres em Portugal*. Lisbon: CESIS, CITE.

Richardson, D., and V. Robison. 2008. *Introducing Gender and Women's Studies*. Basingstoke: Palgrave Macmillan.

Rubery, J. (2014). "From Women and Recession to Women and Austerity." In *Women and Austerity: The Economic Crisis and the Future for Gender Equality*, edited by M. Karamessini and J. Rubery, 17–36. London: Routledge.

Smith, M., and P. Villa. 2010. "The Ever-Declining Role of Gender Equality in the European Employment Strategy." *Industrial Relations Journal* 41 (6): 526–543.

Torres, A., B. Coelho, I. Cardoso and R. Brites. 2012. "A Mysterious European Threesome: Workcare Regimes, Policies and Gender". *International and Multidisciplanry Journal of Social Sciences* 1 (1): 31–61.
Torres, A., B. Coelho, and M. Cabrita. 2013. "Bridge Over Troubled Waters." *European Societies* 15 (4): 535–556.
Torres, A., B. Haas, N. Steiber, and R. Brites. 2007. *First European Quality of Life Survey: Time use and work-life options over the life course.* European Foundation for Improvement of Living and Working Conditions. Luxembourg, Office for Official Publications of the European Communities.
Torres, A., J. L. Castro, F. V. Silva, S. A. e Inglez. 1999. Políticas Sociais e a questão do acolhimento das crianças em Portugal. *Revista Cadernos de Política Social Redes e Políticas de Solidariedade* 1 (1): 14–35.
Torres, A., P. C. Pinto, D. Costa, B. Coelho, D. Maciel, T. Reigadinha and E. Theodoro. 2018. *Igualdade de Género ao Longo da Vida: Portugal no Contexto Europeu.* Lisbon: FFMS.
Venn, S., K. Davidson, and S. Arber. 2011. "Gender and Ageing." In *Handbook of Sociology of Aging: Handbooks of Sociology and Social research,* edited by Jr. Settersten, A. Richard and J. L. Angel, 71–82. New York: Springer.
Wall, K. (Coord.), V. Cunha, S. Atalaia, L. Rodrigues, R. Correia, S. V. Correia and R. Rosa. 2016. *Livro Branco—Homens e Igualdade de Género em Portugal.* Lisbon: CITE.

CHAPTER 4

What Law Has Joined: Family Relations and Categories of Kinship in the European Court of Human Rights

Linda Hart

Introduction

What is a family? What must family relations be "made of" to merit legal protection from a State? How and to what extent are family relations protected by human rights principles and international human rights law? To be recognised by law, does a family need to be built on a heterosexual relation between a woman and a man, on marriage, or on blood relations? In Europe today, what constitutes or does not constitute a family is subject to many things, depending on the context: subjective opinion, personal and collective beliefs, social movements, civil society activism, political decision-making, legislation, and sometimes going to court in national and international tribunals. One would not think that something so mundane, personal, and micro-level as family relations might cause so much passion, debate, disagreement, bureaucracy, and adjudication. Here, let us see how different aspects of family relations as socio-legal phenomena tie together.

Family law is an area of national legislation in each State governing, for example, how and under what circumstances children become legally related to their parents, what makes a marriage valid, who may marry whom and to what extent adults are responsible for supporting and maintaining their spouses and children. Family law and human rights law relevant to family issues are mostly the terrain of lawyers who practice law in real-life situations, and legal scholars who study and teach law and the development of legal

L. Hart (✉)
Faculty of Social Sciences, University of Helsinki, Helsinki, Finland
e-mail: linda.hart@alumni.helsinki.fi

doctrine. The intersection of family law and human rights law also provides a fascinating and multidisciplinary field of inquiry for sociologists (see, e.g., Ammaturo 2017; Johnson 2014, 2013 and 2016; Hart 2016) and anthropologists (see Dembour 2006, 2010; Hart 2018), as it deals with who is seen to relate to whom, what kinds of care-related and financial consequences this has in everyday life, and how different aspects of family relations are protected by human rights norms.

In family law in general and in the case law of the European Court of Human Rights (ECtHR) in particular, the convergence of biological, legal, and social relations emerges as a norm and a cultural ideal (Hart 2009). In many legal disputes and cases, one of these elements is absent, contested, or sought after. In this chapter, it is argued that what law has joined, cannot easily be undone in the legal realm. Thus, a legally recognised relation such as one established at birth tends to be protected and would in only very limited circumstances be dismantled.[1] On the other hand, even when the facts of who gave birth to whom are not disputed, a legally recognised relation between a mother and a child needs a pre-existing legal framework to become officially recognised.[2]

This chapter gives an overview of how family relations, something that sociologists of families and intimate lives and anthropologists of kinship study in their fields, are subject to human rights litigation and argued to be protected in Europe today by human rights law stemming from the European Convention on Human Rights (ECHR). This regional human rights treaty lays the foundation to the work of the European system of human rights protection, functioning within the Council of Europe[3] and the European Court of Human Rights, an international human rights court where States can be challenged on their adherence to the ECHR. In this chapter, judgements from the ECtHR act as examples of where human rights protection according to the ECHR extends to regarding the "right to respect to family life" (Article 8 ECHR) and the "right to marry" (Article 12 ECHR). The judgments are not analysed from the perspective of legal scholars, but to illustrate how concepts within the anthropological study of kinship come to life in contemporary human rights litigation. The concepts utilised in introducing sociologically and anthropologically interesting case law are alliance, consanguinity, and filiation (Lévi-Strauss 1958; see also Hart 2016).

Family Law and Human Rights in Europe

Marie-Bénédicte Dembour (2006), both an anthropologist and a legal scholar, has provided a sophisticated socio-legal analysis of case law of the ECtHR as an arena of competing approaches to human rights as a goal of social justice. She looked at ECHR case law from realist, utilitarian, Marxist, particularist, and feminist perspectives, showing how human rights law are applied to a wide range of issues. Furthermore, she characterised four "schools" of human rights: given, perhaps by God (natural), agreed upon between people (deliberated), fought for within conflicts in society (protest school) or talked about (discursive school) (Dembour 2006, 254–255, see also Dembour 2010, 11). These approaches may be of help in understanding how the applicants in ECtHR cases and the States they challenge argue their positions and how historical and social change bring about new issues that are argued to be covered by the human rights principles written in the ECHR. For example, rights to recognised forms of family relations for same-sex couples have been and still are, to some extent, a contentious field of human rights litigation in Europe. Thus, these issues have made it to the human rights agenda through being talked about, fought for, and agreed upon.

How is it, then, that legal disputes end up as case law in an international human rights tribunal and even as landmark cases influencing future legislation in Member States of the Council of Europe? In all cases that end up in the ECtHR based in Strasbourg, France, "domestic remedies" must have been exhausted, meaning that a case must have gone through the appeal opportunities available in the legal system of the State in question. If the applicant(s) take their case to the ECtHR and the case is evaluated as well-founded and admissible from a legal point of view, the ECtHR delivers a judgement on the case. The judgement given offers an evaluation on whether the rights protected by the European Convention that must have been evoked by the applicants have been violated. In addition, if a right enshrined in the ECHR is interpreted in a way that challenges existing case law, the respondent State should modify its legislation to be compatible with the new interpretation of the ECHR. Sometimes cases are brought to the ECtHR due to "strategic litigation": non-governmental organisations might seize the opportunity brought by a particular case, and support and help the applicant(s) in making a complaint to the ECtHR (Hodson 2011, 2014 and Johnson 2016, 179). This is how many cases dealing with lesbian, gay, bisexual, and transgender (LGBT) rights have managed to bring about legal change: through organised legal activism and not just individual-level complaints.

The ECHR was drafted soon after the Second World War by Western European States. After the Cold War and the breakdown of the Soviet Union, the Council of Europe expanded and today it comprises many Member States also beyond geographical Europe. The rights written down in the ECHR have been subject to "dynamic interpretation", which is also called "evolutive" and "contextual" (see, e.g., Johnson 2013, 84–85). Due to this, the ECHR has been interpreted by the ECtHR to cover many issues that were not originally in its remit. Rights of sexual and gender minorities in different matters, not just family life, are a good example of this.

Article 8 of the European Convention on Human Rights, the founding human rights treaty of the Council of Europe, says that

> Everyone has the right to respect for his private and family life, his home and his correspondence

What the ECHR says about family life in terms of human rights protection relates primarily to the civil right to the protection of privacy and the right to not be subjected to State interference in who one lives and sets up home with, forms a family with and corresponds. Based on the wording of Article 8 of the ECHR, the ECtHR makes a distinction between the "right to respect for private life" and the "right to respect to family life". Both areas have given rise to a large body of case law during the more than 60 years of existence of the ECHR. Respect for the home and correspondence are also covered by Article 8, but these two fields of application have produced less case law than respect for private life and family life. The historical context of the right to respect for private and family life, the home and correspondence refers to the persecution faced by groups such as Jews and political dissidents during the Second World War. Indeed, in the preparatory works of the ECHR, the context is governmental interference in one's private and family life, home, and correspondence (European Commission of Human Rights 1956). It is only in later case law that Article 8 of the ECHR has become subject to the recognition of the diversity of family relations among many other themes (Hart 2016).

As to the right to marry, there is Article 12 of the ECHR, which says that

> Men and women of marriageable age have the right to marry and to found a family, according to the national laws governing the exercise of this right.

This Article has produced less case law than Article 8, and as its wording suggests, applies only to the freedom to marry. Thus, no right to divorce as such may be inferred from it, and existing case law does not support it. Furthermore, at least so far, the right to marry has been interpreted only to mean marriage for different-sex couples, even though relationship recognition for same-sex couples in the form of civil unions has been interpreted as an evolving new human rights norm.[4]

The wordings of both Articles need to be first understood in their historical context after the Second World War, when issues of gender equality, sexual orientation, or gender identity were not on the mainstream European human rights agenda. It is only later that these human rights principles have been evoked and applied to issues of gender, legal sex, and individual-level gender identities. Furthermore, the word "family" does not stand there as a concept of its own, as it only appears as "family life" in the ECHR. For example, it is not characterised as an institution in need of protection from the State, like in the Universal Declaration of Human Rights,[5] a global human rights declaration, even though this understanding underpins the ECHR, too.

These shifts in historical contexts illustrate how what family life, family relations and the concept of family mean in a "European culture of human rights" (see, e.g., Ammaturo 2017, 39), is subject to historically rooted and changing interpretations of human rights principles. The notion of family relations in the ECtHR encompasses biological (bio-genetic), legal (State-recognised), and social (lived-out) relations on a "commonsensical" and easily applicable level. They cover most of the tangible aspects related to family relations and provide the subject matter for adjudicating what is important in each case. However, this three-level approach leaves the gendered aspects of these relations untouched. A fourth, gendered dimension of family relations is also relevant (Hart 2009).

For the purposes of this chapter, family relations as socio-legal entities are defined as "State-recognised privileged personal relations between individuals that embody or emulate genealogical principles of prohibited degrees of relationships and genetically reckoned descent" (Hart 2016, 86). What people regard as their own family relations or those of others is not always subject to genetic or legal proof, and there may be variation in the sexuality, legal sex, and gender identities of the persons involved. However, for a family to exist as a legally recognised entity in the eyes of a State, there needs to be at least one relation between two subjects, either that of alliance (adult-adult) or filiation (adult-child). A privileged status distinguishes family relations from other close relations important to a person in her or his private life, and this affects, for example, being responsible for maintaining children or a spouse or the transmission of property.

Alliance, Consanguinity, and Filiation

The sociological study of families can hardly be untangled from the anthropological study of kinship. Indeed, having a look at the protection of family life in a human rights context benefits from the distance that anthropological analysis provides. From the perspective of anthropology of kinship, relatedness rests on two main types of relations: alliance and filiation, also known as affinity and descent (see Déchaux 2002). Alliance refers to the act of joining two previously unrelated individuals or groups together, often through marriage or some other form of recognised union for enjoying sexual relations, pooling wealth, forming a household, and possibly raising children. As a form of alliance, marriage connects two adults who become spouses to each other, but it also connects two groups, as a marriage turns the spouses' family members into in-laws.

Filiation refers to a legally recognised relation between a parent and a child, and this may be created through birth (mother–child), recognition (assumption of paternity in marriage, a legal act of recognition by an unmarried father, or recognition of a mother's female partner's legal parenthood through marriage or other means if allowed by the State in question) or adoption, which may happen within a family unit between a child and a step-parent, or outside a family, when a previously unrelated child is adopted by a couple or a single individual. Kinship terminology makes it possible to articulate how people relate to each other, and it helps in articulating incest prohibitions (who may not marry and have sexual relations with whom), transmission of wealth, and power relations between generations and genders.

Family law in a particular State provides codification of kinship rules and kinship terms. Kinship systems in the sense of the anthropological study of kinship do not exist only in "other" cultures—the Euro-American kinship system, by and large and with some national variation when it comes to kinship terms, is one way of reckoning kin relations (see Schneider 1968). One may start with incest prohibitions: who is allowed to marry whom. In many States, cousins are allowed to marry each other. Brothers and sisters are not, stepbrothers and step-sisters neither. Likewise, uncles are not allowed to marry their nieces and aunts are not allowed to marry their nephews. At the advent of civil unions and marriage for same-sex couples, prohibitions structured in a similar manner to these have been carried over to apply to same-sex marriages as well.

Claude Lévi-Strauss (1908–2009), a French social theorist and anthropologist, characterised human kinship with the help of the notions of alliance, consanguinity, and filiation. In an essay on applying structural analysis from linguistics based on the thought of Ferdinand de Saussure, he names the simplest structures of kinship as relations between siblings, spouses, and parents and children. This is linked to his key thesis according to which the prohibition of incest (who is not allowed to marry whom) is the threshold between nature and culture. Incest prohibitions, which vary from one culture to another, lay down the principle of "exogamy" ("marrying out"), according to which men exchange their sisters[6] with men from other groups, leading to the alliance of two groups through a marital union where the spouses are not siblings. When these unions produce children, relations of filiation are created between parents and children. Lévi-Strauss calls this the basic "element of kinship" (Lévi-Strauss 1958, 56).

The main argument of Lévi-Strauss (1958) is that alliance, not filiation, is the foundation of kinship, as it is a relation of exchange between two kin groups. The principle of exogamy, "marrying out" motivates kin groups to enter into relations with other kin groups through the exchange of spouses for the sake of reproduction and the exchange of both material and immaterial goods. Kinship terminology consists of arbitrary linguistic signs that differ from one language and culture to another. Even though kinship terminology and linguistic signs are important in naming the actors, it is the relations between these signs and persons that are most important (Lévi-Strauss 1958, 57). This idea that kinship systems consist of arbitrary meanings instead of "objective" relations resonates with contemporary debates in sociology, anthropology, gender studies, and other disciplines about the notion of family and how it is defined in different contexts. For example, since the advent of same-sex marriage and family formation, it is nowadays more intelligible than before to say that there are two mothers or fathers in the same family unit.

If sex and gender are not rigid and defining characteristics in defining family relations, close personal relations fall in two categories: intimate adult-adult relations (alliance) and parent-child relations (filiation). In Lévi-Strauss' words in an English translation of *Structural Anthropology*:

> In order for a kinship structure to exist, three types of family relations must always be present: a relation of consanguinity, a relation of affinity, and a relation of descent – in other words, a relation between siblings, a relation between spouses, and a relation between parent and child.
>
> Claude Lévi-Strauss (1967, 43)

Alliance (affinity), consanguinity, and filiation (descent) are anthropological categories through which almost any empirical context such as ECtHR case law may be discussed (Hart 2016). This distinction is helpful for analysing ECtHR case law from a sociological and anthropological perspective to dissect the empirical context of biological, legal, social, and gendered relations in the context of human rights law. Alliance refers to intimate relations, unions, and marriages between two adults. Consanguinity acts as the category for analysing the role of shared origins, "blood relations" and maternity and paternity to the extent that they are governed by it. Filiation is often established based on consanguinity, but may take many other forms such as adoption, the use of donated gametes and in some cases, surrogate pregnancies.

Alliance: Cohabitation, Marriage, and Civil Unions

Alliance often precedes filiation in the construction of a family unit. Within European human rights law, the right to marry a person of one's choice is regarded as a fundamental human right as long as the couple are of the right legal sex (es), adults age and not too closely related. The details of criteria vary somewhat from one State to another. In contrast, the question of divorce is not subject to much attention in human rights conventions or human rights law. The ECtHR has examined weighty politico-moral issues such as abortion, divorce, and the definition of marriage as very sensitive matters. Some case law on abortion and divorce exists, but ECtHR jurisprudence on the matter is limited to specific points related to these matters. For example, as regards divorce, the ECtHR ruled in *Andrzej Piotrowski v. Poland* (2016)[7] and in *Babiarz v. Poland* (2017)[8] that the ECHR does not oblige Member States to offer divorce and that an individual right to divorce is not guaranteed.

In the ECHR, the right to marry as according to Article 12 is heavily subject to the legislation in the Member State in question ("... according to the national laws governing the exercise of this right"). This means that Member States are free to decide through their legislative bodies what constitutes marriage, and in the last instance, whether they offer divorce or not. Therefore, divorce has not really materialised as a human rights issue on the international human rights agenda. Divorce has been legalised in all European States, sometimes through a referendum or other forms of canvassing public opinion. However, its conditions vary from one State to another. Thus, human rights institutions have been in many cases relieved of taking a stance whether there is a human right to divorce or not.

The advent of same-sex civil unions[9] in the late 1990s and continuing into the 2000s and 2010s, and the subsequent wave of legalising same-sex marriage in many States,[10] some of which first legislated civil unions and then same-sex marriage, constitutes a process of undoing and "de-gendering" marriage as a restrictive social institutions (see Théry 1993; Barker 2012, 121; Ball 2014, 136) in many legal and political contexts. This may be understood as the expansion or redefinition of the concept of marriage. This emphasises the contractual nature of marriage as a civil institution, and the sex of the persons entering a marriage contract is not of issue as long as prohibited degrees and age limits are not transgressed.

Judging by how gender-neutral marriage has become a legal reality in many European States in recent years, it may be said that alliance is seen quite differently now compared to how it was seen a few decades ago. The ECtHR also acknowledges this, to a certain extent: since *Schalk and Kopf v. Austria* (2010) same-sex couples, not just different-sex couples, have been acknowledged to share family life from the perspective of European human rights protection. Furthermore, in the case of *Oliari and others v. Italy* (2015) it was required that states must offer some form of civil partnerships for same-sex couples to form unions. This may be through legislation offering same-sex partnerships or through legislation offering such partnerships to all couples as a form of "lightweight marriage". However, the ECtHR has not been interpreted to include an obligation for Member States of the Council of Europe to institute gender-neutral marriage. The question is left to state legislatures, different political landscapes, and decision-making processes.

Consanguinity: Maternity by Birth and Paternity by Marriage or Recognition

Same-sex civil unions and gender-neutral marriage have paved the way for acknowledging different forms of parental relations, such as gender-neutral step-parent adoption. Also, gamete donation and medically assisted reproduction offer possibilities for couples and individuals in different situations to become parents. However, these practices are not mere technological procedures, as they involve serious ethical considerations, their availability varies from one State to another and they are limited by sexed reproduction in one way or another. For example, surrogacy remains a difficult issue for human rights adjudication. Shared genetic origin, consanguinity, is not the only criterion for establishing filiation, but it figures in the background and gives rise to legal cases of its own.

The judgement *Marckx v. Belgium* (1979)[11] is a temporally distant but in many ways a very illuminating case dealing with the recognition of family relations in the case law of the ECtHR. In Belgium in the 1970s, an unmarried woman who gave birth had to "adopt" her own child to become the child's legally recognised parent. In Belgium in those times a child born out of wedlock was administratively in the situation of a foundling. The case illustrates that not even the act of giving birth automatically creates a legal mother–child relation without a pre-existing legal framework for recognising it. From the perspective of human rights protection, the outcome of the case in favour of the mother and the child meant that children born to unmarried mothers and children born in wedlock were to be treated the same way in the recognition of filiation by birth. Also, Belgian legislation at the time was lagging behind other European States in these matters, so the changes demanded by the ECtHR were not hugely controversial.

In *Marckx v. Belgium,* the ECtHR emphasised that different forms of families should be legally recognised, focusing on the family unit created by a mother and a child she has given birth to. In a way, the case of *Marckx* illustrates the idea of the "core family" of a mother and child(ren) put forward by Martha Fineman, an American feminist legal scholar, who argues that "the mother-child formation would be the 'natural' or core family unit—it would be the base entity around which social policy and legal rules are fashioned" (1995, 5–6). This notion is useful when applied to *Marckx v. Belgium*: a child's parental relations are built around her or him, beginning from maternity based on giving birth, adding paternity to it through the assumption of paternity in marriage or through an act of recognition by an unmarried father. In some cases, these ties are not established or are legally severed, and adoption takes place. Today, in some States in Europe, the female partner of a woman giving birth may also be recognised as the parent of the child through a process of recognition or intra-familial adoption.

Whereas *Marckx* was a story of liberation and affirmation, the cases of *Odièvre v. France* (2003)[12] and *Kearns v. France* (2008)[13] illustrate the themes of giving birth anonymously and subsequent adoption. *Odièvre* also illustrates the question of origins. In *Odièvre*, an adult woman was searching for information on her origins as she had been adopted as a child after being born to a woman who gave birth to her anonymously. In *Kearns*, a foreign woman came to France to give birth anonymously and gave the child away, but regretted her decision and tried to get the child back after the consideration period granted to her. In *Odièvre*, the practice of privacy and the secret to origins meant that Ms Odièvre was able to obtain some non-identifying biographical information of her birth mother and birth family but was not granted access to identifying information. Ms Kearns, in her case, appealed to her distressing situation giving birth in a foreign country and not understanding the full ramifications of her actions when agreeing to give her child away for adoption. In both cases, relations created and confirmed with the force of law prevailed: when an adoption has taken place, it is very rarely undone. What had been joined by law would not be undone, or uncovered.

The judgements of *Johnston v. Ireland* (1986)[14] and *Keegan v. Ireland* (1994)[15], in turn, provide a perspective into unmarried paternity, even more invisible in some not-so-distant times and locations. In *Johnston*, a man had left his wife and started cohabiting with a new female partner with whom he had a child. As divorce was not possible in the Republic of Ireland at the time, it was impossible for him to be fully recognised as the father of the child born of this relationship. The ECtHR did not find a violation of the rights of the parents as to their inability to marry due to Mr Johnston being unable to obtain a divorce and remarry. In *Keegan*, a child was born of a short relationship to an unmarried woman who gave the baby up for adoption. Mr Keegan, the father of the child, would have wanted to be recognised as the father and to care for the child. This was not possible as he had no standing in the adoption procedure due to being an unmarried father and thus completely unrecognised as a legal parent in Ireland at the time.

The situation of unmarried women giving birth some decades ago was not easy, but in many ways unmarried fathers were even more ignored in establishing legal family relations in situations of disagreement or dispute. In *Marckx, Johnston* and *Keegan* what was at stake was not really that their bio-genetic or social claims to establishing a relation of filiation with the child in question would have been doubted. Rather, the law in place in their respective contexts had been designed to sideline both unmarried mothers and fathers. Without a pre-existing legal framework and a logic of seeing also unmarried women and men as parental subjects, establishing filiation was either cumbersome or close to impossible. In *Keegan*, too, what was joined by law, meaning the adoption of the child, could not be undone. The mother had given the child up for adoption, and the legal act of adoption was not to be reversed as the relation of filiation between the adoptive parents and the child had been given the weight of law. In situations where consanguinity, meaning bio-genetic relations, exists, it is not the sole basis of legally recognised filiation without social and/or legal frameworks backing it up.

Filiation: Adoption, Assisted Reproduction, and Surrogate Pregnancies

Adoption, medically assisted reproduction, and surrogacy are fields of case law where the constitution of relations of filiation, family law, and human rights arguments collide at their barest. Medically assisted reproduction and surrogacy are also fields that are subject to dynamically changing case law in the ECtHR. Adoption may take place in many different situations: by a social step-parent within a family unit to recognise an existing relation, or by a different-sex couple, a single person or a same-sex couple in order to create new parent-child relations when children have been given away, taken into permanent State care or orphaned. Different forms of adoption have also been subject to important judgements in the ECtHR, shedding light on different sub-categories of adoption.

Adoption is a rather clear example of the "What law joins…" principle, as after the required administrative process of placing a child with her or his new parent(s) has taken place, there are very few circumstances, if any, where this legal relationship of filiation would be taken apart. Adoption is and cannot really be a "right" in itself—rather, the cases concerning adoption and Article 8 of the ECHR deal with a right to apply for adoption and to be evaluated by relevant authorities as a potential adoptive parent. In the ECtHR, there have been cases where the national administrative and legal system has taken the criterion of non-heterosexual identity of an applicant willing to adopt as a single person as a bar to being considered as an adoptive parent.[16] Adoptive parents are evaluated according to many criteria, and positive outcomes in individual cases cannot be guaranteed.

In Member States of the Council of Europe, a person's sexual orientation is not a valid criterion for dismissing an adult as a prospective adoptive parent.[17] So far, providing legislation that allows same-sex couples to adopt has been left to Member States to decide. In the context of same-sex couples, what has materialised also in ECHR case law is intra-familial adoption, meaning the recognition of a female partner of a woman giving birth as a legal parent, or step-parent adoption within a family in which a child or children are legally related to only one parent. In ECHR case law, same-sex couples are protected from discrimination compared to different-sex couples in step-parent adoption, but only when unmarried couples are compared to each other and married couples to each other (see Nozawa 2013). Thus, step-parent adoption may take place in families formed by both different-sex and same-sex couples, and in addition to existing legislation, the status and views of a possible preexisting legal parent to the child(ren) may play a role in the process.[18] There is no case law on joint adoption by same-sex couples and allowing it is not required from Member States.

Assisted reproduction is also a field where relations of filiation are created. Different-sex couples are often given treatment with their own gametes (sperm and eggs), and the convergence of bio-genetic, legal, and social relations is not up for dispute. However, sometimes donated sperm or eggs may be required, and this is where legislation differs from one State to another. Some practices and techniques are not allowed by law in all States. Sperm donation and assisted reproduction through insemination are widely accepted in Member States of the Council of Europe. In several States, assisted reproduction by insemination (and if needed, in vitro fertilisation) are available to single women and female couples, whereas in some States fertility treatments for women without a male partner are prohibited by law. Furthermore, egg donation and subsequent in vitro fertilisation are not legal in all Member States. *S.H. and others v. Austria* (2011)[19] acts as an example of this, and the ECtHR did not rule that all forms of assisted reproduction must be allowed in all Member States. In all States, the availability of different forms of medically assisted reproduction within public healthcare also differs, sometimes also by marital status and legal sex.

Furthermore, as *Evans v. the United Kingdom* (2006)[20] demonstrates, human rights issues dealing with assisted reproduction are not always associated with the marital status, legal sex, and sexual orientation of the adults seeking treatments, but with the problematics of the beginning of life itself. In *Evans*, a woman had sought in vitro fertilisation together with her husband. They separated during the process and she would have wanted to try to get pregnant with embryos left over from the treatments. However, her male ex-partner had the right, also according to the ECtHR, to veto the use of embryos created with his genetic material.

Last but not least, disputes concerning surrogate pregnancies have produced important ECHR case law in recent years. Surrogacy is banned in one way or another in many European States, and as a rule, remunerated commercial surrogacy treatments are not available in Western and Northern Europe. Surrogacy has given rise to an abundance of difficult legal cases both in Europe and elsewhere, especially when things have not gone according to plan. In ECHR case law, the case law available deals mainly with cross-border surrogacy, meaning that the treatments and the services related to it have taken place in the United States, Ukraine, or some other State where commercial surrogacy is practised. The cases then deal with the administrative and legal procedures of creating legally recognised relations of filiation between the children born of a surrogate pregnancy and the commissioning parents who return to their home country with the children.

In *Mennesson v. France* (2014) and *Labassee v. France* (2014)[21] the crux of the matter was that in the eyes of French law, the children born in the United States were not legally related to them at all and they did not possess French citizenship, as all children born in the United States become U.S. citizens. In these cases, the ECtHR ruled that the right to respect for private life of the children had been breached under Article 8 of the ECHR, but not the right to family life of the parents. As surrogacy is banned in France, the parents had contravened French law and public policy by obtaining surrogacy services abroad. However, as the resulting children ended up living in a legal limbo vis-à-vis their parents, there should have been a mechanism to improve their legal standing and to recognise their relation of filiation to the parents they were living and growing up with. In other cases dealing with surrogacy the ECtHR has been of the opinion that in cases where it is possible to establish a relation of filiation between a commissioning father acting as a sperm donor in the surrogacy process, it is not unjustified to require the partner of the biological father to establish her (or his, national legislation allowing) parental relation to the child through intra-familial adoption.[22]

Conclusion

The understandings people hold of their own and other people's family relations, family law in different States and international human rights law intersect in many ways. It is possible to study the intersection of family relations and law in many different contexts, of which the European Court of Human Rights and its case law provides just one among many. Reading ECtHR case law from a sociological perspective with the help of anthropological notions makes it possible to see different layers of what family relations are made of: shared bio-genetic substance, social relations, and recognised or disputed legal relations. Added together, the layers give weight to one another. Examples from the ECHR show that different combination of bio-genetic, social, legal, and gendered relations give rise to different kinds of legal disputes and human rights claims. Human-made rules and categories matter: despite possible bio-genetic evidence to the contrary, a legally created or enforced family relation is rarely undone. New forms of legislation, on the other hand, may bring about new forms of family relations.

From a sociological point of view, structures such as kinship systems or law produce concepts that can be applied to real-life situations. Sex, gender, and generation are the most important structures, and family law operates with kinship terminology in both national legal structures and interactions between people. To say that something is a structure or a concept does not mean that their content does not evolve through time. However, especially when it comes to adjudicating what is right, wrong or in need of human rights protection in a court of law language and the way it might lag behind changing understandings of family life is important.

The concepts of alliance, consanguinity, and filiation have been chosen here to illustrate how mundane and contemporary forms of family relations may be viewed with the help of tools from classical social and anthropological theory. From the point of view of the categories of both legal sex and social gender identities, alliance can be rather easily conjugated into a gender-neutral relation. In recent years, cases in the ECtHR focused on different forms of civil unions and the possibility of same-sex marriage have been scrutinised within the remit of Article 12 (right to marry) of the ECHR. So far, the ECtHR has not ruled that same-sex marriage is a human right flowing from Article 12 but has taken other steps towards wider relationship recognition regarding same-sex couples.

Filiation, meaning legally recognised parental relations between adults and children, is more complicated from the perspective of sex and gender. All over Europe the woman giving birth to a child is in most cases directly recognised as the legal mother of the child, and the parental relation of the other parent, male or female, is structured in relation to the birth mother. Thus, filiation starts from the mother–child dyad, proceeding to the recognition of paternity or other parentage through an existing union or an act of recognition. A mother may recede her legal maternity and thus a child's parental relations may be organised anew, with the help of a father-child relation, recognition of a female parent and/or a set of adoptive relations. Understandings of reckoning and naming spouses, parents and children may be in flux, but a great deal of the social and legal structures behind language of kinship change very slowly.

Notes

1. See *X and Others v. Austria* [GC], no. 19010/07, ECHR 2013.
2. *Marckx v. Belgium*, 13 June 1979, Series A no. 31.
3. The Council of Europe is an intergovernmental organisation which acts as the regional human rights system in Europe. The Council of Europe (CoE) is distinct from the European Union (EU). However, ratifying the European Convention of Human Rights is a key membership criterion for Member States of the European Union. This includes, for example, the decriminalisation of homosexuality.
4. *Oliari and Others v. Italy*, nos. 18766/11 and 36030/11, 21 July 2015.
5. Article 16, Universal Declaration of Human Rights: *(1) Men and women of full age, without any limitation due to race, nationality or religion, have the right to marry and to found a family. They are entitled to equal rights as to marriage, during marriage and at its dissolution. (2) Marriage shall be entered into only with the free and full consent of the intending spouses. (3) The family is the natural and fundamental group unit of society and is entitled to protection by society and the State* (Universal Declaration of Human Rights).
6. Even though Lévi-Strauss talks about men exchanging their sister in his theory, he has later stressed that the main import of the theory is the making linkages between different kin groups, and not the patriarchal structure of men being actors and women being commodities. See Lévi-Strauss (2000).
7. *Andrzej Piotrowski v. Poland*, no. 8923/12, 22 November 2016.
8. *Babiarz v. Poland*, no. 1955/10, 10 January 2017.
9. In October 2019, civil unions but not marriage was available for same-sex couples in Andorra, Croatia, Cyprus, Czech Republic, Estonia, Greece, Hungary, Italy, Liechtenstein, Slovenia, and Switzerland (Lipka and Maschi 2019).
10. In October 2019, same-sex marriage was legal in Austria, Belgium, Denmark, Finland, France, Germany, Iceland, Ireland, Luxembourg, Malta, Netherlands, Norway, Portugal, Spain, Sweden, and the UK (England and Wales, Northern Ireland, Scotland) (Lipka and Maschi 2019).
11. *Marckx v. Belgium*, 13 June 1979, Series A no. 31.
12. *Odièvre v. France* [GC], no. 42326/98, ECHR 2003-III.
13. *Kearns v. France*, no. 35991/04, 10 January 2008.
14. *Johnston and others v. Ireland*, no. 9697/82, 18 December 1986, Series A no. 112.
15. *Keegan v. Ireland*, no. 16969/90, 26 May 1994, Series A no. 29.
16. *Fretté v. France*, no. 36515/97, ECHR 2002-I and *E.B. v. France* [GC], no. 43546/02, 22 January 2008. For a closer analysis of these two cases, see Hart (2009).
17. See previous note.
18. See *X and Others v. Austria* [GC], no. 19010/07, ECHR 2013.
19. *S.H. and Others v. Austria* [GC], no. 57813/00, ECHR 2011.
20. *Evans v. the United Kingdom*, no. 6339/05, 7 March 2006.
21. *Mennesson v. France*, no. 65192/11, ECHR 2014 (extracts) and *Labassee v. France*, no. 65941/11, 26 June 2014. For similar cases, see *Foulon and Bouvet v. France*, nos. 9063/14 and 10410/14, 21 July 2016 and *Laborie v. France*, no. 44024/13, 19 January 2017.
22. *C v. France* and *E v. France*, nos. 1462/18 and 17348/18, 19 January 2019.

References

Ammaturo, Francesca Romana. 2017. *European Sexual Citizenship: Human Rights, Bodies, Identities*. Cham: Palgrave Macmillan/ Springer Nature.
Andrzej Piotrowski v. Poland, no. 8923/12, 22 November 2016.
Babiarz v. Poland, no. 1955/10, 10 January 2017.
Ball, Carlos A. 2014. *Same-Sex Marriage and Children: A Tale of History, Social Science and Law*. Oxford: Oxford University Press.
Barker, Nicola. 2012. *Not the Marrying Kind: A Feminist Critique of Same-Sex Marriage*. Basingstoke: Palgrave MacMillan.
Déchaux, Jean-Hugues. 2002. "Paradoxes of Affiliation in the Contemporary Society." *Current Sociology* 50 (2): 229–242.
Dembour, Marie-Bénédicte. 2006. *Who Believes in Human Rights? Reflections on the European Convention*. Cambridge: Cambridge University Press.
Dembour, Marie-Bénédicte. 2010. "What Are Human Rights? Four Schools of Thought." *Human Rights Quarterly* 32 (1): 1–20.
European Commission of Human Rights. 1956. *Preparatory Work on Article 8 of the ECtHR*. Information Document prepared by the Secretariat of the Commission (*travaux préparatoires*). Web publication: www.echr.coe.int/LibraryDocs/Travaux/ECHRTravaux-ART8-DH(56)12-EN1674980.pdf. Accessed 6 January 2019.
European Convention for the Protection of Human Rights and Fundamental Freedoms, ETS No.005, 11 April 1950. https://www.coe.int/en/web/conventions/full-list/-/conventions/treaty/005. Accessed 24 June 2020.
Evans v. the United Kingdom, no. 6339/05, 7 March 2006.
Fineman, Martha Albertson. 1995. *The Neutered Mother, the Sexual Family and Other Twentieth Century Tragedies*. New York: Routledge.
Foulon and Bouvet v. France, nos. 9063/14 and 10410/14, 21 July 2016.
Hodson, Loveday. 2011. NGOs and the struggle for human rights in Europe.
Hart, Linda.2009. "Individual Adoption by Non-Heterosexuals and the Order of Family Life in the European Court of Human Rights." *Journal of Law and Society* 36 (4): 536–557.
Hart, Linda. 2016. *Relational Subjects: Family Relations, Law and Gender in the European Court of Human Rights*. Publications of the Faculty of Social Sciences. Helsinki: Unigrafia.
Hart, Linda. 2018. "Anthropology Meets Human Rights Rationality: Limits of Family Life in the European Court of Human Rights." *European Societies* 20 (5): 816–834.
Hodson, Loveday. 2014. "Activists and Lawyers in the European Court of Human Rights: The Struggle for Gay Rights." In *Rights and Courts in Pursuit of Social Change*, edited by Dia Anagnostou, 181–204. Oxford: Hart Publishing.
Johnson, Paul. 2013. *Homosexuality and the European Court of Human Rights*. Abingdon: Routledge.
Johnson, Paul. 2014. "Sociology and the European Court of Human Rights." *The Sociological Review* 62 (3): 547–564.
Johnson, Paul. 2016. *Going to Strasbourg: An Oral History of Sexual Orientation Discrimination and the European Court of Human Rights*. Oxford: Oxford University Press.
Johnston and others v. Ireland, no. 9697/82, 18 December 1986, Series A no. 112.
Kearns v. France, no. 35991/04, 10 January 2008.
Keegan v. Ireland, no. 16969/90, 26 May 1994, Series A no. 29.

Labassee v. France, no. 65941/11, 26 June 2014.
Laborie v. France, no. 44024/13, 19 January 2017.
Lévi-Strauss, Claude. 1967. *Structural Anthropology*. New York: Anchor Books. [Translation of Lévi-Strauss, Claude. 1958. *Anthropologie structurale*. Paris: Plon].
Lévi-Strauss, Claude. 2000. Postface. *L'Homme* 154–155: 713–722.
Lipka, Michael, and David Masci. 2019. *Where Europe Stands on Gay Marriage and Civil Unions*. Pew Research Center. Accessed January 12, 2020, https://www.pewresearch.org/fact-tank/2019/10/28/where-europe-stands-on-gay-marriage-and-civil-unions.
Marckx v. Belgium, 13 June 1979, Series A no. 31.
Mennesson v. France, no. 65192/11, ECHR 2014 (extracts).
Nozawa, Junko. 2013. "Drawing the Line: Same-Sex Adoption and the Jurisprudence of the ECtHR on the Application of the "European Consensus" Standard under Article 14." *Merkourios: Utrecht Journal of International and European Law* 29 (77): 66–75.
Odièvre v. France [GC], no. 42326/98, ECHR 2003-III.
Oliari and Others v. Italy, nos. 18766/11 and 36030/11, 21 July 2015.
Radcliffe-Brown, A. R. 1941. The Study of Kinship Systems: Presidential Address. *Journal of the Royal Anthropological Institute* 71 (1–2): 1–18.
Schneider, David. 1968. *Kinship: A Cultural Account*. Chicago: University of Chicago Press.
S.H. and Others v. Austria [GC], no. 57813/00, ECHR 2011.
Théry, Irène. 1993. *Démariage: justice et vie privée*. Paris: Odile Jacob.
Universal Declaration of Human Rights. 1948. Resolution 217 A (III) of 10 December 1948, General Assembly of the United Nations. Accessed November 10, 2020. https://www.un.org/en/universal-declaration-human-rights/index.html.

CHAPTER 5

Family Demography and Values in Europe: Continuity and Change

Detlev Lück, Kerstin Ruckdeschel, Anna Dechant, and Norbert F. Schneider

INTRODUCTION

Some characteristics of family lives and family demography in Europe have remained particularly stable throughout the last century, while others have changed rapidly. Both, the persisting aspects and the main pathways of change show common patterns throughout Europe (and beyond). There are remarkable differences in the timing and speed of these changes; however, even these differences show common patterns (Schneider 2011). Values and cultural-normative conceptions of how families and family biographies should look like often mirror the structural manifestations of families and of family demography.

Reciprocal influences cause this interrelation: Factual family demographic situations shape the subjective perceptions, expectations, and evaluations of the people experiencing them. The subjective views, again, strongly affect individual behaviour. Accordingly, on the macro-level, statistically predominant

---

D. Lück (✉) · K. Ruckdeschel · A. Dechant · N. F. Schneider
Federal Institute for Population Research (BiB), Wiesbaden, Germany
e-mail: detlev.lueck@bib.bund.de

K. Ruckdeschel
e-mail: kerstin.ruckdeschel@bib.bund.de

A. Dechant
e-mail: anna.dechant@bib.bund.de

N. F. Schneider
e-mail: norbert.schneider@bib.bund.de

© The Author(s), under exclusive license to Springer Nature Switzerland AG 2021
A.-M. Castrén et al. (eds.), *The Palgrave Handbook of Family Sociology in Europe*, https://doi.org/10.1007/978-3-030-73306-3_5

or predominantly perceived family patterns create according cultural conceptions, and vice versa. Consequently, cultural differences between countries, regions, and social milieus are key factors in the explanation of relevant differences in family-related behaviour and demographic outcomes. Furthermore, cultural developments are key factors in understanding changes in family lives and in family demography. This contribution introduces main approaches to explaining the continuities and changes of family demography in Europe from a cultural perspective and indicates their strengths and limitations. We focus on theoretical approaches that have been highly influential in empirical research in sociology throughout Europe.

The question of the degree to which social and demographic behaviour are driven by cultural factors—in contrast to structural factors on the one hand (including political, economic, and other contexts) and to agency on the other hand—has always challenged sociology and demography studies, since the answer has highly relevant implications. In particular, the prediction of future trends and the identification of policies that are able to influence this future depend on the knowledge of to what degree values, norms, habits, and other normative conceptions determine our behaviour. Furthermore, they depend on the knowledge of what determines these conceptions. However, cultural concepts are often only "backgrounded" in demographic concepts as they seem to be difficult to operationalise in demographic models (Bachrach 2014).

In focussing on cultural change, we concentrate on cultural concepts underlying models of demographic change. We start with a short introduction on related terminology and theoretical concepts that form the basis of relevant approaches, outlining a few peculiarities of debates on culture. We proceed by pointing out a few aspects of family lives in Europe that have remained particularly stable throughout the last century, despite all changes occurring. We then focus on the main historic patterns of change in family lives. In alignment with the temporal division in modernisation on the one hand (which is the transformation from agricultural to industrial societies and the complex set of related processes, such as urbanisation, secularisation, and the replacement of religious belief by rational reflection) and late modernity on the other hand, and we assign each theoretical approach to one of these two eras. In the context of modernisation, we refer to the concept of the First Demographic Transition, the Value of Children approach, the modernisation theory, and the establishment of the nuclear family. In the context of late modernity, our discussion includes the concept of the Second Demographic Transition, the individualisation shift thesis as well as an overview of further sociological approaches to changing gender roles and pluralisation of family lives, ideas regarding the change of family relations as well as concepts of life course change. A further chapter refers to theories on cross-cultural differences. Finally, in a short conclusion, we discuss the importance of including cultural aspects in studies on family demography.

Terminology, Conceptions, Causal Mechanisms, and Operationalisations

Cultural approaches suffer from a set of specific interrelated challenges. As these need to be kept in mind when evaluating them and the according empirical evidence, they are outlined here before we turn to the approaches as such.

One core challenge of any scientific debate on culture is that it uses a large variety of terms and of underlying theoretical concepts. These range from values, attitudes, and preferences, social roles, norms, and expectations to everyday knowledge, understandings, representations, schemas, conceptions, frames, scripts, and habits (for more detailed overviews of a few of these concepts, see e.g., Lamont and Small 2008; Leung and Morris 2015). In part, the empirical phenomena the concepts aim to describe are roughly the same. However, even if they are distinguishable from a theoretical perspective, they are often not distinguishable empirically, which has to do with two further challenges:

First, the methodological operationalisations are rarely precise enough to allow one interpretation only. In survey research, a common operationalisation would be to ask whether a respondent agrees or disagrees with a certain normative statement or generally across a number of similar statements. Another example is the Inglehart Index (Inglehart 1977), which is based on a ranking of four political goals according to the respondent's evaluation of their importance. Whether such an indicator measures a value, a preference or something else remains debatable. Secondly, even if it is clear which concept an indicator is measuring, findings based on this indicator may reflect a different phenomenon than it appears. Most of the cultural concepts are strongly correlated. The subjective perception of society expecting mothers to be homemakers, for example, will empirically be strongly correlated to the personal attitude that mothers should *not* be reduced to that role. For these reasons, decisions on how to interpret an empirical finding, which concept to refer to and which term to use are difficult and, to some degree, arbitrary. This makes it harder for debates to be related and for each theoretical approach to be tested empirically.

Nevertheless, for the theoretical debate the question is relevant because certain concepts suggest certain causal mechanisms of *how* factual family demography affects culture and vice versa. Being unable to discuss the similarities and differences here systematically, we suggest three dimensions for indicating how concepts vary:

1. Concepts may refer to (a) a micro-phenomenon, assigned to individuals (e.g. a personal attitude), (b) a macro-phenomenon, assigned to societies or groups (e.g. a social norm), or (c) both at the same time (e.g. a value).
2. Concepts may refer to (a) a general phenomenon that potentially affects all kinds of behaviour in almost any situation (e.g. a value) or (b) a

specific phenomenon that is very much linked to one particular issue (e.g. an attitude).
3. Concepts may refer to (a) a personal evaluation of an actor (ego) themselves (e.g. an attitude), (b) an expectation based on the perceived evaluation of others (alter) (e.g. a norm), or (c) an implicitly underlying, potentially subconscious assumption or routine (e.g. a habit).

The causal mechanisms are rarely empirically studied within sociology, probably due to the methodological restrictions described above. They are rather addressed in theoretical debates, suggesting why mutual influences are likely to exist. We give two examples of these theoretical approaches.

One example comes from the sociology of knowledge: Berger and Luckmann's theory of the social construction of reality (Berger and Luckmann 1966) argues that people who are interacting with each other within a given societal or social context create mental representations of each other's actions through the repeated mutual experience of these actions. Over time and with increasing experience and habituation, these turn into reciprocal roles that structure further interactions. By making these habituated mental representations available to others, they become institutionalised. Then, a shared intersubjective knowledge—or rather, believed knowledge—is created: a knowledge of how people (supposedly) act, who takes which role and who is entitled, responsible or obliged to do what. A social process of interaction and socialisation constructs reality. For the present context, this means that repeatedly performed and mutually experienced factual family demography creates routines, expectations, and roles concerning family and family relations. These again prompt the ways in which individuals interact.

A second example is focussed predominantly on how cultural conceptions affect individual behaviour and the factual family demography. The answer offered by the theory of Frame Selection (Esser 2002, 2009; Kroneberg 2006) has its roots in rational choice theories and represents an attempt to link these to cultural-constructive approaches: People either make decisions based on rational reflections of costs and benefits or they rely on non-reflective routines, called "scripts". The latter happens if the situation in which an actor finds himself oder herself matches a culturally pre-defined category of situations, called a "frame". The better the situation matches, the more likely the selection of the automatic-spontaneous mode of action over the reflecting-calculating mode. Each frame is linked to at least one script that is then activated. In this context, this means that if an individual feels familiar with a family-related situation, they will more or less unconsciously decide to follow an according routine. The aggregation of individual behaviour, then, is reproducing and shaping macro-conditions, including culture. There are at least two examples of the adoption of this model on family-related issues: Esser (2002) has applied the model to the choice (not) to divorce and Jan Eckhard (2014) has applied it to the decision (not) to have children.

Most approaches are focussed on one direction of the reciprocal causal relation. Authors of some publications have assumed a one-way causal impact, mostly from subjective normative conceptions on demographic behaviour (e.g. Hakim 2003). However, these need to be regarded as simplifications of a rather multi-dimensional complex reciprocal relationship.

Continuities

Between the phases of change, described in the following two chapters, patterns of family lives have often remained rather stable for several decades. A few aspects of family lives have even remained particularly stable throughout all recent history and across all of Europe. These include the fact that, in most people's subjective perceptions, family has remained one of the most important spheres of life, if not the most important one. There is also a notable orientation towards the monogamous couple relationship as the aspired living arrangement as well as the fact that satisfaction with a relationship is the best predictor for overall life satisfaction. Finally, they include a general tendency within the division of paid work and unpaid care work between men and women in couple relationships, which has only gradually shifted (Schneider 2011). These continuities are seldom addressed in research. However, to understand the stability of these patterns, cultural-normative conceptions may be even more relevant than for the processes of change.

Change in the Era of Modernisation

Family demography in Europe and the Western world has undergone fundamental changes, particularly in the late nineteenth and early twentieth centuries, in the process of industrialisation, urbanisation, and modernisation. In our view, the most comprehensive description of the changes within family demography in this era is labelled the Demographic Transition.

The Demographic Transition

The Demographic Transition (Notestein 1945) describes a process of four phases that societies usually go through during the transition from agricultural to industrial societies. They start at a high level of mortality, because levels of prosperity and medical care are low. At the same time, these societies have relatively high fertility rates—on average, around four to five births per woman in Western Europe, and higher in most other regions. These processes are balanced in such a way that the size of the population remains roughly stable. With the industrialisation process, nutrition and sanitation improve. Consequently, mortality decreases, particularly childhood and infant mortality, which results in a strong increase in the population. With some delay, the fertility level adjusts to the new situation: The number of births per woman decreases to approximately two or slightly above. With the decreasing fertility level, population growth ends.

This transition has been observed to follow similar paths throughout Europe. Accordingly, the thesis that it marks the transition from agricultural to industrial societies is well accepted (Myrskylä et al. 2009). However, the causal mechanisms behind the Demographic Transition are controversial, particularly regarding the fertility decline (Bulatao 2001; Hirschman 1994; Mason 1997). Therefore, it is not certain which role culture plays within this process. Researchers tend to find that cultural and structural factors contribute to this process, with the exact mechanisms varying by country. Nevertheless, the concept of the Demographic Transition does not emphasise cultural influence specifically. However, it is helpful as a reference for the cultural approaches focussing on specific changes within this era as well as the concept of the Second Demographic Transition, described later.

The Value of Children Approach

The question of how to explain the fertility decline linked to modernisation is debated not only in demography but also in sociology. Here, in particular, the answers rooted in the Value of Children approach (Hoffman 1975; Hoffmann and Hoffmann 1975; Nauck 2006, 2014) are influential.

According to this approach, a decision to have or not to have children, as well as deciding on a certain number of children, is based on the goals that individuals or couples intend to reach by having children, consciously or otherwise. Various authors distinguish different kinds of values that may be associated with children, such as "economic utility", "social comparison, competition" or "stimulation, novelty, fun" (Hoffmann and Hoffmann 1975). The associated values vary individually but also between societies and developmental states of societies, depending, for example, on the predominant types of occupation or the cultural evaluation of parenthood. In less developed societies, economic utility and a corresponding increase in social status are important reasons for having children. In a society with a high level of prosperity and welfare, health insurance, social security and pension systems and a small agricultural sector, the need for schooling and the importance of tertiary education make children costly rather than economically valuable. Accordingly, in an industrial or post-industrial highly developed society, children can no longer provide the achievement of the same goals. Other reasons for having children become more relevant, such as emotional stimulation and affection, self-development or the availability of social ties later in life. Following this approach, a few children are enough to achieve the "late modern" values connected to them. Accordingly, with some delay, social status also becomes linked to a lower number of children.

The Value of Children approach is one of several examples of the complex interplay between structural and cultural changes as well as between societal context and agency. In essence, the economic transformation of societies modifies the cultural-normative evaluations of children and of numbers of children. These, again, impact couples' decisions about the number of children they want to have. This certainly can explain the fertility decline linked to the Demographic Transition. It also can explain changes in fertility in other historic phases as well as cross-cultural differences in fertility (Nauck 2006). The approach is insofar restricted as it assumes that couples make rational decisions (even if these are influenced by cultural ascriptions) regarding the number of children they have, which certainly is not necessarily the case.

Modernisation and the Establishment of the Nuclear Family

In the course of the modernisation process, a distinct pattern of family demography emerges, starting in the late nineteenth century and reaching its peak in the post-war years between 1950 and 1965. This pattern involves the nuclear family as well as a standard life course and family life cycle as universal standards, at least in Western Europe, the USA, and other regions of the Western world. The pattern includes a close linkage and biographically fast realisation of heterosexual monogamous partnerships, marriage, cohabitation, parenthood with approximately two children, a complementary gender-specific division of paid work and care work and little support by public childcare. Simultaneously, strong social norms are established, defining this pattern as the only legitimate and strongly normatively expected track. Theories on the emergence of the nuclear family have been discussed in sociology, particularly from a functionalist perspective (Parsons and Bales 1956), which is hardly supported today, in light of the re-increasing diversity of family forms and trajectories. Rather well accepted are theoretical reflections about the standardisation of life courses (Kohli 2007). The emergence of these patterns is furthermore well empirically described by historic research.

In the centuries before industrialisation, the predominant form of household arrangement in Europe was a married couple with children plus other relatives, maidservants, and farmhands, all of whom would operate a common farm or crafts workshop. The household usually represented both a business and a private living arrangement, which could be considered a "family". At the same time, it could be a place for home-schooling and even jurisdiction. The married couple was the centre, with the husband the unquestioned head of the household. Hierarchies were strict (Cavallo 2010; Shorter 1976). Only those men who had the means to run their own businesses—who had inherited a farm or who had their own workshop and master craftsman's diploma—received the allowance from their liege or guild to marry. Overall, the church only allowed married couples to have children. A strict institutional regulation of family trajectories, reinforced by strong religious cultural norms, was intended to avoid the birth of children who could not be provided for. Family was very much an economic matter. Children who could not be provided for by the household business were often sent away as maidservants or farmhands to other households where they were needed. Siblings or other relatives without an allowance to marry or without husbands or wives were also accepted into the household, as there were few other places they could go (Cavallo 2010). Wives would have many births. However, hardly more than half of the children born would live to adulthood, so the average number of children living in a household was not necessarily much higher than in early industrial ages (Shorter 1976).

Industrialisation and urbanisation forced people to find new living arrangements. Since the majority of people made their living as manual workers in industrial production in bigger cities, most households no longer had servants. Paid work and private living were rather separated; household and family became a sphere of their own and a counterbalance against the strain of industrial work. Marriage, children, and household size were economically relevant only in terms of consumption and household production, no longer in terms of economic production. For example, there was no need to take in unmarried siblings into the household, and households condensed to nuclear families. The number of children born declined, as they tended to live past childhood and required investments into their education rather than acting as a support for the subsistence of the household. Many changes appeared to be mainly driven by economic structures; cultural change was best visible within family relations. Marriage continued to be a standard living arrangement. However, it became perceived as a civil contract rather than a sacrament of the church. Romantic love replaced "fitting" as main criterion for choice of partner. With children's schooling and other responsibilities being delegated to other institutions, families were able to focus on and expand their remaining responsibilities, particularly those for primary socialisation and providing emotional closeness to its family members (Kertzer and Barbagli 2001, 2002).

A particularly interesting process of change that occurred simultaneously was the emergence of complementary gender roles. With paid work and private households as two physically separate spheres, it became possible to distinguish the two and meaningfully divide responsibilities for tasks inside and outside the household. Principally, there was now a reason to split these tasks, since the separation of spheres and the reduction of child labour introduced a problem of reconciling paid work and childcare. However, at the turn of the nineteenth to the twentieth century, when the complementary division of responsibilities was established as a social norm, the large majority of couples were unable to afford to have a housewife not contributing to the household income—this practice was only common in the 1950s. So, the bourgeois arrangement of gender roles started as a practice of the economic elite and took roughly 50 years to diffuse through society, much in line with the economic means to afford such arrangements. Interestingly, complementary gender roles have been promoted partially in the spirit of liberating women from the patriarchal hierarchy that would define the husband as absolute head of the household in every sphere: Ascribing women a "natural" competence for childcare and empathy was a feminist act in the sense that women at least received some responsibility of their own. Accordingly, what we would consider conservative or "traditional" gender roles today were rather perceived as progressive or "modern" gender roles at the time. Nevertheless, the strong proclamation of a supposedly natural particularly strong emotional bond between a biological mother and her child is certainly one of the most far-reaching social constructions of reality of the industrial age (Hardyment 2007; Schütze 1986).

The well-known sociological theories on modernisation formulated at the time offer illustrations of this process of social construction. Émile Durkheim, for example, does not only offer a theoretical reflection on the decline of household and family sizes with his "law of contraction" (Durkheim [1892] 1965). He also offers a quite favourable analysis of the complementary gender roles in "De la division du travail social" (Durkheim [1893] 2014), arguing that the modernisation process provokes a reorganisation of social relationships from similarity to complementarity, which creates mutual dependence. It is also suggested explicitly that in heterosexual relationships women specialise in affection and men in intellectual reflection (idem). In a similar but more elaborate way, Talcott Parsons and Robert Bales (1956) claimed that the formation of the nuclear family as the dominant (and eventually, only) family form was the necessary outcome of modernisation. The complementary gender roles appear as a functional necessity. Parsons defines the husband's responsibility to hold the "instrumental" and the wife's responsibility to hold the "expressive" role. Higher effectivity and efficiency have, in one way or another, served the conclusion that complementary gender roles were increasing necessarily over the course of social change. Efforts to frame the nuclear family and complementary division of work intellectually may illustrate how deeply the evolution of family demography was culturally established as well as contributing to a process of constructing cultural conceptions.

Continuity and Change in the Era of Late Modernity

When analysing social change in general, sociological analyses tend to identify a turning point in the mid-1960s. Here, the process of industrialisation was moving forward and entering a phase of post-industrialisation, with the service sector gaining more importance than industrial production. Many labels have been applied to the era of societal change starting here, such as "post-modernisation" or the "second modernity". Remarkably, family demography also took a completely new direction of change in the mid-1960s that persists today.

The Second Demographic Transition

The most comprehensive description of the changes within family demography in this era is labelled the Second Demographic Transition (Lesthaeghe 1995; van de Kaa 1987). The concept relates to the thesis of the (First) Demographic Transition. The latter is the characteristic transformation of family demography of societies entering the industrial era, as described before. The industrial era is typically linked to an increase in prosperity in the long run. This is the starting point for the value change from materialism to post-materialism described by Ronald Inglehart (1977, 2018). The value change, again, causes fundamental changes in family demography, as Ron Lesthaeghe (1995) and Dirk van de Kaa (1987) describe. Accordingly, every society entering the industrial age and experiencing the Demographic Transition will typically, after it has reached a certain level of prosperity, experience the *Second* Demographic Transition a few decades later.

The theory of value change by Inglehart (1977, 2018) suggests that values are biographically developed in adolescence according to needs that are unfulfilled at the time. The values developed will focus on needs of survival ("materialism") as long as survival cannot be taken for granted. They will focus on less fundamental issues of well-being ("post-materialism") if—always at a young age—a safe home and the reliable provision of food are nothing to be concerned about. With the increase of prosperity and welfare, the societal conditions for the development of values change. This happened quite late in the industrial age, as the two world wars continued to impose existential threats on people; this situation was only reached in the mid-1960s, after a decade of stable peace and strong increase in prosperity, and post-war generations of post-materialists appeared. Through the gradual demographic exchange of generations, societies undergo a gradual shift from materialism to post-materialism, introducing new orientations towards individual self-fulfilment, hedonism, emancipation, women's rights, environmental protection, etc., although at different paces and manifesting at different intensities across various social segments of societies.

Such fundamental cultural changes affect family biographies and family forms: Fundamental changes in family demography can be observed in Europe starting in the mid-1960s and persisting today. The theoretical link between the two is encompassed by the concept of the Second Demographic Transition by Dirk van de Kaa (1987, 1994, 2002) and Ron Lesthaeghe (1995; Lesthaeghe 1995, 2010).

The empirical analysis of the transformation and its theoretical interpretation has evolved over the course of decades. Core theses are that "the principal demographic feature of this second transition is the decline in fertility from somewhat above the 'replacement' level of 2.1 births per woman […] to a level well below replacement" (van de Kaa 1987) and that the Second Demographic Transition is characterised by four sub-processes (van de Kaa 1987):

- the weakening of marriage as the only type of family structure, resulting from high divorce rates and a rise in cohabitation,
- a shift in family relations from 'king-child with parents' to 'king-pair with child',
- a shift from preventive contraception to self-fulfilling contraception,

- The uniform family (the conjugal family) starts giving way to more pluralistic forms of families.

The four sub-processes mainly represent shifts in individual orientations due value change. In interaction with given institutional and legal structures, these cause a large number of demographic changes, such as decreasing marriage rates, a stop of the decline and eventually a renewed increase of the age at marriage, rise in premarital cohabitation, increasing divorce rates, increasing share of couples cohabiting without the intention to marry, a loosened link between sexual intercourse and fertility, a loosened temporal link between marriage and childbearing, decline in fertility below the replacement level, rise in non-marital fertility, and an increase in the heterogeneity of family forms.

Given that it refers to value change as a driving force, the concept of the Second Demographic Transition could be considered a genuine cultural approach. However, structural contexts also play an important role, because value change as such has economic structural causes. The concept has been strongly influential in empiric research to date, at least in terms of demography. However, there has also been increasing criticism, particularly because the concept lacks a clear gender perspective (Bernhardt 2004). Several authors argue that the dynamics of family demography rather mirror a change in power relations between women and men (Cherlin 2016; Esping-Andersen and Billari 2015; Goldscheider et al. 2015). Furthermore, it can be argued that family relations have, in recent decades, been shifting back from "king-couple with child" to "king-child with parents" (see section on "Dehierarchisation of family relations and increasing requirements for parenting").

Changing Gender Roles, Declining Birth Rates and Pluralisation of Family Lives in Sociological Perspectives

Several sociological theoretical approaches have been implemented to address the de-standardisation of the nuclear family, declining birth rates and other family demographic changes, for a long time. Here, we introduce a few influential examples. Sociological theories (and lately, the demographic debate) are usually strongly focussed on the change of gender roles in the division of paid work and care work. This process is of major importance for families' everyday lives and individuals' life courses in Europe; it implies, for example, stronger career orientation among women, somewhat stronger engagement of men in childcare, less uneven power relations and legal equalisation. In many ways, gender is a sociological research topic of its own. Since this contribution is focussed on family demography, the following analyses are limited to those that *also* address gender role change, in addition to the demographic transitions described above.

A popular theoretical frame is the thesis of an individualisation shift in "second modernity" by Beck and Beck-Gernsheim (Beck 1992; Beck and Beck-Gernsheim 1993). The authors suggest that in late modernity, the awareness emerges that modernisation and technological innovation may have negative implications, such as social inequality or pollution. Accordingly, a naive trust in any modernisation trend is exchanged for critical reflection. Within this process, a shift in accelerated individualisation also occurs: Individuals are released from traditional ascriptions and normative expectations related to, for example, origin, social class, or sex. Accordingly, they can choose life-course tracks on their own regarding partnerships, children, careers, and so on. Female emancipation is one important outcome, and fertility declines because parenthood becomes one biographical option among others. However, the freedom to design one's own life course comes with the obligation to do so: With the loss of a normative standard life course, orientation is lost and replaced by the burden of decision making. Individuals become self-responsible and held responsible for the outcomes of their decisions. This is rarely experienced as freedom, particularly since information that would be necessary to make a *well-informed* decision is often lacking. The failure of individual life-course decisions is a permanent risk that people need to take on. A partnership may break up, parenthood may intervene with career aspirations and education goals or career tracks may fail. Further difficulties emerge with partnership formation when two individually planned life courses need to be coordinated. Consequently, the individual choice of life courses leads to a larger variety of family forms and family life cycles, partly because it reflects a variety of individual preferences (such as those of unmarried or voluntary childless couples) and partly because unintended outcomes are experienced (such as single parents or stepfamilies).

Similar argumentations come, for example, from the thesis of the "deinstitutionalization of the nuclear family" (Tyrell 1988), describing change of families as a loss of the family's character as an institution. It argues that the family in the mid-twentieth century could be regarded institution regulated by a set of social norms and regulations to ensure that families fulfil certain societal needs. However, legal regulations and cultural norms have weakened, leaving individuals with fewer and much less restrictive conventions for how to conduct their family lives. State, church, and culture exercise little influence anymore. Complementary to the "deinstitutionalization" thesis, several microlevel approaches emphasise agency and the dynamic processes of individually designing family arrangements, life courses, and couples' careers. The Family Configurations approach (Aeby et al. 2019; Widmer and Jallinoja 2008), for example, is focussed on individuals' construction of personal networks over the life course, with early adulthood and life course transitions as decisive phases. These processes lead to individually highly heterogeneous networks that are subjectively regarded as "family". The Doing Family concept (Jurczyk et al. 2019) refers to the concept of Doing Gender (West and Zimmerman 1987)—that describes gender as a result of social construction—and argues that family can be understood as a permanent process of social construction. It involves coordination between the individual lives of the family members ("balance management") as well as the symbolic construction of togetherness.

Quite similarly, the concept of Family Practices (Morgan 2011a, b) takes the perspective that family consists of the daily acts of individual people, creating togetherness between them and other family members and thereby creating a family. These practices are embedded in other sets of practices as well as macro-level contexts. However, they are not determined in that respect; they are fluid, in the sense of constantly changing. These approaches mirror a strong focus of current European family sociology on family as a dynamic process of social construction and reconstruction, highly dependent on micro-level interactions and subjective understandings. They give room to cultural influence as well as influence of other macro-level contexts, in which construction processes are embedded. However, the outcomes appear less predictable than according to other theoretical approaches.

Dehierarchisation of Family Relations and Increasing Requirements for Parenting

Among the recent historic changes in the context of family sociology, highly important changes are occurring in family relations, although these have received appropriate attention in terms of research and theoretical debate rather late. The changes concern all family relations, including those between partners and spouses as well as between parents and children. Here, at least two major processes have been observed: a process of dehierarchisation of family relations and a process of increasing requirements for parenting.

Dehierarchisation implies that hierarchies between sexes and between generations decline. The distribution of power becomes more equal. Husbands no longer (should) have power over their wives. Parents are no longer entitled to command and expect obedience from their children in the same ways they used to; instead of punishment, instructions need to be repeated patiently. When asked by their children, parents need to explain their decisions and instructions. This process is neither restricted to the twentieth century but has been, with interruptions, ongoing at least since the modernisation era. This process certainly has changed people's everyday lives in a more profound way than many of the demographic changes discussed earlier. In the following, we discuss a few particularly well recognised theoretical concepts describing and interpreting these trends.

Anthony Giddens (1993) suggests that the change of intimate sexual relations is characterised by the emergence of "pure relationships" with the sole purpose of fulfilling the partners' needs for intimacy. They are liberated from traditions and the duty to fulfil social expectations, such as marriage or procreation. Love in the pure relationship is confluent in the sense that it is not taken for granted but under permanent evaluation as to whether it is still mutual, equal, and mutually satisfying. The relationship lasts only as long as it is considered rewarding by both partners. Breaking up is not a taboo, but rather the logical consequence of the relationship losing its purpose. The analysis is quite similar to the identification of individualised life courses by Beck and

Beck-Gernsheim (Beck 1992; Beck and Beck-Gernsheim 1995). It is in line with research confirming that intimacy and romantic love gain new qualities and relevance in late-modern couple relationships (Singer 2009). Despite this general convergence towards more equal relationships and increasing freedom of choice in intimacy, social inequalities associated with gender, social class, and ethnicity still shape these trends (Jamieson 1999).

Another well-accepted analysis comes from François de Singly (1996), who suggests that the understanding of couples' lives is transforming from a "couple fusionnel" ("fusion couple") to a "couple fissionnel" ("associative couple"). The typology is characterised by varying degrees of individual autonomy and fusion. According to the concept of the fusion couple, living as a couple implies loosing one's individual identity, particularly for women. The individual is merged in the couple, which then will present itself towards third people always as "we" and "us", ignoring individual perceptions, moods, attitudes, desires, activities, and planning. In the associative couple, however, partners remain individuals who insist on maintaining individual perspectives and retaining autonomy. Here, couple life implies permanent coordination and negotiation between these two perspectives, which can be challenging and threaten relationships. Separating is considered a legitimate strategy for dealing with incompatible interests and relationship problems. Similarly to Giddens, de Singly also observes a shift from task-orientation to relationship-orientation in the self-conception of couples.

A concept that focuses on parent–child relation rather than couple relation is the proposal of a shift from "command households" to "negotiation households" by de Swaan (1982) and Du Bois-Reymond (1995, 1999). Its core thesis is that households—particularly the parent–child relation—shift from management through command to management through negotiation. The unequal distribution of power fades, as does the belief in obedience and duties. In the negotiation household, all family members, both parents and children, participate in decision-making processes and are equally entitled to express their views. Decisions are made based on the most convincing rationale, not on an uneven power relation.

Increasingly egalitarian processes in relationships do not occur linearly or universally. Research finds that social differentiation and inequality among partners still exist and may be remarkably resistant to change (Jamieson 1999). Traditional and modern attitudes, in that respect, may coexist (Grunow et al. 2018; Knight and Brinton 2017). However, as a general trend in the last decades, the thesis of an increase in egalitarian relationships can be accepted.

Not only are parents losing their absolute authority over their children, but they are also confronted with increasing requirements regarding parenting. There is an increasing supply of pedagogic and medical knowledge with implications for parenting as well as a greater supply of expert advice. This leads to an increasing social expectation that parents stay informed and follow the advice offered based on the most recent scientific state of the art. This concerns all aspects of child care, from women's nutrition during pregnancy to the choice of occupational careers of the adolescent child; parenting undergoes a trend of "educationalisation" (Furedi 2002; Hardyment 2007).

Another aspect makes parenting more demanding in late modernity. It mainly derives from the increasing emphasis on the individual responsibility, as described by the individualisation thesis: Successful child development is increasingly considered the parents' responsibility. Whether a child is well educated, in good health, successful at school, talented in terms of sports or music, has good friends, finds a nice partner, participates in rewarding hobbies, and achieves a promising career—parents are increasingly expected to be concerned about all of these factors and feel responsible if things turn out badly. Accordingly, parents care about their children's development in many more ways than they did in the early twentieth century, or even in pre-industrial times (Furedi 2002; Kaufmann 1990).

Life Courses and Family Careers

Since the mid-twentieth century, the average age at first marriage and first birth have been increasing. This is an almost universal trend across Europe that has continued to date (Billari et al. 2008).

One driving force is the change of occupation and the rising importance of tertiary education. This leads to increasing shares of young adults attending colleges and universities, which implies longer educational biographical phases. A second driving force in recent decades is the uncertainty of labour markets: After education is finished, entering the labour market and finding an adequately paid job has recently been harder for many European generations, compared to the 1960s. This has consequences for the entire life course: Children tend to move out of their parents' houses, find steady life partners, move in together, marry and have children at later ages: The structure of life courses has shifted. This shift has revealed a new life course phase known as "post-adolescence", consisting of people in their early (or even late) 20s who are legally adults but economically dependent on their parents and not fully socially self-responsible, e.g. because they are attending university. Additionally, there is a larger heterogeneity of life courses, with a relevant share remaining without partners, partly by coincidence, partly by choice. Lifelong monogamous marriage is typically replaced by sequences of monogamous relationships as well as phases of singlehood. The postponement of marriage and first birth in the life course has artificially decreased common demographic period indicators, such as total marriage rates and total fertility rates, and thereby has given a more drastic impression of the demographic changes in Europe than what has actually occurred (Bongaarts and Feeney 2008).

Cross-Cultural Differences

The processes of change described in the past sections have more or less been observed all over Europe. However, countries and regions have experienced them at very different levels and in different decades (Schneider 2011). Among the common trends, the patterns regarding which countries are leading change and which are following have repeated themselves: Scandinavia and the North-West of Europe are often in the front, countries in Southern Europe are rather late and post-communist societies in Eastern Europe are experiencing many transitions with strong delays, shortly after the fall of the Iron Curtain (Billari et al. 2008). This suggests that there are common explanations for temporal delays that can be found in economic or institutional settings, e.g. in the stage of industrialisation or post-industrialisation. They can also be found in cultural differences, such as predominant religious denominations. As many examples in this section (e.g. the Value of Children approach or the value change to post-materialism) have shown, both can be hard to distinguish and are certainly strongly interrelated.

The difficulties in identifying causes and consequences in cross-cultural comparisons of historic changes have led many authors to merely describe the differences in typologies and deliberately forego clear analyses of causal mechanisms. A particularly prominent typology is the distinction of welfare regimes by Esping-Andersen (1990), which, however, is more concerned with policies than with family demography and family relations. It has been criticised for ignoring gender aspects (Lewis 1992). In response to Esping-Andersen, other typologies have been developed focussed on family and gender, particularly gender regimes (Pascall and Lewis 2004; Sainsbury 1999). An early example is the typology suggested by Ilona Ostner and Jane Lewis (1995), differentiating between strong, medium, and weak male breadwinner states.

Birgit Pfau-Effinger (1996, 2004) suggests a particularly meaningful typology, especially in terms of a cultural perspective. Her typology of Gender Arrangements provides a theoretical framework as well as a suggestion for an empirical research agenda. Based on macro-level research, Pfau-Effinger distinguishes five arrangements (or cultural models) of sharing paid work and care work between women, men and the state in Western Europe. These are: "(1) the family-economy model", which implies family businesses in which paid work and care work are provided jointly within the same household, "(2) the housewife model of the male breadwinner marriage, (3) the part-time career model of the male breadwinner marriage, (4) the dual breadwinner model with external child care, and (5) the dual breadwinner model with partner-shared child care" (Pfau-Effinger 2004). This work seems exemplary and appropriate for understanding cross-national differences in two ways. First, it combines structural and cultural influences theoretically to explain cross-national differences by suggesting that the cultural context ("gender culture") and the institutional-structural settings ("gender order") are typically balanced and reinforce one another. Secondly, Pfau-Effinger's model allows and empirically identifies social change in such a way that a given society may change its gender arrangement over time. This is certainly true not only for gender arrangements but for other aspects of family relations and of family demography as well.

Conclusion

Families and family demography in Europe have repeatedly undergone profound changes. In recent history, two major trends are observable: first, the formation of the nuclear family and a standard family life cycle as societal standards during the industrialisation era until the mid-twentieth century, and second, an increasing diversity of living arrangements and family trajectories as well as socially accepted family forms, which started in the mid-1960s. Within the latter trend, a core transition in recent decades is the detachment of parenthood and marriage. Both trends were accompanied by according processes of cultural change. For both trends, or at least for aspects of them, sociology has offered explanations that draw on culture as a driving force, but not the only driving force.

No simple answers have been found to the question of whether structure affects culture or vice versa. There is little empirical evidence disentangling the two. Research and theoretical debate rather tend to converge on the insight that the causal relationship is reciprocal. The legal regulation and factual availability of, for example, assisted reproductive technologies (ART) will certainly be affected by the previously established social acceptance of using ART and, at the same time, affect the social acceptance in the present and near future. Identifying cause and effect appears to be an obsolete endeavour. In studying particular historic processes of social change in particular societies, it certainly may be worthwhile to identify contradictions and influences between structural settings, social acceptance, and behaviour, maybe even in more differentiated ways. In terms of general assumptions, contemporary approaches mostly assume a reciprocal influence between culture and structure and a tendency of mutual correspondence, as in the example of Pfau-Effinger's (2004) Gender Arrangements. What can be stated with certainty is that the influence of culture is highly relevant, even though not quantifiable. However, it interacts strongly with structural influences, so that research approaches should not look for purely cultural explanations in an isolated way.

A similar conclusion can be drawn regarding the relationship between cultural and structural factors on the one hand and agency on the other. The debate on this relationship has become less controversial since most approaches have assumed agency to be restricted by structural and cultural boundaries, which in return are reproduced and eventually changed through individual actions. A progressive social group may, by introducing a new behavioural pattern (e.g. cohabitation without marriage), challenge existing habits, norms, and regulations regarding such behaviour. An initial weakening of norms may encourage others to adopt the novel behaviour, which again weakens opposed norms and, eventually, changes legal regulations and policies, which again will support diffusion through society. Debates have mostly been limited to the degree to which boundaries or agency deserve to be emphasised (e.g. Morgan 2011a; Widmer and Jallinoja 2008). However, here again we can conclude that we are facing complex reciprocal causal interrelations and interactions.

Cultural aspects are a major part of family lives and family demography and need to be taken into account to fully describe related patterns and their changes. They are also vital to a full understanding of the causal mechanisms behind cross-national differences or social change. However, inasmuch as the picture would be incomplete without looking at culture, it would equally be incomplete by looking at culture only.

References

Aeby, G., J.-A. Gauthier, and E. D. Widmer. 2019. "Beyond the Nuclear Family: Personal Networks in Light of Work-Family Trajectories." *Advances in Life Course Research* 39: 51–60. https://doi.org/10.1016/j.alcr.2018.11.002.

Bachrach, C. A. 2014. "Culture and Demography: From Reluctant Bedfellows to Committed Partners." *Demography* 51 (1): 3–25. https://doi.org/10.1007/s13524-013-0257-6.

Beck, U. 1992. *Risk Society: Towards a New Modernity*. London: Sage.

Beck, U., and E. Beck-Gernsheim. 1993. "Nicht Autonomie, Sondern Bastebiographie: Anmerkungen zur Individualisierungsdiskussion am Beispiel des Aufsatzes von Günter Burkart." *Zeitschrift für soziologie* 22 (3): 178–187.

Beck, U., and E. Beck-Gernsheim. 1995. *The Normal Chaos of Love*. Cambridge: Polity Press.

Berger, P. L., and T. Luckmann. 1966. *Social Construction of Reality: A Treatise in the Sociology of Knowledge*. London: Penguin Books.

Bernhardt, E. 2004. "Is the Second Demographic Transition a Useful Concept for Demography?" *Vienna Yearbook of Population Research* 1: 25–28. https://doi.org/10.1553/populationyearbook2004s25.

Billari, F. C., A. C. Liefbroer, and D. Philipov. 2008. "The Postponement of Childbearing in Europe: Driving Forces and Implications." *Vienna Yearbook of Population Research* 2006: 1–17. https://doi.org/10.1553/populationyearbook2006s1.

Bongaarts, J., and G. Feeney. 2008. "The Quantum and Tempo of Life-Cycle Events." *Vienna Yearbook of Population Research* 2006: 115–151. https://doi.org/10.1553/populationyearbook2006s115.

Bulatao, R. A. 2001. "Introduction." In *Population and Development Review: 27 : Supplement. Global Fertility Transition*, edited by R. A. Bulatao and J. B. Casterline, 1–14. New York, NY: Population Council.

Cavallo, S. 2010. "Family Relationships." In *Cultural History of Childhood and Family: The Early Modern Age*, vol. 3, edited by S. Cavallo and S. Evangelisti, 15–32. Oxford: Berg.

Cherlin, A. J. 2016. "A Happy Ending to a Half-Century of Family Change?" *Population and Development Review* 42 (1): 121–129. https://doi.org/10.1111/j.1728-4457.2016.00111.x.

De Singly, F. 1996. *Le Soi, le couple et la famille*. Paris: Nathan.

De Swaan, A. 1982. "Uitgaansbeperking en uitgaansangst. Over de verschuiving van bevelshuishouding naar onderhandelingshuishouding [A Ban on Going Out May

Lead to Fear in the Streets. The Shift from Command Household to Negotiation Household]." In *De mens is de mens een zorg*, edited by A. de Swaan, 81–225. Amsterdam: Meulenhoff.
Du Bois-Reymond, M. 1995. "The Modern Family as a Negotiating Household: Parent-Child Relations in Western and Eastern Germany and in the Netherlands." In *Childhood and Youth in Germany and The Netherlands: Transitions and Coping Strategies of Adolescents*, edited by M. Du Bois-Reymond, R. Diekstra, K. Hurrelmann, and E. Peters, 127–160. Berlin: Walter de Gruyter.
Du Bois-Reymond, M. 1999. "Conflict and Negotiation in the Family." In *Models of Conflict Resolution*, edited by H. I. Sagel-Grande and M. V. Polak, 79–93. Antwerpen and Apeldoorn: E.M. Meijers Inst.
Durkheim, É. [1892] 1965. "The Conjugal Family: transl. George Simpson." *American Journal of Sociology* 70 (5): 527–536. https://doi.org/10.1086/223929.
Durkheim, É. 2014 (orig. 1893). *The division of labor in society*. (Ed. by S. Lukes.) London: Free Press.
Eckhard, J. 2014. "Theoretical Explanations of Increasing Childlessness—Divergent Approaches and the Integrating Potential of the Frame Selection Theory." *Comparative Population Studies* 39 (1): 49–72. https://doi.org/10.12765/CPoS-2014-01en.
Esping-Andersen, G. 1990. *The Three Worlds of Welfare Capitalism*. Princeton, NJ: Princeton University Press.
Esping-Andersen, G., and F. C. Billari. 2015. "Re-theorizing Family Demographics." *Population and Development Review* 41 (1): 1–31. https://doi.org/10.1111/j.1728-4457.2015.00024.x.
Esser, H. 2002. "Ehekrisen: Das Re-Framing der Ehe und der Anstieg der Scheidungsraten." *Zeitschrift für soziologie* 31 (6): 472–496.
Esser, H. 2009. "Rationality and Commitment: The Model of Frame Selection and the Explanation of Normative Action." In *Raymond Boudon: A Life in Sociology; Essays in Honour of Raymond Boudon*, edited by M. Cherkaoui, 207–230. Oxford: Bardwell.
Furedi, F. 2002. *Paranoid Parenting: Why Ignoring the Experts May Be Best for Your Child*. Chicago: Chicago Review Press.
Giddens, A. 1993. *The Transformation of Intimacy: Sexuality, Love and Eroticism in Modern Societies*. Stanford, CA: Stanford University Press.
Goldscheider, F., E. Bernhardt, and T. Lappegård. 2015. "The Gender Revolution: A Framework for Understanding Changing Family and Demographic Behavior." *Population and Development Review* 41 (2): 207–239. https://doi.org/10.1111/j.1728-4457.2015.00045.x.
Grunow, D., K. Begall, and S. Buchler. 2018. "Gender Ideologies in Europe: A Multidimensional Framework." *Journal of Marriage and the Family* 80 (1): 42–60. https://doi.org/10.1111/jomf.12453.
Hakim, C. 2003. *Models of the Family in Modern Societies: Ideals and Realities*. Aldershot: Ashgate.
Hardyment, C. 2007. *Dream Babies: Childcare Advice from John Locke to Gina Ford*. London: Frances Lincoln.
Hirschman, C. 1994. "Why Fertility Changes." *Annual Review of Sociology* 20: 203–233. https://doi.org/10.1146/annurev.so.20.080194.001223.
Hoffman, L. W. 1975. "The Value of Children to Parents and the Decrease in Family Size." *Proceedings of the American Philosophical Society* 119 (6): 430–438.

Hoffmann, L. W., and M. L. Hoffmann. 1975. "The Value of Children to Parents." In *Psychological Perspectives on Population*, edited by J. T. Fawcett, 19–76. New York: Basic Books.

Inglehart, R. 1977. *The Silent Revolution: Changing Values and Political Styles Among Western Publics*. Princeton: Princeton Legacy Library, Princeton University Press.

Inglehart, R. F. 2018. *Cultural Evolution: People's Motivations are Changing, and Reshaping the World*. Cambridge: Cambridge University Press.

Jamieson, L. 1999. "Intimacy Transformed? A Critical Look at the 'Pure Relationship." *Sociology* 33 (3): 477–494. https://doi.org/10.1177/S0038038599000310.

Jurczyk, K., B. Jentsch, J. Sailer, and M. Schier. 2019. "Female-Breadwinner Families in Germany: New Gender Roles?" *Journal of Family Issues* 40 (13): 1731–1754.

Kaufmann, F.-X. 1990. *Zukunft der Familie: Stabilität, Stabilitätsrisiken und Wandel der familialen Lebensformen sowie ihre gesellschaftlichen und politischen Bedingungen. Perspektiven und Orientierungen. Schriftenreihe des Bundeskanzleramtes*, vol. 10. München: Beck.

Kertzer, D. I., and M. Barbagli, eds. 2001. *The History of the European Family, Vol. 1: Family Life in Early Modern Times 1500–1789*. New Haven: Yale University Press.

Kertzer, D. I., and M. Barbagli, eds. 2002. *The History of the European Family, Vol. 2: Family Life in the Long Nineteenth Century 1789–1913*. New Haven: Yale University Press.

Knight, C. R., and M. C. Brinton. 2017. "One Egalitarianism or Several? Two Decades of Gender-Role Attitude Change in Europe." *American Journal of Sociology* 122 (5): 1485–1532. https://doi.org/10.1086/689814.

Kohli, M. 2007. "The Institutionalization of the Life Course: Looking Back to Look Ahead." *Research in Human Development*, 4(3–4): 253–271.

Kroneberg, C. 2006. *The Definition of the Situation and Variable Rationality: The Model of Frame Selection as a General Theory of Action*. Sonderforschungsbereich 504 No. 06–05. Mannheim.

Lamont, M., and M. L. Small. 2008. "How Culture Matters: Enriching our Understanding of Poverty." In *The Colors of Poverty: Why Racial and Ethnic Disparities Exist*, edited by A. C. Lin and D. R. Harris, 76–102. New York, NY: Russell Sage.

Lesthaeghe, R. 1995. "The Second Demographic Transition in Western Countries: An Interpretation." In *International Studies in Demography. Gender and Family Change in Industrialized Countries*, edited by K. O. Mason and A.-M. Jensen [Papers Presented at a Seminar Organized by the Committee on Gender and Population of the International Union for the Scientific Study of Population and held in Rome, January 1992], 1998th ed., 17–62. Oxford: Clarendon Press.

Lesthaeghe, R. 2010. "The Unfolding Story of the Second Demographic Transition." *Population and Development Review* 36 (2): 211–251. https://doi.org/10.1111/j.1728-4457.2010.00328.x.

Leung, K., and M. W. Morris. 2015. "Values, Schemas, and Norms in the Culture–Behavior Nexus: A Situated Dynamics Framework." *Journal of International Business Studies* 46 (9): 1028–1050. https://doi.org/10.1057/jibs.2014.66.

Lewis, J. 1992. "Gender and the Development of Welfare Regimes." *Journal of European Social Policy* 2 (3): 159–173. https://doi.org/10.1177/095892879200200301.

Mason, K. O. 1997. "Explaining Fertility Transitions." *Demography* 34 (4): 443–454.

Morgan, D. H. J. 2011a. "Locating 'Family Practices." *Sociological Research Online* 16 (4): 174–182. https://doi.org/10.5153/sro.2535.
Morgan, D. H. J. 2011b. *Rethinking Family Practices*. Basingstoke: Palgrave Macmillan.
Myrskylä, M., H.-P. Kohler, and F. C. Billari. 2009. "Advances in Development Reverse Fertility Declines." *Nature* 460 (7256): 741–743. https://doi.org/10.1038/nature08230.
Nauck, B. 2006. "Value of Children and Fertility Strategies in Cross-Cultural Comparison. Ideal Family Size and Targeted Fertility in Eleven Societies." In *Social Development and Family Changes*, edited by C. Gomes, 300–344. Newcastle, UK: Cambridge Scholars Press.
Nauck, B. 2014. "Value of Children and the Social Production of Welfare." *Demographic Research* 30: 1793–1824. https://doi.org/10.4054/DemRes.2014.30.66.
Notestein, F. W. 1945. "Population—The Long View." In *Food for the World*, edited by T. W. Schultz, 36–57. Chicago: University of Chicago.
Ostner, I., and J. Lewis. 1995. "Gender and the Evolution of European Social Policies." In *European Social Policy: Between Fragmentation and Integration*, edited by P. Pierson and S. Leibfried, 1–40. Washington, DC: The Brookings Institution.
Pascall, G., and J. Lewis. 2004. "Emerging Gender Regimes and Policies for Gender Equality in a Wider Europe." *Journal of Social Policy* 33 (3): 373–394. https://doi.org/10.1017/S004727940400772X.
Pfau-Effinger, B. 1996. "Analyse internationaler Differenzen in der Erwerbsbeteiligung von Frauen. Theoretischer Rahmen und empirische Ergebnisse." *Kölner Zeitschrift für Soziologie und Sozialpsychologie* 48 (3): 462–492.
Pfau-Effinger, B. 2004. "Socio-Historical Paths of the Male Breadwinner Model—An Explanation of Cross-national Differences." *The British Journal of Sociology* 55 (3): 377–399. https://doi.org/10.1111/j.1468-4446.2004.00025.x.
Parsons, T., and R. F. Bales. 1956. *Family. Socialization and interaction process*. (Edited by James Olds.) Abingdon, Oxon: Routledge.
Sainsbury, D. 1999. *Gender and Welfare State Regimes*. Oxford: Oxford University Press.
Schneider, N. F. 2011. "The Future of the Family in Europe: Diversity and Convergence." In *Family, Ties and Care: Family Transformation in a Plural Modernity*, edited by H. Bertram and N. Ehlert, 225–239. Opladen: Budrich.
Schütze, Y. 1986. *Die gute Mutter: Zur Geschichte des normativen Musters "Mutterliebe". Theorie und Praxis der Frauenforschung*, vol. 3. Bielefeld: Kleine.
Shorter, E. 1976. *The Making of the Modern Family*. London: Collins.
Singer, I. 2009. *The Nature of Love: The Modern World*. 2nd ed., Irving Singer Library: v.3. Cambridge: MIT Press.
Tyrell, H. 1988. "Ehe und Familie: Institutionalisierung und Deinstitutionalisierung." In *Die "postmoderne" Familie: Strategien und Familienpolitik in einer Übergangszeit*, edited by K. Lüscher, F. Schultheis, and M. Wehrspaun, 145–156. UVK.
Van de Kaa, D. J. 1987. "Europe's Second Demographic Transition." *Population Bulletin* 42 (2): 3–55.

Van de Kaa, D. J. 1994. *The Second Demographic Transition Revisited: Theories and Expectations*. Den Haag.

Van de Kaa, D. J. 2002. *The Idea of a Second Demographic Transition in Industrialized Countries. Paper presented at the Sixth Welfare Policy Seminar of the National Institute of Population and Social Security, Tokyo, Japan, 29 January 2002.* Retrieved from http://www.ipss.go.jp/webj-ad/WebJournal.files/population/2003_4/Kaa.pdf.

West, C., and D. H. Zimmerman. 1987. "Doing Gender." *Gender & Society* 1 (2): 125–151.

Widmer, E., and R. Jallinoja, eds. 2008. *Beyond the Nuclear Family: Families in a Configurational Perspective*. Population, Family, and Society, vol. 9. Bern: Lang.

CHAPTER 6

The Configurational Approach to Families: Methodological Suggestions

Eric D. Widmer

This chapter provides insights into addressing empirical research on families as configurations in which neither the family's boundaries nor the set of roles under consideration is taken for granted (Jallinoja and Widmer 2008). From this perspective, families are analysed as large networks of interdependencies that extend well beyond households or the roles and statuses associated with the nuclear family. The following pages contain some methodological suggestions that can be applied to advance the understanding of family configurations. The importance of using dilemmas to uncovering the logics behind family identification and functional interdependences among family members is emphasised.

The configurational approach posits that families are networks of interdependencies formed among human beings; in other words, a family comprises a structure of mutually oriented and functionally dependent persons (Elias 1978). Being interdependent means that one configuration member's practices and decisions have important consequences for those of other members. Individuals are interdependent in a family configuration because each fulfils some of the others' needs for emotional support, financial and practical resources or social recognition (Quintaneiro 2004). Therefore, each person becomes a resource and a constraint for other configuration members, whether directly or indirectly. Thus, rather than cohesive groups bounded by the limits of

---

E. D. Widmer (✉)
Department of Sociology, University of Geneva, Geneva, Switzerland
e-mail: eric.widmer@unige.ch

the household, families are process-oriented networks of functional interdependencies in which individuals not only cooperate, but also hinder each other voluntarily and involuntarily (Widmer 2016). Indeed, in a configurational perspective, what makes individuals interdependent are the functions they have for each other. Such functions relate with economic, practical and emotional support, sociability, sex, identity orientation and cognitive significance, among other dimensions for which contributions of significant others are needed, Functional interdependencies then set specific balances of power, as the power differential between individuals is a translation of the balance of functions they have for one another (Connolly and Dolan 2011).

Individuals in families are linked through functional balance and balance of power. In families, as in other configurations, no party has total control over another and "power games" unfold regarding the distribution of resources in terms of time, money, sociability, or support (Elias 1978). The outcomes of such power games are in most cases unintended, as they are the results of "the interweaving of countless individual interests and intentions" (Elias 1994: 389; Newton 1999). Therefore, the pattern of interdependencies characterising family configurations is also largely unintended. In turn, such large configurations of interdependencies define the family's boundaries, as well as the distinction between insiders and outsiders. Such processes make understanding spouse, parent–child and sibling relationships difficult—if not impossible—without considering the pattern of interdependencies to which such dyads belong (Widmer 2016).

Researchers who focus on configurational issues should consider methods that can best reveal dimensions such as the importance of identification with a family, its set of functional interdependencies and its balance of tensions and power. Relational sociology, under the guidance of Norbert Elias, Georg Simmel, and others (Donati 2010; Elias 1978; Emirbayer 1997; Simmel 2015) has theorised and empirically considered various processes that shape all human groupings in a variety of ways beyond families. This chapter contains some methodological suggestions that may enhance the design of future studies on family configurations. We assume that understanding the family from a configurational perspective means unfolding the set of patterns that makes it unique among human configurations (Widmer 2016). Accordingly, this chapter describes methodological strategies followed by some European family sociology studies conducted in close connection with activities organised by the European Sociological Association on Families and Intimate Lives' Research Network 13. The selection of reviewed studies is not intended to be complete or representative. Rather, its purpose is illustrative: based on a small number of examples, we aim to emphasise a few methodological principles that may be valuable for future research.

This chapter's main argument is that using dilemma-sensitive methods constitutes a valuable entry point for the understanding of family configurations. Sociology as a discipline has developed an interest in a variety of dilemmas generated by the unexpected and often undesirable collective consequences of the aggregation of individual actions (Kollock 1998). Indeed, individuals are usually embedded in situations to which numerous others contribute. Therefore, the individuals' pursuit of their goals is embedded in uncontrollable collective dynamics. When negative, these dynamics have been described as vicious circles (Quintaneiro 2004) or social double binds (Elias 1993). On the emotional side, dilemmas translate into ambivalence, which is defined as a tension felt by an individual who faces a dilemma when, for instance, their relations with other group members are filled with love and anger or when an individual wishes to achieve autonomy and group identity simultaneously (Lüscher 2002). According to Lüscher (2011: 197), ambivalence entails "oscillating between polar contradictions of feeling, thinking, wanting or social structures, contradictions that appear temporarily or permanently insolvable".

The configurational perspective on families developed from a genuine interest in such situations because dilemmas and the ambivalence they generate are likely to reveal core configurational processes. Indeed, a focus on dilemmas and ambivalence facilitates researchers' tracing the chains of interdependences and power balances that bind family members together. Consider, for instance, the case of an elderly man who requires increasing care. Some of his family members might wish to send him to a care facility or institution that provides him with the expected services to alleviate their own burden. However, such a situation entails the cost of moving him to a more distant area, so visiting him frequently is no longer possible. Neither of the available options is desirable, and the family members might have distinct opinions and personal reasons for promoting one option over another, leading to ambivalence and interpersonal tensions. Some might recommend letting the ageing man move out and not seeing him on a regular basis anymore, whereas others might insist upon keeping him at home. The situation might result in a great deal of relational ambivalence among family members. They might blame each other for not doing enough or taking advantage of the situation, whereas the elderly man might consider his family members ungrateful or intrusive. The overall situation reveals the unintended consequences of the aggregation of various individual interests and strategies, as well as the balance of power and tensions unfolding among family members. In configurational terms, ambivalence (Lüscher 2002, 2011) is found in the power-loaded interventions of third parties in matters often understood initially as private to a person or a single relationship. Such interventions are likely to increase stress and conflict across networks of family interdependences (Widmer and Lüscher 2011). Looking for dilemmas and ambivalence therefore makes it possible to delineate the patterns that shape interdependencies in family configurations.

Family Weness

Setting a family's boundaries and collective identity might shape one such dilemma. How does a person conform to the collective definition of family as an individual embedded in a complicated life? At critical points in their lives, many individuals need to redefine their families. Marriage, parenthood, divorce, and widowhood are occasions in which new family boundaries are established, with possible tensions and clashes. A wedding, for instance, is an occasion that defines family insiders and outsiders, and the new partners implement several strategies, often with unexpected consequences (Castren and Maillochon 2009). In studies inspired by the structural-functional perspective, family boundaries and family weness were a non-issue, as the nuclear family, defined by the borders of the household, was considered a self-evident unit in any analysis or understanding of the family (Parsons and Bales 1955). We have stressed elsewhere (Widmer 2016) that, although the structural-functional perspective has lost traction in family sociology, researchers' use of household composition to define family boundaries has remained prominent, as the distinctions between single-parent families, stepfamilies, same-sex families and nuclear families shows. The configurational perspective challenges this conventional approach to families, which focuses on the household unit. Such criteria are administrative and disregard how various individuals create and understand families through their daily practices and interactions. In their book *The Established and the Outsiders*, Elias and Scotson (1994) coined the term *family configurations oriented towards the mother* by tracing the boundaries of family configurations according to interdependences existing among individuals beyond households. In other words, the use of household composition to identify family units and study family diversity disregards the complex set of family processes and interdependencies that constantly define family (Widmer 2016).

Cherlin and Furstenberg (1994) made this point long ago in a review paper on stepfamily research. They reported that according to empirical research conducted in the United States, a majority of children who faced the separation of their parents defined their significant family members in full or partial contradiction with household membership, generating a series of dilemmas and ambivalences regarding who was a family insider and who was an outsider. Overall, research on stepfamilies has stressed the variety of extant relational arrangements within the household and in connection with external family members (Ganong and Coleman 2012). Methodological attempts to capture family interdependencies using household structures have overlooked such dilemmas and ambivalence by applying a formal criterion to an informal issue. Indeed, if household membership is relevant enough for administrative tasks, it is cumbersome for systematic research on interdependencies. After all, what matters most in family research, as Burgess and Locke (1945) emphasised, is not the administrative classification of households, but family interactions (i.e. functional interdependencies among family members). Therefore, rather than using household composition as a decisive criterion to identify family groupings, the configurational perspective employs data collection methods that are sensitive to lay definitions of the concept of the family. For instance, what happens when family weness does not correspond to living arrangements, such as in stepfamilies? What strategies and consequences does such a dilemma entail? How do individuals in stepfamilies deal with the nuclear family normative model? What about cases in which parents and children have contradictory definitions of their significant family members?

There is a growing emphasis in research on various family configurations that serve as alternatives to the nuclear family defined by marriage and household membership (e.g. Budgeon and Roseneil 2004; Widmer 2016; Widmer and Jallinoja 2008). In configurational family research empirical analysis begins from the perspective that what makes family is the inclusion of individuals in a "we" or "weness"—that is, a co-constructed feeling of being part of a family (Castren 2019; Castren and Widmer 2015; Elias 1994). Such a "we" is based on individuals' feelings of intimacy, as well as the commitments they develop over time (e.g. Weeks 2007). The ways in which these configurations embody mechanisms of family member exclusion or inclusion have received increasing attention. To understand how identification with a family group unfolds, a series of configurational studies asked respondents to report their significant family members. The Family Network Method (FNM) is a validated instrument used on various populations (Oris et al. 2016; Wall et al. 2018; Widmer 2016; Widmer et al. 2013). Following previous work on lay definitions of family (Furstenberg 1987; Levin 1993; Milardo 1989; Pasley 1987), it first asks respondents to identify their significant family members. The term "family" is deliberately left undefined to elicit personal definitions of the concept. Participants are instructed that the term "significant" refers to people in their families who have played positive or negative roles in their lives during the past year. First, the participants list all significant family members. Then, they are asked to provide the status of each member (e.g. father, mother, partner, and sibling) and their socio-demographic profile.

Such methods provide lists of family members of various statuses (e.g. fathers, mothers, children, siblings, aunts, uncles, cousins, stepparents) that can be subsumed into a small number of types using cluster analyses (Kaufmann and Rousseeuw 1990), a multivariate statistical method that enables researchers to find groups in data automatically. The diversity of definitions of family in middle adulthood can be summarised using a limited number of distinct types. In a study of 300 women with children in a variety of family situations (Widmer et al. 2006), the most populated family configuration was almost exclusively centred on the partner and the children and therefore was identified as the type "*Nuclear family*". All other configurations, however, extended well beyond the limits of the household. *Friend/family configurations* focused on individuals who were considered family members but were not related by blood, marriage or partnership. *In-law configurations* had a strong orientation towards the partner and the in-laws. The partner and the partner's mother were over-represented, as were other in-law relationships. *Brother and sister configurations* included the respondent's siblings and their children and current partners. *Kinship configurations* included a variety of individuals related by blood and marriage, such as partners, parents, children, uncles, aunts, nieces, nephews, cousins, and grandparents. *Beanpole configurations* referred to families in which several generations co-existed, with only a few family members in each of them (Bengtson et al. 1990). They focused on blood relatives, with the inclusion of members of various generations, particularly grandparents from the mother and father's sides. By definition, they were vertically oriented rather than horizontally oriented, unlike the *brother and sister configurations*. Respondents who had *without partner configurations* did not include the present partner as a significant family member, although the partner lived, as in all other cases, within the same household as the female respondent and her child. In contrast, *post-divorce configurations* included the female respondents' former male partners and their relatives, as well as the new male partner and his relatives (his children and, in some cases, his female ex-partner).

Individuals make choices about family boundaries that arise from the intersection of social norms about what legitimately constitutes a family (see the later section on *leitbilder*), and their own practices and interdependencies (see the next section). Two individuals living in the same household featuring a divorce and a remarriage might therefore define their family in conflicting ways. For instance, one might belonging to the *without partner configuration*, and the other might belong to a *nuclear family configuration*. Therefore, as Cherlin and Furstenberg (1994) emphasised regarding post-divorce families, if a researcher asks individual members of any household who is part of their family, each member will provide a different answer. This is a major dilemma that family members must resolve: How can they be a family together if they define family quite differently? Indeed, family boundaries defined as real are real in their consequences (Merton 1995; Thomas and Thomas 1970).

The constitution of family weness has much to do with how individuals construct their life trajectories (De Carlo et al. 2014; Widmer 2016). Family weness is the result of a life-course cumulative process in which various decisions concerning marriage, fertility, separation, and divorce, as well as migration and job orientations, play out. Widowhood, separation, and divorce are associated with individuals' reorganisation of their family ties (Silverstein and Giarrusso 2010). Widowed and divorced people have a larger proportion of extended kin and friends compared to married people (Cornwell 2011). Compared to married individuals, widowed individuals are more likely not only to develop relationships with siblings, but also to receive support from them (Ha 2008). Therefore, their personal networks are heterogeneous, which translates directly into their family weness (Girardin and Widmer 2015). Because they are especially at risk of losing significant ties with their children, divorced men sometimes seek to compensate such losses by investing in other ties (Campbell et al. 1999). Childless individuals also invest in alternative family ties such as with siblings, diverse extended kin or friends who become family insiders because they possess important emotional support potential (Schnettler and Wöhler 2013).

Interestingly, weness dilemmas become even clearer when researchers decrease the maximum number of family members that can be cited, which is a methodological tool intended to force respondents to make choices under constraints related to their significant others (Girardin et al. 2018). Interdependencies and the tensions they generate are also revealed by the comparison of various individual interviews with adults and children stemming from the same family configuration (Brannen 2013; Castren 2019), as well as differences between descriptions provided by respondents in a variety of interview settings (e.g. individual interviews using the FNM and its derivatives, narrative interviews, focus groups). Researchers should also be aware of the difference between private and public interviews. The interview, whether it occurs in the presence of other family members or in private with the interviewer, can be used to disentangle interdependencies (Castren and Widmer 2015). Indeed, qualitative research can make unique contributions to configurational family analysis, as it can delve deeper into personal understandings of patterns of interdependencies compared to quantitative formal methods.

A clear example of a qualitative approach to family weness is provided by negotiations surrounding the family name in marriage. A variety of strategies stem from Castren's (2019) empirical study in Finland, which we review in brief here. Castren began by emphasising the dilemma caused among young couples by the issue of the family name. Specifically, this entailed the desire to share a surname with future children (emphasising family weness), which contrasted with the desire to seek an individual identity and favour gender equality by keeping one's birth name. Castren's study was therefore built on a predefined dilemma that served as an indicator of the tensions and power relationships present in new families in Finland. In methodological terms, the study conducted joint interviews of both partners in each couple, because such interviews enable researchers to observe partners in the midst of the decision-making process. The point was not only to collect accounts from two people, but also to observe how interdependencies are shaped in interactions.

In addition, the analysis heavily relied on Jokinen's (2005) earlier conceptualisation of gender reflexivity in Finland, which, according to Castren (2019), offered the means to investigate how couples' awareness of gendered expectations and inequality influenced negotiations about names. Configurational studies often use typologies or conceptual models to develop their cases and increase their generalisability (Lück et al. 2017; Widmer 2006; Zartler 2014). The study's results revealed three patterns of reasoning regarding the marital name. In the first, the woman's taking the man's name at marriage was taken for granted, as though it were self-evident. Changing names was seen as intimately linked with becoming "us", a new family unit, of which the shared surname was a valued symbol. The existence of gender-specific expectations and their heterosexual foundations were not reflected, and people did what they were supposed to do as women and men according to the conventional understanding of proper gender roles and family. In the second pattern, the symmetric position of women and men under Finland's current name law was acknowledged and was seen as giving couples the right to choose. However, it was considered the woman's choice rather than the man's choice. The second pattern drew on reasoning that highlighted the marital name as an issue that partners decided individually in principle but which was, in practice, a matter of the woman's choice to keep or change her name. In the third pattern, the discourse on names recognised women and men's equivalent positions in relation to the marital name and led to a decision that was difficult to make when partners were drawn to the one-name-for-a-family model, as only one name could be chosen to represent the family unit being formed. In the cases described by Castren (2019), ambivalences in family relationships were central. Such ambivalences took the shape of a dilemma for young couples, especially among women: How does one combine gender equality, and the family as a collective identity superseding individual orientation and interests? The three patterns of weness revealed by this empirical study enable the reader to understand the balance of tensions and power that Finnish couples face in direct connection with their social context. Such understanding is precious, as it indicates future conflicts and ambivalences that are likely to accompany husbands and wives throughout their lives together in Finland. Alternative settings in which ambivalences are present can be emphasised, such as the unequal inclusion of family members in typical family celebrations such as weddings, birthdays, or funerals, as well as the study of gifts and celebrations (Castren and Maillochon 2009). Such methodological approaches are likely to reveal various ways in which family boundaries and weness are shaped. In all such cases, a focus on the persons excluded and the reasons given by the interviewees for such exclusions is likely to highlight the balance of tensions and power that shapes family boundaries and weness.

Looking for Patterns of Interdependency

For many years, family researchers have been interested in collective processes and patterns of interactions. System-oriented sociology researchers considered families groups rather than configurations and therefore promoted methodological approaches that considered families as wholes or sub-systems and measured them accordingly (Olson et al. 1983; Parsons and Bales 1955). Individuals appeared only subsequently and were usually considered only as incumbents of roles and functions. Such theorisation had considerable empirical consequences, especially for measurements. For example, family system cohesion was measured using true–false answers to statements such as "Family members consult other family members on their decisions" (Olson et al. 1983). Such indicators have validity problems when applied to many contemporary families. In fact, if such scales were used to interview subjects living in step-households, the reports of all household members would include different sets of people. Interestingly, major current social surveys often limit their inquiry of families to within household dynamics. For instance, when the division of family work is measured, only the division between coresident partners is often considered (e.g. ISSP Group 2016).

Understanding families as configurations enables researchers to seek methods that demonstrate the patterns of interdependencies that link family members together. Family interdependences are needs that individuals can only fulfil in relation to other members. As noted above, such interdependencies create dilemmas that are indicative of the overall balance of tensions and power at the root of daily interactions and long-term ties in families. From that perspective, the positive dimensions of family interactions should be considered in relation to the negative dimensions, given that resources are scarce and their allocation and exchange are embedded in power relations. Popular concepts in family research such as family bond, family solidarity and family support emphasise the positive impact of family interactions and the ways families create and sustain cohesion. Such concepts ignore conflict and violence. Family researchers should keep in mind that all human configurations feature an ever-shifting balance of tensions and power (Elias 1978; Elias 2013). Such a balance should be examined by identifying together positive and negative patterns of relationships and meanings (Simmel 2015), rather than by focusing on single variables or factors. Indeed, dilemmas and ambivalences are never created by single forces, such as a drive towards autonomy in relationships. Contradictions necessitate the rise of at least two opposite forces, and often many more, such as when one family member's drive towards autonomy collides with the solidarity and equality expectations of other family members. Therefore, methods designed to uncover patterns in dilemmas and contradictions rather than single dimensions of family interactions are crucial to the configurational perspective on families. Stepfamily research, for instance, stresses the ambivalence present in the relationships between child, mother, father, stepfather, and stepmother because of the dilemmas that co-parenting among several adults in divorce chains generates (Finch and Mason 1993; Hetherington 2003; Hetherington and Stanley-Hagan 2002). Similarly, ambivalence between adult siblings or adult children and their parents generated by intergenerational relationships and elderly care has been documented extensively by social gerontologists (Connidis and McMullin 2002; Lüscher 2002). In both cases, a configurational approach goes beyond dyadic analysis and seeks patterns of interdependences and their embeddedness in social structures and the life-course (Widmer 2016).

A series of studies using social network questions examined families in several countries from that perspective (Oris et al. 2016; Wall et al. 2018; Widmer et al. 2013). In all such surveys, a set of questions about emotional support and conflict among listed family members was used in accordance with the FNM (Widmer 1999). Emotional support was typically measured using questions such as the following: "Who would give emotional support to X (i.e., each individual included in the respondent's family configuration, considered one by one) during routine or minor troubles?" Conflict was investigated with the following question: "Each family has its conflicts and tensions. In your opinion, who makes X (i.e., each individual included in the respondent's family configuration, considered one by one) angry?" Respondents had to evaluate not only their own family relationships, but also those among all their significant family members (Widmer et al. 2013). Each set of responses is transformed into a matrix such as the one presented in Table 6.1, which shows responses given by one respondent in a study of middle adulthood parents in Switzerland about the provision of emotional support (Widmer et al. 2012).

In this matrix, each dependency is represented by 1. An absence of dependency leads to a 0, and interdependence (both actors being dependent of each other) is represented by 1 at the two possible intersections between the actors. For instance, because the respondent's son and the respondent's mother are interdependent for emotional support, there is a 1 in the intersection of the rows of the son and the columns of the mother. Note that the dependencies are directional: the lower and upper halves of the matrix can be different, revealing cases in which only one actor is dependent on the other. This is reflected in the fact that the nephew, for instance, is dependent on the respondent, but the respondent is not dependent on the nephew.

The respondents' configuration of Table 6.1 includes 10 persons (including herself) from three generations living in different households, with the inclusion of a partner, children, in-laws, stepchildren and parents, relatives, etc. Network methods enable researchers to understand the chain of interdependencies connecting key family members. For instance, rather than asking each respondent to provide an overall assessment of family cohesion, one can operationalise cohesion of ties within one's family network by its density; that is, the number of existing connections divided by the number of pairs of family members cited by the respondent (i.e. potential connections; see Wasserman and Faust 1994). Answers to such questions can also be used to provide a visual representation of family interdependencies as evidenced by Fig. 6.1. Socio-metric matrices and their corresponding graphs offer visualisation capturing the chains of interdependencies linking family members together. In Fig. 6.1, there are 27 arcs (i.e. someone available to help someone else in case she or he needs it) from the potential 90 arcs existing among 10 persons (10 × 9). As in other configurational studies using social network methods (Widmer 2016; Widmer et al. 2013), arrows point to persons providing resources, which is consistent with the conceptualisation of ties as dependencies. Socio-metric graphs are of great value to configurational research because they enable researchers to visualise family interdependencies. The graph in Fig. 6.1 in particular reveals a rather dense configuration of support, with the respondent playing a major role. However, the partner's daughters have no connection with members of the respondent's family except for their father. In contrast, the partner's mother is integrated in the respondent family by an interdependence with her.

Table 6.1 Matrix representation of interdependencies in one family configuration

	Respondent	Partner	Son	Father	Mother	Nephew	Mother of Partner	Daugther of Partner	Daugther of Partner	Friend
Respondent	0.0	1.0	0.0	0.0	1.0	0.0	0.0	0.0	0.0	0.0
Partner	1.0	0.0	0.0	1.0	1.0	0.0	1.0	1.0	1.0	1.0
Son	1.0	1.0	1.0	1.0	1.0	0.0	0.0	0.0	0.0	0.0
Father	1.0	1.0	0.0	0.0	0.0	0.0	0.0	0.0	0.0	0.0
Mother	1.0	0.0	1.0	0.0	0.0	0.0	0.0	0.0	0.0	0.0
Nephew	1.0	0.0	0.0	1.0	0.0	0.0	0.0	0.0	0.0	0.0
Mother of Partner	1.0	1.0	0.0	0.0	0.0	0.0	0.0	0.0	0.0	0.0
Daugther of Parther	0.0	1.0	0.0	0.0	0.0	0.0	0.0	0.0	0.0	0.0
Daugther of Partner	0.0	1.0	0.0	0.0	0.0	0.0	0.0	0.0	0.0	0.0
Friend	1.0	1.0	0.0	0.0	0.0	0.0	0.0	0.0	0.0	1.0

118   E. D. WIDMER

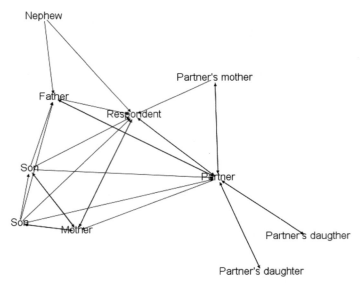

Fig. 6.1 Support relationships in the respondent's family configuration (arrows point to resource individuals)

The dilemma facing this female respondent is revealed when one considers the other face of supportive interdependencies (i.e. the conflict relationships). Figure 6.2 reports conflict interactions between family members according to her. In this case, the arrows point towards individuals who are sources of anger for others, always from the perspective of the respondent. The configuration seen from that angle is quite different. Indeed, the density of conflict is much lower than the density of support, corresponding to the general case of family configurations. Interestingly, this female respondent captured almost all negative interactions in the family configurations, except for two that focused on her mother. Figures 6.1 and 6.2 show she is the person in charge of many things in the family with consequently great centrality in conflict, including tense relationships with her partner's two daughters, who were unconnected with her for support. This relates to patterns we have described as overload, which is typical for women burdened with family responsibilities (Aeby et al., forthcoming; Sapin et al. 2016). This pattern presents an interesting paradox: the person helping most is also the one who creates the most conflict and tension within the family configuration.

Such patterns are present in all age groups and life situations where critical resources are lacking (Aeby et al., forthcoming; Girardin et al. 2018; Sapin et al. 2016). Let us consider old age as an example using the *Vivre-Leben-Vivere* data, a large representative survey of residents in Switzerland aged 65 and older (Oris et al. 2016). Family configurations in which all the

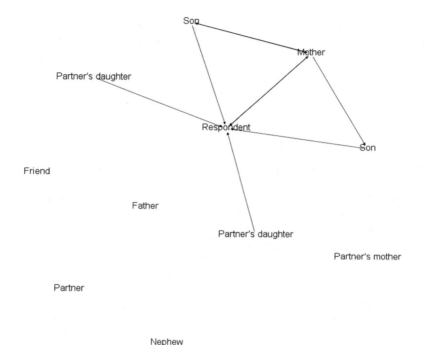

Fig. 6.2 Conflict relationships in the respondent's family configuration (arrows point to conflict-generating individuals)

members are strongly interconnected through long-lasting and intimate relationships, with frequent contacts and exchanges of various resources (high density of connection), often trigger a significant level of tension and conflict (Girardin et al. 2018). Although ensuring effective support and trust, tight interdependence among family members enhances individual expectations, claims, and obligations because of the increasing collective nature of normative control and support (Coleman 1988), with likely negative consequences including family interference (Johnson and Milardo 1984) and threat to individual autonomy (Cornwell 2011). Therefore, dense support, with its strong underlying normative pressure, creates tension and conflict if expectations and obligations are not respected, or if individuals claim too much autonomy. Thus, dense family configurations are not solely supportive but also a source of stress and conflict (Widmer 2016). Negative feelings about family members were developed by individuals in family configurations where the activation of intergenerational ties was not met by sufficient resources, such as when the income of the family was low or the health of the ageing respondent was rather poor (Girardin et al. 2018).

This example emphasises that collecting family network data helps scholars understand the balance of tensions and power that individuals face when dealing with the dilemma of helping a family member and interfering with her or his life (Widmer et al. 2009). Network methods are largely adaptable to a survey context and therefore make it possible to provide detailed information on family configurations in large representative samples. Such methods are an entry point to the understanding of family weness and interdependencies at a population level. Despite some of their limitations associated with the time-consuming process of collecting such data, especially when information is requested from all network members, social network methods are optimal for dealing with patterns of interdependencies when analysing family relationships. They provide a graphical representation of interdependencies that is extremely valuable in this regard.

Such methods also help relate family sociology with the expanding world of social network research. The idea that the pattern of social ties in which actors are embedded has important consequences for those actors has been stressed by sociology since its origin (Freeman 2004). Starting in the 1930s, theoretical and methodological developments first associated with the figure of Jakob Moreno (1934) made it possible for social scientists to develop a body of empirical studies uncovering such patterns in a variety of social settings, such as the job market and industrial relations, affiliations to parties and clubs, and international affairs (Scott 2002). Although anthropologists' work on kinship systems using social network analysis has been extensive (Scott 2002), the use of social network analysis of family issues in Western societies has remained for a number of decades rather limited. One exception was the seminal work of Elisabeth Bott (1957), who related couples' internal divisions of roles and labour to the pattern of relationships they develop with friends and kin. However, such attempts at linking family issues with social networks were quite limited until early 2000, with a few notable exceptions (i.e. Milardo 1988, 1989; Stein et al. 1992). Although such studies focused on the connection between families and their networks, the configurational perspective went a step further by considering families as networks (Widmer 2016). Such a configurational perspective relates well with work on personal networks from a life-course perspective with its emphasis on linked lives unfolding through time (Antonucci and Akiyama 1987; Bidart and Lavenu 2005; Giele and Elder 1998), although life-course researchers who rather consider relationships as resources do not generally share its focus on power relationships, ambivalence, and dilemmas. Such interest in the dark side of relationships is to some extent explained by the large set of obligations associated with family life, especially intergenerational relationships, which make them in many instances prone to ambivalence and dilemmas (Girardin et al. 2018; Lüscher 2002). Indeed, personal network research from a life-course perspective does not develop an exclusive focus on family ties, whereas the configurational perspective of families obviously does.

Going Deeper into Interdependencies

Formal approaches stemming from network analysis are a major avenue for a configurational approach to families. Qualitative methods are complementary because they provide a more in-depth understanding, from the actors' perspectives, of the various meanings given to interdependencies. Grounded theory and other fully inductive approaches have achieved a high level of visibility in the social sciences in recent decades. However, one may be sceptical about their merits for configurational studies because it is doubtful that many respondents will deliberately emphasise their functional dependencies on others in interviews. What a number of qualitative empirical studies using such inductive approaches rather show is that respondents tend to stress autonomy and independence as key principles of their private and family lives, following normative imperatives of late modernity concerning intimate relationships (e.g. Mason et al. 2007). Because autonomy in intimate relationships and family harmony have achieved such normative premium, the social desirability to stick with them in fully open interviews is high. To examine the patterns of interdependencies that individuals develop in their family interactions, researchers are helped by prior conceptual models and typologies (Widmer 2016). Therefore, to achieve a configurational understanding of families, deductive qualitative methods (Gilgun 2005), which stress key questions about configurations and use conceptual models, are preferable even though such questions and models may not be the ones that directly develop in the minds of the interviewees when they are first asked to describe their family lives or intimate relationships.

Scholars can achieve a deeper understanding of interdependencies through a number of methods in qualitative research. In general, the focus of qualitative interviews on dilemmas is advisable: interviewers might ask respondents to list issues or conflicts that they meet in their daily life or in critical transitions in relation with solidarity practices and group memberships, as well as how they try to solve such issues. Such emphasis on ambivalent situations is in line with the understanding of family configurations as sets of actors made interdependent by their needs for each other's assets and resources. Researchers may ask respondents how they think the other family members understand dilemmas. They may conduct multiple interviews on the same set of issues with a variety of family members to find out how their interlocking perspectives may create misunderstandings that then reverberate upon all members' interdependencies. It is obviously difficult for a researcher to interview a large number of family members, especially when such members are linked by anger and conflict, but having two or three of such members makes it already possible to go deeper in the understanding of family weness and interdependencies. An alternative to individual interviews is to conduct focus groups on a predefined list of dilemmas. This was done when dealing with the definition of *family* by asking members of family configurations to talk about their understanding of such dilemmas in front of the other (Castren and Widmer 2015).

It is worth noting that unfolding family interdependencies can also be achieved to some extent by understanding family practices. *Doing family* (Morgan 2011a) is an inherent part of configurational processes. Outstanding research has been done on such practices, especially in the UK, which is relevant for the configurational perspective (Finch 2007; Jamieson 2004; Mason et al. 2007; Smart 2007; Smart and Shipman 2004). Morgan and colleagues indeed stress the importance of studying family practices, that is what family members do together in terms of sociability, meals, family work and other regular activities, in relation with the biographies of family members and their social position in terms of gender and social class. Many functional interdependencies indeed unfold in daily activities: when people do things together they become interdependent. Interestingly, "families we live by", i.e. individuals' conceptions of the right ways to be a family (Gillis 1997; Gillis 2015), are yardsticks by which actual family practices are understood. By developing family narratives, individuals link their family experiences with more general patterns of social meanings about relationships. In that sense, paying attention to how family members narrate "family" is key to the "doing family perspective" (Morgan 2011a) and resonates with the configurational perspective and its focus on patterns of interdependencies, which also focus on the ways in which individuals foster connections with others through the construction of shared symbols and meanings (Elias 1989). Of course, such narratives usually provoke ambivalences and dilemmas, due to the conflicting norms or contradicting family experiences that individuals have to accommodate (Connidis and McMullin 2002; Finch and Mason 1993; Lüscher 2002; Mason et al. 2007). In contrast to the family practice approach, the configurational approach has developed a focus on the complex networks of functional interdependencies and the balance of power and tension within which such family practices and experiences unfold.

THE NUCLEAR FAMILY AS A *LEITBILD*

In general, individuals belonging to social classes or groups that experience threats of losing prestige and power tend to develop alternative representations of reality that position them in a higher status (Elias 2013). By contrast, individuals from well-established groups tend to secure their positions by reinforcing norms and values re-presenting them as better or morally superior to outsiders. This process, as stressed by Elias (2013) and Elias and Scotson (1994), may concern the family in relation to a variety of situations. Indeed, research has stressed the importance of the nuclear family as a *leitbild* or guiding image; that is, the socially ideal way of being a family, including its gender and intergenerational order (Pfau-Effinger 2004). Lück et al. (2017) further stress that *leitbild* expresses an idea or conception of how things in a certain context should be, work, or appear. It can have the character of a role model to emulate or of an ideal or a vision for which to strive. Accordingly, in configurational terms, *leitbild* can be seen as patterns of idealised interdependencies that exert a strong normative influence.

Defining the family *leitbild* in Germany, Lück and colleagues stated, "*People may envision that a 'normal' family consists of three to five people, including a man and a woman, both being married to each other, with the man being two to four years older and around 10 cm taller than his wife, including also one to three children, all common biological children of the couple, all about 30 years younger than their parents and about two years apart from each other*". This normative definition of a "true" family matters because it creates tensions and ambivalences in the way individuals experience their family practices (Finch 2007), which eventually contribute in unexpected ways to the shaping of their family configurations by downgrading some family situations or twisting in specific ways the perceptions and understandings that individuals have of their family reality.

In that respect, Zartler's (2014) seminal paper stressed the way parents and children individually deal with the representation of the so-called right family in Austria. A normative script was inherent in the accounts of children and parents she interviewed, irrespective of their family structure. When describing nuclear families, respondents referred to them as "normal" and "functional", in sharp contrast to other family forms classified as below standard. Complementarity in the care for children between parents was regarded as the most prominent benefit connected with nuclear families, and alternatives were considered to lack this crucial feature (Zartler 2014). According to Zartler, missing complementarity between father and mother was described as a source of feeling socially excluded. Single parents and their children were confronted with negative connotations and therefore ascribed deficiency to themselves and their family situation. Alternatively, as Zartler pointed out, individuals in post-divorce configurations developed imitation strategies that aimed at minimising visible differences between lone parents and nuclear families, with individuals trying to conceal the specifics of their family interdependences. A third set of strategies aimed at compensation and were based on efforts to integrate "missing" attributes of family, whereas a fourth set of strategies, according to Zartler, aimed at drawing boundaries between single-parent and nuclear families. Interestingly, parents and children of the same family configuration might not develop the same strategy, creating tensions that become part of the process shaping their family configuration: the use of different strategies by children and parents provided the basis for inconsistencies or incompatibilities. Overall, the idealisation of the nuclear family is an expression of the exclusion of non-nuclear family configurations from the realm of normality in line with the family *leitbild*. Castren and Widmer (2015) confirmed this trend. In a qualitative study on family weness in Switzerland, they found strong evidence of attempts by a large share of divorced mothers to recreate a nuclear family with a new partner by emphasising the current household as the natural family unit and disregarding interdependencies to their previous partnership as irrelevant or below normative standards.

Zartler (2014) used a qualitative approach focused on specific questions for both children and parents that address who is part of the family, what they like and do not like about their family, and how they spend their time during the week and on weekends. In all cases, Zartler's methodology has similarities with the methodology of the Family Network Method and its extensions (Widmer 2016). The in-depth interviews made it possible to delineate strategies underlying some of the answers regularly given in response to quantitative surveys. Providing responses that go beyond the nuclear definition of family is indeed often associated with a social cost to be paid. The nuclear family *leitbild* is not an artefact from the past, destined to disappear, but an institutionalised norm ranking families and therefore individuals embedded in them from closest to furthest away from the ideal. Indeed, the nuclear family *leitbild* has not lost its power of exclusion and status ranking in late modernity. Marriage continues to signal social status throughout Western societies (Cherlin 2010), which may explain its long-lasting popularity. Such a type of "family display" (Finch 2007) may be more easily studied over time than other dimensions of family configurations because they can be found in artefacts such as drawings, diaries, or letters available for various historical periods. These data sources make it possible to develop process-oriented analysis through historical time of family as a symbol (Elias 1989).

Away from Social Expectations

The configurational perspective has developed methodological approaches to estimate how similar a family configuration is to *leitbilder*. In many cases, a family configuration creates a sense of being "out of the ordinary" (Widmer 2019). First, such configurations are called extraordinary because they do not include a person whose status is defined by social norms as outside the nuclear family or the ties normatively defined as close family. In the sample of older individuals (Girardin and Widmer 2015; Oris et al. 2016), 33% of those who had a partner did not include the partner on the list of their most significant family members, and 20% of individuals who had a child did not include children on the list (Girardin and Widmer 2015). Even the closest family connections are dependent on "doing family" (Morgan 2011b) in family configurations rather than fully depending on family normative obligations. Second, they may be "extraordinary" because they include individuals who are usually family outsiders (Elias and Scotson 1994). For instance, if the inclusion of a partner or children is commonplace, the inclusion of an aunt or uncle in the circle of significant family members is something that happens much less often. Consider the case where a respondent indicates her family includes the following members: *Partner, Daughter, Daughter, Father, Brother, Partner's sister, Partner's sister, Partner's father, Partner's mother, Partner's sister's partner, Partner's sister's partner, Partner's sister's daughter, Partner's sister's son, Partner's sister's son*. Much of the emphasis is on the partner's relatives, which is quite unusual, because a partner's siblings are seldom included as significant family members, and their children even less so. It reveals an unexpected orientation of family weness towards ties created by partnership, whereas blood ties become of secondary importance. Another situation is one in which no one is considered a significant family member. Overall, individuals in many situations develop family configurations that do not correspond to the nuclear family *leitbild*. They do so for a variety of reasons, mostly associated with the unfolding of their life-courses (Widmer 2016). Studying family lists such as the one above is a straightforward way of appreciating the extent to which family configurations as defined by respondents are in tension with the nuclear family model. Qualitative inquiries about the reasons given by respondents for inclusion or exclusion of specific family members are fruitful methods for further understanding the ways family configurations are shaped.

Conclusion

The configurational approach sees families in the light of other configurations constituting societies (Elias 1978). Rather than stressing families as solidarity groups or sets of personal practices and interactions, it defines families as process-driven networks of functionally interdependent individuals. Overall, this chapter makes several suggestions to researchers who wish to study families as configurations. One critical methodological suggestion relates to the choice of key dilemmas shaping families. Identifying situations where tension exists between hard-to-reconcile functional interdependencies is crucial for the understanding of family configurations. For instance, tensions among individuals concerning group membership versus personal autonomy and between *leitbild* and everyday practices provide key information on the processes shaping families. Focusing on such dilemmas enables researchers to understand the balance of tensions and power in family configurations.

Research methods drawn from social network analysis are critical for configurational studies. Such methods are indeed adjusted to the empirical assessment of chains of functional interdependencies and their corresponding balance of power and tensions. They should be used to look for patterns of interdependencies beyond dyads and the household. Indeed, dilemmas and ambivalence are understandable only when several colliding social forces are considered together rather than independently from each other. Formal methods of data collection enabling quantitative research designs to study family configurations are now available, making it possible to implement the configurational perspective in large representative surveys. However, qualitative research has unique contributions to make to configurational analysis of family, because it can go deeper into personal understandings of dilemmas than formal quantitative methods can. Interdependencies and the tensions they generate are revealed by the comparison of a variety of individual interviews stemming from the same family configuration, as well as by differences between descriptions provided by respondents in a variety of interview settings. In all cases, because the configurational perspective seeks to uncover the balance of tensions and power that structure families, a fully inductive process of quantitative or qualitative research is not advisable. Indeed, respondents may not be eager to talk voluntarily about the dilemmas and ambivalence present in their family lives. In addition, unfolding patterns of interdependencies turns out to be easier for researchers who use prior conceptual models and typologies, sometimes coming from outside family sociology. Therefore, it is preferable to use a kind of semi-deductive analysis in close connection with the fundamental issues raised by the configurational perspective on families.

The configurational perspective considers social relationships as functional interdependencies. It is to note however that this perspective is critical to the structural-functional understanding of families (Widmer 2016). Such understanding assumed that a predefined set of functions such as the one presented in the AGIL model (Parsons and Bales 1955), plays out across so-called family sub-systems. It also claims that the family as an institution functions for the good of all its members and of society. In a configurational perspective, functions performed by family members for each other cannot be defined a priori using abstract conceptualisations and hence should be uncovered empirically; functional interdependences do not connect cohesive sub-systems, but individuals with their own, and possibly contradicting, orientations; they do not necessarily unfold for the common good of all family members and society but rather translate into power fights and the domination of some family members on others; the dominance of one institutional model of family at the societal level, such as the nuclear family, is not seen as proof of its functional superiority but rather as the result of the balance of power and tensions characterising social groups located in time and place.

Many limitations are obviously associated with the current state of configurational studies on families. Because they are still few, they offer very limited results about the interplay between family configurations and crucial social structures such as social class, ethnicity, citizenship, and gender, not to mention state intervention. In other words, existing studies have only marginally been able to address the importance of such factors. Such limitations might be overcome by future large surveys designed using a configurational perspective if enough methodological expertise, institutional motivation, and financial resources are available to conduct them internationally, which remains to be seen.

References

Antonucci, Toni C., and Hiroko Akiyama. 1987. "Social Networks in Adult Life and a Preliminary Examination of The Convoy Model." *Journal of Gerontology* 42 (5): 519–527.

Bengtson, Vern L., Carolyn J. Rosenthal, and Louis E. Burton. 1990. "Families and Aging: Diversity and Heterogeneity." In *Handbook of Aging and Social Sciences*,

edited by Robert H. Binstock, and Linda George, 263–287. San Diego, CA: Academic Press.
Bidart, Claire, and Daniel Lavenu. 2005. "Evolutions of Personal Networks and Life Events." *Social Networks* 27 (4): 359–376.
Bott, Elizabeth, 1957. *Family and Social Networks*. London: Tavistock.
Brannen, Julia. 2013. Life story talk: Some reflections on narrative in qualitative interviews. *Sociological Research Online* 18 (2): 48–58.
Budgeon, Shelley, and Sasha Roseneil. 2004. "Editors' Introduction: Beyond the Conventional Family." *Current Sociology* 52 (2): 127–134.
Burgess, Ernest W., and Harvey J. Locke. 1945. *The Family: From Institution to Companionship*. New York: The American Book Company.
Campbell, Lori D., Ingrid Arnet Connidis, and Lorraine Davies. 1999. "Sibling Ties in Later Life: A Social Network Analysis." *Journal of Family Issues* 20: 114–148.
Castrén, Anna-Maija, and Eric D. Widmer. 2015. "Insiders and Outsiders in Stepfamilies: Adults' and Children's Views on Family Boundaries." *Current Sociology* 63: 35–56.
Castrén, Anna-Maija. 2019. "Becoming "Us": Marital Name, Gender, and Agentic Work in Transition to Marriage." *Journal of Marriage and Family* 81 (1): 248–263.
Castrén, Anna-Maija, and Florence Maillochon. 2009. "Who Chooses the Wedding Guests, the Couple or The Family? Individual Preferences and Relational Constraints in France and Finland." *European Societies* 11 (3): 369–389.
Cherlin, Andrew J. 2010. *The Marriage-go-Round: The State of Marriage and the Family in America Today*. Vintage.
Cherlin, Andrew J., and Frank F. Furstenberg. 1994. "Stepfamilies in the US: A Reconsideration." *Annual Review of Sociology* 20: 359–381.
Coleman, James S. 1988. "Social Capital and the Creation of Human Capital." *American Journal of Sociology*, 94, Supplement: Organizations and Institutions: Sociological and Economic Approaches to the Analysis of Social Structure, S95–S120. The University of Chicago Press.
Connidis, Ingrid Arnet, and Julie Ann McMullin. 2002. "Sociological Ambivalence and Family Ties: A Critical Perspective." *Journal of Marriage and Family* 64 (3): 558–567. https://doi.org/10.1111/j.1741-3737.2002.00558.x.
Connolly, John, and Paddy Dolan. 2011. "Organisational Centralisation as Figurational Dynamics: Movements and Counter-Movements in the Gaelic Athletic Association." *Management & Organizational History* 6 (1): 37–58. https://doi.org/10.1177/1744935910387026.
Cornwell, Benjamin. 2011. "Independence Through Social Networks: Bridging Potential among Older Women and Men."*The Journals of Gerontology, Series B: Psychological Sciences and Social Sciences* 66: 782–794.
De Carlo, Ivan, Gaëlle Aeby, and Eric D. Widmer. 2014. La variété des configurations familiales après une recomposition: choix et contraintes. *Revue Suisse De Sociologie* 40 (1): 9–27.
Donati, Pierpaolo. 2010. *Relational Sociology: A New Paradigm for the Social Sciences*. Routledge.
Elias, Norbert. 1978. *What Is Sociology*. London: Hutchinson.
Elias, Norbert. 1989. "The Symbol Theory: An Introduction, Part One." *Theory, Culture & Society* 6 (2): 169–217.
Elias, Norbert. 1993. *Engagement et distanciation*. Paris: Fayard (1ère éd. 1983).
Elias, Norbert. 1994. *The Civilizing Process*. Vols 1 and 2. Oxford: Blackwell.

Elias, Norbert. 2013. *Studies on the Germans: Power Struggles and the Development of Habitus in the Nineteenth and Twentieth Centuries*. University College Dublin Press.
Elias, Norbert, and John L. Scotson. 1994. *The Established and the Outsiders*.Vol. 32. Sage.
Emirbayer, Mustafa. 1997. "Manifesto for a Relational Sociology." *American Journal of Sociology* 103 (2): 281–317.
Finch, Janet. 2007. "Displaying Families." *Sociology* 41(1): 65–81.
Finch, Janet, and Jennifer Mason. 1993. *Negotiating Family Responsibilities*. London: Routledge.
Freeman, Linton C. 2004. "The Development of Social Network Analysis." *A Study in the Sociology of Science*, BookSurge, LLC, Southern California.
Furstenberg, Frank F. 1987. "The New Extended Family: The Experience of Parents and Children After Remarriage." In *Remarriage and Stepparenting: Current Research and Theory*, edited by Kay Pasley and Marilyn Ihinger-Tallman, 42–61. New York: Guilford.
Ganong, Lawrence H., and Marilyn Coleman. 2012. *Stepfamily relationships*. Springer-Verlag New York.
Giele, Janet Z., and Glen H. Elder, Jr. 1998. "Life Course Research: Development of a Field." *Methods of Life Course Research: Qualitative and Quantitative Approaches* 5–27.
Gilgun, Jane F. 2005. "Qualitative Research and Family Psychology." *Journal of Family Psychology* 19 (1): 40.
Gillis, John R. 1997. *A World of Their Own Making: Myth, Ritual, and the Quest for Family Values*. Harvard University Press.
Gillis, John R. 2015. "Marriage of the Mind." *Journal of Marriage and the Family* 66 (4): 988–991.
Girardin, Myriam, and Eric D. Widmer. 2015. "Lay Definitions of Family and Social Capital in Later Life." *Personal Relationships* 22 (4): 712–737.
Girardin, Myriam, Eric D. Widmer, Ingrid Arnet Connidis, Anna-Maija Castrén, Rita Gouveia, and Barbara Masotti. 2018. "Ambivalence in Later-Life Family Networks: Beyond Intergenerational Dyads." *Journal of Marriage and Family* 80 (3): 768–784.
Ha, Jung-Hwa. 2008. "Changes in Support from Confidants, Children, and Friends Following Widowhood." *Journal of Marriage and Family* 70: 306–318.
Hetherington, E. Marvis, and Margaret Stanley-Hagan. 2002. "Parenting in divorced and remarried families." In Marc H. Bornstein (Ed.), *Handbook of parenting: Being and becoming a parent* (p. 287–315). Lawrence Erlbaum Associates Publishers.
Hetherington, E. Mavis. 2003. "Intimate Pathways: Changing Patterns in Close Personal Relationships Across Time." *Family Relations* 52: 318–331.
ISSP Research Group. (2016).*International Social Survey Programme: Family and Changing Gender Roles IV - ISSP 2012. GESIS Data Archive, Cologne. ZA5900 Data file Version 4.0.0*.
Jamieson, Lynn. 2004. "Intimacy, Negotiated Non-Monogamy and the Limits of the Couple." *The State of Affairs: Explorations in Infidelity and Commitment*, 35–57.
Johnson, Michael P., and Robert M. Milardo. 1984. "Network Interference in Pair Relationships: A Social Psychological Recasting of Slater's Theory of Social Regression." *Journal of Marriage and the Family* 46 (4): 893–899.
Jokinen, Eeva. 2005. *Aikuisten arki* [Everyday Life of Adults]. Helsinki: Gaudeamus.

Kaufmann, Leonard, and Peter J. Rousseeuw. 1990. *Finding Groups in Data: An Introduction to Cluster Analysis*. New York, NY: Wiley.

Kollock, Peter. 1998. Social dilemmas: The anatomy of cooperation. *Annual review of sociology* 24 (1): 183–214.

Levin, Irene. 1993. "Families as Mapped Realities." *Journal of Family Issues* 14 (1): 82–91.

Lück, Detlev, Sabine Diabaté, and Kerstin Ruckdeschel. 2017. "Cultural Conceptions of Family as Inhibitors of Change in Family Lives: The 'Leitbild' Approach." In *Family Continuity and Change: Contemporary European Perspectives*, edited by Vida Česnuitytė, Detlev Lück, and Eric D. Widmer, 61–86. London: Macmillan Palgrave.

Lüscher, Kurt. 2002. "Intergenerational Ambivalence: Further Steps in Theory and Research." *Journal of Marriage and Family* 64 (3): 585–593. https://doi.org/10.1111/j.1741-3737.2002.00585.x.

Lüscher, Kurt. 2011. "Ambivalence: A 'Sensitizing Construct' For the Study and Practice of Intergenerational Relationships." *Journal of Intergenerational Relationships* 9 (2): 191–206.

Mason, Jennifer, Vanessa May, and Lynda Clarke. 2007. "Ambivalence and the Paradoxes of Grandparenting." *The Sociological Review* 55 (4): 687–706.

Merton, Robert K. 1995. "The Thomas Theorem and the Matthew Effect." *Social Forces* 74 (2): 379–422.

Milardo, Robert M. 1988. *Families and Social Networks: An Overview of Theory and Methodology*. Thousand Oaks, CA: Sage.

Milardo, Robert M. 1989. "Theoretical and Methodological Issues in the Identification of the Social Networks of Spouses." *Journal of Marriage and the Family* 51: 165–174.

Moreno, Jacob L. 1934. *Who Shall Survive? A new Approach to the Problem of Human Interrelations*. Beacon House.

Morgan, David. 2011a. *Family Practices*. Palgrave MacMillan.

Morgan, David. 2011b. "Locating 'Family Practices'." *Sociological Research Online* 16 (4): 14.

Newton, Tim. 1999. "Power, Subjectivity and British Industrial and Organisational Sociology: The Relevance of the Work of Norbert Elias." *Sociology* 33 (2): 411–440. https://doi.org/10.1177/S0038038599000243.

Olson, David H., Hamilton I. McCubbin, Howard Barnes, Andrea Larsen, Marla Muxen, and Marc Wilson. 1983. *Families: What Makes Them Work*. Beverly Hills, CA: Sage.

Oris, Michael, Marthe Nicolet, Eduardo Guichard, Christophe Monnot, and Dominique Joye. 2016. "Surveying the Elderly, Capturing Vulnerability. The VLV (Vivre-Leben-Vivere) Survey." In *Surveying Vulnerability, Surveying Vulnerable Populations. Ten Experiences Across the Swiss Society*, edited by Michael Oris, Caroline Roberts, Dominique Joye, and Michèle Ernst Stähli. New York, NY: Springer Series Life Course Research and Social Policies.

Parsons, Talcott, and Robert Freed Bales. 1955. *Family: Socialization and Interaction Process*. New York: The Free Press.

Pasley, Kay. 1987. "Family Boundary Ambiguity: Perceptions of Adult Stepfamily Family Members." In *Remarriage and Stepparenting: Current Research and Theory*, edited by Kay Pasley and Marilyn Ihinger-Tallman, 206–225.

Pfau-Effinger, Birgit. 2004. "Socio-historical Paths of the Male Breadwinner Model– an Explanation of Cross-national Differences 1." *The British Journal of Sociology* 55 (3): 377–399.
Quintaneiro, Tânia. 2004. "The Concept of Figuration or Configuration in Norbert Elias' Sociological Theory." *Teoria and Sociedade* 12: 54–69.
Sapin, Marlène, Eric D. Widmer, and Katia Iglesias. 2016. "From Support to Overload: Patterns of Positive and Negative Family Relationships of Adults with Mental Illness Over time." *Social Networks* 47: 59–72.
Schnettler, Sebastian, and Thomas Wöhler. 2013. "On the Supporting Role of Friendship for Parents and Non-Parents in Later Life. A Comparative Analysis Using Data from the Three Waves of the German Aging Survey." In *Vielfalt und Zusammenhalt: Verhandlungen des 36*, edited by M. Löw. Kongresses der Deutschen Gesellschaft für Soziologie in Bochum 2012.
Scott, John, ed. 2002. *Social Networks: Critical Concepts in Sociology*. Vol. 4. Taylor & Francis.
Silverstein, Merril, and Roseann Giarrusso. 2010. "Aging and Family Life: A Decade Review." *Journal of Marriage and Family* 72: 1039–1058.
Simmel, Georg. 2015. *Soziologie: Untersuchungen über die formen der vergesellschaftung*. BoD–Books on Demand.
Smart, Carol. 2007. *Personal life: New Directions in Sociological Thinking*. Cambridge, UK and Malden, MA: Polity.
Smart, Carol, and BeccyShipman. 2004. "Visions in Monochrome: Families, Marriage and the Individualization Thesis." *The British Journal of Sociology* 55 (4): 491–509.
Stein, Catherine H., Ellen G. Bush, Ronald R. Ross, and Marcia Ward. 1992. "Mine, Yours and Ours: A Configural Analysis of the Networks of Married Couples in Relation to Marital Satisfaction and Individual Well-being." *Journal of Social and Personal Relationships* 9: 365–383.
Thomas, William I., and Dorothy Swayne Thomas. 1970. "Situations Defined as Real Are Real in Their Consequences." *Social Psychology Through Symbolic Interaction*, 154–155.
Wall, Karin, Eric D. Widmer, Jacques-Antoine Gauthier, Vida Česnuitytė, and Rita Gouveia, eds. 2018. *Families and Personal Networks: An International Comparative Perspective*. London: Macmillan Palgrave.
Wasserman, Stanley, and Katherine Faust. 1994. *Social Network Analysis: Methods and Applications*. Cambridge University Press.
Weeks, Jeffrey. 2007. *The World We Have Won: The Remaking of Erotic and Intimate Life*. Routledge.
Widmer, Eric D. 1999. "Family Contexts as Cognitive Networks: A Structural Approach of Family Relationships." *Personal Relationships* 6 (4): 487–503.
Widmer, Eric D. 2006. "Who are My Family Members? Bridging and Binding Social Capital in Family Configurations." *Journal of Social and Personal Relationships* 23 (6): 979–998.
Widmer, Eric D. 2016. *Family Configurations. A Structural Approach to Family Diversity*. London, Routledge (Reedition), First Edition, 2010.
Widmer, Eric D. 2019. "Qui sont les membres de ma famille? Liens manquants, liens inattendus, et qu'ils nous révèlent des configurations familiales." *Revue de l'Institut international de psychanalyse et de psychothérapie Charles Baudoin* 65: 63–76.
Widmer, Eric D., Gaëlle Aeby, and Marlène Sapin. 2013. "Collecting Family Network Data." *International Review of Sociology* 23 (1): 27–46.

Widmer, E., Nicolas Favez, Gaëlle Aeby, Ivan De Carlo, and Minh-Thuy Doan. 2012. *Capital Social et coparentage dans les familles recomposées et de première union.* Sociographe. Université de Genève, Archives ouvertes.

Widmer, Eric D., Francesco Giudici, Jean-Marie Le Goff, and Alexandre Pollien. 2009. "From Support to Control. A Configurational Perspective on Conjugal Quality." *Journal of Marriage and Family* 71 (13): 437–448.

Widmer, Eric D., and Riitta Jallinoja. 2008. *Beyond the Nuclear Family. Families in a Configurational Perspective.* Bern: Peter Lang.

Widmer, Eric D., Jean Kellerhals, and René Levy. 2006. "Types of Conjugal Interactions and Conjugal Conflict: A Longitudinal Assessment." *European Sociological Review* 22 (1): 79–89.

Widmer, E. D., and Lüscher, Kurt. 2011. "Les relations intergénérationnelles au prisme de l'ambivalence et des configurations familiales." *Recherches familiales* 1: 49–60.

Zartler, Ulrike. 2014. "How to Deal With Moral Tales: Constructions and Strategies of Single-Parent Families." *Journal of Marriage and Family* 76 (3): 604–619. https://doi.org/10.1111/jomf.12116.

CHAPTER 7

Visual Family Research Methods

Irena Emilija Juozeliūnienė

INTRODUCTION

The objective of this section is to demonstrate how visual methods can be applied in the research of families and intimate lives. Researching with images has become a routine practice for many sociologists researching family configurations, relationships, and practices. This involves a wide use of photographs, video recordings, drawings, family albums, ego-centric maps; researchers choose one visual method or use it interchangeably with others in mixed-methods research. Family researchers emphasise the advantages of visual methods; however, there are also those sceptical about that. The latter encourage researchers to evaluate the specificities of visual methods and warn researchers against the risks arising when entering new word-image research areas. Below, the author will discuss the origins of visual sociology and will demonstrate the value of visual methods in family research. Further on, the author will focus on the technique in the field of visual methodology, which are particularly relevant in family research, i.e. on using drawings, photographs, video recordings, and participant-led maps. The author will draw attention to the advantages and disadvantages of using visual methods in family research and will discuss the questions related to visual research ethics.

I. E. Juozeliūnienė (✉)
Department of Sociology, Vilnius University, Vilnius, Lithuania

Going Beyond the Contraposition of Language and Vision

Historically, sociology has not remained unaffected by the contraposition of language and vision. The 'linguistic turn' was followed by the 'visual turn' and later, social scientists undermined the strict division between the word and the image and began searching for the theoretical footing in the studies of the visual, and researching with the visual.

The 'linguistic turn', which took place in the 1960s, marked the transformation of sociology. Social scientists invited to rally around the analysis of the 'text' (e.g. Derrida) and the 'discourse' (e.g. Foucault) as the models of culture and social practice. Western modernity institutionalised the layers of sociological inquiry as 'rational'/ 'emotional', 'true'/ 'imaginary', and these pragmatically separated and unequal domains implied that visuality was merely an aid to our rational understanding of reality or even an obstacle. In the era of the 'absorption of image by discourse' (Mitchell 1995: 28), visual information played only the role of supplementing or illustrating the text. The visual attracted more attention in the history of art, but even in art the visual was considered as an image of a certain narrative.

The digital revolution and the subsequent pictorial transformations in culture enhanced the focus on the issues of how social reality is mediated by both the linguistic and the visual. The rise of image culture was followed by the attempts to theorise the visual and the sensual in general. For instance, scholars argued that the importance of the visual to contemporary Western societies is an essential part of the wider analysis of the shift from modernity to postmodernity. They even claimed that 'the modern world is very much a "seen" phenomenon' (Jenks 1995: 1–2) and that 'seeing comes before words' (Berger 1972: 7). Everything is best summarised by Mirzoeff's (1998: 1) remark that the visual is central to postmodernity not simply because visual images are part of everyday life or because we are used to thinking about the world visually, but, most importantly, because we started interacting with the experiences totally shaped by the visual images.

In order to discover the theoretical footing in the studies of the visual, social scientists started applying a wide range of methodologies that had an impact on the sociological thinking about the social world and the new space for sociological research (for the 'visual turn', see Thomson 2008; for the 'pictorial turn', see Mitchell 1995; for the 'iconic turn', see Bartmanski 2014). The researchers did not place the study of the visual on an equal footing with the study of images, but rather considered it as a study of how social reality was observed. They aimed at including visuality into the master categories of sociological analysis of reality and worked on creating an integrative framework to overcome the word/image contraposition.

Linking the Visual with Sociological Thinking

The spread of visual research in sociology is linked to the emergence of visual social studies as an independent field in the 1980s and with visual sociology in the 1990s. Visual social studies paved the ground for discussions between empiricists and symbolists. Empirical visual sociologists' beliefs were the opposite of those who focused on symbolic (typically semiotic) analysis of visual texts (e.g. photos, films, drawings, cartoons, advertisements, etc.), therefore, visual sociology, considered as qualitative methodology, was described as a 'two-headed beast separating the empirical from the symbolic' (Harper 2000: 24). The discussions have led to the formation of a newly integrative visual sociology with one foot in the old traditions in the context of visual ethnography, documentary photography, and semiotics, and with the other in the experimental thinking found in social sciences and humanities at that time. Ethnography and photojournalism are considered as the origins of visual sociology. Bateson and Mead's work *'Balinese Character'* (1942) and Becker's paper *'Photography and Sociology'* (1974), where he argued that the photograph should be linked with sociological consciousness, are noteworthy. In their works, Harper (2002), Chaplin (1994), Knowles and Sweetman (2004) thoroughly discussed the origins of visual methods and summarised the research studies carried out by using these methods.

The scholars have a two-fold approach towards the visual (see Thomson 2008; Rose 2014). The first is related to visual culture and is largely manifested in literature, art history, philosophy, history, and social sciences. Social scientists elaborate on 'the sociology of the visual' by working with visual materials which already exist. They aim at investigating the production, methods of use, interpretations, and social effects of visual artefacts (e.g. online archives, YouTube and video games, websites, newspapers, magazines, advertising, films, book illustrations, maps, photographs, paintings, cartoons, etc.) and use different methodologies such as semiology, psychoanalysis, and discourse analysis for the purpose.

The second approach is referred to as 'visual sociology', or, to be more specific, as 'visual research methods', and is firmly established in social sciences. In this case, the images are actively used in doing research, alongside with other sorts of data normally generated by interviews or ethnographic fieldwork. Visual research methods involving the production of visual images are used as a means of eliciting an answer to a research question which may have little to do with the visual *per se*. While Thomson (2008: 8) argues that these approaches can be combined, Rose (2014: 10) notes that until recently 'there has been remarkably little dialogue between social scientists using visual research methods as a way of answering research questions, and visual culture scholars who study found images'.

Flick (2002) claimed that visual sociology came into existence in order to critically interpret visual representations. Data collection characterised by the use of photographs (see Harper 2002; Wagner 1978), family albums (see

Spence and Holland 1991), drawings (see Levin and Trost 2000), ego-centred map methods (see Samuelsson et al. 1996; Spencer and Pahl 2006) in research established itself very quickly and became widespread. Visual material was actively used in many ways in various research studies, such as 'image-based research' (Thomson 2008; Prosser 2000), 'creative', or 'arts-based research' (Buckingam 2009; Knowles and Cole 2008; Vist 2019). Researching with visual material was given the names of 'visual elicitation' (Varga-Atkins and O'Brien 2009) and 'graphic elicitation' (Bagnoli 2009; Crilly et al. 2006). See Prosser and Loxley (2008) for a discussion of using various visual methods.

At the end of twentieth century, the transition towards the 'voice' led to an interest in visual research and opened a qualitatively new space for sociological analysis of various aspects of family life. Family sociologists aimed at expanding scientific knowledge by looking for the perspectives of 'others' by gender, sexuality, age, race, ethnicity and, by doing this, introduced the 'silenced voices' as an object of analysis. Researchers went beyond the search for an 'authentic' voice of the informants and acknowledged the existence of a variety of 'voices', the origins whereof depend on the variety of positions from which the participants speak. Using ethnographic methodology, researchers re-engaged in the art of listening (Back 2007) and in the analysis of idioms as an 'instrument' for understanding the encounters and experiences of children (Nolas et al. 2019).

The Value of Visual Methods for Family Research

Family researchers raised the question as to which methods could serve best for the most precise elicitation of the 'voices' (Alanen 1992; Lewis 2010; Thomson 2008). Visual research using drawings, photographs, cartoons, maps, cameras, etc. seemed particularly sensitive to the discussions about 'giving a voice' to children, migrant families, and queer identity partnerships and were expected to work well when social networks or other phenomena under study were not amenable to articulation in words. The transition towards 'voicing' determined the fact that it was the whole process of the production of visual artefacts that generated the data for analysis rather than the visual material per se. The focus was rather on participants' own meanings than on interpreting visual products on the basis of pre-existing theory (see Thomson 2008).

The rise of researching with images echoed the transition towards researching 'with' rather than 'about' or 'on' participants in order to keep power balance and enable the interviewees' participation (Morgan et al. 2002). There have been concerns about the spontaneous processes of creating visual images as an act of elicitation of a researcher-participant dialogue, while the image itself was described as a useful hint for the researcher, as an 'opener' and 'ice breaker' during the interviews (Morrow 1998). In addition, visual research methods provided the means for highlighting the social meanings stemming from the person's account, also for analysing personal experiences in the wider social context (Gabb 2010) and for talking about private issues in public (Finch 1987).

Family researchers claimed that visual methodology offered advantages in studying family relations (e.g. a couple, parent-child, intergenerational) and family change (e.g. divorce, re-marriage, migration). These topics were considered too sensitive in order to ask research participants respective direct questions, while researching with images allowed the researchers to avoid ethical and emotional difficulties encountered during participants' narratives of their personal experiences (Brannen et al. 2000; Angell et al. 2014). It was expected that visual methods should enable researchers to desensitise and depersonalise the situations in the focus of the research projects as well as to uncover the 'unrecognised, unacknowledged or "unsayable" stories' (Leitch 2008: 37).

The sections below focus on the technique in the field of visual methodology, which are particularly relevant in family research, i.e. on using drawings, photographs, video recordings, and participant-led maps in sociological analysis of families and intimate lives.

USING DRAWINGS IN FAMILY RESEARCH

Lots of research based on drawings have long been used in psychology, especially in clinical and therapeutic settings. Mostly, research was carried out with standardised tests (see Linesch 1994). Relatively few studies invited the participants to be co-interpreters or narrators of their images (Leitch and Mitchell 2007). More therapeutically oriented methods, like those of kinetic family drawings and regressed family drawings, were employed to encourage discussions, for example on the relationships within schoolchildren's families to explore the impact of losing a father (Burns and Kaufman 1970; Furth 1988).

The 'Draw a Family Test' is an example demonstrating the way family researchers performed the analysis of drawings to better understand children's views on their families. This method was applied by Isaacs and Levin (1984) in the longitudinal analysis of the changes in a child's relationship with his/her parents after one parent leaves the household. The researchers applied the 'Draw a Family Test' to clarify the aspects of power redistribution in the family and the changes in family composition, and the way these changes are reflected in children's drawings.

A child was given a sheet of paper and a pencil and asked to draw a picture of his/her family. After completing the drawing, the child was asked to identify the people he/she had drawn. The changes in the drawings from the first and second periods were analysed with a focus on (1) family composition, (2) the size of the figures, and (3) the change in creativity/constriction. Family composition was taken into account in order to clarify which individuals the child considers as part of his/her family and whom the child includes/excludes from family drawings in the first year after his/her parents' separation and respectively in the second year. It was believed that the relative size of the figures drawn reflected power relationships in the child's family. The researchers compared the size of the parents in each drawing within each period of time. The change in creativity/constriction was analysed by noting the change in the degree of details of human figures, their clothing, in the differentiation between the sexes, and in the integrity of body parts of the human figures (Isaacs and Levin 1984: 5–6).

The drawing has been the central tool for researchers, due to the fact that it is an easily available form of resource and is attractive to research participants. Despite the lack of a universally recognised method for data analysis as well as the divergence of opinions in relation to the reliability and validity of data interpretation, children and young people's drawings were the forerunners of a large quantity of research used for educational, diagnostic, and therapeutic purposes. Family drawings produced by children have been widely used in exploring children's views on their family transitions such as divorce or remarriage. For example, the size of the figures in drawings, the inclusion/exclusion of parents, siblings, the grouping of figures were analysed in order to measure the children's adaptation to different family settings, like having a stepfather, a single parent, or living in a complex stepfamily (Roe et al. 2006). The 'Colour the Family Drawing Test' was designed for the analysis of the colours in children's family drawings in order to study the perception of their family relationships in 'harmonious' as opposed to 'conflicting' families for cross-cultural comparison purposes (Biasi et al. 2015).

The 'Draw And Write' method and the methodological development of the 'Draw, Write and Tell' research method are the examples of the methodologies in the area of visual research have been changing during the last five decades (Angell et al. 2014). The creative research method known as 'Draw And Write' was developed in 1972 and has been widely used by researchers working with children in order to study social and health-related issues. It was argued that the drawing and writing activities enabled the participation of the informant and helped shape a wider picture of the views of the informant; moreover, they were suitable for a broad range of people in different age groups and with different abilities. The method was used as a means of collecting data with pictures and text, or as a 'warm up exercise'.

By their involvement in the search for creative methods allowing the 'voicing' of research participants, family researchers started using family drawings as a means of data collection in researching 'with' participants. The 'Draw, Write and Tell' method was developed in an attempt to resolve some of the issues identified in the 'Draw And Write' methodology (Angell et al. 2014). Substantial improvements of the original method included the conceptual framework, analysis, and interpretation of the data. More specifically, the improvements were the following: granting children the right to comment on the situations which affected them, the inclusion in the 'tell session' of open questions addressed to children, the construction of the 'commentary' by using all data streams, and the use of children's written and verbal interpretations, preferably in the form of direct quotes. The research procedure is the following:

> In the classroom, the researcher reads a simple story and shows pictures on large picture boards to a group of children. The children might be given clarifications, if necessary. The children are asked to draw pictures and create texts to finish the story. Finally, the children are individually invited in a separate room to talk about it. The researcher starts the conversation with a positive comment about the child's drawing and asks the child how, in the child's opinion, the story should finish. It is proposed that during the research one researcher should undertake all the classroom activities and data collection in order to ensure consistency. When analysing the data, the drawing, the text and the interview material is combined into a written 'commentary'. The commentaries are coded until saturation. (Angell et al. 2014: 6–7)

Drawings may also serve as an independent means of data collection and may be used in combination with other research methods. Leitch (2008) presents a series of research studies on how drawings are given the central focus in large-scale, smaller-scale, and ethnographic-type of participatory studies 'with' children and young people. However, in family research the data obtained by using the drawings made by the informant could be combined with the data from other methods for the purpose of adding a new dimension to the previously described individual experience. For example, in their study of examining the descriptions of families after separation and re-partnering, with a focus on family boundaries, Castren and Widmer (2015) employed written family descriptions and drawings made by the members of each stepfamily, namely the mother, the new partner, and the child. In their analysis of inclusive, exclusive, and mixed family descriptions, the authors focused on the examination of constructing the family we-ness and creating the family boundaries generated by mutual interdependences. In family research, drawings are combined with concentric circles (Elden 2012), 'emotion maps' (Gabb and Singh 2015), and 'family trees' (Gabb 2005).

Family researchers can also use special sets of drawings and vignettes prepared for the purpose of depicting family groupings and family change (Brannen et al. 2000; Gabb 2010; Rigg and Pryor 2007) to elicit an interview about family conceptualisations. For example, Rigg and Pryor (2007) explored children's understanding of family groupings using third-party scenarios and vignettes. They sought to examine which kind of relationships young people consider as family relationships.

The interview consisted of three sections. In the first section, three open-ended questions were used to obtain the definition of the family and the explanations of why family is important, and to identify, based on the verbal descriptions, family structures. The second section consisted of 13 vignettes depicting family groupings and containing various scenarios (e.g. a married/cohabiting couple without children, non-residential related person, a same-sex couple, etc.). The third section included nine vignettes focusing on family change. The researchers highlighted the ways in which family conceptualisations were shaped by developmental influences, family structure experiences, and cultural background (Rigg and Pryor 2007: 20–21).

Family Photography and Filming

Photographs commonly appear as a part of research projects and are widely supported by the scientific community (Wagner 1978; Harper 2002; Rose 2014; Prosser and Schwartz 2000). The use of photographs in research is considered as a very innovative and productive way of 'voicing' informants, but it is also a complex one, in which the inventory, performance, and the role of the researcher has a significant influence on data. Moreover, there is still no clearly established methodological framework for discussing the methods of use of photography in social science research, particularly in family research. According to Becker (2002: 11) photos are a valuable way of conveying 'real, flesh and blood life'. However, others argue that, as far as social researchers are concerned, it is not the visual content of a photograph that matters but rather how it is made and interpreted in the context of a specific project. In this case, visual material per se is used as a means for achieving a certain purpose. As Knowles and Sweetman (2004: 6) put it, the emphasis is on 'what it is that visual methods are able to achieve' rather than on what photographs inherently are.

Social scientists widely use photographs, photo-essays, and videos in participatory research 'with' children and young people to elicit their perspectives on the environment (Morrow 2001), school life (Mitchell and Weber 2000), and kinship (Mason and Tipper 2008), also to explore their migrant or refugee experiences with the focus on the family, friendship, and school (de Block and Buckingham 2007); participatory filmmaking as a research methodology has been designed to support the inclusion of children with disabilities as co-researchers (Benjamin-Thomas et al. 2019). Participatory research with photographs and video diaries has already been recognised as a methodology, empowering participants to represent themselves better in the studies of family change, gender roles in families, family communication, space sharing in households, and 'voicing' queer identities. For example, Steiger (1995) researched the impact of children on family dynamics as well as the identity of the woman-as-mother. She used family photographs made by both herself and research participants, including children. Steiger wanted to ensure that her pictures should not only show what she experienced but should also reflect the point of view of family members (e.g. she asked the participants the pictures of which objects they wanted to be taken, and at what place). In the photo-elicitation interview, the informants were asked to choose a series of photographs which illustrated their feelings best. While combining photography with interviewing, she compared the circumstances of Swiss families having their first child and belonging to different social classes; by using this method, she revealed the meanings of family changes.

When exploring life in a shared household, Heath and Cleaver (2004) gave a disposable camera to each member of a household of the chosen composition, and asked them to make a visual record of what they considered as significant and meaningful aspects of living in shared spaces. They received three types of photographs: illustrations of events and activities in which household members were interacting with broader groups of friends and colleagues (e.g. playing golf); everyday activities in a domestic space (e.g. cooking, shared meals); thought-provoking abstract photographs (e.g. bedrooms and bathrooms, shirts drying on a wash line). The researchers concluded that the analysis of photographs in their own right did not add much to the data received through sketches, notes, and structured interviews, meanwhile the invitation of participants to describe each image and to explain the significance of the image for them proved as a useful exercise.

Technological change associated with cameras, films, storage, and display has affected the perception of family photography and its use in social interactions. While personal photographs, digital or otherwise, still serve as memory tools, they can also be used as public signifiers of individual or group identity. Chalfen (2000) points out that self-representation became a central theme in the area of leading a 'normal' family life or demonstrating it as such. He coined the term 'home mode' for visual/pictorial communication to define the snapshots and the peculiarities of making them and introduced a descriptive framework for the qualitative study of the series of snapshots in the area of family photography. Holliday (2004) shows the way in which the processes of creating video diaries (narrativisation of identity, reflecting the selection, editing and refining) is important in the research of performative nature of queer identities, i.e. self-representation and the representation of intimate relationships.

The research study by Janning and Scalise (2015) describes how the processes of taking, organising, and sharing of family photographs affect people's feelings towards their family roles and reveal the pressure on people to present, via the photographs, an idealised version of their family both to themselves and others. The participants were asked to show family photographs (in their chosen format) and to pick one or more photos which, in their opinion, represented their family well. These pictures then served as visual references during the interviews and as reminders of participants' family members, events, and feelings.

Social scientists employ autoethnography to study family issues, photographs being a significant part of the research study. For example, Taylor (2019) offers a daughter's emotional geography of fatherlessness to discuss men's involvement in fathering. The author introduces a process of examining interconnections of spatial and familial absence and loss through memories, photographs, and mobile 'go-along' interviews. She shows the experience of silently leading a fatherless childhood in a paternalistic community village.

Family Mapping

The map as a technique is used to explore the nature of relationships and networks developed as a tool for the assessment of family therapy. Maps were often used in combination with family tree diagrams, the techniques the roots of which stem from family counselling and therapeutic assessment (see Hartmann 1995; Bowen 1978). An overview of the methods used in sociological analysis of families and intimate lives is presented below.

'My Family Map'. The method is an example of the research technique developed by Levin (1993) in her sociological research studies of stepfamilies. The method of defining one's family from the perspective of an individual was based on defining the 'family' as a concept, and it varied among different individuals and in different periods of time and space. The Kvebaek's sculpture technique developed in family therapy and Jorgenson's method of studying newly-wed couples with small children as well as Levin's earlier research work with divorced families have been an inspiration for the three-step family mapping method. The method enabled the 'voicing' of interviewees and gave access to individuals' views on what/who constituted one's family at the time of study. This method offered a relatively rapid way of moving into emotional areas of relationships and posed the challenge of talking about them. Moreover, the method ensured the participation of the interviewee in the research, while the three-step structure of researching (family list, family map, and interview) provided a 'within method triangulation'. The procedure of the research is the following:

> The first step (family list) starts with a question: "When do you think of your family, who do you think of? Make a list of those whom you consider as your family." The interviewee writes the names on a sheet of paper and reads the names or relationships aloud. The list can be changed at any time during the interview. During the second step (the family map), the interviewee is asked to place each family member, symbolized by circular (for female) and triangular (for male) pieces of paper, on a large sheet. The interviewee starts with himself/herself and then places the others based on how close or how distant one feels they are to him/her. During the third step (the verbal interview), the interviewee identifies family members, gives explanations about relationships between himself/herself and the family members and provides more information than is given on the map. (Levin 1993: 87–89)

The method was used to interview both adults and children. The research with adults normally involved the use of figures (circles and triangles), while the research with children was done with drawings (Levin and Trost 2000). Consequently, the participant-led map technique did not differ from the usage of drawings in family research. Maps or drawings were used both as a means of getting the view of the participants' conceptualisation of their family and as means of starting researcher-participant communication.

Levin's method was used in researching a variety of families. In Norway, Bolstad (1995) used this method to examine family conceptualisation in case of the parents who were forced to give up their children to foster-care. In Lithuania, Juozeliūnienė (2014) used the 'My Family Map' method to study transnational family conceptualisations and children's views on their families while staying in childcare institutions under state custody. The family map presented in Fig. 7.1 comes from the research study of conceptualising families in childcare homes carried out by the author and her student within the network of testing mapping methods when researching vulnerable families in Lithuania.

Rūta[1] is a 15-year-old girl whose parents are deceased, living at a care home. In her family map, she noted her relatives and her late mother, father, and grandmother. She also noted her late grandfather, although she had never seen him. Her closest relationship is with her aunt Kamilė whom she calls by name. Rūta says: 'I have been communicating with her since my childhood, she loves me very much, she is like a mother to me, I may say. She hugs and consoles me'. Her other aunt is more distant, therefore she does not call her by

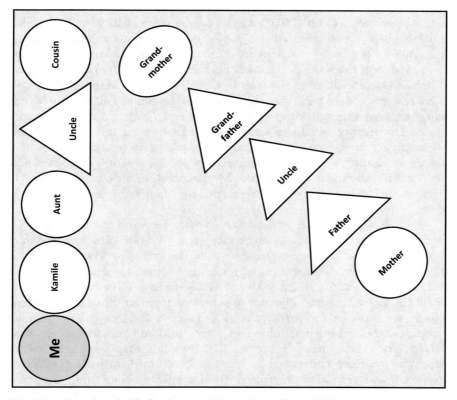

Fig. 7.1 Rūta (aged 15) family map (*Source* Radavičiūtė 2013)

name. She noted one uncle closer to herself because he often visits Rūta at the care home, 'unlike that other uncle'. She considers the other uncle as '<...> a certain relative, but I do not keep much contact with him. He sometimes comes'. She included him in the family maps, but only among the deceased members. Her female cousin is a very important person for her because she calls her often, comes and invites her for a visit. Rūta has more relatives but did not include them in the family map because she rarely keeps contact with them and does not want them to cause her pain. This is what they sometimes say to her: '<...> you will be like your mother: a drunkard and unemployed' (Radavičiūtė 2013).

'My Family Map' method was extended by Juozeliūnienė (2014) to a four-stage mapping method. It contains the stages of making a list, ranking the items on the list in the order of significance to the informant, making a map, and conducting the interview. This extension of the mapping method opened the possibilities to study the informant's own understanding of 'proper parenting' and transnational mothering/fathering, to determine transnational children's identities, to highlight the views on bi-national family relationships, and to examine the ways bi-national and transnational families are done and displayed.

'Emotion Map'. Gabb (2010) developed the participatory method which visually mapped the affective geography of family interactions. Doucet's techniques of portraying the household in analysing gender roles and responsibilities among heterosexual couples, later extended by Dunne in the study of lesbian households, were the basis of Gabb's 'Emotion Map'. The method offers new ways of studying the relationships of the couple and the family, this being achieved through mapping the nature and quality of everyday experience. The method produces visual data in its own right, but its greatest advantage lies in the facilitation of in-depth qualitative interviews on where affective encounters took place alongside with the discursive data around family relationships and everyday life. By generating data on related everyday practices, this method focuses on the materiality, temporality, and emotionality of family lives.

The techniques of the method are suitable for both parents and children irrespective of their age or literacy skills. A floor plan of the family home is produced by the researcher before the interview alongside with a set of coloured emoticon stickers representing happiness, sadness, anger, and love/affection. The informant is asked to designate a coloured sticker to each family (in the wide sense) member to represent them on the map. Different colours are used for the participant, their partner, children (if any), family, friends, pets, etc. Then the informant places coloured stickers on the floor plan to signify the change of emotions. The 'Emotion Map' grants the insight into family routines, encourages to visualise the normally invisible patterns of behaviour, and gives a point of departure for talking about family dynamics and affective household space. The stickers aimed at signifying an exchange of emotions, while the in-depth interview that followed provided the basis for getting the data about the complexity of feelings and their dynamics signified on the map (Gabb 2010: 44–45).

Catherine's 'emotion map' (see Fig. 7.2) was produced during the family session arranged to solve the husband/father's anger outbreaks and was aimed at 'improving family communication' (Gabb and Singh 2015). The drawings of 'my family' and 'emotion maps' were used to facilitate personal reflection, family conversation, and 'give voice' to Catherine. In the map, the major conflict venue was the 'mud room' (hallway), an area where Dad (yellow) and Richard (green) would typically get anger outbreaks. The family members

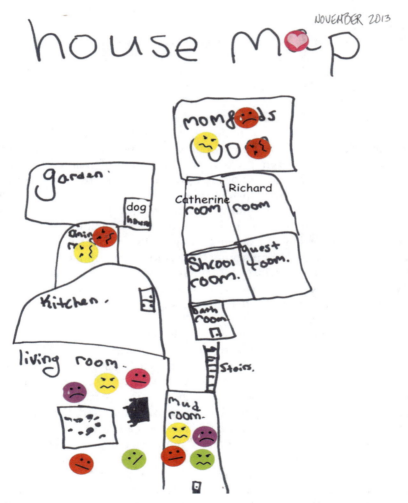

Fig. 7.2 Catherine (aged 10) emotion map. Yellow = Dad; red = Mum; Catherine = purple; Richard = green (*Source* Gabb and Singh 2015: 191)

listened while Catherine explained the map and described how she experienced the events. The emotion map and Catherine's explanations opened a conversation about how differently the members of the family positioned themselves in conflict situations.

As the research studies (Gabb 2010; Gabb and Singh 2015) show, the 'emotion map' has the potential of providing the information about the existing relationships and of facilitating the displays of parenting scenarios, and of highlighting the 'educational dimension' through encouraging informants to think about solving family problems proactively. The sharing of individual emotion maps between the couple and among family members demonstrated their potential and possible further uses in researching intimate lives of the families.

The map of concentric circles. The circles (or ego-centred) maps, based on the physical distance symbolising emotional proximity and remoteness, are widely applied when studying research participants' social networks. The 'Five Field Map' (Samuelsson et al. 1996) consists of six concentric circles divided into five sectors named family, relatives, formal contacts, school, and friends/neighbours. The map in question is an update of the original version of the map used by Pattison in clinical work with families which aimed at measuring the structure (number of important persons) and composition (relative size of the different sectors and distribution of children/adults and males/females) of the networks of the children from different family settings. Proximity is measured by evaluating how closely to the centre of the map the informant places his/her important persons. Negative contacts, conflicts, and dissatisfaction are marked on the map by specific signifiers. The previous techniques of using physical distance to symbolise emotional proximity and remoteness were limited to measuring the relationships within the family, while the 'Five Field Map' considers the family as part of the individual's social network. Later, the 'Four Field Map' was developed further. Based on the 'Five Field Map,' it was adapted by omitting the 'formal contacts' domain (Sturgess et al. 2001).

Typically, the procedure included the following steps: the participant was given a blank map consisting of six concentric circles and divided into five sectors as well as a list of symbols for men (filled triangles), women (filled circles), boys (unfilled triangles), and girls (unfilled circles) with the abbreviations of the most usual persons like mother, father, stepfather, grandparent, uncle, teacher, schoolmate, etc. The participant was told that the centre represents the participant himself/herself and was asked to draw the symbols of those persons who were important for him/her in the different sectors, starting with the family and continuing clockwise. The most important persons were placed in the inner circle, while the least important ones were placed in the fourth circle; the outer ring represented negative contacts (i.e. for placing the persons who the child felt he/she was on bad terms with). The definition of an 'important' person was left at the participant's discretion. When the participant filled in the map, he/she was asked about any conflicts or broken relationships among the persons on the map. If any, the relationships were marked by the lines with the symbols indicating the type of problem. Further, the participant was asked whether or not he/she was happy with the relationships in each sector. This was marked by an 'S' (for satisfaction) and 'D' (for dissatisfaction) in a box at each sector (Samuelsson et al. 1996: 331–332).

The network map provided an immediate understanding of the informant's family situation. It became a starting point for the dialogue with the informant about his/her social relationships. The properties of the informant's network map were studied by comparing the maps of different samples of informants, and by correlating the map variables with other instruments measuring social interaction.

Spencer and Pahl (2006) used the map of concentric circles when exploring personal communities in order to reveal the interaction of a range of the 'given' and 'chosen' relationships of individuals representing different forms and styles of suffusion in their lives. Their concern was to unpack the 'negotiated specificities' of actual relationships (Finch and Mason 1993) with a focus on friendship and friend-like relationships to determine the type of social suffusion—or the blurring of roles—between friends and family. The researchers avoided dividing the circles into sectors in order to prevent the advance requirement to attribute the relationships with a specific person to only one relational category of family, relatives, school, friends, and neighbours.

Before the interview, the researchers asked the informants to make a list of up to 20 people who were 'important' to them at that specific moment and to arrange the names on the map in the order of importance, placing the names in the appropriate circle at a certain distance from the centre. The informants' understanding of a family member, a friend, family-like, and friend-like relationships were explored throughout the interview by discussing the way in which the names were attributed to specific circles, by exploring the normative expectations about commitments related to the roles of community members in providing various forms of social support, by comparing relationships with family members and friends, and by analysing the strategies of the formation of selected friendships. Asking questions about one's significant life events such as divorce, their consequences, coping strategies, etc. enabled the researchers to explore the relative salience of 'chosen' and 'given' relationships. At the end of the interview, the researchers asked the informants to consider the maps of their personal communities and to review them. This gave the informants a chance to reflect on the importance of different relationships and to make changes (Spencer and Pahl 2006: 46–47).

The map of ego-centred set of relationships and the subsequent interviews revealed four main types of friendship scenarios (basic, intense, focal, broad) and four friendship modes (bounded, serial, evolving, 'ruptured') as well as six distinctive forms of personal communities (friend-like, friend-enveloped, family-like, family-dependent, partner-based, and professional-based) which reflect different forms of the suffusion of relationships.

Elden (2012) showed how the map of concentric circles could be usefully combined with the 'draw-your-day' exercise in the study of childcare. The point of departure of the first method is the 'relationships' of care, while that of the second method is the 'doing' of care. The mixing of visual methods helped the child and the researcher narrativise practices and relationships of care.

Elden began researching practices and activities by means of 'draw-your-day' exercise. The child was given a large piece of paper divided into four squares and was asked to draw his/her day focusing on either a particular day or a 'regular' day (or both). In the first square, the child was asked to draw something that happened in the morning; the second focused on lunchtime; the third on the afternoon; and the last square on the evening. While the child was drawing, the researcher asked the child about the people in the drawings and their actions and also about the meanings attributed to them. Further, the child was asked to draw himself/herself in the inner circle of the map of concentric circles and then to draw the individuals 'who take care of you', 'who you take care of', and 'who are important to you' in the surrounding circles. It was expected that this second method should reveal the relationships surrounding the child (Elden 2012: 5–6).

Methodologically Complex Visual Family Research

Prosser (2008) argues that in order to achieve its potential, visual research requires creative work that draws on the combined strengths of interdisciplinary mixed-methods research. The mixing of visual methods alongside other methods is becoming common in researching families and intimate lives. The researchers working within the mixed-methods framework state that using different methodological tools during the research process allows drawing a multi-layered picture of family life. The research studies presented below are the few examples of complex visual family research methodology.

In their research study whereby they investigated the meanings which children attach to the concepts of care primarily in relation to family life, Brannen et al. (2000) carried out a questionnaire-based survey, conducted focus-group discussions and interviews using family maps for locating significant persons and also used family trees and vignettes. The mixing of visual methods during the interviews with children coming from different types of household settings allowed the researchers to present the evidence concerning the children's usual views on what constitutes a family and family life, more specifically the children's views on what families 'are' in practice and what families 'ought to' look like, and whom they consider as their significant persons within the families and beyond their households and kin, and what the variations in significant person's networks are in the context of family change.

Mason and Tipper (2008) used photo-elicitation, concentric circles and drawings to analyse how children actively create and define kinship and relatedness. The researchers gave the children cameras prior to the interviews and asked them to take photographs of those 'who mattered' to them, or of the places and things which they associated with those who mattered to them. The photographs were used in the subsequent interviews as elicitation material to identify the significant persons and to clarify how the children defined and experienced kinship. Some children chose to draw their family or relatives. The mixing of methods allowed to explore practices, perceptions, and experiences involved in children's kinship and to reveal the different modes of 'reckoning' kinship, more specifically, the layers of understanding and of doing kinship that intersect each other and interact with one another.

Merla and Nobels (2019) used the 'emotion map' suggested by Gabb (2010) in the four-stage analysis of 'multi-local residentiality' and 'multi-local living' of children in post-divorce families alongside with specific participatory methods: The 'Socio-Spatial Network Game' and the 'Go-Along Method'. The map with the other two innovative methods enabled, among others, the analysis of children's family networks, their spatial configuration, the dwelling practices and mobility.

A Critical Glance at Using Visual Methods in Family Research

The penetration of visual methodologies into family research has to sides. Some researchers welcome the application of visual methods in family research and emphasise their advantages and the new opportunities opening for researchers, while others, on the contrary, are concerned with new challenges which the researchers studying families and people's intimate lives encounter. For example, Prosser (2008) uses the metaphor of 'the darker side' of visual research to indicate a few things: (1) the paradigm polarisation and 'wall building' between visual researchers, (2) their claims regarding the supremacy of methodological skills and theoretical knowledge over visual research in order to fully understand social reality by visual means, and (3) the researchers' inability to understand the limitations of one's own perspective and to recognise the benefits of adversative ideas.

Without undermining the opportunities of methodologically mixed research and emphasising the importance of integration of words and images in the field of sociological research of families and intimate lives, Smart (2009) expressed reservations regarding the borrowing from other fields of the methodologies used for the analysis of visual material and claimed that at least those methodologies should not be used which had not been integrated into the theoretical model of the research project.

The sceptically minded researchers expressed their critical opinion towards different aspects of researching with visual material. They argued that researchers' attempts to reveal specific meanings through visual methods raised the questions of reliability, validity, and truthfulness of visual research data. Researchers were being rebuked for the lack of clarity about the wider picture of researching with visual material: for the terms they used, often failing to distinguish between the type of visual artefacts, and for the lack of clarity as to whether they had been generated by the researcher or the participant (Bravington and King 2018). The sceptics also claimed that visual researchers saw visual methods as a single entity and were unable to differentiate between the methods designed for different purposes (Buckingham 2009). Mitchell (2006: 62) examined the idea of using drawings for the 'voicing' of children and argued that 'current claims about the suitability of visual methods for research with children may be tied to both adult-ist and North Americancentric assumptions about drawings and about children'.

The use of visual methodologies in family research raised the question of the ethical guidelines for researching with visual material. Some visual researchers note that so far there are no clear and established ethical guidelines in visual research (see Prosser et al. 2008: 3), while others argue that the researchers who use some kind of visual methods can and should apply the general principles of ethical research. More specifically: research shall ensure the integrity, quality, and transparency; research staff and participants shall be fully informed about the purpose, methods, and use of research data; confidentiality of information and anonymity of respondents shall be respected; the participants' participation in the research shall be voluntary, any damage and conflicts of interests shall be avoided (Rose 2014: 329).

Working with visual material may require compliance with specific ethical standards. For example, Rose (2014: 331–340) considers three areas — consent, anonymity, and copyright — as being particularly problematic for visual research. Consent forms are expected to include a short description of what participants should do (e.g. make a family map, make photos) and the researcher's intended methods of use of the visual material. Verbal or written consent forms should be signed by all participants at the beginning of the research project. The author notes that recognisability is in an obvious conflict with confidentiality and anonymity when using visual materials produced by the informants or found by the researchers during research studies. However, she argues that anonymity is not necessarily obligatory when using image-based research methods; anonymity is something to be carefully considered in the process of a specific research project. Finally, copyright refers to the ownership of a specific visual image. The researcher has to obtain a permission to reproduce visual materials in any presentations or publications.

Professional associations draft visual research guidelines meant for researchers. For example, the National Centre for Research Methods (NCRM) offered a valuable review to assist researchers in identifying what ethical issues might arise in undertaking visual research and how these might be addressed (Wiles et al. 2008). The authors outline the approaches to research ethics and discuss the way they influence legal regulation and practice, specify the factors influencing ethical issues and decision-making. Drawing on practical illustrations from research projects, the authors explore the core ethical issues of consent, confidentiality and anonymity associated with research using photographs, films, and videos and discuss the ethical issues raised in relation to the construction and consumption of images.

The ethical issues of ensuring confidentiality in the publication or in the dissemination of visual works have also been noted by Backett-Milburn and McKie (1999). Visual research practices highlighted the ethical implications of involving children in the research and enabling them to negotiate on their participation by letting them refuse to draw (Horstman et al. 2008) or by offering them such refusal strategies as taking a book to read (Pridmore and Lansdown 1997).

Komulainen (2007) notes that 'voicing' methodologies raise specific requirements for researchers' agentic potential and their ability to 'listen' to the voices of participants. The visual material produced by the informants communicates back with the informant and may reveal the 'hidden' knowledge about their relationships with close people. The emerging memories and newly conceived relationships may have an impact on the emotional well-being of research participants. Researchers have to observe the emotional reactions of the informant and prevent any negative emotional effect produced by the research. The researcher has to consider such ethical behaviour as avoiding to cross the line when asking the informant about his/her family and intimate relationships, informing the participant about the possibility to give no answer to the disturbing questions or even terminate the interview at any time. It is also important that interviews are finished only after all emotions subside (Levin 1993; Juozeliūnienė 2014).

Summarising, visual family research methods are gaining importance. Researching with images opens new opportunities in the research of families and intimate lives, however sometimes researchers convert empirical data into theoretical considerations, diagrams, and models too quickly. Visual research is especially sensitive to research ethics, because visual methods enable the 'voicing' of participants. Researchers have different moral attitudes towards what is right and wrong as well as different abilities to create the researcher-researched person interaction favourable for the research, and to have an insight into the relationship of experiences with the wider social context. Using M.C. Esher's drawings ('Two hands' and 'Hand and Sphere') as visual metaphors Prosser (2008: 10) gives perfect examples of what, in his opinion, a visual research should look like. The drawings speak about close relationships between the researcher and the person being researched and the contextualisation of these relationships in a wider inter-disciplinary discourse.

NOTE

1. All names and identifying details in this chapter have been changed to protect confidentiality.

References

Alanen, Leena. 1992. *Modern Childhood? Exploring the 'Child Question' in Sociology.* Jyvaskyla: University of Jyvaskyla.

Angell, Catherine, Jo Alexander, and Jane A. Hunt. 2014. "'Draw, Write and Tell': A Literature Review and Methodological Development on the 'Draw and Write' Research Method." *Journal of Early Childhood Research* 5: 1–12.

Back, Les. 2007. *The Art of Listening.* Oxford: Berg.

Backett-Milburn, Kathryn, and Linda McKie. 1999. "A Critical Appraisal of the Draw and Write Technique." *Health Education Research* 14: 387–398.

Bagnoli, Anna. 2009. "Beyond the Standard Interview: The Use of Graphic Elicitation and Arts Based Methods." *Qualitative Research* 9 (5): 547–570.

Bartmanski, Dominik. 2014. "The Word/ Image Dualism Revisited: Towards an Iconic Conception of Visual Culture." *Journal of Sociology* 50 (2): 164–181.

Bateson, Gregory, and Margaret Mead. 1942. *Balinese Character: A Photographic Analysis.* New York: New York Academy of Sciences.

Becker, Howard S. 1974. "Photography and Sociology." *Studies in the Anthropology of Visual Communication* 1 (1): 3–26.

Becker, Howard S. 2002. "Visual Evidence: A Seventh Man, the Specified Generalization, and the Work of the Reader." *Visual Studies* 17: 3–11.

Benjamin-Thomas, Tanya Elizabeth, Debbie Laliberte Rudman, Jeshuran Gunaseelan, Vinod Joseph Abraham, Debra Cameron, Colleen McGrath, and Samuel Prasanna Vinoth Kumar. 2019. "A Participatory Filmmaking Process with Children with Disabilities in Rural India: Working Towards Inclusive Research." *Methodological Innovations*, September-December, 1–14.

Berger, John. 1972. *Ways of Seeing.* London: British Broadcasting Corporation, and Harmondsworth: Renguin.

Biasi, Vleria, Paolo Bonaiuto, and James M. Levin. 2015. "The 'Colour Family Drawing Test': Assessing Children's Perception of Family Relationships." *Studies on Mental Health and Cross-Cultural Comparisons. Health* 7: 300–307.

Bolstad, Synnøve Thoresen. 1995. Fra Moedreness Synsvinkel. *Social Work Reports*, 17.

Bowen, Murray. 1978. *Family Therapy in Clinical Practice.* Northvale, NJ: Jason Aronson Inc.

Brannen, Julia, Ellen Hepinstall, and Kalwant Bhopal. 2000. *Connecting Children: Care and Family Life in Later Childhood.* London: Routledge.

Bravington, Alison, and Nigel King. 2018. "Putting Graphic Elicitation into Practice: Tools and Typologies for the Use of Participant-led Diagrams in Qualitative Research Interviews." *Qualitative Research* 1: 1–18.

Buckingham, David. 2009. "Creative Visual Methods in Media Research: Possibilities, Problems and Proposals." *Media, Culture and Society* 31 (4): 633–652.

Burns, Robert C., and S. Harvard Kaufman. 1970. *Kinetic-Family-Drawings (K-F-D).* New York, NY: Brunner/Mazel.

Castren, Anna-Maija, and Eric D. Widmer. 2015. "Insiders and Outsiders in Stepfamilies: Adults' and Children's Views on Family Boundaries." *Current Sociology* 63 (1): 35–56.

Chalfen, Richard. 2000. Interpreting Family Photography as Pictorial Communication. In *Image-based Research: A Sourcebook for Qualitative Researchers*, edited by Jon Prosser, 214–234. London: Routledge.

Chaplin, Elizabeth. 1994. *Sociology of Visual Representation*. London: Routledge.
Crilly, Nathan, Alan F. Blackwell, and P. John Clarkson. 2006. "Graphic Elicitation: Using Research Diagrams as Interview Stimuli." *Qualitative Research* 6 (3): 341–366.
de Block, Liesbeth, and David Buckingham. 2007. *Global Children, Global Media. Migration, Media and Childhood*. London: Palgrave Macmillan.
Eldén, Sara. 2012. "Inviting the Messy: Drawing Methods and 'Children's Voices.'" *Childhood* 20 (1): 66–81.
Finch, Janet. 1987. "The Vignette Technique in Survey Research." *Sociology* 21: 105–114.
Finch, Janet., and Jennifer Mason. 1993. *Negotiating Family Responsibilities*. London: Routledge.
Flick, Uwe. 2002. *An Introduction to Qualitative Research*. Thousand Oaks, CA: Sage.
Furth, Gregg M. 1988. *The Secret World of Drawings—Healing Through Art*. Boston: Sigo.
Gabb, Jacqui. 2005. "Lesbian M/Otherhood: Strategies of Familial-Linguistic Management in Lesbian Parent Families." *Sociology* 39 (4): 585–603.
Gabb, Jacqui. 2010. *Researching Intimacy in Families*. London: Palgrave Macmillan.
Gabb, Jacqui, and Reenee Singh. 2015. "The Uses of Emotion Maps in Research and Clinical Practice with Families and Couples: Methodological Innovation and Critical Inquiry." *Family Process* 54 (1).
Harper, Douglas. 2000. "An Argument for Visual Sociology." In *Image-Based Research: A Sourcebook for Qualitative Researchers*, edited by Jon Prosser, 24–41. London: Routledge.
Harper, Douglas. 2002. "Talking About Pictures: A Case for Photo Elicitation." *Visual Studies* 17 (1): 13–26.
Hartmann, Ann. 1995. "Diagrammatic Assessment of Family Relationships." *Families in Society* 76 (2): 111–122.
Heath, Sue, and Elizabeth Cleaver. 2004. "Mapping the Spatial in Shared Household Life: A Missed Oportunity?" In *Picturing the Social Landscape: Visual Methods and the Sociological Imagination*, edited by Caroline Knowles and Paul Sweetman, 65–78. London and New York: Routledge.
Holliday, Ruth. 2004. "Reflecting the Self." In *Picturing the Social Landscape: Visual Methods and the Sociological Imagination*, edited by Caroline Knowles and Paul Sweetman, 49–64. London and New York: Routledge.
Horstman, Maire, Susie Aldiss, Alison Richardson, and Faith Gibson. 2008. "Methodological Issues When Using the Draw and Write Technique with Children Aged 6 to 12 Years." *Qualitative Health Research* 18: 1001–1011.
Isaacs, Marla B., and Irene Levin. 1984. "Who's in My Family? A Longitudinal Study of Drawings of Children of Divorce." *Journal of Divorce* 7 (4): 1–21.
Janning, Michelle, and Helen Scalise. 2015. "Gender and Generation in the Home Curation of Family Photography." *Journal of Family Issues* 36 (12): 1702–1725.
Jenks, Chris. 1995. "The Centrality of the Eye in Western Culture." *In Visual Culture*, edited by Chris Jenks, 1–12. London: Routledge.
Juozeliūnienė, Irena. 2014. *Žemėlapių metodai vaizdu grįstame tyrime*. Vilnius: Vilniaus universiteto leidykla.
Knowles, Caroline, and Paul Sweetman, ed. 2004. *Picturing the Social Landscape: Visual Methods and the Sociological Imagination*. London: Routledge.

Knowles, J. Gary, and Ardra L. Cole. 2008. *Handbook of the Arts in Qualitative Research: Perspectives, Methodologies, Examples and Issues*. London: Sage.

Komulainen, Sirkka. 2007. "The Ambiguity of the Child's 'Voice' in Social Research." *Childhood* 14 (1): 1–28.

Leich, Ruth, and Simon J. Mitchell. 2007. "Caged Birds and Cloning machines: How Student Imagery 'Speaks' to Us About Cultures of Schooling." *Improving Schools* 10: 53–71.

Leitch, Ruth. 2008. "Creatively Researching Children's Narratives Through Images and Drawings." In *Doing Visual Research with Children and Young People*, edited by Pat Thomson, 37–57. London and New York: Routledge.

Levin, Irene. 1993. "Family as Mapped Realities." *Journal of Comparative Family Studies* 14 (1): 82–91.

Levin, Irene, and Jan Trost. 2000. "Step Family as Dyads—Direct and Indirect Relationships." *Journal of Comparative Family Studies* 31 (2): 139–153.

Lewis, Ann. 2010. "Silence in the Context of 'Child Voice.'" *Children and Society* 24 (1): 14–23.

Linesch, Debra. 1994. "Interpretation in Art Therapy Research and Practice: The Hermeneutic Circle." *The Arts in Psychotherapy* 3: 185–195.

Mason, Jennifer, and Becky Tipper. 2008. "Being Related: How Children Define and Create Kinship." *Childhood* 15 (4): 441–460.

Merla, Laura, and Bérengère Nobels. 2019. "Children Negotiating Their Place Through Space in Multi-local, Joint Physical Custody Arrangements." In *Families in Motion: Ebbing and Flowing Through Space and Time*, edited by Lesley Murray, Liz McDonnell, Tamsin Hinton-Smith, Nuno Ferreira, and Katie Walsh, 79–95. Emerald publishing.

Mirzoeff, Nicholas. 1998. "What is Visual Culture?" In *The Visual Culture Reader*, edited by Nicholas Mirzoeff, 3–13. London: Routledge.

Mitchell, Lisa M. 2006. "Child-Centered? Thinking Critically About Children's Drawings as a Research Method." *Visual Anthropological Review* 22 (1): 60–73.

Mitchell, William John Thomas. 1995. *Picture Theory: Essays on Verbal and Visual Representation*. Chicago: University of Chicago Press.

Mitchell, Claudia, and Sandra Weber. 2000. "Picture This! Class Line-ups, Vernacular Portraits and Lasting Impressions of School." In *Image-based Research: A Sourcebook for Qualitative Researchers*, edited by Jon Prosser, 197–213. London: Routledge.

Morgan, Myfanwy, Sara Gibbs, Krista Maxwell, and Nicky Britten. 2002. "Hearing Children's Voices: Methodological Issues in Conducting Focus Groups with Children Aged 7–11 Years." *Qualitative Research* 2: 5–20.

Morrow, Virginia. 1998. *Understanding Families: Children's Perspectives*. London: National Children's Bureau.

Morrow, Virginia. 2001. "Using Qualitative Methods to Elicit Young People's Perspectives on their Environments: Some Ideas for Community Health Initiatives." *Health Education Research* 16 (3): 255–268.

Nolas, Sevasti-Melissa, Vinnarasan Aruldoss, and Christos Varvantakis. 2019. "Learning to Listen: Exploring the Idioms of Childhood." *Sociological Research Online* 24 (3): 394–413.

Pridmore, Pat, and Richard Lansdown. 1997. "Exploring Children's Perceptions of Health: Does Drawing Really Break Down Barriers?" *Health Education Journal* 56: 219–230.

Prosser, Jon. 2008. *The Dark Side of Visual Research*. Working Paper. Available at www.manchester.ac.uk/realities.
Prosser, Jon, and Andrew Loxley. 2008. "Introducing Visual Methods." *NCRM Methodological Review*. Available at www.ncrm.ac.uk/research/outputs/publications/.
Prosser, Jon, and Dona Schwartz. 2000. "Photographs Within the Sociological Research Process." In *Image-based Research: A Sourcebook for Qualitative Researchers*, edited by Jon Prosser, 115–130. London: Routledge.
Prosser, Jon, Andrew Clark, and Rose Wiles. 2008. *Visual Research Ethics at the Crossroads*. National Centre for Research Methods/Realities Working Paper. Available at https://epints.ncrm.ac.uk/535/.
Prosser, Jon, ed. 2000. *Image-Based Research. A Sourcebook for Qualitative Researchers*. London: Routledge.
Radavičiūtė, Dovilė. 2013. *Šeima globos namų auklėtinių požiūriu*. Bakalauro darbas, apgintas Vilniaus Universitete.
Rigg, Andrea, and Jan Pryor. 2007. "Children's Perceptions of Families: What Do They Really Think?" *Children and Society* 21: 17–30.
Roe, Amy E. C., Laura J. Bridges, Judy Dunn, and Thomas G. O'Connor. 2006. "Young Children's Representations of Their Families: A Longitudinal Follow-Up Study of Family Drawings by Children Living in Different Family Settings." *International Journal of Behavioral Development* 30: 529–536.
Rose, Gillian. 2014. *Visual Methodologies. An Introduction to Researching with Visual Materials*. London: Sage.
Samuelsson, Margareta, Gunilla Thernlund, and Jerker Ringstrom. 1996. "Using the Veeld Map to Describe the Social Network of Children: A Methodological Study." *International Journal of Behavioral Development* 19: 327–345.
Smart, Carol. 2009. "Shifting Horizons: Reflections on Qualitative Methods." *Feminist Theory* 10 (5): 295–308.
Spence, Jo, and Patricia Holland, ed. 1991. *Family Snaps: The Meaning of Domestic Photography*. London: Virago.
Spencer, Liz, and Ray Pahl. 2006. *Rethinking Friendship: Hidden Solidarities Today*. Princeton, NJ: Princeton University Press.
Steiger, Ricabeth. 1995. "First Children and Family Dynamics." *Visual Studies* 10 (1–2): 28–49.
Sturgess, Wendy, Judy Dunn, and Lisa Davies. 2001. "Young Children's Perceptions of Their Relationships with Family Members: Links with Family Setting, Friendships, and Adjustment." *International Journal of Behavioral Development* 25 (6): 521–529.
Taylor, Lisa. 2019. "Losing a Father in an Ex-industrial Landscape: A Researcher's Emotional Geography." In *Families in Motion: Ebbing and Flowing Through Space and Time*, edited by Lesley Murray, Liz McDonnell, Tamsin Hinton-Smith, Nuno Ferreira, and Katie Walsh, 177–194. Emerald publishing.
Thomson, Pat, ed. 2008. *Doing Visual Research with Children and Young People*. London: Routledge.
Varga-Atkins, Tünde, and Mark O'Brien. 2009. "From Drawings to Diagrams: Maintaining Researcher Control During Graphic Elicitation in Qualitative Interviews." *International Journal of Research and Method in Education* 32 (1): 53–67.
Vist, Torill. 2019. "Toddler Encounters as Aesthetic Interviews? Discussing an Arts-Based Data Gathering." *Qualitative Inquiry* 25 (7): 604–614.

Wagner, Jon. 1978. "Perceiving a Planned Community." In *Images of Information*, edited by Jon Wagner, 85–100. Beverly Hills, CA: Sage.

Wiles, Rose, Jon Prosser, Anna Bagnoli, Andrew Clark, Katherine Davies, Sally Holland, and Emma Renold. 2008. *Visual Ethics: Ethical Issues in Visual Research*. ESRC National Centre for Research Methods Review Paper. https://eprints.ncrm.ac.uk/421/1/MethodsReviewPaperNCRM-011.pdf.

PART II

Welfare State and Family Policy Regimes in Europe

Edited by Katarzyna Suwada

CHAPTER 8

Family Transformations and Sub-replacement Fertility in Europe

Irena E. Kotowska, Monika Mynarska, and Anne H. Gauthier

INTRODUCTION

Persistent sub-replacement fertility, initially observed in a growing number of European countries and subsequently also in other developed countries, is without historical precedent and has become a global phenomenon. In 1990 the share of the world's population living in countries with fertility below 2.1 births per woman was slightly less than 25%. In 2019 it accounted for nearly 50% (United Nations 2019). Moreover, from 1990 to 2019 the total number of countries with very low fertility, that is below 1.5 children per woman, increased from eight to 25, with 13 of them being in Europe.

Demographic developments in Europe and elsewhere are increasingly recognised a crucial factor for the sustainability of societies (European Commission 2006, 2009). Fertility decline along with the continuous and

---

I. E. Kotowska (✉)
Institute of Statistics and Demography, Warsaw School of Economics, Warsaw, Poland
e-mail: iekoto@sgh.waw.pl

M. Mynarska
Institute of Psychology, Cardinal Stefan Wyszyński University in Warsaw, Warsaw, Poland
e-mail: m.mynarska@uksw.edu.pl

A. H. Gauthier
Netherlands Interdisciplinary Demographic Institute (NIDI-KNAW), University of Groningen, Den Haag, The Netherlands
e-mail: gauthier@nidi.nl

© The Author(s), under exclusive license to Springer Nature Switzerland AG 2021
A.-M. Castrén et al. (eds.), *The Palgrave Handbook of Family Sociology in Europe*, https://doi.org/10.1007/978-3-030-73306-3_8

remarkable lengthening of the life span, and major streams of in- and out-migration are having profound effects on the age structure of societies. The demographic consequences of sub-replacement fertility, i.e. a population decline, advanced population ageing, and comprehensive changes of family and household structures, place fertility change among the most debated demographic issues (Luci-Greulich and Thevenon 2013; Sobotka et al. 2019). Political interest in policies to raise fertility is furthermore increasingly declared by governments, mostly in Europe and Asia. In 2015, 62% of them have already implemented measures aimed at stimulating fertility (United Nations 2018).

In this chapter, we focus on the European countries—forerunners in the fertility decline. We describe the fertility trends across the continent (section "Patterns of Low and Very Low Fertility") and discuss them in relation to new and diverging patterns of family-related behaviours and new ways of 'doing family' that have emerged in the recent five decades (section "Low Fertility and Family Transformations"). We provide some interpretation of the reasons for the sub-replacement fertility in Europe, commenting on its possible future developments (section "The Drivers of Fertility and Family Changes in Europe"). We also discuss the role of policies in shaping these developments (section "Policy Responses to Low Fertility and Changes in Families"). The chapter closes with reflection on research and data necessary for designing efficient evidence-based policies (section"Towards Better Understanding of Family Transformations and Evidence-Based Policies: Research Challenges and Data Needs").

Patterns of Low and Very Low Fertility

Fertility rates have declined strongly in Europe during the past 50 years, from about 2.6 children per woman on average in the early 1960s to about 1.6 today (see Fig. 8.1). However, the speed of this change and the current level vary widely across European regions. This diversity is important since it has not only shaped different political discourses on demography (as will be seen in section "Policy Responses to Low Fertility and Changes in Families") but it has also been accompanied by different trends in family formation (section "Low Fertility and Family Transformations").

The decline in fertility started in Northern Europe in the late 1960s and countries of Western Europe rapidly joined this trend in the next decade. By far, this decline came somewhat unexpectedly as the expectation was that in modern societies fertility would stabilise around the replacement level of around two children per woman (van de Kaa 1987). The below-replacement fertility, observed in various European countries in the 1970s, was therefore considered to be a temporary phenomenon. This however turned out not to be the case. In contrast, during the next decade additional European countries joined the downward fertility trend. Nordic and Western European countries were followed by countries of Southern Europe in the 1980s. The rapid

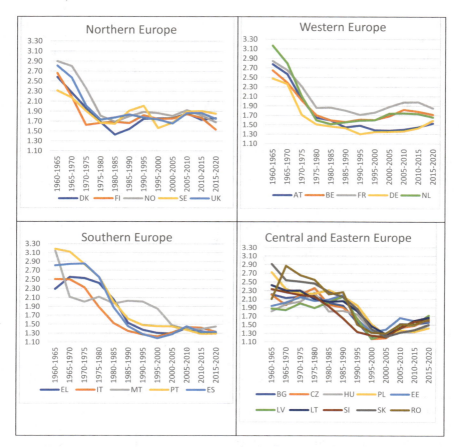

Fig. 8.1 Period total fertility rates by regions in Europe, 1960–2020 (*Source* UN fertility data)

fertility decline observed in post-socialist countries since 1990 completed the picture. At that point, it has become evident that the replacement fertility level cannot be considered a glass floor for the fertility decline. In particular, while in some countries fertility did stabilise around 1.5 children per woman, in others (mainly Southern and Eastern Europe), it did so even below 1.3, labelled the lowest-low fertility (Kohler et al. 2006; Lesthaeghe 2020).

The above trends of fertility decline result from changes in the reproductive behaviour of the younger generations (younger birth cohorts). In the 1970s and 1980s, the quantum decline in Northern and Western Europe resulted from falling progression to third and subsequent births in the cohorts born between 1940 and 1955 (with the exception of Western Germany, Switzerland, and the Netherlands where decreasing first-birth rates contributed to this change). In countries joining this trend in the next decades, it was driven by falling either first-birth rates (Southern Europe) or second birth-rates (Central and Eastern Europe) among women born between 1955 and 1970 (Zeman et al. 2018). Also childlessness has been growing in these birth cohorts in most European countries. Among women born around 1970, approximately one woman in five has never had children in Austria, Germany, or Switzerland, as well as in Italy and Spain (Sobotka 2017). Incidence of childlessness remains much lower in the post-socialist countries, but it has also been growing among women born in youngest cohorts (ibidem).

In recent years, some fertility recovery has been observed. This is however mostly due to some recuperation at later ages resulting from increasing age-specific fertility among women aged 30 and more. The recuperation process also differs by European regions and across countries. In the Northern countries and in some Western countries, the fertility recuperation came nearly to the end in the 2000s already while in Central and Eastern Europe this process just started. Also countries of Southern Europe, where childbearing postponement approached its limits, show signs of the moderate recuperation (Frejka 2011).

These trends all point towards a common downward in fertility but also a clear regional gradient in terms of timing and intensity of fertility changes. In particular, they have resulted in a divide of European countries between those with persisting low fertility and even the lowest-low fertility and those where the period TFR did not fall below 1.5. Moreover, these two groups of countries reveal also diverse patterns of fertility changes. Here, the countries of Southern, Central and Eastern Europe deserve attention since, in their cases, the gap between desired and achieved fertility is the largest (Kohler et al. 2006; Sobotka 2017). This distinction is crucial for understanding dynamics of fertility and family changes across different regions. It also seems central in the discussion on whether and under what circumstances, we can expect to witness fertility recovery in Europe.

Low Fertility and Family Transformations
Demographic Markers of Changes

Childbearing decisions, which result in sustained below-replacement fertility, need to be considered in relation to other demographic transitions over one's life-course. Especially, the behaviours that define the transition to adulthood are crucial for family formation. The 'old' pattern of the transition to adulthood observed till the 1970s and labelled as 'early, contracted and simple', evolved into the new one in the 1980s: 'late, protracted and complex' (Billari and Liefbroer 2010). This shift reflects changes in all demographic markers of the transition to adulthood manifested by the postponement of leaving parental home, forming partnership and becoming a parent, and the de-institutionalisation of union formation as well as increasing union instability. Research indicates however that transitions to adulthood are becoming increasingly diverse not only between European countries but also within countries and between social groups (Perelli-Harris et al. 2010; Schwanitz 2017).

When key demographic markers of transition to adulthood are considered, the most profound changes can be observed in patterns of union formation and their relation to parenthood (Billari and Liefbroer 2010; Perelli-Harris et al. 2010; Perelli-Harris and Lyons-Amos 2015; Lesthaeghe 2020). The general trend in transitions to partnership is manifested by decline in marriage accompanied by a rise in unmarried cohabitation and non-co-residential partnerships and the postponement of a first union. The postponement is much stronger for marriage than for cohabitation. This trend started in Northern and Western Europe and initially contributed to the deepening of historically rooted differences of marriage patterns between the West and East. In Central and Eastern Europe, the decline in the propensity to marriage and delays in marriage started in the 1990s but with great intensity. However, the old East–West divide at the Hajnal's line (from Triest to Saint Petersburg, Hajnal 1965) still remains today with women on the eastern side of the line still marrying at younger ages than women on the western side. In the eastern region, some reversals of retreat from marriage after 2010 can be noticed.

Since the 1970s cohabitation has been increasingly chosen as a way of starting a first union, initially in the Nordic countries and France and later in other European countries. Diffusion of cohabitation is the most advanced in Northern and Western Europe, while some countries of Southern and Central and Eastern Europe are on the other extreme. In 2000–2004, in the former group more than half of women aged 25–29 being in union for at least one year were in cohabitation while in the latter group that share did not surpass 30% except for Spain (Lesthaeghe 2020). Beside the diverse spread of cohabitation in Europe its status vis-à-vis marriage and—most importantly—parenthood has also changed (Sobotka and Toulemon 2008; Perelli-Harris and Lyons-Amos 2015; Di Giulio et al. 2019). On the one hand, in most countries premarital cohabitation delays marriage, but it has not become its alternative yet. In contrast, the advanced postponement in first marriage in Italy and Spain results from shifts in timing of direct marriage without premarital cohabitation. Moreover, even though in some countries expecting a baby remains a relevant incentive for converting cohabitation into marriage (Flanders, Italy, Poland, Romania, Slovakia) the overall uptrend in non-marital childbearing can be observed. The trend started in Scandinavia in the mid-1960s and was diffused gradually across Europe. The Southern Europe and several countries of Central-Easter Europe have been its late followers of the 1990s. Currently, more than half of births are given outside marriage in Nordic countries, and one in four in Poland and Lithuania. Only few countries present a lower share of non-marital births (e.g. Greece, Belarus, North Macedonia). While the trends related to cohabitation and extramarital childbearing are diversified across countries, they illustrate the increasing contribution of non-marital unions to partnership formation and fertility as well as the weakening association between marriage and fertility.

In addition to the growing relevance of cohabitation for partnering and re-partnering, marriages are increasingly ending in divorce. In result, partnerships have become more exposed to dissolution. In Northern and Western Europe divorce rates started to rise at the turn of 1960s and 1970s. However, forerunners in marriage dissolution were some republics of the Soviet Union, where the trend began in the mid-1960s already. Currently, these countries show high levels of marriage instability. Southern and most of the Central Europe countries experienced this change since the 1990s. A majority of them display still relatively low divorce rates now. This high cross-country heterogeneity in exposure to divorce is expected to be reduced in the future (Sobotka and Toulemon 2008).

The above changes in partnership behaviour in Europe, characterised by postponement, the gradual retreat from marriage, the rise of cohabitation and the diversity of unions lived, and the declining stability of marriages, provide the context for the transformation of childbearing behaviours. A pronounced delay in a transition to parenthood is indicative of transforming childbearing patterns in Europe, constitutive for fertility changes since the 1970s. A rising mean age of women at first birth has changed the timing of births (tempo) and has influenced the total number of children born (quantum), contributing to the fertility decline below replacement (Kohler et al. 2006; Frejka and Sobotka 2008; Beaujouan and Toulemon 2019).

To sum up, in contemporary Europe, family-related behaviours have become highly complex and depict increasingly diverse family biographies. As the result, childbearing occurs in a wider variety of family constellations. Even though the most common form of the nuclear family is still the married couple with one or two children, other family forms have become more frequent: cohabiting couples, single parents, reconstituted families, couples without children, and same-sex couples (Parke 2013). The number of non-resident families—living apart by choice or circumstance—is also growing. Increasing people's mobility, in particular due to employment or job searching outside a place of residence, makes family arrangements even more complex. They are often characterised by the absence of some family members (partner, parents, and/or children) for remarkable time periods which contributes to the organisation of family life, in particular as regards sharing housework and care duties. Moreover, different family forms are practised by individuals over their life course, contributing to the de-standardised and dynamic family biographies. In this diversified demographic picture, also ways of 'doing family' have significantly changed.

Changing Ways of 'Doing Family'

Changing patterns of family-related demographic behaviours have also been accompanied by changes in the organisation of family life, including family relations, gender roles, and family values. An increasing 'family fluidity' reflects a fundamental shift in the social organisation of intimacy and social contacts, increasing individualisation and growing diversity of the partnership forms (Daly 2005; Hantrais 2006; Saraceno 2008). Moreover, extended longevity results in the verticalisation of kinship networks (they include more generations); however, this process is moderated by the postponement of childbearing. Due to delayed childbearing, the age gap between generations is becoming relatively large and the likelihood that multiple generations are alive at the same time is reduced. Similarly, the linked lives of subsequent generations are lasting longer than ever. Low fertility impacts the size of subsequent generations and reduces horizontal ties (slimming of kinship networks). Union dissolution also reduces the networks of relatives while re-partnering has the opposite effect (Saraceno 2008; Dykstra 2010), but resulting in more complex, 'patchwork' relations between 'old' and 'new' family members. The evolution of kinship relationships transforms the nature of kinship ties and exchanges within and between generations, challenging the established norms about filial responsibilities, shaped by country-specific economic, cultural, and institutional settings (Daly 2005; Saraceno 2008; Hagestad and Dykstra 2016).

The family changes have been closely interrelated with women's growing commitment to the labour market. Women's participation in the labour force along with their steady increase in educational attainment constitute a core of the societal transformation witnessed in developed countries in the second half of the twentieth century. The two processes imposed the gradual shifts in responsibilities for economic provision to the family, housework and care between women and men, accompanied by increasing recognition of gender roles (Goldin 1990; Bernhardt 1993; Mason 1997). Therefore, to understand family transformations changing demographic patterns need to be described along with evolution of women's and men's roles within and outside the family.

Steadily increasing economic activity of women has broken the traditional gender contract with the normative ascription of breadwinning to men and family caring and household chores to women (Mason 1997; Leira 2002). These strictly defined social roles of men and women through their family responsibilities as regards breadwinning and caregiving have been reflected in gender role specialisation by economic theorising (Becker 1981) and Parsons' male breadwinner family model (Parsons 1955), which presumes a mother's role as a homemaker-carer and a father's role as an economic provider. Both concepts have been increasingly contested. Oppenheimer (1997) has pointed out that pooling resources by spouses/partners makes it possible to better adapt to increasing demands of the labour market. Consequently, the modernised male breadwinner model and the dual-earner family model ('shared roles model') have been formulated (Leira 2002). They have conceptualised on-going and expected changes in sharing economic and care responsibilities within the family. The modernised male breadwinner (female part-time carer) model is based on mothers sequencing employment and family work, while the dual earner assumes both partners are providing income.

Along with growing women's employment, the male breadwinner model has been gradually replaced, first by a model in which a father remains the main economic provider while a mother is perceived a secondary earner with her paid work subordinated to her family duties. Next, the dual-earner model has been more frequently practised. However, a greater involvement of women in paid work outside the household has not been accompanied by parallel shifts in housework and care responsibilities among partners, resulting in the family model with a double burden of women. Decisions as to who provides childcare and who is responsible for household chores remain controversial and contested, however to different extent across countries (Matysiak and Węziak-Białowolska 2016). Such decisions might be even more complicated in patchwork families, where responsibility for own as well as partner's children is involved. An increasing number of same-sex families also poses new challenges to how gender roles in the family are defined.

Altogether, 'living as a family in Europe' (Hantrais 2006) is more complex demographically and increasingly interrelated with women's and men's participation in the labour market and its on-going transformation. While childbearing is strongly linked to other demographic events in one's life-course, the nature of this link has also been changing in recent decades.

The Drivers of Fertility and Family Changes in Europe

In the demographic literature, the Second Demographic Transition Theory (SDT) occupies a key place in having proposed a mechanism linking sub-replacement fertility to changes in partnership and childbearing patterns (van de Kaa 1987, 1994; Lesthaeghe 1995, 2010). However, this mechanism has been increasingly contested. Since the mid-1980s, the correlation between period TFR and various indicators of family dynamics started to reverse (Kohler et al. 2006; Sobotka and Toulemon 2008; Prskawetz et al. 2010). Consequently, in Europe the highest fertility is now observed in countries which are advanced in the postponement and de-institutionalisation of family formation. They show the strongest delays in marriage, high percentages of non-marital births, relatively frequent unmarried cohabitation as well as high divorce rates. In most countries, the lower marriage rates are not related to the increasing proportion of persons who forego family formation and remain childless, but more to the growing share of couples having children outside marriage. In countries where the link between marriage and parenthood is still relatively strong, fertility remains low (e.g. Italy, Greece, Lithuania, Poland, Romania), while in other countries where marriage and childbearing are disconnected, fertility is relatively high in European terms (e.g. Sweden, France, Norway, Belgium, Netherlands).

The reversal in the cross-country macro-level association between fertility and aggregate indicators of family formation and dissolution cannot be explained by a change in causal relationship between fertility and family-related behaviour at the individual level. At the micro-level, behaviours indicative of family de-institutionalisation and destabilisation are still negatively related to childbearing. However, the strength of this relation is lower in countries showing more progress in evolution of gender roles within and outside the family (Prskawetz et al. 2010). Moreover, the recent increase in marriage rates, mostly in Central and Eastern Europe along with some recovery of fertility, seem to indicate relevance of marriage-based family for childrearing. Institutional settings and the social context, including gender roles, remain important for macro-level outcomes.

The SDT conceptual framework includes structural components of market economy and improving living conditions, as well as recognises increasing education attainment of women and their growing economic autonomy as part of societal changes (Van de Kaa 1994). However, when explaining family changes and below-replacement fertility, the emphasis has been given to culture and technology. Ideational changes regarding intimate relationships, fertility and the family have determined new family-related behaviours. Weakening of normative constraints along with better access to effective contraception have imposed fundamental changes in sexual relations and their links with childbearing and marriage. The on-going labour market transformations, in particular since the onset of globalisation in the 1990s, and increasing economic uncertainties have been largely ignored (Bernhardt 2004; Frejka and Sobotka 2008; Perelli-Harris et al. 2010). The critique of the SDT refers also to lacking explicit gender perspective.

The gender perspective appears unavoidable when discussing current fertility trends and family transformations. Contrary to Becker's predictions on the fertility decline following women's labour market involvement, since the mid-1980s in Western countries and 20 years later in Central and Eastern Europe women' employment has been positively associated with fertility. The reversal of correlation between women's employment and fertility has drawn attention on conditions under which mothers' employment can be combined with childrearing (Adserà 2011; Matysiak 2011). Of course, in individual biographies, employment still competes with childbearing for women's time. Yet, in-depth analyses at both micro- and macro-levels point to the macro-context and its role in reconciling competing demands of family and other life domains, and to evolving perceptions of social roles of women and men. In particular, institutional settings with well-developed early childhood education and care services support not only mothers' employment and strengthen their role in economic provision for the family, but also reveal positive effects for fertility.

The scientific discussion on gender roles within and outside the family in the context of changing fertility and family behaviours evolved into a coherent theoretical framework. It provides explanations for fertility decline by referring to the gender revolution as a driving force and the economic, institutional, and cultural contexts for its progress. The framework describes a U-shape relationship between gender revolution and fertility, reflecting on conditions for a possible recovery of fertility.

The first stage of gender revolution is characterised by the growth of labour force participation of women, linked to the transition from the male breadwinner family to the dual-earner family. Women's stronger attachment to paid work has been accompanied by increasing social acceptance for employment of women and the declining gender inequalities in individual-oriented social institutions while gender inequity in family-oriented social institutions still persists (McDonald 2000). At this stage, mothers are still perceived as a primary carer, in particular for small children, and men's involvement in home and childcare responsibilities is low. As this involvement increases, men's role transforms from a primary family provider to an economic provider (primary or secondary) and the involved, caring partner and father. These developments are attributed to the second stage of the gender revolution. Until men's contribution to domestic tasks and care work does not match that of women in paid work, the gender revolution remains incomplete (Esping-Andersen 2009; Esping-Andersen and Billari 2015; Goldscheider et al. 2015). However, the transition to the dual-earner–dual-carer model requires also increasing social acceptance of women as a primary economic provider in the family. In consequence, other patterns of sharing economic and home responsibilities within the family like the female primary earner or breadwinner-mother models would be more frequent.

The gender revolution is a global process. Its course is highly diversified across countries mostly due to diverse cultural constraints, institutional frameworks, and policy approaches which determine the context for reconciliation of family/private sphere and work/public sphere. Most of the developed countries are—to different extent—advanced in the first phase of the gender transformation while only relatively few countries are starting the second phase (Nordic countries, France). Women's rights and gender equality have been at the centre of political attention since the 1970s, firstly with a focus on women's participation in the labour market. Since the 1990s more attention has been paid to gender equality in both paid and unpaid work and the family life has been recognised as a factor relevant for gender inequalities in the labour market (Lewis 1992; Bernhardt 1993; Gornick et al. 1997). Besides referring to different labour market measures, the family has directly been introduced into research on employment patterns by gender (couples' employment patterns by the presence of children, their number and age) (Hantrais 2006; Del Boca and Wetzels 2007; Matysiak 2011). In parallel, growing attention has been paid to institutional settings depicted by different welfare states and their regulations on the labour market and family policy measures. Besides highlighting relevance of policy measures aimed at reducing gender inequity in family-oriented social institutions (leave regime, childcare provision, flexible working time) claims for direct recognition of changing gender roles in welfare regimes typology have been increasingly voiced (Leira 2002; Lewis 2009).

Policy Responses to Low Fertility and Changes in Families

The very large changes in fertility and patterns of family formation and dissolution described earlier in this chapter have taken place in the midst of major developments in the institutional context and in the political discourses surrounding families. The exact causal relationship between changes in individual-level demographic behaviour and developments of macro-level settings (e.g. politics and policies) is however complex. On the one hand, changes in fertility and families have led governments over the years to adopt policies to reflect the new diversity in family structures and gender roles. On the other hand, these same demographic changes have also led some governments to try to counteract them (e.g. low fertility). And again behind these institutional developments lie important differences between European regions.

Governmental support for families has a long history. Already more than 100 years ago maternity leave schemes were introduced to protect the health of working mothers and their children (Gauthier and Koops 2018). This early support to working mothers was gradually supplemented or replaced, starting from the 1970s, by a package of policies targeted instead at working parents. The introduction of parental leave (which can be shared between parents) perfectly illustrates this trend and marks a major shift away from the earlier breadwinner model to today's dual-earner model. This shift was a milestone in the history of governmental support for families. Not only it moved the discourse away from a strict focus on mother's health and traditional gender roles, but it also embraced the broader issues of gender equality and work-life balance of parents. The recently adopted Directive on work-life balance for parents and carers by the Council of the European Union (Council of the EU 2019) is a good example of this transition towards the dual-earner–dual-carer family.

Today's governmental support for working parents includes comprehensive leave schemes (maternity, parental, paternity leaves), work scheduling arrangements (e.g. time flexibility), and childcare provisions. There are however major regional differences in the nature and extent of this support.[1] At least four clusters of countries can be distinguished. There is first the Nordic countries where governmental support for gender equality has long been engrained in the welfare state. The first parental leave was introduced in 1974 in Sweden and was followed up in all countries with additional measures to encourage fathers to take-up parental leave (e.g. daddy's quota, higher compensation level) and to be equal partners in the caring of their children (Neyer 2013). The second cluster is the Central and Eastern European countries representing a hybrid welfare model. There are large differences between countries in this cluster but they generally share a policy model which provides a very long parental leave (but mostly taken up by the mother) and show significant difficulties in the reconciliation of work and family, in part due to labour market rigidities. This policy model has in fact been criticised for keeping mothers out of the labour market for too long periods of time and therefore of running against the objective of gender equality (Frejka and Gietel-Basten 2016; Ferragina 2019). The third and fourth clusters comprise respectively Western and Southern European countries where despite progress towards gender equality in paid and unpaid work, some obstacles remain including labour market rigidity, unequal childcare provisions (especially for very young children), and a low take-up of parental leave by fathers. In particular, and despite gradual reforms, the Southern European model continues to feature a family-oriented approach to the issue of work–family reconciliation (Riva 2016; Mínguez and Crespi 2017). Recent changes have however further strengthened the support for working parents, while also revealing important within-cluster differences (Escobedo and Wall 2015). For example, while Portugal has been promoting an early return to full-time work for mothers after childbirth, Spain has opted for a more 'choice oriented' model (Wall and Escobedo 2009).

The introduction of family policy measures in the past decades, including in the domain of work-family reconciliation, has pursued various objectives including the promotion of gender equality, the protection of economically vulnerable families (e.g. single parents) and the reduction of social and economic inequalities. At the same time, these same measures have also pursued demographic objectives in some countries and have been viewed as instruments to increase fertility. It is no denying that the steady decline in fertility and the reach of low—and very low—levels of fertility (as described earlier in this chapter) have large consequences on the sustainability of welfare states (e.g. pensions, health care). Governments have not stayed indifferent to this situation. According to the United Nations, a majority of European countries currently view their fertility as too low (United Nations 2018). However, the actual policy response to this situation has resulted in a large East–West divide. In Western Europe, governments have responded to low fertility and related demographic changes in two ways: first by strengthening the measures to support working parents (as difficulties in combining work and family responsibilities continue to be one of the key reasons for the decline in fertility) and second by reforming institutions to adapt to population ageing (Rechel et al. 2013; Gauthier 2015). The latter includes the promotion of lifelong learning and healthy ageing, and the encouragement for later retirement. These reforms, especially to the pension systems, have not been easy to implement. But they are seen as essential to respond to the demographic trends. In Central and Eastern Europe, similar trends have been observed but also a return to more traditional gender values together with pronatalist discourses. This is notably the case in Hungary, Poland, and Russia where governments have introduced a series of financial measures (including baby-bonuses, family allowances, tax release) to promote larger families (Frejka and Gietel-Basten 2016; Sobotka et al. 2019). And while the actual impact of these policies remains a debated issue, the pronatalist and traditional stance adopted in the region has clouded further advances in gender equality and support for the dual-earner/dual-carer model.

As mentioned above, these policies are both the consequences and determinants of changes in the family. They are consequences in the sense that they have been adopted by governments to reflect the rapid increase in female labour force participation and the changing social norms regarding gender equality. But they are also determinants in that they can have an impact on families, for example by supporting further increases in female labour force participation and in the participation of fathers in the caring of children. And despite the common trends reviewed above, strong regional differences also persist not only in governmental support for families, but also in the broader institutional context affecting families including labour market structures and policies, tax structures and gender norms (Matysiak and Węziak-Białowolska 2016). The interplay between welfare state regimes and fertility is thus central and helps explain the fact that the regional differences in the institutional context of families do mirror to a large extent the geographical pattern of fertility decline described earlier (Neyer 2013). At the same time, the recent decline in the Nordic countries—where extensive measures to support working parents are in place—is a clear reminder that emerging new risks, including growing economic uncertainty, social inequalities and environmental concerns, are also shaping people's fertility intentions. This will be calling for reforms to family policies and the welfare regimes to account for these new risks.

Towards Better Understanding of Family Transformations and Evidence-Based Policies: Research Challenges and Data Needs

Changes in family-related behaviours and the family life constitute a fundamental component of on-going societal transformations. They carry also important consequences for individuals, families, and societies. At the micro-level, they strongly influence the (objective and subjective) well-being of individuals and families (their happiness, health, and wealth), and they have a major impact on the linkages between the lives of different generations. At the macro-level, they affect the population dynamics and the population composition as well as families and kinships networks conducive for human capital of Europe's countries and their prospects.

Sub-replacement fertility is a key macro-level outcome of on-going societal transformations. While it is universally witnessed in Europe, it is important to recognise how strong the fertility decline has been in different countries, how far from the replacement level fertility it has dropped and for how long.

In general, the social democratic regime of Nordic countries and the conservative regime of Western Europe (with the exception of Germany, Austria, and Switzerland) seem to be more effective in preventing fertility from dropping to low levels, contrary to welfare regimes of Southern Europe and the post-socialist countries. Even if we acknowledge that sub-replacement fertility constitutes an inevitable outcome of societal transformations (Lesthaeghe 2020), it does not contradict efforts aimed at searching for fertility recovery. The objective of 'promoting demographic renewal in Europe', voiced at the European level (European Commission 2006), calls for measures to support young people in their fertility and family intentions. This is particular the case in countries of Southern and Central and Eastern Europe which reveal a high discrepancy between desired and achieved fertility (so-called fertility gap). And despite recent policy reforms aimed at better reconciliation of work and family, their welfare regimes still display weaker support for the dual-earner–dual-carer family and slower progress towards gender equality in individual- and family-oriented social institutions. Also in countries with period TFR visibly above 1.5 children per women the 'fertility gap' exists, signalling obstacles in fulfilling fertility intentions.

There is increasing evidence about the impacts of family policies on fertility, revealed at the macro- and micro-levels (Thevenon and Gauthier 2011; Luci-Greulich and Thevenon 2013; Sobotka et al. 2019). To address properly obstacles to have children as desired, which differ not only across countries and welfare regimes but also by gender, education, and societal strata, more knowledge is needed at the individual level. To study how family-related events shape the lives of women and men and their family constellations at subsequent stages of their life trajectories, how family structures impact the timing and patterns of relevant events, and how individual lives are interlinked, in particular—lives of subsequent generations, adequate scientific data is needed. Such data can be provided only by longitudinal surveys that take the life-course approach.

In Europe two research infrastructures provide such data: the Survey of Health and Retirement in Europe (SHARE) which is focused on the life course of people aged 50 years and more, and the Generations and Gender Programme (GGP), which focuses on the whole life course with a special emphasis on the younger adults and the childbearing years (respondents aged 18–79 years old). Moreover, the GGP is the only one which is specifically designed to capture demographic change along the key dimensions of demographic change: generations, gender, and family dynamics (Gauthier et al. 2018). Along with cross-sectional data collected in sample-based international surveys like the European Social Survey, the European Value Study, and the International Social Survey Programme (ISSP) they constitute research infrastructures/data resources to study societal transformations in Europe. The research that considers the dimensions of generations, gender, and family dynamics seems pivotal for understanding and responding to sub-replacement fertility. It is also necessary to secure well-being of future generations. Young people are increasingly confronted with various challenges as they enter adulthood and make choices regarding union formation and childbearing. They need to deal with dynamic and unstable labour market prospects, imposed by the labour market transformation with its high demands for digital skills, flexibility and mobility. They are also exposed to different kinds of uncertainty in the globalised world with its environmental and technological challenges as well as societal transformations driven by migration. Diverse chances and barriers faced by young generations in starting their own family and getting economic independence may produce poor outcomes in later life and also result in labour migration, union dissolution, and re-partnering.

Different family forms lived by parents over their life-course determine complex living arrangements for their children. Some of them are associated with more exposure to economic insecurity and poverty. Moreover, a higher risk of separation among lower socio-economic strata as well as the socioeconomic gradient of cohabitation raise concerns about persisting unequal lives of subsequent generations. Disadvantages distinctive for some stages of life may accumulate over the life-course (Anxo et al. 2010; Cahn et al. 2018). To capture these complexities and inequalities is of crucial importance for improving individual opportunities of family members through adequate policy interventions.

Family changes and evolving gender roles challenge relationships between generations, in particular distribution of work and care over the life course between women and men. The slimming kinship networks are important source of different kinds of support for all members. Reconciling paid work and care for children and dependent adults and its impact on intra- and intergenerational exchanges need to be continuously explored in European populations facing advanced ageing. The increasing elderly population constitutes a considerable resource of down support to the younger generations. This calls for more investigation how ascending generations contribute to younger ones, exposed to more diversified, less secure and stable life courses than experienced by their parents.

Note

1. Some of these differences also include those related to the timing in the implementation of parental leave available for parents and its overall design (e.g. duration, payment, eligibility, transferability between parents). Because of space constraints we do not discuss in details these differences.

References

Adserà, Alicia. 2011. "Where Are the Babies? Labor Market Conditions and Fertility in Europe." *European Journal of Population* 27 (1): 1–32.

Anxo, Dominique, Gerhard Bosch, and Jill Rubery. 2010. *The Welfare State and Life Transitions: A European Perspective*. Cheltenham, UK and Northampton, MA: Edward Elgar.

Beaujouan, Éva, and Laurent Toulemon. 2019. "The Delay in Procreation in Europe." *Médecine de la Reproduction* 21 (3): 209–219.

Becker, Gary S. 1981. *A Treatise on the Family*. Cambridge, MA: Harvard University Press.

Bernhardt, Eva M. 1993. "Fertility and Employment." *European Sociological Review* 9 (1): 25–42.

Bernhardt, Eva M. 2004. "Is the Second Demographic Transition a Useful Concept for Demography?" *Vienna Yearbook of Population Research* 2: 25–28.

Billari, Francesco C., and Aart C. Liefbroer. 2010. "Towards a New Pattern of Transition to Adulthood?" *Advances in Life Course Research* 15 (2–3): 59–75.

Cahn, Naomi R., June Carbone, Laurie Fields DeRose, and William Bradford Wilcox, eds. 2018. *Unequal Family Lives: Causes and Consequences in Europe and the Americas*. Cambridge, UK and New York, NY: Cambridge University Press.

Council of the EU. 2019. "Better Work-Life Balance for Parents and Carers in the EU: Council Adopts New Rules," Press Release. https://www.consilium.europa.eu/en/press/press-releases/2019/06/13/better-work-life-balance-for-parents-and-carers-in-the-eu-council-adopts-new-rules/.

Daly, Mary. 2005. "Changing Family Life in Europe: Significance for State and Society." *European Societies* 7 (3): 379–398.

Del Boca, Daniela, and Cecile Wetzels, eds. 2007. *Social Polices, Labour Market and Motherhood*. Cambridge: Cambridge University Press.

Di Giulio, Paola, Roberto Impicciatore, and Maria Sironi. 2019. "The Changing Pattern of Cohabitation: A Sequence Analysis Approach." *Demographic Research* 40 (42): 1211–1248.

Dykstra, Pearl A. 2010. *Intergenerational Family Relationships in Ageing Societies*. Geneva: United Nations Economic Commission for Europe.

Escobedo, Anna, and Karin Wall. 2015. "Leave Policies in Southern Europe: Continuities and Changes." *Community, Work & Family* 18 (2): 218–235.

Esping-Andersen, Gøsta. 2009. *The Incomplete Revolution: Adapting Welfare States to Women's New Roles*. Cambridge: Polity Press.

Esping-Andersen, Gøsta, and Francesco C. Billari. 2015. "Re-theorizing Family Demographics." *Population and Development Review* 41 (1): 1–31.

European Commission. 2006. *The Demographic Future of Europe—From Challenge to Opportunity*. Communication from the Commission. Brussels.

European Commission. 2009. *Dealing with the Impact of an Ageing Population in the EU*. European Comission (Brussels).

Ferragina, Emanuele. 2019. "Does Family Policy Influence Women's Employment?: Reviewing the Evidence in the Field." *Political Studies Review* 17 (1): 65–80.

Frejka, Tomas. 2011. "The Role of Contemporary Childbearing Postponement and Recuperation in Shaping Period Fertility Trends." *Comparative Population Studies* 36 (4): 927–958.

Frejka, Tomas, and Stuart Gietel-Basten. 2016. "Fertility and Family Policies in Central and Eastern Europe After 1990." *Comparative Population Studies* 41 (1).
Frejka, Tomas, and Tomáš Sobotka. 2008. "Overview Chapter 1: Fertility in Europe: Diverse, Delayed and Below Replacement." *Demographic Research* S7 (3): 15–46.
Gauthier, Anne H. 2015. "Social Norms, Institutions, and Policies in Low-Fertility Countries." In *Low Fertility and Reproductive Health in East Asia*, edited by Naohiro Ogawa and Iqbal H. Shah. Springer.
Gauthier, Anne H., Susana Laia Farinha Cabaço, and Tom Emery. 2018. "Generations and Gender Survey Study Profile." Longitudinal and Life Course Studies 9 (4): 456–465.
Gauthier, Anne H., and Judit C. Koops. 2018. "The History of Family Policy Research." In *Handbook of Family Policy*, edited by Guðný Björk Eydal and Tine Rostgaard, 11–23. Edward Elgar.
Goldin, Claudia. 1990. *Understanding the Gender Gap. An Economic History of American Women*. Oxford: Oxford University Press.
Goldscheider, Frances, Eva Bernhardt, and Trude Lappegård. 2015. "The Gender Revolution: A Framework for Understanding Changing Family and Demographic Behavior." *Population and Development Review* 41 (2): 207–239.
Gornick, Janet C., Marcia K. Meyers, and Katherin E. Ross. 1997. "Supporting the Employment of Mothers: Policy Variation Across Fourteen Welfare States." *Journal of European Social Policy* 7 (1): 45–70.
Hagestad, Gunhild O., and Pearl A. Dykstra. 2016. "Structuration of the Life Course: Some Neglected Aspects." In *Handbook of the Life Course*, edited by Jeylan T. Mortimer, Michael J. Shanahan and M. Johnson, 131–157. New York: Springer.
Hajnal, John. 1965. "European Marriage Patterns in Perspective." In *Population in History. Essays in Historical Demography*, edited by D.V. Glass and D.E.C. Eversley, 101–143. New Brunswick, NJ: Aldine Transaction.
Hantrais, Linda. 2006. "Living as a Family in Europe." In *Policy Implications of Changing Family Formation*, edited by Linda Hantrais, Dimiter Philipov and Francesco C. Billari, 117–181. Council of Europe Publishing.
Kohler, Hans Peter, Francesco C. Billari, and José Antonio Ortega. 2006. "Low Fertility in Europe: Causes, Implications and Policy Options." In *The Baby Bust: Who Will Do the Work? Who Will Pay the Taxes?*, edited by F. R. Harris, 48–109. Lanham, MD: Rowman & Littlefield.
Leira, Arnlaug. 2002. *Working Parents and the Welfare State. Family Change and Policy Reform in Scandinavia*. Cambridge University Press.
Lesthaeghe, Ron. 1995. "The Second Demographic Transition in Western Countries: An Interpretation." In *Gender and family change in industrialized countries*, edited by K.O. Mason and A.M. Jensen, 17–62. Oxford: Clarendon Press.
Lesthaeghe, Ron. 2010. "The Unfolding Story of the Second Demographic Transition." *Population and Development Review* 36 (2): 211–251.
Lesthaeghe, Ron. 2020. "The Second Demographic Transition, 1986–2020: Sub-replacement Fertility and Rising Cohabitation—A Global Update." *Genus* 76 (1): 10.
Lewis, Jane. 1992. "Gender and the Development of Welfare Regimes." *Journal of European Social Policy* 2 (3): 159–173.
Lewis, Jane. 2009. *Work-family Balance, Gender and Policy*. Cheltenham, UK and Northampton, MA: Edward Elgar.

Luci-Greulich, A. and Olivier Thevenon. 2013. "The Impact of Family Policy Packages on Fertility Trends in Developed Countries." *European Journal of Population* 29 (4): 387–416.
Mason, Karen O. 1997. |"Gender and Demographic Change: What Do We know?" In *The Continuing Demographic Transition*, edited by G. W. Jones, R. M. Douglas, J. C. Caldwell, and R. M. D'Souza. Oxford: Clarendon Press.
Matysiak, Anna. 2011. *Interdependencies Between Fertility and Women's Labour Supply.* New York: Springer.
Matysiak, Anna, and Dorota Węziak-Białowolska. 2016. "Country-Specific Conditions for Work and Family Reconciliation: An Attempt at Quantification." *European Journal of Population* 32 (4): 475–510.
McDonald, Peter. 2000. "Gender Equity, Social Institutions and the Future of Fertility." *Journal of Population Research* 17 (1): 1–16.
Mínguez, Almudena Moreno, and Isabella Crespi. 2017. "Gender Equality and Family Changes in the Work–Family Culture in Southern Europe." *International Review of Sociology* 27 (3): 394–420.
Neyer, Gerda. 2013. "Welfare States, Family Policies, and Fertility in Europe." In *The Demography of Europe*, edited by Gerda Neyer, Gunnar Andersson, Hill Kulu, Laura Bernardi and Christoph Bühler, 29–53. Springer.
Oppenheimer, Valerie Kincade. 1997. "Women's Employment and the Gain to Marriage: The Specialization and Trading Model." *Annual Review of Sociology* 23: 431–453.
Parke, Ross D. 2013. *Future Families: Diverse Forms, Rich Possibilities.* Chichester, West Sussex: Wiley.
Parsons, Talcott. 1955. "The American Family: Its Relations to Personality and the Social Structure." In *Family Socialization and Interaction Process*, edited by Talcott Parsons and Robert F. Bales. Glencoe, IL: The Free Press.
Perelli-Harris, Brienna, and Mark Lyons-Amos. 2015. "Changes in Partnership Patterns Across the Life Course: An Examination of 14 Countries in Europe and the United States." *Demographic Research* 33 (6): 145–178.
Perelli-Harris, Brienna, Wendy Sigle-Rushton, Michaela Kreyenfeld, Trude Lappegård, Renske Keizer, and Caroline Berghammer. 2010. "The Educational Gradient of Childbearing within Cohabitation in Europe." *Population and Development Review* 36 (4): 775–801.
Prskawetz, Alexia, Marija Mamolo, and Henriette Engelhardt. 2010. "On the Relation Between Fertility, Natality, and Nuptiality." *European Sociological Review* 26 (6): 675–689.
Rechel, Bernd, Emily Grundy, Jean-Marie Robine, Jonathan Cylus, Johan P. Mackenbach, Cecile Knai, and Martin McKee. 2013. "Ageing in the European Union." *The Lancet* 381 (9874): 1312–1322.
Riva, Egidio. 2016. "Familialism Reoriented: Continuity and Change in Work–Family Policy in Italy." *Community, Work & Family* 19 (1): 21–42.
Saraceno, Chiara. 2008. "Patterns of Family Living in the Enlarged EU." In *Handbook of Quality of Life in the Enlarged Union*, edited by Jens Alber, Tony Fahey, and Chiara Saraceno, 47–72. London and New York: Routledge.
Schwanitz, Katrin. 2017. "The Transition to Adulthood and Pathways Out of the Parental Home: A Cross-National Analysis." *Advances in Life Course Research* 32: 21–34.

Sobotka, Tomáš. 2017. "Childlessness in Europe: Reconstructing Long-Term Trends Among Women Born in 1900–1972." In *Childlessness in Europe: Contexts, Causes, and Consequences*, edited by Michaela Kreyenfeld and Dirk Konietzka, 17–53. Cham: Springer.

Sobotka, Tomáš, Anna Matysiak, and Zuzanna Brzozowska. 2019. "Policy Responses to Low Fertility: How Effective Are They?" *UNFPA Technical Division Working Paper Series* Working Paper 1, May 2019.

Sobotka, Tomáš, and Laurent Toulemon. 2008. "Changing Family and Partnership Behaviour: Common Trends and Persistent Diversity Across Europe." *Demographic Research* 19 (6): 85–138.

Thevenon, Olivier, and Anne H. Gauthier. 2011. "Family Policies in Developed Countries: A 'Fertility-Booster' with Side-Effects." *Community, Work & Family* 14 (2): 197–216.

United Nations. 2018. *World Population Policies 2015*. Department of Economic and Social Affairs, Population Division (New York).

United Nations. 2019. *World Population Prospects, Highlights*. Department of Economic and Social Affairs, Population Division (New York).

Wall, Karin and Anna Escobedo. 2009. "Portugal and Spain: Two Pathways in Southern Europe." In *The Politics of Parental Leave Policies*, edited by Sheila Kamerman and Peter Moss. The Policy Press.

van de Kaa, Dirk J. 1987. "Europe's Second Demographic Transition." *Population Bulletin* 42 (1): 1–59.

van de Kaa, Dirk J. 1994. "The Second Demographic Transition Revisited: Theories and Expectations." In *Population and Family in the Low Countries 1993: Late Fertility and Other Current Issues*, edited by G. Beets et al., 81–126. Pennsylvania/Amsterdam: Swets and Zeitlinger, Berwyn.

Zeman, Krystof, Éva Beaujouan, Zuzanna Brzozowska, and Tomáš Sobotka. 2018. "Cohort Fertility Decline in Low Fertility Countries: Decomposition Using Parity Progression Ratios." *Demographic Research* 38 (25): 651–690.

CHAPTER 9

Reexamining Degenderisation: Changes in Family Policies in Europe

Steven Saxonberg and Dorota Szelewa

INTRODUCTION

Starting in the early 1990s a debate arose about gendering welfare states. This led to widespread agreement that traditional welfare typologies failed to take into account how welfare policies influence gender relations; however, little agreement emerged as to what the optimal gender-based typology should be. Eventually, the familialisation-defamilialisation typology became the most prominent during the next decade. Back in 2013 Saxonberg (2013) published his article 'From Defamilialization to Degenderization: Toward a New Welfare Typology', which criticised this typology and offered an alternative. The article basically had 3 goals: first to criticise welfare typologies that are based on regime types rather than social policies; second to propose an alternative typology to the familisation-defamilisation typology that had become dominating; and third, to show how this new typology could be applied in practice by looking at family policies among European countries.

S. Saxonberg (✉)
Faculty of Social and Economic Sciences, Comenius University, Bratislava, Slovakia
e-mail: steven.saxonberg@fses.uniba.sk

Department of Social Policy and Social Work, Masaryk University, Brno, Czech Republic

D. Szelewa
UCD School of Social Policy, Social Work and Social Justice, University College Dublin, Dublin, Ireland
e-mail: dorota.szelewa@ucd.ie

© The Author(s), under exclusive license to Springer Nature Switzerland AG 2021
A.-M. Castrén et al. (eds.), *The Palgrave Handbook of Family Sociology in Europe*, https://doi.org/10.1007/978-3-030-73306-3_9

This chapter re-examines the typology in several ways. First, it will take up some of the main criticisms that the typology has received. Second, it will re-examine the European countries to see how their family policies have changed since the original article was published. In doing so, we will speculate as to whether there is a trend towards greater genderisation or degenderisation.

THE BACKGROUND

Before re-examining the typology, we will remind the reader of the main arguments of the original article. The article noted that Esping-Andersen's (1990) *The Three Worlds of Welfare Capitalism* sparked a big debate on welfare typologies. His book encouraged feminist scholars to criticise his typology for leaving out gender aspects of social policy and they pointed out that he did not include such matters as unpaid household work (i.e. Lewis 1993; Sainsbury 1994). In addition, feminists criticised his typology for making decommodification the main goal since the goal of the mainstream women's movement in most Western countries had been the commodification of women (i.e. the ability for women to enter the labour market, not leave it) (i.e. Hervey and Shaw 1998; Jenson 1997).

Even though many typologies have emerged, the most common one has become the familialisation-defamilisation typology. The article criticised this typology for being too ambiguous, for not clearly enough describing the goals of mainstream feminist movements and for relying on outcomes rather than policies.

Too Ambiguous and Not the Right Goals

The familialisation/defamilialisation dichotomy has the advantage that it allows for a parallel to Esping-Andersen's scale of degrees commodification and decommodification. This makes it easier to present a clear alternative to Esping-Andersen's measurement of welfare regimes.

In Esping-Andersen's typology decommodified workers gain bargaining power vis-à-vis their prospective employers, because if they are not forced to work for economic reasons, the employees must offer good conditions in order to induce people to enter the labour force and accept their job offers. Similarly, theoretically defamilialised women gain power vis-à-vis their male partners (if they are in a heterosexual relationship), because if daycare takes care of their children, mothers can work and therefore are no longer dependent on their male partners' incomes to survive.

Despite these advantages, the defamilialisation typology suffers from a lack of clarity. While decommodification implies the degree in which one is able to survive without selling one's labour power on the labour market and commodification implies the degree to which one is forced to sell one's labour power on the labour market, it is much more difficult to delimit the meaning of 'defamilialisation'. Taken literally, the term implies the goal of policymaking should to encourage parents to put their children into formal childcare as soon the child is born, since responsibility for childcare would be taken *away* (i.e. *de*-familialising) from the family. Of course, in practice nobody seriously advocates such policies.

Nevertheless, this term leaves a certain ambivalence on how to categorise parental leaves. For example, if defamilialisation implies that responsibility for chid raising moves outside of the family, then it means that daycare is always something 'good', while fathers going on parental leave is something 'bad' since father leaves are 'familialising' in the sense that a family member is taking care of the child. Yet, if we are to reach the goal of mainstream feminism of eliminating gender roles, then father leaves should be considered something 'good'.

Scholars face dilemmas in trying to get around this problem. Thus, Lister (1994, 37) defines defamilialisation, as 'the degree to which individuals can uphold a socially acceptable standard of living independently of family relationships, either through paid work or social security provision'. The problem is that according to this definition both parental leaves that encourage fathers to share equally in the leave time and those that encourage the mother to stay at home for long periods can both be 'defamilialising'. Both types of leaves enable women to 'uphold a socially acceptable standard of living independently of family relationships', but they have radically different influences on gender relations. If the parental leave is based on the income replacement principle, so fathers do not lose much money if they stay at home and the leave has a long father's quota, then the generous leave will encourage an increase in gender equality and a decrease in gender roles. This is because fathers would have incentives for sharing the parental leave periods rather equally with mothers. However, if the leave pays a generous amount of money, but at a flat rate and it does not include father quotas, then it will indeed allow mothers to 'uphold a socially acceptable standard of living independently of family relationships', but it will also encourage a continuation of separate gender roles, in which the mother is responsible for raising the children and the father is responsible for having a job. Thus, two policies could encourage the exact opposite types of changes in gender roles and yet still fall under the category of 'defamilialisation'.

Since in practice, scholars have been unsure of how to measure parental leave policies in terms of defamilialisation, they have often come up with much different results in their typologies. In fact, they are not even able to reach an agreement as to whether familialisation is bad and defamilialisation is something good. For example, Daly and Schweiwe (2010, 187) see paternal leave as something positive but *at the same time* familialising. Similarly, Leitner (2003) praises Sweden for having familialising regime as does Saraceno (2016). Since its type of familialisation is 'optional' (Leitner 2003) it is actually superior to defamilialising regimes. Saraceno (2016) calls it 'supported familialism' and does not clearly state whether or not it is superior to defamilialisation. Thus, not surprisingly, scholars vary greatly in how they rank the countries on scales of defamilialisation. Some see Sweden as being 'familialised' (e.g. Daly and Schweiwe 2010; Leitner 2003), while others see the country as being defamilialised (e.g. Hantrais 2004). To take another country, Hantrais (2004) considers the UK to be partially defamilialised, while O'Connor et al. (1999) classify the UK as 'familialist', Leitner (2003) labels the country defamilialist and Esping-Andersen (1999) considers the country to be 'non-familialist'.

These examples show the problems in interpreting family policies within the framework of defamilialisation, which lead to many different classification systems, although they were supposedly all based on the same or similar definitions of defamilialisation. Another problem is that typologies based on defamilialisation can only be applied to certain types of policies, as will be discussed later in this chapter. Directly below we discuss the second main criticism of the defamilialisation discourse, which is that it bases itself on the concept of regimes rather than basing itself on actual policies.

Policies or Regimes?

Above we discussed the problems that defamilialisation has in dealing with parental leaves, but it also has problems in dealing with daycare. This discourse has relied on Esping-Andersen's strategy of basing typologies on regime types rather than policies. The regime-type approach includes welfare contributions made by markets as well as the public sector. Concretely, in the regime-type tradition this means, for example, that one examines the percentage of pre-school children attending daycare rather than public daycare policies. However, cultural norms as well as policies can influence decisions about whether to go on parental leave and whether to send children to daycare (e.g. Pfau-Effinger 2000; Duncan and Strell 2004). Since in some countries the private sector can also provide services even without any public support, it shows that the percentage of children attending is also influenced by socio-economic factors, such as whether a large and relatively wealthy group of middle-class women emerges who can afford to pay for expensive private childcare, etc.

The article from 2013 argued that it is important for social scientists to be able to separate policies from outcomes, so that we can analyse what influence certain types of policies have in different types of settings. A certain kind of policy might lead to much different results in two different countries if each country has great differences in the cultural norms and in their socio-economic conditions. As Saxonberg and Szelewa (2007) note, even if the UK and Poland might have had similar kinds of laissez-faire policies in the 2000s, the outcomes of these policies were much different in both countries. While market-oriented, residual-liberal welfare policies led to relatively high fertility rates and high female labour-market participation rates in countries such as the UK (Boje 2007; Esping-Andersen 1990; Gornick 1999; Korpi 2000), such policies had the opposite effect in a country like Poland. The Anglo-Saxon countries have a rather large upper middle class, which is able to afford private alternatives for childcaring. Meanwhile a relatively large pool of low-paid immigrant workers exists in these countries that are willing to take care of children of the middle and lower middle classes for a low fee. In a post-communist country like Poland, however, the middle class is much smaller and less wealthy, while the pool of cheap immigrant labour is also much smaller. Consequently, women in Poland cannot afford to leave the labour market when they no longer have access to publicly financed daycare and instead leave the reproductive market (Saxonberg and Sirovátka 2006; Saxonberg and Szelewa 2007). Thus, policy recommendations based on the British experience are unlikely to achieve similar results when applied in the Polish socio-economic context. On the contrary, they are likely to lead to a drop in fertility rates and female employment.

So, if we use a typology based on policies, then Poland and the UK wind up in the same group, but if we use a typology based on results (i.e. regime types), then the two countries would fall into different categories. If our goal were merely normative, to say which countries are better to live in, then the regime-type kind of typology would be enough. But if we as social scientists want to influence society by being able to present plausible policy recommendations, then we need to base our typologies on policies and then analyse how different types of policies influence outcomes differently in different countries that have different cultural norms and different socio-economic conditions. Consequently, we do not follow the approach of scholars, such as Saraceno (2016) who support the regime-type tradition in stating that familialism and defamilialisation are based on cultural attitudes and values instead of only policies. Instead, we argue that we should have a typology of policies and then investigate how the different cultural values interact with policies in different countries.

GENDERISATION AND DEGENDERISATION

The genderisation/degenderisation proposal came about because it seemed to fall into place with what the mainstream feminist discourse was *really* about: i.e. the desire to eliminate gender roles. Books and articles appeared in the 1990s on the theme of *gendering* social policies, so it only made sense to base a new typology on the extent that policies encourage degenderisation (i.e. the elimination of gender roles) or genderisation (i.e. the strengthening of gender roles). A famous example is the anthology that Diane Sainsbury (1994) edited, entitled *Gendering Welfare States*. Since feminist scholars were writing about the need to genderise social policies and their main goal has been to eliminate gender roles (e.g. Orloff 2009; Lister 2003) then it makes more sense to talk about the degree in which policies encourage degenderisation rather than the degree in which they encourage defamilialisation.

Consequently, the article defined 'genderising' as *policies that promote different gender roles for men and women*. 'Degenderising', by contrast, were *policies that promote the elimination of gender roles*. Even though the article criticised Leitner (2003) for applying the familialisation/defamilialisation and it also criticised the label of 'optional familialisation', it did support her differentiation between implicit and explicit policies, as such differentiation recognised varieties of ways that state can influence or not gender relations. Rather than differentiate between implicit and explicit familialisation, the degenderising article differentiated between implicit and explicit genderising policies. It noted that some policies openly aim to reinforce separate gender roles. Meanwhile, other, more market-oriented policies implicitly support the continued existence of gender roles, because given the patriarchal starting point we cannot expect fathers to share in the leave times unless encouraged to do so through family policies. The article also argued that market-oriented family policies are likely implicitly to reinforce separate gender roles, because many women are unlikely to be able to afford child-caring facilities without state support.

An additional argument in favour of the genderisation/degenderisation typology is that in contrast to the familialisation/defamilialisation typology, one can apply it to almost any type of social policy. Even though the article itself concentrated on family policy, it argued that it could be applied to all types of social policies. Thus, the article argued for having a holistic view of social policies rather than looking at them in isolation from each other. Thus, it claimed that we should not limit ourselves by looking 'at the level of the trees rather than the wood' (Powell and Barrientos 2011, 75).

This chapter proceeds by presenting the original genderisation/degenderisation model—that is by discussing the criteria that were used. Then the following section takes up the criticisms that the typology received. Finally, based on the criteria of the typology, we analyse what changes have taken place since the 2013 article appeared.

Operationalising Genderisation Typologies of Family Policy

As the original article concentrated on family policy as an example of how the typology could be applied, this chapter briefly recaps the way in which the typology was operationalised. It concentrated on the level of paid parental leave and state support for childcare.

Genderising Parental Leave

Parental leave policies that aim to degenderise family relations would need to encourage fathers to share equally—on the average—in parental leave time. In our view this does not mean that mothers and fathers must share the leave time exactly equally in each case. If we eliminate gender roles and one's gender no longer can predict how long or if one will go on parental leave, then we will have come a long way in eliminating gender roles. Once gender no longer plays a role, then in some cases we might expect the fathers to stay at home longer than the mothers and in other cases mothers would stay at home longer than the fathers.

Given the unequal starting points in which culturally mothers are expected to go on leave more than are fathers and economically fathers often have higher incomes than the mothers, two types of policies can do the most to promote the degenderisation of parental roles. First, since fathers often have higher incomes than the mothers, fathers are likely to conclude that they cannot 'afford' to go on parental leave if they think their loss of income would be too great. Therefore, the leave should be based on the income-replacement principle, so that the loss of income is minimised for the parent who goes on leave. The state could, however, provide a minimum, lump sum payment for those parents with low incomes or who are unemployed.

Second, since there are cultural constraints on fathers that discourage them from going on parental leave, a certain portion of the leave time should be reserved only for the father. Even if the father would want to go on parental leave, bosses and colleagues are likely to look down upon him and consider him to not be 'ambitious', while they would consider it to be perfectly 'normal' for the mother to go on leave. Therefore, fathers wanting to go on parental leave risk being ostracised.

Following the 2013 article, the main criteria for judging parental leave to be degenderising are that:

- Parental leave is open for both parents and is at least nine months long, so that fathers are likely to share in the leave time, given the fact that mothers at least in contemporary European society often want to stay at home for the first four to six months in order to breast-feed their children.
- The replacement rate is high enough to encourage fathers to go on parental leave even if their salaries are higher than the mother of the child. 'Generous' is defined as paying at least 65% of one's previous income.
- The benefit ceiling is not so low that it discourages fathers in practice from taking parental leave.
- Usually, some kind of father quota exists.

Concerning the issue of the length of parental leave, we can also add that some scholars argue that if the leave is 'too long', it tends to hurt the mothers as it will encourage mothers to stay at home for long periods and keep them longer out of the labour market (Bergmann 2008; Lewis 2009; Morgan and Zippel 2003; Sipilä et al. 2010; Van der Lippe et al. 2010). In contrast, we do not share the opinion that longer leaves necessarily hurt women by encouraging them to stay at home longer. It depends on the type of leaves. If the leave combines father quotas with benefits based on the income replacement principle, then longer leaves can encourage fathers to share more equally in the leave time (see Bergqvist and Saxonberg 2017).

Now that we have operationalised the definition of degenderising family policies, we will operationalise *explicitly* genderising policies. Such policies give strong incentives for mothers to leave the labour market at least during the first two years of a child's birth, without giving incentives for fathers to share in the leave. Again, following Saxonberg (2013), the main policies that encourage this include:

- A maternity leave that reserves at least four months only for the mother and pays a high replacement rate for that period.
- A maternity leave followed by a long, extended leave (usually two to three years). It might be open for fathers. However, it pays a low-flat rate benefit, which discourages fathers from taking the leave.
- A generous maternity leave for mothers, but no paternity leave for fathers other than a short period (up to two weeks) in which the father can assist the mother after the birth of the child.

Meanwhile, parental leave is 'implicitly' genderising if it follows residualist, market-oriented policies. That is, it does not offer any parental leave benefits or only a short maternity leave of four months or less. If one can receive benefits after the initial maternity leave, they are means-tested. This type of policy discourages fathers from sharing in the leave, since the father is more likely to have a higher income than the mother in a given family. However, since the state does not pay mothers to stay at home for long periods, it encourages a gendered division of labour more *implicitly* than explicitly genderising policies.

Genderizing Daycare Policies

The 2013 article argued that daycare policies are *degenderising* when the public sector provides a relatively large number of childcare places children both aged under and over three, or at least the state provides heavy subsidies, so that the private sector could provide affordable childcare services.

Implicitly genderising policies, by contrast, would leave childcare to the market. Therefore, governments would provide low levels of public subsidies for childcare and they provide relatively few childcaring spaces for children. Given the unequal starting point, such policies are implicitly genderising, because although they do not openly promote separate gender roles, if affordable childcare is not available, mothers are much more likely than fathers to have to stay at home with their children.

Explicitly genderising childcare policies allow for some amount of state support for childcare, as they follow the paternalistic Bismarckian tradition. Since they want mothers to be the main carers of young children, *explicitly genderizing* childcare policies do not provide much support for children under three. However, they are much more likely than countries with implicitly genderising policies to support 'kindergartens' for pre-school children aged over three. Furthermore, these facilities are likely to be only open part-time. This comes from the Bismarckian tradition of having pre-school education to help raise the morals of pre-school children or the more humanistic Fröbelian tradition that emphasised the pedagogical and social needs of younger children (Saxonberg 2014).

Unfortunately, it is more difficult to differentiate between policies and results in the case of childcare than for parental leave. If one concentrates on publicly financed childcare, then policies and results will usually be about the same, because in most countries the supply of public daycare is lower than the demand. Furthermore, even if the supply of publicly financed daycare were to exceed the demand during a period, governments would be likely to reduce daycare expenditures. Therefore, we can assume that the actual usage of publicly financed childcare facilities approximates the level of government support. A problem arises in that nowadays it is extremely difficult to get data on the percentage of children attending public daycare. Instead, most governments and international organisations only provide data on the total number/percentage of children attending daycare without differentiating between public and private daycare. As a result, we are usually forced to use this imperfect data, which confuses the differences between policies and outputs.

Some governments might choose to support private childcaring institutions rather than investing money in public institutions. Since subsidies for private institutions still constitute public policy, we should take into account such support. Consequently, the 2013 article recommended using data on governmental spending.

Criticisms of the Degenderisation

This section discusses the three main criticisms that the original article received: (1) it did not take up the child's perspective; (2) it did not consider the intergenerational effect; and (3) the concept should be expanded to include gay relationships.

In our view, one of the best criticisms of the degenderisation concept is that it leaves out the child's perspective (Kurowska 2018). However, this is not just a problem for the degenderisation typology, it has been a problem for the feminist discourse in general in that its focus has been on eliminating gender roles, empowering women, etc. rather than focusing on children. We agree that the child's view is also important even if it has not been central for the feminist discourse. Nevertheless, a growing body of literature indicates that policies that promote gender equality and the elimination of gender roles also have positive effects on children (e.g. Engster and Olofsdotter Stensöta 2011; Bretherton 2010; Kerstis et al. 2018; Ramchandani et. al. 2013; Petts, Knoester, and Waldfogel 2020). When it comes to daycare, studies have also indicated that high quality institutions improve the child's well-being (e.g.

Bengt-Erik Andersson 1992, 2005; Deater-Deckard et al. 1996, 940; Adi-Japha and Klein 2009, Borge et al. 2004). Finally, we should remind the reader that an advantage of the degenderisation paradigm is that it can be applied to *all* types of social policies, since all types of social policies influence gender relations. However, not all social policies influence children. For example, policies aimed at helping the elderly have gender aspects, but not child aspects.

A second criticism has been that the degenderising article neglected the intergenerational effect (Lohnman and Zagel 2016). However, in our view, intergenerational relationships do not present any problem at all for the typology as the typology was designed to deal with *all* types of policies and not be limited to family policy. Family policy was only used as an illustration. For example, when it comes to care for the elderly if the state provides subsidised housing in old-age or retirement homes, this would be degenderising, as would support for home helpers who come to the elderly's home and help them with household chores, preparing meals, bathing, getting dressed, etc.

In this aspect, one could also employ the defamilialising term as well. However, another issue is who takes care of the elderly when they are not in homes or do not have home helpers. This includes the case in which the elderly are normally capable of taking care of themselves, but suffer from a short-term illness. In this case, degenderising policies would pay family members of both sexes a benefit based on the income replacement principle. Even though we do not know of actual cases of this, the policies would be even more degenderising if they have quotas, so some of the caring time is reserved only for male family members (such as the sons, sons-in-law).

Explicitly genderising policies would give benefits only to female family members (such as daughters and daughters-in-law) or would pay a flat benefit, which gives female family members a greater incentive to take time off of work to care for the elderly than it does for male family members. Again, the starting point is that in most families the men earn more than the women, so a flat rate discourages male members from going on leave. Furthermore, culturally the elderly and society generally expect the female family members to do the caring.

Meanwhile, implicitly genderising policies would either leave everything to the market or they would give some benefit to the elderly, who could then decide how to use the money. In the first case the benefits would be implicitly genderising because if left to the market, few male family members would be willing to take time off of work to take care of the elderly, thus putting pressure on the female family members to do so. This is especially the case when the state does not subsidise home helpers or old-age homes, because then many families cannot afford to pay for such alternatives. In the second case, giving money to the elderly is likely to result in a situation in which the elderly keep the money for themselves, as they still expect female family members to take care of them for free.

A third critique of the degenderisation typology is the claim that it must be expanded to take into account gay rights (Hildebrant 2018). However, Hildebrant (2018, 2) mistakenly lists Saxonberg (2013) as being a supporter of the defamilialisation paradigm although Saxonberg's article was clearly a *critique* of the defamilialisation paradigm. Nonetheless, the degenderisation paradigm has no problems dealing with gay couples. Laws that give gay couples the same rights as heterosexual couples are degenderising. This includes family issues, such as the right to live in registered partnerships, the right to get married, the right to adopt children In addition, policies that eliminate legal discrimination of LGBT+ persons from jobs are also degenderising. Again, one of the advantages of degenderisation over defamilialisation is that nothing in the term 'degenderisation' implies that policies need to be linked to the family. The *only* criterion is that policies have to have an influence on gender roles (they either strengthen them or weaken them).

Similarly, policies that openly discriminate against LGBT+ persons are explicitly genderising since they support traditional gender roles, in which men and women have clear roles, pairs are heterosexual, and LGBT+ persons are seen as people who refuse the accept their 'natural' roles in society of how they should behave in their private life. Policies that aim to prevent LGBT+ persons from entering certain professions also have the goal of preserving gender roles, because these policies try to prevent children from being influenced by alternative types of partnerships and gender relations. We have to admit, we cannot conceive of policies that would be implicitly genderising concerning gay rights. Nevertheless, the important point is that it is easy to classify policies towards LGBT+ persons in terms of genderising and degenderising; and one can easily do it in fields outside of the realm of family policy, which is something that the defamilialisation typology cannot do. The case of gay relationships again shows the advantage of the degenderising typology over the defamilialisation typology.

In conclusion, our discussion of the critiques of the degenderisation typology shows that the degenderisation paradigm has no problems dealing with these issues and that it actually deals with these issues much better than does the defamilialisation typology.

One more point: since we see the importance of separating welfare policies from welfare results, we do not take into account cultural or socio-economic aspects, because once again the same policies can have different results based on cultural and socio-economic conditions of each particular country. We think it is important to separate the two so that we can examine how different policies influence outcomes in countries that have different cultural and socio-economic starting points. So, if we are to examine gender relations between countries, then the degederisation typology would only be one aspect of it: it allows us to analyse the policies, but of course outcomes are also influenced by culture and socio-economic conditions.

Changes in Parental Leave

Table 9.1 shows that there have not been great changes in parental leave schemes since the article on degenderisation appeared in 2013. Sweden, Iceland, and Norway still do the most to encourage fathers to share in parental leave because they have insurance-based leaves with father quotas. In addition, both Sweden and Norway have increased the time reserved for fathers, while Iceland has been discussing replacing the 3 + 3 + 3 model with a 5 + 5 + 2 model. This is, in the future the leave period will increase from 9 to 12 months and the amount of non-transferable leave time reserved for each parent will increase from 3 to 5 months, with 2 months remaining to be shared according to the parents' preferences.

A few years before the article came out, Germany had made the jump from implicitly genderising to degenderising parental leave policies as it introduced a parental leave that pays 67% of previous income. This level seems lower than in Sweden and Norway, but since it is based on the *net* salary, while recipients in the Nordic countries must pay taxes on their benefits, the actual benefit level has been similar to the other Nordic countries. However, the government decided against reserving any months for the father and instead introduced an incentive for fathers to take at least two months leave, because if they do their family receives benefits for another two months. Since then the government made a slight reform in that if one's income is above a certain level, one only receives 65% instead of 67% of one's previous income.

Hungary remains a borderline case. It offers an initial 6-month maternity leave which encourages the mother to stay at home for a rather long period and it does not offer a similar paternity leave. In addition, although it offers a two-year leave is available with a 70% replacement rate, the ceiling is rather low at about twice the minimum wage, which greatly dampens the degenderising effect for high-income families. Furthermore, the country also offers a universal three-year flat rate payment for those ineligible for the two-year leave, in line with traditional conservative policies. Even parents taking the two-year insurance-based leave are allowed to utilise the third year of the flat-rate leave, which further encourages mothers to stay at home for longer periods. However, in contrast to Iceland, Sweden, and Norway, no father quota exists and the government has never started campaigns to encourage fathers to go on parental leave. Nevertheless, although the government as become decisively anti-feminist since the article came out and even went to far as to ban gender studies as a university topic, the country's basic family policies remain unchanged.

Among the countries that fell under the category of explicitly genderising in the 2013 article, many of the countries have made adjustments, but except for Austria and Luxembourg none have made major changes. Belgium and Italy have made some slight improvements. One could claim that the Czech Republic has also made some slight improvements in that fathers can take a short leave to help mothers at birth and parents can choose a shorter, higher

Table 9.1 Parental leave schemes in 2019 with changes since 2013

	Maternity leave (length + % of income replacement)	Paternity leave and/or father's quota of parental leave (length + income replacement rate)	Payment of parental leave (income replacement rate and/or flat-rate when applicable)
Degenderizing			
Iceland	Part of parental leave, 13 weeks reserved for mother No change	Part of parental leave 13 weeks reserved for father No change	80% No change
Sweden	Part of parental leave, **3 months (previously 2 months)** reserved for mother plus 7 weeks pregnancy leave **Change: 3 months instead of 2**	10 days at birth, **3 months (previously 2 months)** reserved for father (part of parental leave) **Change: 3 months instead of 2**	80% No change
Norway	Part of parental leave, **15–19 (previously 9 weeks)** reserved for mother **Change: 6 weeks is obligatory**	15–19 weeks **(previously 4)** reserved for the father **Change: 15–19 weeks reserved instead of 4, mother's work no longer a condition**	100% income replacement, for **49 (previously 42)** weeks or 80% if they take **59 (previously 50)** weeks **Change: extension of the leave duration**
Germany 2007	14 weeks, at 100% No change	2 months bonus if father takes at least 2 months of leave (parental leave) No change	65–67% up to 1800 euro for 12 months or 14 months if father takes at least 2 months No change
Hungary	24 weeks at 70% No change	5 days at 100% income replacement No change	70% income replacement No change

	Maternity leave (length + replacement rate)	Paternity leave	Payment of parental leave
Explicitly genderizing			
Belgium	4 weeks at 82% then 11 weeks at 75% No change	Paternity leave: 10 working days, at 100% for 3 days and 82% for 2 days No change Father's quota of parental leave: **4 (previously 3)** months **Change: +1 month of father's quota**	Low flat rate **€750 per month (previously €537)** for 4 months **Change: increased flat-rate payment for longer period**

(continued)

Table 9.1 (continued)

	Maternity leave (length + replacement rate)	Paternity leave	Payment of parental leave
Denmark	18 weeks at 100% **No change**	Two weeks of paternity leave, 100% **No change**	32 weeks at 100%, with a ceiling **No change**
Finland	105 days at **70–90%** **(previously 60–100%)** **Change: the range of replacement rates**	Previously: 18 days at 60–100% **Now: 54 working days (9 weeks),**[a]**Change: longer fathers' leave (up to 54 days), but smaller payment**	158 days at 70% (previously 60%), decreasing for higher income brackets **Change: increase in replacement rate**
Italy	21 weeks at 80% **No change**	Paternity leave: 5 days obligatory (100%) **Change: 1–5 days of paternity introduced since 2013 gradually** Father's quota of parental leave: 5–6 months plus bonus if father takes the leave **No change**	30% when leave is taken for a child under 6 years of age; the leave is unpaid if taken when a child is 6–12 years of age **No change**
Luxembourg	20 weeks (previously 16) at 100% **Change: 4 more weeks**	Paternity leave: 10 working days (2 d. 100% then flat rate) **No change**	The benefit **(replacement wage)** is calculated on the basis of income and hours worked on average during the 12-month period preceding the start of the leave and the leave option chosen.[b] **Change: increased and wage-related benefit**
Austria	16 weeks at 100% **No change**	**Paternity leave:** a new 'family-time bonus' for fathers, i.e. 28 and 31 days (within 91 calendar days) after the birth of the child. There is no job protection during the 'family-time bonus' **Change: introduction of a new scheme**	Flexible flat-rate childcare benefit account and the income-related childcare benefit **Change: introduction of a new scheme**

(continued)

Table 9.1 (continued)

	Maternity leave (length + replacement rate)	Paternity leave	Payment of parental leave
France	16 weeks at 100% **No change**	Paternity leave: 2 weeks (11 working days), at 100% **(previously 2 weeks at birth at 100% for first 3 days,** then up to a max for remaining 11 days) **Change: increase to 100% for the whole leave duration**	The basic benefit is €396 per month if not working; €256 per month if working fewer than half of full-time hours; and €147 per month if working 50–80% of fulltime hours **Change: Decrease in the level of benefit, change in the rules** (previously: flat rate of €521 per month at 3 years per parent)
Czech Republic	28 weeks at 70% (previously 69%)	Paternity leave: 7 calendar days at 70% **Change: introduction of a new scheme (2018)**	There are options to take a shorter period of leave with higher level of payments, or a longer period at a lower level of payment. 2018: shortest possible option: 6 months, longest possible 4 years **Change: introduction of various options of using the leave** (previously: 4 years, low flat rate)
Slovakia	**34 (previously 28) weeks at 75% (previously at 55%) Change**: extended duration, increased payment	No statutory entitlement **No change**	Until child is 3, low flat rate **No change**

(continued)

Table 9.1 (continued)

	Maternity leave (length + replacement rate)	Paternity leave	Payment of parental leave
Implicitly genderizing			
Ireland	A weekly maternity benefit rate of €245 is paid to qualifying persons for 26 weeks; the remaining 16 weeks is unpaid **Change**: introduction of a flat-rate payment (previously 18 weeks at 70% with a maximum plus 14 weeks unpaid)	2 weeks of paternity leave with a weekly paternity benefit payment of €245[c] **Change: introduction of a new scheme (2016)**	18 weeks unpaid (parental leave) plus two weeks of paid leave (individual and non-transferrable) paid at €245 per week
The Netherlands	16 weeks at 100% **No change**	**Paternity leave:** The length of leave is equivalent to the number of working hours per week per partner/father[d] **Change: introduction of a new scheme** (previously: 2 days at birth at 100%) **Father's quota of parental leave:** 26 times the number of working hours per week per parent per child **Change: calculation of leave duration** (previously: each parent received a 3-month unpaid leave)	Unpaid except for civil servants **No change**
Poland	**20 weeks** at 100% or 80% if combined parental leave **Change: duration extended from 16 to 20 weeks**	**Paternity leave:** **2 weeks** pf paternity leave at 100% (gradually from 2010) **Father's quota of parental leave:** **32 weeks** of parental leave (first introduced as 26 weeks from 2014) **Change: both schemes are new**	New parental leave paid at 60% or 80% if taken together with maternity leave **Change: Introduction of a new scheme and payment**

(continued)

Table 9.1 (continued)

	Maternity leave (length + replacement rate)	Paternity leave	Payment of parental leave
Portugal	17 weeks at 100% or 21 weeks at 80%), plus 3 months unpaid except if taken immediately after Initial Parental leave, when paid at 25%. A sharing bonus is allocated: 150 days (21 weeks) paid at 100% of earnings or 180 days (28 weeks) at 83% **Change**: extending the period of payment plus adding a sharing bonus, adding some payment to previously unpaid parental leave scheme	**Paternity leave:** **Previously:** 5 days at birth at 100%, 3 months unpaid **Change:** (earmarked part of parental leave): 25 working days, 15 of which are mandatory, at 100% **Father's quota of parental leave**: 3 months	Unpaid except if taken immediately after Initial Parental leave, when paid at 25% **Change:** adding some payment to previously unpaid leave scheme
Spain	16 weeks at 100% **No change**	**Paternity leave:** 8 weeks at 100% **Change: Extension of duration and increase in payment** (previously: 2 days at birth at 100% paid by employer, 3 years unpaid) **Father's quota of parental leave**: Up to three years after the child's life **No change**	Unpaid **No change**
Switzerland	14 (statutory, 16 provided by many collective agreements) weeks at **80%** (previously 100%) **Change: shorter period of the leave with smaller replacement rate**	No statutory entitlement **No change**	No statutory entitlement **No change**

(continued)

Table 9.1 (continued)

	Maternity leave (length + replacement rate)	Paternity leave	Payment of parental leave
United Kingdom	52 weeks, first 6 weeks paid at 90%, then £148.68 [€166.52] or 90% (whichever is lower) for the next 33 weeks. The remaining 13 weeks are unpaid **Change: extended duration of the leave plus small changes in the benefit level**	**Paternity leave:** 1 or two weeks, with a flat-rate benefit GBP£148.68 [€166.52] per week **Change: this is a new scheme**	Unpaid, **18** (previously 13) per parent per child, up to 4 weeks per year **Change: extension of the leave's duration**

[a]54 days of which the father can take one to 18 days while the mother is on Maternity or Parental leave, but now at 70%, decreasing for higher income brackets
[b]Full-time workers taking the full-time leave option (six months or four months) receive between €2,071.10 per month (the minimum social wage) and €3,451.83 (the minimum social wage increased by two-thirds)
[c]From November 2019: Each parent is entitled to 2 weeks paid parent's leave (€245 pw). This is to be gradually extended to 2 months per parent until 2022
[d]For example, a full-time job of 38 hours per week gives a leave entitlement of 38 hours (i.e. one week). This leave will be extended by a further five weeks from July 2020 onwards
Source This table from Saxonberg (2013) updated on the basis of Koslowski et. al. (2019)

paying leave. Except for Austria, the other countries still clearly belong to the explicitly genderising group. Austria now allows for several types of parental leaves, including the option to choose a Nordic type of degenderising leave. However, since this is just one option among several, we do not consider the country's parental leave policies to be degenderising. Luxembourg is the candidate that comes the closest to moving up to the degenderising category as the parental leave now is partially based on the income replacement principle up to a certain level. However, the system for calculating it remains a bit confusing. In addition, there is no father quota. When the child is born, the father can stay at home with the mother and child for 10 days, but only two days are based on the income replacement principle, with the other days being remunerated at a flat rate.

The implicitly genderising countries have introduced quite a number of changes, but none of them have introduced changes that are great enough to change their categorisation. The country that comes the closest to degenderising is Poland. The country gradually increased the maternity leave from 16 to 26 weeks, which makes it more explicitly genderising. However, it also introduced a 26-week parental leave based on the income replacement principle. In 2015 6 weeks of maternity leave were transferred to the parental leave period. Thus, the total leave time remains 52 weeks (20 + 32 = 52) (Szelewa 2017).

Overall, the new parental leave goes to some extent in the degenderising direction. Nevertheless, the parental leave is clearly geared to the mother rather than trying to induce fathers to share in the leave time. First, there is no earmarked part of the leave that would be reserved for the father. In addition, when the mother begins her maternity leave, she must choose whether she wants to continue to get 100% of her former salary for the first 6 months after which the parents can only receive 60% for the next 6 months, or she can choose to receive 80% for the first 6 months, in which case either parent can receive 80% for the other period as well. So it means that if the mother chooses the 100% rate for the maternity leave, the parental leave payment is only 60% which does not give a great incentive for fathers to share in the leave time.

Portugal has also taken steps in the degenderising direction by introducing a bonus if fathers share in the parental leave and by making part of the paternity leave (15 days) mandatory. Furthermore, the paternity leave has increased from 5 to 25 days. On the whole, the policies cannot be considered degenderising, because the paid period (based on the income replacement principle) is still much too short to induce fathers to stay at home for long periods.

Spain is another country that has made some noteworthy changes in a degenderising direction having introduced an 8-week paternity leave that pays 100% of one's previous salary. Nevertheless, 16 weeks of paid leave for the mother plus 8 for the father is not long enough to encourage the elimination of gender roles, because if some parents to want to keep their children home longer than 24 weeks then these mothers will have an incentive to take up the additional unpaid leave period.

In other words, many explicitly and implicitly genderised countries have taken steps in a degenderising direction, but so far these steps have been too small to cause us to reconsider their categorisation.

Changes in Daycare

In contrast to parental leaves, reforms in daycare policies have led to substantial changes. Table 9.2 shows that there has generally been a large increase in support for daycare. We must be careful in any conclusions, since we do not have data on the percentage of children attending public daycare centres. Since we only have data on the total percentage attending, which includes private daycare institutions, it means that we have not really solved the problem of basing the typology on policies rather than results. We were able to adjust for this somewhat by including data on the percentage of GDP spent on daycare, but even this causes problems because, for example, when a country's GDP rapidly increases, then the portion of GDP spent on daycare might decline even if the actual amount spent on daycare increases.

Table 9.2 Daycare policies

Country	% < 3 in PUBLIC formal childcare (Saxonberg 2013)	% < 3 in formal childcare 2005[a]	% < 3 in formal childcare 2017[b]	Public expenditures on 0–3 as % of GDP 2005[c]	Public expenditures on 0–3 as % of GDP 2015[d]	% aged 3–5 in PUBLIC formal care (Saxonberg 2013)	% aged 3–5 in formal care 2005[c]	% aged 3–5 in formal care 2017[b]	Access to care for 3–5 year olds (Saxonberg 2013)	Access to care for 3–5-year olds 2017[b]	Public pre-school expenditures on children 3%–5% of GDP (Saxonberg 2013)	Public pre-school expenditures on children 3–5% of GDP 2017[b]
Degenderizing												
Denmark	48	73	71.7	0.93	–	82	–	87.7	Full day	Full day	0.61	–
Iceland	38	41	59.7	0.94	0.91	94	–	97.4	Full day	Full day	0.56	0.89
Sweden	33	53	52.7	0.69	1.06	72	100	94.1	Full day	Full day	0.45	0.55
Belgium	30	42	52.9	0.22	0.12	95	100	98.4	Full day	Full day	0.58	0.69
France	23	32	50.5	0.43	0.63	99	68.1	100.0	Full day	Full day	0.67	0.69
Finland	21	27	33.3	0.97	0.59	53	87.7	79.5	Full day	Full day	0.3 (2003)	0.53
Norway	20	33	48.1	0.6	0.67	63		96.9	Full day	Full day	0.3	0.66
Explicitly genderizing												
Czech Rep	10.3	2	6.5	0.12	–	94.7	84.7	87.7	Full day	Full day	0.37	
Hungary	10.1	7	13.8	0.10	0.11	87.8	86.8	92.0	Full day	Full day (most attend part time)	0.7	0.62
Netherlands	8	40	61.6	0.17	0.24	71	–	94.5	Full day (most attend part time)	Full day	0.38	0.36
Italy	6	25	28.6	0.13	0.08	91	90*	93.9	Full day	Full day	0.43	0.48
Slovakia	5.6	3	0.6	0.09	0.08	80.1	73.3	73.9	Full day	Full day	0.42	0.41
Luxemburg	3	22	60.8	0.4		67		87.5	Full day (most attend part time)	Full day (most attend full day now)	0.5 (data only for 2003)	
Spain	5	37	45.8	0.27	0.03	84	97.6	97.1	Full day (most attend part time)		0.5 (data only for 2003)	0.47

Country	% < 3 in PUBLIC formal childcare (Saxonberg 2013)	% < 3 in formal childcare 2005[a]	% < 3 in formal childcare 2017[b]	Public expenditures on 0–3 as % of GDP 2005[c]	Public expenditures on 0–3 as % of GDP 2015[d]	% aged 3–5 in PUBLIC formal care (Saxonberg 2013)	% aged 3–5 in formal care 2005[c]	% aged 3–5 in formal care 2017[e]	Access to care for 3–5 year olds (Saxonberg 2013)	Access to care for 3–5-year olds 2017[b]	Public pre-school expenditures on children 3%–5% of GDP (Saxonberg 2013)	Public pre-school expenditures on children 3–5% of GDP 2017[e]
Germany	2	16	30.3	0.04	0.19	78	87.6	94.6	Full day	Full day	0.36	0.41
Austria	3	4	21	0.25		74	–	89.3	–	Full day (most attend part time)	0.4 (data only for 2003)	
Implicitly genderizing												
Poland	5.1	2	11.6	0		49.9	38.3	81.6	Full day	Full day	0.4	
Portugal	6	30	47.5	0.2	–	–	76.6	90.1	Full day	Full day	0.4	
UK	2	29	33.2	0.28	0.08	60	90.2	100	Mixed	Mixed (most attend part-time)	0.26	0.57

[a]Eurostat database, data for 2005 or similar
[b]Eurostat database, data for 2017 or similar
[c]OECD Family Database, data for 2005 or similar
[d]OECD Family Database, data for 2015 or similar
[e]OECD Family Database, data for 2017 or similar

Taking into account these problems and admitting that we do not have the best possible data, it still seems that the countries that had degenderising daycare policies when the 2013 article appeared, still continue to have such policies. In 5 of 7 countries the percentage of children under 3 attending daycare increased notably (Iceland, Belgium, France, Finland, Norway). Denmark and Sweden faced very slight declines, but they had the highest percentage of children under 3 attending daycare in the previous survey. When it comes to expenditures, the picture is more mixed as the percentage of GDP spent on daycare for children under 3 increased in Sweden and France, but decreased in Belgium and Finland. When it comes to children aged 3–5, the changes were not so great, but Finland and Norway witnessed noticeable increases in attendance. When it comes to expenditures, however, almost all the countries enjoyed large increases in terms of portion of GDP as 5 of the countries had increases of at least 10%. Although no separate data for spending on various age groups could be found for Denmark, the overall spending for early education and care has slightly decreased from 1.32% of GDP in 2005 to 1.23% of GDP in 2015 (OECD Family Database). This implies that some degree of cost-containment probably took place in Denmark, but enrolment levels remained high because they took measures to lower the quality of care (higher children per staff ratios, less rigorous screening of staff education, etc.).[1] Nevertheless, since Denmark is so much ahead of other countries, we would still consider the country's childcare services to be degenderising.

Among those countries that were explicitly genderising according to the 2013 article, all of them except for Slovakia saw increases in the percentage of children attending nurseries. At least in the case of The Netherlands, Luxemburg, and Spain, the increase is large enough that there is good reason to consider their daycare policies for children under 3 to be degenderising. When it comes to expenditure the changes are not so great except for in Spain where the decrease is noticeable. Generally speaking, there was not much change in the percentage of children attending kindergartens, but since the percentage is quite high this strengthens the idea that these three countries could now be considered to have degenderising daycare policies if we would make the mistake of not considering whether the children attend full-time or part-time. It turns out that Luxemburg is the only one of these countries where a large portion of children attend kindergartens full-time. While only 23% of all children at the age of 3 to 5 attended kindergartens full time (at least 30 hours per week) in Luxemburg in 2007, this indicator increased to 63.9% in 2017 (Eurostat SILC). However, a reverse trend took place in Spain, where the share of all pre-school age children attending full-time decreased from 57% in 2007 to 37.9% in 2017 (Eurostat SILC). Meanwhile, in The Netherlands a great majority of children continue to only attend kindergarten part-time. Consequently, when taking into account access to full-time daycare, Luxembourg is the country making the jump from explicitly genderising to degenderising in the area of daycare.

Among those countries that were implicitly genderised in 2013, Poland and Portugal have seen significant increases in children under 3 attending daycare, but the percentage is only high enough in Portugal to consider it to be degenderising. At the same time, although data show some improvement in kindergarten attendance in the UK, the percentage of children attending full-time is relatively small and remains at a similar level (21–22% of all children pre-school age). This level is still too low to allow the UK to make the jump from implicitly genderising to degenderising.

Even if we have to be careful because of the lack of reliable statistics, it seems that 3 formerly explicitly genderising countries and one implicitly genderising country in the area of daycare policies now have made the step up the to degenderising category: Portugal, The Netherlands, Luxembourg, and Spain.

Conclusion

In conclusion, there seems to be a general trend towards increased degenderisation, but the changes have rarely been big enough to force us to reconsider to what category each country belongs. Our study gives reason for cautious optimism. Most countries have made some improvements, but only Luxemburg has made large enough changes to have had one of its policy areas (daycare) move into the degenderising category.

This review of the changes since the 2013 article also indicates that the genderisation typology is still very applicable for analysing family policies. Our discussion of the criticisms of the typology also shows that the typology is capable of taking into account other aspects than traditional family policy. It has no trouble, for example, in analysing gay rights or intergenerational issues. Even though it does not take up children's issues, policies that promote gender equality also seem to promote the child's well-being.

Funding The research was co-funded by the Erasmus+ Programme of the European Union, project number 611572-EPP-1-201 9-1-SK-EPPJ MO-CHAIR.

The European Commission support for the production of this publication does not constitute an endorsement of the contents which reflects the views only of the authors, and the Commission cannot be held responsible for any use which may be made of the information contained therein.

Note

1. We would like to thank Caroline de la Porte and Trine Larsen for sharing this information.

References

Adi-Japha, Esther, and Pnina S. Klein. 2009. "Relations Between Parenting Quality and Cognitive Performance of Children Experiencing Varying Amounts of Childcare." *Child Development* 80 (3): 893–906.
Andersson, Bengt-Erik. 1992. "Effects of Day-Care on Cognitive and Socioemotional Competence of Thirteen-Year-Old Swedish Schoolchildren." *Child Development* 63 (1): 20–36.
Andersson, Bengt-Erik. 2005. "Tidig dagisstart det bästa för de allra flesta barn." *Dagensnyhter*, April 8.
Bergmann, Barbara R. 2008. "Long Leaves, Child Well-Being, and Gender Equality." *Politics Society* 36 (3): 350–359.
Bergqvist, Christina, and Steven Saxonberg. 2017. "The State as a Norm-Builder? The Take up of Parental Leave in Norway and Sweden." *Social Policy and Administration* 5 (7): 1470–1487.
Boje, Thomas P. 2007. "Welfare and Work. The Gendered Organisation of Work and Care in Different European Countries." *European Review* 15 (3): 373–395.
Borge, Anne I. H., Michael Rutter, Sylvana Côté, and Richard E. Tremblay. 2004. "Early Childcare and Physical Aggression: Differentiating Social Selection and Social Causation." *Journal of Child Psychology and Psychiatry* 45 (2): 367–376.
Bretherton, Inge. 2010. "Fathers in Attachment Theory and Research: A Review." *Early Child Development and Care* 180 (1–2): 9–23. https://doi.org/10.1080/03004430903414661.
Daly, Mary, and Kirsten Schweiwe. 2010. "Individualisation and Personal Obligations—Social Policy, Family Policy, and Law Reform in Germany and the UK." *International Journal of Law, Policy and the Family* 24 (2): 177–197.
Deater-Deckard, Kirby, Relana Pinkerton, and Sandra Scarr. 1996. "Child Care Quality and Children's Behavioral Adjustment: A Four-Year Longitudinal Study." *Journal of Child Psychology and Psychiatry* 37 (8): 937–948.
Duncan, Simon, and Monika Strell. 2004. "Combining Lone Motherhood and Paid Work: The Rationality Mistake and Norwegian Social Policy." *Journal of European Social Policy* 14 (1): 41–54.
Engster, Daniel, and Helen Olofsdotter Stensöta. 2011. "Do Family Policy Regimes Matter for Children's Well-Being?" *Social Politics* 18 (1): 81–124. https://doi.org/10.1093/sp/jxr006.
Esping-Andersen, Gøsta. 1990. *The Three Worlds of Welfare Capitalism*. Cambridge: Polity Press and Princeton, NJ: Princeton University Press.
Esping-Andersen, Gøsta. 1999. *Social Foundations of Postindustrial Economies*. Oxford: Oxford University Press.
Gornick, Janet C. 1999. "Gender Equality in the Labour Market." In *Gender and the Welfare States Regimes*, edited by Diane Sainsbury, 210–244. Oxford: Oxford University Press.
Hantrais, Linda. 2004. *Family Policy Matters*. Bristol: Policy Press.
Hervey, Tamara, and Jo Shaw. 1998. "Women, Work and Care: Women's Dual Role and the Double Burden in EC Sex Equality Law." *Journal of European Social Policy* 8 (1): 43–63.
Hildebrant, Timothy. 2018. "The One-Child Policy, Elder Care, and LGB Chinese: A Social Policy Explanation for Family Pressure." *Journal of Homosexuality* 66 (5): 590–608.

Jenson, Jane. 1997. "Who Cares? Gender and Welfare Regimes." *Social Politics* 4 (2): 182–187.
Kerstis, Brigitta, Cecilia Åslund, and Karin Sonnby. 2018. "More Secure Attachment to the Father and the Mother is Associated with Fewer Depressive Symptoms in Adolescents." *Upsala Journal of Medical Sciences* 123 (1): 62–67. https://doi.org/10.1080/03009734.2018.1439552.
Korpi, Walter. 2000. "Faces of Inequality: Gender, Class, and Patterns of Inequalities in Different Types of Welfare States." *Social Politics* 7 (2): 127–191.
Koslowski, Alison, Sonja Blum, Ivana Dobrotić, Alexandra Macht, and Peter Moss. 2019. "International Review of Leave Policies and Research." Available at: https://www.leavenetwork.org/annual-review-reports/.
Kurowska, Anna. 2018. "(De)Familialization and (De)Genderization—Competing or Complementary Perspectives in Comparative Policy Analysis?" *Social Policy & Administration* 52 (1): 29–49. https://doi.org/10.1111/spol.12272.
Leitner, Sigrid. 2003. "Varieties of Familialism: The Caring Function of the Family in Comparative Perspective." *European Societies* 5 (4): 353–375. https://doi.org/10.1080/1461669032000127642.
Lewis, Jane, ed. 1993. *Women and Social Policies in Europe*. Camberley: Edward Elgar.
Lewis, Jane. 2009. *Work-Family Balance, Gender and Policy*. Cheltenham: Edward Elgar.
Lister, Ruth. 1994. "'She Has Other Duties'—Women, Citizenship and Social Security." In *Social Security and Social Change: New Challenges to the Beveridge Model*, edited by Sally Baldwin and Jane Falkingham, 31–44. London and New York, NY: Harvester Wheatsheaf.
Lister, Ruth. 2003. *Citizenship: Feminist Perspectives*. Washington Square, NY: University Press.
Lohnman, Henning, and Hannah Zagel. 2016. "Family Policy in Comparative Perspective: The Concepts and Measurement of Familization and Defamilization", *Journal of European Social Policy* 26 (1): 48–65. https://doi.org/10.1177/0958928715621712.
Morgan, Kimberley J., and Kathrin Zippel. 2003. "Paid to Care: The Origins and Effects of Care Leave Policies in Western Europe.", *Social Politics* 10 (1): 49–85. https://doi.org/10.1093/sp/jxg004.
O'Connor, Julia, Ann Shola Orloff, and Sheila Shaver. 1999. *States, Markets, Families: Gender, Liberalism and Social Policy in Australia, Canada, Great Britain and the United States*. Cambridge: Cambridge University Press.
Orloff, Ann S. 2009. "Gendering the Comparative Analysis of Welfare States: An Unfinished Agenda." *Sociological Theory* 27 (3): 317–343. https://doi.org/10.1111/j.1467-9558.2009.01350.x.
Petts, Richard J., Chris Knoester, and Jane Waldfogel. 2020. "Fathers' Paternity Leave-Taking and Children's Perceptions of Father-Child Relationships in the United States." *Sex Roles* 82 (3): 173–188. https://doi.org/10.1007/s11199-019-01050-y.
Pfau-Effinger, Brirgit. 2000. *Kultur und Frauenerwerbstätigkeit in Europa. Theorie und Empirie des internationalen Vergleichs*. Opladen: Leske und Budrich.
Powell, Martin, and Armando Barrientos. 2011. "An Audit of the Welfare Modelling Business." *Social Policy & Administration* 45 (1): 69–84. https://doi.org/10.1111/j.1467-9515.2010.00754.x.

Ramchandani, Paul G., Jill Domoney, Vaheshta Sethna, Lamprini Psychogiou, Haido Vlachos, and Lynne Murray. 2013. "Do Early Father–Infant Interactions Predict the Onset of Externalising Behaviours in Young Children? Findings from a Longitudinal Cohort Study." *Journal of Child Psychology and Psychiatry* 54 (1): 56–64. https://doi.org/10.1111/j.1469-7610.2012.02583.x.

Sainsbury, Diane, ed. 1994. *Gendering Welfare States*. London: Sage.

Saraceno, Chiara. 2016. "Varieties of Familialism: Comparing Four Southern European and East Asian Welfare Regimes." *Journal of European Social Policy* 26 (4): 314–326.

Saxonberg, Steven. 2013. "From Defamilialization to Degenderization: Toward a New Welfare Typology." *Social Policy & Administration* 47 (1): 26–49.

Saxonberg, Steven. 2014. *Gendering Post-communist Family Policies: A Historical-Institutional Analysis*. Neuviden: Palgrave.

Saxonberg, Steven, and Tomáš Sirovátka. 2006. "Failing Family Policy in Post-communist Central Europe." *Comparative Policy Analysis* 8 (2): 189–206.

Saxonberg, Saxonberg, and Dorota Szelewa. 2007. "The Continuing Legacy of the Communist Legacy." *Social Politics: International Studies in Gender, State & Society* 14 (3): 351–379.

Sipilä, Jorma, Katja Repo, and Tapio Rissainen. 2010. "Introduction." In *Cash-for-Childcare. The Consequences for Caring Mothers*, edited by Jorma Sipilä, Katja Repo and Tapio Rissainen, 1–23. Cheltenham, Northampton: Edward Elgar.

Szelewa, Dorota. 2017. "From Implicit to Explicit Familialism: Post-1989 Family Policy Reforms in Poland." In *Gender and Family in European Economic Policy. Developments in the New Millennium*, edited by Diana Auth, Jutta Hergenhan, and Barbara Holland-Cunz, 129–156. Cham: Palgrave.

Van der Lippe, Tanja, Judith de Ruijter, Esther de Ruijter, and Werner Raub. 2010. "Persistent Inequalities in Time Use Between Men and Women: A Detailed Look at the Influence of Economic Circumstances, Policies and Culture." *European Sociological Review* 27 (2): 164–179.

CHAPTER 10

Familialisation of Care in European Societies: Between Family and the State

Agnieszka Furmańska-Maruszak and Katarzyna Suwada

INTRODUCTION

The aim of the chapter is to describe the organisation of care in four European societies: the Netherlands, Poland, Portugal, and Sweden. Care is perceived here in terms of work as practices and is connected with fulfilling human needs; it requires knowledge and competences, takes time and effort. As such it is the fundamental work that plays a crucial role in the process of reproduction of the society (Daly and Lewis 2000). It is also a universal phenomenon, since in every society there are people who need help in everyday lives and there are people, mostly women, who provide this help. At the same time the organisation of care differs in various social and cultural contexts. It is not only a private matter of families, who are primarily responsible for their members in need, but it is a public and political issue. We intend to outline how care is organised in the European societies keeping in mind the relations between family and the welfare state that are analysed here through the concept of familialisation. Familialisation serves here as a measure to assess to what extent family is supported in its caring obligations. We concentrate here on childcare and care for the elderly in the context of three types of policies: care leaves, formal

---

A. Furmańska-Maruszak (✉) · K. Suwada
Institute of Sociology, Nicolaus Copernicus University, Toruń, Poland
e-mail: afmaruszak@umk.pl

K. Suwada
e-mail: k.suwada@umk.pl

care services and cash benefits. We use both terms—familialisation and familialism—since they are used interchangeably by different authors to describe the same social phenomenon.

Welfare State and Care Arrangements

Mahon (2002) claims that child care has become a central issue to a contemporary welfare state design, mostly because of the emergence of the dual-earner family model, in which both men and women are expected to participate in the labour market. The increasing labour force participation of women, in particular, has been leading to a process of *defamilialisation* of care, which is demonstrated by the greater focus on the institutional care on children. The second important structural change is the process of ageing society that results from low fertility rates and increasing life expectancy (Oláh and Fahlén 2013). These two trends lead to a problem of unmet care needs, which cannot be satisfied only by family and market mechanisms. Thus the organisation of care for children and the elderly has become one of the major challenges for the European welfare states. Today the welfare state is recognised as a significant actor beside the family that provides care for those in need. Yet the extent to which the welfare state supports families in providing care vary in Europe. To assess it, we refer to an axis of familialisation-defamilialisation that was formulated to analyse the impact of the welfare state on family life (Lister 1994; Leitner 2003). Lister defines the term familialisation as 'the degree to which individuals can uphold a socially acceptable standard of living independently of family relationships, either through paid work or social security provision' (Lister 1994, 37). The concept was firstly formulated to describe the situation of women and their dependence on male breadwinner, but later was extended to all relations between family members (Saraceno 2016). Therefore, the axis of familialisation-defamilialisation can be used to describe different models of care provisions and the role of the welfare state in promoting a particular model of care organisation.

In our chapter, we refer to a conceptualisation of familialism of Leitner (2003). In her proposal, familialism should be used to describe those public policies which 'explicitly support the family in its caring function' (2003, 354). The welfare state can support the family in different ways—it can enable an individual to provide care for other family members, or it can (partially) relieve the family from caring obligations. As Leitner notices: 'Whereas the first type of policy puts the family at the centre of care provision, the second one either socializes or "marketizes" the caring function of the family through public social services or market-driven care provision' (2003, 357).

Since in one welfare state there can be different means of supporting family, it is not easy to unambiguously classify a particular welfare state as a familialistic or defamilialistic regime (Leitner 2003; Saraceno 2016). It is important to look rather on actual policies and their effects on the organisation of care, than on welfare states as whole systems. Based on this assumption, Leitner (2003) divides policies into two types: familialistic and defamilialistic. The first ones allow family to provide care personally. These are time rights (e.g. care leaves), cash transfers for caring (e.g. cash benefits or tax reductions) and social rights attached to caregiving. The second type of policies is aimed to unburden family members from their caring obligations through public provision of care, social services or subsidies of care provision through the market. Leitner combines these different policies of two types in one matrix and distinguishes four types of familialism: (1) explicit familialism, (2) optional familialism, (3) implicit familialism, and (4) defamilialism. In the welfare state based on *explicit familialism*, family is not only openly strengthened in caring obligations, but there are also no alternatives to family care, such as public or market care institutions. In the *optional familialism* individuals have a choice to what extent they want to engage in care. They have the right to time to care, but they also have access to public institutions of care. In the *implicit familialism* there is lack of any instruments of support—thus the family needs to provide care because of the lack of alternatives. Finally, in the *defamilialistic model* there is a strong support for state or market provision of care services, but at the same time the family has a limited possibility to personally provide care for its members.

Methodology

In the following analysis, we concentrate on four different European countries. Thanks to a comparative analysis, we can see how different instruments of family policy are implemented in different societies and, consequently, how care organisation looks in various institutional contexts. We decided to concentrate on four countries, which are in different geographical locations in Europe, but are also characterised with a different organisation of family life and paid work. The Netherlands is located in the continental Europe and characterises with a relatively extensive welfare system, high employment rate (in 2019 80.1%[1]), very high part-time employment rate (in 2019 46.8%), and average fertility rate (in 2018 1.59). Sweden, located in the Northern Europe, characterises with an extensive welfare system, high employment rate (in 2019 82.1%), and average part-time employment rate (in 2019 20.9%). It is also known for an extensive family policy and one of the highest fertility rates in Europe (in 2018 1.8). Both Poland and Portugal characterise with weaker welfare systems, but still with different characteristics. Poland is a representative of post-communist European welfare state with rather low employment rate (in 2019 73%), very low part-time employment rate (in 2019 5.9%), and low fertility rate (in 2018 1.46). Whereas Portugal is a Southern European country with an average high employment rate (in 2019 76.1%), low part-time employment rate (in 2019 7.9%), and low fertility rate (in 2018 1.42). All of these countries characterise with different history, culture and religion. At the same time all of them are members of the European Union and as such need to follow the EU rules and comply with the EU directives.

The following analysis comes from desk research based on the literature review and the analysis of legal regulations. Besides the data from databases of Eurostat and the World Bank, we use the data from reports of the International Network on Leave Policies and Research, European Commission, OECD, and Eurofound (European Working Conditions Surveys). We distinguish main instruments of European policies aimed at care organisation and attempt to compare and assess them in terms of their (de)familialistic effects. We focus on three types of instruments: care leaves, formal care services, and cash benefits. Since the policies addressed to childcare are differently designed than the policies addressed to the elderly, we analyse them separately.

Childcare Policies in European Welfare States

In contemporary European societies both women and men are under pressure to combine parenthood with paid work. Yet these two spheres of life often impose on them conflicting expectations that lead to a problem with fulfilling satisfactorily obligations from parenting and paid work (van der Lippe et al. 2006; Oláh and Fahlén 2013). Thus one of the aims of the welfare state is to support parents in their everyday endeavours through family policy instruments. In general the aim of the most European family policies is twofold. On the one hand, they should encourage labour force participation regardless of the individual's family situation. On the other hand, they have to support families by creating conditions, in which children receive care adequate to their age and needs.

Care Leaves for Parents

The general aim of the leaves is to allow parents to take a break in paid work in connection to becoming a parent without losing a job. In this context parental leave should be seen as a familialistic type of instrument in a form of time right that allows parents to fulfil their caring obligations (Leitner 2003). The first leave, called then maternity leave, were introduced in most European countries in 1883 (Gauthier 1999). At the beginning leaves were perceived as an instrument of increasing the well-being of female workers, their loyalty to employers, as well as of improving mothers' and children's health. Later they started to be an encouragement for women to participate in the labour market and an instrument fighting with gender inequalities (Gauthier 1999). Since the postwar period the increase in the length of maternity leaves, as well as the level of benefits connected to them, can be observed. This process was connected with a growing number of women participating in the labour market and the need to support them in reconciliation of paid work with caring obligations.

European countries differently design their parental leave system. Yet according to the EU Maternity Leave Directive from 1992, every woman should have a right to minimum 14 weeks of maternity leave that can be used before and/or after the birth. Two weeks of such leave are obligatory. Its aim is to allow a woman to recover after the delivery and pregnancy. Apart from that European countries offer additional leaves. Besides maternity leave we can distinguish paternity leaves for fathers and parental leaves addressed to both mothers and fathers.

In the four welfare states analysed here, the parental leave systems are differently designed. As it is indicated in the International Review of Leave Policies and Research (Koslowski et al. 2019), the Netherlands offers 16 weeks of fully paid maternity leave, one week of fully paid birth leave for fathers or partners and unpaid 26 weeks of parental leave. In Poland there are: 20 weeks of maternity leave (paid at the level of 80% or 100% of earnings), two weeks of paternity leave only for fathers (paid 100%), and 32 weeks of parental leave that can be shared by both parents (paid 80% or 60%). Additionally, parents can take up to three years of extended leave, which is unpaid or is connected to flat-rate payments for the families with low income. In Portugal parents have a right to 120 or 150 days of initial parental leave paid on the level accordingly 100% or 80%. Six weeks of this leave is reserved for a mother. Additionally, there is five weeks of an obligatory fully paid father-only leave. After using the initial parental leave each parent has a right to three months of unpaid additional parental leave. If this leave is used, one parent gains a right to two years of unpaid childcare leave. Whereas in Sweden each parent has a right to 240 days of parental leave. 195 days is in-come based on the level of 77.6% of earning, the remaining 45 days are flat-rate paid. 90 days of high paid leave are non-transferrable to the other parent, whereas the rest of days can be transferred. Additionally, fathers have a right to ten days of temporary leave in connection with a child's birth or adoption paid on the level of 77.6%.

Trying to understand what effects in terms of familialisation these different arrangements have on the organisation of care, it is crucial to check the length of highly paid leave and also how it fits to other instruments of family policy, in particular the system of institutional childcare. The longest highly paid leave is offered by Sweden (390 days, i.e. 13 months) and Poland (52 weeks, i.e. 12 months). In the Netherlands only mothers can stay less than three months on such a leave, whereas in Portugal the maximum period of such leave is less than five months. In all of these countries, parents can stay home longer, yet it usually connects with the substantial loss of income. Thus the question what alternatives parents have after the period of highly paid leave. To map these alternatives, we look at institutional care and cash benefits. It must be noted that the way parental leave system is designed has also consequences for gender inequalities. We are not getting into discussion about it, although we are aware that long parental leaves without incentives for fathers have a familialistic effect only on mothers (see Chapters 9 and 11 for a more details).

Care Institutions for Children

The public care institutions are the oldest instrument of supporting parents. They firstly appeared at the beginning of the nineteenth century in Europe

(Gauthier 1999). At the same time there are many differences between European welfare states in terms of the development of public childcare, as well as its organisation that have its roots in different national traditions and norms around care (Scheiwe and Willekens 2009; Saxonberg et al. 2012). There have been two main policy motives declared in connection to the development of public childcare in the European states—the need of public education and allowing parents to combine parenthood with paid work. Recently a third argument appeared according to which the institutional care for children is seen as an important instrument decreasing gender inequalities. This approach is linked with full employment policy, in which it is expected that all people in reproductive age engage in paid work. Thus this instrument is mostly addressed to women who are a group at greater risk of resigning from paid work in connection to parenthood (Scheiwe and Willekens 2009). As such the instrument can be seen as defamilialising, because it relieves mothers from care obligations and, thus, promotes gender equality in care within the couple.

Similarly, as in case of parental leaves, the four analysed here countries significantly differ in terms of an access to institutional care for children in preschool age. Poland and the Netherlands are examples of a system in which children around age three move from childcare institutions to educational kindergartens. There is an evident split between childcare and early education. Portugal represents somewhat split system in which the qualifications of practitioners have to be high across all early childhood education and care (ECEC) services, yet the educational guidelines are only set for children over three. In Sweden such division blurs and the education authority is responsible for the whole age range (European Commission/EACEA/Eurydice 2019). Such situation has implications for the access to ECEC services in these countries. In Sweden a place in an ECEC institution is guaranteed when a child is one year old, in Poland when a child is three, whereas in Portugal and the Netherlands when child is four. The incongruence of parental leave system and ECEC services leads to the childcare gap, which is a period when child is uncovered neither by care leave nor a guaranteed place in childcare institution (Ingólfsdóttir and Gíslason 2016). Its length has consequences on how care is organised by the family. In the four analysed countries there is no childcare gap only in Sweden. The highly paid parental leave ends in a thirteenth month, whereas the universal entitlement to public ECEC starts when a child is 12-month-old. It means that Swedish parents are in a comfortable position in which they can easily and with flexibility transit to a situation in which a child regularly attend preschool and they come back to paid work. In three other countries the childcare gap exists and lasts: in Poland for 24 months, in Portugal for 42 months, and in the Netherlands for 45.2 months (Koslowski et al. 2019). The analysis of European Commission (European Commission/EACEA/Eurydice 2019) indicates that in Poland and Portugal the demand for places for early age children is not met. In 2016 in Poland the attendance rate for children aged 0–2 is 12%, whereas in Portugal it is 36% (Koslowski et al. 2019). It means that majority of families have to find other ways to organise care. In the Netherlands, where in 2016 attendance rate for children aged 0–2 is 56%, demand is met only because of a market-driven system and high rates of part-time employment. Such situation allows for the conclusion that these three countries characterise with an implicit familialism in this regard. Since they do not openly enhance parents to stay home with children under three or four, but leave this area unsupported forcing them to find informal sources of care (such as grandparents or other family members) or finance it from private resources. Such situation can have very negative effects on parents who do not have strong family ties, nor economic resources. In this context, only Sweden decided to introduce a strong defamilialistic mechanism, regardless the fact that it also offers parents generous parental leave opportunities.

Cash Benefits

The history of child benefits is long. Prior to 1930s they were mostly limited to low-income and/or large families and were seen mostly in terms of instrument against children's poverty. Between 1930 and 1958 they started to be available for more families, yet there were still some restrictions (e.g. employment-related, excluding children of low-birth order, being means-tested, having different levels for different categories of families). Later more countries decided to introduce universal benefits (Gauthier 1999). Universal benefits are not an instrument aimed only for working parents, so their aim is rather to financially support people and consequently give them resources to provide parental obligations.

The comparative analysis of cash benefits in Europe is very difficult, since there are multiple ways the welfare states support financially parents and families. In the following analysis, we focus only on these cash benefits that have an explicit impact on the organisation of care. We do not include allowances aimed to the poorest families, which main goal is to reduce poverty. Among allowances helping to organise care there are two main types. First one is of universal character and its recipients are all parents. Such financial support can be without restrictions used by parents as they wish. Second one is granted only when special conditions are fulfilled and are aimed at a particular organisation of care. An example of such mechanisms is: a cash for care benefit which is granted for jobless parents of children in early age not attending any ECEC services or a subsidy paid directly to parents to cover the cost of a private childcare institution.

In 2020 in the analysed countries universal child allowance is implemented in the Netherlands, Poland, and Sweden. In the Netherlands it is paid once per quarter and it increases with the age of child (221.49 EUR till child is 5 years, 268.41 EUR per child 6–11 years old, and 316.41 per child 12–17 years old). In Poland the benefit is at the level of 500 PLN (112 EUR) per month until a child is 18, whereas in Sweden it is 1250 SEK (120 EUR) per month until 16 or longer if a child is still in education. In Portugal there is no universal benefit for a child (although there is a child benefit framed as an instrument against poverty). It is difficult to assess the familialistic effect of such benefits on the family. It depends on other factors, such timing, alternative childcare options, including access to childcare institutions or the length of parental leave. In Sweden and in the Netherlands child allowance were introduced in 1940s and have a long tradition. Whereas in Poland child benefit is a new instrument introduced in 2016, but only in 2019 it became universal for each child. Consequently, its introduction is perceived in terms of a turn from implicit familialism to explicit familialism (Szelewa 2017).

When it comes to the second type of benefits distinguished above, the explicitly familialistic mechanism cash-for-care was only introduced in Sweden in between 2008 and 2016, yet it was abolished. It is argued that it has a negative impact on women's employment rates in rural and mixed areas (Giuliani and Duvander 2017). Whereas in the Netherlands, there is a childcare benefit which is granted if both parents work and the child goes to a registered care institution. Its aim is to cover the cost of institutional care for children, so such instrument might be seen as a defamilialistic policy. Yet this benefit is mean-tested, so their defamilialistic effect is rather limited.

(De)Familialisation of Childcare

Taking into considerations all above-mentioned instruments and its effect in terms of familialisation, it is clear that familialistic instruments dominate in the system of the Netherlands, Poland, Portugal, and Sweden. The Netherlands and Portugal characterise with implicit familialism, since they offer rather short highly paid parental leaves and have quite big childcare gaps resulting from the lack of support for institutional childcare for the youngest children. Poland is rather an explicitly familialistic regime, in which parents have a right to long highly paid leave, the institutional care for children under three is limited, but parents have a right to universal childcare benefit. Sweden has the most flexible system, in which there is no childcare gap, each one-year-old child has a right to a place in a care institution and parents can take rather long parental leaves exceeding 12 months. Thus Sweden could be characterised as an optional familialism regime.

CARE FOR THE ELDERLY IN EUROPEAN WELFARE STATES

Care given to a dependent adult differs significantly from childcare. First, it is difficult to predict the duration and intensity of a necessary help provision. Being a natural consequence of physiological aging process, old age infirmity leads gradually to losses of physical, mental, and/or cognitive capacities. However, the loss of capacity is not always irreversible. In some cases, elder people might recover gaining some of their lost capacities back at least for some time. Second, giving care to dependent relatives most often means accompanying them during the last period of their lives. Third, the need to give care to a family member usually arises at the different stage of the career than childcare. People aged 45 to 64 seem to be involved in eldercare the most. When workers age they tend to put more importance on family, their relationships with relatives and close friends and they seem to be less willing to accept problems related to work-life conflict (Thrasher et al. 2016).

The intensity and type of care given to an elderly family member differs according to the degree of their dependency. The extent to which the person loses their capacities of self-care determines the activities of caregivers. These activities might be undertaken by informal caregivers (family members, friends, or neighbours) and by professionals (from social care or healthcare sector) at home or in an institution. A family might be a direct or indirect provider of care performing all caring activities or focusing on the organisation of care. The extent to which a family carries a burden of care depends on the support provided by the state by means of formal care services, carer-friendly employment conditions as well as cash benefits.

Formal Care Services

Provision of formal long-term care (LTC) services is usually divided between social care and healthcare system. Many European countries still lack a separated and integrated long-term care system. LTC services might be provided at home or in institutions. LTC institutions refer to nursing and residential care facilities that provide accommodation and LTC in one to people with moderate to severe functional impairments. LTC at home includes care services together with assisted or adapted living arrangements specially designed for those who need regular help in their own home. It also refers to the use of institutions that help the elderly person stay at home as long as possible. This includes community care, day care centres as well as respite care used on temporary basis (OECD/European Commission 2013).

Taking into account the four analysed countries, formal care services provided both at home and in institutions are much more developed in Sweden and in the Netherlands where spendings on LTC services (covered by government or compulsory insurance schemes) are the highest. In 2017 expenditure both for social and health component amounted to 3.7% of GDP in the Netherlands and 3.2% of GDP in Sweden. The key role of informal care provided by family members goes in line with low spending on LTC services in Portugal (0.5% of GDP) and Poland (0.4% of GDP) (OECD 2019).

The coverage rate of LTC services among people aged 65 and over is therefore the highest in Sweden (16.2%) and the Netherlands (13%). The majority of LTC recipients in Sweden (66%) and in the Netherlands (73%) receive care at home. The OECD data for Portugal and Poland is limited and shows that in 2017 in Portugal 1.9% people aged 65 and over received long-term care within RNCCI (National Network for Long-Term Integrated Care) established in 2006 as a joint initiative of health and social sector. The data for care received only within social care is not available which blurs a bit the whole picture of LTC provided in Portugal. Recently there has been an increase in social care provided to the dependent elderly with in-home services being a priority (Lopes 2017). Despite this growth a lot of care needs is still unmet. The OECD data available for Poland includes only LTC given in institutions and reveals that in 2017 in Poland only 0.9% of people aged 65 or more were provided with this type of care services.

While care received in institutions constitutes a substitute to family care, home help services can both relieve the family from its caring function or support it in performing caring duties (Leitner 2003). Thus, the developed LTC services both in Sweden and in the Netherlands provided mainly at home may indicate both familialisation and de-familialisation trends depending on the role home help plays for informal care provision. In Portugal and Poland the LTC system is not so developed and the burden of care is carried mainly by families who are (unlike in Sweden and in the Netherlands) legally obliged to give care to its dependent members. In Portugal, there has been a recent development of LTC services within the integrated care network and within social care sector enabling Portuguese to improve not only residential care, but primarily home care and care provided in day care centres (Lopes et al. 2018).

Care Leaves

Time rights for working carers are a typical example of familialistic policies. Unlike parents, carers of the elderly have less entitlements to request leave to care for their family members. Leave conditions depend on the labour market arrangements available for the carers. They might be imposed by the state in labour law regulations, via collective agreement or might be entirely the matter for the employers' discretion. Entitlements to care leave might vary according to sectors (e.g. private or public sector) or form of employment (e.g. in the Netherlands self-employed are not entitled to carer's leave provision) (Bouget et al. 2016). There are differences in length and payment of leave as well as the conditions for taking it. The criteria of eligibility vary from countries where care leave might be taken in the case of ordinary illness to countries where it is available in the case of very serious and terminal illness (Koslowski et al. 2019).

In terms of care for a dependent relative one can distinguish between short-term and long-term care leaves. The former are usually related to giving care to a sick person no matter the sickness-related reason is. They last from couple of days to three weeks. Dependency might be related to disability from birth or acquired disability regardless of age and finally might be the result of old age accompanying diseases. Usually the disability scale is used to assess the need for care. In some countries it is based on medical examination and a relevant medical certificate. Care leaves might be paid and unpaid. There are differences between countries in benefit level and entitlements to social security rights. Most often the payment during leave is established as a proportion of previous earnings (usually between 70 and 80%, sometimes 100%). There are countries where care leave is paid at a flat rate or income related and equal to the rate of unemployment benefit. In some cases leave benefit is calculated on the basis of sickness benefit. Leave provisions are usually combined with social security entitlements, but it may vary according to the duration and the type of leave (whether it is paid or unpaid) (Bouget et al. 2016).

Care leaves are provided in the four analysed countries. In Portugal and Poland only short-term care leaves are available. In Poland, the two-week leave is paid (80% of previous earnings), but is eligible only for those who co-reside with a person they care for. In Portugal the leave is unpaid and can be taken for 15 days per year for close relative plus 15 days for severely disabled or chronically ill spouse (Koslowski et al. 2019). In Sweden care leave is provided to give care to a severely ill closely related person. It is paid for up to 100 days and the doctor's certificate is required (Schön and Johansson 2016). In the Netherlands, both short-term and long-term care leaves are available. Short-term leave may be taken for a period equalled double the number of hours worked per week and is paid 70% of wages. Long-term care leave is unpaid available at the maximum duration of six times the weekly working hours. The payment conditions of the leaves may be changed in collective agreements or by the decision of an employer (van der Woude et al. 2016). In Sweden and in the Netherlands not only relatives are recognised as informal carers and are entitled to care leaves. In the Netherlands the group of depended persons for whom an employee is entitled to take care leave has been extended enormously now including not only spouses and partners as well as their children, but also a kinsman in the first and second degree and a person living at the same address as well a person with whom the employee has a social relation (Furmańska-Maruszak and Heeger-Hertter 2019).

Time rights in the form of care leave seem to be the least developed in Portugal. Both Portugal and Poland lack long-term care leaves. In Sweden and in the Netherlands working informal carers are much more supported by the possibility to take leave and adjust its duration. However, despite the availability the take-up of care leaves in these two countries is limited. Although paid, long-term care leave in Sweden is underused probably due to relatively low benefit. In the Netherlands carers taking long-term care leave are not paid and are not insured against sickness, disability and unemployment. Workers prefer to make use of holidays or work part-time in order to balance work and caring duties (van der Woude et al. 2016).

It is much more difficult to decide on the length and the conditions of care leave to make it an efficient element of familialistic policies as the time of care and its intensity is difficult to predict in case of the elderly. Taking into account growing needs for eldercare as well as labour market participation of women, it is important to develop regular entitlements for carers to take short-time paid leave as a minimum. European Commission recommends the introduction of short-term (5 days per year) leave paid at least at sick pay level (European

Commission 2017). Taking into account the four analysed countries, only in Portugal these recommendations have not been put in practice yet.

Cash Benefits

The role of cash benefits is twofold. First, they compensate for extra costs of care required by a dependent person. Second, they replace lost earnings due to care. They might be directly paid to carers or to the dependent person. The person in need of care may use it to support care given by a family member or to pay for care services available on the market. Cash support paid to caregivers is a way of recognising their important social role. Benefits might be provided as a remuneration to family caregivers who are formally employed or might be provided as a means-tested allowance.

Taking into account the four analysed countries cash benefits paid to informal carers are available in Poland (based on state regulation) and with some limitations—in the Netherlands and in Sweden (based on municipalities' regulations). In Poland there are allowances for carers who cannot participate in the labour market due to care given to a disabled adult. The amount of the allowance equals approximately 20% of the minimum wage in Poland and is not sufficient to compensate for the lost earnings. In the Netherlands, generally there are no allowances directly paid to informal carers. The only exception is the personal budget scheme (PBG) within which both professional and informal care can be financed. In practice, the eligibility criteria to pay for informal care within PBG are unclear and in some municipalities almost impossible to be met (van der Woude et al. 2016). In Sweden carers' cash benefits are also provided by some municipalities. The rule is to provide services before cash. Caregivers can receive carers allowance within which municipality employs family member for giving care. Attractiveness of this benefit is limited by selective and discretionary granting restricted to a special situation of a person in need of care (Schön and Johansson 2016).

In the four analysed countries cash benefits paid to a dependent person are available, but they have different characteristics. In Poland cash benefits for a dependent person (nursing supplement financed by social insurance or nursing allowance financed by central budget) are paid to everyone who is 75 or over and in case of younger adults—for those who are disabled. The eligibility criteria are not restricted, but the amount of benefit is relatively low—it is not sufficient to cover extra costs of care (used rather to help the ends meet in the home budget). In Portugal there is only a dependency supplement for the disabled with low income (eligibility is related to the level of dependency). In the Netherlands cash benefits policy depends to a large extent on municipalities. Some cash benefits to pay for care services (e.g. travel costs, unemployment benefit) are available, but the priority is to stay in employment using all flexible arrangement accessible to combine work and care. In Sweden the attendance allowance is available for the disabled who are less than 65 and need assistance for more than 20 hours a week. Attendance allowance might be also paid in the form of municipal cash benefit. In this case the benefit is paid to the dependent person to pay a family member for their help.

(De)Familialisation of Care for the Elderly

Family is a backbone of all long-term care systems in Europe. The way it is supported by public policies differ among the four analysed countries. While in Sweden and in the Netherlands the trend of refamilialisation has been observed, which means that after some defamilialistic trends, family has become to be more openly supported. In Poland and in Portugal the need to support family who has always been the main provider of care has been more pronounced.

It is difficult to find strong defamilialising policies as the development of institutional care has not been a priority in any of the analysed countries. In Sweden home help has been the most pronounced instrument of strengthening the family as a care provider, but also unburdening it to some extent from caring responsibilities. If necessary, cash for care is also available still with services being a priority. Time rights for cares in a form of paid care leaves are accessible and some flexibility in arranging work is also observed. This leads to the conclusion that familialism in Sweden in case of elderly care is optional.

The Netherlands lacks cash for care benefits. Short-term care leave is paid and long-term care leave is unpaid and does not include all social insurance for the carer. The Dutch LTC system is developed with an increasing role of municipality policies. Carers have access to information and training at the local level. Family care is supported in more discretionary way by employers or via social agreements. The most important help to perform care duties and work is related to high usage of part-time work. Caring function of the family is not explicitly enforced. Thus public policies in terms of care for the elderly have more features of implicit familialism.

Portugal has recently started the development of LTC system. Still the coverage rate is very low and formal care services are not sufficient. Short-term care leave is unpaid and long-term care is not available. Cash benefits are only available for the most fragile with the lowest levels of income. Family is not sufficiently supported, but having in mind recent changes and the development of home care, day care and institutional help within the framework of RNCCI, we can say that implicit familialism is slowly becoming more explicit.

Like Portugal, Poland lacks the developed LTC systems and there are long waiting lists to receive care in institutions by the most fragile elderly. Benefits provided to the carer and to the elderly are often considered insufficient. Home help is not developed. Short-term care leave is paid, but long-term leave is not available. Flexibility of work arrangements is not very high and carers do not have any special entitlements in this field. Familialism represented by this type of policies is implicit.

Discussion

Our analysis shows that the familialistic orientation of policies persists in four discussed countries. Implicit familialism is clearly visible in the Dutch and Portuguese system of childcare policies, where there is a huge childcare gap and paid care leaves are short. Parents with a limited support from the state need to organise care for their children. The Dutch parents fill the childcare gap with the instruments available on the market, as well as thanks to combing parenthood with part-time employment. In Poland, we can observe a shift from implicit familialism to explicit familialism, which is connected with recent reforms that prolonged parental leave to 52 weeks and introduced cash benefits. Polish parents have limited possibilities to organise care for children under three outside the family. Only Sweden provides various instruments supporting parents in providing care, therefore the Swedish system is characterised as optional familialism. Similarly in policies aimed at care for the elderly implicit familialism dominates. It is visible in the Dutch and Polish systems, the Portuguese system can be described as a system in transition from implicit to explicit familialism. And only Sweden follows the path of optional familialism. All of these show that even though the European welfare states try to answer the problem of unmet care needs, they still rely on families. Family members, usually women, are seen as the main providers of care in the family and the role of the state is limited to support them.

The above analysis, as well as the application of the concept of familialism to describe the family policy systems, has limitations. First, it must be noted that we consider only three types of instruments. In case of time rights we concentrate on care leaves, but in fact it would be also beneficial to look broader on time rights and include in the analysis flexible working arrangements, such as flexible working time, which gives employees possibilities to adjust working time schedule to their needs and flexible working hours, which allow for adjusting the number of working hours per week. This is an important element of the contemporary welfare state system that helps individuals to combine different obligations resulting from paid work and family life (see: Chung and van der Lippe 2020). Secondly, the concept of familialism has limited possibilities to recognise gender inequalities in the family life, since it focuses on a family as an unit of analysis consequently missing the perspective of an individual. To recognise this dimension, it is better to use the concept of genderisation (discussed in Chapter 9 in this book). This issue is connected with a fact that the concept does not help to acknowledge family diversities and it mostly fits to analyse the situation of nuclear families with heterosexual couples and their biological children. But keeping in mind these limitations, we still argue that the concept is useful to describe the prevailing approach of the European welfare states to a family as a social institution. The European welfare states define their role in terms of supporting families that remain the main providers of care to their members. Additionally, the concept can be used in a more flexible way that allows to assess the impact on family of particular instruments of various public policies.

Acknowledgements The research conducted by Katarzyna Suwada was financed by the National Science Centre of Poland, grant Sonata 10 no UMO-2015/19/D/HS6/02338.

NOTE

1. Data on employment rates come from Eurostat database, available at: https://ec.europa.eu/eurostat/data/database (accessed: 1-09-2020), whereas data on fertility rates from the World Bank database, available at: https://data.worldbank.org (accessed: 1-09-2020).

REFERENCES

Bouget, Denis, Slavina Spasova, and Bart Vanhercke. 2016. *Work-Life Balance Measures for Persons of Working Age with Dependent Relatives in Europe. A Study of National Policies.* Brussels: European Commission.

Chung, Heejung, and Tanja van der Lippe. 2020. "Flexible Working, Work–Life Balance, and Gender Equality: Introduction." *Social Indicators Research* 151: 365–381. https://doi.org/10.1007/s11205-018-2025-x.

Daly, Mary, and Jane Lewis. 2000. "The Concept of Social Care and the Analysis of Contemporary Welfare States." *The British Journal of Sociology* 51 (2): 281–298. https://doi.org/10.1111/j.1468-4446.2000.00281.x.

European Commission. 2017. *Proposal for a Directive of the European Parliament and of the Council on Work-Life Balance for Parents and Carers and Repealing.* Brussels: Council Directive 2010/18/EU.

European Commission/EACEA/Eurydice. 2019. *Key Data on Early Childhood Education and Care in Europe—2019 Edition.* Eurydice Report. Luxembourg: Publications Office of the European Union.

Furmańska-Maruszak, Agnieszka, and Susanne Heeger-Hertter. 2019. "Combining Paid Work and Eldercare in The Netherlands in the Practice of Selected Dutch Organizations." *Olsztyn Economic Journal* 14 (3): 255–270.

Gauthier, Anne H. 1999. "Historical Trends in State Support for Families in Europe (Post-1945)." *Children and Youth Services Review*, Children and Family Policy in Europe 21 (11): 937–965. https://doi.org/10.1016/S0190-7409(99)00062-6.

Giuliani, Giuliana, and Ann Zofie Duvander. 2017. "Cash-for-Care Policy in Sweden: An Appraisal of Its Consequences on Female Employment: Cash-for-Care Policy in Sweden." *International Journal of Social Welfare* 26 (1): 49–62. https://doi.org/10.1111/ijsw.12229.

Ingólfsdóttir, Edda Sigurbjörg, and Ingólfur V. Gíslason. 2016. "Gendered Solutions to the Care Gap Issue in Iceland." *NORA: Nordic Journal of Women's Studies* 24 (4): 220–233. https://doi.org/10.1080/08038740.2016.1241826.

Koslowski, Alison, Sonja Blum, Ivana Dobrotić, Alexandra Macht, and Peter Moss, eds. 2019. "International Review of Leave Policies and Research." Available at: https://www.leavenetwork.org/annual-review-reports/review-2020/.

Leitner, Sigrid. 2003. "Varieties of Familialism: The Caring Function of the Family in Comparative Perspective." *European Societies* 5 (4): 353–375. https://doi.org/10.1080/1461669032000127642.

Lippe, Tanja van der, Annet Jager, and Yvonne Kops. 2006. "Combination Pressure: The Paid Work: Family Balance of Men and Women in European Countries." *Acta Sociologica* 49 (3): 303–319. https://doi.org/10.1177/0001699306067711.

Lister, Ruth. 1994. "'She Has Other Duties'—Women, Citizenship and Social Security." In *Social Security and Social Change: New Challenges to the Beveridge Model*, edited by Sally Baldwin and Jane Falkingham, 31–44. London and New York, NY: Harvester Wheatsheaf.

Lopes, Alexandra. 2017. "Long-Term Care in Portugal. Quasi-Privatisation of a Dual System of Care." In *Long-Term Care for the Elderly in Europe. Development and Prospects*, edited by Bent Greve, 59–74. London: Routledge.

Lopes, Hugo, Céu Mateus, and Cristina Hernández-Quevedo. 2018. "Ten Years After the Creation of the Portuguese National Network for Long-Term Care in 2006: Achievements and Challenges." *Health Policy* 122 (3): 210–216. https://doi.org/10.1016/j.healthpol.2018.01.001.

Mahon, Rianne. 2002. "Child Care: Toward What Kind of 'Social Europe'?" *Social Politics: International Studies in Gender, State & Society* 9 (3): 343–379. https://doi.org/10.1093/sp/9.3.343.

OECD. 2019. *Health at a Glance 2019: OECD Indicators*. Paris: OECD Publishing, https://doi.org/10.1787/4dd50c09-en.

OECD/European Commission. 2013. *A Good Life in Old Age? Monitoring and Improving Quality in Long-Term Care*. OECD Health Policy Studies. Paris: OECD Publishing

Oláh, Livia, and Susanne Fahlén. 2013. "Introduction: Aspirations and Uncertainties. Childbearing Choices and Work-Life Realities in Europe." In *Childbearing, Women's Employment and Work-Life Balance Policies in Contemporary Europe*, edited by Livia Oláh and Ewa Frątczak, 1–27. Basingstoke: Palgrave Macmillan.

Saraceno, Chiara. 2016. "Varieties of Familialism: Comparing Four Southern European and East Asian Welfare Regimes." *Journal of European Social Policy* 26 (4): 314–326. https://doi.org/10.1177/0958928716657275.

Saxonberg, Steven, Hana Hašková, and Jiří Mudrák. 2012. *The Development of Czech Childcare Policies*. Praha: SOCIOLOGICKÉ NAKLADATELSTVÍ (SLON).

Scheiwe, Kirsten, and Harry Willekens. 2009. "Introduction: Path-Dependencies and Change in Child-Care and Preschool Institutions in Europe—Historical and Institutional Perspectives." In *Childcare and Preschool Development in Europe: Institutional Perspectives*, edited by Kirsten Scheiwe and Harry Willekens, 1–22. London: Palgrave Macmillan UK.

Schön, Pär, and Lennarth Johansson. 2016. *ESPN Thematic Report on Work-Life Balance Measures for Persons of Working Age with Dependent Relatives*. Sweden, Brussels: European Commission.

Szelewa, Dorota. 2017. "From Implicit to Explicit Familialism: Post-1989 Family Policy Reforms in Poland." In *Gender and Family in European Economic Policy*, edited by Diana Auth, Jutta Hergenhan, and Barbara Holland-Cunz, 129–251. Cham: Palgrave Macmillan.

Thrasher Gregory R., Keith Zabel, Kevin T. Wynne, and Boris Baltes. 2016. "The Importance of Workplace Motives in Understanding Work-Family Issues for Older

Workers." *Work, Ageing and Retirement* 2 (1): 1–11. https://doi.org/10.1093/workar/wav021.

van der Woude, Froukje, Katrien de Vaan, and Marieke Blommesteijn. 2016. *ESPN Thematic Report on Work-Life Balance Measures for Persons of Working Age with Dependent Relatives. The Netherlands*. Brussels: European Commission.

CHAPTER 11

Who Benefits from Parental Leave Policies? A Comparison Between Nordic and Southern European Countries

Ann-Zofie Duvander and Elisabetta Ruspini

INTRODUCTION

Parental leave is generally understood to be a care measure, intended to give both mothers and fathers the opportunity to spend time caring for a young child, sometimes in addition to periods of maternity or paternity leave (Addati et al. 2014; Koslowski et al. 2020). Parental leave is commonly a longer period of leave where the parents decide themselves how to share it. In addition to other forms of leave, such as leave to care for sick children or other adult family members, it constitutes a major policy component for promoting work-life balance for working parents with caring responsibilities (Hagqvist et al. 2017). In this chapter we ask the fundamental question of which groups of parents benefit from various set-ups of parental leave and whether there are different beneficiaries in different types of welfare states. To pursue these questions, we compare the parental leave set-up in the Nordic and Southern European clusters.

A.-Z. Duvander
Stockholm University, Stockholm, Sweden

Mid University, Östersund, Sweden

A.-Z. Duvander
e-mail: ann-zofie.duvander@sociology.su.se

E. Ruspini (✉)
Department of Sociology and Social Research, University of Milano-Bicocca, Milan, Italy
e-mail: elisabetta.ruspini@unimib.it

© The Author(s), under exclusive license to Springer Nature Switzerland AG 2021
A.-M. Castrén et al. (eds.), *The Palgrave Handbook of Family Sociology in Europe*, https://doi.org/10.1007/978-3-030-73306-3_11

Although the right to parental leave has been established in most countries, large differences continue to exist, also between EU member states (Koslowski et al. 2020; Van Belle 2016; Stewart and Janta 2018). There is considerable variation in terms of eligibility, payment, leave length, and possible flexibility in usage. There are also significant variations in terms of transferability between parents and whether parental leave is a family or individual right (Koslowski et al. 2020). The availability to potential carers is also dependent on criteria such as whether a person is in paid work, if he/she is an employee or self-employed, the sector in which the person works, the length of service, whether he/she is living with the child or not, and sometimes citizenship. Parental leave might also not be accessible to same-sex couples or migrants (EIGE 2020). Some countries aim for a gender-neutral leave policy (e.g. Sweden), with all available leave designated as parental leave, while other have leave-systems that identify the mother as primary carer, with a long period of maternity leave before the parental leave (e.g. Italy) (EIGE 2020).

Regular monitoring of parental leave policies by the International Network on Leave Policies and Research shows that policies are constantly developing (see leavenetwork.org). Indeed, changes in the labour market, such as the spread of atypical work (where migrants are over-represented), have increased concerns about parents' access to leave, especially in cases where it is based on definitions of traditional standard employment. Moreover, evolving gender roles and family forms call for coverage and measures for fathers, single parents, same-sex couples, cohabiting couples, and adoptive parents.

According to Duvander et al. (2005, 4–5), parental leave has the potential to structure the gender distribution of paid and unpaid work, childbearing decisions, and poverty risks of families. These outcomes are related to whether such policies support an earner-carer family or whether they support more traditional family types. Even if such divisions between models of family policy are becoming blurred over time and increasingly countries would be defined as mixed models, the set-up of parental leave indicates the possibility to combine work and family for women and men, for well-established and less well-established parents, and for parents living in different family types. Parental leave will thus obviously influence the chances of achieving work-life balance and what form such balance can take.

The key role played by parental leave in the work-life balance process is reaffirmed by the EU Directive on Work-Life Balance for Parents and Carers (Directive 2019/1158). Work-life balance is today a significant challenge. Balancing work and family life is at the forefront of multiple transformations in contemporary societies that have increased the demands from the family and work domains (European Union 2019): population ageing, the increasing number of single parent families, rising levels of female employment and women's career opportunities (IPPR 2015). The changing nature of work, with the expansion of atypical forms of employment poses further challenges: flexible working time brings about both work intensification and work extensification (Lu 2009). For example, job calls, online meetings, or events organised during the parental leave could have negative consequences on family life and childcare (Brandth and Kvande 2019; Duvander et al. 2017). Work-life balance is also a key policy issue and has been given greater priority on the policy agenda of many OECD countries and of the European Union (Fagnani 2011; European Union 2019).

Given these premises, the chapter describes parental leave in the two clusters, considering basic similarities but also differences. Different policy dimensions are taken into account: which groups benefit from various policy characteristics, eligibility for parental leave, and the possibility to achieve work-life balance (WLB) for various groups. We conclude with a discussion of the main characteristics of parental leave in the two clusters.

Nordic Countries

Similar Basis?

The Nordic countries are most often included in the same welfare cluster and defined as generous welfare states with a social democratic orientation. The Nordics have been described as defamilialised as a lot of services and economic transfers are provided so as to solve the work-family conflict. To facilitate the combination of work and family life is also a major aim of the family policy. Indeed women's labour force participation is high in the Nordic countries, also for mothers of young children, a situation often connected to the generous family policy including parental leave and childcare (Oláh 2011). Female labour force participation ranges between 70 (Finland) and 85% (Iceland), which is considerably higher than the European average of around 64%. Another often mentioned, and both investigated and debated outcome, is the relatively high fertility, albeit with variations over time and across countries (Duvander et al. 2019; Oláh 2011; Neyer 2011).

A well-known characteristic of the Nordic cluster is the focus on gender equality, not least expressed through fathers' increased participation in childcare. Fathers' involvement in childcare is sometimes connected to the relatively high fertility with the argument that gender equality will lead to a balanced fertility close to replacement level (Goldscheider et al. 2015). Icelandic fathers are using the largest share of the parental leave, 30% in 2017, closely followed by 29% in Sweden and 20% in Norway, while fathers' take-up rates are lower in Finland and Denmark (less than 11% of the leave) (Nordic Statistics Database). Shared parental responsibility for childcare and economic child support has been at the core of the Nordic development in the last decades (Leira 2006). By now all countries except Denmark have quotas reserved to both the father and the mother, which has been found to increase the sharing of leave (Duvander and Johansson 2012; Cools et al. 2015).

Differences Between the Nordics?

Parental leave provided to both parents is a dominant part of the Nordic family policy and has a relatively long history. It was in all the countries introduced in the 1970s or beginning of the 1980s and the length today is about a year in all countries (except Iceland with 9 months leave). With the exception of the late-comer Iceland the length has also been extended over time (see leavenetwork.org or summary in Duvander et al. 2019). In some countries the parental leave replaced the earlier maternity leave (e.g. Sweden) while in others it was added on to the maternity leave (e.g. Finland), but over time the parental leave has been made available to two parents. The wage replacement during leave is relatively generous ranging from full replacement to about 80% of the income.

However, the variation between the Nordic countries also emerges. For example, a comparison of the parental leave in 19 countries placed Norway and Finland in a choice-oriented cluster while Denmark, Iceland, and Sweden were placed in a cluster with more focus on gender equality (Wall 2007). Such categorisation is likely to change over time when today Denmark is the only Nordic country without a fathers' quota and Iceland the country with largest care gaps between parental leave and available public childcare (Eydal and Rostgaard 2011). The percentage of all children attending public childcare at early age also varies largely between the Nordic countries. In the ages 0–2 years, 66% of Danish children attend public childcare, 59% of Icelandic children, 56% of Swedish children, 55% of Norwegian children but only 28% of Finnish children (Nordic Statistics database, numbers from 2014). The share of children in public childcare is largely dependent on the length of the parental leave and also on flexibility options. In Denmark the parental leave together with the maternity leave is just under one year, it is paid at 100% of previous income and it is very flexible in that it can be used in blocs, can be used part-time, can be combined with work and used until the child is 9 years old (Koslowski et al. 2020).

In Finland the leave is somewhat shorter at 9.5 months with somewhat lower payment (depending on period between 70 and 90% of earlier income). There is some flexibility in when fathers can use their leave but most of the leave (including the maternity leave) has to be used from when the child is born. However, the parental leave in Finland is combined, in a majority of families, with a home care allowance which extends the period at home, thus reducing children's participation in public childcare and women's labour force participation.

In Iceland the leave is shorter: 9 months at 80% of earlier income. The parental leave was dramatically reformed in the beginning of the 2000s: a 3 + 3 + 3 months system was introduced where each parent (father and mother) was entitled to 3 months and 3 months could be shared between them. There is some flexibility in use, but leave can only be used during the first two years of the child's life.

In Norway the leave is approximately one year, but length depends on the chosen level of payment between 100 and 80% of earlier income. Norway was the first country to introduce a quota for fathers and this quota is today 3.5 months (2019). The leave has to be used within three years and there is some flexibility in how it can be combined with work or used part-time.

In Sweden the leave is the longest: 16 months, 13 of which are paid at 78% of earlier income. Perhaps the most flexible system is also found in Sweden where 4/5 of the leave can be used up to the child is 4 years old and the rest up to the child is 12 years old. Leave can partly be used for fathers and mothers together and it is common to extend leave also with unpaid leave, leading to large variations in leave patterns (Duvander and Viklund 2019).

Thus, among the Nordic countries there are quite some variation where Sweden most clearly favours earner-carer families, and Finland so far has taken the route of a 1.5 earner model. Norway has developed towards earner-carer over time, while Iceland had the most dramatic shift towards a gender equal system. Denmark is, as mentioned, most resistant to quotas and gender equality measures but has strong family policy regarding public childcare and women do not work to a lesser extent than in the other Nordic countries.

Despite the difference in length and compensation, in all the Nordic countries the set-up is aimed to support a life course where both women and men get established on the labour market first, and then enter parenthood.

Challenges, for Whom Is Work-Life Balance Facilitated?

Family policy in the Nordics aims at a shared parental responsibility between parents and this is today often phrased as a gender-neutral policy. The tendency towards gender-neutral policy builds on an attempt not to support traditional gender roles and to be inclusive also for same-sex parents, but may hide gender differences in take-up, responsibility, and economic situation. For example, in all countries women still take more parental leave, work more part-time, and have lower income during the childrearing years compared to men. Regarding the gendered income and wage development during the childrearing years there is little sign of progress (Angelov et al. 2016). Gender inequalities during the childbearing and childrearing years have major impact for the rest of the life course, not least at older ages. As an example, women's pensions in Sweden are only 70% of men's pensions (Inspectorate for the Social Insurance 2017b). Thus differences by gender still remain in all Nordic countries and it seems that in the last years men are making progress in their entry into the realms of childcare, while women's economic progress has halted. Men's increased childcare is often connected to the policy scheme where the quotas for fathers seem to be the most efficient tool in increasing their share of leave (Duvander et al. 2019).

The remaining gender differences in multiple areas of society are also indicated in that family policy is not available to all groups to the same extent. Eligibility for parental leave is mainly based on residence and on the parents' prior individual earnings. However, Norwegian fathers are partly dependent on mothers' eligibility through her earnings. In Finland, fathers have until very recently (2017) had to share residence with the mother in order to use the leave. In Iceland and Sweden, fathers' rights are more protected; in Sweden the only requirement for leave take-up is custody over the child, while in Iceland only an agreement with the custodian parent is needed. In Denmark, the father should be in a recognised partnership with the other parent. In all countries, same-sex parents are treated in the same way as other parents, rights being based on legal parenthood status.

The leave can in all countries be shared between the two parents and, with the above-mentioned exceptions, it is thus available to two parents. The reserved parts in the system to each parent will make sure that the entitled parent will take part of the leave, else it is forsaken. Such construction may have beneficial outcomes for gender equality, foremost in sharing the parental leave days but also long term (Duvander and Johansson 2019). But there is less consideration of single parents at the early stages in a child's life. A care gap between when the leave is ended and a guaranteed place in public childcare is created by the reserved months in some of the countries, as the synchronising of the parental leave and public childcare is based on two parents using the leave. Another example is that less leave is used after an early parental separation in Sweden, clearly disadvantaging children of divorced and single parents (Inspectorate for the Social Insurance 2017a). It seems that the gender-neutral and inclusive rights to both parents are prioritised and single parents become a category forgotten in the policy legislation. Another example comes from Iceland where the original aim of parental leave to ensure childcare from *fathers and mothers* was in 2006 changed to *both parents*, thus always assuming two parents (Arnalds et al. 2013).

Another group to make note of are those who have not worked before becoming parents and therefore either receive a low flat rate benefit or a lump sum. These parents are economically disadvantaged and may either have to try hard to find a job early in the child's life, which may be difficult, or will run the risk of being long-term economically marginalised. In most cases that mothers are not active on the labour market, they do the caring and use most of the parental leave. Migrant families are highly overrepresented among those not having worked in Sweden before having children and their use of leave is both less flexible and less shared between parents (Mussino and Duvander 2016). Among migrant fathers the lack of labour market attachment is a major deterrent to using parental leave (Tervola et al. 2017).

The question is then whether the family policy in the Nordic countries will lead to more work-life balance. In a cross country comparison with 22 countries it seems that women, but particularly men, in countries who have promoted gender equality are more sensitive to an unfair division of housework for their experience of work-life conflict (Öun 2013). Studies based on the International Social Survey Programme (ISSP) in 2012 show clear difference in attitudes to the family-work dilemma and these correlate with country policy set-ups (Valarino et al. 2018; Edlund and Öun 2016).

Part-time work may be a way to reduce work family conflict and such rights exist in the Nordic countries for parents of preschool children. However such temporary reduced working hours is mainly used by women and even if correlated with less work family conflict it is also correlated with fears of negative repercussions at the workplace (Grönlund and Öun 2018). In Norway 30% of women aged 25–49 work part-time, compared to 11% of men in the same age group. The numbers are very similar in Denmark, Iceland, and Sweden but lower in Finland where 17% of women aged 25–49 work part-time and only 6% of men (Nordic Statistics Database, numbers from, 2017). The Nordic example thus indicates that work-life balance still and strongly has to be discussed with an explicit gender perspective.

Southern European Countries

Similarities and Some Differences

Southern European countries (Greece, Italy, Spain, Portugal) form a peculiar cluster in the universe of welfare regimes. The four countries all had past experiences of authoritarianism and totalitarian dictatorship and have suffered from economic and industrial delays in the processes of modernisation (early industrialised areas in Italy and Spain constitute an exception) (Moreno 2000). Moreover, in these countries there is a distinctive welfare mix: state/family/church/charity (Rhodes 1996; Petmesidou 1996; Gal 2010). In the welfare state literature this country cluster has been defined as a familialistic welfare regime type (Olah 2015). Familialism describes the centrality of the family unit and stresses the obligations and support that family members owe to both nuclear and extended kin (e.g. Petmesidou 1996; Papadopolous 1998). The specific orientation taken by familialism has been called 'familialism by default' or 'unsupported familialism', a term that expresses the lack of public interventions and services (Saraceno 2016). Southern European policy models have indeed developed on the existence of a widespread support network provided by the family along gender lines (Santos 1994; Naldini 2003). In the Southern European cluster, defamilialisation and demotherisation of care work are low (Mathieu 2016). Traditional gender ideologies and a strong tradition of male breadwinners are among the explanatory factors for both the low fertility rates and the gender gap in employment. In all Southern European countries women, compared to men, work more part-time, have lower incomes, and are less likely to hold high-level jobs. Especially in Greece, Italy, and Spain women's employment lags behind the EU average. However, women's labour market participation is growing, albeit at different speeds, especially among the younger generations. The increase in women's employment has generated a growing demand for paid care (Bouget et al.

2017). The number of dual-career couples is increasing too, a more effective trend in Spain and Portugal than in Italy and Greece (Karamessini 2008; Moreno 2008; Naldini and Jurado Guerrero 2013). Thus, Southern European countries are challenged by the need to articulate transitions towards the dual-earner model, despite heterogeneous socioeconomic situations, traditional gender ideologies, cultural resistance to social change, and a context of economic crisis.

Parental Leave in the Southern European Country Cluster

Southern European countries show, at the same time, relevant differences from the Nordic countries but also a trend towards recognition of the growing diversity of work-life balance needs for working parents (Escobedo and Wall 2015; EU 2019; Koslowski et al. 2020). On the one hand, contrary to what happens in the Nordic country cluster, parental leave to both parents is not a dominant part of the policy systems, the wage replacement during leave cannot be considered as satisfactory, and parental-leave eligibility is still low due to restrictive criteria regarding being in employment, the length of time in current work or whether an individual is in a heterosexual or same-sex partnership (EIGE 2020). A further obstacle to an effective implementation of WLB policies seems to be the still low availability of public early childhood education and care services (Pandolfini 2015). On the other hand, longer periods of paid leave were implemented, as well as public incentives to encourage fathers' involvement in childcare (Crespi and Ruspini 2016). The availability of paid parental leave for same-sex parents is also growing.

In Greece, flexible working arrangements are still limited and parental leave arrangements are unequal between public and private sector (Koukoulis-Spiliotopoulos 2015) and childcare enrolment rates are among the lowest in the EU. However, mandatory enrolment of four-year-olds in kindergarten is being gradually implemented and should apply by 2021 (European Commission 2019—Country Report Greece, 29). Parental leave is added on to 2–3 months of paid maternity leave after the child is born. In the private sector, parental leave is unpaid and the total duration is up to four months per child for each parent. In the public sector, length of leave is up to five years per parent but unpaid, with the exception of parents of three or more children for whom three months of parental leave are fully paid. Parental leave may be taken until the child's sixth birthday. If both parents work for the same private employer, they cannot simultaneously go on leave. It is the mother who overwhelmingly uses leave rights in cases both parents are eligible (Hatzivarnava-Kazassi and Karamessini 2020).

In Italy measures to promote equal opportunities and a work-life balance are fragmented and limited in scope. This negatively affects women's participation in the labour market. Childcare and long-term care services are still underdeveloped, especially in Southern Italy: the share of children under three years of age in formal early childhood education at 29% (2017) is well below the EU average (European Commission 2019—Country Report Italy, 70). In addition to a five months maternity leave, the length of parental leave is six months per parent but the maximum total length of leave per family is ten months. The leave is paid at 30% of earnings when it is taken for a child under six years of age; unpaid if taken when a child is six to twelve years of age. Italy has introduced incentives to encourage fathers to use parental leave. If the father takes at least three months of leave, he can extend his leave to seven months and the total length of leave that can be used by both parents is raised to 11 months. A single parent may take ten months of leave. A good degree of flexibility is provided. Parents can be on leave at the same time (Addabbo et al. 2020).

Portugal and Spain have a more consistent development in their gender-equality orientation and in the expansion of care for children under age three. Spain, in the last two decades, has followed a defamilialisation trend, taking a new direction away from the family/kinship model and towards a dual-earner family model (Valiente 2010; Naldini and Jurado Guerrero 2013). However, compared to Portugal, Spain has a less generous system, offering flexible unpaid part-time parental leave during childhood instead of extending paid parental leave; it also has less extended hours and less subsidised childcare services. In Spain, existing parental leave is an unpaid individual right during the child's first three years. During the first year, return to the same job position is protected; after the first year, job protection is restricted to a job of the same category. The use of unpaid parental leave is fairly low, especially among fathers: fathers made up 8.7% of users in 2018 (Meil et al. 2020). In addition to the unpaid leave there are 16 weeks maternity and 12 weeks paternity leave with full replacement.

Portugal has promoted gender equality and support for dual earner parents: the outcome of this commitment is the high rates of full-time dual-earners, and the high maternal employment rates (Escobedo and Wall 2015). However, even if the coverage of full-time childcare is high, a mismatch between supply and demand occurs in some areas, particularly the largest cities (European Commission 2019—Country Report Portugal, 43). Since 2009, maternity, paternity, and parental leave in Portugal is called initial parental leave, parental leave reserved to the father and additional parental leave. The length of initial parental leave is 4–5 months depending on replacement level, with one month bonus if shared between parents. Parental leave reserved to fathers is one month mandatory leave with full replacement. Additional parental leave is an unpaid leave of three months per parent (that can be paid at 25% of average earnings in some specific cases). Leave may be used up to the child's sixth birthday. Unpaid parental leave can be taken by both parents at the same time; but paid leave can only be taken by one parent at a time. Take-up of additional parental leave is low: it represents about 10.4% of all parental leaves (Wall et al. 2020).

Open Challenges: Who Takes Up, Who Benefits and Who Doesn't

In Southern European countries, there is a tendency to lower take-up rates of parental leave, both among mothers and fathers. In these countries, the proportion of eligible women who takes parental leave is smaller than in the Nordic countries, where most women are employed (Anxo et al. 2007), and the share of fathers taking parental leave remains at low levels despite some partial growth (especially in Portugal and Italy) (Eurofound 2019). This can be explained by various factors. First of all, gender ideologies maintain the traditional gendered division of work. A second factor is that parental leave is typically badly compensated: in Greece, parental leave is mainly unpaid. Italy has one of the lowest compensation ratios in Europe: 30% of basic remuneration until the child's sixth birthday (Eurofound 2019; Addabbo et al. 2020). In Spain, parental leave is unpaid: only two out of 17 regions provide flat-rate benefits to increase the use (Meil et al. 2020). In Portugal, additional parental leave is unpaid, except if taken immediately after initial parental leave, or after the other parent has taken additional parental leave. In these cases, it is paid at 25% of average earnings (Wall et al. 2020).

A third factor to be taken into account is that parental leaves in Southern European countries are not available to all parents as eligibility depends on parents' position in paid work at the beginning of the leave. In Greece, the leave is granted to all employees in the private sector who have completed one year's employment with their present employer (Hatzivarnava-Kazassi and Karamessini 2020). In Italy it is granted to all employed parents, except domestic workers. Self-employed workers are generally entitled to three months, which can be taken only during the child's first year (Addabbo et al. 2020). In Portugal, initial parental leave is granted to all employees with a record of six months of social security contributions (Wall et al. 2020). In Spain, all employed parents are eligible but employees on temporary contracts can only claim leave that is shorter than their contract period. Unemployed and self-employed workers are not eligible (Meil et al. 2020). This raises concern about parents' access to leave, due to increased labour market flexibility and due to the strong connection between migration, precarious work experiences, and unemployment in most European countries.

A further factor is that Southern European countries welfare state provisions are still supplemented with relatively large support from kin networks, particularly in the area of care. There is great reliance on grandparents (especially grandmothers) providing extensive childcare (Mills et al. 2013; Janta 2014). The role of grandparents as informal carers is, in certain cases, institutionally supported. For example, in Portugal grandparents are entitled to take leave from work in order to substitute parents in caring for sick children (Wall et al. 2020). Achieving work-life balance can thus be particularly difficult for parents who lack informal (family) social support and for families whose members have non-standard work contracts or who work in sectors which have atypical working time arrangements (Santero and Naldini 2017).

In recent years, leave policies have overall become more generous and open to new family forms. Same-sex parents are now eligible to parental leave in Italy, Portugal, and Spain, but not yet in Greece (Janta and Picken 2019). Leave policies have also evolved in the direction of promoting the involvement of fathers in leave. However, in Greece fathers are entitled to a leave of two working days after the birth, and in Italy the length of mandatory paternity leave is seven days and a further one day of optional leave is available if the mother transfers part of her maternity leave.

Conclusions

Our aim in this chapter was to describe parental leave policies in two clusters of European countries, the Northern and the Southern ones, and to understand who benefits from the parental leave set-up in the different systems of family policy. We aimed to underline not only similarities within the two clusters but also internal differences.

To start with the Nordics, it is clear that family policy and strong legislation make the combination of work and family possible for the large part of the population. Parental leave is an important prerequisite to improve work-family balance, but such policy has to be accompanied with changes in attitudes towards work and family. Such changes may go hand in hand but also at different speeds. Even if there is some variation between the countries it seems that the overarching aim of policy to facilitate the combination of work and family is actually leading to a more homogeneous parental leave policy set-up, at least when we consider parents that are employed.

The Nordic cluster is also coherent in emphasising gender equality. The development towards gender-neutral policy is meant to be inclusive for both mothers and fathers and for parents in different types of families, but is also hiding gender differences in access to leave and possibilities to benefit from it. An example is the care gap that is created for single parents by reserving a large part of the leave to each parent; a policy aimed at advancing gender equality but which also works to the disadvantage of women who constitute a major part of single parents.

The Nordic countries have policies that can be used in its full flexibility mainly by co-residential parents who are dual earners, and the changing labour market conditions may be an example where reality does not match the policy aims. Thus parents with less stable positions and low earnings are not likely to be able to take advantage of the flexibility in the leave systems.

The Southern European cluster can be defined as a group of countries characterised by a reduced universalism, medium-low defamilialisation and demotherisation of care work. Important changes in legislation have recently been introduced, but they are limited. Family policy still depends to a large degree on family solidarity and is not clearly aiming at the distribution of care responsibilities between women and men. The main winners of this incomplete development are families with two main earners who can combine available family policy with informal care support, while families (and especially women) who work full-time but without a family network able to provide care (such as migrant women) have larger difficulties to reconcile work with their care responsibilities. The risk is that increasing care needs may force women to leave their jobs. Along the well-known heterogeneity in the Southern cluster (Ferrera 1996), the development of family policy is still far from offering universal, gender-equal parental leave policies. There is hetereogeneity also in the Northern cluster but parental leave is more coherently aiming towards a gender equal division of leave and may be seen as universal. The heterogeneity among the Nordic countries may be less visible as a general and inclusive policy is assumed while, in reality, it is less inclusive of for example unemployed parents, fathers not living with children, and mothers who are single parents.

Moreover, while fathers are increasingly benefitting from the leave in the Nordic cluster, father's involvement is in its initial phases in the Southern European cluster. As fathers have mainly advanced their use of leave at the same time as leave length has been extended in the Nordic countries, the same development has not necessarily meant that mothers are losing out on leave availability in the same process.

We thus conclude that even within very different family policy models it is still similar groups who are advantaged, in primis dual-earner families and, especially in the Southern European cluster, parents who can combine available family policy with informal care support coming from the family network. The groups with less access to the benefits of the leave are also similar in the two clusters, mostly single parents and parents with vulnerable employment. These are often parents with immigrant background and in atypical work. It thus seems that in both country clusters it is still the parents most in need of support that are left on the margins of parental leave policies. This is an unavoidable consequence of parental leave being connected to work and employment, but it is still worth pointing out that the groups receiving least support from parental leave are in most need of further support, provided through other dimensions of family policy and/or family solidarity.

References

Addabbo, Tindara, Valentina Cardinali, Sara Mazzucchelli, and Dino Giovannini. 2020. "Italy." In *International Review of Leave Policies and Research 2020*, edited by Alison Koslowski, Sonja Blum, Ivana Dobrotić, Gayle Kaufmann, and Peter Moss. Available at: https://www.leavenetwork.org/lp_and_r_reports/.

Addati, Laura, Naomi Cassirer, and Katherine Gilchrist. 2014. *Maternity and Paternity at Work: Law and Practice Across the World*. Geneva: International Labour Office (ILO).

Angelov, Nicolay, Per Johansson, and Erica Lindahl. 2016. "Parenthood and the Gender Gap in Pay." *Journal of Labor Economics* 34: 545–579.

Anxo, Domenique, Collette Fagan, Mark Smith, Marie-Therese Letablier, and Corrinne Perraudin. 2007. *Parental Leave in European Companies. Establishment Survey on Working Time 2004–2005*. Dublin: European Foundation for the Improvement of Living and Working Conditions.

Arnalds, Ásdís A., Guðný Björk Eydal, and Ingólfur V. Gislason. 2013. "Equal Rights to Paid Parental Leave and Caring Fathers—The Case of Iceland." *Icelandic Review of Politics and Administration* 9 (2): 323–343.

Bouget, Denis, Chiara Saraceno, and Slavina Spasova. 2017. "Towards New Work-Life Balance Policies for Those Caring for Dependent Relatives?" In *Social Policy in the European Union: State of Play*, edited by Bart Vanhercke, Sebastiano Sabato, and Denis Bouget, 155–179. Brussels: ETUI.

Brandth, Berit, and Elin Kvande. 2019. "Workplace Support of Fathers' Parental Leave Use in Norway." *Community, Work & Family* 22 (1): 43–57.

Cools, Sara, Jon H. Fiva, and Lars Johannessen Kirkeboen. 2015. "Causal Effects of Paternity Leave on Children and Parents." *Scandinavian Journal of Economics* 117 (3): 801–828.

Crespi, Isabella, and Elisabetta Ruspini, eds. 2016. *Balancing Work and Family in a Changing Society. The Fathers' Perspective*. Basingstoke: Palgrave Macmillan.

Duvander, Ann-Zofie, and Mats Johansson. 2012. "What Are the Effects of Reforms Promoting Fathers' Parental Leave Use?" *Journal of European Social Policy* 22 (3): 319–330.

Duvander, Ann-Zofie, and Mats Johansson. 2019. "Does Fathers' Care Spill Over? Evaluating Reforms in the Swedish Parental Leave Program." *Feminist Economics* 25 (2): 67–89.

Duvander, Ann-Zofie, and Ida Viklund. 2019. "How Long Is the Parental Leave and for Whom? An Analysis of Methodological and Policy Dimensions of Leave Length and Division in Sweden." *International Journal of Sociology and Social Policy* 40 (5/6): 479–494.

Duvander, Ann-Zofie, Tommy Ferrarini, and Sara Thalberg. 2005. *Swedish Parental Leave and Gender Equality. Achievements and Reform Challenges in a European Perspective*. Arbetsrapport/Institutet för Framtidsstudier.

Duvander, Ann-Zofie, Linda Haas, and Sara Thalberg. 2017. "Fathers on Leave Alone in Sweden: Toward More Equal Parenthood?" In *Comparative Perspectives on Work-Life Balance and Gender Equality. Fathers on Leave Alone*, edited by Margaret O'Brien and Karin Wall, 125–146. Cham: Springer Open.

Duvander, Ann-Zofie, Guðný Björk Eydal, Berit Brandth, Ingólfur V. Gíslason, Johanna Lammi-Taskula, and Tine Rostgaard. 2019. "Gender Equality: Parental Leave Design, Men's Participation and Evaluating Effects." In *Parental Leave and Beyond: Recent Development, Current Issues, and Future Directions*, edited by Peter Moss, Ann-Zofie Duvander, and Allison Koslowski. 187–204. Bristol: Policy Press.

Edlund, Jonas, and Ida Öun. 2016. "Who Should Work and Who Should Care?: Attitudes Towards the Desirable Division of Labour Between Mothers and Fathers in Five European Countries." *Acta Sociologica* 59 (2): 151–169.

EIGE-European Institute for Gender Equality. 2020. *Gender Equality Index 2019. Work-Life Balance. Parental-Leave Policies. Parental-Leave Conditions May Help or Hinder Gender Equality*. Available at: https://eige.europa.eu/publications/gender-equality-index-2019-report/parental-leave-policies.

Escobedo, Anna, and Karin Wall. 2015. "Leave Policies in Southern Europe: Continuities and Changes." *Community, Work & Family* 18 (2): 218–235.

Eurofound. 2019. *Parental and Paternity Leave—Uptake by Fathers*. Luxembourg: Publications Office of the European Union.
European Commission. 2019. *Country Report Greece, Italy, Portugal, Spain 2019*. European Semester: Assessment of progress on structural reforms, prevention and correction of macroeconomic imbalances, and results of in-depth reviews under Regulation (EU) No 1176/2011, Brussels.
European Union. 2019. *Work-Life Balance for All: Best Practice Examples from EU Member States*. Luxembourg: Publications Office of the European Union.
Eydal, Guðný Björk, and Tina Rostgaard. 2011. "Gender Equality Re-visited: Changes in Nordic Child-Care Policies in the 2000s." *Social Policy & Administration* 45 (2): 161–179.
Fagnani, Jeanne. 2011. *Work-Family Life Balance: Future Trends and Challenges*. In OCDE, *The Future of Families to 2030*, 119–188. OCDE Publishing.
Ferrera, Maurizio. 1996. "The 'Southern Model' of Welfare in Social Europe." *Journal of European Social Policy* 6 (1): 17–37.
Gal, John. 2010. "Is There an Extended Family of Mediterranean Welfare States?" *Journal of European Social Policy* 20 (4): 283–300.
Goldscheider, Frances, Eva Bernhardt, and Trude Lappegård. 2015. "The Gender Revolution: A Framework for Understanding Changing Family and Demographic Behaviour." *Population and Development Review* 41 (2): 207–239.
Grönlund, Anne, and Ida Öun. 2018. "Beyond the Mummy Track? Part-Time Rights, Gender, and Career-Family Dilemmas." *Nordic Journal of Working Life Studies* 8 (3): 177–198.
Hagqvist, Emma, Mikael Nordenmark, Gloria Pérez, Sara Trujillo Alemán, and Katja Gillander Gådin. 2017. "Parental Leave Policies and Time Use for Mothers and Fathers: A Case Study of Spain and Sweden." *Society, Health & Vulnerability* 8 (1).
Hatzivarnava-Kazassi, Evi, and Maria Karamessini. 2020. "Greece." In *International Review of Leave Policies and Research 2020*, edited by Alison Koslowski, Sonja Blum, Ivana Dobrotić, Gayle Kaufmann, and Peter Moss. Available at: https://www.leavenetwork.org/lp_and_r_reports/.
Inspectorate for the Social Insurance. 2017a. Föräldrapenninguttag före och efter en separation. En analys av hur separerade föräldrar använde föräldrapenning i jämförelse med de som inte separerade [Usage of Parental Benefit—Before and After Separation Between Parents]. Rapport 2017:11. Inspektionen för socialförsäkringen.
Inspectorate for the Social Insurance. 2017b. Kvinnors och mäns pensioner [Women's and Men's Pensions]. Rapport 2017:8. Inspektionen för socialförsäkringen.
IPPR. 2015. *Who's Breadwinning in Europe?* London: Institute for Public Policy Research.
Janta, Barbara. 2014. *Caring for Children in Europe. How Childcare, Parental Leave and Flexible Working Arrangements Interact in Europe*. Rand Europe. Available at: https://www.rand.org/pubs/research_reports/RR554.html.
Janta, Barbara, and Natalie Picken. 2019. *Leave Policies and Practice for Non-traditional Families*. Luxembourg: Publications Office of the European Union.
Karamessini, Maria. 2008. "Still a Distinctive Southern European Employment Model?" *Industrial Relations Journal* 39 (6): 510–531.
Koslowski, Alison, Sonja Blum, Ivana Dobrotić, Gayle Kaufmann, and Peter Moss, eds. 2020. "International Review of Leave Policies and Related Research 2020." Available at: https://www.leavenetwork.org/annual-review-reports/review-2020/.

Koukoulis-Spiliotopoulos, Sophia. 2015. "Greece." In: European Network of Legal Experts in the Field of Gender Equality, *The Implementation of Parental Leave Directive 2010/18 in 33 European Countries*, pp. 98–106.

Leira, Arlung. 2006. "Parenthood Change and Policy Reform in Scandinavia 1970s–2000s." In *Politicising Parenthood in Scandinavia*, edited by Anne Lise Ellingsaeter and Arlung Leira. Bristol: Policy Press.

Lu, Jinky L. 2009. "Effect of Work Intensification and Work Extensification on Women's Health in the Globalised Labour Market." *Journal of International Women's Studies* 10 (4): 111–126.

Mathieu, Sophie. 2016. "From the Defamilialization to the 'Demotherization' of Care Work. Social Politics." *International Studies in Gender, State & Society* 23 (4): 576–591.

Meil, Gerardo, Irene Lapuerta, and Anna Escobedo. 2020. "Spain." In *International Review of Leave Policies and Research 2020*, edited by Alison Koslowski, Sonja Blum, Ivana Dobrotić, Gayle Kaufmann, and Peter Moss. Available at: https://www.leavenetwork.org/lp_and_r_reports/.

Mills, Melinda, Patrick Präg, Flavia Tsang, Katia Begall, James Derbyshire, Laura Kohle, and Stijn Hoorens. 2013. *Use of Childcare Services in the EU Member States and Progress Towards the Barcelona Targets*. Short Statistical Report No. 1. Rand Europe. Available at: https://www.rand.org/pubs/research_reports/RR185.html.

Moreno, Luis. 2000. "The Spanish Development of Southern European Welfare." In *Survival of the European Welfare State*, edited by Stein Kuhnle, 146–165. London: Routledge.

Moreno, Luis. 2008. "The Nordic Path of Spain's Mediterranean Welfare." CES Working Paper No. 163.

Mussino, Eleonora, and Duvander, Ann-Zofie. 2016. "Use It or Save It? Migration Background and Parental Leave Uptake in Sweden." *European Journal of Population* 32 (2): 189–210.

Naldini, Manuela. 2003. *The Family in the Mediterranean Welfare States*. London: Frank Cass.

Naldini, Manuela, and Teresa Jurado Guerrero. 2013. "Family and Welfare State Reorientation in Spain and Inertia in Italy from a European Perspective." *Population Review* 52 (1): 43–61.

Neyer, Gerda. 2011. "Should Governments in Europe Be More Aggressive in Pushing for Gender Equality to Raise Fertility? The Second 'NO'." *Demographic Research* 24 (10): 225–250.

Oláh, Lidia Sz. 2011. "Should Governments in Europe Be More Aggressive in Pushing for Gender Equality to Raise Fertility? The Second 'YES'." *Demographic Research* 24 (9): 217–224.

Oláh, Lidia Sz. 2015. "Changing Families in the European Union: Trends and Policy Implications." Working Paper, Families And Societies Working Paper Series, n. 44.

Öun, Ida. 2013. "Is It Fair to Share? Perceptions of Fairness in the Division of Housework Among Couples in 22 Countries." *Social Justice Research* 26 (4): 400–421.

Pandolfini, Valeria. 2015. "Families, Care and Work in European Mediterranean Countries: Findings and Lessons from a Comparative Analysis of Work-Life Balance Policies." *Italian Sociological Review* 4 (19): 93–116.

Papadopoulos, Theo. 1998. "Greek Family Policy from a Comparative Perspective." In *Women, Work and the Family in Europe*, edited Eileen Drew, Ruth Emerek, and Evelyn Mahon, 47–57. London: Routledge.

Petmesidou, Maria. 1996. "Social Protection in Southern Europe: Trends and Prospects." *Journal of Area Studies* 9: 95–125.

Rhodes, Martin. 1996. "Southern European Welfare States: Identity, Problems and Prospects for Reform." *South European Society and Politics* 1 (3): 1–22.

Santero, Arianna, and Manuela Naldini. 2017. "Migrant Parents in Italy: Gendered Narratives on Work/Family Balance." *Journal of Family Studies* 26 (1): 126–141.

Santos, Boaventura de Sousa. 1994. "Etats, rapports salariaux et protection sociale à la semi-périphérie – cas du Portugal." *Peuples Méditerranéens* 66: 23–66.

Saraceno, Chiara. 2016. "Varieties of Familialism: Comparing Four Southern European and East Asian Welfare Regimes." *Journal of European Social Policy* 26 (4): 314–326.

Stewart, Katherine, and Barbara Janta. 2018. *Paternity and Parental Leave Policies Across the European Union. Assessment of Current Provision*. EU publications Directorate-General for Employment, Social Affairs and Inclusion.

Tervola, Jussi, Ann-Zofie Duvander, and Eleonora Mussino. 2017. "Promoting Parental Leave for Immigrant Fathers—What Role Does Policy Play?" *Social Politics* 24 (3): 269–297.

Valarino, Isabel, Ann-Zofie Duvander, Linda Haas, and Gerda Neyer. 2018. "Exploring Leave Policy Preferences. A Comparison of Austria, Sweden, Switzerland and the United States." *Social Politics* 25 (1): 118–147.

Valiente, Celia. 2010. "The Erosion of 'Familism' in the Spanish Welfare State: Childcare Policy Since 1975." In *Children, Gender and Families in Mediterranean Welfare States. Children's Well-Being: Indicators and Research*, edited by Mimi Ajzenstadt and John Gal, 129–142. Dordrecht: Springer.

Van Belle, Janna. 2016. *Paternity and Parental Leave Policies Across the European Union*. Santa Monica and Cambridge: RAND Corporation.

Wall, Karin. 2007. "Leave Policy Models and the Articulation of Work and Family in Europe: A Comparative Perspective." In *International Review of Leave Policies and Related Research 2007*, edited by Peter Moss and Karin Wall, 25–43. London: EMAR.

Wall, Karin, Rita B. Correia, and Mafalda Leitão. 2020. "Portugal." In *International Review of Leave Policies and Research 2020*, edited by Alison Koslowski, Sonja Blum, Ivana Dobrotić, Gayle Kaufmann, and Peter Moss. Available at: https://www.leavenetwork.org/lp_and_r_reports/.

CHAPTER 12

Family, Poverty, and Social Policy Interventions

Ryszard Szarfenberg

INTRODUCTION

The chapter aims to convince the reader that while poverty harms families' welfare and well-being, social policy instruments can reduce poverty and therefore social policy has a positive impact on families.

There is a simple theory that poverty has a negative impact on the family, contributing to its disintegration by adding stress, shame, and stigma to family life (Rose and McAuley 2019). Meanwhile, social policy reduces poverty by delivering the resources families living in poverty need. On this basis, we can build a simple argument about the positive impact of social policy on family outcomes, where poverty is a mediator for this relationship.

- Premise 1: poverty harms the family.
- Premise 2: social policy reduces the rate and depth of poverty.
- Conclusion: social policy has a positive impact on the family by reducing poverty.

This argument is based on more general one with three premises: poverty is a social bad, poverty can be eliminated, public policies can help do that (Ravallion 2013). If poverty is the social bad, then it should be bad for family. If public policy can reduce poverty in general, then social policy which is a type

R. Szarfenberg (✉)
Faculty of Political Science and International Studies, Uniwersytet Warszawski, Warszawa, Poland
e-mail: r.szarfenberg@uw.edu.pl

of public policy, should be helpful in alleviating family poverty. The conclusion is that social policy is good for families.

Of course, it is not only poverty that has an impact on family outcomes, and poverty is also affected by many other factors than social policy. Models of poverty determinants can be very complex and include factors at micro- and macro-levels, i.e. market income inequality (wages, hours worked, other income), redistribution through taxation, transfers and social services, macro-economic forces (GDP growth, globalisation, technological change), demographic forces (migration, dependency, single parents, extended families), inequality in skills (education), and labour market institutions such as employment protection or the minimum wage (Diris et al. 2014). The impact of social policy on the family can be mediated through other factors than poverty and also in more direct ways, i.e. through family law, e.g. mandated child support from an absent parent.

The literature on poverty is extensive in economics (Ravallion 2016), as well as sociology (Suter et al. 2017) and the social sciences generally (Brady and Burton 2017; Greve 2019). Social policy and family policy are the main focus of political and policy sciences (Greve 2018; Eydal and Rostgaard 2018). The study of poverty and the family together is a complex and multi-disciplinary subject (Crane and Heaton 2007).

The following section discusses the first premise that poverty harms the family. The third section addresses four types of social intervention that can help families by reducing poverty. The final part of the chapter locates those strategies in the context of the research on the impact of different social policy instruments on poverty. Due to limited space, the chapter does not address the expansion of family policy (Ferragina 2019), the connections between the concepts of policy, social policy and family policy (Zimmerman 1979), as well as issues of multidimensional family poverty (Roelen 2017; Whelan et al. 2014) or causal theories of poverty (Brady 2019). Due to the same reason it is was not possible to elaborate on general literature about relationship between the welfare state and poverty (Marx et al. 2015) or the welfare state and family (Halla et al. 2016), as well as on specific country cases with their different cultures, institutions, economic and social circumstances.

Poverty Is Harmful for Family and Children

The first premise of this chapter is that poverty is harmful to families' welfare and well-being. In this section we will elaborate on this topic to better understand this part of the argument. The concept of poverty, as well as how it is measured, will be explained, and a model of the relationship between poverty and family functioning will be presented.

Poverty is a concept with a very broad array of meanings. Paul Spicker distinguishes twelve clusters of them, with unacceptable hardship at the centre, and divided them into three categories: material conditions (limited resources, need, patterns of deprivation), economic circumstances (standard of living, inequality, economic position), and social relations (social class, dependency, exclusion, lack of basic security, lack of entitlement) (Spicker 2007). From a sociological perspective, the relational cluster, covering concepts such as social exclusion, stigma, and shame, seems to be the most important (Putnam 2020; Spicker 2020).

In the empirical and quantitative research, poverty is mainly understood within material and economic framework as the household's income or expenditures lower than a poverty threshold derived by different methods.[1] Given the plethora of issues involved in empirical research on poverty, researchers must confront and solve numerous methodological problems (Atkinson 1998). One of them is the choice of research unit (whose poverty counts).

Poverty is measured on the level of the household, which is defined as a person or persons, the latter who support themselves together, i.e. combine most of their income and expenses, meeting their needs together, in particular their co-residence housing needs. There is a variety of household types, but many of them comprise one or several families (familial household), such as cohabitated or married childless couples, couples with children, single parents with children, stepfamilies, adult children living together with older parents. Some multi-person households are comprised of individuals that share no family relationships. There is an overlap between concepts of a family and a household, but there are families not living in households, e.g. homeless couples or homeless parents with children, and non-familial households, e.g. single-persons living alone, several young people renting a single flat. The relationship between these two concepts has long been discussed in the literature (Yanagisako 2015).

Another standard assumption in the quantitative research on poverty is that income or expenditure and living standards are equally distributed among household members. Therefore, if a household is considered poor by application of the poverty threshold, all members are poor, and vice versa: none are poor when it is above the poverty threshold. However, several attempts to overcome these limitations have been made by focusing research on the intra-household distribution of material resources (e.g. Bennett 2013).

The mismatch between being income poor and having unmet needs (non-income deprivations) is a first step to fully acknowledge poverty as a non-monetary phenomenon (Whelan et al. 2004; Alkire and Foster 2011). The latest development in this area is a proposal of non-monetary poverty measurement based on Amartya Sen's capability approach (Anand et al. 2020). This is one of the many manifestations of the wider movement towards research within a framework of multidimensional poverty (Beck et al. 2020). In policy practice multidimensional approach is also gaining more attention. In the EU's ten-year strategy 'Europe 2020', there was a separate goal of reducing poverty with the target measured by income poverty, as well as the index of non-income deprivations. If a household representative chose at least four needs from the list of nine[2] as unaffordable, the household considered to be living in severe material deprivation (Whelan and Maître 2012). The third dimension in this approach is the social exclusion measured by very low intensity of work in a household.[3]

Developments in understanding and measuring poverty are important, but the key, at least for the present chapter, is a model explaining the negative impact of poverty on the family. The Family Stress Model (FSM) includes poverty (economic hardship, low income, low assets) as a key factor with a negative impact on several family variables, such as parents' well-being, family functioning, parenting style and practices, child outcomes in the context of low socio-economic position, reduced human and social capital (Park et al. 2002). This model was based on the *social causation perspective*, which maintains that social and economic factors directly influence peoples' emotions, beliefs, and behaviours (Conger and Conger 2008). FSM comprises several causal links, starting from economic hardship (low income, high debt, low assets, negative economic life events) leading to economic pressure (unmet material needs, unpaid debts, painful cutbacks), parental distress (emotional problems, behavioural problems), disrupted family relations (interparental conflict/withdrawal, harsh and inconsistent parenting), and finally to child and adolescent adjustment (emotional, behavioural problems, impaired competence) (Conger and Conger 2008, 67) and/or to relationship quality and stability (Conger et al. 2010). FSM has been empirically validated in the USA (for marital quality and stability see Laxman et al. 2019; Williams et al. 2015), as well as in Europe (Ponnet et al. 2016). The causal relationship between poverty and parenting is a complex issue, however (La Placa and Corlyon 2016).

Data from 30 European countries provide evidence that people who currently experience and perceive economic hardship are less satisfied with their family life, irrespectively of family composition, macro-economic circumstances, and gender (Blom et al. 2019). A comparison of different types of families (nuclear, single-parent and stepfamilies) within the FSM framework in Germany indicated that single-parent families and stepfamilies, in that order, are the most exposed to poverty as measured by the poverty threshold or by subjective feelings of financial strain (Heintz-Martin and Langmeyer 2020). Single-parent families are at a greater risk of poverty due to the lack of a permanent second earner and have greater difficulty combining work and care for children or dependent adults (Nieuwenhuis and Maldonado 2018).

A thorough review of the literature about links between poverty and personal relationships and family leads to the conclusion that there is a 'central tension for families between their participation in the labour market and their caring responsibilities' and the best way to address individual and family poverty is to help them to reconcile this tension (Stock et al. 2014). Another literature review of thirty-nine studies published between 1983 and 2015 in 12 countries found that economic distress negatively influences couple relationships and parenting (Fonseca et al. 2016).

A lot of evidence was accumulated during the last several decades about the negative impact of poverty on children's health, psychosocial development, and academic achievement (Gupta et al. 2007; Van Lancker and Vinck 2019). In the last 10 years, new research has been started on the mechanism by which poverty negatively impacts brain development during childhood (e.g. Luby et al. 2013).

The hypothesis of intergenerational poverty states that there is a higher probability that children from poor families will be poor as adults than children of non-poor parents. FSM researchers from the USA have confirmed that there is a transmission of economic conditions from parent to child (Conger et al. 2012). A general and interdisciplinary model of intergenerational poverty can involve many causal mechanisms: biological, social structure, cultural and status attainment (McEwen and McEwen 2017). So there is a plenty of evidence that poverty hurts family and its members, especially children in the short, medium, and long-term, in one generation and across generations. The reduction of poverty is of key importance in improving family relationships and well-being.

The next sections elaborate the second premise of the argument that societies can reduce poverty.

Four Types of Social Policy Instruments and Family Poverty

A key question to ask is how social policy can reduce family poverty. To answer it, the theory of social policy instruments and the mechanisms of their impact on family poverty will be useful.[4]

Let's start from the assumption that every family unit receives income from different sources to meet its needs by purchasing goods and services. The problem of poverty arises when income is too low to meet the family's needs. The first intuition about possible anti-poverty measures, therefore, is to make family income sufficient by increasing it. There are many sources of income, including both market and non-market forms.[5] The first category comprises incomes from employment, self-employment, and property (capital), e.g. income from renting out a flat or room, income from selling real property. The second category covers incomes from sources which do not directly require something in return, e.g. an income donation from parents to their adult children living independently, from charity or municipal social assistance. Some sources of income can be more generous than others, e.g. wages from employers are received in exchange for work, accounting for why they are usually higher than cash benefits from charity or social assistance.

There is an array of possibilities for social policy interventions aimed at reducing poverty. The first approach is to make market income sources more inclusive and friendly for all families, e.g. by prohibiting discrimination on the grounds of sex, race, etc. by employers. The second approach is based on the assumption that there are basic requirements that must be met in order for one to gain access to market sources of income, e.g. making education obligatory for children and providing it free to all families may help children avoid poverty in the future. The third approach concerns private non-market sources of income such as family itself or charities, e.g. making child support obligatory for absent parents, introducing tax exemptions for charities. The fourth approach is to create public sources of non-market income, e.g. family benefits financed by tax revenues for all children. The first three types are indirect measures, while the fourth is a direct mechanism that influences family income.

Another way to think about anti-poverty social policy is based on the distinction between protection and promotion measures (Dreze and Sen 1989; Ravallion 2013). The first protects families' incomes against negative shocks such as job loss, accidents at work, sickness, and disability, e.g. employment protection legislation, obligatory social insurance, social assistance benefits. The second promotes families' incomes by supporting their efforts to get more income from market sources, especially from employment, e.g. public employment services help families find full-time jobs through job search support, free training for new skills or partially subsidising the cost of employment to employers, to name three.

Combining the above direct-indirect dimension with protection-promotion yields a fourfold typology of anti-poverty social policy instruments (see: Table 12.1).

Table 12.1 Four types of social policy instruments for reducing family poverty

Direct or indirect impact?	*Protection or promotion approach?*	
	Protection against loss of income	*Promotion of income increase*
Direct impact on income	1. Direct protection of income against negative shocks (loss, substantial decrease), e.g. social insurance, minimum wage legislation, indexation of cash transfers	2. Direct promotion of income increases, e.g. lower taxes on low wages, minimum wage introduction or increase, social transfers introduction or increase
Indirect impact on sources of income or on income earner/recipient	3. Indirect protection of income against negative shocks (loss, substantial decrease), e.g. right to renumeration in cash, protection against unfair dismissal, awareness campaigns for employees' rights	4. Indirect promotion of income by influencing its sources/recipients, e.g. employer's obligations enforcement, active labour market programmes for employability (recipient), job placement (recipient), free or subsidised childcare (recipient)

Source The author

There are, however, a number of debates in the literature, media, and politics concerning answers to the questions: who should help families, when and how to get out and stay out of poverty. Below, there is an overview of some of these debates.

- Who: extended family and friends or social professions such as social workers; private companies or churches and charities; charities or municipalities and the state?
- When: before or after poverty has emerged; early when poverty has just occurred or later when there are signs of permanency; when poverty is shallow or when it is deeper?
- How: by stimulating job quality or by promoting the approach 'any work is the best protection against poverty'; by work first approach or by gradually building employability; by cash or in-kind transfers; by contributory, categorical, or income-tested transfers; by information and education or by social transfers; by legal rights or by legal obligations; by economic incentives or by nudges[6]; through a top-down paternalistic approach to families and helping professionals or a bottom-up, participatory and co-producing approach?

These represent fundamental problems discussed in the welfare state and social policy literatures, in the media and political debate about competing ideas, ideologies of welfare, and social policy approaches (for an overview of many of them see: Deacon 2002). One important conceptual development in this literature should be mentioned here: change in emphasis from direct protection to indirect promotion instruments.

These developments culminated in the theoretical advances in social policy literature and new frameworks such as active social policy (ASP) and the social investment paradigm. The activation approach in social policy has been promoted since the 1990s by international bodies such as the European Union and the OECD (Gilbert 2005). In this framework, direct income transfers (mainly unemployment and early retirement benefits) are called passive measures, while instruments such as reskilling, training, and job placement are considered active labour market programmes (ALMPs). ASP was more than an ALMP because it combines them with work incentives in cash transfer schemes (e.g. conditionality, in-work benefits) and childcare services (Bonoli 2013). This type of policy approach can be classified mainly as the indirect promotion of income. It is intended first and foremost to increase family income from work, especially by encouraging the employment of mothers.

In the social investment paradigm, social policy is justified on the grounds of economic efficiency and a return to investment in human capital (Smyth and Deeming 2016). Its focus is more on early education and childcare than on work incentives for mothers receiving direct cash benefits, a fact emphasised in the activation approach. Important goal of this paradigm is to eradicate child poverty and activation approach has an impact on social work and the construction of the problem of poverty in terms of education and activation of child and parent (Schiettecat et al. 2015). There is an evidence that social investment policies have positive outcomes for families with children in OECD countries (Plavgo and Hemerijck 2020).

The implementation of social policy instruments aimed at reducing family poverty is the responsibility of different organisations and their personnel, a large number of whom are social workers who work directly with poor families. Their practices are the subject of interesting literature on social work, which is also a very important topic for sociological research. This is a micro-perspective focused on individual family based on the understanding and mapping of relationships between familial household members and external resources (Vosler 1996; Sanders and Bor 2007).[7]

The sociology of the family and of the institutional interactions in the context of social and family services may contribute to the understanding of families living in poverty and how it affects their responses to and interaction with the above-mentioned social policy instruments offered to them (Hall et al. 2013; Seltzer et al. 2017). Ignoring the social aspects of helping families getting out of poverty in designing social policy may add suffering and end up in a bureaucratic ritualisation and inefficiency (Baumberg 2016; Dubois 2016). Designing better anti-poverty social and family instruments may also be an important contribution of the emerging field of design sociology (Lupton 2018).

The Impact of Social Policy Instruments on Family Poverty

The fifth and final section examines evidence that different social policy instruments decrease family poverty in Europe. Poverty among familial households in Europe has been investigated extensively in recent decades through national and international surveys on household income and living conditions, e.g. ECHP, EU-SILC (e.g. Jenkins 2019). One of the more obvious indicators of familial household poverty is child poverty. Most children live together with adults who support them and with whom they have a biological or de facto parental bond.

However, child poverty in familial households does not include those children who live with parents in different institutions of collective housing, e.g. shelters for homeless mothers with children; or who live in atypical places (e.g. mobile houses) or stay in non-residential areas with at least one parent. We need other indicators for all familial households where there were no children at all, or where there once were but no longer are, i.e. young adult children staying at the parents' home after completing their education, adult children staying and living with older parents, as well as for childless couples, couples after the children have left home, etc.

In addition to the above problems of measuring family poverty by child poverty only, there are also problems with examining the impact on poverty of deliberately designed public interventions. As family poverty is affected by many different factors from different levels through various mechanisms, the challenge for causal analysis is to distinguish the impact of interventions which reduce poverty from the impact of other confounding factors (e.g. the efforts of family members, informal help, economic booms, luck) that somehow exert the same effects. It is also necessary to take into account the costs of the interventions and their possible unintended effects, which also need to be identified (for an overview of the evaluation of social policy, see Greve 2017).

Bearing all these limitations in mind, we will now turn to the results of several comparative studies on the impact of different public policy instruments on child poverty in Europe. Among the direct income instruments are various cash benefits, including ones designed specifically to reach families with children. However, this does not mean that other cash benefits do not reduce child poverty. Pensions also play an important role especially in Southern, Central, and Eastern European countries (Bradshaw and Hirose 2016). In these countries the effectiveness of reducing child poverty (by 30–40%) by means of all benefits is also lower than in Northern Europe (50–60%). In the latter, the impact of pensions on child poverty is negligible. One possible explanation for these differences is that there is a greater share of multi-generational households in the first group of countries. More advanced studies have also found that child benefits ameliorate child poverty, as do other social transfers (Diris et al. 2014).

Material deprivation of children's needs is also an important subject of research. Representatives of households with children were asked whether they were able to meet the specific needs of their children. This approach was used in studies on the impact of various income benefits when controlling for family level factors as well as national level ones (Bárcena-Martín et al. 2017). A study explaining the differences in child deprivation between countries found that child deprivation rises when there is a larger number of children in the household, a single parent, or chronically ill or disabled people in the family. In turn, child deprivation was reduced when parents worked continuously full-time throughout the year, the parents owned a flat and had a higher education. In the case of allowances measured by the share of total expenditure on them in national income, they decreased deprivation of children's needs. However, it was not found that expenditure on benefits aimed at children or the poorer part of the population explained the international variation in child deprivation. A mitigating impact has been also confirmed for old-age and survivors' pensions and sickness and disability benefits, as stated above.

Other cross-sectional and international studies have found that benefits targeted at children have a stronger negative impact on child poverty than do benefits targeted at the households living in poverty (Bárcena-Martín et al. 2018). This is because the former may be provided at a higher level and reach all children from poor families, not just some of them. A study done on four countries (Finland, Germany, UK, and Australia) confirms the importance of rules on combining child support from absent parents with other benefits to reduce child poverty in single-parent families (Hakovirta et al. 2020). For example, the attribution of child support to income-dependent benefits results in lower combined financial support for single parents.

The impact of social policy instruments other than cash benefits aimed at reducing child poverty has also been examined. One such study analysed data from 22 European countries[8] in the period 2006–2015 and found that expenditure on services (benefits in kind) reduced child poverty more than expenditure on cash benefits, though it only studied those benefits aimed at families (Nygård et al. 2019). As regards childcare, i.e. indirect instruments increasing family income from work, simulation studies also confirm their reducing impact on child poverty (Hufkens et al. 2019). The mechanism in this case is as follows: if a mother from a poor family starts working full-time after her child was placed in a quality crèche or kindergarten, the predicted poverty in such a family will decrease due to the rise in the mother's income from work.

Research has also been done on the impact of defamilisation[9] on material deprivation with results about childcare. The results indicated that an extension of childcare services can lower deprivation among families, particularly in countries with high levels of involuntary part-time work (Israel and Spannagel 2019).

As was mentioned in section "Poverty Is Harmful for Family and Children", children are more at risk of poverty in certain household structures, e.g. single parent, large families with more than two children, disabled parents and/or children (Palmer 2011; Shahtahmasebi et al. 2011). The case of single-parent households at risk of poverty is well recognised as work and parenting must be reconciled with only one earner-parent in the household. There is evidence that social policy instruments such as paid parental leave and cash benefits for children are effective in reducing single-parent poverty up to 13 percentage points (Maldonado and Nieuwenhuis 2015).

Poverty is also a greater risk for childless familial households with people with disabilities and older persons. The main instruments for protecting these two groups from financial distress include disability and retirement pensions, a carer allowance, as well as subsidised assistive equipment, and personal and long-term care services. Due to ageing and widespread pension reforms cutting replacement rates, there is concern about the risk of increasing poverty among the elderly in Europe and beyond (for overview see Kwan and Walsh 2018). Some groups of older people, including women, migrants, and those with low-education, are more at risk of poverty (Ebbinghaus et al. 2019).

CONCLUSION

The main argument put forward in this chapter is that poverty harms family as a whole and their members individually, and the harm is long lasting and multi-generational. Social policy instruments designed to reduce family poverty can be understood as a part of a harm-reduction strategy.

The harmful consequences of poverty on marital relationships and parenting style via mechanisms of economic stress were confirmed in the framework of the Family Stress Model, even within an intergenerational poverty perspective. The quantitative and comparative research with a focus on Europe reviewed in this chapter confirms that child benefits, as well as pensions and benefits in kind, e.g. early education and care or paid parental leaves, reduce poverty in familial households both directly and indirectly. They improve the welfare and well-being of family members, including children and their future.

Family poverty and social-family policy should be an important subject for research in European sociology of the family as well as other branches of sociological inquiry.

However, every argument has its weaknesses. Firstly, the evidence that poverty is harmful to many family dimensions should be confronted with evidence that some families respond to financial stressors with bonadaptation, i.e. adaptation that promotes well-being (LeBaron et al. 2020). Secondly, there is a very long tradition of criticising social policy for its biased approach to families living in poverty, e.g. unjust accusations of child abuse and neglect due to their financial situations in the context of child protection services (Bullock 2003; Lambert 2019). Another long-term strand of criticism against social policy highlights its negative side effects, which can also be harmful to the relationships within families, welfare, and social status, e.g. by creating intergenerational state dependence by welfare cultures (Dahl et al. 2014) or incentives to single motherhood (González 2007). Fourthly, the evidence generated in social sciences is only as good as the theories and methods applied to test it empirically. Quantitative evidence can be criticised for philosophical, data and measurement problems, and methodological flaws in causal designs. The numerous failures of replication of previous results in social sciences are likewise a matter for concern (Romero 2019). Fifthly, there is ongoing tension between researchers' political preferences and their choice of concepts, theories, and goals for their research strategies. For instance left-leaning supporters of the extensive and comprehensive welfare state focus their efforts on finding evidence that its anti-poverty effects far outweigh its costs and side effects. This is an example of ideologically driven distortions in the social sciences (Clark and Winegard 2020).

The debate on the positive and negative consequences of different forms of poverty and economic hardship and different social policy instruments on families living in various economic circumstances is far from over. That is only further proof that it will move with us into the future.

Notes

1. There are several methods for determining such a threshold. Absolute one, which is the aggregate market value of the cheapest goods and services which are necessary to fulfil basic needs (food, clothing, shelter) at a minimum level during a specified period and for several types of family (Deeming 2020; Bradshaw and Movshuk 2019). Another, relative one, was developed as an alternative to the basic needs approach (Townsend 1979). It was simplified in research practice to choosing the mean or median of incomes or expenditures, e.g. 50% of the mean (OECD), 60% of the median (EU). A third method is based not on basic needs or a fixed percentile of incomes, but on the opinions of individuals about their economic condition under different levels of income (Flik and van Praag 1991). Poverty thresholds are discussed widely in the economics literature (Ravallion 2016, chapter 4).
2. These items were: to pay their rent, mortgage, or utility bills; to keep their home adequately warm; to face unexpected expenses; to eat meat or protein regularly; to go on holiday; a television set; a washing machine; a car; a telephone.
3. It is defined as the number of persons living in a household where the members of working age worked less than 20% of their total potential during the previous 12 months.
4. There are many explanations of poverty classified recently by Brady into three main groups: behavioural (incentives and culture as main causal factors), structural (the demographic and economic context causes behaviour and poverty), and political (power and institutions cause policy, which has a causal influence on poverty and the relationship between poverty and behaviour) (Brady 2019). Political theories are more relevant to the chapter's argument, because they make explicit the causal role of social policy.
5. OECD developed an internationally agreed framework with detailed description of income, consumption, and wealth (OECD 2013).
6. Nudge is a strategy used to influence human behaviour by changing choice conditions in which people make decisions to improve them for their own good (in the context of poverty see: Anand and Lea 2011).
7. Ecomap is a diagram used as a tool for clinical practice in social work with families and is also a research tool for research on familial relationships, social networks, and social support (e.g. Jacobs Johnson et al. 2017).
8. The countries included Austria, Belgium, the Czech Republic, Denmark, Estonia, Finland, France, Germany, Greece, Hungary, Ireland, Italy, Latvia, Luxembourg, the Netherlands, Poland, Portugal, Slovakia, Slovenia, Spain, Sweden, and the UK.
9. Early definition: 'the degree to which individual adults can uphold a socially acceptable standard of living, independently of family relationships, either through paid work or through social security provision' (Lister 1994, 27).

References

Alkire, Sabina, and James Foster. 2011. "Understandings and Misunderstandings of Multidimensional Poverty Measurement." *The Journal of Economic Inequality* 9 (2): 289–314. https://doi.org/10.1007/s10888-011-9181-4.

Anand, Paul, and Stephen Lea. 2011. "The Psychology and Behavioural Economics of Poverty." *Journal of Economic Psychology* 32 (2): 284–293. https://doi.org/10.1016/j.joep.2010.11.004.

Anand, Paul, Sam Jones, Matthew Donoghue, and Julien Teitler. 2020. "Non-monetary Poverty and Deprivation: A Capability Approach." *Journal of European Social Policy* (August): 095892872093833. https://doi.org/10.1177/0958928720938334.

Atkinson, Anthony. B. 1998. *Poverty in Europe*. Oxford: Wiley-Blackwell.

Bárcena-Martín, Elena, Maite Blázquez, Santiago Budría, and Ana I. Moro-Egido. 2017. "Child Deprivation and Social Benefits: Europe in Cross-National Perspective." *Socio-Economic Review* 15 (4): 717–744. https://doi.org/10.1093/ser/mwx019.

Bárcena-Martín, Elena, M. Carmen Blanco-Arana, and Salvador Pérez-Moreno. 2018. "Social Transfers and Child Poverty in European Countries: Pro-poor Targeting or Pro-Child Targeting?" *Victorian Literature and Culture* 47 (4): 739–758. https://doi.org/10.1017/s0047279418000090.

Baumberg, Ben. 2016. "The Stigma of Claiming Benefits: A Quantitative Study." *Journal of Social Policy* 45 (2): 181–199. https://doi.org/10.1017/s0047279415000525.

Beck, Valentin, Henning Hahn, and Robert Lepenies, eds. 2020. *Dimensions of Poverty*. Vol. 2. Philosophy and Poverty. Cham: Springer International Publishing. https://doi.org/10.1007/978-3-030-31711-9.

Bennett, Fran. 2013. "Researching Within-Household Distribution: Overview, Developments, Debates, and Methodological Challenges." *Journal of Marriage and Family* 75 (3): 582–597. https://doi.org/10.1111/jomf.12020.

Blom, Niels, Gerbert Kraaykamp, and Ellen Verbakel. 2019. "Current and Expected Economic Hardship and Satisfaction with Family Life in Europe." *Journal of Family Issues* 40 (1): 3–32. https://doi.org/10.1177/0192513x18802328.

Bonoli, Giuliano. 2013. *The Origins of Active Social Policy: Labour Market and Childcare Policies in a Comparative Perspective*. Oxford: Oxford University Press.

Bradshaw, Jonathan, and Kenichi Hirose. 2016. *Child Benefits in Central and Eastern Europe—A Comparative Review*. ILO. https://www.ilo.org/budapest/what-we-do/publications/WCMS_532424/lang--en/index.htm.

Bradshaw, Jonathan, and Oleksandr Movshuk. 2019. "Measures of Extreme Poverty Applied in the European Union." In *Absolute Poverty in Europe*, 39–72. Policy Press. https://doi.org/10.2307/j.ctvf3w3zg.7.

Brady, David. 2019. "Theories of the Causes of Poverty." *Annual Review of Sociology* 45 (1): 155–175. https://doi.org/10.1146/annurev-soc-073018-022550.

Brady, David, and Linda M. Burton, eds. 2017. *The Oxford Handbook of the Social Science of Poverty*. Vol. 1. Oxford: Oxford University Press. https://doi.org/10.1093/oxfordhb/9780199914050.001.0001.

Bullock, Candra. 2003. "Low-Income Parents Victimized by Child Protective Services." *Journal of Gender, Social Policy & the Law* 11 (2).

Clark, Cory J., and Bo M. Winegard. 2020. "Tribalism in War and Peace: The Nature and Evolution of Ideological Epistemology and Its Significance for Modern Social Science." *Psychological Inquiry* 31 (1): 1–22. https://doi.org/10.1080/1047840x.2020.1721233.

Conger, Rand D., Katherine J. Conger, and Monica J. Martin. 2010. "Socioeconomic Status, Family Processes, and Individual Development." *Journal of Marriage and Family* 72 (3): 685–704. https://doi.org/10.1111/j.1741-3737.2010.00725.x.

Conger, Rand D., and Katherine Jewsbury Conger. 2008. "Understanding the Processes Through Which Economic Hardship Influences Families and Children." In *Handbook of Families & Poverty*, edited by D. Russel Crane and Tim B. Heaton, 64–81. Thousand Oaks, CA: Sage. https://doi.org/10.4135/9781412976596.n5.

Conger, Katherine Jewsbury, Monica J. Martin, Ben T. Reeb, Wendy M. Little, Jessica L. Craine, Barbara Shebloski, and Rand D. Conger. 2012. "Economic Hardship and Its Consequences Across Generations." In *The Oxford Handbook of Poverty and Child Development*, edited by Rosalind King and Valerie Maholmes. Oxford: Oxford University Press. https://doi.org/10.1093/oxfordhb/9780199769100.013.0002.

Crane, Russel D., and Tim B. Heaton, eds. 2007. *Handbook of Families and Poverty*. Los Angeles: Sage.

Dahl, Gordon B., Andreas Ravndal Kostøl, and Magne Mogstad. 2014. "Family Welfare Cultures." *The Quarterly Journal of Economics* 129 (4): 1711–1752. https://doi.org/10.1093/qje/qju019.

Deacon, Alan. 2002. *Perspectives on Welfare*. Buckingham and Philadelphia: Open University Press.

Deeming, Christopher, ed. 2020. *Minimum Income Standards and Reference Budgets International and Comparative Policy Perspectives*. Bristol: Policy Press.

Diris, Ron, Frank Vandenbroucke, and Gerlinde Verbist. 2014. "Child Poverty: What Can Social Spending Explain in Europe?" *SSRN Electronic Journal* (July). https://doi.org/10.2139/ssrn.2509248.

Dreze, Jean, and Amartya Sen. 1989. *Hunger and Public Action*. Oxford: Oxford University Press.

Dubois, Vincent. 2016. *The Bureaucrat and the Poor*. Routledge. https://doi.org/10.4324/9781315614205.

Ebbinghaus, Bernhard, Kenneth Nelson, and Rense Nieuwenhuis. 2019. "Poverty in Old Age." In *Routledge International Handbook of Poverty*, edited by Bent Greve. Routledge.

Eydal, Guðný, and Tine Rostgaard. 2018. *Handbook of Family Policy*. Edward Elgar Publishing. https://doi.org/10.4337/9781784719340.

Ferragina, Emanuele. 2019. "The Political Economy of Family Policy Expansion." *Review of International Political Economy* 26: 1238–1265. https://doi.org/10.1080/09692290.2019.1627568.

Flik, Robert J., and Bernard M. S. van Praag. 1991. "Subjective Poverty Line Definitions." *De Economist* 139 (3): 311–330. https://doi.org/10.1007/bf01423569.

Fonseca, Gabriela, Diana Cunha, Carla Crespo, and Ana Paula Relvas. 2016. "Families in the Context of Macroeconomic Crises: A Systematic Review." *Journal of Family Psychology* 30 (6): 687–697. https://doi.org/10.1037/fam0000230.

Gilbert, Neil. 2005. "Protection to Activation: The Apotheosis of Work." In *Welfare to Work in Practice: Social Security and Participation in Economic and Social Life*, edited by Peter Saunders. Aldershot: Ashgate.

González, Libertad. 2007. "The Effect of Benefits on Single Motherhood in Europe." *Labour Economics* 14 (3): 393–412. https://doi.org/10.1016/j.labeco.2006.03.001.

Greve, Bent. 2017. *Handbook of Social Policy Evaluation.* Edward Elgar Publishing. https://doi.org/10.4337/9781785363245.
Greve, Bent, ed. 2018. *Routledge Handbook of the Welfare State.* 2nd ed. Abingdon, Oxon and New York, NY: Routledge. https://doi.org/10.4324/9781315207049.
Greve, Bent, ed. 2019. *Routledge International Handbook of Poverty.* 1st ed. New York: Routledge. https://doi.org/10.4324/9780429058103.
Gupta, Rita Paul-Sen, Margaret L. de Wit, and David McKeown. 2007. "The Impact of Poverty on the Current and Future Health Status of Children." *Paediatrics & Child Health* 12 (8): 667–672. https://doi.org/10.1093/pch/12.8.667.
Hakovirta, M. I. A., Christine Skinner, Heikki Hiilamo, and Merita Jokela. 2020. "Child Poverty, Child Maintenance and Interactions with Social Assistance Benefits Among Lone Parent Families: A Comparative Analysis." *Journal of Social Policy* 49 (1): 19–39. https://doi.org/10.1017/s0047279419000151.
Hall, Christopher, Kirsi Juhila, Maureen Matarese, and Carolus van Nijnatten, eds. 2013. *Analysing Social Work Communication.* Routledge. https://doi.org/10.4324/9780203084960.
Halla, Martin, Mario Lackner, and Johann Scharler. 2016. "Does the Welfare State Destroy the Family? Evidence from OECD Member Countries." *The Scandinavian Journal of Economics* 118 (2): 292–323. https://doi.org/10.1111/sjoe.12144.
Heintz-Martin, Valerie K., and Alexandra N. Langmeyer. 2020. "Economic Situation, Financial Strain and Child Wellbeing in Stepfamilies and Single-Parent Families in Germany." *Journal of Family and Economic Issues* 41 (2): 238–254. https://doi.org/10.1007/s10834-019-09653-z.
Hufkens, Tine, Francesco Figari, Dieter Vandelannoote, and Gerlinde Verbist. 2019. "Investing in Subsidized Childcare to Reduce Poverty." *Journal of European Social Policy* (06). https://doi.org/10.1177/0958928719868448.
Israel, Sabine, and Dorothee Spannagel. 2019. "Material Deprivation in the EU: A Multi-level Analysis on the Influence of Decommodification and Defamilisation Policies." *Acta Sociologica* 62 (2): 152–173. https://doi.org/10.1177/0001699318778735.
Jacobs Johnson, Cleo, Jaime Thomas, and Kimberly Boller. 2017. "Ecomapping as a Research Tool for Informal Child Care." *Early Education and Development* 28 (6): 705–714. https://doi.org/10.1080/10409289.2016.1255081.
Jenkins, Stephen P. 2019. "Perspectives on Poverty in Europe. Following in Tony Atkinson's Footsteps." *Italian Economic Journal* 6: 129–155. https://doi.org/10.1007/s40797-019-00112-0.
Kwan, Crystal, and Christine A. Walsh. 2018. "Old Age Poverty: A Scoping Review of the Literature." Edited by Ronnie Donaldson. *Cogent Social Sciences* 4 (1). https://doi.org/10.1080/23311886.2018.1478479.
Lambert, Michael. 2019. "Between 'Families in Trouble' and 'Children at Risk': Historicising 'Troubled Family' Policy in England Since 1945." *Children & Society* 33 (1): 82–91. https://doi.org/10.1111/chso.12309.
Laxman, Daniel J., Brian J. Higginbotham, Stacey S. MacArthur, and ChienTi Plummer Lee. 2019. "A Test of the Family Stress Model Using a Remarriage Sample." *Journal of Divorce & Remarriage* 60 (7): 518–536. https://doi.org/10.1080/10502556.2019.1586230.
LeBaron, Ashley B., Melissa A. Curran, Xiaomin Li, Jeffrey P. Dew, Trevor K. Sharp, and Melissa A. Barnett. 2020. "Financial Stressors as Catalysts for Relational Growth: Bonadaptation Among Lower-Income, Unmarried Couples." *Journal of*

Family and Economic Issues 41 (3): 424–441. https://doi.org/10.1007/s10834-020-09666-z.
Lister, Ruth. 1994. "'She Has Other Duties'—Women, Citizenship and Social Security." In *Social Security and Social Change: New Challenges to the Beveridge Model*, edited by Sally Baldwin and Jane Falkingham. New York and London: Harvester Wheatsheaf.
Luby, Joan, Andy Belden, Kelly Botteron, Natasha Marrus, Michael P. Harms, Casey Babb, Tomoyuki Nishino, and Deanna Barch. 2013. "The Effects of Poverty on Childhood Brain Development." *JAMA Pediatrics* 167 (12): 1135. https://doi.org/10.1001/jamapediatrics.2013.3139.
Lupton, Deborah. 2018. "Towards Design Sociology." *Sociology Compass* 12 (1): e12546. https://doi.org/10.1111/soc4.12546.
Maldonado, Laurie C., and Rense Nieuwenhuis. 2015. "Family Policies and Single Parent Poverty in 18 OECD Countries, 1978–2008." *Community, Work & Family* 18 (4): 395–415. https://doi.org/10.1080/13668803.2015.1080661.
Marx, Ive, Brian Nolan, and Javier Olivera. 2015. "The Welfare State and Antipoverty Policy in Rich Countries." In *Handbook of Income Distribution*, edited by Anthony B. Atkinson and François Bourguignon, 2063–2139. Amsterdam: Elsevier. https://doi.org/10.1016/b978-0-444-59429-7.00024-8.
McEwen, Craig A., and Bruce S. McEwen. 2017. "Social Structure, Adversity, Toxic Stress, and Intergenerational Poverty: An Early Childhood Model." *Annual Review of Sociology* 43 (1): 445–472. https://doi.org/10.1146/annurev-soc-060116-053252.
Nieuwenhuis, Rense, and Laurie C. Maldonado, eds. 2018. *The Triple Bind of Single-Parent Families*. Bristol University Press. https://doi.org/10.2307/j.ctt2204rvq.
Nygård, Mikael, Marja Lindberg, Fredrica Nyqvist, and Camilla Härtull. 2019. "The Role of Cash Benefit and In-Kind Benefit Spending for Child Poverty in Times of Austerity: An Analysis of 22 European Countries 2006–2015." *Social Indicators Research* 146 (3): 533–552. https://doi.org/10.1007/s11205-019-02126-8.
OECD. 2013. *OECD Framework for Statistics on the Distribution of Household Income, Consumption and Wealth*. OECD. https://doi.org/10.1787/9789264194830-en.
Palmer, Michael. 2011. "Disability and Poverty: A Conceptual Review." *Journal of Disability Policy Studies* 21 (4): 210–218. https://doi.org/10.1177/1044207310389333.
Park, Jiyeon, Ann P. Turnbull, and H. Rutherford Turnbull. 2002. "Impacts of Poverty on Quality of Life in Families of Children with Disabilities." *Exceptional Children* 68 (2): 151–170. https://doi.org/10.1177/001440290206800201.
Placa, Vincent La, and Judy Corlyon. 2016. "Unpacking the Relationship Between Parenting and Poverty: Theory, Evidence and Policy." *Social Policy and Society* 15 (1): 11–28. https://doi.org/10.1017/s1474746415000111.
Plavgo, Ilze, and Anton Hemerijck. 2020. "The Social Investment Litmus Test: Family Formation, Employment and Poverty." *Journal of European Social Policy* (September): 095892872095062. https://doi.org/10.1177/0958928720950627.
Ponnet, Koen, Edwin Wouters, Tim Goedemé, and Dimitri Mortelmans. 2016. "Family Financial Stress, Parenting and Problem Behavior in Adolescents." *Journal of Family Issues* 37 (4): 574–597. https://doi.org/10.1177/0192513x13514409.
Putnam, Daniel. 2020. "Poverty as a Social Relation." In *Dimensions of Poverty*, edited by Valentin Beck, Henning Hahn, and Robert Lepienies, 41–55. Cham: Springer International Publishing. https://doi.org/10.1007/978-3-030-31711-9_3.

Ravallion, Martin. 2013. "The Idea of Antipoverty Policy." 19210. NBER Working Papers.
Ravallion, Martin. 2016. *The Economics of Poverty. History, Measurement, and Policy*. Oxford: Oxford University Press.
Roelen, Keetie. 2017. "Monetary and Multidimensional Child Poverty: A Contradiction in Terms?" *Development and Change* 48 (3): 502–533. https://doi.org/10.1111/dech.12306.
Romero, Felipe. 2019. "Philosophy of Science and the Replicability Crisis." *Philosophy Compass* 14 (11). https://doi.org/10.1111/phc3.12633.
Rose, Wendy, and Colette McAuley. 2019. "Poverty and Its Impact on Parenting in the UK: Re-defining the Critical Nature of the Relationship Through Examining Lived Experiences in Times of Austerity." *Children and Youth Services Review* 97 (February): 134–141. https://doi.org/10.1016/j.childyouth.2017.10.021.
Sanders, Matthew R., and William Bor. 2007. "Working with Families in Poverty: Toward a Multilevel, Population-Based Approach." In *Handbook of Families & Poverty*, edited by D. Russell Crane and Tim B. Heaton, 442–456. Thousand Oaks CA: Sage. https://doi.org/10.4135/9781412976596.n26.
Schiettecat, Tineke, Griet Roets, and Michel Vandenbroeck. 2015. "Do Families in Poverty Need Child and Family Social Work?" *European Journal of Social Work* 18 (5): 647–660. https://doi.org/10.1080/13691457.2014.953916.
Seltzer, Michael, Christian Kullberg, and Ilmari Rostila. 2017. *Listening to the Welfare State*. Edited by Michael Seltzer, Christian Kullberg, Søren Peter Olesen, and Ilmari Rostila. Routledge. https://doi.org/10.4324/9781315250472.
Shahtahmasebi, Said, Eric Emerson, Damon Berridge, and Gillian Lancaster. 2011. "Child Disability and the Dynamics of Family Poverty, Hardship and Financial Strain: Evidence from the UK." *Journal of Social Policy* 40 (4): 653–673. https://doi.org/10.1017/s0047279410000905.
Smyth, Paul, and Christopher Deeming. 2016. "The 'Social Investment Perspective' in Social Policy: A Longue Durée Perspective." *Social Policy & Administration* 50 (6): 673–690. https://doi.org/10.1111/spol.12255.
Spicker, Paul. 2007. "Definitions of Poverty: Twelve Clusters of Meaning." In *Poverty: An International Glossary*, edited by Paul Spicker, Sonia Alvarez Leguizamón, and David Gordon. London: Zed Books.
Spicker, Paul. 2020. *Poverty of Nations: A Relational Perspective*. Bristol: Policy Press.
Stock, Laura, Judy Corlyon, Cristina Castellanos Serrano, and Matthew Gieve. 2014. *Personal Relationships and Poverty. An Evidence and Policy Review*. London: The Tavistock Institute.
Suter, Christian, Tugce Beycan, and Laura Ravazzini. 2017. "Sociological Perspectives on Poverty." In *The Cambridge Handbook of Sociology*, edited by Kathleen Odell Korgen, 397–406. Cambridge: Cambridge University Press. https://doi.org/10.1017/9781316418376.039.
Townsend, Peter. 1979. *Poverty in the United Kingdom*. London: Allen Lane and Penguin Books.
Van Lancker, Wim, and Julie Vinck. 2019. "The Consequences of Growing up Poor." In *Routledge International Handbook of Poverty*, edited by Bent Greve, 96–106. 1st ed. New York: Routledge. https://doi.org/10.4324/9780429058103-8.
Vosler, Nancy. 1996. "Families and Poverty: Theory and Research." In *New Approaches to Family Practice: Confronting Economic Stress*, edited by Nancy Vosler,

154–181. Thousand Oaks, CA: Sage. https://doi.org/10.4135/9781483327747.n8.
Whelan, Christopher T., and Bertrand Maître. 2012. "Understanding Material Deprivation: A Comparative European Analysis." *Research in Social Stratification and Mobility* 30 (4): 489–503. https://doi.org/10.1016/j.rssm.2012.05.001.
Whelan, Christopher T., Richard Layte, and Bertrand Maître. 2004. "Understanding the Mismatch Between Income Poverty and Deprivation: A Dynamic Comparative Analysis." *European Sociological Review* 20 (4): 287–302. https://doi.org/10.1093/esr/jch029.
Whelan, Christopher T., Brian Nolan, and Bertrand Maître. 2014. "Multidimensional Poverty Measurement in Europe: An Application of the Adjusted Headcount Approach." *Journal of European Social Policy* 24 (2): 183–197. https://doi.org/10.1177/0958928713517914.
Williams, Deadric T., Jacob E. Cheadle, and Bridget J. Goosby. 2015. "Hard Times and Heart Break." *Journal of Family Issues* 36 (7): 924–950. https://doi.org/10.1177/0192513x13501666.
Yanagisako, Sylvia J. 2015. "Households in Anthropology." In *International Encyclopedia of the Social & Behavioral Sciences*, edited by James D. Wright, 228–232. Elsevier. https://doi.org/10.1016/b978-0-08-097086-8.12088-4.
Zimmerman, Shirley L. 1979. "Policy, Social Policy, and Family Policy: Concepts, Concerns, and Analytic Tools." *Journal of Marriage and the Family* 41 (3): 487. https://doi.org/10.2307/351620.

PART III

Families as Relationships

Edited by Anna-Maija Castrén

CHAPTER 13

Redefining the Boundaries of Family and Personal Relationships

Rita Gouveia and Anna-Maija Castrén

INTRODUCTION

How do we define who counts as family? Do friends replace relatives? What criteria do we use to consider someone as being close or intimate? Can individuals be connected to others through care and trust, as well as through tension and conflict? How do the children of separated parents build and maintain significant ties across multiple households? What does it mean "to be friends" on Facebook? Can we feel as attached to pets as we are to relatives and friends? What are the challenges of in vitro fertilisation and surrogacy to the sense of "being related to"? These types of questions may arise when witnessing the changes in contemporary societies in the spheres of family, personal life and intimacy. In this chapter, we focus on the research developments which, in recent decades, have contributed to redefining what sociology considers to be family and familial relationships. The aim is to highlight some core debates in conceptualising family less as a pre-given entity and more as comprising multiple kinds of personal relationships.

By moving sociological imaginary away from preconceived notions of family based on the normative expectations of relatedness, such as consanguinity, alliance, genealogical proximity, co-residence and heteronormativity, many

---

R. Gouveia (✉)
Institute of Social Sciences, University of Lisbon, Lisbon, Portugal
e-mail: rita.gouveia@ics.ul.pt

A.-M. Castrén
Department of Social Sciences, University of Eastern Finland, Kuopio, Finland
e-mail: anna-maija.castren@uef.fi

researchers have focused on how individuals relate to others in their everyday lives within a wider setting of personal relationships grounded on feelings and practices of closeness that may or may not overlap with cultural understandings of kinship. The task of accommodating the diversity and complexity of day-to-day relational arrangements with the cultural understandings that the idea of family still occupies in lay knowledge and practices has required a double epistemological movement. On the one hand, such an accommodation requires a reconceptualisation of family life that is less rigid and prescriptive, allowing for more inclusive and plural definitions that are closer to everyday scenarios. On the other hand, it decentres the analytical lens from familial ties of descent and alliance to other meaningful relational contexts and practices in which individuals are embedded in their social and cultural milieu.

Engaging in this cultural and relational turn, many authors have developed concepts and methodologies that enable researchers to capture the "vitality of significant relationships" (Gabb and Silva 2011), while still taking into account the structural and social contexts in which they occur, such as gender, ethnicity and social class inequalities (cf. Jamieson 1998; Wall and Gouveia 2014). Despite the different approaches and methods, they share the common concern of making sense of the relational processes of everyday life by exploring the beliefs, practices and meanings that bind people together or set them apart.

Next, we will briefly outline some core debates that offer fertile ground and inspiration for further developments. We will then introduce the theoretical and methodological developments that instil what we call here the *socio-cultural perspective*, highlighting the relationships instead of the entities in family studies. After briefly discussing some of the most recent research fields, we conclude with some reflections on European research trends.

From Institutional to Individual Perspective

Since the mid-twentieth century in particular, family sociologists have paid attention to the impact of societal transformations associated with urbanisation, geographical mobility, industrialisation and the widespread use of ICT (information and communications technology), for example, on the individual's sociability and personal life (Allan 2008). It is said that the demographic transformations that have taken place throughout Europe at an increasing rate since the late 1960s reflect changing patterns of behaviour in the realms of partnership, parenting and gender-work relations (e.g. Roussel 1989). In the light of the new societal and relational dynamics, acknowledged as being the second demographic transition (Lesthaeghe 2010), the hegemony of the structural-functionalist model of the nuclear family (Parsons 1943) as the most prevalent family form has deteriorated. The changes were noted, for example, in contributions focusing on the interactions in familial relationships that cemented new norms in family life (Kellerhals et al. 1993 [1984]) and as the "deinstitutionalisation" of the family (Roussel 1989).

In the 1980s, research highlighted the importance of the individual's emotional investment as being fundamental to family life, the detraditionalisation of the life course and the role of negotiation in personal and familial relationships (e.g. Roussel 1989; Kellerhals et al. 1993 [1984]; Beck 1992 [1986]). Ulrich Beck's book on the emergence of a *new modernity* (1992 [1986]) discussed in length the social surge of individualisation as a liberation from historically prescribed social forms and commitments, and as a loss of stability with respect to faith and guiding norms. The new or reflexive modernisation that was taking place in the "Western" welfare states toned down the traditional parameters of industrial society, such as class culture and consciousness, gender and family roles. This led families to become sites of continuous juggling of multiple ambitions among occupational necessities, educational constraints and parental duties. According to Beck, a type of *negotiated family* emerged, in which individuals "enter into a more or less regulated exchange of emotional comfort, which is always cancellable" (ibid., 87–89, 128).

In addition to Beck who, together with Elisabeth Beck-Gernsheim, published several core texts (1995, 2002), the nature of family, intimacy and personal relationships in late/post/reflexive modernity also gained ground in the 1990s and early 2000 in the works of other prominent sociological thinkers (Giddens 1992; Bauman 2003). Although using different foci and conceptual tools, these authors shared a generally common narrative regarding the nature and drivers of social change in family and personal life in "Western" societies. Changes in personal life were interpreted as a consequence of the strengthening of reflexivity in individuals as actors and agents of their own biographies and relational worlds. This idea of the *solo* individual liberated from the chains of traditions and social institutions, but caught up in other structural constraints such as the employment market, was the basis of analysis in individualisation theories, which pervaded both scientific and political discourses on these matters (Beck 1992 [1986]). Maintaining a somewhat optimistic stance, Giddens attributed the changes in people's life situations and biographies to the transformations in the nature of self-identity and intimate relationships, the latter becoming more equal and democratic (Giddens 1992). Based on electivity, mutual disclosure and trust, the so-called *pure relationship* provided individuals with a sense of ontological security in order to face the social uncertainties and risks that characterised modern times (Giddens 1992). However, the increase in the significance of subjective perspectives, personal choices and decisions in intimate relationships rendered the different kinds of family constellations impossible to identify objectively (Beck and Beck-Gernsheim 2002, 204). Thus, for Beck and Beck-Gernsheim (ibid., 203–204), in the era of changing institutions, the family was characterised as a zombie category, dead but alive, similarly to class and neighbourhood.

Theorisation on individualisation turned out to be extremely influential in the field of family and personal relationship studies. Misunderstandings and simplifications of the original arguments were not avoided (see Beck and

Beck-Gernsheim 2002, 202), but a growing body of empirical research also highlighted the fragilities. First, since individualisation theory offered a rather general level of theorisation—often more essayistic than empirical in nature—one critique related to this lacuna. In fact, empirical research pointed out the contradictory evidence on the enduring significance of traditional structures of gender and ethnicity, for example, in family ties and other close relationships based on care, commitment and support (Finch and Mason 1993). Far from being immune to social constraints, an individual's sociability and intimacy embody both "traditional" and "modern" practices and beliefs, and continue to be shaped by social inequalities associated with gender, social class and ethnicity. Another controversial aspect lay in the broad, linear and uniform portrayals of social change, without taking into account the historical and cultural specificities of each society (Allan 2008; Eisenstadt 2000; Smart and Neale 1999). Although susceptible to multiple criticisms, individualisation theories stimulated sociologists of family and personal relationships towards conceptual and methodological developments in the field.

Theoretical and Methodological Frameworks for (Re)Defining Relational Boundaries: Families, Intimacy and Personal Life

Contributions stemming from the intersection between the sociologies of family, friendship, gender and personal life share the proposition of extending the framework within which contemporary transformations in the realm of families, intimacy and personal life may be analysed. Although they will be presented separately here, we want to emphasise that many of them emerged concomitantly, in dialogue with and mutually influencing each other, even if they were driven by specific concerns, mobilised different concepts and applied distinct methodologies.

An innovative approach to capturing family dynamics, developed by David Morgan (1996, 2011a, b), looked at *doing* family instead of *being* family by focusing on the family practices of everyday life. By moving the use of the term *family* as a noun towards the use of *family* as an adjective, this approach allowed for a more inclusive and fluid conceptualisation of what *family* means beyond the limits of blood, law and household structures. Instead of being obsessed about defining family, Morgan emphasised the valuable knowledge that researchers could gain from looking at the "little fragments of daily life, which are part of the normal taken-for-granted existence of practitioners" (1996, 190). These constitute "sets of practices which deal in some way with the ideas of parenthood, kinship and marriage and the expectations and obligations which are associated with these practices" (1996, 11). Thus, planning holidays, organising festivities, the distribution of domestic tasks, taking care of loved ones and so many other so-called mundane activities, rituals and occasions are impregnated with values, ideas and boundaries about family, i.e.

family meanings. In the same vein, Finch (2007) applied the term *displaying* to refer to how people enact their family and other close relationships in their lived experiences. The term *display* refers to "the process by which individuals, and groups of individuals, convey to each other and to relevant others that certain of their actions do constitute 'doing family things' and thereby confirm that these relationships are 'family' relationships" (Finch 2007, 67). Another important tool that was derived from this approach, and which was already being used in the late 1980s by Finch and Mason (1993), is the notion of "negotiation". As a noun and verb, *negotiation* and *negotiating* have since fallen into the "goes-without-saying premise" in the vocabulary of family sociology, sometimes to the extent that it is unclear what it exactly means. However, analytically rigorous work has been conducted that seeks to differentiate, for example, between explicit and implicit negotiation in couple relationships (Wiesmann et al. 2008).

Similarly, in the field of the sociology of everyday life (which is interested in "lives as lived"), Kaufmann (1992, 2005), for example, focused on how partners reinvent or reproduce their inherited family cultures and gender beliefs within the couple while managing the laundry; or how family meanings are built and contested by social actors when shopping for groceries, cooking or participating in family meals (see also DeVault 1991). Consequently, this epistemological movement also requires methodological diversification as these practices and displays would hardly be captured by classical household characterisations or quantitative surveys. Within this approach, research embodies a strong qualitative lens that can entail a wide spectrum of methodologies, including ethnomethodology, visual methods, time-use surveys and/or narrative analysis.

Thus, methodologically innovative sociological research has highlighted the different ways in which familial and intimate relationships emerge in interaction. For example, in analysing everyday kin relations in France, Weber (2013; see also Déchaux 2008) investigated "practical kinship" from three perspectives, highlighting feelings of symbolic affiliation (lineage), the network of active kin relations in which people are embedded (kin group or kindred) and the sharing of everyday life, resources and the domestic division of labour (*maisonnée*). Weber's conceptualisation brings together the individual and social aspects of family belonging that are present in references to blood relatives and in the sharing of economic resources in everyday life. The last aspect brings forward the spatial and material elements that are intertwined in the formation and maintenance of relationships and allows us to investigate the various ways of sharing daily life, domesticity and spatial closeness that diverge from household-based family stereotypes. For example, such circumstances apply to communal living arrangements (Törnqvist 2019) as well as to situations of live-in care workers such as nannies and *au pairs* (Eldén and Anving 2019) or carers of the elderly (Näre 2011).

A focus on materiality in close connection with the relational embeddedness of the self (originating in the symbolic interactionism tradition of Mead

[1934] and Cooley [1922]) was captured by the sociology of personal life in the framework of relationality. This approach takes a further step in decentralising the status of family in the sociological imaginary, by broadening the spectrum of relationships on the grounds of personal life. The concept of personal life entails "all sorts of families, all sorts of relationships and intimacies, diverse sexualities, friendships, and acquaintanceships" (Smart 2010, 188) and also brings in the examination of "things", the inanimate objects that are part of everyday life. This conceptualisation opens up other ways of looking at connectedness through relationality, i.e. by focusing on the active work of building, maintaining and negotiating meaningful relationships over time and place (Finch and Mason 1993, 2013). Consequently, researchers should make use of methodologies and concepts that grasp the complexity of meanings, feelings and practices that sustain connectedness with others in day-to-day lives. Empirical research in this area uses a conceptual toolbox, which includes memory, imaginary, embeddedness and biography as complementary analytical devices (Smart 2010). A good example of the use of this toolbox is Mason's work on how individuals experience, interpret and construct family resemblances by carrying out qualitative interviews, including home observations, exploring the meanings of objects, such as photos and drawing family trees in collaboration with the interviewees (Mason and Davies 2010; also Mason 2018).

Another influential analytical tool for theorising relationships relies on the work of Lynn Jamieson who, in her book *Intimacy* (1998), criticised the unidimensional and poorly developed notion of intimacy proposed and popularised by individualisation theorists. While Giddens's concept of intimacy (1992) was defined as a distinctive type of relationship characterised by self-disclosure and equality, and inherently a matter of the private sphere, Jamieson offered a more nuanced insight into intimacy as comprising multiple dimensions and entailing different practices, in which self-disclosure is only one possible form (Jamieson 1998, 2005). Thus, these practices can entail both expressive and instrumental care, and rather than being inherently based on equality grounds, they are still regulated by social asymmetries (Jamieson 1999, 2005). Like Morgan's ideas on family practices (1996, 2011a, b), research on intimacy benefits from looking at the ways in which people "do intimacy" and display their intimacy repertoires in various settings, such as families, parent-child relationships, couples, sexual relationships, friendships and other relational environments in which people create such a sense of close connection (Jamieson 2011). For example, in her research on couples, Gabb (2008) highlighted how intimacy is embodied through material and symbolic meanings built through touch, gestures and other displays of affection, as well as through the exposure of nudity, or the appropriation of domestic space.

Jamieson also elaborated on the role of boundaries and boundary work in personal life. Drawing on the notion of the anthropologist Fredrik Barth (1969), boundary work refers to the processes through which individuals create social divisions of sociability between those who are considered to be intimates and those who are out of the intimate circle (Jamieson 2005). Building intimacy often (but not always) requires boundary work, meaning that people are actively engaged in drawing relational boundaries through their discourses, actions and interactions. Moreover, the boundaries between intimates and non-intimates intersect with other structural boundaries, such as those associated with gender, age, social class, ethnicity and sexuality, which reconfigure and are reconfigured by the former (Jamieson 2005). As analytical tools, the notions of boundary and boundary work have been frequently applied to the study of post-separation family relationships. The prevalence of separation and re-partnering has contributed to the loosening of household-based family boundaries, particularly for children whose parents and siblings may live in two or more households (e.g. Allan et al. 2011; Ihinger-Tallman 1988; Smart et al. 2011). The idea of family boundaries reflects inclusion and exclusion, but it also allows for varying degrees of flexibility in constructing boundaries (Allan et al. 2011). In step-family contexts, for example, mechanisms of inclusion and exclusion can vary between adults and children (Castrén and Widmer 2015), which indicates the importance of subjective sense-making on the one hand (also Déchaux 2002) and of the relational context that constrains the individual on the other, in terms of defining emotional closeness and intimacy. We will return to the notion of boundary work as a useful analytical tool later when looking at the online vs. offline divide in personal networks.

The boundary question is closely linked to the line that is drawn between friends and kin, which some authors claim to be more artificial than exemplificative of lived experience (Pahl and Pevalin 2005; Pahl and Spencer 2004; Wall and Gouveia 2014; Allan 2008). Conceptualising the individual's relational embeddedness as personal communities (Wellman 1988), Pahl and Spencer (2004) investigated the process of suffusion between family and friends. According to these authors, the boundaries between family and friends are becoming increasingly blurred, as certain friends are perceived and trusted as having family-like qualities and immersed in "family-like" practices of care and support (ibid.). Friends can be embedded in the networks of kin ties and integrated into family gatherings and routines. But the opposite is also true, as some relatives can also be considered to be friends, which is quite common, for example, among siblings and as individuals grow older (e.g. parents who consider their adult children to be friends). Considering non-kin as family depends on the relational qualities of the bond, such as duration, positive role and shared history, as well as on the structural embeddedness of the individuals according to age, gender, education and family circumstances (Wall and Gouveia 2014; also Luotonen and Castrén 2018). The intensity and contours of such processes vary between different countries (Wall et al. 2018), which confirms the interplay between interpersonal dynamics and macro-social factors, such as welfare state arrangements and socio-economic contexts.

The categorical difference between friendship and kinship was particularly questioned under the umbrella of queer studies and in research on the personal relationships of individuals living non-heteronormative lives. The pioneering work of American anthropologist Kath Weston (1991) on the gay and lesbian community in San Francisco in the 1980s was highly influential in this field. The life histories of gay men and lesbians revealed that while some of them combined their relatives (e.g. parents) with friends in their family networks, many of them reported tension, hostility, disruption and distance with the members of their families of origin, also designated as *families of fate*, which often resisted to their non-heteronormative sexualities and identities. Thus, individuals built their *families of choice* based on practices of love, commitment, care and support, by integrating a multiplicity of ties, such as relatives, friends, lovers and ex-lovers. On the one hand, this perspective criticised the predominance of the heteronormative framework and the related enduring primacy of standard conjugal and parental dyads in the sociological intellectual imaginary (Roseneil and Budgeon 2004; Roseneil 2007). On the other hand, it contested the naturalisation and dichotomisation of gender, sexual, body and family categories (Weeks et al. 2001). These contestations have been particularly mobilised in more recent research on the challenges faced by trans and non-binary people in their families, intimate relationships and citizenship (Santos 2018). Sensitive analytical tools must be used when individuals are non-monogamous and non-heterosexual, are not living with a partner under the same roof and do not have children, and when investigating how gender non-conforming individuals build their personal relationships in transphobic contexts. How do individuals who defy traditional categories manage to build meaningful and close ties? These are the kind of issues the "queering" gaze proposes to address by enlarging the doorways of analysis in the realms of intimacy beyond heteronormativity.

The configurational approach (see Chapter 6) is another relationally-oriented perspective that distances itself from pre-defined relationship categories and family as a fixed entity. This approach was methodologically inspired by social network analysis and has been applied in several national contexts throughout Europe (see Widmer et al. 2004; Widmer 2010; Castrén and Ketokivi 2015; Jallinoja and Widmer 2011; Wall and Gouveia 2014; Česnuitytė 2012). Drawing on Norbert Elias' concepts of configuration/figuration and interdependency (Elias 1978 [1970], 2010 [1991]), families and personal networks are seen as constellations of significant ties linked by mutual emotional, material and identity interdependencies, as well as by conflict and ambivalence (Widmer 2010). Four theoretical assumptions guide this approach (Widmer et al. 2008). First, the rejection of aprioristic criteria set by an outside observer to define who is considered to be a significant family member or an important person in an individual's life. Second—and bridging with the life course approach that highlights linked lives (Elder et al. 2003)—assuming that a change in a person's life will impact the lives of those with whom they are interdependent (also Elias 1978), key dyad dynamics (parent-child, couples, friends) can only be understood in terms of their relational embeddedness. For example, the conjugal quality and sexuality of partners are highly influenced by the composition and interference of the personal configurations of couples (Ammar et al. 2014; Vesela 2017). Third, the approach involves the understanding of both personal perspectives and group formations as being mutually constituted. It does not ignore the ways in which constellations of relationships structure individual selves, nor the impact of personal choices, motives and identities on these constellations. Fourth, the integration of time and space as configurations evolve over biographical, generational and historical times and are situated in geographical, structural and political-historical contexts (Widmer et al. 2008; Wall et al. 2018). This concern with the temporal and spatial contextualisation of configurations provides an analytical framework in which to capture social differentiation processes and inequalities that shape the composition and structure of personal and family relationships. For example, Girardin and Widmer (2015) found that family configurations and social capital in old age are the result of a combination of an individual's agency and structural constraints as resources associated with social class, family and health conditions are limited and unevenly distributed among the elderly population.

As a transversal topic to all the approaches introduced above, friendship captures many of the core elements of contemporary personal relationships: it highlights the importance of individual sense-making and emotional investments, as well as the relational embeddedness that engenders constraint in an individual's actions. Although friendship has gained sociological ground, particularly since the turn of the twenty-first century, its importance in personal life and as a research topic is not "new" (Blouin 2016). In the mid-twentieth century, community studies focused on working-class sociability or the gendered patterning of friendship was tapping into the relevance of friends in private and public spheres (see Adams and Allan 1998). In a narrative of increasing deinstitutionalisation, democratisation and electivity in personal relationships, friendship was considered to be the perfect representation of these features. However, studies have shown that, as in the case of kin relations, relationships with friends are constrained by context (Adams and Allan 1998). Friendship regulated by life course dynamics (Fischer and Oliker 1983) is shaped by an individual's transitions and events, such as entering into a partnership (Kalmijn 2003) or retirement (Cozijnsen et al. 2010). Furthermore, social structures such as gender, age and social class impact the development and maintenance of friendship ties and their salience is regulated by homophily mechanisms (Adams and Allan 1998; Policarpo 2015).

The relevance of friendship ties is a consequence of individuals having increasing relational flexibility (Allan 2008). The meanings of friendship are plural, configuring different profiles or *repertoires*, and are sustained by a diversity of practices or *modes* (Spencer and Pahl 2006). For example, Policarpo (2015) showed the plurality of friendship repertoires in a Portuguese context and constructed a typology on the basis of multiple meanings attributed to friends. While some friends were ascribed a family meaning (*family-oriented*), others were based on the sense of "being there" on a regular basis (*presence-oriented*); or on the grounds of trust (*trust-oriented*) or self-disclosure and unconditional support (*self-oriented*). Moreover, these repertoires were varyingly associated with certain social profiles according to gender, age, marital status and education, which illustrates the socially-constructed nature of friendship that is often assumed to be purely elective (idem).

Recent Research Settings Generating Redefinitions of Boundaries

Some emerging social scenarios benefit from the relational framework outlined above as they challenge the normative assumptions of relatedness and demand active and constant boundary work. We will briefly discuss three recent research settings from this perspective.

Technologically-mediated communication, particularly social networking sites (SNS), represents one of these settings. The ways in which online and offline relationships interact and practices of intimacy take place in a virtual environment are better understood from the perspective of their embeddedness in personal relationships. Getting in touch with old friends, deciding whether to share family pictures with co-workers or whether to unfriend or block a person in a virtual environment are common experiences that entail reconciling different facets of self-identity and reflecting on the boundaries between private and public spheres, intimacy and distance, offline and online. However, rather than promoting a radically new way of relating to others, as is often proclaimed by mediacentric discourses, technologically-mediated communication offers other relational affordances and demands for creating, sustaining, reinventing and disrupting personal relationships (Policarpo 2019). Thus, there is a relational continuum between online and offline personal bonds and practices of intimacy.

The ability to bridge time and space that is offered by virtual environments did not erode pre-existing relationships in which individuals are embedded, nor did developing intimacy exempt individuals from engaging in some degree of co-presence and material and physical practices of closeness (Jamieson 2013). Also, far from democratising relationships, personal life in SNS is regulated by new and enduring dynamics of social inequality. Focusing on Facebook, Lambert (2013) suggested the term *intimacy capital* to acknowledge the process of accumulating intimacy on this platform, which requires cultural, social and technical skills that are not evenly distributed within and across societies. Another important virtual relational terrain in which intimacy is strongly shaped by structural contexts is online dating applications. For example, the strategies of self-presentation to attract others are impregnated with new and old social representations of masculinity and femininity (Casimiro 2015).

Medically-assisted procreation (MAP), including in vitro fertilisation, egg, sperm, embryo donation and surrogacy, is another field that challenges the cultural understandings of family. The use of MAP and the discussion around the sharing and non-sharing of genetic material, biological and legal connections, nurturing and pregnancy, have raised a debate on the meanings of *being related to* within both lay and scientific communities. Useful tools for understanding this topic are offered by cultural anthropologists, such as Schneider, on American kinship (1968 [1980]) and more recently, Carsten (2000, 2004) and Edwards and Strathern (2000), on relatedness. Briefly, their approach to kinship studies denied the idea of there being given or fixed rules related to as facts and, instead, underlined the social construction of kinship by focusing on how people make sense of their relationships and practices of kinning and de-kinning. Such reasoning resonates with the notions of the boundary work and mechanisms of exclusiveness and inclusiveness discussed above.

Hand-in-hand with the normative weight of genealogical rules sustained by blood and alliance, another well-rooted principle has gained ground in the representations and practices of kin as a result of the penetration of biomedical discourse in the expert and lay spheres: the primacy of the genetic link (Nordqvist 2017). Nordqvist (2017) investigated how parents and grandparents of children conceived through egg, sperm and embryo donation build family bonds in the light of ideas about genes and genetic relationships. The author used the term "genetic thinking" to describe the process by which relationships are rendered meaningful in everyday life through a reinvention of what it means "to be related to", which is the result of a complex negotiation of not being genetically related but perceived and loved as such. Again, the relationality toolbox of the sociology of personal life (Smart 2011) represents a powerful instrument for tapping into these complex processes (Nordqvist 2019). The ways in which social actors in MAP are able to feel connected to significant others, how they build their shared memories, ascribe family resemblances, create family secrets or reflect on imaginaries of being a "proper family", can be captured with the idea of the embeddedness in significant personal relationships. In the case of surrogacy, another analytical layer is added to the processes of relatedness: the body and the involvement of a third actor, the gestational mother. In fact, it is not only the gestational mother but also her family who are implicated. For example, Imrie and Jadva (2014) showed how perceptions of the relatedness of surrogates, their partners and their children were complex and diverse, illustrating different meanings and experiences attached to the genetic/gestational link. In some cases, the children of surrogate mothers would refer to the born child as *surro sister* or *surro brother*, others as *cousins*, while other children would not acknowledge or establish any close relationship (Imrie and Jadva 2014).

Another growing body of theoretical and empirical research focuses on the relationship between animals and humans (or non-human and human animals) by recognising the importance of pets or companion animals in people's lives and revealing the meanings and practices that sustain this bond. Again, the boundaries of family and intimacy are in focus, although, in this case, are direct at the inclusion of non-human beings. Although humans and animals have coexisted for thousands of years, the nature of their relationship has changed following the cultural movement from an anthropocentric and materialistic worldview towards more egalitarian, ecological and zoocentric values (Inglehart 1977). The presence of pets in households and their engagement in everyday family practices led us to speculate about the extent to which pets could be considered to be family members. A wide spectrum of positions acknowledges the family membership of pets by referring to these relational settings as *multispecies households* or *more-than-human families* (Irvine and Cilia 2017), *post-human families* (Charles 2016), *hybrid households* (Franklin 2006) or *furry families* (Power 2008).

Although not necessarily attributing them with the same status as humans, and still operating in the context of a power differential, individuals can develop the same kind of feelings that they develop with their significant human others, such as emotional attachment, care and a sense of responsibility. Moreover, companion animals actively enact and shape intimacy and family practices, such as domestic routines, leisure activities, emotional displays of affection or space appropriation. Some practices reflect the attribution of a kind of personhood and agency to companion animals as individuals talk to and attribute personality traits and intentions to their pets, build emotional bonds, such as kindness and empathy, with and through their companion animals, but also violence and abuse. Others, such as childless couples or singles, may create ties with companion animals as a compensatory mechanism, while some pets are key actors during critical events and transitions, such as grief, disease, unemployment or an empty nest. Although it is debatable whether relationships between humans and animals can be equivalent to those among humans, it is undeniable that for some people, animals can blur the boundaries of intimacy, and in some cases, the boundaries of family. Moreover, as in human relationships, the nature and intensity of this bond are contingent upon life course events and power relations. Thus, the place and nature of such relationships evolve over time and space.

Conclusion: Critique and Reflections on European Trends

In this chapter, we have discussed some of the main developments that have contributed to the redefinition of familial relations as personal relationships. Such a perspective on contemporary sociability and relational behaviour can be characterised as socio-cultural; it highlights relational practices and the meanings that individuals ascribe to these practices as historically changing and inherently intertwined with the wider societal and social changes in Europe and other "Western" societies since the early twentieth century. It questions the usefulness of pre-defined relational categories and emphasises boundary work. In many ways, it implies new outlets for discussing and studying family and relationships and instigating critique. Indeed, some of the core debates have raised critical discussions among the community of family sociologists who are highlighting the potential risks of shifting away from the notion of family. For example, during the launch of the journal *Families, Relationships and Societies* in 2012, Rosalind Edwards and Val Gillies (2012) cautioned about the social and political implications of moving away from using the notion of "family" and replacing the term with broader conceptualisations of personal life, intimacy and kinship. According to them, theorising family life on the grounds of the "personal" encompasses the risks of overshadowing the political and public dimensions of family (e.g. in policy-making), as well as the danger of ignoring the weight of normative expectations on the ways that individuals organise and perceive their family life. Moreover, theorising family with a focus on the personal life "risks becoming trapped in the pivot around a reflexive, responsibilised self, disconnecting from other meanings and significances captured through the term 'the family'" (idem, 67). In response, Vanessa May (2012) stressed that the term *personal* is inherently relational and emphasised that one of the cornerstones of the sociology of personal life is precisely the interplay between the public and private sphere (idem). Furthermore, the focus of the sociology of personal life is on the embeddedness and connectedness of individuals within their meaningful relationships and within their differentiated socio-cultural surroundings. Thus, as academic endeavours, family sociology and the sociology of personal life should not be juxtaposed but should rather enrich each other (May 2012, 420).

In 2011, Morgan offered insightful views that resolved some of the controversies when evaluating the potentials, limitations and influences of his "family practices" approach. He highlighted the similarities and differences between various approaches, applying a relational perspective and proposed that the analytical question that could be posed concerns the place or position of "family" within our research frameworks and study designs. This may vary from a central focus (e.g. family practices) to approaches in which family is the major but not exclusive focus of interest (e.g. intimacy, personal life) or to those approaches in which family is an important but not always a key consideration (e.g. caringscapes) (Morgan 2011b, 7).

As noted, the socio-cultural perspective primarily relies on qualitative methods. Even when applying more structured tools to empirical research, in many ways it is *qualitatively driven* (Mason 2006) in the sense that it distances itself from fixed prior conceptions of an individual's ultimate motives and behavioural drivers. In contrast, the research orientations that follow from economics and the seminal work of Gary Becker (1991 [1981]), and from the evolutionary perspective (cf. Salmon and Shackelford 2008)—both prominent approaches in contemporary family research—have very different starting points in addressing the ultimate reasons behind people's behaviour. While the Beckerian perspective adopts a rational choice approach to the family and emphasises individuals as actors seeking to maximise their personal gains in the marriage market, or when balancing family and work, for example (Becker 1991 [1981]), the evolutionary perspective returns to the consideration of human biology, of the ancestral history of humans and of the forces that have shaped not only the human's physical but also mental characteristics that influence family relationships (Salmon and Shackelford 2008, 4). For example, evolutionary psychology draws on natural selection as a process that shapes adaptations that "contributed to ancestral individuals' ability to survive and reproduce in competition with other members of their species" (ibid.). In the contemporary academic scrutiny of family and intimate relations, these three approaches—socio-cultural, rational choice and evolutionary—are combined and intertwined to some extent.

To conclude with some reflections on the advance of the socio-cultural perspective, we will briefly look at the biannual interim meetings organised by the Research Network of the Sociology of Families and Intimate Lives of the European Sociological Association (ESA-RN13) over the last decade (2010–2018). In fact, already changing the network's name from sociology of *family* to sociology of *families and intimate lives* indicates a change in response to the pluralisation of family structures, practices and representations and to the fact that the notion of family excluded other significant intimate relationships. In the titles of the sessions, a theoretical and empirical trend can be detected. Although, to some extent, they are conditional to the conference themes, terms and concepts such as "intimate", "doing", "everyday routines", "practices", "change and stability", "configurations", "networks", "diversity", "making families", "constructing" and "diversity" have increasingly gained ground. For us, this reflects the prevalence of the relational or socio-cultural sociological gaze over multiple topics and national European contexts.

Compared to the rational choice and the evolutionary perspectives on contemporary families, the socio-cultural perspective is the only perspective that puts weight on the individual's subjective perceptions of their significant others. It is our impression that the importance of such emphasis is likely to increase in future. The social conditions of life continue to change due to political conflicts, technological developments and global health and environmental crises, for example, which influence all spheres of life and make life trajectories and the organisation of family life increasingly fragile. Against such background, demarcating significant family relations without including the individual's own perspective will likely become even more complex than it is today.

Acknowledgments Rita Gouveia was granted a post-doc scholarship funded by FCT-Grant SFRH/BPD/116958/2016, MCTE.

References

Adams, Rebecca G., and Graham Allan, eds. 1998. *Placing Friendship in Context*. Cambridge: Cambridge University Press.
Allan, Graham. 2008. "Flexibility, Friendship, and Family." *Personal Relationships* 15 (1): 1–16.

Allan, Graham, Graham Crow, and Sheila Hawker. 2011. *Stepfamilies*. Basingstoke: Palgrave Macmillan.
Ammar, Nadia, Jacques-Antoine Gauthier, and Eric D. Widmer. 2014. "Trajectories of Intimate Partnerships, Sexual Attitudes, Desire and Satisfaction." *Advances in Life Course Research* 22: 62–72.
Barth, Fredrik. 1969. *Ethnic Groups and Boundaries. The Social Organization of Culture Difference*. Oslo: Universitetsforlaget.
Bauman, Zygmunt. 2003. *Liquid Love: On the Frailty of Human Bonds*. Cambridge: Polity Press.
Beck, Ulrich. 1992 [1986]. *Risk Society: Towards a New Modernity*. London: Sage.
Beck, Ulrich, and Elisabeth Beck-Gernsheim. 1995. *The Normal Chaos of Love*. Cambridge, MA: Wiley Blackwell.
Beck, Ulrich, and Elisabeth Beck-Gernsheim. 2002. *Individualization: Institutionalized Individualism and Its Social and Political Consequences*. London: Sage.
Becker, Gary. 1991 [1981]. *A Treatise on the Family*. Enlarged ed. Boston: Harvard University Press.
Blouin, Jennifer. 2016. "Eternal Perspectives in Nineteenth-Century Friendship Albums." *The Hilltop Review* 9 (1): Article 7.
Carsten, Janet, ed. 2000. *Cultures of Relatedness: New Approaches to the Study of Kinship*. Cambridge: Cambridge University Press.
Carsten, Janet. 2004. *After Kinship*. Cambridge: Cambridge University Press.
Casimiro, Cláudia. 2015. "Self-Presentation in the Portuguese Online Dating Scene: Does Gender Matter?" In *Online Courtship—Interpersonal Interactions Across Borders*, edited by I. Alev Degim, James Johnson, and Tao Fu, 71–95. Amsterdam: Institute of Network.
Castrén, Anna-Maija, and Kaisa Ketokivi. 2015. "Studying the Complex Dynamics of Family Relationships: A Figurational Approach." *Sociological Research Online* 20 (1). http://www.socresonline.org.uk/20/1/3.html. https://doi.org/10.5153/sro.3539.
Castrén, Anna-Maija, and Eric D. Widmer. 2015. "*Insiders and Outsiders* in Stepfamilies: Adults' and Children's Views on Family Boundaries." *Current Sociology* 63 (1): 35–56.
Česnuitytė, Vida. 2012. "Changing Family Model, Social Capital and Caring: How to Reconcile? The Case of Lithuania." *Sociologia e Politiche Sociali* 15: 75–104.
Charles, Nickie. 2016. "Post-human Families?: Dog-Human Relations in the Domestic Sphere." *Sociological Research Online* 21 (3): 1–12.
Cooley, Charles H. 1922. *Human Nature and the Social Order*. Revised ed. New York: Charles Scribner's Sons.
Cozijnsen, Rabina, Nan L. Stevens, and Theo G. van Tilburg. 2010. "Maintaining Work-Related Personal Ties Following Retirement." *Personal Relationships* 17: 345–356.
Déchaux, Jean-Hugues. 2002. "Paradoxes of Affiliation in the Contemporary Society." *Current Sociology* 50 (2): 229–242.
Déchaux, Jean-Hugues. 2008. "Kinship Studies: Neoclassicism and New Wave. A Critical Review." *Revue Française de Sociologie* 49: 215–243.
Devault, Marjorie. 1991. *Feeding the Family: The Social Organization of Caring as Gendered Work*. Chicago: Chicago University Press.

Edwards, Jeanette, and Marylin Strathern. 2000. "Including Our Own." In *Cultures of Relatedness: New Directions in Kinship Studies*, edited by Janet Carsten, 149–167. Cambridge: Cambridge University Press.

Edwards, Rosalind, and Val Gillies. 2012. "Farewell to Family? Notes on an Argument for Retaining the Concept." *Families, Relationships and Societies* 1(1): 63–69.

Eisenstadt, Shmuel N. 2000. "Multiple Modernities." *Dædalus: Journal of the American Academy of Arts and Sciences* 129 (1): 1–30.

Eldén, Sara, and Terese Anving. 2019. *Nanny Families: Practices of Care by Nannies, au Pairs, Parents and Children in Sweden*. Bristol: Bristol University Press.

Elder, Glen. H., Monica Kirkpatrick Johnson, and Robert Crosnoe. 2003. "The Emergence and Development of Life Course Theory." In *Handbook of the Life Course*, edited by Jeylan T. Mortimer and Mickael J. Shanahan, 3–19. New York: Kluwer Academic/Plenum Publishers.

Elias, Norbert. 1978 [1970]. *What Is Sociology?* London: Hutchinson.

Elias, Norbert. 2010 [1991]. *The Society of Individuals*. Dublin: UCD Press.

Finch, Janet. 2007. "Displaying Families." *Sociology* 41 (1): 65–81.

Finch, Janet, and Jennifer Mason. 1993. *Negotiating Family Responsibilities*. London: Routledge.

Finch, Janet, and Jennifer Mason. 2013. *Passing on: Kinship and inheritance in England*. London and New York: Routledge.

Fischer, Claude S., and Stacey J. Oliker. 1983. "A Research Note on Friendship, Gender, and the Life Cycle." *Social Forces* 62: 124–133.

Franklin, Adrian S. 2006. "Be(a)ware of the Dog: A Post-humanist Approach to Housing." *Housing, Theory and Society* 23 (3): 137–156.

Gabb, Jacqui. 2008. *Researching Intimacy in Families*. Basingstoke: Palgrave Macmillan.

Gabb, Jacqui, and Elizabeth B. Silva. 2011. "Introduction to Critical Concepts: Families, Intimacies and Personal Relationships." *Sociological Research Online* 16 (4): 23.

Giddens, Anthony. 1992. *The Transformation of Intimacy: Sexuality, Love and Eroticism in Modern Societies*. Cambridge: Polity Press.

Girardin, Myriam, and Eric D. Widmer. 2015. "Lay Definitions of Family and Social Capital in Later Life." *Personal Relationships* 22: 712–737.

Ihinger-Tallman, Marylin. 1988. "Research on Stepfamilies." *Annual Review of Sociology* 14: 25–48.

Imrie, Susan, and Vasanti Jadva. 2014. "The Long-Term Experiences of Surrogates: Relationships and Contact with Surrogacy Families in Genetic and Gestational Surrogacy Arrangements." *Reproductive Biomedicine Online* 29 (4): 424–435.

Inglehart, Ronald. 1977. *The Silent Revolution: Changing Values and Political Styles Among Western Publics*. Princeton, NJ: Princeton University Press.

Irvine, Leslie, and Laurent Cilia. 2017. "More-Than-Human Families: Pets, People, and Practices in Multispecies Households." *Sociology Compass* 11: 1–13.

Jallinoja, Riitta, and Eric D. Widmer, eds. 2011. *Families and Kinship in Contemporary Europe: Rules and Practices of Relatedness*. Basingstoke: Palgrave Macmillan Studies in Family and Intimate Life.

Jamieson, Lynn. 1998. *Intimacy: Personal Relationships in Modern Societies*. Cambridge: Polity Press.

Jamieson, Lynn. 1999. "Intimacy Transformed? A Critical Look at the Pure Relationship." *Sociology* 33: 477–494.

Jamieson, Lynn. 2005. "Boundaries of Intimacy." In *Families in Society*, edited by Linda McKie and Sarah Cunningham-Burley, 189–206. Bristol: Policy Press.
Jamieson, Lynn. 2011. "Intimacy as a Concept: Explaining Social Change in the Context of Globalization or Another Form of Ethnocentrism?" *Sociological Research Online* 16 (4): 15.
Jamieson, Lynn. 2013. "Personal Relationships, Intimacy and the Self in a Mediated and Global Digital Age." In *Digital Sociology*, edited by Kate Orton-Johnson and Nick Prior. London: Palgrave Macmillan.
Kalmijn, Matthijs. 2003. "Shared Friendship Networks and The Life Course: An Analysis of Survey Data on Married and Cohabiting Couples." *Social Networks* 25 (3): 231–249.
Kaufmann, Jean-Claude. 1992. *La Trame Conjugale: Analyse du Couple par Son Linge*, Paris: Nathan.
Kaufmann, Jean-Claude. 2005. *Casseroles, amour et crises. Ce que cuisiner veut dire*. Paris: Armand Colin.
Kellerhals, Jean, Pierre-Yves Troutot, and Emmanuel Lazega. 1993 [1984]. *Microsociologie de la famille*. Deuxième édition corrigée. Paris: Presses Universitaires de France.
Lambert, Alex. 2013. "Intimacy and Social Capital on Facebook: Beyond the Psychological Perspective." *New Media & Society* 18 (11): 2559–2575.
Lesthaeghe, Ron J. 2010. "The Unfolding Story of the Second Demographic Transition." PSC Research Report No. 10-696, January.
Luotonen, Aino, and Anna-Maija Castrén. 2018. "Understandings of Family Among Wives and Husbands: Reconciling Emotional Closeness and Cultural Expectations." *European Societies* 20 (5): 743–784.
Mason, Jennifer. 2006. "Mixing Methods in a Qualitatively-Driven Way." *Qualitative Research* 6 (1): 9–25.
Mason, Jennifer. 2018. *Affinities: Potent Connections in Personal Life*. Cambridge: Polity Press.
Mason, Jennifer, and Katherine Davies. 2010. "Experimenting with Qualitative Methods: Researching Family Resemblances." In *Understanding Social Research: Thinking Creatively About Method*, edited by Jennifer Mason, Katherine Davies, and Angela Dale, 27–48. London: Sage.
May, Vanessa. 2012. "Are we Really Saying Farewell to Family? A Response to Edwards and Gillies "Farewell to family?"". *Families, Relationships and Societies* 1 (3): 415.
Mead, George H. 1934. *Mind, Self and Society from a Standpoint of a Social Behaviourist*. Chicago: Chicago University Press.
Morgan, David. 1996. *Family Connections: An Introduction to Family Studies*. Oxford: Polity Press.
Morgan, David. 2011a. *Rethinking Family Practices*. Basingstoke: Palgrave Macmillan.
Morgan, David. 2011b. "Locating 'Family Practices'." *Sociological Research Online* 16 (4): 14.
Näre, Lena. 2011. "The Moral Economy of Domestic and Care Labour: Migrant Workers in Naples, Italy." *Sociology* 45 (3): 396–412.
Nordqvist, Petra. 2017. "Genetic Thinking and Everyday Living: On Family Practices and Family Imaginaries." *The Sociological Review* 65 (4): 865–881.

Nordqvist, Petra. 2019. "Un/Familiar Connections: On the Relevance of a Sociology of Personal Life for Exploring Egg and Sperm Donation." *Sociology of Health and Illness* 41 (3): 601–615.

Pahl, Ray, and David J. Pevalin. 2005. "Between Family and Friends: A Longitudinal Study of Friendship Choice." *The British Journal of Sociology* 56 (3): 433–450.

Pahl, Ray, and Liz Spencer. 2004. "Personal Communities: Not Simply Families of 'Fate' or 'Choice'." *Current Sociology* 52 (2): 199–221.

Parsons, Talcott. 1943. "The Kinship System of the Contemporary United States." *American Anthropologist* 45 (1): 22–38.

Policarpo, Verónica. 2015. "What Is a Friend?: An Exploratory Typology of the Meanings of Friendship." *Social Sciences* 4 (1): 171–191.

Policarpo, Verónica. 2019. "The Personal Life of Facebook: Managing Friendships with Social Media." *Families, Relationships and Societies* 8 (3): 445–461.

Power, Emma. 2008. "'Furry Families': Making a Human–Dog Family Through Home." *Social & Cultural Geography* 9 (5): 535–555.

Roseneil, Sasha. 2007. "Queer Individualization: The Transformation of Personal Life in the Early 21st Century" *Nordic Journal of Women's Studies* 15 (2/3): 84–99.

Roseneil, Sasha, and Shelley Budgeon. 2004. "Cultures of Intimacy and Care Beyond 'the Family': Personal Life and Social Change in the Early 21st Century." *Current Sociology* 52 (2): 135–159.

Roussel, Louis. 1989. *La famille incertaine*. Paris: Editions Odile-Jacob.

Salmon, Catherine A., and Todd K. Shackelford. 2008. "Toward an Evolutionary Psychology of the Family." In *Family Relationships: An Evolutionary Perspective*, edited by Catherine A. Salmon and Todd K. Shackelford, 3–15. Oxford: Oxford University Press.

Santos, Ana C. 2018. "Heróis no armário: homens trans* e pessoas não binárias prestadoras de cuidado." *Ex Aequo* 38: 33–47.

Schneider, David M. 1968 [1980]. *Kinship: A Cultural Account*. Chicago: University of Chicago Press.

Smart, Carol. 2010. *Personal Life: New Directions in Sociological Thinking*. Cambridge: Polity Press.

Smart, Carol. 2011. "Relationality and Socio-Cultural Theories of Family Life." In *Families and Kinship in Contemporary Europe: Rules and Practices of Relatedness*, edited by Riitta Jallinoja and Eric D. Widmer, 13–28. Basingstoke: Palgrave Macmillan Studies in Family and Intimate Life.

Smart, Carol, and Bren Neale. 1999. *Family Fragments?* Cambridge: Polity Press.

Smart, Carol, Bren Neale, and Amanda Wade. 2001. *The Changing Experience of Childhood: Families and Divorce*. Cambridge: Polity Press.

Spencer, Liz, and Ray Pahl. 2006. *Rethinking Friendship: Hidden Solidarities Today*. Princeton: Princeton University Press.

Törnqvist, Maria. 2019. "Living Alone Together: Individualized Collectivism in Swedish Communal Housing." *Sociology* 53 (5): 900–915.

Vesela, Jana. 2017. *Adverse Socio-Professional Events and Couple's Vulnerability: Exploratory Analyses of the Role of Conjugal Configurations*. PhD diss., Université de Genève. https://doi.org/10.13097/archive-ouverte/unige:112445. https://archive-ouverte.unige.ch/unige:112445.

Wall, Karin, and Rita Gouveia, R. 2014. "Changing Meanings of Family in Personal Relationships." *Current Sociology* 62 (3): 352–373.

Wall, Karin, Eric D. Widmer, Jacques-Antoine Gauthier, Vida Česnuitytė, and Rita Gouveia, eds. 2018. *Families and Personal Networks: an International Comparative Perspective*. London: Palgrave Macmillan.
Weber, Florence. 2013. *Penser la Parenté Aujourd'hui: La Force du Quotidien*. Paris: Éditions Rue d'Ulm.
Weeks, Jeffrey, Brian Heaphy, and Catherine Donovan 2001. *Same Sex Intimacies*. London: Routledge.
Wellman, Barry. 1988. "Structural Analysis: From Method and Metaphor to Theory and Substance." In *Social Structures: A Network Approach*, edited by Barry Wellman and Stephen D. Berkowitz, 19–61. Cambridge: University Press.
Weston, Kath. 1991. *The Families We Choose: Lesbians, Gays, Kinship*. New York: Columbia University Press.
Widmer, Eric D. 2010. *Family Configurations: A Structural Approach to Family Diversity*. London: Ashgate.
Widmer, Eric D., Jean Kellerhals, and René Levy. 2004. "Quelle pluralisation des relations familiales?: Conflits, styles d'interactions conjugales et milieu social." *Revue française de Sociologie* 45 (1): 37–67.
Widmer, Eric D., Anna-Maija Castrén, Riitta Jallinoja, and Kaisa Ketokivi. 2008. "Introduction." In *Beyond the Nuclear Family: Families in a Configurational Perspective*, edited by Eric D. Widmer and Riitta Jallinoja, 1–10. Bern: Peter Lang.
Wiesmann, Stephanie, Hennie Boeije, Anneke Van Doorne-Huiskes, and Laura Den Dulk. 2008. "'Not Worth Mentioning': The Implicit and Explicit Nature of Decision-Making About the Division of Paid and Domestic Work." *Community, Work & Family* 11 (4): 341–363.

CHAPTER 14

Money in Couples: The Organisation of Finances and the Symbolic Use of Money

Lars Evertsson and Charlott Nyman

INTRODUCTION

In this chapter, we focus on one specific area of couple and family life—money, finances and consumption. How financial resources in couples are handled and allocated is interesting from a family sociological perspective, but also from a policy perspective. For instance, money and consumption can be shared unequally between family members, resulting in different levels of financial security and material standard, perhaps even poverty, for individual family members. From a broader social scientific perspective, the study of money in couples can provide a better understanding of the more abstract aspects of couple relationships and of how more overarching social processes may impact couples and families.

A metaphor we often use in teaching that helps to illustrate the complexity of money in couples is money as 'Janus-faced'; money in couples has different sides or 'faces'. The one face or side entails the everyday handling and prioritising of money and consumption and the consequences of different ways of handling money. This side focuses on control, decision-making and allocation of money and consumption, and how these are connected to the exercising of power, normative and ideological expectations and conflicts of interest within

---

L. Evertsson
Mid Sweden University, Östersund, Sweden
e-mail: lars.evertsson@miun.se

C. Nyman (✉)
Department of Sociology, Umeå University, Umeå, Sweden
e-mail: charlott.nyman@umu.se

© The Author(s), under exclusive license to Springer Nature Switzerland AG 2021
A.-M. Castrén et al. (eds.), *The Palgrave Handbook of Family Sociology in Europe*, https://doi.org/10.1007/978-3-030-73306-3_14

couples. This side emphasises the challenges that finances pose for a couple's life together.

The other side or face of money in couples emphasises the more symbolic role of money in constructing couple relationships. The ways couples handle money—share and merge it (or keep it separate), and attitudes towards money—can be expressions of, but also contribute to building love, commitment and trust. They can also influence gender equality and experiences of fairness in couple relationships. For most of those who have lived in a couple relationship, both of these sides—the practical everyday aspects of money as well as the more symbolic aspects of it—will be familiar. As researchers, we have the possibility of making an analytical distinction between the two, but also of seeing connections between them. That is what we will do in this chapter. In the first part of this chapter, we review some basic elements and concepts that are central to the study of money in couples. In the second part, we show some of the symbolic meanings of money in couples.

We will make a few clarifications before we continue. Throughout the chapter, we will use the term couple, instead of the term family. Our reason for doing so is partly because much of the research usually focuses on couples as opposed to the 'family' (though the term family is often used); research seldom includes children or relatives/kin. This is also the reason for not using the term household. Unless there exists a specific reason to do so, we will not distinguish between married or as-married cohabiting couples here, since the latter has become quite common in much of Europe and resembles married couples in significant ways that are relevant to the research. The term couple in this chapter often refers to heterosexual couples, reflecting the focus of most of the research on the topic. The field of money in couples contains many related subtopics and aspects, and can be referred to with different terminology, for instance intra-household allocation, financial organisation, money in marriage. For the sake of simplicity, we will usually use the term 'money in couples' to refer to the large and encompassing field of inquiry.

The Establishment of a Research Field—Money in Couples

It was in the 1980s, due in large part to the work of Jan Pahl (1980, 1983, 1989) that research on money in couples started to become established as a field of inquiry within sociology. Pahl's work expanded on, both in scope and methodologically, the research of others before her, most notably Edwards (1981; also, e.g., Rowntree 1954; Blood and Wolfe 1960; Land 1969; Saflios-Rothschild 1970). Pahl's (1989) major contributions in the early days of research on money in couples were that she (1) updated the field of study to fit in with the profound changes that were taking place in society regarding, for instance, women's increasing participation in paid labour, (2) opened up for scrutiny the 'black box' of the family, within which processes regarding the transfer and handling of money in couples are often invisible, and (3) linked social and economic processes and changes outside of the couple to social and economic processes and changes within the couple. Pahl's study contributed to a shift in researchers' focus on the couple as a singular unit to instead focusing on the situation of the individuals that comprise couples.

The early theoretical perspectives and analytical concepts that were developed by Pahl (and others) during the 1980s and 1990s have stood the test of time and are still at the core of research on money in couples. The focus is still on the intra-household allocation of money and consumption and the social and economic factors and processes involved in how couples manage, control and share money and consumption. Changes in families regarding their composition, organisation and values (Daly 2005) and women's increasing participation in paid work have contributed to a broadening of the scope of research to include a greater variety of empirical questions, types of couples and countries (e.g. Díaz et al. 2007; Knudsen and Wærness 2009; Singh and Morley 2011; Burgoyne et al. 2011; Raijas 2011; Laporte and Schellenberg 2011; Bisdee et al. 2013; Coelho 2014; Evertsson and Nyman 2014; Lyssens-Danneboom and Mortelmans 2014; Addo 2017; Eroğlu 2020; Ibragimova and Guseva 2017; Lott 2017; Huang et al. 2019).

Central Concepts and Theoretical Perspectives in Research on Money in Couples

Management, Control and Power

From the point at which money enters the household to the point at which it leaves in the form of consumption, 'processes of control and management of money intervene' (Bennett 2013, 585). Management refers to the day-to-day decision-making and handling of money and financial matters and the implementation of previously made financial decisions. This includes seeing to it that bills are paid and other necessary expenditures taken care of, transferring money between accounts and purchasing food and other necessities for the family (Edwards 1981; Pahl 1989; Fleming 1997). The scope for management and for decision-making about routine matters on a day-to-day basis is circumscribed by previously made overarching decisions about finances. Because of women's and men's different positions in society and in families, women and men may experience couple finances differently. In couples where money is tight for instance, managing money is often a straining task held by women, while men tend to manage money when there is more of it (Vogler 1998).

Control can be exercised at different stages, for example when money enters the household and/or when decisions are made about financial matters (Goode et al. 1998). The distinction between control and management may be difficult to discern, for both the couples themselves and researchers. The manager of money may have some degree of control because of their management skills (Iversen 2003), and Pahl (1989) found that managers could perceive themselves as having control. Edwards (1981) described management as being more a matter of facts while control is more a matter of perceptions regarding freedom to spend money on personal consumption, feeling a need to justify personal spending to one's partner or feeling free to spend money on something one's partner may disapprove of. Other researchers see control as influence, or 'say', over decision-making processes related to the organisation, use and allocation of money and consumption. Control can also be used to influence which management system should be used (Fleming 1997; Vogler and Pahl 1994).

The concept of control is fluid and complicated, but important. Control entails having influence over major financial decisions such as loans and major purchases. However, control can be exercised at different levels so that decisions made about overarching financial matters (such as savings, investments and debt, but also major purchases such as a house or a car) will set limits for how money is handled in the day-to-day running of the household. Having control means having influence over what consumption is prioritised and which is not and may reflect the preferences of the partner with more control. Control also entails influencing which financial matters are discussed by partners and which are not regarded as important. Control is not necessarily held by one partner *or* the other, *nor* is it necessarily shared equally by both partners.

In order to discuss management and even more so control in couples, it is necessary to discuss power. An important theoretical perspective that has been used to understand power in couple relationships is the resource theory of power (Blood and Wolfe 1960). This theory states that when both partners' financial contributions are equal, they have equal power, and in couples where one partner contributes more money, that partner will have more power in financial matters. Money is seen as the most important source of power; however, other resources such as status and education can also be important power resources (Eroğlu 2020). Men's (often) higher income and access to other power resources such as education and status grant them a power advantage over a female partner, leading to a power imbalance. The partner having more control over money and finances can then explicitly and openly, or implicitly and subtly, restrict his/her partner's access to money and economic room to manoeuvre. Though a large number of studies have found support for the resource theory of power, this approach has been criticised for overlooking cultural and ideological factors and thereby regarding couples' ways of handling money as isolated from wider systems such as gender inequality in the labour market; it has also been criticised for seeing resources as randomly distributed or as personal/couple characteristics rather than being connected to larger patterns in society and the labour market (Roman and Vogler 1999).

An institutional perspective instead sees individuals and couples as embedded within (different) cultural and structural contexts that restrict and influence individual actions in different ways. This perspective includes the importance of gender ideology and of country context (which are often connected to each other) for understanding money management and financial inequality in couples (Yodanis and Lauer 2007; Nyman et al. 2013). Gender ideology refers to beliefs held about women and men and their (expected) roles in a couple relationship. At one end of the spectrum is a traditional gender ideology (or discourse) that constructs the man as the main breadwinner and the woman as responsible for the domestic sphere. At the other end is an egalitarian gender ideology of co-providing and equal sharing (Roman and Vogler 1999). Couples and individuals in couples can be placed somewhere within this spectrum. Research on money in couples has found gender ideology to be important for understanding the allocation of money, consumption and power in couples (Nyman 1999; Roman and Vogler 1999; Yodanis and Lauer 2007; Nyman et al. 2013; Eroğlu 2020). A qualitative comparative study discusses how gender ideology in the form of welfare regime and policy is reflected in gender ideology on the individual/couple level (Nyman et al. 2013). Yodanis and Lauer (2007), in a quantitative comparative study, also found that gender ideology on a country/cultural level influences this on the couple level: 'The overall level of economic inequality in a country also shapes the likelihood of having equal versus unequal money arrangements in marriage.... Within a context that practices and supports economic inequality, couples themselves are more likely to practice economic inequality' (Yodanis and Lauer 2007, 581).

Research has found that women's well-being increases when their financial power in the couple increases (Kulic et al. 2019). Shared control in the form of decision-making has also been shown to result in better living conditions for the household in general (Cantillon et al. 2016; Maksymovych 2017). Money is a common source of conflicts between partners and conflicts about money can be intense and difficult to resolve (Stanley et al. 2002; Miller et al. 2003; Oggins 2003; Dew and Stewart 2012; Kaittila 2012, 2018). Using data from the European Social Survey 2004/2005 from 23 European countries, Kaittila (2012) found that equal contribution to household decision-making was associated with lower levels of conflicts. A qualitative study by the same author found that dissatisfaction with unequal practices was associated with a higher level of conflict (Kaittila 2018). Similarly, Dew and Stewart (2012) found that equal levels of economic power lead to a lower level of conflict in couples. Finally, Dew et al. (2012) found that financial disagreements in married couples were the strongest types of disagreements and a strong predictor of divorce.

Power and the Social Meaning of Money

Money in couples needs to be defined, implicitly or explicitly, and how money is defined will be influenced by who has the power to define it. Depending on the source—salary from paid employment, Christmas bonus, gifted money, child benefit, lottery winnings, inheritance—money can be assigned different meanings and be earmarked for different uses (Zelizer 1989, 1994). From this theoretical perspective, money is seen as heterogeneous, not merely as a neutral medium of exchange. Definitions of ownership of money are important for perceptions about who has the right to exercise control over it and ultimately how money can be used; the partner with more power has the possibility to define money and consumption in ways that benefit himself/herself (or those of other family members) (Nyman 1999, 2003).

One important aspect of the social meaning of money is the ownership of it (Pahl 1989; Zelizer 1989, 1994; Burgoyne 1990; Nyman 2003). Money can be defined as 'my' or 'your' money—belonging to the person who earned it— or as 'our' money—belonging to the couple. Defining ownership of money in couples is complicated by two (potentially) conflicting norms or discourses in couples—the norm that the earner of money owns it and the norm of sharing in couples (Burgoyne 1990). As shown in a qualitative study of Swedish couples, the collective needs of the family/couple may lead to 'my' money being redefined as belonging to the family, or vice versa—the specific needs of a family member may cause 'family' money to be defined as belonging to (and be used for) an individual family member's needs (Evertsson and Nyman 2014). In this sense, money is social and relational in that how it is defined and used are influenced by context and relationships, such as the couple relationship (Zelizer 1989, 1994; Nyman 2003; Burgoyne and Kirchler 2008).

The entitlement and power associated with being the owner of money are strong (Burgoyne 1990; Elizabeth 2001). Owning money is seen as granting a legitimate right to exercise control over it: 'ownership confers the entitlement to dictate how that money is utilized' (Elizabeth 2001, 401). The partner seen as owning money will (implicitly or explicitly) have more control over it and thereby be able to exercise greater influence over what kind of consumption money should be used for and over defining whose consumption it is—mine, yours or ours.

A Typology of Money Management

A typology over allocation systems developed by Pahl (1989, and earlier by Edwards 1981) was an attempt to 'tease out the distinction between control and management of household income, or decision-making versus lower level organization' (Bennett 2013, 585). Pahl's typology was not the first, but is the typology that has been most widely used. It has been further developed by others (including Vogler and Pahl 1994; Pahl 2005; Vogler 2005) and remains one of the major contributions to the field. Pahl's different categories take into account control and management and look at the consequences of the different management systems for partners' personal consumption. The typology includes:

- Whole wage—one partner hands over all or almost all of his/her wages to one partner who is then responsible for managing the household's

finances, freeing the other partner from this responsibility. The earner handing over his/her wages may keep a sum for personal use. A non-earning partner (traditionally the woman) often has little or no control over finances or access to money for personal consumption.
- Housekeeping allowance—the main breadwinner (traditionally the man) hands over a sum of money to his/her partner which serves as an allowance with which to take care of daily purchases and expenses. The earner retains control over the rest of his/her wages. A non-earning partner (traditionally the woman) often has little or no control over or access to money for personal consumption.
- Pooling—the individuals' incomes are combined into a single 'pool' of money which is in theory equally accessible to both partners. The pool can be managed and controlled by either partner or both equally. Spheres of financial responsibility are joint.
- Partial pooling—a portion of each individual's income is pooled to be used for joint expenses. The pool can be managed and controlled by either partner or both equally. The portion that is kept separate is seen as owned and controlled by the earner, and can be used at his/her discretion.
- Independent management—each earner retains his/her earnings and full control over them. Expenses are kept separate and joint expenses are divided up/shared between partners.

The housekeeping allowance and whole wage systems are based (implicitly or explicitly) on a main-breadwinner model where one partner (traditionally the man) brings in all or the main part of the household's income. In these systems (and in pooling below), couples 'operate more or less as single economic units in which individual autonomy is to some degree subordinated to the needs of the couple as a collective unit' (Pahl 2008, 580).

Pooling (sometimes referred to as joint pooling) is the system that has been the focus of much of the research. Pooling entails that earnings from both partners are combined into a pool that both partners have access to. Expenditures and consumption (joint and personal) are paid for from the joint pool. A majority of couples have joint accounts (Addo and Sassler 2010) and money is regarded as 'ours'. In its purest form, no 'my' or 'your' money exists. This system has by many researchers been found to be very common in married and as-married couples in a number of countries (e.g. Vogler and Pahl 1994; Fleming 1997; Nyman 2002; Díaz et al. 2007; Yodanis and Lauer 2014; Lott 2017; Ibragimova and Guseva 2017). Pooling is often seen as a system that has the potential to promote equality in access to money since it allows a non-earning or lower earning partner equal access to household money. However, pooling can also lead to poorer access for the non-earning or lower earning partner (usually the woman) since this partner may feel less entitlement to spending pooled money (Nyman 1999; Pahl 2005). Pooling can also lead to unequal access to personal spending money for women when minor consumption for the family (such as smaller purchases for the household or for children) becomes a 'grey zone' since such consumption is not defined as joint. Women then tend to pay for this kind of consumption since it falls within their (gendered) sphere of responsibility which includes shopping for the home and for children. This in turn may result in less money available for their own personal consumption (Nyman 1999). Vogler et al. (2008) found that pooling leads to equal access only when both partners are in full-time employment and see themselves as co-providers with shared responsibility for breadwinning, illustrating the importance of gender ideology. Pooling can also obscure unequal sharing since equal sharing may be expected and taken for granted and thereby not a matter on the agenda for discussion (Hertz 1986; Wilson 1987a, b; Burgoyne 1990; Nyman 1999; Dema-Moreno 2009).

During the last few decades, researchers have paid more attention to individualised systems of money management—partial pooling and independent management. Both of these are characterised by a large degree of individual control over money and personal spending and a desire to keep individuals' finances separate so that individuals in couples operate, to some degree, as two separate and autonomous economic units (Vogler et al. 2008; Coelho 2014; Evertsson and Nyman 2014). In couples using partial pooling, pooled money is used to pay for joint expenses while the remaining money is held back and regarded as the individual's money. The amount held back can be large or small. In independent management, partners keep their own earnings separate and are often responsible for different areas of household expenses. Couples using independent management value autonomy and control over their money, strive towards equality and fairness in their relationship and tend to define equality as partners' equal contributions towards collective expenditures (Elizabeth 2001; Van Eeden-Moorefield et al. 2007; Ashby and Burgoyne 2008; Evertsson and Nyman 2014).

Individualised money management systems—partial pooling and independent management—are more common in countries in which individualised attitudes and forms of couplehood are more accepted (Lauer and Yodanis 2011). These are more likely to be used by de-institutionalised couple forms such as cohabiters (Burgoyne et al. 2006; Vogler et al. 2008; Lott 2017), non-cohabiting LAT ('living-apart-together') couples (Burgoyne et al. 2011; Lyssens-Danneboom and Mortelmans 2014), reconstituted/blended families and remarried couples (Van Eeden-Moorefield et al. 2007; Raijas 2011; Lott 2017; Eickmeyer et al. 2019), same-sex couples (Burns et al., 2008) and in newly married couples (Pahl 2005; Burgoyne et al. 2006; Lott 2017). Couples with gender egalitarian beliefs and income homogamy are also more likely to use an individualised system (Çineli 2020). This trend towards using such a system is seen as related to a diversification of family forms (Beck-Gernsheim 1998), to an erosion of the male-breadwinner ideology and women's increased financial independence (Lott 2017) and as part of the broader trend towards companionate intimate relationships that are characterised by autonomy and individualism (Lauer and Yodanis 2011; Kan and Laurie 2014). In couples with an individualised attitude toward couple relationships, partners are less likely to see themselves as an interdependent unit (Lauer and Yodanis 2011) and may prioritise individual needs and desires, which are likely to be reflected in the money management system used (Pahl 2005; Vogler 2005).

Individualised systems of money management may seem to be in sharp contrast to norms about equity, fairness, equality and togetherness in couples (Burgoyne 1990). And yet, couples that use them have been found to also value and strive towards an equal yet committed relationship. Individualised management systems may be a way for couples to negotiate conflicting norms of jointness and autonomy (Fleming 1997; Ashby and Burgoyne 2008). Especially for women, individualised systems may be a means by which to negotiate jointness of finances rather than a goal in and of itself (Singh and Morley 2011). Van Eeden-Moorefield et al. (2007) suggest that independent management is used by women as a means by which to gain more influence over and autonomy in financial matters within the couple relationship. Couples using independent management try to negotiate a balance between jointness and autonomy by using one of two strategies (Brines and Joyner 1999; Nyman 1999, 2003; Elizabeth 2001). One strategy entails partners' *equal* (50–50) contribution to joint expenses. When expenses are shared equally, the lower earner will have less of their own income left after contributing to joint expenses, resulting in lower access to personal spending money and a lower standard of living (Pahl 2005; Burgoyne et al. 2006). The other strategy entails *equitable* sharing of joint expenses so that each partner contributes the same percentage of their income to joint expenses. This strategy emphasises equal outcomes in terms of equality of access to personal spending money, but also means that one partner will contribute more of their own money to joint expenses. Independent management may also be a way for women to avoid financial dependence on a partner, and a way to protect and maintain their financial independence, thereby safeguarding their possibilities to exit a relationship (Hobson 1990; Burgoyne and Morison 1997; Nyman and Reinikainen 2007).

Independent management can potentially 'undermine the traditional inequalities within marriage and create egalitarian relationships' (Elizabeth 2001, 401–402). Partial pooling and independent management have the potential of allowing each partner (some degree of) financial autonomy and control. However, the lack of sharing of money with one's partner that is (theoretically) inherent in individualised systems of money management could lead to one partner having a considerably lower standard of living than the other if that partner has a lower income and/or more individual expenses (e.g. debt) that reduce money available for personal spending. Research has shown that the non-/lower earning partner may have poorer access to money, especially when incongruence in income is accompanied by a discourse of earner entitlement or when no sharing between partners is expected (Nyman 1999; Elizabeth 2001; Pahl 2008; Vogler et al. 2008). This may contribute to greater financial power for the higher earner (Pahl 2005; Burgoyne et al. 2006).

Reflecting on the State of Research on Money in Couples

The work discussed above has formed a theoretical and conceptual platform for the study of money in couples that is still used today and the concepts discussed above are still the focus of much of the contemporary research on money in couples. Theoretical assumptions and analytical concepts have of course developed, been refined and expanded in order to raise and answer new questions. However, they have also been challenged.

Researchers have pointed out weaknesses of the different versions of a typology of money management. For example, the categories do not always provide a good 'fit' in relation to the ways couples actually organise finances (Snape et al. 1999; Evertsson and Nyman 2014). Also, the categories of the typology are sometime indistinguishable from each other (Wilson 1987a, b). A great deal of research done during the last few decades has expanded its scope to take into account new forms of couple relationships and how these relate to attitudes towards money and sharing, marriage and couplehood, changing gender roles and ideologies, etc. The once so common nuclear family, consisting of a married heterosexual couple with children and with a male breadwinner, is no longer the only relevant form of couplehood. In many countries, a dual-earner/dual-breadwinner model is the norm or becoming more common, and a variety of new types of families and couples (e.g. LAT, same-sex couples, reconstituted) have become increasingly common in most countries in Europe and North America. A typology may not be able to capture the empirical variation found in these and other (new) forms of couples, and there is a need to continue to develop the typology in order to keep up with changes in society. Despite these weaknesses, we argue that the typology has provided, and still provides, a good methodological and analytical starting point for research, especially for comparative cross-national studies.

A typology can provide only a limited understanding of money in couples since it lacks the theoretical and analytical capacity to address the double and contradictory nature of money in couples, that which we at the beginning of this chapter referred to as its Janus face. Money and consumption can be unequally shared; this can be an expression of power and a source of tension and conflicts. However, money and consumption can also express love, commitment and trust. We argue that research must strive towards investigating the different faces of money in couples and develop theoretical and analytical concepts to understand the interconnection between them. So far, the aim of much of the research has been to investigate inequalities in women's and men's control over and access to money and consumption. Despite the weaknesses and gaps, the research thus far has been important for understanding how power may work and why gender inequality persists in couples. In the next section, we will explore the other face of money in couples—how money and finances can be used to construct couplehood, express love and commitment and assign meaning to acts and actions in couples.

Symbolic Meanings and Uses of Money in Couples

The picture that much of the research has painted is one of unequal (and gendered) access to money and consumption; money as a source of conflict and gender inequality and couple finances is an arena for the playing out of power. However, if we look past these concrete, somewhat problematic aspects, we can gain sight of some of the more symbolic aspects of money and finances in couples. As the field of research has matured, researchers have expanded their focus to include a greater variety of questions about couple relationships. In the remainder of this chapter, we will explore some of these. We will show how money can be used as a symbolic tool to construct the couple relationship. In this respect, money can act as a window into the interaction and processes that take place in couples.

Money in Everyday Life as an Arena for the Construction of Couplehood

The construction of couplehood can be found, we argue, in the many significant as well as the seemingly insignificant daily decisions, practices and behaviours that take place in couple relationships, intentionally or unintentionally. Couple relationships are constituted, experienced and afforded meaning through everyday events and practices (Gabb and Fink 2015). The day-to-day handling of money can in this respect be seen as an important aspect of how couples construct and assign meaning to their relationship (Halleröd et al. 2007; Stocks 2007).

Some couples construct and form their relationship according to traditional scripts about couple, family and gender. However, an increasing number of non-traditional (de-institutionalised) couple relationships lack a clear script, or reject 'traditional' scripts used by their parents, for how to form their couple relationships and financial practices, and are left to their own imagination for finding ways of making their life as a couple work. Whether couples adhere to traditional scripts or seek to revise, reinterpret or reinvent them, the role of money in the construction of couple relationships is considerable (Steuber and Paik 2014). As noted by Ibragimova and Guseva (2017), money and finances are a part of the construction and enactment of the couple's relationship. Ways of handling money are a central and unavoidable part of couples' lives together and must be 'worked out'. It is in this 'working out' of ways to handle money that it acquires a symbolic role and can create and convey meaning (Evertsson and Nyman 2014). The organisation and handling of money can offer couples and the individuals in them the possibility to express, build and strengthen love, commitment and trust. Below, we will illustrate a few of the ways that money can be used in the process of constructing couple relationships.

Expressing Togetherness

A central aspect of couplehood is togetherness and solidarity (Nyman 1999; Elizabeth 2001; Evertsson and Nyman 2014). Upon entering into a relationship, couples meet a number of explicit and implicit norms and expectations about couple relationships in general, and more specifically, about how to organise their finances; these expectations form the script by which couples organise their relationship. Knudson-Martin and Mahoney (1998, 82) describe the complexity involved; couples 'enter into relationships with egalitarian ideals and with expectations that both wives and husbands will work outside of the home. These factors propel couples toward equality. On the other hand, men and women continue to enter relationships with traditional gender expectations and with unequal resources and power, thus making actual achievement of equality difficult'.

Pooling money can be used to express and strengthen the ideals of togetherness, team effort and equity. In an interview study of ten Swedish couples, Nyman (1999) found that most of the couples regarded the family as a unit and both partners' incomes as belonging not to the individuals who earned them, but to the family. The family was seen as 'a joint project for which they worked together as a team' (Nyman 1999, 774). This perception of the sharing of money and consumption can be both an expression of and contributing to establishing a sense of commitment in the couple. And indeed, the sharing and pooling of money are by many seen as at the heart of what it means to be a couple. A qualitative study of the role of money in the construction of Spanish couples (Díaz et al. 2007) found that pooling money binds together partners and is seen as necessary for being a real couple. In several of the couples in this Spanish study, (the idea of) an egalitarian couple relationship was valued despite the man being the main breadwinner and the partner who exercised considerably more control over 'joint' money. The fact that both partners contributed with their salaries to a joint pool allowed these couple to feel like a 'real' couple, but also to construct themselves as an egalitarian couple, despite gender inequalities (as perceived by the women).

The Meanings of Merging Money

Treas (1993) found that some degree of pooling or merging income in couples for example in the form of having joint bank accounts can contribute to forming a 'we' identity and the couple as a collective unit, which may promote relational commitment. Research on the banking practices of couples shows that the kinds of bank accounts held by partners can be a reflection of, but also a creator of meaning. A study of young American cohabiting and LAT couples shows how the merging of money can be an indication and expression of commitment to and belief in the future of the relationship: 'when couples engage in joint financial practices they may be doing so as a matter of dedication' (Addo 2017, 84). The intertwining of finances is one way of building relationship-specific capital and a couple-level identity, and in this process, joint bank accounts can act as a sort of scaffolding upon which to build commitment and dedication (Addo 2017). Steuber and Paik (2014) found in their study of young American (engaged and non-engaged) cohabiters that the merging of finances in the form of joint banking was seen as an important relational behaviour in couples and that committed partners were more prepared to incur the costs of merging finances. Burgoyne et al. (2010) also found that trust and mutual commitment can be expressed and strengthened through the use of joint bank accounts.

The merging of finances can express satisfaction and trust in the relationship, contribute to relationship stability and signal long-term plans. A Swedish qualitative study of couples using an individualised money management system found that LAT and same-sex cohabiting partners expressed trust and commitment by granting access to and insight into each other's finances. They entrusted their partner with access to banking passwords and financial documents, provided insight into financial activities and allowed each other to voice opinions about how individual money was handled (Evertsson and Nyman 2014). These acts can be seen a 'soft' merging of partners' finances. They can also provide couples with the possibility to reconcile the tension between the egalitarian ideology that money in couples should be shared equally and the individualistic ideology that individuals own the money they earn (Burgoyne 1990; Elizabeth 2001; Nyman and Dema 2007; Huang et al. 2019). Having joint finances stresses togetherness, signals trust and signifies equity since it turns individual income into joint money, which entails a loss of control over own money. However joint finances can also conceal discrepancies in partners' economic contributions to the household and neutralise questions of equality, equity, control and allocation, keeping them off the agenda for discussion (Singh 1997; Treas 1999; Burgoyne et al. 2010; Huang et al. 2019).

Symbolic Consumption to Build Couple Relationships—A Few Examples

Couples can (re)define money and use consumption in a symbolic way to express love and commitment. Drawing on our own qualitative research on Swedish couples, we present two illustrative examples. First, we present Frida, a woman in her 30s who re-defines a large personal inheritance by making it visible and accessible for consumption for her family (Nyman 2003). In another study, we found that Swedish same-sex and LAT couples, practising individualised management, create room for symbolic joint consumption by relinquishing control over their own money (Evertsson and Nyman 2014).

Frida received a large inheritance which she defined as her own. This money had special meaning and was kept separate (in a separate personal bank account) from the couple's pooled money for several years. Keeping her money separate gave Frida full ownership and control over it, which was her intention. However, keeping it separate also kept it hidden out of sight and 'invisible' to the rest of the family. As Frida came to see the relationship as stable and lasting, she started to redefine 'her' money as family money. By redefining the inherited money and using it to treat family members to 'extras', Frida made her financial contribution visible and was 'in effect telling her family (husband) that she sees them as a unit, that she trusts them and believes in their future life together' (Nyman 2003, 88). By re-defining her inheritance and using the money for her family in an obvious manner, the symbolic value of her actions was made visible, thereby increasing the status and power that this money bestows (Gullestad 1984).

The re-defining of own money as belonging to the partner or to the couple can be a way of strengthening and manifesting support and love towards one's partner. In an interview study of how independent management was practised in Swedish LAT and same-sex couples, interviewees were prepared to re-define their own money and relinquish control over it in order to facilitate 'symbolically important joint consumption, that is, consumption that was seen as an expression of love and commitment or as an investment in the future or quality of the couple relationship' (Evertsson and Nyman 2014, 75). Symbolically important consumption could be things for the shared home such as a pet dog or a car. However, it could also be shared experiences, such as a dream vacation together that would create joint experiences and memories and thereby strengthen the bond between partners. In this study, money that 'on paper' was owned and controlled by the earner was re-defined as the couple's or the partner's money. This contributed to a weaving together of partners' individual finances and a blurring of the line between individual money and consumption, which illustrates the social and relational nature of money. Couples' desire to express love and commitment prompted them to re-define money from 'mine' to 'yours' or 'ours' in order to facilitate symbolically important consumption. At the same time, the symbolically important consumption that the re-defining of money made possible served as an investment in the future, quality and strength of the couple relationship.

The Symbolic Importance of the Source of Money

The source of money—who earns it and where it comes from—is important for how it is assigned meaning. In couples subscribing to a traditional male-breadwinner ideology, a wife's larger contribution to couple finances can cause friction. In an American study (Wilson and Stocks 2007), an inheritance to the wife, Elizabeth, was used to cover the couple's day-to-day expenses, which made her the breadwinner. This departure from a traditional responsibility for breadwinning challenged the male-breadwinner ideology held by both Elizabeth and her partner and contributed to marital instability. When her husband's income and thereby the proportion he contributed to household finances increased, he was seen by his wife and himself as the main breadwinner which leads to a decrease in tension and a strengthening of the relationship.

Another couple from the same study illustrates that when different gender ideologies are held by partners, views on money may be at odds with each other. This was the case for another couple in which the wife's slightly higher income deprived her husband of the role of main breadwinner and the more traditional division of responsibility he desired. His dissatisfaction with the situation, combined with his wife's strong need to contribute financially and have control over her money, contributed to a non-traditional financial situation and irreconcilable tensions (Wilson and Stocks 2007). For this couple, the challenge to the male-breadwinner ideal and the deviation from expectations regarding partners' relative contribution to couple finances were too great to handle.

Foreshadowing the findings in more contemporary work, Stamp (1985), McRae (1987), and Tichenor (1999, 2005) found that more income contributed by the women, in relation to a male partner, can be too much of a departure from gendered expectations in couples with a male-breadwinner ideology. Women who earned more than their husbands (or who worked in higher status jobs, or both) challenged (albeit unintentionally) normative gender expectations about male breadwinning. Higher-earning wives expressed dissatisfaction over their husband's failure to live up to their traditional obligations as main earner. In order to restore balance, higher-earning women may relinquish control over money in order to compensate for the reversal in breadwinning roles. Tichenor (1999, 2005) also found that women's higher earnings seldom translated into more power for them since women tended to downplay the discrepancy in partners' incomes. Money and the reversed financial roles in these couples serve to uphold a conventional understanding and practising of couplehood, gender, financial practices and the allocation of power in couples. In an interview study on financial decision-making in Spanish couples, Dema-Moreno (2009, 45) found that 'earning or working less did not, on the whole, cause men any loss of influence in decision making nor did it induce them to reduce their expenses as it did in the women's cases'. She found that in couples where wives earned more than her husband, women established strategies to avoid challenges to the man's role as breadwinner. These strategies involved 'overvaluing the contribution made by the man and underestimating that of the women. Some couples disguised the fact that the woman earned more. In others there were separate expenses, so that each member's wages were used to pay for different kinds of items' (Dema-Moreno 2009, 45).

The work of Tichenor and Dema-Moreno (and others) illustrates how money and gender norms are related and shows 'how normative gender expectations constrain interactions between spouses and how spouses in these unconventional marriages struggle to construct appropriate gender identities that are more or less consistent with the conventional expectations that men should be breadwinners and women should be homemakers' (Tichenor 2005, 191). Similar results were found in an Australian study by Blom and Hewitt (2020), based on Australian Household, Income and Labour Dynamics data.

They investigated relationship satisfaction in female-breadwinner households and found that respondents were most satisfied with the relationship when they were in a male-breadwinner/female-homemaker relationship. There is no direct and given association between income earned and power over financial decision-making since gender seems to intervene. These examples also highlight the significance of partners' relative contribution to couple finances. Being the higher earner does not seem to mean for women what it traditionally has meant for men—a source of power that can be used in bargaining for more power over decision-making, at least not in couples with a traditional male-breadwinner ideology. Instead of altering the power balance between women and men in couples, women who earn more than their male partner may find ways of contributing to reproducing men's greater power over financial decision-making in couples. These findings challenge the relevance of the resource theory of power and highlight the importance of gender and gender ideology for how money is perceived and handled in couples.

With the examples above, we have tried to show how money in couples can, to borrow Addo's (2017) illustrative term, serve as a scaffolding upon which to construct and assign symbolic meaning to the couple relationship. We have also, we hope, illustrated the complexity and the ambiguous and Janus-faced nature of money in couples. On the one hand, couples can share money and consumption in ways that conform to and strengthen the ideas they associate with couplehood, such as love, equality/equity, fairness, trust, commitment and togetherness. On the other hand, financial practices adopted by couples can be difficult to reconcile with normative and couple-based ideals and expectations about couplehood.

Concluding Discussion

We have limited our overview here mainly to the sociological research, which has meant that the rich body of literature from other disciplines that have shown an interest in the topic, such as economics, marketing and psychology, have unfortunately been excluded. In one respect, summarising the central aspects of the topic of money in couples is quite simple. Ideas, principles and practices for how couples handle (control, manage, allocate) money and consumption vary according to a number of factors. Couples are seldom comprised of two equal partners in regard to financial (and other) power. In heterosexual couples, the woman is often the financially weaker partner, with smaller chances of influencing couple finances. For this reason, regarding the couple as a financial unit can conceal a great deal of what goes within the 'black box' of couple finances. Much of the research reviewed illustrates, implicitly or explicitly, the gendered ideas and gender inequality that (still) characterises money in couples. From a policy perspective, this is important and points to the need to take women's and men's power and bargaining positions into account. Policies that strengthen women's financial strength, for instance by strengthening their ties to paid employment and/or ensure that they have their own income over different stages of the life course, are important for their influence on couple finances. Social, labour market and family policies that compensate women for loss of income in connection with childbirth and that protect their position in the labour market over the life course can encourage greater equality in partners' influence over financial matters in couples. However, as we have seen, this is not enough to ensure that partners have equal power in financial matters or equal access to money and consumption. Ideas and norms about the financial (and other) roles, responsibilities and needs of women and men in couples are also important for how money is controlled, managed and allocated. Gender clearly matters.

From a family sociology perspective, how couples perceive and organise their couple relationships in general, and their finances more specifically, is interesting. How money in couples is perceived and handled is influenced by (and influences) ideas and ideals about couple relationships, notions of gender and the complex workings of power. Perceptions and the handling of money can be a tool used to create meaning, to express love, commitment and belief in the couple's future together. They can be used to create new scripts for how to perceive and organise finances in couple or to reproduce or revise old ones. We refer to this complex character of money in couples as 'Janus-faced' because money in couples includes the negotiation of power *and* love, owning *and* sharing, 'me' *and* 'we'. The ways that couples regard, handle and talk about money and consumption can be intentional—but also (and often) unintentional—*expressions of* love, trust and commitment. At the same time, they can serve to *create and strengthen* love, trust and commitment. It may be for this very reason that couples are prepared to accept what appears to be (in the eyes of researchers) asymmetries regarding access to money, consumption and power. Or perhaps couples feel that a power imbalance in one area of a couple's life, such as finances, is offset by the (perhaps reversed?) power balance in other areas. This aspect unfortunately falls outside of the scope of this chapter. The unlikely and seemingly contradictory mix of power and love regarding money may also be one reason for the difficulty couples sometimes have in acknowledging the existence of conflicts about money as well as for the difficulty involved in resolving them.

On writing this chapter, we have had the opportunity to reflect on the blind spots, on what is still left to do in research on money in couples. One such blind spot is the fact that most studies are 'snapshots' of how money is handled in couples. Research has paid surprisingly little attention to how foreseeable (e.g. parenthood, empty nest, retirement) and non-foreseeable (e.g. unemployment, illness, marital problems) critical life events influence money in couples over the life course. Surprisingly little research on money in couples has included children, children's perspective or outcomes for children or the role of children for the management of money. The role of family networks and the financial support and/or costs that these entail have also been under-researched. Few studies have addressed the relevance of changed circumstances over the life course, and almost none (if any) longitudinal studies exist. Yet another blind spot in research is the role of marital/relationship quality for how couples organise finances. Also, little systematic research has been done to investigate non-heterosexual couples and newer de-institutionalised forms of couple relationships. We also look forward to research that regards couples' ways of perceiving and handling money from a variety of social/political perspectives and in a variety of cultural contexts.

References

Addo, Fenaba R. 2017. "Financial Integration and Relationship Transitions of Young Adult Cohabiters." *Journal of Family and Economic Issues* 38 (1): 84–99.
Addo, Fenaba R., and Sharon Sassler. 2010. "Financial Arrangements and Relationship Quality in Low-Income Couples." *Family Relations* 59 (4): 408–423.
Ashby, Katherine J., and Carole B. Burgoyne. 2008. "Separate Financial Entities?: Beyond Categories of Money Management." *The Journal of Socio-Economics* 37 (2): 458–480.
Beck-Gernsheim, Elisabeth. 1998. *Was kommt nach der Familie? Einblicke in neue Lebensformen*. München: Verlag C. H. Beck.
Bennett, Fran. 2013. "Researching Within-Household Distribution: Overview, Developments, Debates, and Methodological Challenges." *Journal of Marriage and Family* 75 (3): 582–597.
Bisdee, Dinah, Tom Daly, and Debora Price. 2013. "Behind Closed Doors: Older Couples and the Gendered Management of Household Money." *Social Policy and Society* 12 (1): 163–174.
Blom, Niels, and Belinda Hewitt. 2020. "Becoming a Female-Breadwinner Household in Australia: Changes in Relationship Satisfaction." *Journal of Marriage and Family* 82 (4): 1340–1357.
Blood, Robert O., and Donald M. Wolfe. 1960. *Husbands and Wives: The Dynamics of Family Living*. New York, NY: Free Press.
Brines, Julie, and Kara Joyner. 1999. "The Ties That Bind: Principles of Cohesion in Cohabitation and Marriage." *American Sociological Review* 64 (3): 333–355.
Burgoyne, Carole B. 1990. "Money in Marriage: How Patterns of Allocation Both Reflect and Conceal Power." *The Sociological Review* 38 (4): 634–665.
Burgoyne, Carole B., and Erich Kirchler. 2008. "Financial Decisions in the Household". In *The Cambridge Handbook of Psychology and Economic Behaviour*, edited by Alan Lewis, 132–154. Cambridge: Cambridge University Press.
Burgoyne, Carole B., and Victoria Morison. 1997. "Money in Remarriage: Keeping Things Simple—And Separate." *The Sociological Review* 45 (3): 363–395.
Burgoyne, Carole B., Victoria Clarke, Janet Reibstein, and Anne Edmunds. 2006. "'All My Worldly Goods I Share with You'? Managing Money at the Transition to Heterosexual Marriage." *The Sociological Review* 54 (4): 619–637.
Burgoyne, Carole B., Janet Reibstein, Anne Mary Edmunds, and David Anthony Routh. 2010. "Marital Commitment, Money and Marriage Preparation: What Changes After the Wedding?" *Journal of Community & Applied Social Psychology* 20 (5): 390–403.
Burgoyne, Carole B., Victoria Clarke, and Maree Burns. 2011. "Money Management and Views of Civil Partnership in Same-Sex Couples: Results from a UK Survey of Non-heterosexuals." *The Sociological Review* 59 (4): 685–706.

Burns, Maree, Carole B. Burgoyne, and Victoria Clarke. 2008. "Financial Affairs? Money Management in Same-Sex Relationships." *The Journal of Socio-Economics* 37 (2): 481–501.
Cantillon, Sara, Bertrand Maître, and Dorothy Watson. 2016. "Family Financial Management and Individual Deprivation." *Journal of Family and Economic Issues* 37 (3): 461–473.
Çineli, Beyda. 2020. "Money Management and Gender Equality: An Analysis of Dual-Earner Couples in Western Europe." *Family Relations* 69 (2): 803–819.
Coelho, Lina. 2014. "My Money, Your Money, Our Money: Contributions to the Study of Couples' Financial Management in Portugal." *RCCS Annual Review* 6 (6): 83–101.
Daly, Mary. 2005. "Changing Family Life in Europe: Significance for State and Society." *European Societies* 7 (3): 379–398.
Dema-Moreno, Sandra. 2009. "Behind the Negotiations: Financial Decision-Making Processes in Spanish Dual-Income Couples." *Feminist Economics* 15 (1): 27–56.
Dew, Jeffrey P., and Robert Stewart. 2012. "A Financial Issue, a Relationship Issue, or Both? Examining the Predictors of Marital Financial Conflict." *Journal of Financial Therapy* 3 (1): 43–61.
Dew, Jeffrey P., Sonya Britt, and Sandra Huston. 2012. "Examining the Relationship Between Financial Issues and Divorce." *Family Relations* 61 (4): 615–628.
Díaz, Capitolina, Sandra Dema, and Marta Ibáñez. 2007. "The Intertwining of Money and Love in Couple Relationships." In *Modern Couples Sharing Money, Sharing Life*, edited by Janet Stocks, Capitolina Díaz, and Björn Halleröd, 100–142. London: Palgrave Macmillan.
Edwards, Meredith. 1981. "Financial Arrangements within Families: Empirical Results and Tax Implications." *Children Australia* 6 (3): 16–19.
Eickmeyer, Kasey J., Wendy D. Manning, and Susan L. Brown. 2019. "What's Mine Is Ours? Income Pooling in American Families." *Journal of Marriage and Family* 81 (4): 968–978.
Elizabeth, Vivienne. 2001. "Managing Money, Managing Coupledom: A Critical Examination of Cohabitants' Money Management Practices." *The Sociological Review* 49 (3): 389–411.
Eroğlu, Şebnem. 2020. "Are Movers More Egalitarian than Stayers? An Intergenerational Perspective on Intra-Household Financial Decision-Making." *International Migration Review* 54 (1): 120–146.
Evertsson, Lars, and Charlott Nyman. 2014. "Perceptions and Practices in Independent Management: Blurring the Boundaries Between 'Mine,' 'Yours' and 'Ours'." *Journal of Family and Economic Issues* 35 (1): 65–80.
Fleming, Robin. 1997. *The Common Purse: Income Sharing in New Zealand Families*. Auckland: Auckland University Press.
Gabb, Jacqui, and Janet Fink. 2015. "Telling Moments and Everyday Experience: Multiple Methods Research on Couple Relationships and Personal Lives." *Sociology* 49 (5): 970–987.
Goode, Jackie, Claire Callender, and Ruth Lister. 1998. *Purse or Wallet?: Gender Inequalities and Income Distribution Within Families on Benefits*. London: Policy Studies Institute.
Gullestad, Marianne. 1984. *Kitchen-Table Society: A Case Study of the Family Life and Friendships of Young Working-Class Mothers in Urban Norway*. Irvington-on-Hudson, NY: Columbia University Press.

Halleröd, Björn, Capitolina Díaz, and Janet Stocks. 2007. "Doing Gender While Doing Couple: Concluding Remarks." In *Modern Couples Sharing Money, Sharing Life*, edited by Janet Stocks, Capitolina Díaz, and Björn Halleröd, 143–155. London: Palgrave Macmillan.

Hertz, Rosanna. 1986. *More Equal than Others: Women and Men in Dual-Career Marriages*. Berkeley: University of California Press.

Hobson, Barbara. 1990. "No Exit, No Voice: Women's Economic Dependency and the Welfare State." *Acta Sociologica* 33 (3): 235–250.

Huang, Yangtao, Francisco Perales, and Mark Western. 2019. "To Pool or Not to Pool? Trends and Predictors of Banking Arrangements Within Australian Couples." *PloS One* 14 (4): e0214019.

Ibragimova, Dilyara, and Alya Guseva. 2017. "Who Is in Charge of Family Finances in the Russian Two-Earner Households?" *Journal of Family Issues* 38 (17): 2425–2448.

Iversen, Vegard. 2003. "Intra-Household Inequality: A Challenge for the Capability Approach?" *Feminist Economics* 9 (2–3): 93–115.

Kaittila, Anniina. 2012. "Monetary Conflicts Within Co-residential Unions: A Comparative Perspective." *Research on Finnish Society* 5: 19–28.

Kaittila, Anniina. 2018. "Why Do Conflicts Over Money Occur Between Partners? Exploring the Explanations of Childbearing Adults in Finland." *Journal of Family Studies* 26 (4): 511–527.

Kan, Man Yee, and Heather Laurie. 2014. "Changing Patterns in the Allocation of Savings, Investments and Debts Within Couple Relationships." *The Sociological Review* 62 (2): 335–358.

Knudsen, Knud, and Kari Wærness. 2009. "Shared or Separate? Money Management and Changing Norms of Gender Equality Among Norwegian Couples." *Community, Work & Family* 12 (1): 39–55.

Knudson-Martin, Carmen, and Anne Rankin Mahoney. 1998. "Language and Processes in the Construction of Equality in New Marriages." *Family Relations* 47 (1): 81–91.

Kulic, Nevena, Alessandra Minello, and Sara Zella. 2019. "Manage Your Money, Be Satisfied? Money Management Practices and Financial Satisfaction of Couples Through the Lens of Gender." *Journal of Family Issues* 41 (9): 1420–1446.

Land, Hilary. 1969. *Large Families in London: A Study of 86 Families*. London: G. Bell & Sons Ltd.

Laporte, Christine, and Grant Schellenberg. 2011. "The Income Management Strategies of Older Couples in Canada." Statistics Canada Analytical Branch Studies Working Paper, no. 335.

Lauer, Sean R., and Carrie Yodanis. 2011. "Individualized Marriage and the Integration of Resources." *Journal of Marriage and Family* 73 (3): 669–683.

Lott, Yvonne. 2017. "When My Money Becomes Our Money: Changes in Couples' Money Management." *Social Policy and Society* 16 (2): 199–218.

Lyssens-Danneboom, Vicky, and Dimitri Mortelmans. 2014. "Living Apart Together and Money: New Partnerships, Traditional Gender Roles." *Journal of Marriage and Family* 76 (5): 949–966.

Maksymovych, Sergii. 2017. "Decision-Making in the Household and Material Deprivation." CERGE-EI Working Paper Series, no. 604.

McRae, Susan. 1987. "The Allocation of Money in Cross-Class Families." *The Sociological Review* 35 (1): 97–122.

Miller, Richard B., Jeremy B Yorgason, and Jonathan G. Sandberg. 2003. "Problems that Couples Bring to Therapy: A View Across the Family Life Cycle." *The American Journal of Family Therapy* 31 (5): 395–407.
Nyman, Charlott. 1999. "Gender Equality in 'the Most Equal Country in the World'? Money and Marriage in Sweden." *The Sociological Review* 47 (4): 766–793.
Nyman, Charlott. 2002. *Mine, Yours or Ours?: Sharing in Swedish Couples*. Diss. Umeå universitet, sociologiska institutionen.
Nyman, Charlott. 2003 "The Social Nature of Money: Meanings of Money in Swedish Families." *Women's Studies International Forum* 26 (1): 79–94.
Nyman, Charlott, and Sandra Dema. 2007. "An Overview: Research on Couples and Money." In *Modern Couples Sharing Money, Sharing Life*, edited by Janet Stocks, Capitolina Díaz, and Björn Halleröd, 7–29. London: Palgrave Macmillan.
Nyman, Charlott, and Lasse Reinikainen. 2007 "Elusive Independence in a Context of Gender in Sweden". In *Modern Couples Sharing Money, Sharing Life*, edited by Janet Stocks, Capitolina Díaz, and Björn Halleröd, 41–71. London: Palgrave Macmillan.
Nyman, Charlott, Lasse Reinikainen, and Janet Stocks. 2013. "Reflections on a Cross-National Qualitative Study of Within-Household Finances." *Journal of Marriage and Family* 75 (3): 640–650.
Oggins, Jean. 2003. "Topics of Marital Disagreement Among African-American and Euro-American Newlyweds." *Psychological Reports* 92 (2): 419–425.
Pahl, Jan. 1980. "Patterns of Money Management Within Marriage." *Journal of Social Policy* 9 (3): 313–335.
Pahl, Jan. 1983. "The Allocation of Money and the Structuring of Inequality Within Marriage." *The Sociological Review* 31 (2): 237–262.
Pahl, Jan. 1989. *Money and Marriage*. London: Macmillan Education Ltd.
Pahl, Jan. 2005. "Individualisation in Couple Finances: Who Pays for the Children?" *Social Policy and Society* 4 (4): 381.
Pahl, Jan. 2008. "Family Finances, Individualisation, Spending Patterns and Access to Credit." *The Journal of Socio-Economics* 37 (2): 577–591.
Raijas, Anu. 2011. "Money Management in Blended and Nuclear Families." *Journal of Economic Psychology* 32 (4): 556–563.
Rowntree, Griselda. 1954. "The Finances of Founding a Family." *Scottish Journal of Political Economy* 1 (3): 201–232.
Roman, Christine, and Carolyn Vogler. 1999. "Managing Money in British and Swedish Households." *European Societies* 1 (3): 419–456.
Saflios-Rothschild, Constantina. 1970. "The Study of Family Power Structure: A Review 1960–61." *Journal of Marriage and Family* 32 (4): 539–552.
Singh, Supriya. 1997. *Marriage Money: The Social Shaping of Money in Marriage and Banking*. Sydney: Allen & Unwin.
Singh, Supriya, and Clive Morley. 2011. "Gender and Financial Accounts in Marriage." *Journal of Sociology* 47 (1): 3–16.
Snape, Dawn, Donna Molloy, and Marion Kumar. 1999. "Relying on the State, Relying on Each Other." Research Report no. 103. Department of Social Security, London.
Stamp, Peggy. 1985. "Research Note: Balance of Financial Power in Marriage: An Exploratory Study of Breadwinning Wives." *The Sociological Review* 33 (3): 546–557.

Stanley, Scott M., Howard J. Markman, and Sarah W. Whitton. 2002. "Communication, Conflict, and Commitment: Insights on the Foundations of Relationship Success from a National Survey." *Family Process* 41 (4): 659–675.
Steuber, Keli Ryan, and Anthony Paik. 2014. "Of Money and Love: Joint Banking, Relationship Quality, and Cohabitation." *Journal of Family Issues* 35 (9): 1154–1176.
Stocks, Janet. 2007. "Introduction: The Role of Money in 'Doing Couple'." In *Modern Couples Sharing Money, Sharing Life*, edited by Janet Stocks, Capitolina Díaz, and Björn Halleröd, 1–6. London: Palgrave Macmillan.
Tichenor, Veronica. 1999. "Status and Income as Gendered Resources: The Case of Marital Power." *Journal of Marriage and the Family* 61 (3): 638–650.
Tichenor, Veronica. 2005. "Maintaining Men's Dominance: Negotiating Identity and Power When She Earns More." *Sex Roles* 53 (3–4): 191–205.
Treas, Judith. 1993. "Money in the Bank: Transaction Costs and the Economic Organization of Marriage." *American Sociological Review* 58 (5): 723–734.
Treas, Judith. 1999. "Marriage Money: The Social Shaping of Money in Marriage and Banking." *Contemporary Sociology* 28 (3): 298–299.
van Eeden-Moorefield, Brad, Kay Pasley, Elizabeth M. Dolan, and Margorie Engel. 2007. "From Divorce to Remarriage: Financial Management and Security Among Remarried Women." *Journal of Divorce & Remarriage* 47 (3–4): 21–42.
Vogler, Carolyn. 1998. "Money in the Household: Some Underlying Issues of Power." *The Sociological Review* 46 (4): 687–713.
Vogler, Carolyn. 2005. "Cohabiting Couples: Rethinking Money in the Household at the Beginning of the Twenty First Century." *The Sociological Review* 53 (1): 1–29.
Vogler, Carolyn, and Jan Pahl. 1994. "Money, Power and Inequality Within Marriage." *The Sociological Review* 42 (2): 263–288.
Vogler, Carolyn, Michaela Brockmann, and Richard D. Wiggins. 2008. "Managing Money in New Heterosexual Forms of Intimate Relationships." *The Journal of Socio-Economics* 37 (2): 552–576.
Wilson, Gail. 1987a. *Money in the Family*. Aldershot: Avebury.
Wilson, Gail. 1987b. "Money: Patterns of Responsibility and Irresponsibility in Marriage." In *Give and Take in Families: Studies in Resource Distribution*, edited by Julia Brannen and Gail Wilson, 136–152. Boston: Allen and Unwin.
Wilson, Frank, and Janet Stocks. 2007. "The Meaning of Breadwinning in Dual-Earner Couples." In *Modern Couples Sharing Money, Sharing Life*, edited by Janet Stocks, Capitolina Díaz, and Björn Halleröd, 72–99. London: Palgrave Macmillan.
Yodanis, Carrie, and Sean Lauer. 2007. "Economic Inequality in and Outside of Marriage: Individual Resources and Institutional Context." *European Sociological Review* 23 (5): 573–583.
Yodanis, Carrie, and Sean Lauer. 2014. "Is Marriage Individualized? What Couples Actually Do." *Journal of Family Theory & Review* 6 (2): 184–197.
Zelizer, Viviana A. 1989. "The Social Meaning of Money: 'Special Monies'." *American Journal of Sociology* 95 (2): 342–377.
Zelizer, Viviana A. 1994. *The Social Meaning of Money*. New York, NY: Harper Collins.

CHAPTER 15

Sibling Relationships: Being Connected and Related

Eva Gulløv and Ida Wentzel Winther

INTRODUCTION

There are many ways of being a sibling and sibling relations can change considerably as children grow up and throughout their adult lives. When reading historical and cross-cultural descriptions of sibling relations, it becomes evident that ideals and norms are far from universal (e.g. Cicirelli 1994; Montgomery 2009; Weisner and Gallimore 2008; Davidoff 2012). Sibling configurations have many forms; expectations and obligations vary, as do the experiences of being, having and getting siblings in childhood as well as later in life. In this chapter, we will focus on siblingships in childhood and argue that it is necessary to consider this variation when exploring what siblingship means in individual children's lives, for family relations more generally and for family research.

What does siblingship imply in different contexts? Do children consider all the other children they live with their siblings, even if they do not share biological parents? Are there varying degrees of siblingship? And is it possible

E. Gulløv · I. W. Winther (✉)
University of Aarhus, Aarhus, Denmark
e-mail: idwi@edu.au.dk

E. Gulløv
e-mail: evag@edu.au.dk

E. Gulløv
University of Agder, Kristiansand, Norway

© The Author(s), under exclusive license to Springer Nature Switzerland AG 2021
A.-M. Castrén et al. (eds.), *The Palgrave Handbook of Family Sociology in Europe*, https://doi.org/10.1007/978-3-030-73306-3_15

to stop being siblings? We find such broad, rhetorical questions a productive outset for a culturally sensitive exploration of what siblingship entails. Sibling relations are integrated into family life and vary as much as families do. In most contemporary European societies, a large number of adults change partners with consequences for the relations of the children: children from previous relationships become part of the same household, children who have previously lived together can be separated and many children grow up with several groups of children as they commute between different households. Nevertheless, siblingship is still often conceptualised in the light of a nuclear family model, as reflected, for example, in everyday expressions such as 'half-siblings', 'bonus siblings' and 'real siblings'. In research, there is likewise a tendency to explore siblingship in relation to the nuclear family rather than investigating more broadly what it means to be siblings in various cultural and social contexts.

In this chapter, we present a possible framework for such a broader exploration. Inspired by the fields of family and childhood research, we argue for an approach that empirically explores the everyday practices, routines, dependencies and emotions that constitute contemporary ways of being and having siblings. Through examples drawn from a qualitative research project investigating children's understandings of siblingship in Denmark, we highlight the knowledge not only on siblingships but also on family life more generally, provided through children's perceptions. The project we refer to was conducted 2011–2014 by the authors with Charlotte Palludan and Mads M. Rehder to investigate siblingship in contemporary Danish society (Winther et al. 2015; Gulløv et al. 2015; Palludan and Winther 2017; Rehder 2016; Winther 2015, 2019, 2020). The study involved 93 children from all over Denmark and focused on their perceptions and experiences of sibling relations, paying particular attention to everyday practices and emotional aspects.

We will begin by positioning our approach to siblingship in relation to studies and discussions within the fields of social studies of family and childhood. On the basis of our study from Denmark, we then present an analytical framework for studying contemporary siblingship and discuss its contribution to the existing corpus of family research.

SOCIAL STUDIES OF FAMILY RELATIONS

Siblingship is closely tied to the family, so it is relevant to start with a few points raised by family researchers. First of all, the family is not a static institution; it is culturally and historically variable. This provides the jumping-off point for much contemporary historical, sociological and anthropological family research. The historian John Gillis (1996) has pointed out how, in the North American context he focuses on, the family has become an almost mythological entity, greatly influencing people's expectations of themselves and those closest to them. Making a distinction that is also relevant in a European context, he differentiates between 'the families we live with' and 'the families we live by', stressing how we evaluate our specific family situations and experiences in the light of strong cultural ideals about family relations and family life. The myth that the family is a blood-related, strongly connected and loyal unit lives on, despite significant changes in family patterns over the last 100 years. From a multigenerational, cohabiting kin group, the nuclear family model of a heterosexual couple living with two or three biological children gradually became the norm strongly supported by influential sociologists of the time, like Talcott Parsons (1943). This cultural model still stands as a point of reference for family life—a model 'we live by'—despite the sweeping changes in contemporary family practices and forms as well as in sociological thinking (e.g. Beck-Gernsheim 2002).

Over the last fifty years, ways of living, gender roles and working life have changed, as have cultural views of family life, family relations, parenthood, children and their roles and duties. Today, a range of family forms exists (in Denmark, for example, there are officially 37 different types of family [Danmarks Statistik 2018]) and, despite the continued reference to the nuclear family as the norm, statistics show that fewer Europeans get married and an increasing number of marriages ends in divorce (e.g. Eurostat news 06/07/18). This has the consequence that families split up and children are separated from some family members, connected with others and obliged to relate to newcomers. Furthermore, the fertility rate has substantially declined, and many children live in single-parent homes or with their parent's new partners—all of which has implications for the form and experience of sibling relations (Oláh 2015). This being the case, a growing body of sociological and anthropological family studies addresses issues of separation, divorce and single or shared parenting and care with an open-minded interest in the ways family relations and structures are constituted through and in actions, processes and practices (e.g. Ahlberg 2008; Eldén and Anving 2018; Widmer 2010; Heaphy and Einarsdottir 2012; Castrén and Widmer 2015; Heath et al. 2017; Mason 2018; Merla 2018).

Despite its interdisciplinary nature, this body of research has in common its rejection of an understanding of families as fixed and biologically given entities. Instead, family relations are seen as dynamic and transformative, simultaneously reflecting historical currents of society and people's ways of enacting and interpreting their personal relationships. With such an approach, the notion of family practice or, to use the British sociologist David Morgan's term, the 'doings' of family (1996), becomes central, emphasising the active role played by family members as well as fluidity and change in everyday family life. Such doings are culturally and historically embedded, meaning that not only people's actions but also the family as an institution is changeable and diverse (e.g. Gillis 1996; Smart and Neale 1998; Mogensen and Olwig 2013). The British anthropologist Janet Carsten has suggested a focus on 'relatedness' instead of the notion of 'family'. Her point is that 'biology does not constitute an immutable basis for relations' (Carsten 2000, 2). As a result, rather than kinship and genealogy, she emphasises the need to pay close attention to the lived experiences of relations in specific cultural settings (2000, 2004). In line with this view, Widmer (2010) argues for a configurational perspective on families tracing the complex patterns of emotional, cognitive and practical interdependencies among people who perceive themselves as relatives. A further point emphasised in recent studies is that family relations also are formed by people that families meet and interact with in everyday life, such as friends, nannies, childcare professionals and social workers (e.g. Davies and Heaphy 2011; May and Nordqvist 2011; Heath et al. 2017; Eldén and Anving 2018). It is important to note that, over time, such outsiders can become insiders. Family relationships are not defined by fixed positions and static roles—rather, they depend on mutual social recognition and actions that support them. The classificatory divisions are not always rigid or stable.

Although the focus in the approaches outlined above is on practices and personal experiences, it is important to stress that what constitutes the family is not solely defined by the individual; cultural classifications and social judgements are part of the picture. As the British sociologist Carol Smart emphasises, a person's way of practising family relations reflects his or her personal history, but it also reflects the cultural and social conditions (2007). It follows that specific practices—but also relationships—are not perceived as relevant in every situation; they can be activated or pushed into the background depending on specific circumstances, social and individual interests, as well as more general classifications and ideas of relevance.

Some scholars have raised the point that the distance to psychological studies, found in some parts of family studies, has resulted in a lack of interest in the emotional aspects of family life. Feelings of connectedness, longing, loyalty and love, as well as guilt, frustration, doubt, anger and sorrow, are not only part of an individual's experience of family relations, but a constitutive dimension of family life as such (e.g. Smart 2007; Widmer 2010; Davies 2011a; Frykman 2016; Mason 2018). And probably, they play an even more important role when family relations are not supported by well-established categories, structures and norms. When membership can be challenged, doubts may arise. As we will return to when presenting our own study, this is very much the case when children experience drastic changes in family constellations, such as members that leave or die, new arrivals, new homes and relations. In short, the family is a complex and varied phenomenon that must be explored with close attention to the historical and cultural circumstances, as well as to everyday practices and the different perspectives, feelings and experiences that individual members may have.

The Relevance of Children's Perspectives

It follows from the points presented above that the family will be perceived and practised differently depending on the position one occupies. Whether one is a child or parent makes a difference in terms of what one can do and how one experiences everyday life as well as the boundaries of the family (see, for instance, Edwards et al. 2006; Mason and Tripper 2014; Castrén and Widmer 2015; Kousholt 2019)—a fact that has caused an explicit interest in studying children's perceptions of family life and relationships. From this perspective, critical voices have argued that family research has all too often been based on parents' words and actions rather than exploring family life through the practices of all members, regardless of age. Children do not necessarily have the same experiences and conceptions as their parents or siblings, but there is a risk that diverging perspectives, conflicts of interest and different experiences will be lost in approaches that treat adult perspectives as more important than those of children and see the family as a unit rather than a framework of individuals structured in various power relations (Davies 2015; Haugen 2008; Højholt et al. 2012; Gulløv et al. 2015; Hammen 2016).

We suggest that children's experiences of and perspectives on family relations are not only of interest in themselves, but also provide important knowledge of the family as institution, that is, the dynamics, priorities, and the social and emotional complexities that constitute contemporary family life (Castrén and Widmer 2015; Winther 2019). This point is all the more relevant as the position of children, in a historical perspective, has moved from the periphery to the centre of societal attention, making their emotional state a major concern and responsibility of parents and their viewpoints worth listening to (Elias 1998; Gilliam and Gulløv 2019). In general terms, children's well-being has become the prime indicator of a family's condition and status. This shift can be seen, for example, in the way parents relate to not only their children but also each other—and not only when married, but also when separated, as Smart has shown (2004). Although legislation varies among the European countries, parental custody has generally changed from being given to only one of the parents to be a shared obligation for both. This means that even when divorced, parents remain obliged to relate as family members for the sake of their child (Smart et al. 2001; van Krieken 2005). Children have become the defining centre of families, and their well-being and points of view are therefore an important element in the legal handling of family matters, in parent's ways of organising their lives and therefore also in family research. In our study, the centrality of children's well-being for family life is apparent in a number of ways, one of them being the importance attached to children's views regarding newcomers to the family. In the case of divorced parents meeting new partners and establishing new households comprising the children of both parties, children's feelings and interrelationships may be vital for the longevity of the new relationship (Gulløv et al. 2015). In short, families have changed from parents with children to children as constitutive parts of families (Elias 1998)—a fact that we find makes the inclusion of children's perceptions and viewpoints an indispensable part of family research and directs the scientific approach to focus on reciprocity and mutual dependencies among all family members. Such exploration can increase our understanding of not only the children's positions and roles, but also the dynamics and conditions of contemporary family life. This focus on children's perceptions and agency seems to be particularly fertile when their everyday lives are divided between two or more homes and families. As children often provide the link connecting the new households, their experiences of the various modes of practising family life can provide valuable insights into the values, dynamics and organising principles of the family as an institution in a given society (see, for instance, Mayall 1994; Morgan 1996; Palludan and Winther 2017; Mason and Tripper 2008, 2014; H. Davies 2011a, b; K. Davies 2015; Marschall 2017; Merla 2018).

Sibling Studies in the Field of Social Science

Building directly on these points, our project '(Ex)changeable siblingship' sought to move away from an understanding of parents as the prime agents of family life and instead look at both vertical (child/adult) and horizontal (child/child) relationships, with a particular focus on the latter (Gulløv et al. 2015; Winther et al. 2015). Searching the existing literature, however, we were surprised to find how little siblingship has been studied in the field of social studies. Apparently, siblingship has not been generally considered as a field of interest in itself, nor as contributing to a general understanding of the family as institution or seen, as argued by Fine, as a regular social problem (Fine 2007). However, some noteworthy works do exist showing the importance of siblingship not only for individuals' identities, agency, social encounters, socialisation processes and gender roles, but also for family life as such. Exploring siblingships in various cultural and historic settings, some studies thus demonstrate the diversity in notions of brothers and sisters as well as the differences in perceptions of rights, obligations, feelings and roles in sibling relations throughout life (e.g. Song 2010; Cicirelli 1994; Oris et al. 2007; Weisner and Gallimore 2008 [orig. 1977]; Davidoff 2012). Other typically ethnographic or interview-based studies focus more on the significance of children's 'strategic interactions' for their lateral relations and show their active contribution to the construction, negotiation and contestation of sibling relations (see, for example, Mauthner 2002; Edwards et al. 2006; Punch 2007, 2008; McIntosh and Punch 2009; H. Davies 2011a, b; K. Davies 2015). A few theoretical contributions argue that siblingship should be explored as a social (con)figuration, a network of interdependent individuals. Rather than taking point of departure in the nuclear family form, the view is to explore the various ways people classify each other as siblings and what kind of dependencies such classification involves. By such an approach, relational aspects such as rivalry, conflict, solidarity and affection can be studied sociologically that is as part of wider power-dynamics and distributions of resources rather than as individual psychological dispositions (Buisson 2007; Fine 2007; Widmer 2010).

In continuation of these studies emphasis on context, agency and social interdependencies, we will argue that any study of sibling-practices has to take these dimensions into account. Combined with the previously outlined points concerning the importance of everyday practices for the constitution of family relations, the diversity of contemporary European family forms and children's centrality to the very definition of family, we argue that consideration of children's perspectives and relationships, including their relationships to other children, is vital in developing an understanding of contemporary family life.

Replacing a Normative Terminology

It follows from the discussions referred to above that, just as 'the family' has no fixed form, siblingship is not a stable or easily demarcated phenomenon. Sibling groups are contextually defined and varying family forms affect the specific sibling figuration as well as the interactions and practices that take place. They change over time in shape, intensity and character and it varies who is included in the category. In our study, we found that some of our informants stressed the importance of siblings sharing biological parents; others emphasised the importance of growing up together. Biological bonds are often prominent in public discourses, legal frameworks and administrative practices, which support a specific understanding of what 'real siblingship' is. Yet we also find that this understanding is continuously challenged and co-exists with other understandings and ways of practising sibling relationships. Siblingships are changeable (or, to use our preferred term, (ex)changeable); that is, they change over time in form, kind, classification and content and must therefore be empirically investigated.

When reading popular handbooks on contemporary family life, and more particularly on sibling relations, we have been struck by the way this fluidity is neglected despite the variety in family forms. We have also been surprised by the problem-centred terminology, not least in psychological advice discourses. Families can be 'healthy', but whenever they 'break up' or arrange cohabitation in other ways, it seems to give cause for concern. Some family members seem to be more 'real' than others, as indicated in phrases such as 'half-brother', 'bonus sister', 'stepmother' and 'broken family'—a terminology we also find ever-present in our interviews with parents and children, regardless of their own family form. This reflects the existence of a widespread idea of the nuclear family as normal and healthy—or in Gillis's terms, as the ideal family 'we live by' (Gillis 1996), despite the empirical reality. To explore contemporary ideas of siblingship across the many ways families are organised and lived, the first step must be to insist on a vocabulary that does not implicitly valorise one form by referring to other arrangements as resulting from breaks, fractures and fragments (Smart and Neale 1998). The discourse itself emphasises the destruction of something complete.

As a way to avoid reproducing such normative understandings, we found it productive to conceptualise sibling groups as either 'long and wide' or 'short and narrow'. Aware that this division does not cover all forms of sibling groups,[1] it functioned as an analytical tool that enabled us to focus on variations in relationships in a more open-minded way while still paying attention to the implications of different family forms. 'Long and wide' siblingship indicates a group of children who do not all share the same biological parents. There can be a considerable age difference between the youngest and the eldest child (indicated by 'long'), as their parents may have more sets of children or live with someone who has children from previous partnerships (in our material, for example, one sibling group ranges from 4 to 32 in age). In this type of siblingship, children will rarely cohabit with all their siblings. In the cases where adults have formed new families several times, there will often be many children (indicated be 'wide'). These might feel more or less related depending on the family history and organisation, the frequency of meetings and the relationships between the adults. An example in our study is a 14-year-old girl who has 12 other children in her family group and does not live with any of them. She regards some of these children as her 'real' siblings while others are just acquaintances that she does not feel attached to and does not include in the drawing of her family that we ask all our young informants to make. Her vocabulary reflects the conventional understanding of blood relations as the most important, yet it is clear from her narrative that this phrasing does not match the way she experiences her relationships.

The 'short and narrow' sibling group consists of children who live in the same residence, share parents and are often few in number with a narrow age span. Among these children, we rarely find any hesitation concerning who they regard as their siblings.

Below are two drawings from our archives representing, respectively, a 'short and narrow' (Fig. 15.1) and a 'long and wide' (Fig. 15.2) sibling group.

We have found this differentiation between two kinds of sibling groups a productive basis for analysing how family relations are experienced and practised. It helps us avoid regarding the nuclear family as the norm and instead see how siblingships, as well as family relations in general, are constituted through what the German sociologist Norbert Elias calls human figurations—that is,

Fig. 15.1 Sibling group 'short and narrow'

Fig. 15.2 Sibling group 'long and wide'

networks of interdependent persons (Elias 1970). As pointed out by other scholars working with a figurational approach, we find a need to empirically study who is regarded as significant family members and what this implies (Buisson 2007; Widmer 2010). To understand siblingship and family life, we need to explore the way family members classify, connect and relate—not only as a reflection of a cultural classification of bonds between them, but also as a result of their practical, material and emotional interdependence. It makes a difference to the relations whether the family group consists of a small cohabiting group, sharing and caring for one another on an everyday basis, or encompasses several households with a range of people who are more or less in touch with one another. It not only affects the individual's experiences and feelings, but also the kinds of social obligations, exchanges, everyday chores, routines, opportunities and limitations that are to be found among a group of siblings.

Birth order may serve as an illustration of the insights to be gained by paying closer attention to variations in the figuration. In popular psychological literature on child development (e.g. Leman 2009 [1985]), birth order is often described as significant for the formation of personality. Such an understanding implicitly draws on the nuclear family model and makes little sense in relation to a family whose composition has changed over the years. In 'long and wide' families, where new households have been established, where new partners and children might have been added, and where some children come and go while others may have moved out, birth order is not a stable structure with clear positions. In such family formations, a child can become a little brother as a teenager, an uncle to a child his own age and he can be the eldest child in his father's new household and the youngest in his mother's. Positions shift and change, making it difficult to determine unequivocal psychological sibling profiles. Thus, by looking at sibling relations from a figurational perspective, the focus shifts from being implicitly rooted in the nuclear family towards a more open and empirically based investigation of the social and emotional interdependencies that occur between people defining themselves as being 'family'. Sibling relations change as children grow up, move between households, have to relate to the children of a parent's new partner or to new babies with this partner, and have to face the fact that older siblings move out. Their relations can be stable or fragile, fixed or unpredictable, engendering various forms and degrees of uncertainty, changeability and interdependencies.

Exploring Everyday Practicalities

In order to explore the nature and implications of siblingships, it is pertinent to look at interdependencies occurring in everyday life. On the basis of our research on sibling relations in a Danish context,[2] in the following sections we discuss certain aspects we have found particularly important when analysing siblingships, as well as family relations more generally. Presenting a few examples from our study, we will first highlight the way sibling relations are formed and shaped through everyday practicalities, routines and material aspects. We then address emotional dynamics and discuss how they reflect tensions between family ideals and the many and complex figurations characterising contemporary family realities.

Everyday Practicalities and Routines

Inspired by the theoretical points raised above, we propose an approach that examines sibling relationships as a social practice formed through everyday routines and practices. Classifications, hierarchies, privileges, expectations and values are expressed and upheld through repeated acts, routinised bodily movement and arrangements of objects that often go unnoticed (Ehn and Löfgren 2010; Winther 2018). Commonplace activities like watching YouTube, playing computer or football, eating, brushing one's teeth, going to school, having trivial quarrels or simply hanging out frame and influence children's view of themselves in relation to their siblings, their notion of what it is possible to do and say and their sense of the similarities and differences between them. Acts, rhythms and routines maintain a kind of order that allows continuity without reflection. The shared material décor of the home is likewise an element that influences the form and type of relationship among siblings. This is seen, for example, when Frederikke (aged 18) reflects on her relationship with her elder brother, who recently moved out: 'Before going to sleep at night, we would knock on the wall until either he shouted good night or I shouted goodnight. Because the wall, you can just knock on it … His lamp, you could usually hear when he switched it on or off. So I'd be able to hear when he went to bed. The walls are very thin (…)'. Material conditions, like the thickness of walls and the layout of rooms, and rhythms and rituals, such as bedtime and knocked codes, are all part of what shapes and routinises a relationship. When disturbed, as when one part moves out, the relationship must be redefined.

This becomes apparent when specifically examining 'long and wide' relationships. Although all family relationships change in character over time, 'long and wide' sibling relationships are generally characterised by a quite complex rhythmic pattern as family members move in relation to each other. Instead of a limited number of household routines (when and where to eat, do homework, get ready to go to school, etc.), various rhythms may intersect as family members have different obligations, agreements and considerations. Some children may move between households on a regular basis while others stay put, and elder siblings may have a range of commitments outside the home. The various patterns may challenge synchronicity and hence physical and emotional intimacy between siblings. When everyday routines fail to ensure regular encounters and shared activities, it is up to the individual child to stay in touch with siblings and establish intimacy when physically separated. An active effort is needed. While this may strengthen the relationship, it also makes it more vulnerable and fragile than the taken-for-granted certainty of short and narrow siblingship, stabilised as they are by well-known categories and positions as well as physical proximity, and mundane chores and routines of everyday life.

Commuting Between Sibling Groups and Family Regimes

In our interviews with children in 'long and wide' sibling groups, we find a special kind of interdependency between those siblings who commute together between parental households. These trips, with all the coordination and practical tasks they involve, seem to become ritualised loci of emotional and embodied experiences (Winther 2015). Travelling together means sharing planning, routes and waiting time. Even though the journey between homes might be filled with quarrels, it evidently also contributes to the relationship and offers an opportunity for siblings to share their reflections on life in their common home(s). The physical and practical conditions have implications for the nature of the emotional bonds.

The children not only travel between two geographical locations; they travel between families, parents, siblings and homes. They travel between the rules, logistics and routines characterising each household. And they travel between different kinds of experiences and perceptions of who is included in their family and siblingships, and how family life is performed. They must regularly reorient themselves socially and practically and implement different strategies to help them do just that, as manifested, for example, in what they pack, and how they arrange their belongings at each place.

Moving between homes alters the sibling figuration in both households, not only when a child arrives but also when it leaves. During an interview with Cornelius, aged seven, he jumps to the window and shouts to his peers, who are calling him from the street: 'I can't play right now. I'm being interviewed. I'm a divorced child, you know'. His parents, who are both present, seem quite surprised as Cornelius has lived with them both all his life. He explains that when his two elder sisters (from his mother's previous partnership) are at their father's place, he has to do without them—and hence is 'a divorced child'. Thus, it is not only the children who actively commute between households that experience a difference in their everyday lives but also those left behind. As well as having to adapt to a new rhythm whenever his sisters leave or reappear, he also has to do so with his brother Eigil who lives full-time in the household. The whole group of siblings is involved in different temporal dynamics. It makes a difference to all relations to be part of a two-child-figuration or one of four. It is in this sense we see sibling relations as 'ex-changeable'.

Materiality Matters

Sibling relations are embedded in and expressed through materiality: the more children in a household, the greater the number of things likely to be present—some of which being personal belongings, many that are shared or circulated. Rooms are often personal but may also be shared, as are jackets, toys, bikes and beds, or they are handed down from elder to younger siblings as a material indicator of the relationship. Objects give common experiences and references, but may also cause conflict. Access to and allocation of resources may be interpreted as fair expressions of equality or as symbols of disparate positions and power relations (Palludan and Winther 2017).

Things are part of the relational order and are therefore included in the narratives we encounter when the children and young people in our study characterise a particular relationship. We are told about room sizes, about who gets new things and who gets them second-hand; we are shown whose photo is on the wall; and we hear about how grandparents distribute presents. There is a conspicuous focus on the symbolic meanings of things with regard to sibling relations and thus their social importance.

Conflicts over things seem to be widespread; in all our interviews, the young informants describe quarrels and feelings of annoyance and unfairness when, for instance, siblings disturb the privacy of their room, destroy their personal belongings or have specific rights, privileges or resources that the informant does not. Previous experiences or hopes and expectations of getting or not getting certain things or privileges thus have an impact on the ways siblings interpret one another's intentions, relations and positions. In general, parents seem quite aware of the symbolic dimension of materiality and try to figure out ways to distribute resources in a fair and just manner. In the Danish context, age appears to be the most legitimate argument for the distribution of possessions and it seems that all informants accept this as a just and impersonal principle. The older you are, the bigger, the newer, the more expensive the material resources you seem to be entitled to.

Again, we find that specific circumstances are at play in some of the 'long and wide' families because different rules and principles might apply in different households in relation to children's possessions, pocket money, chores, duties and privileges. For instance, we meet Liv (aged 11), who spends equal time in the respective homes of her father and her mother. A few years earlier, her father's partner had moved into his house with her daughter, Nanna, who is slightly younger than Liv. Of great concern to the girls as well as their parents, the two girls did not get along and there have been many conflicts and arguments between the two. This seems partly caused by the fact that they have very different material conditions, reflecting their respective parents' principles regarding upbringing and resources. Nanna's father is quite generous when it comes to his daughter. She rarely stays with him, but when they meet he often gives her the newest computer games, expensive phones, clothes and pocket money—against Nanna's mother's wishes. Neither of Liv's parents are able or willing to match this, with the result that Nanna has a lot more material belongings than Liv. The example indicates how material conditions can complicate a relationship when conventional criteria, such as age, are not applied as the main principle for allocating resources. In short, established systems of privilege collide when sibling groups are brought together and new figurations are formed. In these changeable structures, privileges and positions are open to negotiation—a fact that becomes particularly important in cases where the relationship is not supported by a long shared history, everyday routines and proximity or the certainty given when no one doubts the nature of the relation.

Emotional Complexities

In general, siblingship is described in the interviews as a kind of relation that, ideally, needs no further consideration—an understanding likely supported by the conventional idea that 'real' siblingship cannot be broken. Siblings 'are just there, and they're nice to have. And you can talk to them and stuff, be with them and you know ...', as one boy (Nicolai, 11) tells us. Some of the children describe siblings as providing a sense of emotional security: a feeling of having someone who is 'always there for you', that you are 'never alone' or 'completely isolated'. Attentiveness and accessibility are central dimensions—also among siblings who do not live together or are not biologically related. Even in the absence of physical proximity, the relation entails an ideal perception of the sibling as someone who takes an interest in your life and backs you up. Yet, conflicts also seem to be a pervasive feature of siblingship (see also Edwards et al. 2006). Siblings argue and have conflicts over rights, status, power and privileges, simultaneously marking both distinctions and common ground. Louise, aged 19, describes her relation to her sister: '… you always feel that you have someone close to you, and someone who can help you – you never feel, you know, all alone … We know each other really well, and because we love each other so much, we also fight a lot'. Louise has lived with her elder sister all her life and she stresses how the closeness of their relationship also causes friction. Similarly, Liv, whom we presented above, describes how her feelings have changed. As mentioned, there have been many conflicts and arguments between Liv and Nanna, but the arguments have gradually lessened and they have grown closer to the extent that Liv now considers Nanna her sister:

> … I mean, when you're siblings, you can get really mad at one another, and then, well, you know … you still love each other, inside, and when you're friends you have to be a little more careful … siblings, they're just … a lot closer than friends; I mean, you're just so much closer. Even if I haven't known Nanna for as long as I have some of my friends, it's like, me and Nanna are still closer than I am with them …

However, sibling relations are not only close and intimate, they may also give rise to feelings of insecurity, guilt, jealousy, distance or doubt. Particular circumstances, such as a lack of time spent together, lack of concern, unequal parental attention, bitter conflicts or drastic changes in the figuration, may generate uncertainty—not only regarding the nature of the relationship, but the very existence of it. In our material, there are several examples where children describe such anxieties and some recount experiences of either rejecting or being rejected by someone they had considered their sibling. The experience of belonging together is entangled with concerns over the nature and depth of this relation. For some, doubt is the prominent feeling; for others, siblings are just a fact of life.

When examining siblingships from the point of view of children coming from various forms of family, we find a range of emotional dynamics reflecting the complex kinds of interdependencies present in contemporary family life. Ordinary practices such as doing chores, spending spare time together, commuting between households and sharing objects evoke composite feelings of emotional intimacy and limited physical proximity, solidarity and annoyance, similarity and distance, frustration and longing. Practical, material everyday matters are intertwined with moral and symbolic orders in ways that influence how siblings view themselves and each other. Presumably, sibling relations have always been complex, being subject to the wider family organisation. However, this seems to be especially true when relations receive little support in the way of synchronised routines, well-established categories and norms. The more complex the organisation, the more it is up to the individuals themselves to establish equal and reciprocal relationships. In this way, the 'family we live with' are much more complex than the 'family we live by'.

Conclusion: Siblingship as Practical and Sensitive Relations

In popular books, films, adverts, etc., siblings are generally presented as biologically connected and relatively straightforwardly positioned in relation to one another: the relation between elder brother and younger sister for example. In line with other researchers arguing for a more relational approach, we have in this chapter argued that it is not always that simple (see, for instance, Fine 2007; McIntosh and Punch 2009). Siblings may or may not be biologically connected, and the importance of their various connections is culturally constructed and may be performed quite differently in diverse cultural and social settings. Siblingships come in many shapes and sizes, depending on family form and individual members' specific perceptions and investments. Inspired by a theoretical emphasis on family doings and social interdependencies, we have in this chapter criticised common-sense understandings of siblingship for uncritically reproducing rather than exploring particular ideas of family relations and instead argued for a more open and empirically based approach able to capture the diversity of siblingship as a phenomenon.

In our empirical study of siblingship in contemporary Denmark, we have time and again been struck by the variation in figurational forms, but also in the temporal dynamics and modes of interdependencies. Sibling relations alter as children grow up or changes in the family's composition occur, but we also find alterations in a minor scale in everyday life as children follow different rhythms, have different hobbies, do separate chores, hang out with each their friends or commute between households. In these movements, the children often put a lot of effort into maintaining relationships with siblings and overcoming any obstacles. However, sibling relations are not determined by the children alone. Parents' organisation of family life—and their notions of what good siblingship entails—establishes a context for children's (inter)actions, as do social conventions and cultural understandings—a context where there might be limited room for the individual to manoeuvre and define relations in personal ways.

As such, the organisation of families plays a significant role in how children interrelate. Some sibling groups are relatively short and narrow: the family only includes few children who are close in age. Other sibling groups are longer and wider, encompassing many children. The complexity of the family organisation is significant in determining the conditions for everyday relations among siblings—that is, what they can do and the amount of time they spend together. This, in turn, has implications for the way they see each other; the identity work at play; the classifications, positions and memories; and, not least, their willingness to invest in the relationship. In this way, siblingship and family form are inseparable in both everyday life and for research. When exploring what it means to be connected and related as siblings, it is necessary to take into consideration the various ideas of and modes of organising contemporary family life, as well as the everyday practices that constitute it. It hereby becomes evident how horizontal relations are formed and framed by the family institution as such, but also that these relations are themselves a vital part of the social and emotional dynamics taking place in any family. In this way, siblingship is a crucial though often overlooked dimension in family research.

Notes

1. It should be noted that this division is analytical and does not cover all forms of sibling groups. 'Long and narrow' groups are also found, e.g. when a couple have few kids over a long period, as are 'short and wide' groups, e.g. seen in foster care. We nevertheless find that the rough division helps to underline how the complexity of the form of the sibling group impacts their relations.
2. The study included 93 children/young people, 12 parents, two youth workers and nine child experts. We conducted interviews with 65 children/young people between the ages of 6 and 20, usually in their homes. They came from various social segments and geographical places, some living in rural areas, some in urban, and the majority having parents who had separated. Fourteen of them were interviewed several times, and in the great majority of cases, we interviewed more than one child from the same siblingship. In addition, we conducted interviews with four groups of four children (aged 9–13) at a leisure centre and participant observations of twelve children (aged 7–12) at four counselling sessions for children with divorced parents. We received permission to follow some of the informants with a camera, filming the activities they engaged in with their siblings, such as sports events, hanging out together in the evenings, visiting cafes, communicating on social media and travelling between homes. This footage was made into a film (Winther and Rehder 2014). For more details on methods, see Winther et al. (2015).

References

Ahlberg, Jenny. 2008. *Efter kärnfamiljen: Familjepraktikker efter skismässa*. Örebro: Örebro Universitet.
Beck-Gernsheim, Elisabeth. 2002. *Reinventing the Family: In Search of New Lifestyles*. Cambridge: Polity Press.
Buisson, Monique. 2007. "La fratrie comme configuration." In *Les fratries. Une démographie sociale de la germanité*, edited by Michael Oris, Guy Brunet, Eric Widmer, and Alain Bideau, 259–291. Bern: Peter Lang SA.
Carsten, Janet. 2000. "Introduction: Cultures of Relatedness." In *Cultures of Relatedness. New Approaches to the Study of Kinship*, edited by Janet Carsten, 1–37. Cambridge: Cambridge University Press.
Carsten, Janet. 2004. *After Kinship. Cambridge*: Cambridge University Press.
Castrén, Anna-Maija, and Eric Widmer. 2015. "Insiders and Outsiders in Stepfamilies: Adults' and Children's Views on Family Boundaries." *Current Sociology* 63 (1): 35–56.

Cicirelli, Victor. 1994. "Sibling Relationships in Cross-Cultural Perspective." *Journal of Marriage and Family* 56 (1): 7–20.
Danmarks Statistik. 2018. Børn og deres familier 2018, 33. https://www.dst.dk/Publ/bornfam.
Davies, Hayley. 2011a. "Affinities, Seeing and Feeling Like Family: Exploring Why Children Value Face-to-Face Contact." *Childhood. A Journal of Global Child Research* 19 (1): 8–23.
Davies, Hayley. 2011b. "Sharing Surnames: Children, Family and Kinship." *Sociology* 45 (4): 554–569.
Davies, Katherine. 2015. "Siblings, Stories and the Self: The Sociological Significance of Young People's Sibling Relationships." *Sociology* 49 (4): 679–695.
Davies, Katherine, and Brian Heaphy. 2011. "Interactions That Matter: Researching Critical Associations." *Methodological Innovations* 6 (3): 5–16.
Davidoff, Leonore. 2012. *Thicker than Water—Siblings and Their Relations, 1780–1920*. Oxford: Oxford University Press.
Edwards, Rosalind, Lucy Hadfield, Helen Lucey, and Melanie Mauthner. 2006. *Sibling Identity and Relationships. Sisters and Brothers*. London and New York: Routledge.
Ehn, Billy, and Orvar Löfgren. 2010. *The Secret World of Doing Nothing*. Berkeley: University of California Press.
Eldén, Sara, and Terese Anving. 2019. *Nanny Families: Practices of Care by Nannies, Au Pairs, Parents and Children in Sweden*. Bristol: Bristol University Press.
Elias, Norbert. 1970. *What Is Sociology?* New York: Columbia University Press.
Elias, Norbert. 1998. "The Civilizing of Parents." In *The Norbert Elias Reader*, edited by Johan Goudsblom and Stephen Mennell, 189–211. Oxford: Blackwell.
Eurostat News. https://ec.europa.eu/eurostat/web/products-eurostat-news/-/DDN-20180706-1?inheritRedirect=true.
Fine, Agnès. 2007. "Les fratries en Europe. Aperçu sur quelques orientations de recherché en anthropologie". In *Les fratries. Une démographie sociale de la germanit*é, edited by Michael Oris, Guy Brunet, Eric Widmer, and Alain Bideau, 47–79. Bern: Peter Lang SA.
Frykman, Jonas. 2016. "Done by Inheritance. A Phenomenological Approach to Affect and Material Culture". In *Sensitive Objects—Affect and Materiel Culture*, edited by Jonas Frykman and Maja Povrzanovic Frykman, 153–179. Lund: Nordic Academic Press.
Gilliam, Laura, and Eva Gulløv. 2019. "Children as Potential: A Window to Cultural Ideals, Anxieties and Conflicts." *Children's Geographies*, published online August 5. https://doi.org/10.1080/14733285.2019.1648760.
Gillis, John Randall. 1996. *A World of Their Own Making: Myth, Rituals, and the Quest for Family Values*. New York: Basic Books.
Gulløv, Eva, Charlotte Palludan, and Ida Winther. 2015. "Engaging Siblingships." *Childhood. A Journal of Global Child Research* 22 (4): 506–519.
Hammen, Ida. 2016. *Slægtskabelser - en undersøgelse af relationer mellem familieplejeanbragte børn, deres forældre og plejeforældre*. Roskilde: Roskilde Universitetsforlag.
Haugen, Gry Mette D. 2008. "Children's Perspectives on Everyday Experiences of Shared Residence: Time, Emotions and Agency Dilemmas." *Children and Society* 24: 112–122.
Heath, Sue, Katherine Davies, Gemma Edwards, and Rachael Scicluna. 2017. *Shared Housing, Shared Lives: Everyday Experiences Across the Lifecourse*. London and New York: Routledge.

Heaphy, Brian, and Anna Einarsdottir. 2012. "Scripting Civil Partnership: Interviewing Couples Together and Apart." *Qualitative Research* 13 (1): 53–70.
Højholt, Charlotte, Marianne Hedegaard, Karin Aronsson, and Oddbjørg Skjær Ulvik, eds. 2012. *Children, Childhood and Everyday Life: Children's Perspectives*. Charlotte, NC: Information Age Publishing.
Kousholt, Dorthe. 2019. "Children's Everyday Transitions: Children's Engagements Across Life Contexts." In *Children's Transitions in Everyday Life and Institutions*, edited by Marianne Hedegaard and Marilyn Fleer, 145–165. London: Bloomsbury Academic.
Leman, Kevin. 2009 [1985]. *The Birth Order Book: Why You Are the Way You Are*. Grand Rapids, MI: Revell Books.
Marschall, Anja. 2017. "When Everyday Life Is Double Looped." *Children and Society* 31: 342–352.
Mason, Jennifer. 2018. *Affinities*. Cambridge: Polity Press.
Mason, Jennifer, and Becky Tipper. 2008. "Being Related: How Children Define and Create Kinship." *Childhood. A Journal of Global Child Research* 15 (4): 441–460.
Mason, Jennifer, and Becky Tipper. 2014. "Children as Family Members." In *Handbook of Child Research*, edited by Gary B. Melton, Asher Ben-Arieh, Judith Cashmore, Gail S. Goodman, and Natalie K. Worley, 153–168. London: Sage.
Mauthner, Melanie L. 2002. *Sistering: Power and Change in Female Relationships*. Basingstoke: Palgrave Macmillan.
May, Vanessa, and Petra Nordqvist. 2011. *Sociology of Personal Life*. Basingstoke: Palgrave Macmillan.
Mayall, Berry, ed. 1994. *Children's Childhoods: Observed and Experienced*. London: Falmer Press.
McIntosh, Ian, and Samantha Punch. 2009. "'Barter', 'Deals', 'Bribes' and 'Threats' Exploring Sibling Interactions." *Childhood. A Journal of Global Child Research* 16 (1): 49–65.
Merla, Laura. 2018. "Rethinking the Interconnections Between Family Socialization and Gender Through the Lens of Multi-local, Post-separation Families." *Sociologica* 12 (3): 47–57.
Mogensen, Hanne Overgaard, and Karen Fog Olwig, eds. 2013. *Familie og slægtskab. Antropologiske perspektiver*. København: Forlaget Samfundslitteratur.
Montgomery, Heather. 2009. *An Introduction to Childhood. Anthropological Perspectives on Children's Lives*. Malden: Wiley-Blackwell.
Morgan, David. 1996. *Family Connections—An Introduction to Family Studies*. Cambridge: Polity Press.
Oláh, Livia Sz. 2015. "Changing Families in the European Union: Trends and Policy Implications." *Families and Societies*. Working Paper Series no. 15. Stockholm: Stockholm University.
Oris, Michael, Guy Brunet, Eric Widmer, and Alain Bideau, eds. 2007. *Les fratries. Une démographie sociale de la germanité*. Bern: Peter Lang SA.
Palludan, Charlotte, and Ida Wentzel Winther. 2017. "'Having My Own Bedroom Would Be Really Cool'—Children's Bedrooms as the Social and Material Organizing of Siblings." *Journal of Material Culture* 22 (1): 34–50.
Parsons, Talcott. 1943. "The Kinship System of the Contemporary United States." *American Anthropologist* 45 (1): 22–38.
Punch, Samantha. 2007. "'I Felt They Were Ganging up on Me': Interviewing Siblings at Home." *Children's Geographies* 5 (3): 219–234.

Punch, Samantha. 2008. "'You Can Do Nasty Things to Your Brothers and Sisters without a Reason': Siblings' Backstage Behaviour." *Children and Society* 22: 333–344.
Rehder, Mads Middelboe. 2016. "Søskendenærvær. Et fænomenologisk inspireret studie af unge adskilte søskendes hverdag med afsæt i teknologier, materialiteter og kropslige erfaringer." Doctoral thesis, Department of Education, Aarhus University.
Smart, Carol. 2004. "Changing Landscapes of Family Life: Rethinking Divorce." *Social Policy and Society* 3 (4): 401–408.
Smart, Carol. 2007. *Personal Life*. Cambridge: Policy.
Smart, Carol, and Bren Neale. 1998. *Family Fragments?* Cambridge: Polity Press.
Smart, Carol, Bren Neale, and Amanda Wade. 2001. *The Changing Experience of Childhood: Families and Divorce*. Cambridge: Polity Press.
Song, Miri. 2010. "Does 'Race' Matter? A Study of 'Mixed Race' Siblings' Identifications." *Sociological Review* 58 (2): 265–285.
van Krieken, Robert. 2005. "The 'Best Interests of the Child' and Parental Separation: on the 'Civilizing of Parents'." *Modern Law Review* 68 (1): 25–48.
Weisner, Thomas S., and Ronald Gallimore. 2008 [1977]. "Child and Sibling Caregiving." In *Anthropology and Child Development. A Cross-Cultural Reader*, edited by Robert A. Levine and Rebecca S. New, 264–270. Malden, MA: Blackwell Publishing.
Widmer, Eric. 2010. *Family Configurations. A Structural Approach to Family Diversity*. Farnham: Ashgate.
Winther, Ida Wentzel. 2015. "To Practice Mobility: On a Small Scale." *Culture Unbound: Journal of Current Cultural Research* 7: 215–231.
Winther, Ida Wentzel. 2018. "Det upåagtedes etnografi – feltvandring og sanselige metoder som etnografiske tilgange i undersøgelsen af 'ik' noget'." In *Etnografier*, edited by Michael Hviid Jacobsen and Hanne Louise Jensen, 297–323. København: Hans Reitzels Forlag.
Winther, Ida Wentzel. 2019. "Delebørn." In *Hvad vi deler – Antropologiske perspektiver på deling som socialt fænomen*, edited by Anders Sybrandt Hansen and Susanne Højlund, 75–93. Århus: Aarhus Universitetsforlag.
Winther, Ida Wentzel. 2020. "Thrown into and out of Togetherness. Children's Experiences of Living Apart and/or Living Together with Their Family." In *Exploring Materiality in Childhood: Body, Relations and Space*, edited by Maarit Alasuutari, Marleena Mustola, and Niina Rutanen, 103–120. London: Routledge.
Winther, Ida Wentzel, and Mads Middelboe Rehder. 2014. "Film: (Ex)Changeable Siblingships. Experienced and Practiced by Children and Young People in Denmark." https://dpu.au.dk/en/research/research-projects/previous-research-projects/exchangeable-siblingship/.
Winther, Ida Wentzel, Charlotte Palludan, Eva Gulløv, and Mads Middelboe Rehder. 2015. *Siblings: Practical and Sensitive Relations*. Copenhagen: Danish School of Education, Aarhus University.

CHAPTER 16

"It's a Balance on a Knife-Edge": Expectations of Parents and Adult Children

Bella Marckmann

INTRODUCTION

What, if anything, do adult children expect from their parents, and what, if anything, are parents' expectations of adult children? Intergenerational relationships are important for both individuals and society, but also more complex than earlier (Kalmijn 2014; van Gaalen 2007). Children are a primary source of support for older individuals, and even generous welfare states rely on families to fill the care gap threatening to arise due to ageing populations (Starr and Szebehely 2017). While increased longevity means 'longer years of shared lives' (Bengtson 2001), families are also smaller and geographically more dispersed than earlier; therefore, much depends on the quality of each relationship and whether parents and adult children have built strong emotional bonds in the years after the children leave home and before the parents grow old.

At the same time, we know relatively little about how people build and maintain such bonds, as relationships between parents and adult children are somewhat under-examined in qualitative sociology compared to other types of interpersonal relationships, with notable exceptions such as Finch and Mason (1993), Attias-Donfut and Segalen (2002), and Brannen (2016). Much of what we know comes from the extensive, mainly survey-based, literature examining intergenerational resource transfers and generalised norms, with studies typically including the emotional quality of the relationship as one variable among others (e.g. Albertini and Kohli 2013; Dykstra 2018). In qualitative

B. Marckmann (✉)
Danish Evaluation Institute, Copenhagen, Denmark

sociology, a substantial literature examines the relationship dynamics of couples (e.g. van Hooff 2016; Gabb and Fink 2017) and families with young children (e.g. McCarthy et al. 2017). In comparison, how parents and children actively produce, maintain, or change their relationships has had relatively little academic interest.

This chapter uses qualitative interview data from 34 Danish men and women aged between 20 and 90 to examine relations between parents and adult children. The aim is to identify contemporary cultural ideals influencing the relationships between parents and their adult children in a Nordic welfare state that supports generational independence and provides citizens with a range of options to cover their care needs. The analysis focuses on the expectations of parents and their adult children towards each other and on how people interpret their interactions as contributing to either closeness or distance in the relationship.

The analysis shows that parents and adult children engage in similar 'relationship work' as do participants in other types of personal relationships, but also that, unlike for example in friendships, the relationships remain clearly asymmetric even after the children have reached adulthood, as much more specific and culturally legitimate expectations apply to parents than to adult children. The so-called Goldilocks principle comes into play in the sense that the parents must strike a balance between maintaining a lifelong emotional engagement in their children and respecting their adult children's autonomy.

Intergenerational Relationships Today

The demographic, economic, and cultural changes of recent decades have contributed to make intergenerational relationships both more important and more challenging. Demographically, increased longevity and lower birth rates cause increasingly vertical family ties. In other words, each person on average has fewer intra-generational relationships, that is, siblings and cousins, than earlier generations did, but more inter-generational relationships, i.e. are more likely to have living parents and grandparents into adulthood and to live to see their own grandchildren and great-grandchildren (van Gaalen 2007). Economically, governments and individuals experience pressures, as population ageing requires a shrinking workforce to provide for growing numbers of elderly (Bloom et al. 2010). Culturally, trends of individualisation emphasising self-realisation and individual choice mean that relationship formation and parenthood have become matters of choice, in principle and practice, to an unprecedented degree (Hagestad 2003; Beck and Beck-Gernsheim 2018 [1995]).

These trends exacerbate the importance of and the challenges related to intergenerational relationships, both on the aggregate and personal levels. On the aggregate level, a 'care gap' threatens to open between the number of care-dependent elderly and the number of carers available to provide either paid or unpaid care (e.g. Pickard 2015). On the personal level, more people have living parents—and often grandparents—well into their own adulthood, and we can expect to live more years as adult children of living parents than as parents of dependent children (Hagestad 2003). When the average family has fewer children than earlier, each parent-child relationship carries a greater weight, for better or for worse. Each child may benefit from more of the parents' resources—time, attention, and material goods—but will also have fewer siblings with whom to share the eventual burden of care for ageing parents. In addition, studies indicate that for adult children engaged in caregiving, it is important to be able to frame this as a choice, motivated by affection, rather than as an obligatory responsibility or duty (Brandt 2013; Funk 2015). In this context, the emotional quality of intergenerational relationships is crucial as a predictor for caregiving behaviour and as an important factor in the health and well-being of both parents and adult children (Antonucci et al. 2011; Merz et al. 2009; Pillemer and Suitor 2006; Swartz et al. 2011).

In spite of its importance, we know little about how intergenerational relationship quality comes about, improves or deteriorates, and how parents and adult children perceive the processes and interactions involved; the analysis in this chapter will address these questions. Thomas Scheff states, "in all human contact, if bonds are not being built, maintained, or repaired, they are being damaged" (Scheff 1997, 76). We know that a variety of personal and situational characteristics correlate with self-reported relationship quality, and that high relationship quality can coexist with both conflict and ambivalence (van Gaalen et al. 2010; Antonucci et al. 2011; Kalmijn et al. 2019). From the literature on friendship and couple relationships, we know that people engage in continuous, deliberate activities to maintain these (Canary and Stafford 1994; Dindia and Baxter 1987; Fehr 1996; Gabb and Fink 2017). This 'relationship work' includes activities such as spending time together, talking, gift-giving, exchange of practical help, and building up a mutual 'deep knowledge' of each other (Jamieson 1998; Nitchovski 2018; Strikwerda and May 1992). Likewise, the concept of kin-keeping is well known in the literature on broader kinship networks (e.g. Di Leonardo 1987). Fewer studies examine relationship work in connection with relationships between parents and adult children. Finch and Mason (1993) demonstrate how family members develop mutual commitments through large and small exchanges of support. However, higher frequency of interaction does not necessarily contribute to the closeness of the relationship, as interactions can also damage the relationship (see, e.g., van Gaalen et al. 2010). Whether interactions between parents and adult children strengthen or weaken their bond depends, among other things, on how the participants interpret it. This in its turn may vary based on personal characteristics of the participants (Connidis and Barnett 2018; Fingerman et al. 2020), but also reflects broader cultural ideals about what intergenerational relationships should look like, and what parents and children may reasonably expect of each other. The present study supplements this literature.

Generational ideals today are contested, with some supporting traditional perceptions of family ties as obligatory and indissoluble and others favouring the ideal of 'elective affinities' (Beck-Gernsheim 1998; Scharp and Thomas 2016), with family ties seen as similar to other types of personal relationships—friends, romantic partners, etc. At the same time, the dissemination of insights from psychology and related sciences through both popular science and government discourse emphasises the importance of childhood and parents' responsibility for children's development (Lee et al. 2014; Rose 1990; Zelizer 1994). In this perspective, intergenerational relations are very different from e.g. friendships, in that they are initially asymmetrical in their outset, with the child completely dependent on the parents. Overall, parents and adult children today face a plethora of competing and sometimes conflicting opinions and ideals. The question, then, is what these macro-tendencies look like when translated into concrete intergenerational interactions in a specific context.

The Institutional Context for Intergenerational Relationships in Denmark

The case of Denmark is interesting because it is on the extreme end of the spectrum as regards formal generational independence. The Scandinavian welfare model has been characterised as 'optional familialism' in that it provides families with a range of options to cover their care needs, enabling most people to choose between affordable high-quality professional child and elder care or state-subsidised family care options (Leitner 2003; Liversage 2017). In countries such as Germany, Italy, and Spain, parents and adult children are legally obliged to support one another (Herlofson et al. 2011; Hagestad and Dykstra 2016; Hämäläinen et al. 2020), and in other countries, such as the UK and USA, the cost of education and care causes de facto generational interdependency (Goldrick-Rab et al. 2016; Kim and Waldfogel 2020). Less so in Scandinavia, where state-funded higher education and affordable child and elder care allow generations to be largely financially independent (Esping-Andersen 1990; Leitner 2003; Rostgaard 2014). Danish youth leave home at the average age of 21, and less than 2% of adults share a household with the older generation, though this percentage has risen slightly following the recent economic crisis (Stehouwer 1970; Andersen 2017). While the institutional framework allows for a high degree of generational independence, the welfare state has not replaced the family, as intergenerational relations in Denmark remain generally close and informal exchanges are frequent (Bordone 2012; Brandt 2013).

However, this state of affairs is of relatively recent date. As in Europe generally, unprecedented economic growth in the decades between 1950 and 1970 accompanied major changes in the economy, in the institutional structure and in family patterns and norms. In 1960, women made up 26% of the workforce; in 1970, 39% and in 2019, 48%, making the 'dual earner-dual carer' family model the norm (Rostgaard 2014). Geographical mobility and urbanisation occurred as the agricultural workforce dropped from 300,000 in 1939 to 30,000 in 1970, and especially young people migrated to the cities in search of work and education (Ringsmose and Hansen 2005). As women increasingly worked outside the home, and older people found themselves without children living nearby, the state met the need for alternative care provision by legislation on day care provision for children in 1964 and home help for the elderly in 1968 (Ringsmose and Hansen 2005; Clotworthy 2017). The changes associated with the second demographic transition gained widespread acceptance both formally and informally (Sobotka 2008; Lesthaeghe 2014). The formal changes include the legal recognition of cohabitation and the institutionalisation of same-sex unions (Syltevik 2010, 2014; Fernández and Lutter 2013). The informal changes include a general culture of sexual permissiveness (Therborn 2004; Liefbroer and Billari 2010) and widespread acceptance of formerly marginalised practices such as homosexuality, abortion, divorce, and single parenthood (Halman et al. 2011; Minkov et al. 2013; Masterson and Hoobler 2015).

Data and Methods

The analysis draws on 34 semi-biographical interviews conducted as part of the project 'The Moral Economy of Families – Intergenerational Exchanges and Normative Expectations', funded by the Danish Council for Independent Research.

Recruitment aimed at maximum variation across gender, age, and socio-economic position in order to explore narratives of individuals with different biographical experiences (Daatland et al. 2011; Liefbroer and Billari 2010). Life course research shows that biographies are patterned, i.e. that while one's location in time, space, and the socio-economic structures does not determine one's trajectory through life, people in similar positions have more similar experiences than people in widely different positions (Hareven 1994). By varying the sample by age and gender, I aimed at investigating normative expectations of men and women who grew up both before and after the advent of the welfare state and the accompanying shifts in family patterns. I aimed for variation across socio-economic position by sampling interviewees with different occupational positions and from different geographical areas, since both of these characteristics are strongly associated with unequal distributions of resources and advantages (Connelly et al. 2016; Jakobsen et al. 2017) (Table 16.1).

Participants self-selected via web survey, flyers in libraries and sports facilities and a final round of cold calling. Interviews lasted from 1½–3 hours and took place in participants' homes or on university premises. All quotes are pseudonymised, and other names have been replaced with appropriate terms, i.e. [daughter]. For ethical reasons, only one member of each family participated: as the interviews touched on potentially sensitive issues, I wanted to

Table 16.1 Interview participants

Age	Women	Men
20–29	**Lindy.** Health care trainee, rents house in small town. Single, no children. Parents, grandparents alive **Nina.** Student, owns house in small town. Cohabiting, no children. Parents alive	**Eric.** Skilled worker, lives in house owned by partner in small town. Cohabiting, no children. Parents, one grandmother alive
30–39	**Saadia.** Social worker, owns apartment in big city. Mother alive **Lettie.** Civil servant, shares rented apartment in big city. Single, no children. Parents, one grandmother alive **Marie.** Student, owns apartment in big city. Cohabiting, expecting 1st child. Parents, one grandmother alive	**James.** Sales executive, owns apartment in big city. Divorced, 1 child. Parents, paternal grandparents alive
40–49	**Kathy.** Social worker, owns house in big city. Married, 3 children. Parents alive **Rebecca.** Service worker, owns house in big city. Father alive **Holly.** Nurse, retired on disability pension, rents apartment in medium city. Divorced, remarried, 3 children, 2 stepchildren. Mother alive **Karen.** Researcher, owns house in big city. Married, 1 child. Parents alive	**Andrew.** System analyst, owns house in medium city. Married, 3 children. Parents, one grandmother alive **Robert.** Skilled worker, rents house in rural area. Divorced, remarried, 2 children. Parents alive **Mel.** Journalist, owns house in rural area. Married, 3 children. Parents alive
50–59	**Sally.** Mid-level manager, owns house in big city. Married, 2 children. Mother alive **Leslie.** Lawyer, owns house in big city. Divorced, 2 children. Father alive **Barbara.** Lawyer, owns house in medium city. Divorced, 2 children. Parents alive **Alexa.** Part-time social worker, rents apartment in big city. Divorced, 2 children. Parents alive **Mary.** Teacher, owns house in big city. Married, 3 children and 2 stepchildren. Parents alive **Vanessa.** Health care worker, owns house in big city. Divorced, remarried, 2 children, 2 stepchildren. No parents **Susan.** Skilled worker, owns house in small town. Married, 2 children. Mother alive	**Martin.** Engineer, owns house in medium city. Married, 2 children. No parents **Larry.** Skilled worker, owns house in medium city. Divorced, 2 children. Mother alive **Norman.** Scientist, owns house in rural area. Married, 2 children. Mother alive

(continued)

Table 16.1 (continued)

Age	Women	Men
60–69	**Sarah.** Service worker, retired, owns house in small town. Single, no children	**Paul.** Lawyer, owns house in big city. Widowed, remarried, 2 stepchildren **Maurice.** Journalist, retired, rents apartment in big city. Divorced, 1 child, 3 grandchildren **Ernest.** Skilled worker, rents house in big city. Married, 2 children, 5 grandchildren
70–79	**Liza.** Teacher, retired, owns house in medium city. Widowed, remarried, 2 children and 4 stepchildren, 13 grandchildren **Kirsty.** Skilled worker, retired, owns house in small town. Married, 3 children, 6 grandchildren **Gina.** Factory worker, retired, owns house in small town. Divorced, 3 children, 5 grandchildren, 1 great-grandchild	**John.** Artist, semi-retired, owns co-op apartment in big city. Married, 3 children, 9 grandchildren
80–89		**Jerry.** Clerk, retired, rents apartment in big city. Widowed, 2 children, 4 grandchildren, 1 great-grandchild

make sure that the participants did not feel that I was positioning myself to judge between different interpretations of events.

Interviewing from the position of cultural insider it is challenging to encourage participants to verbalise phenomena that 'go without saying'. The interviews used a combination of free narrative and elicitation techniques to meet this challenge. The first half of the interviews was conducted as a modified version of Bertaux' open biographical approach, a strategy of minimal researcher intervention encouraging the participant to construct 'spontaneous narratives' (Bertaux 2003; Bertaux and Kohli 1984; Liversage 2009, 2012; Schütze 1983). I started out asking participants to 'tell me about your family', leaving them to define the term 'family' and, thereby, gaining insight into their categorisations. The downside to this approach is that interviews can go in widely different directions. In order to ensure some points of comparison across interviews, I used three different elicitation techniques in the second half of the interview. Firstly, I asked the participants to place their family members within a relationship diagram of concentric circles. Secondly, I asked them to reflect on three survey questions about intergenerational norms from the European Values Study; and thirdly I asked them to react to two vignettes. This strategy allowed the participants to talk about norms and expectations both in general terms and contextualised by their personal experience. All interviews were audio-recorded and transcribed verbatim, and I read and listened to each interview in its entirety several times. I used NVivo for thematic coding and constructed code trees based on themes such as expectations, emotions, and kinship categories. I coded relatively long interview sequences to preserve the context.

In the interviews, the participants talk about a wide range of relationships, including those with grandparents, siblings, cousins, friends, and neighbours. For this analysis, I draw only on those parts of the interviews concerning relationships between parents and adult children. The interviewees describe parent-child relationships in different contexts. They talk, of course, mostly about their own experiences as parents and adult children, but also about those parent-child relationships that come within their experience at second hand, for instance through their perception of their partners' or friends' relationships with their parents and adult children, or their own parents' relationships with their parents. Since the purpose of the analysis is to identify cultural ideas about what intergenerational relationships ought to be, both first-hand and second-hand accounts are relevant in that they can throw light directly or indirectly on what the interviewee considers appropriate or inappropriate, what 'goes without saying', and what they feel the need to justify or explain to the interviewer.

Accessing phenomena such as cultural ideals and normative expectations is methodologically challenging, as many are unused to or uncomfortable talking about such (cf. Clark 1997). I have found it useful to look at two types of accounts in the interview. One, *explicit reflections on expectations and obligations*, both as they relate to particular persons and to generalised norms ('I expect X of my children' or 'Parents should not expect Y of their children'), and two, *descriptions of concrete interactions and interpretations thereof*. The latter corresponds to what Hochschild (1994) calls 'magnified moments', i.e. narrative sequences in which participants describe a situation to exemplify or illustrate something about their relationships. In several cases, the two types of accounts merge into one another, as a general reflection follows a concrete example, or vice versa. The latter type, I have further coded into descriptions of bond-maintaining and bond-damaging interactions. This does not mean that the relationships described fall neatly into the categories 'harmonious' or 'conflicted', as in many cases interviewees give examples of both types of interaction with the same person at different times or in different situations. The stories are windows into some of these bond-modifying micro-interactions. Some stories are very specific, describing in detail a concrete interaction that occurred on one occasion, others are more general, referring to a state of affairs over a longer period, for instance 'that time when I was going through the divorce'. In the analysis, I have asked the following questions: How do the interviewees describe and interpret their interactions, and what are the differences between the stories told by children and those told by parents?

In the following, I look first at both parents' and children's descriptions of their interactions and identify similarities and differences in their expectations of each other. In the second part of the analysis, I take a closer look at narratives of adult children actively distancing themselves from their parents and at the cultural ideal implied in these narratives.

Symmetries and Asymmetries in Parents' and Adult Children's Mutual Expectations

Visits, phone calls, informal meals, shared activities, and mutual help with practical tasks are the building blocks of relationship maintenance as described by both parents and adult children in the sample. Across differences, participants describe these small interactions as the building blocks of close relationships. For example, Martin describes his relationship with his daughters:

> We see each other frequently, and we're close, I'd say (…) we go to the theatre or concerts, and when they come here for a weekend it's maybe taking a drive to see something, or going for a walk, ordinary things, sometimes just sitting and reading the paper or watching a movie together. (…) So far we haven't had a year without spending part of the summer vacation together, and when [daughter] needed her apartment painted, we packed the car with sleeping bags and paint and ladders and spent a couple of days painting her place. Likewise, they helped us renovate the mud room, and now we're planning to fix the driveway and they've said they're available (…) it comes completely naturally, we don't need to ask for it. (Martin, 58)

Many interviewees describe clearly asymmetrical interactions without framing it as a problem. It is often obvious that more money flows from parents to children than vice versa—as when Martin and his wife bring the materials along when helping paint their daughter's apartment—but few participants explicitly highlight this. Another asymmetry is apparent when the adult children, as many do, mention their parents as trusted sounding boards and sources of advice in important decisions:

> My parents allow me the space (…) to test my arguments and my thoughts (…) in a non-judgmental conversation. (…) [My mother] knows me really well, so she can ask the right questions, those questions that only someone can ask who has known you for many years, who knows your strengths and weaknesses and your fundamental values in life. (Marie, 31)

Marie and others highlight the importance of parents' deep knowledge of their children, which makes them a safe haven for the sharing of doubts, or a source of advice, whether it be for large decisions or smaller practical problems. This type of conversations is valued by children and parents both, but from different perspectives. On their part, parents do not seek advice of their children, nor share confidences in the same way, but they appreciate being involved in the children's lives and the trust implied:

My kids are free to do anything they want. I don't expect them to do anything for my sake. Naturally, I want them to stay on a good, productive course and be decent, kind people, but what they want with their work and lives and partners and families (…) we can't decide for them. We can be there if they want to talk, and they do talk to us. You hear a lot these days about how close families used to be and how fragmented they are now, but I think it's totally the other way around. I never had that kind of conversations with my parents about this kind of thing as I have with my children. I never really talked about girlfriends with my parents, or stuff like family planning and the like, we'd never discuss that. It's a much closer relationship. (Norman, 54)

These stories portray a relationship in which parents and adult children choose to spend time together because they enjoy each other's company, and where adult children trust their parents enough to allow them insight into very personal aspects of their lives. In these interviews, it is highly unclear who has helped whom with what and when, and neither is it perceived as relevant by the involved parties to use terms reminiscent of obligations or a 'quid pro quo' exchange logic. On the contrary, when asked, several participants, like Norman, explicitly reject the idea of obligation in personal relationships and emphasise the importance of relationships rooted in voluntary emotional bonds and a desire to spend time together. For example, when asked about her expectations for when her children leave home, Saadia says:

I'd hope they'd want to come home for dinner every Sunday – I know I can't expect it, but I hope that they'll want to. And that they'd do it because they enjoyed it, not see it as a dreary obligation, for all the world not a dreary obligation, but that they want to see me, see their parents. That's my dream scenario, absolutely. (Saadia, 35)

Saadia draws a distinction between hope and expectation. Adult children's behaviour towards their parents is the object of hope, but not expectation, as when both Saadia and Norman explicitly reject the idea of expecting their children to do anything for the sake of their parents. The emphasis on voluntariness and enjoyment, indeed, makes the idea of obligation almost absurd—you cannot make another person want something as a matter of duty.

Parents do have expectations, which Norman refers to in passing as 'naturally', as something that almost goes without saying. However, these are less about what the children should or should not *do* in relation to their parents, but more about what the children should *be* ('good, productive (…) decent, kind people')—i.e. the adult moral identity that parents expect their children to manifest. Martin articulates a similar perspective:

One thing that makes me happy now that they are grown up is to see that they can fend for themselves. That they can navigate both financially and in relation to other people, it sounds a bit old-fashioned, but seeing that they are making good. (…) It means a lot to me, to both of us, to see that they are well-rounded people, doing what they want and that they have been able to cope with education, money and the like, and that they are getting along with others. (Martin, 58)

The primary expectation of the parents is for children to develop into self-reliant, responsible, self-determined adults capable of making their own decisions. The hope that the children's self-directed choices will include staying emotionally close to their parents, spending time with them and involving them in their personal concerns, asking for their advice, etc., is downplayed in comparison.

Sally's interview captures the asymmetry in the parents' expectations and those of adult children. The mother of two young adults, Sally articulates the asymmetric expectations very explicitly:

> I demand a totally different level of acceptance from my parents of myself as a person and my actions than I demand of my children. [The children] don't have to accept me, and there's an inequality in that relationship, I'd do much more for them than they'd do for me, and that is totally OK, because that is inherent in that unconditional love. I don't think the love I have for my parents is unconditional, but my love for my children is. (Sally, 51)

However, the material also contains stories of relationship work that fails and becomes relationship damage. These stories, as we shall see, are asymmetrical in another way, as the large majority comes from the perspective of the child and very few from that of the parents.

Susan is the one example in the material of a parent talking at length about a relationship with a child that has, if not failed outright, at least become more distant and troubled than she would like:

> My daughter doesn't come home as much as she used to do (…) So that makes me a bit sad. But, you know, she doesn't have the same need to stay in touch as I do, at the present time (…) With her it's a bit more 'out of sight, out of mind', you know. I don't think she thinks that much about, how much we think about her and how she's doing and her life (…) We're not that fond of her boyfriend. So that's a bit tiresome. (…) But she says she's happy to be where she is, because that's what worries us, you know, whether she's okay. But she says she is. (Susan, 52)

Susan goes into some detail explaining how she and her husband have tried unsuccessfully to establish a good relationship with the daughter's boyfriend, and how she worries that her daughter feels caught in the middle. It is worth noting that Susan does not use terms that imply moral censure of her daughter or say that the daughter has failed to live up to expectations. Susan does not describe herself as disappointed or angry, but as 'a bit sad' and 'worried'. In this way, she downplays the possible interpretation of her daughter's actions as deliberate distancing behaviour, while still making it clear that the distance between them is not of her choosing.

Susan is the only parent in the material who describes an ongoing ambivalence in the relationship with an adult child. A few parents mention conflicts that have taken place many years in the past—typically interpreted as 'teenage rebellion' on the part of the children—but no parents tell stories of actively distancing themselves from their children. Apparently, parents engaging in distancing behaviour are unwilling to talk about it in interviews. It may be that it is hard to give a justified account of why you would want to distance yourself from your adult child. This is consistent with the widespread cultural perception that the burden of responsibility for the quality of the relationship lies with the parent, not the (adult) child, an unhappy relationship hence reflecting badly on the parent more than on the child.

Distancing Oneself from Under-Involved and Over-Involved Parents

If parents are reluctant to describe ambivalent relationships with their children, the reverse is not the case. The material contains several narratives told from the perspective of adult children who explain why they distance themselves from their parents to some degree. The stories about children distancing themselves from parents fall into two main groups: stories about the under-involved and the over-involved parent.

Far from demonstrating deep knowledge of their children, the under-involved parents show little or no interest in spending time with or listening to them, as when Holly describes her relationship with her father after her parents' divorce, leading eventually to her decision to cut off contact with her father:

> When I came to see him, when I was in high school, he could never remember what grade I was in or whether English was my favorite subject or what my hobbies were, and he kept everlastingly on about his new wife's children and grandchildren. She had a son and that's what he always wanted, and he never had one, since he had us three girls, and it was like he was much more interested in his new family than in the rest of us, and I simply got so tired of that. (...) I didn't want him to meet my children (...) and I'd taken breaks from him before, and whenever I took up the contact it has been the exact same thing, and I remember that my first husband used to say that I was always so sad after visiting my father. (...) So, I reached a point when I said, 'no, and definitely not with my children'. (Holly, 43)

It is interesting that Holly does not describe a father who has in any obvious way mistreated her or failed to provide for her material needs, or even keep in touch. Holly explains her sadness as caused by her father's failure to display that deep knowledge of and interest in her, which other adult children so appreciate in their parents. For Holly, the fact that her father talks 'everlastingly' about his new family makes his failure to engage with her worse, since it shows that he is capable of paying attention when he wants to, but does not show it in relation to herself and her sisters.

Holly's story is typical in that many stories about conflicted or ambivalent relationships have elements of favouritism, where one child perceives that a sibling or stepsibling receives more attention or more help from the parents, that the parents take sides in conflicts between siblings, or—as in Mary's account—her husband's parents favour their biological grandchildren:

> [My husband's mother] has always been very close with [my stepsons] and spent a lot of time with them. (…) his parents give much bigger presents to [my stepsons] than to [my daughter and son], they really favour them. And it's not very charming I think, because they could easily afford it. (…) We try to laugh at it and say 'what a strange present' and so on. But [my daughter] isn't very close to [my husband's parents]. She said, when she got married in the spring, that she didn't want them at her wedding, she saw no reason to have them. (Mary, 55)

The grandparents' display of under-involvement justifies distancing behaviour on the part of Mary's daughter. Like Holly, Mary does not problematise the low degree of involvement so much as the favouritism involved, which highlights the fact that the parents could act differently if they chose.

On the other extreme, the over-involved parents overstep their role as the non-judgemental sounding board when they fail to recognise their adult children's choices—of a partner, as in Susan's case, or of a job, as when Marie describes her partner deciding to quit a prestigious, but stressful, job in order to become a teacher:

> [My partner] keeps a certain distance to his parents. It makes sense to me that one might do that if one's parents have a judgmental attitude to the choices their children make. [His father] is something of a know-it-all when it comes to living one's life in the most optimal way, and he doesn't hesitate to tell my partner if he thinks he is making the wrong choices. That makes one feel less like sharing one's thoughts and the choices one makes, because there's always the risk that one might be told that 'you shouldn't have done that', or 'that was dumb', or 'what the hell were you thinking'. For example, quitting a good job. A good job in the sense that, in a company where my partner had really interesting tasks and he made good money, but he just didn't thrive in that environment, and it made him ill. (…) And his father's comment was, and he keeps saying that, is that it was a stupid decision. (Marie, 31)

Marie's father-in-law fails to recognise his son's ability to make his own choices or to acknowledge their legitimacy. As a result, the son withdraws from the relationship and, unlike Marie, does not involve his parents in major life decisions. Both parents and adult children acknowledge the danger of over-involvement. Himself a grandfather, Ernest warns other parents:

> When your children meet someone, friends, classmates, boyfriends, it's hard for parents to control. You can't. That is, it's a balance on a knife-edge, I almost said, and better not miss your step, because you damn well risk losing your child. Better help in another way than begin to forbid and reject and, because it can go horribly wrong. (...) And apart from that, welcome the boyfriend. The classmate, the friend, welcome them, treat them well, and still, talk with your child, because you risk losing your child if you go on trying to control too much. (...) And if you love and want your child, you need to love and want the boyfriend, or the son-in-law. (Ernest, 62)

Again, the expectations for parents and children are asymmetrical. The parents have a delicate balance to tread between on the one hand staying involved, entering into their children's concerns and making themselves available as a trusted resource and sounding board, and on the other hand not judging the children's choices if they turn out different from those the parents would make. Both too much and too little involvement can damage the bond and make the children draw back from the relationship.

THE GOLDILOCKS PRINCIPLE OF PARENTING: NEITHER TOO HOT NOR TOO COLD

A pattern emerges where much more specific and legitimate expectations pertain to parents than to adult children. Parents avoid articulating any expectations that concern the children's behaviour or emotions towards themselves as parents. If children have any obligations, they are towards their own self and potential, and parents may reasonably expect that their children make good choices and eventually become self-determined adults—not so much in order to avoid becoming a burden on their parents as in order to fulfil the cultural ideal of the self-determining individual. Adult children are not *expected* to visit their parents regularly, nor to ask the parents' advice or consult their wishes in important decisions, nor to show their parents love and gratitude unless motivated by authentic emotions; that is, unless the children freely *choose* to do so.

In contrast, children expect of their parents much that relates closely to the parents' behaviour and emotions towards the children themselves. Children expect that their parents should identify with their concerns, should rejoice in their joys and grieve with their sorrows, and should furthermore recognise the absolute right of their adult child to make his or her own decisions about important matters. Economists use the term 'Goldilocks economy' to describe a balanced market. The concept draws on the story of Goldilocks and the three bears to describe something 'not too hot, not too cold, but just right'. The asymmetrical character of expectations means that a similar

'Goldilocks principle' pertains to the balance parents have to tread between over- and under-involvement. In short, children expect unconditional and life-long love and respect from their parents and are disappointed if the parents fail to manifest such love, whereas parents take their children's love and respect, if forthcoming, as a precious gift and are grateful for it.

As we have seen, some parents and children share expectations, with both parties seeing the asymmetrical exchanges as appropriate and 'just right', while in other cases, different perceptions give rise to mismatched expectations and increased distance in the relationship. Why does the asymmetrical expectations seem appropriate to some parents and not others? Part of the answer might lie in the different frames of reference available to parents and adult children. Parents may be more likely to draw on historical frames of reference, comparing themselves with their own parents and grandparents, while the children are more likely to compare their relationships to their parents with those which they see practised by contemporaries—friends, siblings, or significant others (Gullestad 1996; Hagestad 2003). This discrepancy in the frames of reference may give rise to mismatched expectations. The foregrounding of emotional closeness and the ideal of the self-determining adult both are comparatively recent as pervading cultural ideals, and some parents may find themselves caught in expectations they are unsure how to fulfil, as they struggle with adapting their own frames of reference, which took shape in a more austere epoch (Jenks 2002; Trifan et al. 2014). Without being conclusive, the stories of Holly, Susan and Marie's father-in-law, are all consistent with this hypothesis, as they all involve family histories of social mobility, with the younger generations growing up in relatively affluent conditions and participating more in higher education compared to the older generations.

In some ways, the accounts of distancing behaviour presented here appear to be evidence of individualisation, as they presuppose the general acceptance of the idea that relationships, family ones included, are subject to individual choice (cf. Beck-Gernsheim 1998). In other ways, the accounts highlight the degree to which individuals are embedded in relational networks and make their choices with at least as much attention to these as to their personal preferences (cf. Jamieson 1998). Parents and children rarely negotiate their relationships in a vacuum, but within a complex web of other relationships. Holly evaluates her father's behaviour to herself in comparison with his behaviour to his stepchildren and to her sisters; she discusses it with her husband and makes her final decision to cut off contact with reference to the consequences for her own children. Susan's feelings about her daughter's boyfriend inescapably colour the mother-daughter relationship, etc.

Looking at the accounts in a life course perspective, certain phases appear to be especially salient (cf. Hagestad 2003). Many accounts of bond-damaging interactions resulting in distant and ambivalent relationships refer to events that take place during those years of emerging adulthood when children leave the parental home and make the first important decisions for their own lives, such as a choice of a partner and career. These choices contribute in important ways to whether the child will become a self-determined adult and so are of close concern to both children and parents. As long as children live at home, it may be easier for parents to negotiate the balance between over-and under-involvement. Taking a close interest and keeping in touch with one another's concerns is both more legitimate and less of an effort when sharing a household. Living apart also means interactions happen less frequently, making each interaction potentially more fraught with meaning, as both parents and children have fewer 'data points' from which to extrapolate the current state of their relationship. A successful interaction in which the parent responds appropriately increases the likelihood that the child will involve their parents next time, while a failed interaction where the child feels either ignored or judged will make them more likely to go elsewhere. The parents' ability to balance in the 'Goldilocks zone' between over- and under-involvement in this phase has implications for the subsequent state of the relationship.

Conclusion

I set out to understand contemporary cultural ideals influencing intergenerational relationships, specifically, the expectations held by parents and adult children in Denmark. The analysis has shown that overall, much more specific and culturally legitimate expectations pertain to parents than to adult children, and a much wider field of legitimate justifications for distancing behaviour is available to the children than the parents. A 'Goldilocks principle' applies to the role of parent, who must strike a balance between maintaining a lifelong emotional engagement in their children and respecting the adult children's autonomy. Parents and adult children maintain their relationship through interactions that are similar to those engaged in by participants of other types of personal relationships: visits, phone calls, shared activities, and mutual help. In many cases, the exchanges are unproblematically asymmetrical, with parents happy to be the trusted sounding board when children want to share their thoughts and considerations, but not all parents are equally successful in navigating the Goldilocks principle. In some cases, these difficulties appear connected to different historical frames of reference, with parents socialised under conditions of greater austerity and greater parental authority. If this is the case, the cultural trends of individualisation, emotionalisation of personal relationships, and the responsibilisation of parents interact with existing structures of social differentiation such as social class and the possession of social resources with very different results on the micro-level, and policy makers and opinion leaders would do well to be aware of this. However, an in-depth analysis of these hypotheses goes beyond the scope of this study.

As mentioned, Denmark is an extreme case in regard to formal generational independence. This raises the question of the generalisability of these findings beyond contemporary Denmark. To what extent should we expect to see the same pattern of asymmetrical expectations in the relationships of parents and adult children in other countries? The answer depends on one's understanding of the relative importance of cultural versus institutional factors in shaping relationship norms. The aforementioned cultural trends are not unique to Denmark but are present in large parts of the world (e.g. Therborn 2004; Rutherford 2011). It may be that the institutional conditions allow parents and children living in generous welfare states to go along with these trends to a larger degree than where the generations depend on each other for support. In addition, the situation in Denmark has come about following a period of practically uninterrupted economic growth and expansion of the welfare state. It will be interesting to see how current trends of public retrenchment and increased austerity will influence intergenerational expectations.

Acknowledgements The research for the chapter was supported by The Danish Council for Independent Research (grant number 1329-00112A). I want to thank the participants in the network and workshop series *Significant others—informal social networks between policy and everyday life* for inspiring discussions of the ideas included in this chapter. Especial thanks to Anna-Maija Castrén, Sara Eldén, and Terese Anving. The workshop series was funded by The Joint Committee for Nordic research councils in the Humanities and Social Sciences (grant number 2016-00258/NOS-HS_4). I want to thank Professor Bente Halkier, University of Copenhagen, as well as the editors of this volume and the anonymous reviewers for constructive comments and helpful advice on earlier drafts of this chapter.

References

Albertini, Marco, and Martin Kohli. 2013. "The Generational Contract in the Family: An Analysis of Transfer Regimes in Europe." *European Sociological Review* 29 (4): 828–840.

Andersen, Nadja. 2017. "Under samme tag som svigermor." https://www.kl.dk/nyheder/makro-analyseenheden/danmark-i-forandring/flere-danskere-bor-undersamme-tag-som-svigermor/ Accessed on January 22, 2020.

Antonucci, Toni C., Kira S. Birditt, Carey W. Sherman, and Sarah Trinh. 2011. "Stability and Change in the Intergenerational Family: A Convoy Approach." *Ageing & Society* 31 (7): 1084–1106.

Attias-Donfut, Claudine, and Martine Segalen. 2002. "The Construction of Grandparenthood." *Current Sociology* 50 (2): 281–294.

Beck, Ulrich, and Elisabeth Beck-Gernsheim. 2018 [1995]. *The Normal Chaos of Love*. New York: Wiley.

Beck-Gernsheim, Elisabeth. 1998. "On the Way to a Post-familial Family: From a Community of Need to Elective Affinities." *Theory, Culture and Society* 15 (3–4): 53–70.

Bengtson, Vern L. 2001. "Beyond the Nuclear Family: The Increasing Importance of Multigenerational Bonds: The Burgess Award Lecture." *Journal of Marriage and Family* 63 (1): 1–16.

Bertaux, Daniel. 2003. "The Usefulness of Life Stories for a Realist and Meaningful Sociology." In *Biographical Research in Eastern Europe. Altered Lives and Broken Biographies*, edited by Robert Miller, 39–52. Oxon: Routledge.

Bertaux, Daniel, and Martin Kohli. 1984. "The Life Story Approach: A Continental View." *Annual Review of Sociology* 10 (1): 215–237.

Bloom, David E., David Canning, and Günther Fink. 2010. "Implications of Population Ageing for Economic Growth." *Oxford Review of Economic Policy* 26 (4): 583–612.

Bordone, Valeria. 2012. "Social Norms and Intergenerational Relationships." In *The Family, the Market or the State? Intergenerational Support Under Pressure in Ageing Societies*, edited by Gustavo De Santis, 159–178. Dordrecht: Springer.

Brandt, Martina. 2013. "Intergenerational Help and Public Assistance in Europe: A Case of Specialization?" *European Societies* 15 (1): 26–56.

Brannen, Julia. 2016. *Fathers and Sons: Generations, Families and Migration*. Basingstoke: Springer.

Canary, Daniel J., and Laura Stafford. 1994. "Maintaining Relationships Through Strategic and Routine Interaction." In *Communication and Relational Maintenance*, edited by Daniel J. Canary and Laura Stafford, 3–22. San Diego: Academic Press.

Clark, Candace. 1997. *Misery and Company: Sympathy in Everyday Life*. Chicago: University of Chicago Press.

Clotworthy, Amy. 2017. "Empowering the Elderly? A Qualitative Study of Municipal Home-Health Visits and Everyday Rehabilitation." PhD diss., Det Humanistiske Fakultet, Københavns Universitet.

Connelly, Roxanne, Vernon Gayle, and Paul S. Lambert. 2016. "A Review of Occupation-Based Social Classifications for Social Survey Research." *Methodological Innovations* 9: 2059799116638003.

Connidis, Ingrid Arnet, and Amanda E. Barnett. 2018. *Family Ties and Aging*. Los Angeles: Sage.

Daatland, Svein Olav, Katharina Herlofson, and Ivar A. Lima. 2011. "Balancing Generations: on the Strength and Character of Family Norms in the West and East of Europe." *Ageing and Society* 31 (7): 1159.

Di Leonardo, Micaela. 1987. "The Female World of Cards and Holidays: Women, Families, and the Work of Kinship." *Signs: Journal of Women in Culture and Society* 12 (3): 440–453.

Dindia, Kathryn, and Leslie A. Baxter. 1987. "Strategies for Maintaining and Repairing Marital Relationships." *Journal of Social and Personal Relationships* 4 (2): 143–158.

Dykstra, Pearl A. 2018. "Cross-National Differences in Intergenerational Family Relations: The Influence of Public Policy Arrangements." *Innovation in Aging* 2 (1): igx032.

Esping-Andersen, Gosta. 1990. *The Three Worlds of Welfare Capitalism*. Princeton: Princeton University Press.

Fehr, Beverley. 1996. *Friendship Processes*. Sage Series on Close Relationships, Vol. 12. Thousand Oaks: Sage.

Fernández, Juan J., and Mark Lutter. 2013. "Supranational Cultural Norms, Domestic Value Orientations and the Diffusion of Same-Sex Union Rights in Europe, 1988–2009." *International Sociology* 28 (1): 102–120.

Finch, Janet, and Jennifer Mason. 1993. *Negotiating Family Responsibilities*. London: Routledge.

Fingerman, Karen L., Meng Huo, and Kira S. Birditt. 2020. "A Decade of Research on Intergenerational Ties: Technological, Economic, Political, and Demographic Changes." *Journal of Marriage and Family* 82 (1): 383–403.

Funk, Laura. 2015. "Constructing the Meaning of Filial Responsibility: Choice and Obligation in the Accounts of Adult Children." *Families, Relationships and Societies* 4 (3): 383–399.
Gabb, Jacqui, and Janet Fink. 2017. *Couple Relationships in the 21st Century: Research, Policy, Practice.* Cham: Springer.
Goldrick-Rab, Sara, Robert Kelchen, Douglas N. Harris, and James Benson. 2016. "Reducing Income Inequality in Educational Attainment: Experimental Evidence on the Impact of Financial Aid on College Completion." *American Journal of Sociology* 121 (6): 1762–1817.
Gullestad, Marianne. 1996. "From Obedience to Negotiation: Dilemmas in the Transmission of Values Between the Generations in Norway." *Journal of the Royal Anthropological Institute* 2: 25–42.
Hagestad, Gunhild O., 2003. "Interdependent Lives and Relationships in Changing Times: A Life-Course View of Families and Aging." In *Invitation to the Life Course: Towards New Understandings of Later Life*, edited by Richard Settersten, 135–159. Oxon: Routledge.
Hagestad, Gunhild O., and Pearl A. Dykstra. 2016. "Structuration of the Life Course: Some Neglected Aspects." In *Handbook of the Life Course*, Vol. II, edited by Michael J. Shanahan, Jeylan T. Mortimer, and Monica Kirkpatrick Johnson, 131–157. Cham: Springer.
Halman, Loek, Inge Sieben, and Marga van Zundert, eds. 2011. *Atlas of European Values. Trends and Traditions at the Turn of the Century.* Leiden: Brill.
Hämäläinen, Hans, Antti O. Tanskanen, Mirkka Danielsbacka, and Bruno Arpino. 2020. "Short-Term Reciprocity Between Adult Children and Parents: A Within-Person Investigation of Longitudinal Data." *Advances in Life Course Research* 44: 100337.
Hareven, Tamara K. 1994. "Aging and Generational Relations: A Historical and Life Course Perspective." *Annual Review of Sociology* 20 (1): 437–461.
Herlofson, Katharina, Gunhild Hagestad, Britt Slagsvold, and Anne-Mette Sørensen. 2011. "Intergenerational Family Responsibility and Solidarity in Europe." Multilinks Project. Norwegian Social Research (NOVA). (104 Multilinks Project).
Hochschild, Arlie Russell. 1994. "The Commercial Spirit of Intimate Life and the Abduction of Feminism: Signs from Women's Advice Books." *Theory, Culture & Society* 11 (2): 1–24.
Jakobsen, Katrine, Kristian Jakobsen, Henrik Kleven, and Gabriel Zucman. 2017. "Wealth Taxation and Wealth Inequality: Evidence from Denmark 1980–2014." In Manuscript. https://editorialexpress.com/cgi-bin/conference/download.
Jamieson, Lynn. 1998. *Intimacy: Personal Relationships in Modern Societies.* Cambridge: Polity Press.
Jenks, Chris 2002 [1996]. "The Postmodern Child." In *Children in Families: Research and Policy*, edited by Julia Brannen and Margaret O'Brien, 13–25. London: Routledge.
Kalmijn, Matthijs. 2014. "Adult Intergenerational Relationships." In *The Wiley-Blackwell Companion to the Sociology of Families*, edited by Judith Treas, Jacqueline Scott, and Martin Richards, 385–403. Hoboken: Wiley-Blackwell.
Kalmijn, Matthijs, Suzanne G. de Leeuw, Maaike Hornstra, Katya Ivanova, Ruben van Gaalen, and Kirsten van Houdt. 2019. "Family Complexity into Adulthood: The Central Role of Mothers in Shaping Intergenerational Ties." *American Sociological Review* 84 (5): 876–904.

Kim, Soohyun, and Jane Waldfogel. 2020. "Elder Care and the Role of Paid Leave Policy." In *Handbook on Demographic Change and the Lifecourse*, edited by Jane Falkingham, Maria Evandrou, and Athina Vlachantoni. Cheltenham: Edward Elgar Publishing.

Lee, Ellie, Jennie Bristow, Charlotte Faircloth, and Jan Macvarish. 2014. *Parenting Culture Studies*. Basingstoke: Springer.

Leitner, Sigrid. 2003. "Varieties of Familialism: The Caring Function of the Family in Comparative Perspective." *European Societies* 5 (4): 353–375.

Lesthaeghe, Ron. 2014. "The Second Demographic Transition: A Concise Overview of Its Development." *Proceedings of the National Academy of Sciences* 111 (51): 18112–18115.

Liefbroer, Aart C., and Francesco C. Billari. 2010. "Bringing Norms Back In: A Theoretical and Empirical Discussion of Their Importance for Understanding Demographic Behaviour." *Population, Space and Place* 16 (4): 287–305.

Liversage, Anika. 2009. "Vital Conjunctures, Shifting Horizons: High-Skilled Female Immigrants Looking for Work." *Work, Employment and Society* 23 (1): 120–141.

Liversage, Anika. 2012. "Gender, Conflict and Subordination Within the Household: Turkish Migrant Marriage and Divorce in Denmark." *Journal of Ethnic and Migration Studies* 38 (7): 1119–1136.

Liversage, Anika. 2017. "Twice as Many Helpers: Unpacking the Connection Between Marriage Migration and Older Labour Immigrants' Access to Family Support." *Migration Letters* 14 (1): 50–62.

Masterson, Courtney R., and Jenny M. Hoobler. 2015. "Care and Career: A Family Identity-Based Typology of Dual-Earner Couples." *Journal of Organizational Behavior* 36 (1): 75–93.

McCarthy, Jane Ribbens, Rosalind Edwards, and Val Gillies. 2017. *Making Families: Moral Tales of Parenting and Step-Parenting*. London: Routledge-Cavendish.

Merz, Eva-Maria, Nathan S. Consedine, Hans-Joachim Schulze, and Carlo Schuengel. 2009. "Wellbeing of Adult Children and Ageing Parents: Associations with Intergenerational Support and Relationship Quality." *Ageing and Society* 29 (5): 783.

Minkov, Michael, Vesselin Blagoev, and Geert Hofstede. 2013. "The Boundaries of Culture: Do Questions About Societal Norms Reveal Cultural Differences?" *Journal of Cross-Cultural Psychology* 44 (7): 1094–1106.

Nitchovski, Pavel. 2018. "'Hello, Clarice.' (A Step) Towards a Philosophical Account of Intimacy." Thesis submitted to the faculty at the University of North Carolina at Chapel Hill.

Pickard, Linda. 2015. "A Growing Care Gap? The Supply of Unpaid Care for Older People by Their Adult Children in England to 2032." *Ageing & Society* 35 (1): 96–123.

Pillemer, Karl, and J. Jill Suitor. 2006. "Making Choices: A Within-Family Study of Caregiver Selection." *The Gerontologist* 46 (4): 439–448.

Ringsmose, J., and M. B. Hansen. 2005. *Fælles sprog og ældreplejens organisering i et historisk perspektiv*. Odense: Syddansk Universitet.

Rose, Nikolas. 1990. *Governing the Soul: The Shaping of the Private Self*. London: Taylor & Frances/Routledge.

Rostgaard, Tine. 2014. *Family Policies in Scandinavia*. Berlin: Friedrich-Ebert-Stiftung, Western Europa/North America.

Rutherford, Markella B. 2011. *Adult Supervision Required: Private Freedom and Public Constraints for Parents and Children*. New Brunswick: Rutgers University Press.
Scharp, Kristina M., and Lindsey J. Thomas. 2016. "Family 'Bonds': Making Meaning of Parent-Child Relationships in Estrangement Narratives." *Journal of Family Communication* 16 (1): 32–50.
Scheff, Thomas J. 1997. *Emotions, the Social Bond, and Human Reality: Part/Whole Analysis*. Cambridge: Cambridge University Press.
Schütze, Fritz. 1983. "Biographieforschung und narratives Interview." *neue praxis* 13 (3): 283–293.
Sobotka, Tomáš. 2008. "Overview Chapter 6: The Diverse Faces of the Second Demographic Transition in Europe." *Demographic Research* 19: 171–224.
Starr, Madeleine, and Marta Szebehely. 2017. "Working Longer, Caring Harder—The Impact of 'Ageing-in-Place' Policies on Working Carers in the UK and Sweden." *International Journal of Care and Caring* 1 (1): 115–119.
Stehouwer, Jan. 1970. "Relations Between Generations and the Three-Generation Household in Denmark." In *Readings in Kinship in Urban Society*, 337–366. Oxford: Pergamon.
Strikwerda, Robert A., and Larry May. 1992. "Male Friendship and Intimacy." *Hypatia* 7 (3): 110–125.
Swartz, Teresa Toguchi, Minzee Kim, Mayumi Uno, Jeylan Mortimer, and Kirsten Bengtson O'Brien. 2011. "Safety Nets and Scaffolds: Parental Support in the Transition to Adulthood." *Journal of Marriage and Family* 73 (2): 414–429.
Syltevik, Liv J. 2010. "Sense and Sensibility: Cohabitation in 'Cohabitation Land'." *The Sociological Review* 58 (3): 444–462.
Syltevik, Liv J. 2014. "Cohabitation from Illegal to Institutionalized Practice: The Case of Norway 1972–2010." *The History of the Family* 20 (4): 515–529.
Therborn, Göran. 2004. *Between Sex and Power: Family in the World 1900–2000*. London: Routledge.
Trifan, Tatiana Alina, Håkan Stattin, and Lauree Tilton-Weaver 2014. "Have Authoritarian Parenting Practices and Roles Changed in the Last 50 Years?" *Journal of Marriage and Family* 76 (4): 744–761.
van Gaalen, Ruben I. 2007. "Solidarity and Ambivalence in Parent-Child Relationships." Utrecht University Repository: Utrecht University.
Van Gaalen, Ruben I., Pearl A. Dykstra, and Aafke E. Komter. 2010. "Where Is the Exit? Intergenerational Ambivalence and Relationship Quality in High Contact Ties." *Journal of Aging Studies* 24 (2): 105–114.
Van Hooff, Jenny. 2016. *Modern Couples? Continuity and Change in Heterosexual Relationships*. London: Routledge.
Zelizer, Viviana A. 1994. *Pricing the Priceless Child: The Changing Social Value of Children*. Princeton: Princeton University Press.

PART IV

Parental Arrangements, Parenting and Child Well-Being

Edited by Claude Martin and Almudena Moreno Mínguez

CHAPTER 17

Non-Parental Childcare in France, Norway, and Spain

Gerardo Meil, Vicente Diaz-Gandasegui, Jesús Rogero-García, and Pedro Romero-Balsas

INTRODUCTION

This chapter examines non-parental childcare for children under three years old in France, Norway, and Spain, countries with different public policies classified in the academic literature as different welfare regimes. Specifically, the chapter reviews the participation of pre-school services, non-parental relatives, and professional care providers in caring for children from 0 to 3 years old. Particular attention is paid to social class in different actors' role in each country. Therefore, the chapter contributes doubly to the academic literature: firstly with its novelty, consisting in new findings on the various agents' participation in childcare in each country, and secondly analysing the effect of specific public policies in the different strategies adopted by diverse social groups.

The chapter begins with a description and contextualisation of the different family policies and parents' working conditions in France, Norway, and Spain,

---

G. Meil (✉) · J. Rogero-García · P. Romero-Balsas
Universidad Autónoma of Madrid, Madrid, Spain
e-mail: gerardo.meil@uam.es

J. Rogero-García
e-mail: jesus.rogero@uam.es

P. Romero-Balsas
e-mail: pedro.romero@uam.es

V. Diaz-Gandasegui
Universidad Carlos III de Madrid, Madrid, Spain
e-mail: vdgandas@polsoc.uc3m.es

© The Author(s), under exclusive license to Springer Nature Switzerland AG 2021
A.-M. Castrén et al. (eds.), *The Palgrave Handbook of Family Sociology in Europe*, https://doi.org/10.1007/978-3-030-73306-3_17

establishing the main hypotheses of the research. Thereafter the methodology is explained and the main outcomes of the research grounds for the conclusions discussed in the final section.

Non-Parental Childcare and the French, Norwegian, and Spanish Labour Markets

Family policy directed to children under 3 years old is an essential element in supporting work-life balance, achieving gender equality and enhancing parents' and children's well-being. As a paramount mechanism in welfare state design, such policies define the public agenda and structurally impact in social and family organisation as well as national demographics and economies (Soss and Schram 2007). Nonetheless, public investment in family benefits and policies, including child day care, varies widely across the three countries analysed (Eurostat 2020). Whereas in Spain investment is half the EU mean (1.2% compared to 2.3% of GDP), in France (2.4%) it is similar to other European Union countries and in Norway (3.2%) is nearly a full percentage point higher.

The most relevant childcare mechanism in the earliest stages of a child's life is parental leave. Its design establishes how responsibilities are shared both inside the domestic sphere and between families and the state. For many decades Norway has provided long parental leave that beginning in 2009 is formally shared equally by the two parents, who together have 45 weeks after childbirth at 100% of their salary or 56 weeks at 80%. Fifteen to 19 weeks are reserved exclusively to each, whilst the rest can be distributed at will. However, this divisible part is most often used by mothers (Kvande and Brandth 2017), reinforcing traditional roles due primarily to social inertia and the existing gender salary gap. In France mothers have 16 and fathers 2 weeks of leave at 100% of their salary (Boyer and Fagnani 2019). In Spain maternity and paternity leave were provided by the same criteria as in France, whilst beginning in 2017 paternity leave began to be gradually increased, targeting 16 weeks by 2021 (Meil et al. 2019). After that time, in both countries each parent is entitled to another leave up to the child's third birthday. In Spain it is not remunerated, whereas in France parents are eligible for a child-rearing benefit of up to €580/month depending on the number of children, income level, and the number of hours parents shave off their work week (Fagnani 2020).

After parental leave, pre-school is the most relevant caring strategy to meet family needs, as it softens the work-life balance conflict, further an egalitarian family model and reduce childhood poverty (Korpi 2000; Leira 2002; Rindfuss et al. 2007). Policies which propose an alternative to family care have a substantial impact on gender equality, as in their absence care is assumed by women, typically mothers, hindering their employability and the distribution of household tasks (Brandth and Kvande 2009). The 'substitution thesis' (Tobío 2012) contends that when care services acquire a social commitment, families' and particularly mothers' responsibility declines, enabling them to join the labour market without creating conflicts around childcare tasks.

Spain's investment in childcare services is smaller than in the other two countries, although in terms of percentage of GDP (0.5 vs 0.4%) it is higher than the European mean and close to the figure in France (0.6%). Norway, which has instituted universal pre-school from the age of 1, invests significantly more in that regard. Scandinavian countries have the most 'de-familialised' welfare states characterised, according to Leitner (2003), by public policies that provide families explicit support in the form of alternative childcare, thereby enabling women to join the labour market. Mediterranean countries are the most family-dependent, family members with parents and other relatives assuming the primary responsibility for childcare (Leitner 2003; Wall and Escobedo 2013). These are countries in which social policy is scant and erratic and, despite progress in recent years, families and especially mothers and grandparents bear much of the responsibility for care provision (Leon and Migliavacca 2013). France's conservative welfare state model lies in-between, sharing some of the features of Mediterranean welfare states, although its family policies are more fully developed, with considerable state intervention in childcare. French family policies pursue pro-natalist aims that co-exist with other objectives, such as freedom of choice on childcare and the creation of female employment, particularly beginning in the 70s with the identification of the need to take measures to favour work-family balance (Fagnani and Math 2011). Nonetheless, the ambivalent architecture of French family policies has not generated satisfactory conciliation mechanisms, for relatives' provision of care or informal agreements continue to weigh heavily in the strategies adopted by many families (Fagnani and Math 2011). Before the 2008 crisis, 15% of French children between the ages of 4 months and 2 years were cared for by their grandparents, especially among lower income households in cities with a population of under 100,000 and areas with a smaller proportion of pre-school facilities (Blanpain 2006). A higher percentage of French grandparents engage in care when mothers are employed, devoting more time when the latter have fixed working hours and on weekdays, although more hours are invested by those who provide care on weekends and Wednesdays (when formal childcare services close) (Kitzmann 2018).

Thévenon and Solaz (2013) discuss employment ratios by sex from 1970 to 2012 in 30 OECD countries, France, Norway, and Spain among them. They observed progress in the three countries in equalling employment ratios and hours of paid employment between men and women. Nonetheless, women had 3.6 percentage point higher unemployment than men in Spain, whereas in Norway the difference was 0.6 points and in France just 0.3 points (Eurostat 2020). Men devoted more time to paid work in all three countries, although Norwegian males invested the least. The number of hours parents spend in paid work may be deemed an indirect indication of the time not devoted to childcare. Despite long working hours, however, Spanish mothers do not reduce the time spent caring for their children (Gauthier and DeGusti 2012).

Another labour market feature relevant to childcare is part-time employment. Although it is more common among women in all three countries, substantial differences can be identified. Part-time work is fairly widespread in Norway (20.3%) among both men (10.6%) and women (31.2%), whereas it is less common in France (16.1%) and Spain (13.7%), although also with wide gender gaps. Whilst close to 6% of French and Spanish men work part-time, 27% of French and 23% of Spanish women work part-time. Norwegian mothers have adapted more readily to family needs than their partners, leading to a rise in 'new traditional families' in which mothers work part-time and fathers full-time (Børve and Bungum 2015).

Spanish women collectively entered the labour market decades later than in Norway and France and work-life-balance mechanisms, which made their way onto the public agenda much later, are less fully developed. In that regard, the Spanish model was termed by Leitner (2003) as 'unsupported or implicit familism', referring to public policies characterised by uneven aims and scope and a labour market where long working hours are poorly coordinated with educational institutions. In the Mediterranean and particularly in the Spanish model, caring for pre-school children has frequently been shouldered by mothers and grandparents, particularly grandmothers, who act as 'shock absorbers' (Moreno et al. 2015) in the clash between public and private life. Nonetheless, education policy has undergone change in recent decades, with initiatives tending to favour work/family balance and questioning the country's adherence to an 'implicit familism' model (Valarino et al. 2018). Public education for 3 to 6 year-old has been universally instituted and the number of places for 0 to 2 year-olds has risen substantially, albeit with different types of public funding (Rogero-García and Andrés-Candelas 2019).

Although France, Norway, and Spain have significantly raised the number of public pre-school places in recent years, their enrolment rates differ widely. In France and Spain, moreover, the public offering is supplemented by private institutions, with the concomitant segmentation of care along the lines of household income. In contrast, since 2009 in Norway pre-school from ages 1 to 3 is universal and as public and private institutions are government-regulated and publicly funded, they are similarly priced. Norway has invested heavily in pre-school to favour conciliation and prepare children for elementary education and beyond (Elizalde San Miguel et al. 2015).

In France the number of early childcare (public or chartered) institutions (*crèches* and *écoles maternelles*) has risen significantly since the 80s, with universal enrolment from the age of 4 now ensured. Pre-school education has recently pursued three aims: to favour conciliation, to enhance women's participation in the labour market, and to create jobs (Fagnani and Math 2011). Optionality, a constant feature in the French model, has both beneficial and adverse implications. On the one hand, it provides families freedom of choice about how they wish to care for their children, depending on their resources and preference. On the other, however, it spawns social and gender inequalities, as most of the public funding earmarked for parents (normally mothers) to care for their children (*Allocation parentale d'Education*) goes to low-income families. The options are for one of the parents to stay at home to care for the child or children or to choose among the various childcare formulas in place. The choice of one alternative or the other, i.e., pre-school or professional care providers in or outside the home (*assistants maternelles agréées*), depends on a number of factors such as the number of children or household income. Choices are consequently determined by internal and external conditions that limit the decision adopted by families. Mothers with low incomes or qualifications tend to opt more frequently to care for their children at home, whereas those with higher incomes or qualifications choose pre-school or professionals who care for their children individually or in groups (Fagnani and Math 2011).

In Norway the universality of childcare services for 1 year-olds onward has also co-existed with family choice of the care strategy they deem most suitable. Norwegian optionality enables parents to waive entitlement to a place in pre-school for children between the ages of 12 and 24 months in exchange for a cash benefit known as 'cash for care'. Nonetheless, that alternative to formal care, as in France, entails polarising families and citizens, as 'cash for care' is chosen primarily by low-income mothers and families (Aassve and Lappegård 2009). The Nordic system, which seeks universality and the furtherance of equality, is therefore openly contradicted by the social and gender inequalitiesfostered by the application of this measure (Thévenon and Luci 2012).

Although the Norwegian, French, and to a lesser extent Spanish models are geared to enhancing parents' childcare options (Wall and Escobedo 2013, Escobedo and Wall 2015), the extent and directionality of the investment in family policies are critical to the actual distribution of parental childcare responsibilities (see Table 17.1).

Research Hypotheses

In line with the foregoing, the overall hypothesis is that the participation of non-parental agents in caring for children under 3 years of age depends essentially on the public childcare policies and labour market conditions in place. On those grounds, the expectation is (H1) that de-familialisation is greater in Norway in the light of the generalised use of leaves during a child's first year, universal pre-school from then on and more favourable working hours and salaries. More extensive use of pre-school education and professional non-parental carers (private non-parental carers and day-care centres) is expected in France (H2), given the fairly high public investment in such services. The widespread use of these resources can be explained by the shorter parental leaves available and the fairly infrequent recourse to grandparents as care supporters. In Spain (H3) more family involvement is expected due to the short duration of paid leaves, low and fragmented public investment in conciliation and a higher proportion of parents with unstable employment than in the other two countries analysed. The impact of social class (H4) is expected to

Table 17.1 Characteristics of family policies for 0 to 3 year-olds

Country	Welfare State Model	% GDP in public investment in family benefits and policies	Organisational principle	Family policies for children aged 0–3
Norway	Scandinavian/'de-familialised' model	3.2	Quasi-universality, optionality	Universal well paid leaves until 1st year Universal pre-school education from the age of 1
France	Conservative / optional familistic model	2.4	Non-universality, conditioned optionality	Mothers well paid leaves until 4th months High coverage of public pre-school education from birth
Spain	Mediterranean/unsupported familistic model	1.2	Non-universality, highly conditioned optionality	Universal well paid leaves until 4 months Partial coverage of public pre-school education

Source Formulated by the authors

affect the use of non-family caring agents, particularly for services not publicly funded.

DATA AND METHODOLOGY

The information used in this study was sourced from the 2016 edition of the European Union's *Survey on Income and Living Conditions* (EU-SILC), harmonised for the participating European countries. The present analysis focuses on participation rates in non-parental childcare. The population covered by the survey includes households and the individuals comprising them in the respective countries. The SILC contains items on care for children from 0 to 12 years old living in the respondent's household. Here, the observational unit was children 0, 1, or 2 years old at the time of the interview, and those who were 2 on 31 December of the year prior to when data were collected if the interview was conducted in the first half of the year. The sample therefore includes information on children who, whilst aged 3 at the time of the interview, were eligible for enrolment in pre-school institutions.

The dependent variables were (1) agent participation (yes/no) in childcare for at least 1 hour in a typical week; and (2) the mean number of hours of care provided by each agent or activity per week. The care providers analysed included the following.

1. *Pre-schools*. This includes pre-school per se and other public or private socio-educational services typically offering care for children under the age of 3, with or without governmental authorisation (pre-school or equivalent including kindergarten and nursery school: Eurostat 2017). Their educational classification is ISCED Level 0. The indicator includes the total time spent at the institution, with no distinction drawn between educational and general nursery services. Care may be full or part-time, or even for only a few hours (INE 2019).
2. *Day-care centres*. This category covers all manner of non-pre-school care organised or controlled by a public or private entity. It consequently refers to activities held outside the educational domain that may overlap with the schedule of non-compulsory schooling. Such care may be based on an agreement between parents and the carer (often the parents' employee) or day-care centre or consist in structured family-based care, nursery services or similar, and rendered in or outside the carer's home (as in structured family-based care). The category also includes qualified carers subject to institutional organisation and control, even when paid for by parents directly, such as in France's *assistantes maternelles* (Eurostat 2017).[1]
3. *Professional care providers*. These are carers paid by parents and include nannies, baby-sitters, and 'au pairs'. The service may be rendered either in the child's or the carer's home, full- or part-time or even for a few hours, providing it is routine[2] (INE 2019). It includes neighbours or friends paid to care for the children.
4. *Others, unpaid*. This category refers to unpaid childcare provided by grandparents, other non-parental relatives, friends, neighbours, and similar. It refers to care provided on a routine basis in the child's or the relative's, friend's, or neighbour's home either full or part-time, or even for only a few hours.

The independent variables used were the child's age (0–1; 1–2; 2–3), yearly household equivalent income (€0 to 17,000; €17,001 to €24,000; over

€24,000), and the couple's employment status (both work, only the father works, only the mother works or both are unemployed). The procedure deployed consisted, firstly, in a systematic comparison of the childcare indicators in France, Norway, and Spain based on SILC 2016. The indicators included the intensity of each agent's participation in childcare measured as the number of weekly hours and the usage rates of each care agent, both overall and in the population groups defined by the independent variables. Secondly, the outcomes were then reviewed with reference to the academic literature on childcare and the family policies in place for children aged 0–3 in each country.

Whilst the SILC data are harmonised and inter-comparison is deemed appropriate, they are subject to limitations that should be borne in mind. Firstly, the number of cases under the variable care provided by professional carers was very small in some categories, rendering analysis less rigorous. More specifically, in Norway just five children from 0 to 12 and only two between the ages of 0 and 3 received such care. Spain reported 20 cases and France 68. Although in earlier editions the small caseload under the item on paid care in the child's home in Norway prompted some researchers to attribute it to coding errors (Keck and Saraceno 2011), the similarity of the findings in subsequent editions would appear to confirm the reliability of its depiction of the situation in Norway. In addition, since the pre-school data should be interpreted as usage but not enrolment rates, they supplement but do not replace institutional information (Keck and Saraceno 2011).

Results and Discussion

The findings revealed wide differences in the way childcare is organised for children from 0 to 3 in the three countries analysed, both in terms of the types of resources deployed and the degree of de-familialisation. Those differences, particularly pronounced in the first two years of a child's life, although narrowing considerably in the third, revealed the shortcomings in the welfare regime models or degrees of familism discussed earlier (Wall and Escobedo 2013).

Norwegian parental leavepolicies in the first year and institutional childcare beginning in the second have a significant effect on care patterns. Whereas parents engaged in childcare in the first year, seldom resorting to non-parental intervention, 61.5% of the children in the second year and 88.3% in the third attended pre-school an average of 34.8 hours per week, approximately the same number devoted by adults to full-time work (Table 17.2).That would corroborate hypothesis 1 (H1), according to which pre-school is infrequent in the child's first year due to the duration and generosity of leaves during that period (Kvande and Brandth 2017), whereas it is widely used thereafter due to state investment. Even though the Scandinavian country was the one with the highest fraction of 12–24-month-old children in pre-school, the percentage of use was not universal, perhaps because of the polarisation generated by 'cash

Table 17.2 Percentage of children receiving non-parental care during at least 1 hour in a typical week and mean number of hours by agent, child's age and country

		Child's age	Spain	France	Norway	X^2 Sig
Pre-school services	Percentage	0–1 year	7.0	51.7	1.2	0.000
		1–2 years	38.5	53.8	61.5	0.000
		2–3 years	68.9	59.1	88.3	0.000
		Total	42.8	56	58.7	0.001
	Hours/week		27.6	31.4	34.8	0.000
Professional care providers	Percentage	0–1 year	2.6	5.5	0	0.089
		1–2 years	2.1	10.1	1.3	0.005
		2–3 years	1.4	13.2	0	0.000
		Total	1.9	10.9	0.4	0.000
	Hours/week		22.8	31.5	34.2	0.131
Relatives	Percentage	0–1 year	14.9	18.3	6.2	0.010
		1–2 years	20	19.7	7.5	0.000
		2–3 years	14.4	20.2	5.3	0.000
		Total	16.1	19.7	6.2	0.000
	Hours/week		26.2	14.9	9.6	0.000

Source Calculated by the authors from SILC 2016 database

for care' policies in this regard, as contended by Aassve and Lappegård (2009). Care for children not enrolled in pre-school was assumed to be provided primarily by mothers, as use of other non-parental care options was of scant significance. Participation by a hired employee was unusual and the extended family was involved in caring for only 6.2% of the children.

In France, the use of formal non-parental care is less widespread than in Norway, although it begins earlier, since parental leave is not designed to cover universally and with a satisfactory replacement wage the baby's first year of life (Fagnani 2020). Non-parental care, prevalent after the expiration of maternity leave, was characterised by a diversity of care providers. Whilst 56% of the children benefited from early childcare services, a significant 19.7% were cared for by the extended family and 10.9% by professional care providers. The higher proportion of the professional care provider option in France compared to Norway or Spain is explained by the fact that such services are partly subsidised by French but neither Norwegian nor Spanish authorities. Those findings partially endorse hypothesis 2 (H2): the use of pre-school services and professional care providers is high, but due to substantial public investment in conciliation mechanisms, extended family participation was expected to be lower. Whilst in France early childcare services and hired carer hours (with a mean of 31.4) were similar in most cases to nearly a full working week (with a mean of 31.5 hours), family-based care was considerably less intense (14.9 hours). Such care therefore supplemented rather than substituted formal care. Those data may be explained, in part, by the peculiar practice of defining Wednesday as a non-school day, along with France's fairly low percentage of part-time workers (Kitzmann 2018). As in Norway and Spain non-parental care involvement grew with the child's age and was widespread in their third year.

In the vast majority of Spanish families parents, primarily mothers (Rogero-García and Andrés-Candelas 2019), cared for their baby in its first year, despite the absence of paid leave after the 4-month maternity leave (to which holiday time is routinely added) and even though 62%[3] of mothers had paid employment. Non-parental care at that age, when in place, was provided by relatives, primarily grandparents (Meil et al. 2018), in 14.9% of cases, with only 7% provided by early childcare services and just 2.6% by professional care providers. Those findings consequently confirm hypothesis 3 (H3), further to which family participation (taking parents and grandparents together) was greater than in the other countries analysed. Sources other than the SILC led to somewhat higher non-parental care values. According to official statistics on pre-schooling, 10.9% of babies under 1 year of age were enrolled in pre-school in 2017/2018 (MEFP 2019, 25), in addition to those in unofficial day-care centres.[4] The use of early childcare services rose substantially in the child's second year, to 38.5% (a value consistent with the schooling rate at that age), as did extended family assistance, to 20%. The vast majority (68.9%) of children received non-parental care in their third year of life, especially in early childcare institutions, whilst the percentage cared for by relatives declined to 14.4% and by professional care providers to 1.4%. The mean time spent in early childcare institutions was 27.6 hours, much lower than in the other two countries, whilst the mean time devoted by grandparents and other relatives was similar (26.2 hours). Those data suggest that in Spain grandparental care substitutes for, rather than supplements, formal care (Meil et al. 2018).

The findings confirmed that different agents' participation in childcare was conditioned by both the family's social position and the type of social policy in place (Table 17.2), corroborating hypothesis 4 (H4). In Norway where access to pre-school is universal, it was not conditioned by household income level but rather by the time available to mothers. There, income differences did not explain the use of formal childcare resources, although around 60% of the children whose mothers had no paid employment were not enrolled in pre-school. Rather, households received a so-called cash for care transfer, whereas when the father was the sole member of the couple unemployed, only 37.7% of the children were not enrolled. Those data denote significant sex segregation. Resorting to relatives for care, whilst infrequent, was more common among low-income, low schooling level households where one of the parents worked part-time (data not shown in Table 17.2[5]).

In France, for the reasons discussed above and despite the public subsidies in place, access to early childhood services was tightly conditioned by income: in the highest income bracket households the percentage of children attending pre-school was double the percentage among those from households in the lowest (69.2% compared to 34.2%). The differences were even wider for care provided by professionals, who were hired by 18.3% of the highest income families and only a notional 2.7% in households with low incomes. Those findings are consistent with the correlation between income and childcare resources reported by Fagnani and Math (2011) and with the higher frequency observed in dual-earner households and among women with a high level of schooling and a stable job.

In Spain, although with narrower differences than in France, use of preschool services or professional care providers was also highly conditioned by household income level and the mother's employment status. A total of 61.9% of children from high-income households attended pre-school/daycare centres and 7.9% were cared for by an employee, compared to 35.5% and 0.4%, respectively, among low-income families. Unsurprisingly, then, formal care was more widespread among dual-earner households, where women had a high level of schooling and a stable job. It was likewise more common when only the mother was employed, but not when only the father had a paid job, denoting sex segregation, as it was also observed in Norway.

The extended family did not appear to be the primary caregiver in any of the welfare regimes studied at any of the ages reviewed. Nonetheless, compared to Norway's Scandinavian or de-familialised model, in both the French conservative or optional familistic model and Spanish Mediterranean or implicit familistic model (to use Leitner's typology) care provided by the extended family was relatively important for a significant minority of parents. In Spain and Norway that type of assistance was found in low-income families when the mother was employed (especially when employment was part-time). In France, in contrast, family involvement was greater at higher income levels and when the mother worked, according to Blanpain's (2006) findings. That circumstance is related to the substitutional nature of the care provided by Spanish grandparents ('shock absorbers' to use Moreno et al.'s [2015] term), whose time invested in caring for their grandchildren was roughly comparable to the time the children spent at pre-school. In France, in contrast, grandparental care was supplementary to formal care, accounting as it did for many fewer hours per week (Table 17.3).

Conclusions

The breakdown of the male breadwinner model has generated conflicts between work and family responsibilities. Governmental measures and resources (primarily parental leave and childcare services) instituted with different degrees of public funding to help families settle those conflicts have seldom formed part of consistent and systematic policy (EIGE 2019). The wide diversity of responses to such challenges has led to the formulation of different welfare regimes (Esping-Andersen 1990; Ferrera 1996) or degrees of familism (Leitner 2003). Nonetheless, the findings for the three countries analysed as examples of distinctly different approaches to confronting the challenges of work-life balance posed to families with small children show that with the evolution of public policy and family practices the differences underlying

Table 17.3 Percentage of 0- to 3-year-old children receiving non-parental care by agent, household income, parental employment status and country

		Spain	France	Norway
Pre-school services	**Household yearly equivalent income**			
	€0–€17,000	35.5	34.2	49.7
	€17,001–€24,000	51.0	66.0	65.2
	€24,001 and over	61.9	69.2	58.7
	Sig	*0.000*	*0.000*	*0.361*
	Couple's employment status			
	Both employed	50.8	74.5	63.3
	Father only employed	30.9	28.6	38.7
	Mother only employed	49.9	38.4	62.3
	Both unemployed	17.3	23.1	42.8
	Sig	*0.000*	*0.000*	*0.001*
Professional care providers	**Household yearly equivalent income**			
	€0–€17,000	0.4	2.7	
	€17,001–€24,000	2.7	11.6	
	€24,001 and over	7.3	18.3	
	Sig	*0.000*	*0.000*	
	Couple's employment status			
	Both employed	3.1	16.8	
	Father only employed	0.0	1.1	
	Mother only employed	0.0	3.6	
	Both unemployed	0.0	0.0	
	Sig	*0.009*	*0.000*	
Relatives	**Household yearly equivalent income**			
	€0–€17,000	17.7	14.2	21.4
	€17,001–€24,000	17.4	19.7	8.4
	€24,001 and over	7.4	25.2	5.4
	Sig	*0.045*	*0.000*	*0.060*
	Couple's employment status			
	Both employed	19.7	26.2	5.2
	Father only employed	13.5	6.3	5.5
	Mother only employed	10.2	16.2	14.4
	Both unemployed	0.9	6.0	5.7
	Sig	*0.000*	*0.000*	*0.523*

Insufficient cases
Source Calculated by the authors from SILC 2016 database

the formulation of such typologies have narrowed since they were first introduced. The present analysis therefore confirmed a pattern of cross-national convergence and divergence from traditional welfare regimes, as noted by Escobedo and Wall (2015). A further outcome is that revisiting traditional typologies may lead to defining models differently, depending on the perspective adopted or the policy analysed (Wall and Escobedo 2013). In the light of the complexity and constant change involved, then, specific family policies and their impact on society must be routinely reviewed.

Whereas Norway continues to support de-familialised care and France an optional familistic model (Leitner 2003), Spain is no longer characterised by the unsupported or implicit familism prevailing at the turn of the century. Whilst parental care predominates during a child's first year, that is no longer the norm for all mothers. As their children grow, parents tend to resort more frequently to non-parental care. Among 2-year-olds the inter-model differences narrow substantially. Resorting to relatives instead of professional carers for childcare is a minority option in both familistic models analysed, although it is more common than in Norway's de-familialised model. Patterns in France and Spain differ, however: in Spain, especially in low-income families, relatives devote considerable time to childcare, substituting for formal services (findings consistent with other authors' results: Meil et al. 2018; Rogero-García and Andrés-Candelas 2019), in France relatives provide only supplementary assistance, primarily in more affluent households.

One key factor in the use of non-parental care is affordability. With social spending cutbacks and the growing liberalisation of welfare services in many countries in recent years, universal criteria on protection for families with small children have been forsaken and cost-free services subjected to proof of need (specific income level and/or employment status). Whilst Norway has not been so affected, in France (Fagnani 2020) and Spain (Ibáñez y León 2014) formal care is partially subsidised according to certain criteria and far from free for all families. As a result, access to formal care is strongly conditioned by income level, but inversely to the usual criteria for benefits: the lower the income, the lower is the access to formal care. That stands as proof of the failure of non-universalist public policy to ensure access to formal childcare. Consequently, children born into disadvantaged families face two drawbacks practically from birth. First, they are less likely to reap the cognitive and developmental benefits of quality pre-school, which straightens their opportunities for educational success. And second, their mothers encounter greater difficulties to land and/or keep a job, a circumstance detrimental to household finances that raises the likelihood of poverty.

Funding This work was supported by the Ministerio de Economía y Competitividad under Grant CSO2017-84634R.

Notes

1. Such care is often provided by the social welfare system, particularly for children under the age of 3. The category covers care for children too young to be at school or pre-school as well as children attending school or pre-school and cared for 1 day a week when schools are closed. It may be provided on a full- or a part-time basis or even for just a few hours. Cultural and sporting activities (clubs, for instance) are not included, inasmuch as they are not deemed to be childcare services but children's leisure time activities. Day care for children with special needs is included (Eurostat 2017).
2. Here 'professional' is understood to mean a person for whom childcare is a job or paid activity: it infers nothing about their qualifications or the quality of the care provided.
3. Value drawn from a review of the microdata for the INE's 2018 fertility survey (*Encuesta de Fecundidad*).
4. Such differences may be due to the SILC data collection timetable. Since the fieldwork was performed in the three first quarters only, it very likely gathered a smaller proportion of children under the age of 1 than if it had been distributed uniformly across all four quarters.
5. For reasons of space, the data in Table 17.2 were broken down by the most significant independent variables only.

References

Aassve, Arnstein, and Trude Lappegård. 2009. "Childcare Cash Benefits and Fertility Timing in Norway." *European Journal of Population* 25 (1) (February): 67–88. https://doi.org/10.1007/s10680-008-9158-6.

Blanpain, Nathalie. 2006. "Garder et faire garder son enfant." In *Données sociales - La société française*, 77–83. Institut national de la statistique et des études économiques. https://www.insee.fr/fr/statistiques/fichier/1371999/donsoc06h.pdf.

Børve, Hege Eggen, and Brita Bungum. 2015. "Norwegian Working Fathers in Global Working Life." *Gender, Work & Organization* 22 (4) (July): 309–323. https://doi.org/10.1111/gwao.12086.

Boyer, Danniele, and Jeanne Fagnani. 2019. "France Country Note." In *15th International Review of Leave Policies and Research 2019*, edited by Alison Koslowski, Sonja Blum, Ivana Dobrotić, Alexandra Macht, and Peter Moss. https://www.leavenetwork.org/lp_and_r_reports/.

Brandth, Berit, and Elin Kvande. 2009. "Gendered or Gender-Neutral Care Politics for Fathers?" *The Annals of the American Academy of Political and Social Science* 624 (1) (July): 177–189. https://doi.org/10.1177/0002716209334119.

EIGE (European Institute for Gender Equality). 2019. *Eligibility for Parental Leave in EU Member States*. Luxembourg: Publications Office of the European Union. https://doi.org/10.2839/919049.

Elizalde San Miguel, Begoña, Vicente Díaz Gandasegui, and Magdalena Díaz Gorfinkiel. 2015. "Crisis y estado de bienestar en el cuidado de menores: reflexiones conceptuales a partir de un estudio comparado de España y Noruega." *Revista de Economía Crítica* 20 (Segundo semestre): 120–134. https://www.revistaeconomiacritica.org/sites/default/files/4-Elizalde-Diaz-Diaz_Crisis-y-estado-del-bienestar-cuidado-menores_0.pdf.

Escobedo, Anna, and Karin Wall. 2015. "Leave Policies in Southern Europe: Continuities and Changes." *Community, Work & Family* 18 (2): 218–235. https://doi.org/10.1080/13668803.2015.1024822.

Esping-Andersen, Gøsta. 1990. *The Three Worlds of Welfare Capitalism.* Oxford: Polity Press.

Eurostat. 2017. *Methodological Guidelines and Description of EU-SILC Target Variables. 2016 Operation (Version May 2017).* https://circabc.europa.eu/sd/a/165c80b9-5631-4f5b-b847-29c638715c0e/DOCSILC065%20operation%202016%20VERSION%2022-05-2017.pdf.

Eurostat. 2020. "Population and Social Conditions." Last updated October 30, 2020. https://appsso.eurostat.ec.europa.eu/nui/show.do?dataset=spr_exp_ffa&lang=en.

Fagnani, Jeanne. 2020. "Reasons for the Decrease in the Number of Beneficiaries of Parental Leave Benefit in France: Exclusion, Self-exclusion and Disaffection." *Revista del Ministerio de Trabajo, Migraciones y Seguridad Social* 146: 101–115.

Fagnani, Jeanne, and Antoine Math. 2011. "The Predicament of Childcare Policy in France: What Is at Stake?" *Journal of Contemporary European Studies* 19 (4) (December): 547–561. https://doi.org/10.1080/14782804.2011.639990.

Ferrera, Maurizio. 1996. "The 'Southern Model' of Welfare in Social Europe." *Journal of European Social Policy* 6 (1) (February): 17–37. https://doi.org/10.1177/095892879600600102.

Gauthier, Anne H., and Berenice DeGusti. 2012. "The Time Allocation to Children by Parents in Europe." *International Sociology* 27 (6) (November): 827–845. https://doi.org/10.1177%2F0268580912443576.

Ibáñez, Zyab, and Margarita León. 2014. "Early Childhood Education and Care Provision in Spain." In *The Transformation of Care in European Societies*, edited by Margarita León, 276–300. New York: Palgrave Macmillan.

INE (Instituto Nacional de Estadística). 2019. *Encuesta de condiciones de vida. Metodología.* Madrid: INE. https://www.ine.es/daco/daco42/condivi/ecv_metodo.pdf.

Keck, Wolfang, and Chiara Saraceno. 2011. "Comparative Childcare Statistics in Europe. Conceptual and Methodological Fallacies." *Carlo Alberto Notebooks* (229). https://www.carloalberto.org/wp-content/uploads/2018/11/no.229.pdf.

Kitzmann, Morgan. 2018. "Les grands-parents: un mode de garde régulier ou occasionnel pour deux tiers des jeunes enfants." *Études et Résultats*, 1070, Drees. https://drees.solidarites-sante.gouv.fr/IMG/pdf/er1070.pdf.

Korpi, Walter. 2000. "Faces of Inequality: Gender, Class and Patters of Inequalities in Different Types of Welfare States." *Social Politics: International Studies in Gender, State and Society* 7 (2) (Summer): 127–191. https://doi.org/10.1093/sp/7.2.127

Kvande, Elin, and Berit Brandth. 2017. "Individualized, Non-Transferable Parental Leave for European Fathers: Migrant Perspectives." *Community, Work and Family* 20 (1): 19–34.

Leira, Arnlaug. 2002. *Working Parents and the Welfare State. Family Change and Policy Reform in Scandinavia.* Cambridge: University Press.

Leitner, Sigrid. 2003. "Varieties of Familialism: The Caring Function of the Family in Comparative Perspective." *European Societies* 5 (4): 353–375. https://doi.org/10.1080/1461669032000127642.

Leon, Margarita, and Mauro Migliavacca. 2013. "Italy and Spain: Still the Case of Familistic Welfare Models?" *Population Review* 52 (1): 25–42. https://doi.org/10.1353/prv.2013.0001.

MEFP (Ministerio de Educación y Formación Profesional). 2019. *Sistema estatal de indicadores de la educación 2019*. Secretaría General Técnica del Ministerio de Educación y Formación Profesional. https://www.educacionyfp.gob.es/dam/jcr:627dc544-8413-4df1-ae46-558237bf6829/seie-2019.pdf.

Meil, Gerardo, Irene Lapuerta, and Anna Escobedo. 2019. "Spain Country Note." In *15th International Review of Leave Policies and Research 2019*, edited by Alison Koslowski, Sonja Blum, Ivana Dobrotić, Alexandra Macht, and Peter Moss. https://www.leavenetwork.org/lp_and_r_reports/.

Meil, Gerardo, Jesús Rogero-García, and Pedro Romero-Balsas. 2018. "Grandparents´ Role in Spanish Families. Work/Life Balance Strategies." *Journal of Comparative Family Studies* 49 (2) (Spring): 163–177. https://doi.org/10.3138/jcfs.49.2.163.

Moreno Fuentes, Francisco Javier, Pau Marí-Klose, Angie Gago, Svein Olav Daatland, Erling Barth, Arnlaug Leira, Inés Calzada and Eloísa del Pino. 2015. "New Social Risks and Welfare State Reforms in Norway and Spain." Estudios/Working Papers GIGAPP, WP-2015-01. https://www.gigapp.org/administrator/components/com_jresearch/files/publications/WP-2015-01.pdf.

Rindfuss, Ronald R., David Guilkey, S. Philip Morgan, Øystein Kravdal, and Karen Benjamin Guzzo. 2007. "Child Care Availability and First-Birth Timing in Norway." *Demography* 44 (2) (May): 345–372. https://doi.org/10.1353/dem.2007.0017.

Rogero-García, Jesús, and Mario Andrés-Candelas. 2019. "Cuidado y violencia familiar hacia la primera infancia en España." *Documento de trabajo 2.3 VIII Informe FOESSA*, coordinated by Guillermo Fernández Maíllo. Madrid: Fundación Foessa.

Soss, Joe, and Sandford F. Schram. 2007. "A Public Transformed? Welfare Reform as Policy Feedback." *American Political Science Review* 101 (1) (February): 111–127. https://doi.org/10.1017/S0003055407070049.

Thévenon, Olivier, and Angela Luci. 2012. "Reconciling Work, Family and Child Outcomes: What Implications for Family Support Policies?" *Population Research and Policy Review* 31 (6) (December): 855–882. https://doi.org/10.1007/s11113-012-9254-5.

Thévenon, Olivier, and Anne Solaz. 2013. "Labour Market Effects of Parental Leave Policies in OECD Countries." OECD Social, Employment and Migration Working Papers, no. 141. OECD Publishing. https://doi.org/10.1787/5k8xb6hw1wjf-en.

Tobío, Constanza 2012. "Reciprocity and Solidarity in Intergenerational Relationships: France, Norway and Spain in Comparative Perspective." *Papers* 97 (4): 849–873. https://dx.doi.org/10.5565/rev/papers/v97n4.246.

Valarino, Isabel, Gerardo Meil, and Jesús Rogero-García. 2018. "Family or State Responsibility? Elderly and Childcare Policy Preferences in Spain." *International Journal of Sociology and Social Policy* 38 (11/12): 1101–1115. https://doi.org/10.1108/IJSSP-06-2018-0086.

Wall, Karin, and Anna Escobedo. 2013. "Parental Leave Policies, Gender Equity and Family Well-Being in Europe: A Comparative Perspective." In *Family Well-Being*, edited by Almudenta Moreno Mínguez, 103–129. Dordrecht: Springer.

CHAPTER 18

Sharing the Caring Responsibility Between the Private and the Public: Childcare, Parental Choice, and Inequality

Michel Vandenbroeck, Wim Van Lancker, and Jeroen Janssen

INTRODUCTION: CHILDCARE MATTERS

Children are increasingly cared for by people other than their parents. Across European countries, the numbers of children under three being full-time enrolled in formal childcare services rose almost continuously since the turn of the century. Many countries report pre-school participation rates of almost 100% of children between three and five years old. This has changed the nature of parenthood and parenting, and according to a substantial body of research, to the betterment of children (Engle et al. 2011).

There is now a robust body of evidence on the benefits of participating in early childhood education and care (ECEC) services for children's cognitive and non-cognitive outcomes. The attention for the educational potential of ECEC originated with three famous US-based longitudinal studies on poor children attending high-quality ECEC, as these studies for the first time showed that not only these children fared better in school, but also that the effects are still noticeable in their adult lives. This knowledge laid out the

---

M. Vandenbroeck (✉) · J. Janssen
Department of Social Work and Social Pedagogy, Ghent University, Ghent, Belgium
e-mail: michel.vandenbroeck@ugent.be

J. Janssen
e-mail: jerojans.Janssen@UGent.be

W. Van Lancker
Centre for Sociological Research, University of Leuven, Leuven, Belgium
e-mail: wim.vanlancker@kuleuven.be

scientific foundation for the importance of public investment in the early years (e.g. Barnett 2011). Today there is also robust evidence from diverse European longitudinal studies on the impact of high-quality ECEC on children's cognitive and socio-emotional development as well as on their school readiness, learning outcomes and later-life educational and labour market achievement (see Vandenbroeck et al. 2018 for an overview). It has now been generally accepted in academia as well as in European policy that early childhood care and education can contribute to equalising opportunities for children, can alleviate poverty for parents, and can foster social cohesion in local communities (European Commission 2018; OECD 2015). However, one should be cautious in assuming that ECEC is like a magic wand that will save the world one child at a time. Morabito et al. (2013) argued that the equalising potential of ECEC is all too often based on studies that compare poor children who attended ECEC with equally poor children who did not attend. As a result, based on these studies one could draw conclusions on the beneficial impact of ECEC for this particular group of children, but not about the equalising impact vis-à-vis middle class or rich children. In addition, Morabito et al. (2018) found that comprehensive policies combining high-quality ECEC with a home visiting programme may also yield paradoxical effects, serving middle-class families better than poor families. These cautions should not lead us astray from the fact that high-quality ECEC is good for children. It should however help us understand that ECEC will not necessarily reduce inequalities between children, and that the benefits of ECEC are conditional on specific quality and accessibility criteria. These conditions are far from being met by childcare systems all across Europe (Vandenbroeck and Lazzari 2014). The problem is this: In Europe (as well as in other OECD countries), poor families tend to have less access to ECEC services than higher-income families. Moreover, if they do have access, children from poor families are more often enrolled in ECEC of poorer quality compared with their better-off peers. If children coming from disadvantaged background are less likely to participate in high-quality ECEC, the benefits are reaped by children who were already advantaged in the first place. The phenomenon that better-of families tend to benefit more from government investment than disadvantaged families is referred to as a Matthew Effect, a term coined by the sociologist Robert K. Merton. In popular discourse, this is often succinctly summarised as the rich get richer, the poor stay poor. The observation that a Matthew Effect prevails in ECEC provision is bad news. Not only does it mean that caring responsibilities are not shared by the private and the public domain for all families alike, it also means that social inequalities in access to quality nonparental care are likely to exacerbate inequalities in childhood, which would jeopardise the objective of public investments in ECEC.

In this chapter, we first document the problem of accessibility by focusing on the enrolment gap by socio-economic status of the family. Secondly, we look at explanations for these gaps, discussing the role of parental choice and preferences as well as structural barriers. Third, we briefly consider the issue of quality with a focus on the ECEC workforce. The findings we present here seem to point in the direction of ECEC as a public service, sharing the care responsibilities between the private and the public domains, if one wishes to attribute an equality of opportunities mission to ECEC.

Unequal Take-Up

Many recent studies have documented persistent inequality in the take-up or use of formal ECEC services in the majority of European countries (Pavolini and Van Lancker 2018; Van Lancker and Ghysels 2016; Van Lancker 2013). In split systems, where childcare for the youngest children is separated from preschool for the older children, this gap is wider in childcare than in preschool (Vandenbroeck 2019). Consequently, we will primarily focus on childcare in this chapter. Parents from a low socio-economic status, measured by educational attainment, social class, or family income, tend to have less access to formal childcare services for under threes compared with higher status families. In 2015, the European Commission launched a feasibility study for a Child Guarantee and in that framework the inequalities in access for children from poor families, single-parent families, Roma families, and for children with special educational needs were documented in the then 28 Member States (Vandenbroeck 2019; Frazer et al. 2020). All EU Member States face lower enrolment rates for children from ethnic minorities, refugee children, children with special needs and children from poor families, compared to the general population (a notable exception is Malta). Inequality in enrolment is also observed in countries with generous welfare systems and high overall enrolment rates such as Denmark (78% of children from ethnic minorities compared to 95% of the majority population), albeit to a lesser extent than in many other countries. For children from single-parent families, the picture is slightly different: several countries do not have specific data (e.g. Estonia); in many Member States, single parents encounter difficulties to use ECEC (e.g. Belgium) while in others their enrolment rate exceeds that of dual parent families (e.g. Austria). Although inequalities in enrolment by socio-economic status are an almost universal phenomenon, the extent of the gap differs across countries. Van Lancker and Ghysels (2016) examined the difference in formal childcare use for under threes by educational attainment of their mother in Europe, the USA, and Australia. They observe an inverse relationship between average enrolment rates and inequality in enrolment. In general, countries with the highest levels of enrolment (Denmark, Iceland, Sweden) report relatively low levels of inequality in enrolment by educational level of the mother. In contrast, countries with low levels of enrolment (the Czech Republic, Poland, Romania, Bulgaria, the UK) generally report high levels of inequality. There are however notable exceptions to this rule. Countries such as France, the Netherlands, or Belgium combine relatively high enrolment rates with wide socio-economic gaps in enrolment. The results indicate that when demand exceeds supply and there is a shortage in the number of available places, securing a slot in childcare for the youngest children becomes more difficult for disadvantaged families. Some examples that may illustrate the gap: in Austria, the average enrolment rate for 0–4 years is 47%, yet in households at risk of poverty it is only 32%; in Spain, 56% of children in 5th quintile between 4 and 6 years attend ECEC, compared to 31% in the 1st quintile; in Croatia, only one out of four children from households that are recipients of social assistance attend Kindergarten; in Portugal, just over one child out of three in the bottom third incomes is enrolled in preschool, compared to 94% of the general population (Vandenbroeck 2018). Moreover, children from a disadvantaged background may be more often enrolled in childcare settings from poorer quality than their more affluent peers (Dowsett et al. 2008; Gambaro et al. 2015; Stahl et al. 2018).

A Matter of Choice?

Historically, scholars have long been concerned with parental preferences and choice mechanisms to explain socio-economic differences in the use of quality ECEC. Several well-cited studies in late twentieth and early twenty-first centuries framed inequalities observed as being the result of cultural differences in parenting practices or family characteristics. Examples are the assumption that immigrant mothers have a cultural preference for home care, that poor families have less knowledge about quality criteria, or that families living in precarious conditions attach more importance to practical criteria (opening hours, distance) while middle-class families were believed to attach more importance to quality issues (Himmelweit and Sigala 2004; Kim and Fram 2009; Shlay et al. 2005; Sylva et al. 2007). As Meyers and Jordan (2006) state, childcare choices can be understood as accommodations—"to family and employment demands, social and cultural expectations, available information, and financial, social and other resources" (p. 64)—that often reproduce other forms of economic and social stratification. It is for instance assumed that migrant groups do not enrol their child for cultural reasons and that this may explain differences between as well as within countries. Pavolini and Van Lancker (2018) examined the question to what extent "cultural" (demand-side) or "structural" (supply-side) factors were best able to explain inequality in childcare enrolment among families with a youngest child under six. Culture was measured as the share of the population adhering to traditional norms on motherhood. The analyses showed that in countries with more traditional norms on motherhood, overall childcare use was lower for all families. In contrast, in countries with structural constraints in the availability or affordability of childcare places children growing up in disadvantaged families were affected most. This basically means that cultural norms, and parental preferences as well, are important to take into consideration when examining overall childcare use. But the explanatory power of cultural factors for explaining *inequities* in access is low; problems in terms of childcare provision such as a shortage in the number of places or parental fees are much better suited.

A more detailed study in Flanders showed that the unmet needs of childcare are twice as high among families with a migration history than among natives, and higher among poor families compared to non-poor families (Teppers et al. 2019).

Today, childcare is increasingly seen as a commodity and—as a result—countries across the globe have again stressed parental choice and parental responsibilities in relation to ECEC. Parents are considered as consumers, who are expected to critically compare the childcare services on offer, and to duly consider quality, price, and practicalities. From 2005, the Dutch Childcare Act profoundly reorganised Dutch childcare: funding shifted from supply-side funding through the local authorities to demand-side funding through employers and tax reductions, resulting in a substantial increase in market approaches and the advent of corporate business (Akgunduz and Plantenga 2014). Between 2003 and 2010 the share of non-profit providers in the Netherlands diminished from 60 to 30% and has continued to decrease since (Van der Werf et al. 2020). In 2006, the British Child Care Act made local authorities the "last resort" in organising childcare, to be turned to only when private providers do not deliver (Penn 2013). Since the enforcement of the Act on Service Vouchers in Social Welfare and Health (569/2009) in 2009, many Finnish municipalities have begun to provide ECEC vouchers for families. As a result, the private ECEC sector has expanded especially during the past decade, and now accounts for 17% of all ECEC provision (Ruutiainen et al. 2019). In France, between 2013 and 2017, 25% (2013) to half (2017) of the growth in childcare places was due to "micro-crèches", which are almost all private initiatives. In 2016, 58% of all newly created childcare places in France belonged to private for-profit organisations, financed through demand-side funding (called *CMG de la Paje*) rather than the traditional supply-side funding (called *Prestation de Service Unique*) (Haut Conseil de la famille, de l'enfance et de l'âge 2018). Today two French private for-profit providers (People&Baby and Babilou) own, respectively, 550 and 700 childcare centres. In all of these cases, the shift from public to private responsibilities is legitimised by a discourse on parental choice and the belief that the market is inherently fair. It is argued that parents will make rational choices based on preferences, price, and quality and that the supply will follow the demand.

However, that is not what empirical studies show. Already in the late 1980s and early 1990s, US-based studies showed that the market of childcare is an imperfect market, since the necessary conditions can never be ensured, the lack of perfect information being the most striking difference between a child care market and the idealised perfect market (Walker 1991) and these were later corroborated by European studies (Plantenga 2013). In addition, given that the costs of childcare are primarily staff costs, defined among others by staff qualifications and adult–child ratio's, the possibilities of enhancing profit and productivity without jeopardising quality are extremely limited (Gallagher 2018; Lloyd 2013). One of the main reasons why parents cannot be assumed to be critical "choosers" of child care is that they cannot rate the quality of the service when it is most critical, namely when parents are absent and staff is caring for the children. It should therefore not come as a surprise that the appreciation of ECEC quality by parents differs substantially from the appreciation of trained observers (Cryer and Burchinal 1997). Information asymmetry explains adverse selection and low average childcare quality. Childcare markets fail to perform like perfect markets, first because of a public interest in child care: childcare is indeed of public interest as it is invested both by needs of parents and by different policy domains (employment, equal opportunities, education) and can thus not be left to be defined by the market. Second, they fail to perform as markets for the inability of parents to make judgements about quality. Janssen, Spruyt, and Vandenbroeck (2021) concur for the Dutch-speaking community of Belgium: childcare quality and parent satisfaction are hardly related to each other.

The context of Flanders (the Dutch-speaking community of Belgium) offers an interesting site to study such assumptions, as it is a region with high overall enrolment of children (55% of all children below the age of three regularly attend child care), and the vast majority of places using means-tested parental fees (Kind en Gezin 2019). In that context, a unique study closely monitored the process quality in a stratified random sample of 400 childcare groups (200 centre based and 200 home based). The study looked at process quality, using CLASS Infant (Hamre et al. 2014) and CLASS Toddler (La Paro et al. 2012) observation schemes by trained observers. It simultaneously did a survey of all parents attending these groups, resulting in data on the search process and appreciation of 3172 parents, meaning a response rate of 64,8% (see Janssen et al. 2021; Janssen et al., forthcoming; Vandenbroeck et al. 2016 for details about the study). Questionnaires gathered insights in parents' childcare decision-making and their experiences while searching for a childcare place. The questionnaires allowed to distinguish demographic groups based on home language, family composition, country of birth, and employment status. Finally, parents' overall satisfaction and their satisfaction with the communication process were assessed. The study showed that parents make childcare arrangements because of practical circumstances (work or vocational activities) as well as for educational reasons, such as the socialisation of children, a smooth transition to preschool and support for children's intellectual development. When "choosing" a particular child care place, both practical convenience and quality concerns mattered, such as impressions of child care staff, and well-being of other children in the setting. Interestingly, the importance of practical versus educational concerns was hardly associated with family demographic characteristics (one exception is that home language is associated with the importance of childcare costs). While the study found that children from multilingual parents attend childcare of lower quality, remarkably, these parents engaged most in educational reasoning. Compared to others, they motivated childcare enrolment significantly more in terms of children's intellectual and behavioural development and (pre)school readiness. The study shows that the unequal take-up is not the only problem. It shows that investing in additional childcare places without ensuring equal quality, constructs an new inequality problem in trying to solve the previous one, related to unequal choice options. Indeed, language barriers were associated with significantly more difficulties in locating formal childcare resources. Monolingual Dutch-speaking families have 2.17 greater chance of experiencing childcare options than foreign-speaking families and 1.54 greater odds of choice than multilingual Dutch-speaking families. The same pattern of disadvantage reoccurred once other variables were controlled for. In addition, we found no significant differences for different groups of parents in the criteria used for "choosing" a particular place, except that financial constraints are more important for families with migrant backgrounds. In general, parents were quite satisfied with their "chosen" childcare and multilevel regression models showed that differences in satisfaction—insofar that they exist—are related to variables on the personal level (e.g. choice options) as well as on the level of childcare settings (e.g. childcare type). Childcare characteristics have less explanatory power than personal characteristics and childcare quality in particular explains only a very small margin of the variance in parental satisfaction (Janssen et al., forthcoming). In sum, there is no empirical reason to assume that parents choose child care for its quality nor that "choice" is a concept that can be assumed to be "fair". And it is also abundantly clear that in this study parental satisfaction could not be regarded as a quality criterion. Hence, the market of childcare is not a perfect market, and a turn towards marketisation may affect first and foremost the most disadvantaged families.

Structural Barriers

Erica Burman (1997) noted a few decades ago that the language of "choice" implies an equality of access to the market that denies actual structural positions of disadvantage. In the Child Guarantee feasibility study, it was revealed that one of the most salient structural positions of disadvantage is a structural lack in number of childcare places and an unequal geographical distribution of the places that are available (Vandenbroeck 2019). In several European Member States where the responsibility of ECEC was devolved regionally, it is usually the case that poorer regions have less ECEC places available. Geographical disparities may be very significant in some countries, such as Croatia, due to municipalities setting different priorities and standards. In Croatia, the poorest counties have the lowest enrolment rates. This is also the case for the different Austrian Bundesländer. In Italy, enrolment for the children below three years of age is a mere 1.2% in Calabria, compared to 25.6% in Emilia Romagna. In Spain, there are significant disparities across the Autonomous Communities. In the Netherlands, it was documented that the privatisation of childcare increased the number of places in affluent urban neighbourhoods, while it decreased in lower income neighbourhoods and rural areas (Noailly et al. 2007). In Flanders, Van Lancker and Vandenbroeck

(2019) found that higher average incomes in a municipality are associated with more available childcare places and that this is not only the case when comparing all municipalities, but often also when comparing neighbourhoods within cities. The lack of available places entails waiting lists (e.g. in metropolitan areas in the Netherlands, Belgium, or Latvia) that affect especially those who have more difficulty in subscribing a long time before their actual child care needs. This is the case for parents with precarious employments, as well as for migrant parents, who are not always able to navigate red tape and often complex admission procedures. In sum, inequalities in enrolment are to a very large extent due to inequalities in availability.

In addition to availability issues, affordability is an important explanatory factor as well. According to Eurostat data, 50% of the non-users of childcare in the European Union mention costs as the main reason not to enrol their child. According to comparative data drawn from the OECD Library (2020), parental fees often vary widely by socio-economic status of the household. In Cyprus for instance, the cost of ECEC represents on average 15% of net family income, but for poor and single-parent families this is 61.5 and 67.7%, respectively. In Spain, ECEC represents 5.6% of the disposable income for dual-earner families, but 15.1% for single-parent families. In Croatia, parent fees may vary between 8 and 16% of net income, according to varying municipal standards. In Estonia, a shortage of municipal centres is countered by private provision, yet parental fees are significantly higher in these private ECEC centres. In England, parents of children with special needs risk being charged three to four times the hourly rates for non-disabled children. In the Czech Republic, the growing "childminding groups" are becoming the main response to the lack of available places and they have high parental fees as well as poorer educational and hygienic quality standards. As a result, some countries have considered to offer a limited number of days (or hours) of free ECEC to all children of a specific age group, a typical example being England. It needs to be noted that the introduction of the entitlement for free years of preschool in England was not accompanied by sufficient subsidies, resulting in an increase of parental fees above wages and inflation as well as an increased closure of nurseries and childcare providers. Moreover, the English policy of offering a free year of ECEC has mainly reduced income for ECEC provision yet failed in attracting a more precarious population (Campbell et al. 2019). There are also interesting exceptions, In Luxemburg, Iceland, and the Scandinavian countries, for instance, there is hardly a difference in the burden of childcare on the household budget according to income and some countries (e.g. Malta, Slovenia, Latvia) offer free ECEC from a relatively early age. It needs to be noticed, however, that free ECEC does not necessarily mean that there are no costs that withhold families in poverty to enrol their child, considering costs for clothing, transportation, school canteens, or educational materials and in some countries, the entitlement is not available for refugee children.

Other structural barriers include priorities that are set by the provision. Typically, in split systems, the ECEC for the youngest children is considered as "child care" and intended to be for women at work. It is part of a labour and gender policy, rather than conceptualised as an educational environment in its own right. As a result, ECEC for the youngest children is more scarce than preschool places and priorities are set, favouring employment (e.g. in Germany, Romania, Spain, and the UK). All too often, the staff in these services lack the expertise to work with families in poverty, with Roma families, or with children with additional educational needs. A notable exception is Slovenia that has introduced a rather comprehensive system of trained Roma assistants (Samardzic-Markovic 2014).

In contrast, structural barriers to childcare enrolment are less important in countries with a legal entitlement to a place in childcare (which is the case in Denmark, Sweden, Finland, Norway, Germany, Estonia, Latvia, and Slovenia), a high share of publicly organised or subsidised facilities, and importantly, in which accompanying policies such as parental leaveentitlements are in synch with the usual admission age to childcare (Van Lancker and Ghysels ; Pavolini and Van Lancker 2018). This also means that in order to keep inequality at bay, governments need to devote sufficient resources to childcare (Van Lancker 2018).

SHARING THE CARING RESPONSIBILITIES

While availability and affordability are essential conditions for ECEC in general and childcare in particular to realise its potential towards children, parents, and societies, they are not sufficient conditions. Quality is a crucial pillar of proper childcare policies because only above-average quality can yield the expected results in terms of child development (Morabito et al. 2018; Slot et al. 2016). In contrast, we know that poor quality childcare may even be harmful for children (e.g. Gunnar et al. 2010). Most important in this regard is so-called process quality, defined as the quality of the interactions between adults and children and among children that are significant for the impact on children's development. It is generally assumed that it consists of two broad dimensions. The first is emotional quality and it is about building secure relations, trust, and a feeling of safety, thanks to the sensitivity and responsivity of the adult. The second is the educational support and that concerns the facilitation of exploration of the child (i.e. scaffolding), or the language support, the quality of feedback given to the child. It is regrettable to notice that most studies using in-depth observations of this process quality find that while emotional quality is average to good, the educational quality is significantly lower and often below what is needed to expect beneficial impact (Cadima et al. 2016; Hamre et al. 2014; Jamison et al. 2014; La Paro et al. 2014; Slot et al. 2016).

The European Commission (2018) adopted a comprehensive framework, based on an extensive literature review, defining five quality dimensions: accessibility, workforce, curriculum, monitoring, and governance. The bulk of the recommendations (eight out of 22) are about the workforce (pre-service training, in-service training, and working conditions), indicating its significance. As several studies (e.g. Eurofound 2015; Urban et al. 2012) have shown, higher qualifications are associated with better quality and improved child outcomes. Studies have also indicated that a lack of pre-service training may be compensated by training and sustained professional development (Fukkink and Lont 2007; Peleman et al. 2018). However, according to an OECD report (2019), status, remuneration, qualifications, in-service training, and working conditions are all below what is needed to safeguard the necessary quality in many of the OECD countries. As a result, most OECD countries face a shortage of staff, while needing to expand their childcare offer. This may lead to a downwards quality trend. Indeed, as countries wish to expand the number of childcare places and increase accessibility but cannot—or do not wish to—foresee the necessary budget, they may find it hard to engage the necessary staff. As a result, they may be inclined to lower (rather than raise) the expectations for childcare staff, hoping to engage less qualified personnel. A typical example of this policy is to be found in France (yet not only there). The "micro-crèches" (small, mostly private, child care centres) have fewer quality regulations, lower expected staff qualifications and lower wages, yet in 2016, 58% of all newly created childcare places in France belonged to such private for-profit organisations (Haut Conseil de la famille, de l'enfance et de l'âge 2018). It has been documented (e.g. Lloyd 2013; Van der Werf 2020) that countries who expanded their childcare provision through privatisation have also lowered the qualification of the workforce, their working conditions. Inadequate working conditions tend to lead to higher turn-over (especially for the better qualified staff members) and that is detrimental for the quality on offer (e.g. Early et al. 2007).

Obviously, there are also countries that have a standing tradition in providing fair access to high-quality ECEC for all children. Sweden, Malta, and Slovenia are among the many examples of systemic approaches that succeed in combining quality and quantity. It is probably not a coincidence that these are examples in which the public function of ECEC is stressed and where approximately 1% of GDP is spent in ECEC (OECD 2020) and where ECEC in general and childcare in particular are considered as a public good and framed as an entitlement, either for the general population (e.g. in Sweden and Slovenia) or for specific vulnerable target groups. The Swedish curriculum (Skolverket 2019) is quite explicit about what this means. It starts by claiming that the preschool is part of the school system and rests on the basis of democracy. It argues that education needs to be "equivalent", meaning that education should take into account the different conditions and needs of children and be adapted to all children in the preschool. This means that education cannot be structured in the same way everywhere and that the resources of the preschool should not be distributed equally. Common to these countries is the idea that ECEC is an entitlement and that public authorities (be it national or local) are responsible to enable families to make use of that entitlement.

Discussion

We now know that ECEC in general and childcare for the youngest children in particular have beneficial effects on the development of children and that these effects may last way beyond primary and secondary school. Therefore, ECEC is increasingly framed as one of the means to realise equal opportunities and create more fair and inclusive societies. It is therefore worrying to notice that children from poor families are less often enrolled in childcare and when they are, they are more often to be found in childcare from lower quality than their more affluent peers.

There is an increasing awareness that availability, affordability, and quality of early childhood education in general and childcare in particular are cornerstones of family policies. They are essential conditions for family policies that are beneficial for all children and for children in difficult situations in particular. This vision is backed by robust evidence and acknowledged by international NGO's (see also the Sustainable Development Goal 4) and policy levels, such as the European Commission.

However, it is to be noticed that the reality of the childcare landscape somewhat differs from this vision. European countries highly differ in the extent to which they see childcare as a private affair, favouring concepts of parental choice, and seeing childcare as a commodity on the one side and as a public responsibility and an entitlement for families on the other side. These fundamental options (and hybrid variations in between) mark the financing system, the options families have, but also the degrees of inequality in enrolment. As a result, childcare risks to reinforce the existing gap, and the expected benefits of childcare investment for disadvantaged children may fail to materialise.

In addition, important differences in process quality remain and the educational quality of many childcare places does not always match the required standards to expect the beneficial effects on children's development. For children who live in a stimulating and nurturing home environment, this means a loss of opportunities, yet not necessarily a dramatic impact on their later academic achievement. For children living in more deprived home environments, this may mean that they miss an essential opportunity to catch up. In that sense, the educational gap risks to be structurally organised before the compulsory education begins.

The recent stream of privatisation and commodification of childcare (and its shift from supply-side to demand-side funding) may hinder the public responsibility over quality issues (such as the workforce) and risks to put more emphasis on parental "choice", masking the structural inequalities where "choice" in reality only exists for some.

References

Akgunduz, Y. E., and J. Plantenga. 2014. "Childcare in the Netherlands: Lessons in Privatisation." *European Early Childhood Education Research Journal* 22 (3): 379–385.
Barnett, W. S. 2011. Effectiveness of Early Educational Intervention. *Science* 333 (975–978): 975–978.
Burman, E. 1997. "Psychology: Market, Metaphor and Metamorphosis." *Culture & Psychology* 3 (2): 143–152.
Cadima, J., S. Barros, T. Ferreira, V. Coelho, C. Peixoto, A. I. Pinto, and M. Pessanha. 2016. "Variations of Classroom Quality in Infant Classrooms in Portugal." EARLI SIG-5, Porto.
Campbell, T., L. Gambaro, and K. Stewart. 2019. *Inequalities in the Experience of Early Education in England: Access, Peer Groups and Transitions*. London: Centre for Analysis of Social Exclusion, London School of Economics.
Cleveland, G. 2008. *If It Don't Make Dollars, Does That Mean That It Don't Make Sense? Commercial, Nonprofit and Municipal Child Care in the City of Toronto*. Toronto: Department of Management, University of Toronto Scarborough.
Cryer, D., and M. Burchinal. 1997. "Parents as Child Care Consumers." *Early Childhood Research Quarterly* 12: 35–58.
Dowsett, C. J., A. C. Huston, A. E. Imes, and L. Gennetian. 2008. "Structural and Process Features in Three Types of Child Care for Children from High and Low Income Families." *Early Childhood Research Quarterly* 23: 69–93.
Early, D. M., K. L. Maxwell, M. Burchinal, S. Alva, R. H. Bender, D. Bryant, and N. Zill. 2007. "Teachers' Education, Classroom Quality, and Young Children's Academic Skills: Results from Seven Studies of Preschool Programs." *Child Development* 78: 558–580.
Engle, P., L. C. H. Fernald, H. Alderman, J. Behrman, C. O'Gara, A. Yousafzai, and Global Child Development Steering Group. 2011. Child Development 2. Strategies for Reducing Inequalities and Improving.
Eurofound. 2015. *Working Conditions, Training of Early Childhood Care Workers and Quality of Services—A Systematic Review*. Luxembourg: Publications Office of the European Union.
European Commission. 2018. *Council Recommendation on High Quality Early Childhood Education and Care Systems. SWD(2018) 173*. Brussels: European Commission.
Frazer, H., A.-C. Guio, and E. Marlier. 2020. *Feasibility Study for a Child Guarantee. Intermediate Report*. Luxemburg: LISER.
Fukkink, R. G., and A. Lont. (2007). "Does Training Matter? A Meta-Analysis and Review of Caregiver Training Studies." *Early Childhood Research Quarterly* 22: 294–311.
Gallagher, A. 2018. "The Business of Care: Marketization and the New Geographies of Childcare." *Progress in Human Geography* 42 (5): 706–722.
Gambaro, L., K. Stewart, and J. Waldfogel. 2015. "A Question of Quality: Do Children from Disadvantaged Backgrounds Receive Lower Quality Early Childhood Education and Care?" *British Educational Research Journal* 41 (4): 553–574.
Ghysels, J., and W. Van Lancker. 2010. "De terugkeer van het Mattheüseffect? De casus van de kinderopvang in Vlaanderen." *Tijdschrift voor Sociologie* 31 (2): 151–163.

Gunnar, M. R., M. J. Van Ryzin, and D. Phillips. 2010. "The Rise in Cortisol in Family Day Care: Associations with Aspects of Care Quality, Child Behavior and Child Sex." *Child Development* 81 (3): 851–869.

Hamre, B. K., K. M. La Paro, R. C. Pianta, and J. LoCasale-Crouch. 2014. *Classroom Assessment Scoring System. Manual. Infant.* Baltimore: Paul H. Brookes.

Haut Conseil de la famille, de l'enfance et de l'âge. 2018. *L'accueil des enfants de moins de trois ans. Tome I: Etat des lieux.* Paris: HCFEA.

Henly, J., and S. Lyons. 2000. "The Negotiation of Child Care and Employment Demands Among Low-Income Parents." *Journal of Social Issues* 56 (4): 683–706.

Himmelweit, S., and M. Sigala. 2004. "Choice and the Relationship Between Identities and Behaviour for Mothers with Pre-School Children: Some Implications for Policy from a UK Study." *Journal of Social Policy* 33 (3): 455–478.

Hofferth, S., and D. Wissoker. 1992. "Price, Quality and Income in Child Care Choice." *Journal of Human Resources* 27 (1): 70–111.

Jamison, K. R., S. Q. Cabell, and J. LoCasale-Crouch. 2014. "CLASS-Infant: An Observational Measure for Assessing Teacher-Infant Interactions in Center-Based Childcare." *Early Education and Development* 25 (4): 553–572.

Janssen, J., B. Spruyt, and M. Vandenbroeck. (2021). Is Everybody Happy? Exploring the Predictability of Parent Satisfaction with Childcare in Flanders. *Early Childhood Research Quarterly* 55: 97–106.

Janssen, J., B. Spruyt, Van drooghenbroeck, and M. Vandenbroeck. Forthcoming. "Is Everybody Happy? Exploring the Predictability of Parent Satisfaction with Childcare in Flanders." *Early Childhood Research Quarterly.*

Kind en Gezin. 2019. *Jaarverslag 2018.* Brussel: Kind en Gezin.

Kim, J., and M. S. Fram. 2009. "Profiles of Choice: Parents' Patterns of Priority in Child Care Decision-Making." *Early Childhood Research Quarterly* 24: 77–91.

La Paro, K. M., B. K. Hamre, and R. C. Pianta. 2012. *Classroom Assessment Scoring System. Manual. Toddler.* Baltimore: Paul H. Brookes.

La Paro, K. M., A. C. Wiliamson, and B. Hatfield. 2014. "Assessing Quality in Toddler Classrooms Using the CLASS Toddler and the ITERS-R." *Early Education and Development* 25 (6): 875–893.

Lloyd, E. 2013. "Childcare Markets: An Introduction." In *Childcare Markets. Can They Deliver an Equitable Service?*, edited by E. Lloyd and H. Penn, 3–18. Bristol: Policy Press.

Magnuson, K. A., and J. Waldfogel. 2005. "Early Childhood Care and Education: Effects on Ethnic and Racial Gaps in School Readiness." *The Future of Children* 15 (1): 169–196.

Meyers, M. K., and L. P. Jordan. 2006. "Choice and Accommodation in Parental Child Care Decisions." *Community Development* 37 (2): 53–70.

Morabito, C., D. Van de gaer, J. L. Figueroa, and M. Vandenbroeck. 2018. "Effects of High Versus Low-Quality Preschool Education: A Longitudinal Study in Mauritius." *Economics of Education Review* 65: 126–137.

Morabito, C., M. Vandenbroeck, and R. Roose. 2013. "The Greatest of Equalisers: A Critical Review of International Organisations' Views on Early Childhood Care and Education." *Journal of Social Policy* 42 (3): 451–467.

Moss, P. 2013. "Need Markets Be the Only Show in Town?" In *Childcare Markets. Can They Deliver an Equitable Service?*, edited by E. Lloyd and H. Penn, 191–208. Bristol: Policy Press.

Noailly, J., S. Visser, and P. Grout. 2007. *The Impact of Market Forces on the Provision of Childcare: Insights from the 2005 Childcare Act in the Netherlands*. Den Haag: Centraal Planbureau.
Organisation for Economic Co-operation and Development. 2015. *Starting Strong IV. Monitoring Quality in Early Childhood Education and Care*. Paris: O.E.C.D.
Organisation for Economic Co-operation and Development. 2019. *Good Practice for Good Jobs in Early Childhood Education and Care: Eight Policy Measures from OECD Countries*. Paris: OECD.
Organisation for Economic Co-operation and Development. 2020. *Education at a glance. OECD Indicators*. Paris: OECD.
Peleman, B., A. Lazzari, I. Budginaite, H. Siarova, H. Hauari, J. Peeters, and C. Cameron. 2018. "Continuous Professional Development and ECEC Quality: Findings from a European Systematic Literature Review." *European Journal of Education* 53 (1): 9–22.
Peyton, V., A. Jacobs, M. O'Brien, and C. Roy. 2001. Reasons for Choosing Child Care: Associations with Family Factors, Quality, and Satisfaction. *Early Childhood Research Quarterly* 16: 191–208.
Penn, H. 2013. "Childcare Markets: Do They Work?" In *Childcare Markets. Can They Deliver an Equitable Service?*, edited by H. Lloyd and H. Penn, 19–42. Bristol: Policy Press.
Plantenga, J. 2013. "Local Providers and Loyal Partners: Competition and Consumer Choice in the Dutch Childcare Market." In *Childcare Markets. Can They Deliver an Equitable Service?*, edited by E. Lloyd and H. Penn, 63–77. Bristol: Policy Press.
Ruutiainen, V., M. Alasuutari, and K. Karila. 2019. "Rationalising Public Support for Private Early Childhood Education and Care: The Case of Finland." *British Journal of Sociology of Education, On line first*. https://doi.org/10.1080/01425692.2019.1665497.
Samardzic-Markovic, S. 2014. *Inclusion from the Start. Guidelines on Inclusive Early Childhood Care and Education for Roma Children*. Brussels: Council of Europe – UNESCO.
Shlay, A., H. Tran, M. Weinraub, and M. Harmon. 2005. "Teasing Apart the Child Care Conundrum: A Factorial Analysis of Perceptions of Child Care Quality, Fair Market Price and Willingness to Pay by Low-Income, African-American Parents." *Early Childhood Research Quarterly* 20: 393–416.
Skolverket. 2019. *Curriculum for the preschool Lpfö 18*. Stockholm: Frizes kundservice.
Slot, P., M.-K. Lerkkanen, and P. Leseman. 2016. *The Relations Between Structural Quality and Process Quality in European Early Childhood Education and Care Provisions: Secondary Analyses of Large Scale Studies in Five Countries*. Utrecht: Utrecht University - CARE project.
Stahl, J. F., P. S. Schober, and C. K. Spiess. 2018. "Parental Socio-Economic Status and Childcare Quality: Early Inequalities in Educational Opportunity?" *Early Childhood Research Quarterly* 44: 304–317.
Sylva, K., A. Stein, P. Leach, J. Barnes, and L. E. Malmberg. 2007. "Family and Child Factors Related to the Use of Non-Maternal Infant Care: An English Study." *Early Childhood Research Quarterly* 26 (1): 118–136.
Teppers, E., W. Schepers, and T. Van Regenmortel. 2019. *Het gebruik van en de behoefte aan kinderopvang voor baby's en peuters jonger dan 3 jaar in het Vlaamse Gewest*. Leuven: Steunpunt Welzijn, Volksgezondheid en Gezin.

Thomason, A. C., and K. M. La Paro. 2009. "Measuring the Quality of Teacher-Child Interactions in Toddler Child Care." *Early Education and Development* 20 (2): 285–304.

Pavolini, E., and W. Van Lancker. 2018. "The Matthew Effect in Childcare Use: A Matter of Policies or Preferences?" *Journal of European Public Policy* 25 (6): 878–893.

Urban, M., M. Vandenbroeck, K. Van Laere, A. Lazzari, and J. Peeters. 2012. "Towards Competent Systems in Early Childhood Education and Care. Implications for Policy and Practice." *European Journal of Education* 47 (4): 508–526.

Van Lancker, W. 2013. "Putting the Child-Centred Investment Strategy to the Test: Evidence for the EU27." *European Journal of Social Security* 15 (1): 4–27.

Van Lancker, W., and J. Ghysels. 2016. "Explaining Patterns of Inequality in Childcare Service Use Across 31 Developed Economies: A Welfare State Perspective." *International Journal of Comparative Sociology* 57 (5): 310–337.

Van Lancker, W. 2018. "Reducing Inequality in Childcare Service Use Across European Countries: What (If Any) Is the Role of Social Spending?" *Social Policy & Administration* 52 (1): 271–292.

Vandenbroeck, M. 2019. *Feasibility Study for a Child Guarantee. Policy Paper on Early Childhood Education and Care. Unpublished Report.* Brussels: European Commission.

Vandenbroeck, M., S. De Visscher, K. Van Nuffel, and J. Ferla. 2008. "Mothers' Search for Infant Child Care: The Dynamic Relationship Between Availability and Desirability in a Continental European Welfare State." *Early Childhood Research Quarterly* 23 (2): 245–258.

Vandenbroeck, M., F. Laevers, H. Hulpia, M. Daems, B. Declercq, J. Janssen, and C. Van Cleynenbreugel. 2016. *MeMoQ Deelrapport 14. Samenvatting van de nulmeting.* Brussel: Kind en Gezin; Gent: UGent; Leuven: KU Leuven.

Vandenbroeck, M., and A. Lazzari. 2014. "Accessibility of Early Childhood Education and Care: A State of Affairs." *European Early Childhood Education Research Journal* 22 (3): 327–335.

Vandenbroeck, M., K. Lenaerts, and M. Beblavy. 2018. *Benefits of Early Childhood Education and Care and the Conditions for Obtaining Them.* Brussels: European Expert Network on Economics of Education.

Van der Werf, W. 2020. *Diversiteit, inclusie en kwaliteit in het hybride kinderopvangstelsel in Nederland.* Utrecht: Universiteit Utrecht.

Van der Werf, W. M., P. L. Slot, P. N. Kenis, and P. P. M. Leseman. 2020. "Hybrid Organizations in the Dutch ECEC Privatized and Harmonized System: Relations with Quality of Education and Care." *Early Childhood Research Quarterly* 53: 136–150.

Van Lancker, W., and Vandenbroeck, M. 2019. *De verdeling van de kinderopvang in Vlaanderen en in de centrumsteden: spanning tussen de economische en sociale functie van kinderopvang.* Leuven: KU Leuven; Gent: UGent.

Walker, J. R. 1991. "Public Policy and the Supply of Child Care Services." In *Economics of Child Care*, edited by D. M. Blau, 51–77. New York: Russell Sage Foundation.

Yuen, G. 2013. "Tinkering with Early Childhood Education and Care: Early Education Vouchers in Hong Kong." In *Childcare Markets. Can They Deliver an Equitable Service?*, edited by H. Lloyd and H. Penn, 79–95. Bristol: Policy Press.

CHAPTER 19

Shared Parenting After Separation and Divorce in Europe in the Context of the Second Demographic Transition

Lluís Flaquer

Introduction

In the last decades one of the major innovative developments in the area of postdivorce family arrangements has been the rise and emerging institutionalisation of shared parenting after separation and divorce. Simply stated, this new form of custody involves that after the breakup of a marriage or partnership with children there is no single custodial parent, as it was mostly frequent in earlier days, but it is rather based on an arrangement by which both parents share the responsibility for major decisions as well as they take an equitable part in the caring of children. To the great majority of the millennial generation this setup may seem an obvious and common-sense strategy and yet the question is why this plain idea took so much time to be seriously considered and why even nowadays its implementation generates in some countries heated debates. In fact, this is a very complex issue that needs to be examined from a multidisciplinary approach.

To begin with, one of the difficult challenges to confront is the variety of terminology used to refer to shared parenting after separation and divorce in different disciplines and countries.[1] One of the most popular expressions is joint physical custody (JPC), with the caution that it must be carely distinguished from joint legal custody, another similar term but with a quite different meaning. If joint legal custody refers to a custodial arrangement

L. Flaquer (✉)
Universitat Autònoma de Barcelona, Bellaterra, Spain
e-mail: lluis.flaquer@uab.cat

© The Author(s), under exclusive license to Springer Nature Switzerland AG 2021
A.-M. Castrén et al. (eds.), *The Palgrave Handbook of Family Sociology in Europe*, https://doi.org/10.1007/978-3-030-73306-3_19

where both parents share the right and the obligation of making most important choices about the life of their children, including school and education, religious practice, and health care, JPC must be seen as a type of living arrangement and it has mainly to do with time and residence (Smyth 2017; Solsona et al. 2020). It means that the child spends a significant amount of time with each parent, ideally half and half, by alternating between separate households and that each of them plays an important part in child-rearing and in the daily care of the child (Kurki-Suonio 2000; Halla 2009; Turunen 2015). Historically, the development of joint legal custody took place prior to that of JPC and this marked important differences between them (Kurki-Suonio 2000; Halla 2009). While both types of joint custody make a good contribution to the ideal of shared parenting, JPC generally takes for granted joint legal one, but the opposite is not the case. In fact, JPC always goes together with joint legal custody, but the reverse is not necessarily true (Braver and Lamb 2018; Steinbach et al. 2020). In order to clarify the confusion that this diverse terminology might imply, in this chapter the expression JPC is used in cases where we are dealing with custody as a living arrangement (shared parenting time) and shared parenting after separation and divorce where both aspects of joint custody are involved.

All definitions are confronted with the determination of the amount of time that children should spend with each parent so that a custody arrangement is to be qualified as JPC. If there is no dispute about the notion that in JPC all children should have frequent contact and a close relationship with both parents, descriptions may diverge as to the share of time spent by children with father and mother. This applies not only to the legal definitions used in different national jurisdictions, but also to those pertaining to research literature reviews and meta-analyses. Beyond the ideal of full parity, guidelines in different legal systems relating to the percentage of total time spent by children with each parent to qualify as JPC are usually vague and unexplicit. There is a lack of agreement regarding research definitions on criteria to distinguish between sole custody and JPC. A number of researchers believe that the line of demarcation for the distinction between sole and JPC arrangements must be drawn at a minimum of around 35% of the child's time with each parent (Nielsen 2011, 2014, 2017, 2018; Braver and Lamb 2018). However, other authors are less strict in the definition of JPC and they contend that children's time with each parent should be at least in the range of 25–50% (Smyth 2017; Steinbach 2019).

The purpose of this chapter is the study of the development and institutionalisation of JPC in Europe. Its main thesis is that the significance of JPC must be seen against the backdrop of the progress of gender equality. The growth of JPC is understood in the context of the Second Demographic Transition (SDT), a theoretical framework that in its recent versions emphasises female education and gender equality as the main drives for momentous changes in the area of the family and population (Esping-Andersen and Billari 2015). The chapter explores the availability of comparable quantitative data on the prevalence of JPC as well other relevant indicators on its trends with the aim of offering clues on the position of countries in the transition process. This approach unfortunately excludes the coverage of the rich literature based on the results of qualitative research.

This chapter consists of six different sections including this *Introduction*. The second section delves into the significance of JPC in the context of the SDT, which is driven by a push for gender equality. In particular, the rise of JPC is explained by the decline of the male breadwinner family model and the shift towards a new dual-earner and dual-carer one and by the replacement of the traditional judicial presumption that the mother shall have sole and exclusive custody by a gender-neutral one. The third section focuses on different national experiences of five selected European countries (Germany, Spain, England and Wales, France, and Sweden) in relation to the progress of JPC. The fourth section deals with the relationship between the prevalence of JPC and patterns of gender equality in Europe. A scatter plot and a table are included to summarise the results of analysis. The fifth section focuses on outcomes for children living in JPC in relation to other postseparation arrangements. Finally, the *Conclusion* highlights the existence of wide disparities among European countries concerning the development of JPC, presses for the collection of comparable data and warns that policy reforms cannot be applied across the board.

The Significance of Shared Parenting After Divorce in the Context of the Second Demographic Transition

The Second Demographic Transition (SDT) provides a comprehensive analytic framework in which it is possible to understand the nature and the development of shared parenting after separation and divorce. Original proponents of the SDT theory such as Ron Lesthaeghe and Dirk van de Kaa (1986) contended that new developments in the last decades of the twentieth century brought about a disjunction between marriage and procreation, marriage and parenthood postponement, the rise of alternative forms of partnerships and living arrangements, parenthood outside marriage and, last but not least, sustained subreplacement fertility (Lesthaeghe 2010, 2014; Zaidi and Morgan 2017). Newer versions of the SDT are emphasising women's growing economic independence as a main driver of family transformation but also as an amplification factor of financial inequalities. The development of this process results in a marked divergence of children's destinies (McLanahan 2004).

Esping-Andersen and Billari concur with McLanahan's analysis in that women are spearheading a new social order and they posit their emancipation as the driving force setting in motion the transition process. They particularly stress that "the rise of female education is a key factor behind the move away from the traditional equilibrium" (Esping-Andersen and Billari 2015, 11). In their view, two foremost family changes stand out in the SDT, i.e. the decline of fertility and the loss of partnership stability and they set the diffusion of gender-egalitarian norms as the goal leading to a new normative equilibrium (Esping-Andersen and Billari 2015).

In this sense, we can conceive the SDT as a process in which gender equality is diffused from pioneering and minority sections of the population to the society as a whole. This is a long-standing cycle involving the replacement of a great many institutions such as traditional family models, outdated patriarchal norms, archaic welfare-state models, etc. by new, emerging values based on gender equality.

In Western societies in the decades following the start of the SDT,[2] we have witnessed not only the eclipse of housewife figure as a life career, but also the collapse of the Parsonian family (Esping-Andersen 2009). Esping-Andersen refers to the male breadwinner/female homemaker family model, a famous analytical construct that dominated family research during the second half of the twentieth century. It is doubtless that the long-standing hegemony of the male breadwinner family model is currently on the wane. Family breakup is a privileged moment for disclosing the parental norms of an era (Hachet 2016). The prevalence of different types of child custody tends to mirror dominant models of family organisation. While sole legal custody may be taken as a reflection of the traditional family model by which the children were cared for by the mother at home while the father's main responsibility was earning money, the development of JPC in many European countries can be interpreted as an expression of the decline of the male breadwinner family model (Creighton 1999; Crompton 1999; Lewis 2001; Flaquer et al. 2017). The distribution of tasks between the breadwinning husband and the caring wife in postseparation families is nowadays increasingly out of touch with reality in a society where most mothers from intact families are economically active and a growing number of fathers are taking care of their children at home (Melli and Brown 2008; Lewis et al. 2008; Gracia 2014; Flaquer et al. 2016; Flaquer et al. 2020; Steinbach et al. 2020).

In the Anglo-American legal tradition, the common award of child custody to mothers harks back to the Custody of Infants Act approved by the British Parliament in 1839 under the advocacy of Caroline Norton, an English social reformer. This marked a turning point in the history of divorce, since earlier on child custody was mostly granted to the father, and introduced the so-called *Tender Years* presumption by which mothers were awarded the custody of children under the age of 7 while fathers were deemed responsible for their financial maintenance. In 1873 this presumption was extended to children until the age of 16 (Wroath 1998; Katz 1992; Hartenstein 2016).

This family law principle was based on the concern that mothers were intended to be natural and primary caretakers as they were the best equipped to meet the physical and emotional needs of their children. Well until the late 1960s, judicial courts routinely allocated custody to mothers based on the notion that they had superior, "natural" nurturing abilities and a biological connection to their infants (Mason 1994; Artis 2004; Hartenstein 2016).

Whether it was regarded as a legal presumption or it was rather expressed as a rule of thumb, maternal preference had been solidly entrenched for many decades and even a long time after its formal abolition it was still applied by a number of judges as an unwritten presumption not only in England but elsewhere (Klaff 1982; DiFonzo 2014). This stance was especially noticeable with regard to younger children and it reflected a common stereotype that a young child healthy development required maternal care. This made nearly impossible for fathers to get custody of a child. From the 1970s this trend was gradually replaced with a gender-neutral presumption named the Best Interest of the Child Standard (Stamps 2002; Hartenstein 2016).

JPC can be taken as an ideal interpretation of the best interests of the child, a paramount principle in family law (Kurki-Suonio 2000). Its development reveals a gradual progress of the child centrality in family policy (Lewis 2006) and is parallel to the rise of a long-lasting movement for father involvement in the care of children (Lamb 2000; Marsiglio et al. 2000). One of the reasons why the *Tender Years* presumption came to lose its dominance was the emerging evidence on the benefits of father involvement provided by ongoing research. A number of prominent developmental psychologists were able to demonstrate that fathers, in the same way as mothers, were capable of becoming primary carers if they had the opportunity to come to interact with young children from the very beginning (Lamb 2013).

National Experiences of JPC in a Selection of European Countries

The purpose of this section is to present and discuss an overview of the situation of JPC in a selection of European countries through their national experiences. Unfortunately, available evidence is patchy, heterogeneous, and fragmented, it is hard to get enough comparable information enabling to devise a common analytical framework and therefore it is quite difficult to describe comparative patterns and characteristics from different countries.

This section will discuss accessible research and data concerning JPC from five major European countries, i.e. Germany, Spain, England and Wales, France, Sweden. The criteria under which the countries under consideration have been selected are the following: the existence of easily available sources in English or other major European languages on the subject as well as relevant information about legislative reforms and policy debates and their social and political context. In particular, a couple of indicators are used in order to better characterise the profiles of each country, i.e. (1) the educational gradient of fathers and mothers opting for JPC in relation to parents from other post-separation living arrangements and (2) the percentage of contested cases in separation or divorce procedures involving children (Perelli-Harris et al. 2010; Haux et al. 2017; Fransson et al. 2016, 2018b).

In Germany the debate on shared parenting (*Wechselmodell*) focuses on an issue widely regarded to be one of the most contentious in the country today

(Busse 2018). As of today, despite intensive public discussion in the last few years, no presumption of JPC was approved. A court order or an explicit agreement for this arrangement is required. Family courts stimulate parents to reach mutual agreements on key points by means of seeking mediation or consultation from the Youth Welfare Office (*Jugendamt*). Whereas married parents are granted (legal) joint custody right away, the unmarried ones are required to make an agreement at the *Jugendamt* or to seek a joint custody order from a family court. Since 1st February 2017 family courts are allowed to decide on JPC, even without both parents' consent, provided that the best interest of the child is taken into consideration (Kreidler-Pleus 2018; Maydell and Plitzko 2019).

Using data drawn from the 7th wave of Relationships and Family Panel (Pairfam) (2014/2015—children aged 9–17) one can estimate the prevalence of different custody models in Germany. Only about 4% of separated parents are living in a JPC arrangement in a strict sense (60:40%). Another 5% of separated parents are living in an asymmetrical two-home arrangement and about 7% of them are single fathers. Only in 3 out of 10 single-mother households children have regular weekly contact with their fathers. In Germany educational gradients for JPC parents are positive in contrast to those from single mothers whose children have little or no contact to their fathers, where the opposite is true. However, single mothers with children having a regular contact to their fathers have a gradient tending to zero. This important finding suggests that in this country the latter is the reference living arrangement (Walper 2016, 2018; Walper and Lux 2016).

Spain is one of the EU countries where the growth of JPC has been more intense in the last decade. JPC as a new form of custody was introduced for the first time in the Spanish legislation in 2005. The impact of this legal reform was greater than expected because since 2010 it was established as the reference custody in a few Northeastern regions with civil legislation powers such as Aragon, Catalonia, Navarre, and the Basque Country (Escobedo et al. 2012; Solsona and Ajenjo 2017; Flaquer et al. 2017).

In the last decade there has been a significant growth of divorce cases involving JPC in Spain where they have shifted from 9.6% of annual divorces with children in 2007 to 33.9% in 2018. However, one can observe striking regional disparities with percentages ranging from higher than 45% in the Northeast to lower than 25% in the South. Little information is available about the percentage of JPC cases in relation to the total number of legal separations filed from unmarried parents with children. However, there is every indication that for the latter percentages of JPC judicial rulings are much lower because the percentage of contested separation proceedings is higher than as much as double[3] (Solsona and Spijker 2016; Solsona and Ajenjo 2017; Solsona et al. 2020; Flaquer and Becerril 2020).

Using Spanish HBSC data 2014,[4] it is estimated that in Spain about one out of every 20 children (5%) lives in JPC. This kind of family arrangement is mostly prevalent among the middle classes and among parents with higher educational attainments. Likewise, mothers from two-home arrangements were the most eager to have a job and they had higher employment rates than the rest (Flaquer et al. 2017).

Although in the UK there are two different jurisdictions, i.e. England and Wales and Scotland, most of the available information about JPC refers to the former and, therefore, the following discussion is almost restricted to it. There is a growing consensus among British researchers on the need for improving data collection methods in order to better study the characteristics and practices of separated parents as well as the outcomes of their children (Bryson et al. 2017; Haux et al. 2017). The absence of statistical information on the prevalence of postseparation parenting and contact matters because it prevents researchers from interpreting properly the constraints faced by families and, if there is no clear-cut baseline, it is not possible to observe change through time. This possibly reveals a lack of policy interest and of political will (Haux et al. 2017).

When the Children Act 1989 introduced the concepts of parental responsibility and residence orders in England and Wales, JPC was mentioned for the first time. However, it was only meant as an unusual order made in exceptional circumstances (Hayden 2011). In a Green Paper on Parental Separation, which preceded the approval of *Children and Adoption Act 2006*, a presumption of JPC was specifically ruled out (HM Government 2004). During the passage through parliament proposals to introduce a legislative presumption of minimum contact were debated and subsequently rejected, while reforms aimed at maximising contact when in the best interests of the child were enacted (Fehlberg et al. 2011a). Finally, in the *Children and Families Act 2014*, a presumption that parental involvement is in the best interests of the child was included but its significance has been largely symbolic (Haux et al. 2017).

In accordance with legal provisions, in the UK there is a growing emphasis on postseparation private child arrangements and maintenance without state intervention. All divorcing or separating parents are legally encouraged to make essential arrangements for the children, and most of them come to some sort of mutual agreement. This implies that in some cases of postseparation the court is not issuing any residence orders and it is not directly involved in the making of arrangements. As far as litigation is concerned, only about 10% of divorcing or separating parents are dealing with the courts in the process of making child residence or maintenance arrangements. This small percentage of cases is usually deemed to be high conflict (Peacey and Hunt 2008; Fehlberg et al. 2011b; Nikolina 2015; Haux et al. 2017). However, this low figure has been recently challenged by Cafcass, an official source, which revealed that 38% of separating parents go to court.

Summing up, one can consider the policy towards JPC in England and Wales as rather passive and geared towards the privatisation of agreements on family arrangements. In general, the mainstream attitude of public opinion is not very much supportive of JPC as a living arrangement and most researchers discussing the matter remain cautious and reluctant to advance towards more radical and progressive reform. Legislating on JPC is not seen as the best solution as it involves the risk of imposed judicial arrangements (Fehlberg et al. 2011a).

France is one of the pioneering nations in relation to the development of JPC. Even if the legal concept of "alternating residence" was not introduced in the French legislation until 2002, a research monograph had already been published as early as in 1994, which stimulated public debate and paved the way for reform (Neyrand 2009, 2010; Escobedo et al. 2012; Hachet 2016).

Using personal income tax statements as a source, in 2016 about 400,000 children under 18 lived in JPC in France. Since 2010 the share of children in JPC has doubled and in 2016 it came to reach a 2.7% of all children. The proportion of children living in shared residence increases steadily with age and it reaches its zenith at 3.8% for the group of children 11–14 years. The mean age of children living in two-homes in 2016 was 10.5 years (Bonnet et al. 2015; Cretin 2015; Algava et al. 2019). An important finding is that the living conditions of households with children in JPC are better than those from the average of households with children. Children in JPC are more likely to live in well-off families than in other kinds of households. Child poverty rates of children in JPC are a half of those for all children (11% vs 22%). A similar advantageous position also occurs in two of living arrangements where two-home children usually live, i.e. families headed by a couple or by a single parent (Algava et al. 2019).

Sweden is undoubtedly the European leader in JPC and accordingly there is a great wealth of information available concerning this living arrangement (Fransson et al. 2018b). In particular, the growth in JPC has been steady in the last decades rising from about 1% of children in postseparation families in the mid-1980s to 35% in the present so that it is now almost as common as the traditional sole mother care. For some authors it has already become the norm and its increase is one of the most outstanding family developments occurred in the last two decades (Bergström et al. 2013; Fransson et al. 2018a).

Most of explanations concerning the growing progression of JPC in Sweden have to do with the character of Swedish family policies in connection with gender equality (Fransson et al. 2016; Fritzell et al. 2020). In Sweden there is a long-standing tradition of family policies taking for granted that both parents are participating in the labour market while they are also caring for their children. Since 1974 both parents have had access to paid parental leave and fathers use a substantial proportion of it (24% in 2012). Accordingly, father involvement is also relatively high (Bergström et al. 2013). In line with these policies, Sweden has the highest female labour force participation among the Eurostat countries, i.e. 81% in 2018.[5] Swedish family policies support the dual earner-carer model and therefore both mothers and fathers are financially independent and self-sufficient. Attitudes toward gender equality in parenting are also sustained by the bulk of the population, which provides a large consensus on family values and policy strategies. In the last decades the male breadwinner has been replaced by an involved caring father (Engster and Stensöta 2011; Fransson et al. 2016).

Even if, technically, in Sweden there is not a written and formal presumption of JPC, yet societal values are clearly supporting gender equality. Since 1998 the Swedish courts may rule for JPC, even when one parent or both do not agree on sharing, if the judge finds that it is the best decision because it is in the best interest of the child (Turunen 2017; Fransson et al. 2018b; Fritzell et al. 2020). Despite this discretionary power of the family courts, only about 9% of parents are resorting to judicial litigation, but other authors report a figure as low as 2%, which is a very modest one in relation to other countries (Fransson et al. 2016, 2018b). This not only indicates that in Sweden JPC is becoming the norm, but also that there is a great social and cultural consensus over the model.

One of the recent scientific discoveries is that in Sweden very little differences are currently found between the shares of parental high education for both intact families and JPC in contrast to households with one single custodial parent, where their percentage is much lower (Fransson et al. 2018a). However, JPC was a less common postseparation arrangement among families with a migrant background and among those in the lowest income category (Bergström et al. 2013; Fransson et al. 2018b). This is indicative that JPC is becoming the norm as their parental profiles resemble more and more the mainstream population of parents with children.

Patterns of JPC in Relation to Gender Equality in a European Comparative Perspective

I have reviewed thus far a selection of representative countries having various and distinct features concerning JPC with the purpose to present and discuss certain issues regarding possible factors underlying its growth and progress. Another approach to be explored to diagnose the situation of JPC and to monitor its evolution is comparative analysis. This is a perspective widely used in public policy enabling to undertake a descriptive and explanatory quantitative analysis of the patterns and development of a particular phenomenon using a larger sample of countries. Given the existing wealth of comparable indicators in many fields, the European Union is an appropriate institutional setting for such kind of analyses. However, regarding the study of JPC, the review of the literature available in different countries shows the difficulties in finding equivalent and comparable indicators necessary for keeping track of the progress of JPC. As it has been mentioned above, data on the prevalence of JPC in EU countries are extracted from various sources and are based on different statistical indicators, which make it difficult to draw valid comparisons. The only source in relation JPC covering most of the EU countries is the HBSC database (see End Note No 4). One prominent feature of these surveys is that informants about the family situation and school context are the school-aged children themselves. Behaviours and practices reported by adolescents are seen through their eyes rather than through the official categories.

In the 2001–2002, 2005–2006, and 2009–2010 editions the questionnaire included a question on «Do you have another home or another family, such as the case when your parents are separated or divorced?» and inquired about the presence of close family members living in the second home (father, mother, stepfather, stepmother, grandfather, and grandmother), as well as the number of [step]brothers and [step]sisters staying there. Likewise, another question was asked on «How often the child stays in the second home» . Those children answering «Half of the time» were deemed to live in a symmetrical JPC arrangement. It appears that in the two last editions (2013–2014 and 2017–2018) questions on the second home have unfortunately been discontinued from the mandatory core questionnaire (Steinbach et al. 2020).

Various indicators of prevalence have been estimated for all HBSC countries using pooled data from 2001, 2006, and 2010 waves, and these are the only comparative data available so far (Steinbach et al. 2020).[6] HBSC surveys were representative of 11-, 13-, and 15-year-old children being the school class the initial sampling unit. Given the scope of this chapter, I have only selected data from EU countries, with the exception of Cyprus and Lithuania, where information was missing, and I have chosen as a main indicator the percentage of children reporting symmetrical JPC in relation to all families, which yields a quite conservative estimate of prevalence (Steinbach et al. 2020). Steinbach et al. (2019) suggest the idea that the progress of JPC seems to be the result of increasing gender equality, and therefore the analysis of a possible relationship between a measure of gender equality and the development of JPC is most relevant (Flaquer et al. 2017; Solsona and Ajenjo 2017; Solsona et al. 2020). The inclusion of an index of gender equality is fully justified on the grounds that the state of the art concerning the high prevalence of JPC in Sweden and other Nordic nations shows the importance of family policies for its increase. In particular, most authors highlight the significance of gender equality as a guiding principle in these countries and this is often highlighted as one of the reasons why JPC has developed so intensely (Fransson et al. 2016; Bergström et al. 2019; Fritzell et al. 2020). To test this association, I have used the 2010 Gender Equality Index (GEI), calculated by the European Institute for Gender Equality (EIGE).[7]

Figure 19.1 describes the positions of different EU countries on a coordinate plane by the prevalence of symmetrical JPC and by the Gender Equality Index scores. One can easily see on the scatter plot that there is a positive relationship between both variables. The calculation of the correlation yields a high Pearson coefficient ($R = .788^{**}$).[8] Sweden (3.3%) and to a lesser extent Belgium (2.7%) are clearly outliers and they occupy a unique position in Europe. In the group of leaders, although quite far from Sweden and Belgium, we find the UK and France (1.5%), Finland (1.3%), Denmark (1.2%), the Netherlands, and Ireland (1.0%). The rest of the countries exhibit

Fig. 19.1 Scatter diagram of symmetrical JPC prevalence by gender equality index in the EU countries. CIRCA, 2010 (*Sources* Vertical axis Steinbach et al. (2020) using HBSC data 2002, 2006, 2010; horizontal axis: GEI from EIGE 2010)

prevalences of less than 1.0%. We should not forget that prevalence values correspond to circa 2010 and that advances for some countries (Spain, Italy, Portugal, France) have been dramatic in the last few years. It is a pity that HBSC does not allow the calculations of prevalence with the same methodology any longer. At any rate, this finding suggests and possibly confirms that one of the main drivers for the development of JPC could be the increase in gender equality, and similarly it provides a useful baseline for discussion as well a good starting point for assessing further developments from 2010.

Table 19.1 summarises the results of sections "National Experiences of JPC in a Selection of European Countries" and "Patterns of JPC in Relation to Gender Equality in a European Comparative Perspective". In the third column, it also includes updated GEI data for 2017 and the growth of index values in percentage points between 2010 and 2017. France is the country that shows the greatest scope for growth in 2010–2017 (7.1 p.p.), which is corroborated by information from the national report in section "National Experiences of JPC in a Selection of European Countries". The rest of countries display moderate increases. One of the obstacles blocking the progress of Spain is its high percentage of contested separations. With the exception of Sweden, the rest of countries have positive educational gradients and this is indicative that they find themselves at earlier phases of the transition process.

OUTCOMES FOR CHILDREN

Concerns derived from family instability not only have to do with economic insecurity and child poverty but also with relational vulnerability (Martin

Table 19.1 Table of different indicators of JPC. Selection of European countries for which information is available

Countries	Prevalence of JPC in relation to all families in % (circa 2010)	GEI Index 2010	GEI Index 2017 (Growth in p.p. 2010–2017)	Educational gradients	% of contested cases of separation or divorce
Germany	0.8	62.6	66.9 (4.3)	Positive	Not available
Spain	0.7	66.4	70.1 (3.7)	Positive	23% divorces 59.4% separations
United Kingdom (England and Wales) ([a])	1.5	68.7	72.2 (3.5)	Not available	10–38 %
France	1.5	67.5	74.6 (7.1)	Positive	Not available
Sweden	3.3	80.1	83.6 (3.5)	It tends to 0	2–9%

[a]Data from the three first columns refer to the UK; information from the two last columns refers to England and Wales

1997; Sigle-Rushton and McLanahan 2004; Flaquer 2014). Interest in the evaluation of custody arrangements results from the growing awareness of the distress caused by separation and divorce. In a world increasingly characterised by the centrality of children, child well-being is one of the most genuine touchstones for the quality of living arrangements. If we want to assess the benefits of JPC as a valuable custody arrangement in relation to other post-separation families, it is important to ensure its good performance in terms of children's well-being. In a pioneering article using data from Norway, Breivik and Olweus (2006) compared adolescent's adjustment in four post-divorce family structures and they found that adolescents in JPC were at no higher risk of displaying adjustment problems than their peers from non-divorced families except in the area of school achievement. Many other articles focusing on adolescents follow a similar strategy. Another classical, widely cited article analysed adolescents' adjustment in JPC in relation to sole-custody arrangements by means of a meta-analytic review of earlier work from mostly the 1980s and 1990s with very positive results for JPC concerning general adjustment, family relationships, self-esteem, emotional and behavioural adjustment, and divorce-specific adjustment (Bauserman 2002). This opened up an avenue of meta-analyses in order to be able to keep pace with the assessment of a burgeoning and rapidly expanding literature (Nielsen 2011, 2013a, b, 2014, 2017, 2018; Baude et al. 2016; Steinbach 2019). They cover altogether 250 studies from the 1980s to the present, although some of them may be duplicated in various articles. Finally, it is significant to report a few comparative studies in which groups of countries are jointly analysed (Bjarnason and Arnarsson 2011; Bjarnason et al. 2012; Bergström et al. 2019).

The positive effects of JPC are visible in a number of children's well-being areas such as the following (1) better physical health; (2) lower cigarette smoking rates; (3) reduced alcohol taking and substance abuse; (4) lower levels of aggression, dissatisfaction, depression, and anxiety; (5) better cognitive development and school outcomes; and (6) better relationships with fathers, mothers, and other family members. Even if a few studies have failed to demonstrate some of these favourable claims, none of them has suggested that JPC can harm children. At worst, no significant differences were found between children with different custody arrangements (Braver and Lamb 2018).

A recent meta-analysis regarding children's well-being concludes that JPC is linked to better outcomes than sole physical custody, independent of family income or level of conflict between parents. All studies that examined children's relationships with their parents and other kin found better outcomes for children in JPC (Nielsen 2018). Furthermore, in none of Swedish studies for children aged 3 years or more was children's well-being found to be poorer in JPC than in single parental custody (Fransson et al. 2018b).

One of the concerns of scholars working in this area is that, even if they consistently find an association between particular family arrangements and certain outcomes for children, they do not know for sure what are the specific mechanisms involved in these relationships. There is a lively debate going on concerning the underlying factors producing the well-known results in terms of well-being (Braver and Lamb 2018; Braver and Votruba 2018; Fransson et al. 2018b). One of the preferred explanations is self-selection. It has been known for long that children living in JPC fare better in terms of well-being than those in single parent households (Bauserman 2002). If at the early stages of JPC development meta-analyses reported very positive associations between this custody arrangement and child well-being in most countries, these favourable results were possibly connected to the over-representation of parents with higher educational attainments. However, most international studies using regression models adjust for socioeconomic factors so that outcomes are not unduly influenced by this selectivity. Moreover, most JPC arrangements reported in meta-analyses were wilfully agreed on by parents in uncontested divorce proceedings. With an increasing spread of JPC parents become a more heterogeneous and less selected group, which may mean the erosion of the protective shelter provided by parental higher income and educational attainment (Trinder 2010; Sodermans et al. 2013). Even if most researchers tend to exclude the explanatory weight of self-selection and give support to a causal interpretation of advantageous results (Braver and Votruba 2018), it is nonetheless true that the cumulative heterogeneity of JPC parents may have an impact on the decline of their aggregate levels of family well-being.

Having said that, some analysts may wonder to what extent JPC tends to be a middle-class arrangement. Splitting one household into two homes requires an amount of resources that not everybody has. It is obvious that this process may involve higher costs beyond removal or relocation. Scale economies of the old home will be lost. Both father and mother must have viable independent incomes. If we take for granted that children go to the same school, then the distance between father's and mother's residences is a critical issue and it is not so easy to find affordable accommodation in certain urban areas. Parents must have enough income to provide for two different homes appropriate for children as well as to enjoy family-friendly working hours and work schedules (Nielsen 2013a). In this sense, even if the increase of JPC is driven by changing cultural norms, this progression may be influenced or offset by financial constraints and structural restrictions. Having more or less resources may facilitate or inhibit the prevalence of postseparation arrangements (Vanassche et al. 2017). One of emerging developments in postindustrial societies is an increasing stratification of family structures and it is bound to result in a growth of socioeconomic inequality among children (McLanahan and Percheski 2008; Garriga and Bernardi 2019). However, we know that parental educational gradients for JPC are positive in many countries and this may have a moderating effect for inequality.

A second common explanation is that having a close and intense relationship with both parents as in JPC yields more benefits to children because that is what resembles more to intact families. Utilising all the available skills, abilities, expertise, resources, strengths, opportunities, and social capital of both parents will probably maximise the results with respect to other families that, for whatever reason, they are not doing so. One of the reasons why children in JPC families get better outcomes is because they have more access to social capital from two parents, i.e. all the forms of those available assets and resources likely to enhance individuals' well-being. Another important resource is time as a necessary—but not a sufficient—factor for beneficial father involvement with children. It is essential that parents are thoroughly involved in children's lives if they are meant to have a positive bearing on their development. This not only requires plenty of interaction time with children, but also engagement in their activities on a regular and extensive basis in a variety of specific circumstances and contexts. In order to develop high-quality relationships influencing children's adjustment, fathers as well as mothers need in the first place to have enough time to foster opportunities for dealing with everyday lives routines, having frequent exchanges and sharing common experiences (Lamb et al. 1997; Austin 2011; Braver and Lamb 2012; Braver and Lamb 2018; Baude et al. 2016; Adamsons 2018).

Conclusion

The main conclusion of this analysis of shared parenting after separation and divorce in Europe is that its development results from the slow but steady progress of widespread and comprehensive gender equality. This trend goes hand in hand with various important advances in the framework of the SDT such as the demise of the "tender years presumption", the decline of the male breadwinner family model, and the intensification of children's centrality in the family as well as the increase in father involvement in the care of children. Although we do not yet fully know what are the links and mechanisms between the extension of gender equality and the spread of more equitable family arrangements after separation and divorce, it is most likely that both terms are making progress by means of a virtuous circle.

One of the lessons to be drawn from this chapter is the existence of wide differences among European countries regarding the gradual formation and expansion of JPC. Especially, a visible contrast between the far-flung position of Sweden and Belgium in relation to other countries is obviously noticeable (see Fig. 19.1). One can clearly observe that the bulk of the EU countries having lower JPC prevalences had also smaller GEI scores. Although the EU keeps moving towards gender equality at a snail's pace, it still has a lot of room for improvement. Since 2005, the GEI EU's score has increased by only 5.4 points, but in some countries recent advances have been extraordinary (European Institute for Gender Equality 2019).

In order to advance our understanding of JPC, it is absolutely necessary to have at our disposal equivalent and comparable indicators enabling to make a diagnosis of the situation as well as a prognosis of the future evolution of shared parenting in different countries across Europe.[9] With the purpose of regularly producing updated and comparable data, we badly need a European-wide survey enabling to obtain information, among others, about essential issues for JPC such as (1) prevalences and incidences of JPC; (2) percentages of contested cases of separation and divorce; (3) estimates of positive or negative gradients of parental educational attainment and/or socioeconomic status levels.

An important number of researchers have suggested that we should strive for the creation in the EU of a European cohort panel survey enabling longitudinal analysis (Fransson et al. 2016; Braver and Votruba 2018; Adamsons 2018; Steinbach 2019). The great advantage of cohort panel surveys is that they enable us to observe specific life events such as parental divorce and then to assess what are their long-lasting impacts on children in relation to counterparts from intact families. It may be then possible to ascertain with valid causal inferences from observational data whether children in JPC have similar, better or worse outcomes in terms of well-being than other children in different households or types of custody.

One of the ways in which the transition process of the SDT is expressed is through a permanent clash over different views as well as by opposition and conflict between various groups and sections of the population, including men and women. In many countries this divide is often the result of contrary stances of fathers' and mothers' associations over JPC as an issue (Hachet 2016). In this sense, one of the main conclusions of this chapter is that advocacy of JPC should be accompanied by the promotion of reforms in various fields of gender equality. Empowering women and men in all the areas where they have deficits, enhancing their rights, opportunities, and capabilities, reducing gender income gap, and combatting gender-based violence are the best guarantees for achieving a well-balanced society in which shared parenting after separation and divorce can develop and thrive.

Acknowledgements I would like to express my thanks to the scientific reviewers of the draft for their contribution to the clarification of many complex issues and to the improvement of various aspects of the text. Likewise, I am deeply indebted to Almudena Moreno (University of Valladolid) as well as to Marta Ortega and Carlos Gamero (University of Malaga) for their valuable comments and suggestions.

Notes

1. Its diffusion in recent years in many European countries has been accompanied by the proliferation of a number of different descriptive terms such as shared/joint residence, shared residency, alternating residence, dual residence, shared care, shared/joint custody, shared residential custody, shared-time parenting after separation, two homes and co-parenting after separation and divorce. Equally varied are the words employed in other European languages: résidence alternée (French); Wechselmodell, Pendelmodell, paritätische Doppelresidenz (German); affidamento condiviso (Italian); and custodia compartida (Spanish).
2. New developments corresponding to the SDT trends begin from the 1970s onward (Lesthaeghe 2014).
3. Whereas the percentage of contested cases of divorce is 23%, that of separations is 59,4% (Own calculations with statistical data for 2018 from INE and CGPJ).
4. The Health Behaviour in School-aged Children (HBSC) study is an international alliance of researchers that collaborate on a cross-national survey providing information about the health, health behaviour, well-being as well as social environment of school children from 45 countries covering regions across Europe and North America.
5. Labour Force Survey, Eurostat database, 2020.
6. I would like to express my deep appreciation to Professor Anja Steinbach and her team for letting me use their data on the prevalence of JPC in 37 countries (Steinbach et al. 2020), without which this section of the chapter could not have been drafted.
7. EIGE is an EU autonomous body, established to contribute to and strengthen the promotion of gender equality as a fundamental value of the European Union. GEI provides a composite statistical measure of gender equality developed by EIGE, intended to gauge the progress of gender equality in the EU. It consists of eight domains (work, money, knowledge, time, power, and health), and an additional two satellite indices (intersecting inequalities and violence). The range of score is 1–100 (European Institute for Gender Equality 2013).
8. Correlation is significant at the 0.01 level (2-tailed).
9. As a single example, to the best of my knowledge not a single Eurobarometer has been issued on JPC.

REFERENCES

Adamsons, Kari. 2018. "Quantity Versus Quality of Nonresident Father Involvement: Deconstructing the Argument That Quantity Doesn't Matter." *Journal of Child Custody* 15 (1): 26–34.

Algava, Elisabeth, Sandrine Penant, and Leslie Yankan. 2019. "En 2016, 400 000 enfants alternent entre les deux domiciles de leurs parents séparés." *INSEE Première* No. 1728 (January). Paris: INSEE.

Artis, Julie E. 2004. "Judging the Best Interests of the Child: Judges' Accounts of the Tender Years Doctrine." *Law & Society Review* 38 (4): 769–806.

Austin, William G. 2011. "Parental Gatekeeping in Custody Disputes: Mutual Parental Support in Divorce". *American Journal of Family Law* 25: 148–153.

Baude, Amandine, Jessica Pearson, and Sylvie Drapeau. 2016. "Child Adjustment in Joint Physical Custody Versus Sole Custody: A Meta-Analytic Review." *Journal of Divorce & Remarriage* 57 (5): 338–360.

Bauserman, Robert. 2002. "Child Adjustment in Joint-Custody Versus Sole-Custody Arrangements: A Meta-Analytic Review." *Journal of Family Psychology* 16 (1): 91–102.

Bergström, Malin, Bitte Modin, Emma Fransson, Luis Rajmil, Marie Berlin, Per A. Gustafsson, and Anders Hjern. 2013. "Living in Two Homes- A Swedish National Survey of Well-Being in 12 and 15 Year Olds with Joint Physical Custody." *BMC Public Health* 13: 868.

Bergström, Malin, Emma Fransson, Michael B. Wells, Lennart Köhler, and Anders Hjern. 2019. "Children with Two Homes: Psychological Problems in Relation to Living Arrangements in Nordic 2- to 9-Year-Olds." *Scandinavian Journal of Public Health* 47: 137–145.

Bjarnason, Thoroddur, and Arsaell M. Arnarsson. 2011. "Joint Physical Custody and Communication with Parents: A Cross-National Study of Children in 36 Western Countries." *Journal of Comparative Family Studies* 42: 871–890.

Bjarnason, Thoroddur, Pernille Bendtsen, Arsaell M. Arnarsson, Ina Borup, Ronald J. Iannotti, Petra Löfstedt, Ilona Haapasalo, and Birgit Niclasen. 2012. "Life Satisfaction Among Children in Different Family Structures: A Comparative Study of 36 Western Societies." *Children and Society* 26: 51–62.

Bonnet, Carole, Bertrand Garbinti, and Anne Solaz. 2015. "Les conditions de vie des enfants après le divorce." *Insee Première* No. 1536 (février). Paris: INSEE.

Braver, Sandford L., and Michael E. Lamb. 2012. "Marital Dissolution." In *Handbook of Marriage and the Family*, edited by Gary W. Peterson and Kevin R. Bush, 3rd ed., 487–516. New York, NY: Springer.

Braver, Sandford L., and Ashley M. Votruba. 2018. "Does Joint Physical Custody 'Cause' Children's Better Outcomes?" *Journal of Divorce & Remarriage* 59 (5): 452–468.

Braver, Sandford L., and Michael E. Lamb. 2018. "Shared Parenting After Parental Separation: The Views of 12 Experts." *Journal of Divorce and Remarriage* 59 (5): 372–387.

Breivik, Kyrre, and Dan Olweus. 2006. "Adolescent's Adjustment in Four Post-Divorce Family Structures: Single Mother, Stepfather, Joint Physical Custody and Single Father Families." *Journal of Divorce & Remarriage* 44 (3/4): 99–124.

Bryson, Caroline, Susan Purdon, and Amy Skipp. 2017. *Understanding the Lives of Separating and Separated Families in the UK: What Evidence Do We Need?* London: Nuffield Foundation.
Busse, Johannes Carl. 2018. "The Debate on Shared Parenting in Germany." *Politikon* 36 (April): 66–81.
Creighton, Colin. 1999. "The Rise and Decline of the 'Male Breadwinner Family' in Britain." *Cambridge Journal of Economics* 23 (5): 519–541.
Cretin, Laurette. 2015. "Résidence et pension alimentaire des enfants de parents séparés: Décisions initiales et évolutions." In *Insee Références* «Couples et familles», 41–49. Paris: INSEE.
Crompton, Rosemary, ed. 1999. *Restructuring Gender Relations and Employment: The Decline of the Male Breadwinner*. Oxford: Oxford University Press.
DiFonzo, J. Herbie. 2014. "From the Rule of One to Shared Parenting: Custody Presumptions in Law and Policy." *Family Court Review* 52 (2): 213–239.
Engster, Daniel, and Helena Olofsdotter Stensöta. 2011. "Do Family Policy Regimes Matter for Children's Well-Being?" *Social Politics* 18 (1): 82–124.
Escobedo, Anna, Lluís Flaquer, and Lara Navarro-Varas. 2012. "The Social Politics of Fatherhood in Spain and France: A Comparative Analysis of Parental Leave and Shared Residence." *Ethnologie Française* 42 (1): 117–126.
Esping-Andersen, Gøsta, and Francesco C. Billari 2015. "Re-theorizing Family Demographics." *Population and Development Review* 41 (1): 1–31.
Esping-Andersen, Gøsta. 2009. *The Incomplete Revolution: Adapting to Women's New Roles*. Cambridge: Polity Press.
European Institute for Gender Equality. 2013. *Gender Equality Index Report*. Vilnius, Lithuania: EIGE.
European Institute for Gender Equality. 2019. *Gender Equality Index 2019, Work— Life Balance Gender Equality Index Report*. Luxembourg: Publications Office of the European Union.
Fehlberg, Belinda, Bruce Smyth, Mavis Maclean, and Ceridwen Roberts. 2011a. "Legislating for Shared Time Parenting After Separation: A Research Review." *International Journal of Law, Policy and the Family* 25: 318–337.
Fehlberg, Belinda, Bruce Smyth, Mavis Maclean, and Ceridwen Roberts. 2011b. "Caring for Children After Parental Separation: Would Legislation for Shared Parenting Time Help Children?" *University of Oxford, Family Policy Briefing Paper No 7*.
Flaquer, Lluís. 2014. "Family-Related Factors Influencing Child Well-Being." In *Handbook of Child Well-Being*, edited by Asher Ben-Arieh, Ferran Casas, Ivar Frønes, and Jill E. Korbin, Vol. 4, 2229–2255. Dordrecht: Springer.
Flaquer, Lluís, Almudena Moreno Mínguez, and Tomás Cano López. 2016. "Changing Family Models: Emerging New Opportunities for Fathers in Catalonia (Spain)?" In *Balancing Work and Family in a Changing Society: The Fathers' Perspective*, edited by Isabella Crespi and Elisabetta Ruspini, 65–81. New York: Palgrave Macmillan.
Flaquer, Lluís, Anna Escobedo, Anna Garriga, and Carmen Moreno. 2017. "A igualdade de género, o bem-estar da criança e a residência alternada em Espanha." In *Uma família parental, duas casas. Residência alternada – Dinâmicas e práticas sociais*, edited by Sofia Marinho and Sónia Vladimira Correia, 87–105. Lisboa: Edições Sílabo.

Flaquer, Lluís, and Diego Becerril. 2020. "La ruptura de parejas en cifras: La realidad española." In *La gestión positiva de la ruptura de pareja con hijos*, edited by Francisca Fariña and Pascual Ortuño, 23–35. Valencia: Tirant lo Blanch.

Flaquer, Lluís, Tomás Cano, and Marc Barbeta-Viñas, eds. 2020. *La paternidad en España. La implicación paterna en el cuidado de los hijos*. Madrid: Consejo Superior de Investigaciones Científicas.

Fransson, Emma, Anders Hjern, and Malin Bergström. 2018b. "What Can We Say Regarding Shared Parenting Arrangements for Swedish Children? *Journal of Divorce & Remarriage* 59 (5): 349–358.

Fransson, Emma, Anna Sarkadi, Anders Hjern, and Malin Bergström. 2016. "Why Should They Live More with One of Us When They Are Children to Us Both? Parents' Motives for Practicing Equal Joint Physical Custody for Children Aged 0–4." *Children and Youth Services Review* 66: 154–160.

Fransson, Emma, Sara Brolin Låftman, Viveca Östberg, Anders Hjern, and Malin Bergström. 2018a. "The Living Conditions of Children with Shared Residence—The Swedish Example." *Child Indicators Research* 11 (3): 861–883.

Fritzell, Sara, Michael Gähler, and Emma Fransson. 2020. "Child Living Arrangements Following Separation and Mental Health of Parents in Sweden." *SSM - Population Health* 10: 100511.

Garriga, Anna, and Laura Bernardi. 2019. "Custody Arrangements and Social Inequalities Among Children." *Revue des politiques sociales et familiales* No. 131–132 (2nd and 3rd quarters): 203–217.

Gracia, Pablo. 2014. "Fathers' Child Care Involvement and Children's Age in Spain: A Time Use Study on Differences by Education and Mothers' Employment." *European Sociological Review* 30 (2): 137–150.

Hachet, Benoît. 2016. "La résidence alternée: Pratiques polémiques et normes ambivalentes." *Journal des anthropologues* (144–145): 191–219.

Halla, Martin. 2009. "The Effect of Joint Custody on Marriage and Divorce." IZA Discussion Paper No. 4314. Bonn: Forschungsinstitut zur Zukunft der Arbeit.

Hartenstein, Jaimee L. 2016. "Tender Years Doctrine." In *The Wiley Blackwell Encyclopedia of Family Studies*, edited by Constance L. Shenan. Hoboken, NJ: Wiley.

Haux, Tina, Stephen McKay, and Ruth Cain. 2017. "Shared Care After Separation in the United Kingdom: Limited Data, Limited Practice?" *Family Court Review* 55 (4): 572–585.

Hayden, Adrina. 2011. "Shared Custody: A Comparative Study of the Position in Spain and England." Universitat Pompeu Fabra, Barcelona (Spain): *InDret. 1/2011*.

HM Government 2004. *Parental Separation: Children's Needs and Parents' Responsibilities*. Green Paper Presented to Parliament. Norwich: The Licensing Division, HMSO.

Katz, Sanford N. 1992. "'That They May Thrive' Goal of Child Custody: Reflections on the Apparent Erosion of the Tender Years Presumption and the Emergence of the Primary Caretaker Presumption." *Journal of Contemporary Health Law & Policy* 8 (1): 123–136.

Klaff, Ramsay Laing. 1982. "The Tender Years Doctrine: A Defense." *California Law Review* 70: 335–372.

Kreidler-Pleus, D. 2018. "Family law in Germany: Overview." In *Family Law: A Global Guide from Practical Law*, 4th ed., edited by J. Stewart. London: Sweet & Maxwell Ltd.

Kurki-Suonio, K. 2000. "Joint Custody as an Interpretation of the Best Interests of the Child in Critical and Comparative Perspective." *International Journal of Law, Policy and the Family* 14: 183–205.

Lamb, Michael E. 2000. "The History of Research on Father Involvement: An Overview." *Marriage & Family Review* 29 (2/3): 23–42.

Lamb, Michael E. 2013. "The Changing Faces of Fatherhood and Father-Child Relationships: From Fatherhood as Status to Father as Dad." In *Handbook of Family Theories: A Content-based Approach*, edited by Mark A. Fine and Frank D. Fincham, 87–102. New York: Routledge.

Lamb, Michael E., Kathleen J. Sternberg, and Ross A. Thompson. 1997. "The Effects of Divorce and Custody Arrangements on Children's Behaviour, Development and Adjustment." *Expert Evidence* 5 (3): 83–88.

Lesthaeghe, Ron J. 2010. "The Unfolding Story of the Second Demographic Transition." *Population and Development Review* 36 (2): 211–251.

Lesthaeghe, Ron J. 2014. "The Second Demographic Transition: A Concise Overview of Its Development." *PNAS* 111 (51): 18112–18115.

Lesthaeghe, Ron J., and D. J. van de Kaa. 1986. "Twee Demografisch Transities?" (Two Demographic Transitions?). In *Bevolking: Groeien Krimp (Population: Growth and Decline)*, edited by D. J. van de Kaa and Ron. J. Lesthaeghe. Deventer: Van Loghum Slaterus.

Lewis, Jane, Mary Campbell, and Carmen Huerta. 2008. "Patterns of Paid and Unpaid Work in Western Europe: Gender, Commodification, Preferences and the Implications for Policy." *Journal of European Social Policy* 18 (1): 21–37.

Lewis, Jane. 2001. "The Decline of the Male Breadwinner Model: Implications for Work and Care." *Social Politics* 8 (2): 152–169.

Lewis, Jane. 2006. "Introduction: Children in the Context of Changing Families and Welfare States". In *Children, Changing Families and Welfare States*, edited by Jane Lewis, 1–24 Cheltenham: Elgar.

Marsiglio, William, Randal D. Day, and Michael E. Lamb. 2000. "Exploring Fatherhood Diversity: Implications for Conceptualizing Father Involvement." *Marriage & Family Review* 29 (4): 269–293.

Martin, Claude (1997). *L'après divorce. Lien familial et vulnérabilité*. Rennes: Presses Universitaires de Rennes.

Mason, Mary Ann. 1994. *From Father's Property to Children's Rights: The History of Child Custody in the United States*. New York: Columbia University Press.

Maydell, Marie von, and Nikolaus J. Plitzko. 2019. "Germany – Family Law 2020." Meyer–Köring. ICLG.com. Published 10 September 2019. https://iclg.com/practice-areas/family-laws-and-regulations/germany.

McLanahan, Sara, and Christine Percheski. 2008. "Family Structure and the Reproduction of Inequalities." *Annual Review of Sociology* (34): 257–276.

McLanahan, Sara. 2004. "Diverging Destinies: How Children Are Faring Under the Second Demographic Transition." *Demography* 41 (4): 607–627.

Melli, Marygold S., and Patricia R. Brown. 2008. "Exploring a New Family Form: The Shared Time Family." *International Journal of Law, Policy and the Family* 22 (2) (August): 231–269.

Neyrand, Gérard. 2009. *L'enfant face à la séparation des parents. Une solution, la résidence alternée*. Paris: La Découverte [1st edition, 1994].

Neyrand, Gérard. 2010. "La résidence alternée, una pratique en cours de légitimation." *Études* 2010/10, Tome 413: 331–341.

Nielsen, Linda. 2011. "Shared Parenting After Divorce: A Review of Shared Residential Parenting Research." *Journal of Divorce & Remarriage* 52 (8): 586–609.
Nielsen, Linda. 2013a. "Shared Residential Custody: Review of the Research (Part I of II)." *American Journal of Family Law* 27 (1): 61–71.
Nielsen, Linda. 2013b. "Shared Residential Custody: Review of the Research (Part II of II)." *American Journal of Family Law* 27 (2): 123–137.
Nielsen, Linda. 2014. "Shared Physical Custody: Summary of 40 Studies on Outcomes for Children." *Journal of Divorce & Remarriage* 55 (8): 613–635.
Nielsen, Linda. 2017. "Re-Examining the Research on Parental Conflict, Coparenting, and Custody Arrangements." *Psychology, Public Policy, and Law* 23 (2): 211–231.
Nielsen, Linda. 2018. "Joint Versus Sole Physical Custody: Outcomes for Children Independent of Family Income or Parental Conflict." *Journal of Child Custody* 15 (1): 35–54.
Nikolina, Natalie. 2015. *Divided Parents, Shared Children: Legal Aspects of (Residential) Co-Parenting in England, the Netherlands and Belgium*. European Family Law Volume 39. Cambridge: Intersentia.
Peacey, Victoria, and Joan Hunt. 2008. *Problematic Contact After Separation and Divorce? A National Survey of Parents*. London: One Parent Families/Gingerbread.
Perelli-Harris, Brienna, Wendy Sigle-Rushton, Michaela Kreyenfeld, Trude Lappegard, Renske Keizer, and C. Caroline Berghammer. 2010. "The Educational Gradient of Childbearing Within Cohabitation in Europe." *Population and Development Review* 36 (4) (December): 775–801.
Sigle-Rushton, Wendy, and Sara McLanahan. 2004. "Father Absence and Child Wellbeing: A Critical Review." In *The Future of the Family*, edited by Daniel P. Moynihan, Lee Rainwater, and Timothy M. Smeeding, 116–155. New York: Russell Sage Foundation.
Smyth, Bruce M. 2017. "Special Issue on Shared-Time Parenting After Separation." *Family Court Review* 55 (4): 494–499.
Sodermans, An Katrien, Koen Matthijs, and Gray Swicegood. 2013. "Characteristics of Joint Physical Custody Families in Flanders." *Demographic Research* 28, Art. 29: 821–848.
Solsona, Montse, and Jeroen Spijker. 2016. "Effects of the 2010 Civil Code on Trends in Joint Physical Custody in Catalonia: A Comparison with the Rest of Spain." *Population*-E 71 (2): 297–324.
Solsona, Montse, and Marc Ajenjo. 2017. "Joint Custody: One More Step Towards Gender Equality?" *Perspectives Demogràfiques* (8): 1–4.
Solsona, Montse, Marc Ajenjo, Cristina Brullet, and Amalia Gómez-Casillas. 2020. *La custodia compartida en los tribunales. ¿Pacto de pareja? ¿Equidad de género?* Barcelona: Icaria Antrazyt.
Stamps, Leighton E. 2002. "Age Differences Among Judges Regarding Maternal Preference in Child Custody Decisions." *Court Review* 38 (4) (Winter): 18–22.
Steinbach, Anja. 2019. "Children's and Parents' Well-Being in Joint Physical Custody: A Literature Review." *Family Process* 58 (2): 353–369.
Steinbach, Anja, Lara Augustijn, and Gerrit Corkadi. 2019. "The Prevalence of Joint Physical Custody Arrangements in Post-Separation Families in 38 Western Societies." Poster presented at the PAA Annual Meeting 2019, Austin (Texas, USA), April 2019, Poster Session 3, Marriage, Family, Households, & Unions.

Steinbach, Anja, Lara Augustijn, and Gerrit Corkadi. 2020. "Joint Physical Custody and Adolescents' Life Satisfaction in 37 North American and European Countries." *Family Process* X (X): 1–14.
Trinder, Liz. 2010. "Shared Residence: A Review of Recent Research Evidence." *Child and Family Law Quarterly* 22 (4): 475–498.
Turunen, Jani. 2015. "Shared Physical Custody and Children's Experience of Stress." *Families and Societies Working Papers Series* No. 24.
Turunen, Jani. 2017. "Shared Physical Custody and Children's Experience of Stress." *Journal of Divorce & Remarriage* 58 (5): 371–392.
Vanassche, Sofie, An Katrien Sodermans, Charlotte Declerck, and Koen Matthijs. 2017. "Alternating Residence for Children After Parental Separation: Recent Findings from Belgium." *Family Court Review* 55 (4): 545–555.
Walper, Sabine, and Ulrike Lux. 2016. "Das Wechselmodell nach Trennung und Scheidung in der Diskussion." *Frühe Kindheit* 19 (2): 6–15.
Walper, Sabine. 2016. "Arrangements elterlicher Fürsorge nach Trennung und Scheidung: Das Wechselmodell im Licht neuer Daten aus Deutschland." In Dt. Familiengerichtstag e.V. (Hg.), *Brühler Schriften zum Familienrecht*. 21. Deutscher Familiengerichtstag. Band 19, pp. 99–143. Bielefeld: Gieseking Verlag.
Walper, Sabine. 2018. "Elterliche Sorge und Wohn- bzw. Betreuungsarrangements." In *Familien nach Trennung und Scheidung in Deutschland*, edited by Esther Geisler, Katja Köppen, Michaela Kreyenfeld, Heike Trappe, and Matthias Pollmann-Schult, 16–17. Berlin, Rostock & Magdeburg: Hertie School of Governance, Universität Rostock & Otto von Guericke Universität Magdeburg.
Wroath, John. 1998. *Until They Are Seven: The Origins of Women's Legal Rights*. Winchester, UK: Waterside Press.
Zaidi, Batool, and S. Philip Morgan. 2017. "The Second Demographic Transition Theory: A Review and Appraisal." *Annual Review of Sociology* 43: 473–492.

CHAPTER 20

Subjective Well-Being of Children in the Context of Family Change in Estonia, Poland, and Romania

Dagmar Kutsar and Oliver Nahkur

Introduction

In the context of family change—general decline of the number of marriages, increasing evidence of cohabitations, divorces and separations of parents, and emerging new forms of living (e.g. blended families, families functioning as networks, etc.)—many children in Europe move from one household structure to another during their childhoods. There might be several such changes either increasing or decreasing the number of people with whom the child shares his or her home, with changing patterns of biological and non-biological bonds to the child. Family change uncovers a trend of spreading two adults' households with children where one is a biological and another a non-biological parent for the child. The latter may mean also a partner of the child's biological parent who does not identify him/herself as a step-parent.

Many studies have been carried out concerning the family structural change and its impacts on children's well-being (e.g. Vandewater and Lansford 1998; Amato 2005; Chapple 2013, to name a few). However, because there is no single and generally accepted measure of child well-being, the measures of well-being deficits are most typically used (Chapple 2013). In a seminal analysis made by Amato (2005) about children in the US, he concludes that the impact of family structure on cognitive, social, and emotional functioning of

D. Kutsar (✉) · O. Nahkur
University of Tartu, Tartu, Estonia
e-mail: dagmar.kutsar@ut.ee

O. Nahkur
e-mail: oliver.nahkur@ut.ee

© The Author(s), under exclusive license to Springer Nature Switzerland AG 2021
A.-M. Castrén et al. (eds.), *The Palgrave Handbook of Family Sociology in Europe*, https://doi.org/10.1007/978-3-030-73306-3_20

children is small because children's problems may have many other grounds than only the family type. Still, he argues that children growing up with two continuously married parents are less likely to experience a wide range of problems, both during childhood and in their adulthood. The dominance of Anglophone research on the impact of family structure on child well-being exists, thus the generalisability of these research results has been questioned (Chapple 2013). In the present chapter, we focus on children's subjective well-being in Estonia, Poland, and Romania. These countries belong to the post-communist/Central-Eastern European region where in many aspects, the family change has been the most notable from the 1990s onwards (Oláh 2015), but the change has occurred with different scope.

The way children that experience different living arrangements assess their well-being and what aspects of family life have the major impacts on children's subjective lives, have been loosely studied so far. Research on children's subjective well-being has grown from a 'new' paradigm of understanding children and childhoods (e.g. Qvortrup 1991; Ben-Arieh et al. 2014; James and James 2004), with the view on children as active social agents who are competent according to their age. Thus, children are worth and reliable sources of information about their life experiences (Ben-Arieh 2008; Kutsar et al. 2018; Mason and Danby 2011; Casas 2019). Previous research on children's subjective well-being has shown that the family as the closest life environment is the major determinant of a child's subjective well-being (Ash and Huebner 2001; Henry 1994; Joronen and Astedt-Kurki 2005) compared to neighbourhood and school (Dew and Huebner 1994; Gilman and Huebner 2003; Lee and Yoo 2015). Relations between family members, parenting skills, and many other factors as perceived by a child form the child's subjective family picture that cannot be substituted by adults' opinions or 'guesses' (e.g. Ben-Arieh 2019; Casas 2019). For many western industrialised countries (Bjarnason et al. 2012), including Estonia (Dinisman et al. 2017), there is evidence that children living with two parents assess their well-being higher than children living in other household structures. However, in Romania no household structure differences in subjective well-being were found by Lee and Yoo (2015). Moreover, only in the case of Estonia, there is previous evidence that children living with both parents evaluate their family material and relational well-being higher than children living in a single-parent family and in separated families (Dinisman et al. 2017). We are not aware of any such research evidence about Poland. Keeping family change in the context, the aim of this chapter is to explore subjective well-being in relation to their assessments about family life of children from Estonia, Poland, and Romania living with both birth parents, with a birth and step-parent or with a single parent.

The chapter draws data from the second wave of the International Study of Children's Well-Being "Children's Worlds" (ISCWeB) harmonised dataset of 12-year-old children. ISCWeB is a rich resource of children's assessments about their well-being and living conditions. We chose to focus on Estonia,

Poland, and Romania because they were the only post-communist countries who participated in the ISCWeB second wave in 2013/2014. We ask, whether living in a family with both biological parents; one of them being a step-parent/partner of the biological parent, or living with a single parent, favours the formation of child-friendly atmosphere at home and bolsters child's subjective well-being in child's perceptions. Children defined their household structures by listing all people they live with and answered several questions about relational and material aspects of family life. They also assessed their subjective well-being by answering the question "How satisfied are you with your life as a whole?" Children had an opportunity to define the second 'home' if they had it and its structure because a child may live at times with one parent and another parent, moving between these two. Because of a small number of children commuting between two family nuclei (the birth mother's and father's, who had separated or divorced and formed new households), the chapter will not develop this aspect. We chose to explore twelve years old children's perceptions instead of children of eight and ten years old who also participated in the ISCWeB survey because they have experienced changes in living arrangements with higher probability than younger children.

Family Change—The Context of Children's Subjective Well-Being

Eurostat presents population statistics regarding fertility (including numbers of live births out of the marriage applied also as an indirect indicator of cohabitations), marriages, and divorces. No statistics exist on separations from cohabitation, two-parent families with one of them being a non-biological parent for the child or about blended families that cross the borders of a single household. Thus, the statistics on diversity of household structures is far from complete. Still, the official statistics reveal a diverse picture between the EU countries (e.g. Oláh 2015; OECD 2011; Eurostat 2017) that intrigues researchers to further focus on separate country practices. In many aspects, family change has been the most notable in Central-Eastern European region from the 1990s onwards (see Oláh 2015).

Eurostat (2019) concludes the problems with the family unit as being a changing concept: "… what it means to be a member of a family and the expectations people have of family relationships vary with time and space, making it difficult to find a universally agreed and applied definition. Legal alternatives to marriage, like registered partnerships, have become more widespread and national legislation has changed to confer more rights on unmarried and same sex couples. Alongside these new legal forms, other forms of non-marital relationships have appeared, making it more difficult for statisticians to collect data within this domain that can be compared across countries". However, mapping the changing family structures is possible by drawing data from cross-sectional harmonised international social studies such as European Union Statistics on Income and Living Conditions (EU-SILC) or

European Social Survey (ESS), or last but not least: asking from children about the people they live with (e.g. ISCWeB). Even then, the family structures are not dynamic but snapshots of the measurement moment incorporating invisible structural diversity and its change, where a household (family) member defines the membership when ticking 'right' persons to form the unity for this social study, thus containing some driving forces of a subjective family picture (Kutsar and Raid 2019).

According to Eurostat (2019), the number of marriages per 1,000 persons decreased within the EU countries during recent decades, while the number of divorces increased. An increase in the proportion of children who are born to unmarried couples also occurred. Estonia, Poland, and Romania followed similar trends of family formation and breakup. Between the years 2008–2018, *crude marriage rate* (the number of marriages per 1,000 population) decreased in Poland until 2013, then stabilised around 5.0; the same trend was observed in Romania until 2011 and since 2013 it started to increase, reaching 7.4 in 2018. The latter is the highest among the three countries under observation. In Estonia, the crude marriage rate decreased until 2010 and since then is fluctuating in the range of 4.1–5.2. In this period, the crude marriage rate has stayed above EU-28 average (4.1–4.8) in Romania and Poland, and from 2013 also in Estonia. *Crude divorce rate* (the number of divorces per 1,000 population) has not changed much, but a slight increase occurred between 2008–2018 in Estonia, Poland, and Romania. It was consistently above EU-28 average (1.8–2.0) in Estonia (2.2–2.6) while below it in Poland (1.6–1.8) and Romania (1.4–1.8). *Proportion of live births outside marriage as an indirect indicator of cohabitation* has not changed much between 2008 and 2018 in Estonia (54.1–59.7%) being the highest of the three countries and markedly above the EU average (36.1–42.4%). It is taking a slight increasing trend in Poland (from 19.9% in 2008 to 25% in 2016) and Romania (from 27.4 to 32% respectively). Based on Eurostat's (*various years*) Income and Living Conditions database and EU-SILC data from 2009–2018, *the share of single person households with dependent children* have been above EU-28 average (3.9–4.3) in Estonia until 2013, and below it in Poland (1.9–2.4) and Romania (1.8–2.5). When in 2009–2013 the share of single-person households with dependent children in Estonia increased from 4.8 to 5.9%, then in 2014–2018 it decreased to 3.9–4.2%. However, according to 2011 census data (OECD 2016), single-parent households formed 8.6% from all households in Estonia, 7.7% in Poland, and 5.7% in Romania (EU average 6.8%).

Based on the Income and Living Conditions database, Eurostat establishes that Children in Estonia live less frequently with both married parents, and more frequently with both parents cohabiting or with a single parent compared to children in Poland and Romania. In more detail, in 2009–2018, 51–54% of Estonian children lived with both married parents, being one of the lowest rate among EU countries. The EU-28 average has been 68–72%. In Romania, approximately eight in ten and in Poland two in three children lived with both married parents. However, also in those countries the trend is decreasing. In Romania in 2009 and 2018, 88 and 79% of children lived with both married parents, respectively, the decrease being steepest in 2012. In Poland in 2012 and 2018, 77 and 63% of children lived with both married parents, respectively, the decrease being steepest in 2018. In 2009, every fourth and in 2018 every third child in Estonia lived with cohabiting parents, being the highest rate among European Union countries (in 2018 EU-28 average 15%). The same steady increase is also noticeable in Romania and Poland, 0 to 7% and 11 to 27%, respectively. In Estonia, about nine per cent of children lived with a step-parent according to the 2011 Civil Census (Laes et al. 2013, 33).

In Romania, 10–11% of children lived with single parent and it has not changed in the years 2009–2018 (based on EU-SILC data in Eurostat's Income and Living Conditions database). In Poland, the rate of children living with single parent has decreased in 2009–2018 from 13 to 9%. Until 2014, children in Estonia have been living with single parent less frequently than in EU-28 on average. In 2009, every fifth child in Estonia lived with single parent, but in 2018, it was 15% of the children (EU-28 average 16%). According to Laes et al. (2013), most often (93%) they live with their mother, over half of them have no siblings, and the older the children, the more likely they are to live with one parent (17% of children aged under three and 29% of children aged 12–17).

In sum, living in diverse household structures has been an increasing trend in children's lives in all three countries but the developments have different scope. Family change has been most extensive in Estonia, followed by Poland and then Romania. Among three countries, Estonia has been characterised by the lowest marriage, highest divorce and cohabitation rates, children have least frequently lived with both married parents, and most frequently with both parents cohabiting or with a single parent while Romania has the highest marriage rate, including children most frequently live with both married parents and least frequently with cohabiting parents, and has lowest share of single-parent households. However, some indicators (e.g. crude marriage rate, share of single-person households with dependent children) hint that most recently family change is slowing down or even is taking a reverse trend in these countries.

CHILDREN ASSESS THEIR WELL-BEING AND FAMILY LIFE

Former studies that have explored the relations between child well-being outcomes and family change did not show remarkable differences between the household composition groups (e.g. Vandewater and Lansford 1998; Lee and Yoo 2015; Chapple 2013; Amato 2005) or they showed slight preference of stably married parents raising common children in the same household. Most recently, Ben-Arieh (2019) suggested exploring possible relations between the household composition and subjective well-being: how children evaluate their lives as a whole and with regard to particular aspects of life, in different cultures. With only little previous research (Bjarnason et al. 2012; Dinisman et al. 2017; Lee and Yoo 2015) on this, the present chapter attempts to add research evidence from Estonia, Poland, and Romania using data from the second wave of the International Survey of Children's Well-Being "Children's Worlds" (ISCWeB) in 2013/2014. ISCWeB is a large-scale survey among a representative sample of at least 1,000 children in each age group (8, 10, and 12) globally. It utilises children's perceptions and focuses on their overall life satisfaction and specific domains of their lives, such as the child's home, school, and neighbourhood. Currently, we focus on 12-year-old children's subjective well-being in general and in relation to its material and relational aspects of their family life. In this tabulate, Estonia, Romania, and Poland had 717 (73.4%), 1236 (89.3%), 848 (87.9%) children respectively living with two biological parents, 112 (11.5%), 69 (5%), 57 (5.9%) children, living with biological and step-parent, and 148 (15.1%), 79 (5.7%), 60 (6.2%) children living with single[1] parent.

Children's Overall Life Satisfaction

Looking at children's subjective well-being means hereby measuring how children assess their lives as a whole ("How satisfied are you with your life as a whole?"). We look at it in relation to appraisals of material and relational aspects of family life. It is important to clarify that assessments of subjective well-being are diverted to the positive side of the measurement scale. This normally positive sense of subjective well-being is rather abstract involving both, cognitive and affective appraisals that individuals make about their lives in general (Diener 2009). Cummins (2014) stated that the subjective well-being if measured as a single item is robustly ranging between 60 and 90 on 100 points scale with a mean of 75. Casas (2019) calls it optimistic bias and considers it to be even higher among children than among adults. Children's Worlds study has confirmed this evidence: the highest mean life satisfaction scores in children ranged from 77 out of 100 in South Korea to 95 out of 100 in Romania (Rees and Main 2015). Cummins (2014) proposed a theory of homeostasis of the subjective well-being: people can manage its level alike they manage body temperature—we tend to revert to our baseline after some time whenever any positive or negative event has impacted our lives (Casas 2019). However, if the life event is lasting or if several negative life events cumulate for a longer time, the decline of one's subjective well-being can stabilise on a lower level. In case of children, we suppose that lasting destructive family relationships, child abuse or neglect may cause permanent decline of the child's subjective well-being. According to Cummins (2014, c.f. Casas 2019), whether homeostatic theory tenets apply to children is a pending major test of their validity.

In this chapter, we follow mean assessments of children and show the proportions of children who gave maximum appraisals (10 points on the 0…10 points scale) to their overall life satisfaction. We also highlight the share of children with very low appraisals (0...4 points on the 0...10 points scale). Even when the percentages of children with very low subjective well-being are not high, they deserve attention. These children may face lasting negative life circumstances and may fall into mental health problems, most often this is depression.

Looking more specifically on the three sample countries, 12-year-old children in Romania appear to be the most satisfied with their life as a whole (9.5 points out of 10) followed by Estonia and Poland (8.8 and 8.5, respectively). In all three countries, children's household type seems to matter to their life satisfaction, but not to statistically significant ($p < 0.05$) level.[2] As a slight tendency, children living with two biological parents tend to be more satisfied with their life compared to children living with birth and step-parent in Romania (76 vs 58% gave maximum points) and in Estonia (53 vs 43%). In Poland, these two assessments did not differ (46 vs 47%). We also tabulated the percentage of children who gave low estimate (0...4 points on the scale from 0 to 10) to their life satisfaction. In case of living with biological parents, there were 3% in Estonia, 1% in Romania, and 5% in Poland compared to 6%, 4%, and 6% respectively, who lived with a step-parent. As a general pattern, living with a single parent was related to higher life satisfaction compared to children living with a step-parent. Poland is also outlier here: only 27% of children living with a single parent gave maximum points to their life satisfaction (in Estonia 41% and Romania 64%) while 9% assessed it low (4% in Estonia and 0% in Romania).

Material Well-Being and Overall Life Satisfaction

In the Children's Worlds study children were asked about their satisfaction with things they have and the flat or house where they live; how often they worry how much money their family has, and having a quiet place to study at home. Romanian children were most satisfied with first two material aspects of their family life (75% gave maximum points), and Polish children were least frequently worried about how much money their family had (34% never worried) but instead most frequently agreed that they had a quiet place to study at home (90% totally agreed).

Children's assessments about material aspects of their lives were not related to the household structure in Romania. In Estonia, children living with birth parents were more positive towards the house or flat they live in and having a quiet place to study at home compared to children living in biological and step-parent family or a single-parent family. In Poland, children living with birth parents were more positive towards house or flat they live in compared to children living with a step-parent.

Material aspects are rather important in children's lives. According to regression analysis, *the observed material aspects accounted for 30% of overall life satisfaction variance in the case of children living with biological and step-parent or a single parent, and 21% in the case of living with both birth parents.*

Thus, material aspects of family life matter more in those children's overall life satisfaction who live in step-parent or single-parent household. *Satisfaction with all the things possessing and satisfaction with the house or flat where living in were most influential to children's overall life satisfaction regardless of their household type.* It is apparent that a child as an active social actor needs a decent living place and own things to perform their agency, and family change may uncover risks of meeting the child's needs.

Relational Well-Being and Overall Life Satisfaction

Subjective well-being is a process that receives impacts from relationships with other people, in other words it is context-based. In the Children's Worlds study, children were asked three types of questions concerning relationships in their homes. First, these were frequency-type questions: how often do you talk, have fun, and learn together. In general, the children's assessments did not differ significantly regarding living arrangement. The only exception was 'talking together' in case of Polish children: 30% of children living with step-parent answered that in their family they not at all or once-twice talked in the past week together compared to 13% of children with both birth parents and 16% living with single parents.

Another group of questions were agreement type: whether the child agrees or not with 'I feel safe at home'; 'my parents/carers listen to and take what I say into account'; 'my parents/carers treat me fairly' and 'we have good time together in my family'. Children agreed most with the statement of 'feeling safe at home'—in Poland 90%, in Estonia 83%, and in Romania 74% agreed totally with the statement, without significant difference by household types in Romania and Poland. The exception was Estonia where 7% of children living with a step-parent did not agree with the statement (2% of children with birth parents and 4% living with single parents). Still, 8% of children living with single parents in Romania did not feel safe at home—this is the highest proportion of children feeling not safe at home compared to the same groups in Estonia and Poland. 'My parents/carers listen to me' and 'treat me fairly' show similar pattern of the lowest total agreement across the countries (51–57% agreed totally with the 'listening to question' and 66–74% agreed totally that they are treated fairly). Romanian children's assessments did not differ significantly by household type while children living with birth parents in Estonia and Poland were more positive than children living with a step-parent. Children's appraisal of listening to the child, taking his or her opinion into account and fair treatment reflect new parenting skills of treating a child as a subject and an active social actor who owns personal opinions and social competencies. Paraphrasing Ben-Arieh (2019, 18), fair treatment 'calls for respecting children and their rights and accepting them as human beings, regardless of any differences between them and adults'. In Estonia 73%, in Poland 68% and in Romania 62% agreed totally with the statement 'we have good time together in my family'. Children living with birth parents in Estonia and living with birth parents or single parent in Poland were more positive than children living with a step-parent. In Romania, no significant difference occurred between children living in different household types.

Last but not least, children answered to the questions, 'how satisfied are you with your family life' and 'how satisfied are you with people you live with'. Similarly, to the highest assessments of subjective well-being, Romanian children were most satisfied without significant differences in the mean scores between the household types (82–85% living with birth parents; 74–80% of living with single parent and 70–74% of living in a biological-step-parent household gave maximum 10 points). In Estonia and Poland 62–68% of children with birth parents and 40–49% with step-parents gave the highest assessments to people they live with and their family life. Polish children living with single parents were most critical hereby: only 35% gave maximum appraisal to their family life and 47% were satisfied with people they live with (in Estonia the respective percentages were 52 and 62).

To conclude the patterns of children's appraisals about relationships in their households by country and household type, *it occurs that in almost all of the observed family relational aspects Estonian and Polish children living with birth parents were more positive compared to the children living with biological and step-parent*. Estonian and Polish children living with birth parents were more satisfied with their family life compared to children living in biological-step-parent family or in a single-parent family. They were more satisfied with the people they live with, agreed more that they have a good time together in their family, agreed more often with the statement that their parents/carers listen to them and take what they say into account and treat them fairly compared to children living in biological and step-parent family. In many family relational aspects, Romanian children living with birth parents were also more positive compared to children living in other household types but these differences were not statistically significant.

Next we explore whether and which family relational well-being assessments have significant impacts on overall life satisfaction of children. For this purpose, we first tabulated correlations between family relational aspects and overall life satisfaction and then processed a regression analysis. Regardless of country and family type, among various relational aspects of family life children's overall life satisfaction was most strongly related to their satisfaction with their family life (Table 20.1). However, Romanian and Polish children living with their biological and step-parent were the exceptions. For Romanian children living in biological-step-parent household, overall life satisfaction was most strongly associated with their satisfaction with the people they live with, and in the Polish case with the fair treatment by their parents/carers. *In the case of Estonian and Polish children, different relational aspects of family seem to be more strongly related to their overall life satisfaction for those who live in birth and step-parent or single parent household and less for children living with two biological parents.*

Table 20.1 Correlations between family relational aspects and overall life satisfaction (*Spearman r*)

	I feel safe at home	We have a good time together in my family	How often do family talk together	My parents/ carers listen to me and take what I say into account	My parents/ carers treat me fairly	Satisfaction with the people you live with	Satisfaction with your family life
EE birth parents	0.27*	0.32*	0.15*	0.25*	0.32*	0.33*	0.40*
PL birth parents	0.27*	0.33*	0.21*	0.36*	0.32*	0.41*	0.45*
RO birth parents	0.14*	0.30*	0.24*	0.22*	0.21*	0.24*	0.31*
EE birth and step parent	0.32*	0.49*	0.27*	0.42*	0.52*	0.52*	0.64*
PL birth and step parent	0.34*	0.34*	0.29*	0.39*	0.52*	0.33*	0.38*
RO birth and step parent	0.13	0.28*	0.28*	0.10	−0.02	0.35*	0.30*
EE single parent	0.34*	0.45*	0.27*	0.33*	0.46*	0.39*	0.58*
PL single parent	0.44*	0.36*	0.42*	0.47*	0.44*	0.43*	0.52*
RO single parent	0.06	0.32*	0.21	0.09	0.25*	0.41*	0.43*

*$p < .05$

The regression analysis revealed that children's appraisals of different family relational aspects accounted for 41% of overall life satisfaction variance in the case of children living with a single parent or birth and step-parent when only 25% in the case of children living with birth parents. Thus, the family relational aspects matter more in those children's overall life satisfaction who live in step-parent or single-parent household. More specifically, 'satisfaction with their family life', 'people they live with' and 'having good time together in their family' have the strongest relation to overall life satisfaction in the case of Estonian children living in birth and step-parent household (Table 20.1). Fair treatment by their parents/carers is most strongly related to life satisfaction in the case of Estonian and Polish children living in a biological-step-parent household type. To be listened to and to be taken into account by parents/carers is most strongly related to overall life satisfaction in the case of Estonian children living in birth-step-parent household and Polish single-parent household. Feeling safe at home and frequency of talking together has the strongest relation to overall life satisfaction in the case of Polish children living with a single parent. In the case of Romanian children living with biological and step-parent and/or a single parent, many aspects, for example, feeling safe at home, fair treatment and to be listened to by their parents/carers, frequency of talking together in their family, were not related statistically significantly to overall life satisfaction.[3]

Regression analyses confirmed that *among different family relational aspects children's satisfaction with their family life was most influential to their life satisfaction regardless of their household type. For children living in biological-step-parent household or with a single parent, fair treatment was the next most influential aspect to their life satisfaction.* However, for children living with both biological parents the next most influential aspect to their overall life satisfaction was their satisfaction with people they live with. Following the research evidence from the analysis of children's assessments of their subjective well-being, we suggest that family transitions and change of the household composition is a challenge for children to cope with and for parents to focus on improving their life and parenting skills.

REFLECTIONS AND CONCLUSIONS

Among different life domains, family is a major determinant of children's subjective well-being (e.g. Ash and Huebner 2001; Dew and Huebner 1994; Gilman and Huebner 2003; Henry 1994; Joronen and Astedt-Kurki 2005). We explored the children's assessments about their family life in relation to their subjective well-being in Estonia, Poland, and Romania, in the countries belonging to post-communist/Central-Eastern European region where in many aspects, the family change has been the most notable in the EU from the 1990s onwards (see Oláh 2015). However, going through critical family transitions and living in diverse living arrangements is an increasing trend in children's lives in all three countries but the developments have different scope. Do the diverse household patterns matter for children in their perspectives? The findings show that in general around a half of children in Estonia and Poland, and in Romania about three quarters are totally satisfied with their life (on 0...10 points scale marking 10). It appears that life transitions uncover a challenge: in all three countries children living with birth parents tend to be more satisfied with their lives in general compared to children living with a step-parent or being a part of a single-parent household. However, in Estonia children living with a step-parent are least satisfied with their *family life* compared to Poland where those living with a single parent. Nevertheless, the most general finding confirms that if a child is satisfied with the family life, he or she has also high overall life satisfaction, regardless of the household type. In children's perspectives, fair treatment in a family is an influential determinant of life satisfaction, especially if the child lives with a step-parent in Poland or in Estonia.

In Estonia, where the scope of family change is biggest among the three countries, the appraisals of family relational and material aspects of children living in different household types differ most markedly. In addition to their lowest overall life satisfaction, children living with a step-parent had the lowest satisfaction with their family life and people they live with, house or flat where they live in. They most likely did not agree that they have good time together with their family, that their home is safe, parents/carers treat them fairly and listen to them and take into account what they say; they most likely did not agree that they have a quiet place to study at home. Moreover, children in Estonia who lived with biological and step-parent gave assessments that in almost all different family relational and material aspects were most strongly related to their overall life satisfaction compared to children living with both biological parents or a single parent. In contrast, in Romania where the family change is the lowest, the appraisals of family relational and material aspects of children living in different household types did not differ much. In Poland, standing between Estonia and Romania in terms of scope of family change, the appraisals of family relational and material aspects of children living in different household types differed a bit. In Poland, children living with a single parent had the lowest overall life satisfaction and their assessments in almost all family relational and material aspects were most strongly related to their overall life satisfaction. In sum, it may show that in the process of family change children's perceptions about their family, including its relational and material aspects, will become more important in their overall life satisfaction.

Children favour living with two biological parents. This is most safe for them—91% of Polish, 85% of Estonian, and 74% of Romanian children living with their birth parents totally agreed with the statement. The boundaries of a subjective family of a child in this case are clear and not debated. In Estonia more often than in Poland and Romania, children face separation or divorce of their parents. According to Levin (1994, c.f. Kutsar and Raid 2019, 89–90), the children of separated parents understand family differently. The child may think that he or she belongs to the mother's, father's, or both families, but may also fall in-between without directly belonging to either. The latter may happen if both parents develop new families and the child has one or even two step-parents/partners of their mother and father to cope with. A blended family type is according to Marsolini (2000) a three-part network: it includes the current family, the former family of the parent and the former family of the new partner. For a child, reconstruction of a new subjective family is complicated because of attempts of keeping biological parents in their family framework and accepting a 'new' parent. Castrén and Widmer (2015) found that the mother who lives with the child often drives the reconstruction of family boundaries for children. In the present chapter, we highlighted a research evidence from Poland: only 35% of children in single-parent households were most satisfied with their family life and 9% were really concerned about it. It is most important that separated or divorced parents could be able to continue being parents for the child. First, this needs good life skills of resolving their own problems and tensions, and second, requires very good parenting skills to help the child in saving his or her family unity or refreshing it. But living as a single parent may face several other challenges, for instance related with declining life conditions after the separation or divorce and/or emerging problems of economic coping.

Only 39% of children in Estonia living with a step-parent (against 66% living with birth parents) assessed their family life as totally satisfying; 44% totally agreed that they are listened to and their opinions are taken into account (against 52% of children living with birth parents). Accepting a new adult as a step-parent is a challenge for a child but this is an even bigger challenge for the 'newcomer' in the child's household to become accepted as a 'new parent'. Moreover, also the biological parent is challenged how to manage with the change by taking the child's best interests into consideration.

There is less confusion for a child living in a blended family if the child's parents who live separately can solve their issues in a peaceful manner and communicate in a friendly way. Children value family as a well-functioning network that transcends the boundaries of a single household and encompasses several family nuclei. For example, a child living in a blended family who was actively engaged with father living separately, said, "I like living in that family. I like that everyone loves each other and doesn't fight. That is why it is the best family, I would not change anything!" (Kutsar and Raid 2019, 90). Moreover, separation or divorce of parents may increase the child's quality of life if this ended violence and maltreatment in a child's life. It seems that traditional norms and values associated with a family hamper the development of the family as a network (Kutsar and Raid 2019, 91). The latter can be true also for children living in a single-parent family. Single parenting can capture diverse contexts—it may be the result of a separation, divorce, or death of the other parent or parents never lived together. Polish children who live in single-parent families are least satisfied with their life: 64% of children in Romania, 41% in Estonia and only 27% of children in Poland find they are totally satisfied with life. They are also least satisfied with their family life. What are the concerns of Polish children who live with a single parent? This aspect needs further research.

Family change and living in changing and diverse household structures uncover risks of decreasing subjective well-being of children. It can be less abrupt if parents develop parenting cultures of doing the family and manage family transitions.

The present narrative has a serious limitation: it tries to combine two basic approaches—the family as a unit of change where a household (birth parents/birth and step-parent/single parent) is in the focus and used as a synonym for a family. On the other hand, the focus is put on children's perceptions as units of analysis whose subjective family may not consider all people they live with as their family members or they may include some out of their household. People out of the present household (e.g. a parent living separately from the child) can influence a child's subjective well-being directly or mediated by the present household members and may stay in the child's cognitive map as his or her family member.

Learning about children's perceptions is not an easy task because children can give answers that are not expected or wished by adults. In the current chapter, we learned that the household composition may not be the major determining factor of the child's subjective well-being in case adults are able to manage their own issues and keep good relationships with the child. The analysis of children's perceptions revealed that living with birth parents uncovers less risks of well-being compared to other household types and especially living with the step-parent. This is a strong message from children to adults: listen to your child, be connected and treat him or her fairly, especially in the context of spreading family change across countries as the broader context. Learning about children's perceptions is not an easy task because the items asked from children may not be the most indicative in the child's terms. This is why qualitative approach should accompany quantitative to dig deeper into children's worlds and create new understandings about children's subjective well-being. Moreover, internationally harmonised longitudinal data would be needed to be able to reveal the causality of the relationship between family change and children's (subjective) well-being and also understand the country practices. Last but not least, countries should continue asking children's opinions and prioritise their subjective well-being because learning about children's perceptions helps to create better lives for children and their families.

Acknowledgements This publication was supported by a grant from the Estonian Research Council (PRG700).

Notes

1. Also single grandparents or step-parents are included.
2. In this empirical sub-section, statistically significant ($p < 0.05$) differences are described unless otherwise stated.
3. To some extent, this can be so because of quite small number of respondents (N), ranging between 60 and 80. However, in the case of Polish children living in biological and step-parent or single-parent family, N was about the same size and almost all of these family relational aspects were statistically significantly related to overall life satisfaction.

References

Amato, P. R. 2005. "The Impact of Family Formation Change on the Cognitive, Social, and Emotional Well-Being of the Next Generation." *The Future of Children* 15 (2): 75–96.

Ash, C., and E. S. Huebner. 2001. "Environmental Events and Life Satisfaction Reports of Adolescents: a Test of Cognitive Mediation." *School Psychology International* 22 (3): 320–336.

Ben-Arieh, A. 2008. "The Child Indicators Movement: Past, Present and Future." *Child Indicators Research* 1 (1): 3–16.
Ben-Arieh, A. 2019. "The Well-Being of the World's Children: Lessons from the International Survey of Children's Well-Being." In *Children's Subjective Well-Being in Local and International Perspectives*, edited by Dagmar Kutsar and Kadri Raid, 18–29. Tallinn: Statistikaamet.
Ben-Arieh, A., F. Casas, I. Frønes, and J. Korbin. 2014. "Multifaced Concept of Child Well-Being." In *Handbook of Child Well-Being*, edited by Ben-Arieh, A., F. Casas, I. Frønes, and J. Korbin., 1–27. Dordrecht: Springer.
Bjarnason, T., P. Benstsen, A. M. Arnarsson, I. Borup, R. J. Iannotti, P. Löfstedt, I. Haapasalo, and B. Niclasen. 2012. "Life Satisfaction Among Children in Different Family Structures: A Comparative Study of 36 Western Societies." *Children and Society* 26: 51–62.
Casas, F. 2019. "Are All Children Very Happy? An Introduction to Children's Subjective Well-Being in International Perspective." In *Children's Subjective Well-Being in Local and International Perspectives*, edited by Dagmar Kutsar and Kadri Raid, 6–17. Tallinn: Statistikaamet.
Castrén, A-M., and E. Widmer. 2015. "Insiders and Outsiders in Stepfamilies: Adults' and Children's Views on Family Boundaries." *Current Sociology* 63 (1): 35–56.
Chapple, S. 2013. "Child Well-Being and Single Parenthood Across the OECD." In *Family Well-Being: European Perspectives*, edited by A. Moreno Mínguez, 73–100. Springer: Dordrecht.
Cummins, R. A. 2014. "Understanding the Well-Being of Children and Adolescents Through Homeostàtic Theory." In *Handbook of Child Well-Being*, edited by Asher Ben-Arieh, Ferran Casas, Ivar Frønes, and Jill Korbin, 635–662. Dordrecht: Springer.
Dew, T., and E. S. Huebner. 1994. "Adolescents' Perceived Quality of Life: An Exploratory Investigation." *Journal of School Psychology* 32 (2): 185–199.
Diener, E. 2009. "Assessing Subjective Well-Being: Progress and Opportunities." In *Assessing Wellbeing*, 25–65. Springer: Dordrecht.
Dinisman, T., S. Andresen, C. Montserrat, D. Strózik, and T. Strózik. 2017. "Family Structure and Family Relationship from the Child Well-being Perspective: Findings from Comparative Analysis." *Children and Youth Services Review* 80: 105–115.
Eurostat. 2017. "People in the EU - Statistics on Household and Family Structures." https://ec.europa.eu/eurostat/statistics-explained/index.php/People_in_the_EU_-_statistics_on_household_and_family_structures#Single-person_househ olds. Accessed November 30, 2019.
Eurostat. 2019. "Marriage and Divorce Statistics." https://ec.europa.eu/eurostat/statistics-explained/index.php?title=Marriage_and_divorce_statistics#Fewer_marria ges.2C_more_divorces. Accessed November 29, 2019 and July 22, 2020.
Eurostat. *various years*. "Income and Living Conditions Database." https://ec.eur opa.eu/eurostat/en/web/products-datasets/-/ILC_LVPH02. Accessed November 17, 2019.
Gilman, R., and S. Huebner. 2003. "A Review of Life Satisfaction Research with Children and Adolescents." *School Psychology Quarterly* 18 (2): 192–205. https://doi.org/10.1521/scpq.18.2.192.21858.
Henry, C. S. 1994. "Family System Characteristics, Parental Behaviors, and Adolescent Family Life Satisfaction." *Family Relations* 43 (4): 447–455.

James, A., and A. L. James. 2004. *Constructing Childhood: Theory, Policy and Social Practice*. Basingstoke, UK: Palgrave Macmillan.

Joronen, K., and P. Astedt-Kurki. 2005. "Familial Contribution to Adolescent Subjective Well-Being." *International Journal of Nursing Practice* 11 (3): 125–133.

Kutsar, D., and K. Raid. 2019. "When Traditional Measurement Practices Fail: Who are the Child's Family?" In *Children's Subjective Well-Being in Local and International Perspectives*, edited by Dagmar Kutsar and Kadri Raid, 85–93. Tallinn: Statistikaamet.

Kutsar, D., K. Raid, and K. Soo. 2018. "International Survey of Children's Well-Being—An Opportunity to Develop Child-Centred Statistics." *Quarterly Bulletin of Statistics Estonia* 1: 21–28. https://www.stat.ee/publication-2018_quarterly-bulletin-of-statistics-estonia-1-18.

Laes, T.-L., S. Krusell, A. Reinomägi, and K. Toros. 2013. "The Child in Different Environments". In *Child Well-Being*, edited by Dagmar Kutsar, 13–41. Tallinn: Statistical Office of Estonia.

Lee, B. J. and M. S. Yoo. 2015. "Family, School, and Community Correlates of Children's Subjective Well-Being: An International Comparative Study." *Child Indicators Research* 8 (1): 151–175.

Levin, I. 1994. *Stefamilien – variasjon og mangfold* [The Stepfamily–Variety and Diversity]. Oslo: Aventura.

Marsolini, M. 2000. *Blended Families. Creating Harmony as You Build a New Home Life*. Chicago: Moody Publishers.

Mason, J., and S. Danby. 2011. "Children as Experts in Their Lives: Child Inclusive Research." *Child Indicators Research* 4 (2): 185–189.

OECD. 2011. "Families Are Changing." In *Doing Better for Families*, 17–53. Paris: OECD Publishing.

OECD. 2016. "SF1.1: Family Size and Household Composition." https://www.oecd.org/els/family/SF_1_1_Family_size_and_composition.pdf. Accessed November 30, 2019.

Oláh, L. S. 2015. "Changing Families in the European Union: Trends and Policy Implications." Families and Societies Working Paper Series. https://www.familiesandsocieties.eu/wp-content/uploads/2015/09/WP44Olah2015.pdf. Accessed October 21, 2019.

Qvortrup, J. 1991. *Childhood as a Social Phenomenon: National Report*. Vienna: European Centre for Social Welfare Policy and Research.

Rees, G., and G. Main, eds. 2015. *Children's Views on Their Lives and Well-Being in 15 Countries: An Initial Report on the Children's Worlds Survey, 2013–14*. York, UK: Children's Worlds Project (ISCWeB)

Vandewater, E. A., and J. E. Lansford. 1998. "Influences of Family Structure and Parental Conflict on Children's Well-Being." *Family Relations* 47 (4): 323–330.

CHAPTER 21

Assessment of Parental Potential: Socio-Economic Risk Factors and Children's Well-Being

Judith Lind

Introduction

This chapter deals with the assessment of parental potential, i.e. evaluations of the parenting capacity of people who are aspiring to parenthood, but are not yet parents. In the assessment process, information about candidates and their circumstances is collected and evaluated, with the purpose of deciding whether they are capable of caring for a child.

During research conducted for three different projects on the assessment of parental, or carer, potential in adoption, foster care, and assisted reproduction with donor gametes, I noticed that the socio-economic circumstances of candidates were described as a factor to consider in all three sets of assessment guidelines.[1] I became curious about the assumptions on which the consideration of socio-economic factors in each of the three assessment guidelines was based.

The aim of this chapter is to analyse how the consideration of socio-economic factors is justified in the assessment guidelines, what assumptions form the basis of these justifications and what the potential problems—which presumably can be prevented through the consideration of socio-economic circumstances in the assessment of candidates—are represented to be.

J. Lind (✉)
Linköping University, Linköping, Sweden
e-mail: judith.lind@liu.se

© The Author(s), under exclusive license to Springer Nature Switzerland AG 2021
A.-M. Castrén et al. (eds.), *The Palgrave Handbook of Family Sociology in Europe*, https://doi.org/10.1007/978-3-030-73306-3_21

Assessments of Parental Potential

Assessments of parental potential, or parental vetting, entail the identification of social risk factors, i.e. circumstances or characteristics of individuals, their environment, or living conditions that may increase the likelihood of undesired events, behaviours, or conditions occurring (Hallin 2013). It constitutes an assessment of a parenting situation beforehand, which led Botterell and Mcleod (2016) to refer to parental vetting or licensing as "restrictions on people's freedom to parent a child that the state imposes on them even though they may have never mistreated children" (p. 193). The objective is for the state to reduce the potentially negative effects of parenting that is considered to be poor on both individual children and society. Critiques of parental licensing schemes concern the interest of adults in becoming parents, which Brighouse and Swift (2006) describe as a fundamental, albeit conditional and limited, right. According to De Wispelaere and Weinstock (2012), the cost of denying people the opportunity to parent in order to protect children must therefore be brought into the equation. Furthermore, definitions of circumstances or parents against whom children need to be protected are inevitably informed by dominant political and cultural parenting norms (Blyth et al. 2008; Diekema 2004; Pennings 1999; Quigley 2010). Those whose lives do not conform to such norms risk being discriminated against through policies that serve to regulate reproduction. Using the concept of "stratified reproduction", critical attention has been directed towards "power relations by which some categories of people are empowered to nurture and reproduce", while others, primarily women of colour living in poverty, have been disempowered (Ginsberg and Rapp 1995, 3. See also Roberts 2009; Daar 2017). Rather than regulating individual parenting choices about reproduction, Engster (2010) argues, the state should support people in their parenting task by offering, for example, prenatal care, paid parental leave, good-quality and affordable childcare and public subsidies. It is worth noting that Sweden has many of these child welfare policies in place, which indicates that parental vetting practices and support for parents are by no means mutually exclusive.

The Vetting of Adopters, Foster Carers, and Donor Gamete Recipients

Since the rescinding of policies that enabled the forced sterilisation of individuals, assessments of parental potential have been conducted in Sweden primarily in situations where couples or individuals become parents, or are otherwise entrusted with the care of a child, through the assistance of a state-authorised agency—e.g. through adoption, foster care, or assisted reproduction (Areschoug 2005).

Before an adoption assessment is initialised, prospective adopters must take part in a course of mandatory parental education. The assessment, or home study, comprises several interviews, as a couple and individually, with a social worker, home visits, checks of various records and sometimes meetings with the candidates' social network. The social worker prepares a report and the local social welfare board makes the formal decision to either grant or refuse consent for the candidates to adopt. National adoptions are rare in Sweden. Therefore, prospective adopters contact one of the state-authorised adoption agencies, through which they will eventually be matched with a child in another country (Lind and Lindgren 2017).

Foster care is the primary solution used by Swedish social services to assist children who have been removed from their homes. Reunification with the birth parents is the prioritised goal, but the prioritisation of reunification over stability in placements is increasingly being questioned (Cocozza and Hort 2011; Heimer and Palme 2016).[2] Prospective foster carers contact either municipal social services or one of the many private operators that serve as intermediaries between foster homes and social services to place children in foster care. All foster homes are reimbursed for their expenses and receive an allowance for the care work they do. Candidates who are thought to lack the necessary qualities at an early stage of the process do not undergo a full assessment.[3]

While the assessment of adopters and foster carers is performed by social services, candidates for donor conception are vetted by a fertility clinic. Swedish legislation requires a pre-conception assessment of a candidate's social and psychological circumstances only when gametes from a donor are used, while regional policies link such a requirement to all treatment that is publicly funded (Lind 2020). In donor conception, the legislation demands that the candidates are evaluated by a behavioural scientist. The checking of criminal and other records is not required. In treatment that does not involve the use of donor gametes, candidates commonly only see a fertility doctor, who according to the regional guidelines should ensure that there is no "social or psychological contraindication to parenthood" (Lind 2020, 20).

There are, of course, several differences between the three practices. In contrast to adopters, candidates for donor conception do not assume parental responsibility for a child from another set of parents. Even though gametes from a donor are used, that donor has not previously been responsible for the child who is born as a result of treatment. Indeed, if it had not been for the candidates' decision to have a child, that child would not have come into existence. Foster carers, for their part, assume responsibility for the care of a child, but without necessarily assuming the status of parents. Instead, foster carers perform their parenting task by order of social services. Their contract can easily be cancelled, yet at the same time their services are in high demand. De Wispelaere and Weinstock (2012) argue against the extensive vetting of adopters and foster carers, based on the argument that this will restrict the number of children who can find a family home. Such an argument assumes that there is a public need for more candidates. While this is the case regarding foster carers in Sweden, there is no publicly expressed need for more candidates for adoption or donor conception for that matter. The ratio between supply and demand for candidates in each practice, the payments made by, or to, the candidates, and the figuration of the average candidate in each practice must be taken into consideration, as I will argue, if we want to understand the consideration of socio-economic factors in the assessment of prospective adopters, foster carers, and recipients of Antiretroviral therapy (ART) treatments.

Poverty and Parenthood

Representations of the relationship between socio-economic circumstances, parental behaviour, and outcomes for children are complex. In social epidemiological studies that show a statistical correlation between high rates of poverty, unemployment, welfare dependence, high residence mobility and overcrowding in a specific area or neighbourhood on the one hand, and higher rates of youth criminality, substance abuse, and poor health on the other, parental behaviour has largely been left out of the equation (e.g. Pratt and Cullen 2005; Reiss 2013). When attempts have been made to explain the relationship between socio-economic disadvantages and parental behaviour, economic hardship has been represented as a social stressor, which may lead to parental emotional distress and harsh, inconsistent and/or uninvolved parenting, which in turn may cause child maladjustment (e.g. Conger and Conger 2008; Conger et al. 2010; Neppl et al. 2015). Hence, what is represented as the core problem here is the economic hardship itself.

Parenting support policies of the two last decades, by contrast, build on a slightly different problem representation. Anti-social or criminal behaviour in children has been primarily explained with reference to poor parenting and little attention has been paid to the economic circumstances of the parents (Edwards and Gillies 2011; Littmarck et al. 2018). According to criticism directed at penalising parenting support policies, critiques of poor parenting have transformed into criticism of poor parents (Jensen 2018). Representations of the relationship between poverty and parenting revolve around the question of whether family income is said to determine the investments that parents can make in child-rearing activities that are expected to further a child's academic and social success (e.g. Bradley and Corwyn 2002), or whether there are class-related differences regarding ideas of good parenting, or both. Dominant ideas of good parenthood favour a parenting style that has been labelled *intensive* (Hays 1996). According to Lareau (2003), the *concerted cultivation* favoured by middle-class parents required financial and knowledge resources that the *natural growth* approach of working-class parents did not. According to Dermott and Pomati (2016), the derivation of parenting ideals from middle-class perspectives risks positioning alternative ideas as bad parenting. Related to the assessment of prospective foster carers, adopters, and recipients of ART treatment, the above raises the question of whether poverty is seen as a risk factor because the child may be subjected to material deprivation as a result of it, or whether the socio-economic circumstances of candidates are viewed as a potential source of stress, or whether they are viewed as indicative of the candidates' qualities as parents.

Data and Method

This chapter is based primarily on an analysis of guidelines published by the Swedish National Board of Health and Welfare (NBHW), a government agency under the Ministry of Health and Social Affairs, for the vetting of prospective adopters, foster carers, and candidates for donor conception. The current guidelines for the assessment of candidates in adoption and foster care were published in 2014 and in assisted reproduction with donor gametes in 2016. These constitute the core documents.[4] All three sets of guidelines are preceded or accompanied by published pre-studies or method descriptions. These supporting documents were also consulted, but only one of them (NBHW 2016b) contained sections relevant to the analysis.[5]

The first step in the analysis entailed the identification of sections in which the vetting of candidates was justified, and all sections in which the assessment of the socio-economic circumstances of candidates was mentioned (including income, employment, education, and housing). During this process, I discovered and began to make notes about the many intertextual references (Fairclough 1992) that were made in-between the guidelines, including previous editions, as well as to the NBHW guidelines for child-welfare assessments, the BBIC guidelines. The BBIC guidelines were therefore also analysed.[6]

The guiding question for the second part of the analysis is inspired by the methodology for analysing policy texts introduced by Carol Bacchi (2009), according to which we should interrogate policies by posing the question "what's the problem represented to be?" (WPR). In doing so, WPR analyses policies backwards. Rather than focusing on policy outcomes, WPR contributes to identifying the problems that are represented through the solutions that the policy prescribes. As the assessment guidelines in foster care, adoption and donor conception serve to identify suitable candidates, the problem that is represented through these guidelines is that not all candidates may be suitable to care for a child. Through the identification of risk factors, the various facets of unsuitability are represented. By zooming in on one specific factor, the candidates' socio-economic circumstances, I aim to analyse which facets of unsuitability are represented through the consideration of socio-economic circumstances in the assessment of candidates for parenthood. Problem representations, and the assumptions that underlie them, may be more or less explicit in the policy texts, and analysis requires the consideration of the context in which the policies were introduced. Drawing on results from my previous research—the analysis of adoption assessment reports (Lind and Lindgren 2017), the analysis of reasons for refusal of fertility treatment (Elenis et al. 2020) and focus-group discussions with fertility clinic staff (Lind 2020)—and ongoing research on the recruitment of foster carers, I will discuss the possible assumptions underlying the inclusion of socio-economic factors in the Swedish assessment guidelines in adoption, foster care, and donor conception.

The Official Justification for Vetting in Adoption, Foster Care, and Assisted Reproduction

In order to understand the role of socio-economic factors in the assessment of the candidates for adoption, foster care, and assisted reproduction, we must first examine how the vetting of candidates as such is motivated and justified. In all three sets of assessment guidelines, the candidates are referred to as *sökande* (applicants), couples, individuals, or families, and they are assessed on their suitability to become parents, adoptive parents, or foster carers. With the exception of the mention of single candidates, who are expected to be women, the assessment guidelines are gender neutral in the sense that the assessment criteria are the same for women and men, for prospective mothers and fathers.

According to the guidelines for the assessment of foster carers, the purpose of assessment is to determine the applicants' ability to offer "stable and secure relationships" with a child (NBHW 2014b, 8).[7] The foster-home assessment material that is analysed for this study, the *BRA-fam* manual (NBHW 2014b), is intended for use in the initial assessment of presumptive foster carers. Based on the information collected using the questions given in the *BRA-fam* manual, the social worker is expected to determine whether candidates should be assessed further. Hence, the aim described in the *BRA-fam* manual is to "weed out" unsuitable applicants by focusing on circumstances and factors that would constitute a risk to the placed child (p. 8). In contrast, the purpose of adoption assessments is described as ensuring "that the child will be placed with parents who are well prepared and fit to take care of her/him" (NBWH 2014a, 16), while the explicit purpose of the assessment of applicants for donor conception is to examine the applicant's qualifications and capacity to "provide good circumstances in which the child can grow up" (NBWH 2016a, 9). The latter two sets of wording indicate that the goal of the assessment extends beyond the mere identification of factors that constitute a risk of harm to the child. There are, however, differences in the amount of weight attributed to the interests of the child in these two sets of assessment guidelines.

In the adoption handbook, the best interests of the child are described, in line with article 21 (on adoption) of the UN Convention on the Rights of the Child (hereafter UNCRC, UN 1989), as the paramount consideration. According to the handbook, this means that "[i]f there is doubt that the applicant(s) will be able to meet an adoptive child's special needs, the adults' desire to have a family must come second to the ... child's need for competent parents" (NBHW 2014a, 17). The assessment guidelines for donor conception also refer to the UNCRC. They mention article 3, according to which the best interests of the child shall be "a primary consideration" in all actions concerning children (UN 1989, article 3). Whereas a *paramount* consideration trumps all other considerations, a *primary* consideration is a leading consideration (Archard 2002). Hence, the manner in which the best interests of the child are considered in donor conception leaves room for also considering the interests of other parties involved in the process, primarily the involuntarily childless adults (see also Lind 2019).

The justification for the vetting of candidates in each of these processes is related to the responsibility of society. The adoption handbook refers to the great responsibility assumed by society "when these particularly vulnerable children with special needs receive new parents and new circumstances in which to grow up" (NBHW 2014a, 16). Therefore, the handbook continues, society must ensure that the new parents are well prepared and suitable for taking care of the child (NBHW 2014a). In the assessment guidelines for donor conception, too, the responsibility of society is emphasised: "If society is to contribute actively to parenthood through donor treatment", the guidelines continue, "there shall be requirements for the child to have a secure childhood" (NBHW 2016a, 9). The role of society in foster care is perhaps the most obvious. Through decisions made by social services, children are both separated from their birth families' homes and placed in the care of the foster family. In the *BRA-fam* manual, however, the responsibility of society is not explicitly mentioned, which may indicate that the evaluation of foster homes is perceived as not needing further justification.[8]

To summarise, the welfare of the child plays a prominent role, perhaps even the most prominent, in the explicit justification of the vetting of candidates in each process. In the balancing act between the desires of adults to care for the child and the child's interest in being properly cared for, the latter is ascribed considerable weight. In political arguments, however, the interests of the child are closely linked to those of the state. Proponents of parental licensing argue that harm to children *and* society can be avoided by preventing people who lack the capacity or living conditions material conditions to care for a child from becoming parents (e.g. Mill 1978, 2010; LaFollette 1980; Eisenberg 1994; Westman 1996). Hence, the justification for parental vetting builds on a representation of the acts of having and rearing children as activities that can potentially harm both the children and the wider society.

SOCIO-ECONOMIC CHALLENGES AS A RISK FACTOR IN THE BBIC CHILD-WELFARE ASSESSMENT GUIDELINES

All of the three sets of assessment guidelines in adoption, foster care, and donor conception refer to the NBHW guidelines for child welfare assessments, the so-called BBIC guidelines. BBIC is a Swedish acronym for *Barnets Bästa i Centrum* (The best interests of the child at the centre). Both the current and previous editions of the BBIC guidelines claim to build on the UN Convention on the Rights of the Child (UN 1989) and the Swedish Social Services Act (SFS 2001, 453). They also refer to Urie Bronfenbrenner's ecological systems theory. The fact that assessment guidelines in adoption, foster care, and donor conception contain references to the BBIC guidelines, I argue, has implications for the manner in which the consideration of socio-economic risk factors is introduced in these guidelines. Therefore, I will first discuss the BBIC child welfare assessment guidelines and how socio-economic challenges are represented in them, before returning to the assessment guidelines in adoption, foster care, and donor conception.

In the third edition of the BBIC guidelines (NBHW 2015), as well as in previous and later versions, child abuse and neglect are claimed to be overrepresented in areas that are socio-economically challenged. Parents' education and work are claimed to be important because these influence the financial security and living standards of the family. Furthermore, "[c]hildren who grow up with parents with little or no education and unemployment" are said to be "at increased risk of being subjected to insufficient care and to develop psychosocial problems" (NBHW 2015, 31). Economic stress, long-term poverty, and residence in a socio-economically challenged area are described as risk factors in themselves, because they are associated with children's and young people's poor mental and physical health. A stable household economy and higher education, by contrast, are said to be related to a strong standing on the labour market and good health, and to influence the child's opportunities for stability in their housing situation, activities, and participation in society in general. In contrast, residence in a socio-economically challenged area is claimed to entail a higher risk of criminality and substance abuse, and children who grow up in families that receive welfare benefits are said to be at risk of leaving school with lower grades than other children. The relationship between poverty and social problems is not explicitly described as causal; instead, there is said to be "a relationship" or "correlation" between the two (NBHW 2015, 31). Furthermore, poverty is described as correlating with other factors that constitute additional challenges to parenthood, including single parenthood, unemployment, welfare dependency, a weak anchorage in society, and insufficient language proficiency, all of which are said to potentially make it "difficult to provide necessary care and security for the child" (NBHW 2015, 31).

The BBIC guidelines offer numerous references to publications, mainly reviews and meta-analyses of research studies, to support the representation of the family's housing and finances and the parents' work as important factors to consider in child-welfare assessments. The use of these studies for this purpose is worth discussing for several reasons. Firstly, the majority concern the correlation between socio-economic disadvantages and problematic *child behaviour* at a statistical level, rather than risk factors for *parental behaviour* that is detrimental to the child's well-being at an individual level (cf. Neppl et al. 2015). In fact, one of the few reviews referred to in the BBIC guidelines that is concerned with the correlation between socio-economic challenges and parental child maltreatment explicitly emphasises the fact that most studies demonstrating a concentration of child maltreatment cases in socio-economically disadvantaged neighbourhoods do not account for how these disadvantages affect parental behaviour (Coulton et al. 2007). Several of the studies referred to in the BBIC guidelines were originally used to identify neighbourhoods with a high prevalence of social risk factors in order to inform decisions about preventive measures. Child welfare assessments, however, inform decisions about individual families.

Secondly, the vast majority of the studies cited in the meta-analyses referred to are set in the USA, the UK, or another Anglo-Saxon country, i.e. in a welfare system that differs considerably from the Swedish one, which offers considerably more financial support to children and families, including 13 months of paid parental leave, subsidised childcare, a universal child allowance for all families with children under 18, free-of-charge health and dental care for children, free schooling and attendance at after-school centres, etc. (Engster 2010; Wells and Bergnehr 2014). Hence, the effects of unemployment on a family's financial situation and their ability to provide sufficient care for a child, or the meaning of economic disadvantage, are likely to be different in Sweden than in the USA or the UK.[9]

In addition to these two transferences, from statistical correlations in a particular neighbourhood to individual child welfare assessments and from an Anglo-Saxon to a Swedish welfare political context, the representation of socio-economic risk factors in the BBIC guidelines is also transferred from child welfare assessments to assessments of parental potential. There is an apparent difference between the scope of these two. In a child-welfare case, there is parental performance to evaluate, including the effects that the family's socio-economic circumstances may have already had on the child's situation. In adoption, foster care, and assisted reproduction, however, the effects that such circumstances will have in the future must be estimated beforehand. The studies referred to in the BBIC guidelines demonstrate a correlation between socio-economic challenges and living circumstances that are unfavourable to the child's well-being and development. Through the references made to the BBIC guidelines in the guidelines for the vetting of adopters, foster carers, and candidates for donor conception, this correlation is used to contribute to the identification of candidates who should not be entrusted with the care of a child. I will now move on to analyse the grounds on which socio-economic factors are made relevant in each set of guidelines.

SOCIO-ECONOMIC CHALLENGES AS A RISK FACTOR IN ASSESSMENTS OF PARENTING POTENTIAL

In all three sets of assessment guidelines, the socio-economic circumstances of candidates constitute one of many factors that should be considered, and in none of the guidelines is this factor described as decisive. Furthermore, descriptions of what constitutes socio-economic risk factors and what justifies their consideration in the assessment of candidates are brief, if they exist at all. Below, I will therefore bring my analysis of the explicit justifications for the inclusion of the candidates' socio-economic circumstances in the assessment guidelines into dialogue with figurations of each category of candidate, including information about the payments that are made by and to candidates in each process.

Adoption

In contrast to child welfare assessments, which serve to decide whether support or protection measures are necessary, the vetting of adopters, according to the guidelines, serves to investigate whether the applicants' parenting capacity is sufficient *without* any supportive measures (NBHW 2014a). Unemployment or unstable employment, "economic difficulties", and deficiencies in the housing situation or living environment are listed as "factors that speak, or may speak against suitability" (NBHW 2014a, 106). These factors are described as "important because of their implications for the preconditions to care for an adoptive child and to satisfy her/his needs" (NBHW 2014a, 106). Furthermore, a well-ordered and secure financial situation, secure employment, and job satisfaction are referred to as important in order for work-related problems not to impede "a whole-hearted commitment to an adoptive child" (NBHW 2014a, 106). The section does not contain any references to support these claims.

One explanation for the limited attention paid to socio-economic factors in the guidelines for adoption assessments may be that it is taken for granted that adoption applicants have the financial resources that a transnational adoption requires. Adoption fees range from approximately 15,000 to 28,000 euros, depending on which country the child is adopted from (Adoptionscentrum 2021). Travel expenses are not included in this. Adopters may, however, apply for an adoption grant of approximately 7000 euros from the Social Insurance Agency (2019). When this grant was increased in January 2017, one of the main arguments was that transnational adoption was not affordable for everyone and that the majority of Swedish transnational adopters were middle- or upper-class families (Inspection for Social Insurance (ISI) 2016). While the increase in the grant has reduced adoption costs for adopters, it is not likely to have eliminated the self-deselection of applicants for economic reasons.

Given the figuration of the average adoption applicant as financially secure, it seems reasonable to suggest that consideration of the socio-economic circumstances of adoption applicants does not primarily serve to identify candidates who live in such poverty that their child is at risk of suffering from material deprivation, but rather to ensure that candidates can concentrate on their parenting task. Such an interpretation is supported by a study of 106 Swedish adoption assessment reports for candidates who had been granted consent to adopt (Lind and Lindgren 2017). These candidates were represented as not only suitable adopters and parents, but also as citizens with well-ordered lives. Stability and security in all aspects, including employment and finances, were represented as a prerequisite for a life free from distractions that would allow candidates to prioritise their parenting task over everything else (Lind and Lindgren 2017).

Assisted Reproduction

The assessment guidelines for donor conception contain a whole section entitled "Insufficient ability to provide for oneself and a child and/or serious shortcomings in the housing situation" (NBHW 2016a, 18–19). The knowledge base for this section is claimed to be the BBIC guidelines, and references to the same studies that are referred to in the BBIC guidelines are included in the method description (NBHW 2016b, 7–8). The conclusion drawn by the NBHW is that "children who grow up with parents who are unemployed and who cannot establish themselves on the labour market are at increased risk of being subjected to insufficient care and of developing psychosocial problems" (NBHW 2016b, 8). The same claim is made about children who grow up in inadequate housing situations (NBHW 2016b, 8). The wording of these claims suggests that the correlation between socio-economic challenges and a negative outcome for children is statistical—children living under such circumstances are more likely to receive insufficient care. In the following sentence, however, the relationship was described as causal. "Being a single parent, unemployed, welfare dependent and having a weak link to society can", according to the guidelines, "make it difficult to give children sufficient care and security" (NBHW 2016a, 19).

In contrast to adoption, the costs of assisted reproduction are low for the individual candidate in Sweden because ART treatment is included in the public healthcare scheme. Hence, its accessibility is not dependent on candidates' financial ability to pay for services, and self-deselection for economic reasons can therefore be expected to be low. While consideration of the parenting capacity of candidates at the level of national legislation is limited to the use of donor gametes, at regional level, however, all kinds of publicly funded ART treatment require the evaluation of candidates' parenting capacity. Furthermore, in a previous study, I showed that clinic staff justify the assessment of candidates' parenting capacity equally with reference to the welfare of the child and to the goal of using public funds responsibly. Hence, while the public funding of infertility treatment is intended to make treatment accessible to as many people as possible, the use of public funds as such was used as an argument for making sure that they are not used to create families who cannot cope on their own and will be a burden to society (Lind 2020).

Foster Care

The *BRA-fam* manual for the initial assessment of presumptive foster carers does not include any questions about housing or surroundings. However, it is described as important that the child will have her/his own room and that the foster home is situated in a safe and secure area so that the child can establish "new positive social contacts" (NBHW 2014b, 22). Information about the applicants' finances is said to be collected indirectly through questions about their occupations and transcripts of records from the Enforcement Authority and the Social Insurance Agency, but no specific criteria are mentioned (NBHW 2014b).

While candidates for adoption are presumed to be middle or upper class, and the average Swedish foster home has previously been pictured as a middle-class family (Höjer 2001), the current figuration of the average foster carer is different. When placement in foster care is considered for a child, priority should be given, according to the Swedish Social Services Act (SFS 2001:453, section 6, §5), to families within the child's network. Furthermore, a recommendation that is frequently cited is Höjer's (2001) statement that one of the factors contributing to successful foster care placements is when the socio-economic background of the foster home is similar to that of the child's birth family. Given the fact that a majority of children placed in foster care come from socio-economically challenged homes (Rasmusson and Regnér 2013; Forte 2015), both of these prioritisations require the acceptance of foster carers with less stable socio-economic circumstances.[10] Furthermore, in contrast to transnational adoption, in foster care the ties of the children to their birth families are not permanently severed, and the children are likely to be reunited with their families at some point. Their socio-economic background is therefore not easily reinvented.

The general shortage of foster homes also makes the selection of foster carers dependent upon who the candidates for becoming foster carers are. At a network meeting arranged by the Swedish Association of Local Authorities and Regions, attending social workers unanimously described two categories of average candidates: the immigrant family with insecure or no employment and a shortage of space in their current housing and the family living in rural areas with equally insecure employment and unfinished renovation projects in their homes. In neither case, according to the social workers, could economic motives be excluded (SALAR 2019b).

While adopters pay for the services that will make them parents, and recipients of ART treatment receive those services free—if they fulfil the eligibility criteria for publicly funded treatment—foster carers are paid to serve as parents. In addition to reimbursement for the extra costs associated with the care of the placed child, Swedish foster carers are also paid an allowance. The size of this allowance is determined by the scope and complexity of the care that the child is considered to need. If a foster carer must take time off from her/his employment because care of the child requires full-time attendance for a limited period of time, the carer is also compensated for loss of income (SALAR 2019a). Hence, in contrast to adopters and recipients of ART treatment, foster carers are not expected to be able to manage without public financial support. The payments to foster carers are, however, considered a delicate matter, because they may attract people to fostering for purely economic reasons (Kirton 2001; Hardesty 2018). The *BRA-fam* manual includes a question that addresses the candidates' motives for wanting to become foster carers. The answer options include "The allowance" and "I see it as an opportunity to work from home". Neither of these answers is said to automatically disqualify a candidate (NBHW 2014b, 28). While it is regarded as self-centred and therefore problematic if the allowance is stated as the only motive, this answer is considered acceptable if it is combined with an explicit desire to take care of one's own children together with the foster child in the home as an alternative to working outside the home (NBHW 2014b). The problem that is represented in the guidelines is not primarily candidates who need financial assistance to be able to care for a child, or candidates who are distracted from their care task due to economic stress, but rather candidates who may be suspected of viewing fostering mainly as a source of income and therefore cannot be trusted to genuinely care about the child placed in their charge.

Concluding Discussion

When tracing the origins of eligibility criteria related to socio-economic factors, I discovered that the guidelines for all three practices refer to the NBHW guidelines for child-welfare assessments, the BBIC guidelines. This means that risk factors originally defined for the evaluation of parental performance are transferred to the assessment of the parental potential of presumptive adopters, foster carers, and recipients of ART treatment. Moreover, the majority of studies that constitute the scientific support for taking socio-economic factors into consideration were conducted in the USA and other Anglo-Saxon countries. Hence, their results were transferred from one welfare context to another, quite different, one. Lastly, the studies that support the identification of economic stress, unemployment, and inadequate housing situations as risk factors were primarily conducted with the purpose of identifying how socio-economic disadvantages correlate statistically with problematic child or youth behaviour and poor child well-being, rather than explaining or predicting parental behaviour.

The consideration of socio-economic circumstances in the assessment of candidates for foster care, adoption, and donor conception presumes that such circumstances affect or are indicative of candidates' abilities to care for a child. The questions that this chapter has aimed to address concern the grounds on which these assumptions are made, and what kind of potential problems are represented through the consideration of socio-economic circumstances in the assessment of candidates. In her critical analysis of the ways in which the practices that surround ART treatment in the USA—the high costs and the refusal of treatment to candidates who are not considered eligible—discriminate against women of colour, Judith Daar (2017) asks whether reliance on public assistance serves as a proxy for race or ethnicity in the assessment of candidates. By demanding that candidates are not dependent on public assistance, fertility doctors can maintain, according to Daar, an explicit non-discriminatory stance while at the same time refusing treatment to many African American and Latino candidates. In addition to being a proxy for a racial norm, financial stability as a suitability criterion in assessments of parental potential may also be claimed to serve as a proxy for a middle-class norm. However, such a claim would not do justice to the complexity of the question.

The problem, or unsuitability, that is represented through the consideration of socio-economic circumstances is not the same in the assessment of candidates in adoption, foster care, and donor conception. In the assessment of candidates for adoption and prospective foster carers, what seems to be at stake is their emotional engagement with the child. The potential problem that is represented through the consideration of such circumstances in the assessment guidelines for adoption is instability—rather than challenges—in the financial or housing situation, which is assumed to distract the adopter from focusing entirely on the parenting task. In the assessment of foster carers, in contrast, the potential problem is represented to be candidates for whom the allowance is the primary motive and whose emotional engagement can therefore be questioned. In the assessment guidelines for donor conception, socio-economic disadvantages are represented as a direct threat to a child's well-being as well as a cause, or indicator, of parental unfitness. Thus, it represents the support that is available to socio-economically disadvantaged parents in Sweden as insufficient to achieve good enough care and security for children, and it represents dependence on such support as indicative of deficiencies in parental behaviour that cannot be addressed through financial, or any other, support to the parents, and/or as a factor that defines candidates as undeserving of publicly funded ART treatment.

There is hence not one single answer to the question of which potential problems the consideration of such circumstances in the assessment of candidates is presumed to prevent. This analysis, by considering the assessment guidelines for the evaluation of candidates who aspire to become parents or carers of a child through three different practices alongside each other, and by doing so in light of knowledge about figurations of the average candidate, the candidate supply-and-demand ratio, and the payments made by and to candidates in each practice, has served to illuminate the wide range of assumptions that may underlie considerations of the socio-economic circumstances of candidates. The study results call upon us to be cautious about accepting taken-for-granted claims about indicators of parenting potential, but also warn us not to offer simplified explanations for their origins. Judith Daar (2017) recommends the development of formal written policies for the regulation of access to ART treatments in order to avoid discriminatory practices. Sweden does have national policies and recommendations for the assessment of candidates, not only in assisted reproduction, but also in adoption and foster care. However, policies will inevitably leave considerable room for decision-makers to exercise discretion (Black 2002). Therefore, what is of equal importance is an open and reflective discussion amongst professionals about the assumptions that underlie the consideration of the socio-economic circumstances of candidates, and other criteria, in assessments of parental potential.

NOTES

1. *Preparing for parenthood: Adoption assessments as an institutional process* (Forte—The Swedish Research Council for Health, Working Life and Welfare, grant no. 2015–00542); *The best interests of the child, the reproductive rights of adults, and the responsibilities of the welfare state* (Forte, grant no. 2016–00583), *Recruitment, assessment and matching of foster homes* (Forte, grant no. 2019–01467).
2. As a result of the publicity surrounding the case of a three-year-old girl who died shortly after she was reunified with her birth parents in the spring of 2020, the Swedish government commissioned the NBHW to educate social services on how to work more proactively with adoption for children in out-of-home care (Ministry of Health and Social Affairs 2020).
3. In 2020, the NBHW published a manual for the further evaluation of foster carers—the so-called Foster Home Vignettes (NBHW 2020), which are a translation and adaption of the American *Casey Home Assessment Protocol—Fostering Challenges*. Through interviews based on vignettes that introduce hypothetical situations, candidates are evaluated based on their responses to the vignettes.
4. NBHW (2014a) *Adoption. Handbok för socialtjänsten* [Adoption: Handbook for social services]; NBHW (2014b) *Manual till BRA-fam. En standardiserad bedömningsmetod för rekrytering av familjehem* [Manual for BRA-fam: A standardised evaluation method for the recruitment of foster homes]; NBHW (2016a) *Assisterad befruktning med donerade könsceller. Nationellt kunskapsstöd* [Assisted conception with donated gametes: National recommendations].
5. NBHW (2011) *Initial bedömning vid socialtjänstens rekrytering av familjehem* [Initial assessment in social services' recruitment of foster homes]; NBHW (2016b) *Assisterad befruktning med donerade könsceller. Metodbeskrivning och kunskapsunderlag* [Assisted conception with donated gametes: Method description and knowledge base]; NBHW (2016c) *Förstudie till kunskapsstöd om assisterad befruktning med donerade könsceller* [Prestudy to recommendations regarding assisted conception with donated gametes].
6. NBHW (2015, 3rd) *Grundbok i BBIC. Barns behov i centrum* [Primer on BBIC: Children's needs at the centre].
7. All quotes from Swedish sources have been translated by the author.
8. A report published by the Swedish Health and Social Care Inspectorate in 2017 showed, however, that assessments of foster homes were in some cases incomplete, and in other cases missing altogether (SHSCI 2017).
9. According to UNICEF's (2013) report on child well-being, fewer than 1.5% of Swedish children suffer from material deprivation as measured by the indicators of the UNICEF Child Deprivation Rate.
10. See, for example, the regional recommendations on foster care published by county Gävleborg https://www.regiongavleborg.se/globalassets/samverkan swebben/utveckling-samverkan/valfard-gavleborg/fou-valfard/kunskapsover sikt/kunskapsoversikt-familjehem-fou-valfard.pdf (accessed 3 July 2020).

References

Adoptionscentrum. 2021. *Utlandskontakter*. https://www.adoptionscentrum.se/sv/ Adoption/utlandskontakter/ Accessed 22 April 2021.

Archard, David W. 2002. "Children's Rights." In *The Stanford Encyclopedia of Philosophy*, edited by E. N. Zalta (Summer 2016 Edition). https://plato.stanford.edu/archives/sum2016/entries/rights-children/. Accessed 4 January 2020.

Areschoug, Judith. 2005. "Parenthood and Intellectual Disability: Discourses on Birth Control and Parents with Intellectual Disabilities 1967–2003." *Scandinavian Journal of Disability Research* 7 (3/4): 155–175. https://doi.org/10.1080/15017410500246103.

Bacchi, Carol. 2009. *Analysing Policy: What's the Problem Represented to Be?* Frenchs Forest, NSW: Pearson Addison Wesley.

Black, Julia. 2002. "Regulatory Conversations." *Journal of Law and Society* 29 (1): 163–196. https://doi.org/10.1111/1467-6478.00215.

Blyth, Eric, Vivian Burr, and Abigail Farrand. 2008. "Welfare of the child Assessments in Assisted Conception: A Social Constructionist Perspective." *Journal of Reproductive and Infant Psychology* 26 (1): 31–43. https://doi.org/10.1080/02646830701691301.

Botterell, Andrew, and Carolyn Mcleod. 2016. "Licensing Parents in International Contract Pregnancies." *Journal of Applied Psychology* 33 (2): 178–196.

Bradley, Robert H., and Robert F. Corwyn. 2002. "Socioeconomic Status and Child Development." *Annual Review of Psychology* 53: 371–399. https://doi.org/10.1146/annurev.psych.53.100901.135233.

Brighouse, Harry, and Adam Swift. 2006. "Parents' Rights and the Value of the Family." *Ethics* 117: 80–108.

Cocozza, Madeleine, and Sven E. O. Hort. 2011. "The Dark Side of the Universal Welfare State? Child Abuse and Protection in Sweden." In *Child Protection Systems: International Trends and Orientations*, edited by N. Gilbert, N. Parton, and M. Skivenes, 89–111. New York, NY: Oxford University Press.

Conger, Rand D., and Katherine J. Conger. 2008. "Understanding the Processes Through Which Economic Hardship Influences Families and Children". In *Handbook of Families & Poverty*, edited by D. R. Crane and T. B. Heaton, 64–81. Los Angeles, CA: Sage. https://doi.org/10.4135/9781412976596.n5.

Conger, Rand D., Katherine J. Conger, and Monica J. Martin. 2010. "Socioeconomic Status, Family Processes, and Individual Development." *Journal of Marriage and Family* 72 (3): 685–704. https://doi.org/10.1111%2Fj.1741-3737.2010.00725.x.

Coulton, Claudia J, David S Crampton, Molly Irwin, James C Spilsbury, and Jill E Korbin. 2007. "How neighborhoods influence child maltreatment: A review of the literature and alternative pathways". *Child Abuse & Neglect* 31 (11–12): 1117–42.

Daar, Judith. 2017. *The New Eugenics: Selective Breeding in an Era of Reproductive Technologies*. New Haven, CT: Yale University Press.

Dermott, Esther, and Marco Pomati. 2016. "'Good' Parenting Practices. How Important Are Poverty, Education and Time Pressure?" *Sociology* 50 (1): 125–142. https://doi.org/10.1177/0038038514560260.

De Wispelaere, Jurgen, and Daniel Weinstock. 2012. "Licensing Parents to Protect Our Children?" *Ethics and Social Welfare* 6 (2): 195–205. https://doi.org/10.1080/17496535.2012.682507.

Diekema, Douglas S. 2004. "Parental Refusals of Medical Treatment: The Harm Principle as Threshold for State Intervention." *Theoretical Medicine and Bioethics* 25: 243–264. https://doi.org/10.1007/s11017-004-3146-6.

Edwards, Rosalind, and Val Gillies. 2011. "Clients or Consumers, Commonplace or Pioneers? Navigating the Contemporary Class Politics of Family, Parenting Skills and Education." *Ethics and Education* 6 (2): 141–154.
Eisenberg, Howard B. 1994. "A Modest Proposal: State Licensing of Parents." *Connecticut Law Review* 26 (4): 1415–1452.
Elenis, Evangelia, Agneta Skoog Svanberg, Pia Leandersson, Judith Lind, and Gunilla Sydsjö. 2020. "Access to infertility evaluation and treatment in two public fertility clinics and the reasons for withholding it: a prospective survey cohort study of healthcare professionals". *BMJ Open* 10 (12): http://dx.doi.org/10.1136/bmj open-2020-041538.
Engster, Daniel. 2010. "The Place of Parenting Within a Liberal Theory of Justice: The Private Parenting Model, Parental Licenses, or Public Parenting Support?" *Social Theory and Practice* 36 (2): 233–262.
Fairclough, Norman. 1992. *Discourse and Social Change*. Cambridge: Polity Press.
Forte. 2015. *Barn och unga i samhällets vård. Forskning om den sociala dygnsvården. Forskning i korthet* (4/2015). https://forte.se/app/uploads/2015/02/forskning-i-korthet-barn-och-unga-i-samhallets-vard.pdf. Accessed 8 January 2020.
Ginsberg, Faye D., and Rayna Rapp, eds. 1995. *Conceiving the New World Order: The Global Politics of Reproduction*. Berkeley, CA: University of California Press.
Hallin, Per-Olof. 2013. *Sociala risker – En begrepps- och metoddiskussion*. Malmö: Malmö University Publications in Urban Studies (MAPIUS) 15.
Hardesty, Melissa. 2018. "'It's Not a Job!' Foster Care Board Payments and the Logic of the Profiteering Parent." *Social Service Review* 92 (1): 93–133.
Hays, Sharon. 1996. *The Cultural Contradictions of Motherhood*. New Haven, CT: Yale University Press.
Heimer, Maria, and Joakim Palme. 2016. "Rethinking Child Policy Post-UN Convention on the Rights of the Child: Vulnerable Children's Welfare in Sweden." *Journal of Social Policy* 45 (3): 435–452.
Henkel, Dieter. 2011. "Unemployment and Substance Use: A Review of the Literature (1990–2010)." *Current Drug Abuse Reviews* 4 (1): 4–27. https://doi.org/10.2174/1874473711104010004.
Höjer, Ingrid. 2001. *Fosterfamiljens inre liv* (diss.). Gothenburg: Gothenburg University.
ISI. 2016. Att adoptera – en ekonomisk fråga. En studie om adoptionsbidrag och ekonomiska förutsättningar för adoption. Report 2016:9 https://www.inspsf.se/download/18.6e75aae16a591304896bd3/1565330429821/Att%20adoptera-ISF-Rapport%202016-09.pdf. Accessed 8 January 2020.
Jensen, Tracy. 2018. *Parenting the Crisis. The Cultural Politics of Parent-Blame*. Bristol: Policy Press.
Kirton, Derek. 2001. "Love and Money: Payment, Motivation and the Fostering Task." *Child and Family Social Work* 2001 (6): 199–208. https://doi.org/10.1046/j.1365-2206.2001.00208.x.
LaFollette, Hugh. 1980. "Licensing Parents." *Philosophy and Public Affairs* 9 (2): 182–197.
LaFolette, Hugh. 2010. "Licensing Parents Revisited." *Journal of Applied Philosophy* 27 (4): 327–343. https://doi.org/10.1111/j.1468-5930.2010.00497.x.
Lareau, Annette. 2003. *Unequal Childhoods: Class, Race, and Family Life*. Berkeley, CA: University of California Press.

Lind, Judith. 2019. "The Rights of Intended Children: The Best Interests of the Child Argument in Assisted Reproduction Policy." *Childhood* 26 (3): 352–368. https://doi.org/10.1177%2F0907568219853331.

Lind, Judith. 2020. "Child Welfare Assessments and the Regulation of Access to Publicly Funded Fertility Treatment." *Reproductive BioMedicine and Society Online* 10: 19–27. https://doi.org/10.1016/j.rbms.2020.01.003.

Lind, Judith, and Cecilia Lindgren. 2017. "Displays of Parent Suitability in Adoption Assessment Reports." *Child and Family Social Work* 22 (1): 53–63. https://doi.org/10.1111/cfs.12305.

Littmarck, Sofia, Judith Lind, and Bengt Sandin. 2018. "Negotiating Parenting Support: Welfare Politics in Sweden Between the 1960s and the 2000s." *Social Policy & Society* 17 (3): 491–502. https://doi.org/10.1017/S1474746417000574.

Mill, John Stuart. 1978 [1896]. *On Liberty*. Indianapolis, IN: Hackett.

Ministry of Health and Social Affairs. 2020. *Uppdrag om kunskapshöjande insatser om nationella adoptioner m.m. inom familjehemsvården* (S2020/05272/SOF). https://www.regeringen.se/regeringsuppdrag/2020/06/uppdrag-om-kunskapshojande-insatser-om-nationella-adoptioner-m.m.-inom-familjehemsvarden/. Accessed 8 July 2020.

NBHW. 2011. *Initial bedömning vid socialtjänstens rekrytering av familjehem*. Stockholm: Socialstyrelsen. https://www.socialstyrelsen.se/globalassets/sharepoint-dokument/artikelkatalog/ovrigt/2011-1-11.pdf. Accessed 7 January 2020.

NBHW. 2014a. *Adoption. Handbok för socialtjänsten*. Stockholm: Socialstyrelsen.

NBHW. 2014b. *Manual till BRA-fam. En standardiserad bedömningsmetod för rekrytering av familjehem*. Stockholm: Socialstyrelsen.

NBHW. 2015. *Grundbok i BBIC. Barns behov i centrum*, 3rd ed. Stockholm: Socialstyrelsen.

NBHW. 2016a. *Assisterad befruktning med donerade könsceller. Nationellt kunskapsstöd*. Stockholm: Socialstyrelsen.

NBHW. 2016b. *Assisterad befruktning med donerade könsceller. Metodbeskrivning och kunskapsunderlag*. https://www.socialstyrelsen.se/globalassets/sharepoint-dokument/artikelkatalog/kunskapsstod/2016-12-36-bilaga1.pdf. Accessed 7 January 2020.

NBHW. 2016c. *Förstudie till kunskapsstöd om assisterad befruktning med donerade könsceller*. Accessed 7 January 2020.

NBHW. 2020. *Manual till Familjehemsvinjetter. En standardiserad bedömningsmetod för utredning av familjehem*. https://www.socialstyrelsen.se/globalassets/sharepoint-dokument/artikelkatalog/ovrigt/2020-5-6703.pdf. Accessed 30 October 2020.

Neppl, Tricia K., Jennifer M. Senia, and M. Brent Donnellan. 2015. "Effects of Economic Hardship: Testing the Family Stress Model Over Time." *Journal of Family Psychology* 30 (1): 12–21. https://doi.org/10.1037/2Ffam0000168.

Pennings, Guido. 1999. "Measuring the Welfare of the Child: In Search of the Appropriate Evaluation Principle." *Human Reproduction* 14 (5): 1146–1150.

Pratt, Travis C., and Francis T. Cullen. 2005. "Assessing Macro-Level Predictors and Theories of Crime: A Meta-Analysis." *Crime and Justice* 32: 373–450.

Quigley, Muireann. 2010. "A Right to Reproduce?" *Bioethics* 24 (8): 403–411. https://doi.org/10.1111/j.1467-8519.2008.00722.x.

Rasmusson, Bodil, and Margareta Regnér. 2013. *Ett utvalt hem till ett utvalt barn: Familjehemsutredningar och socialt arbete i praktiken*. Stockholm: Natur & Kultur.

Reiss, Franziska. 2013. "Socioeconomic Inequalities and Mental Health Problems in Children and Adolescents: A Systematic Review." *Social Science & Medicine* 90: 24–31. https://doi.org/10.1016/j.socscimed.2013.04.026.
Roberts, Dorothy. 2009. "Race, Gender, and Genetic Technologies: A New Reproductive Dystopia?" *Signs* 34 (4): 783–804.
SALAR. 2019a. *Ersättningar och villkor vid familjehemsvård av barn, unga och vuxna, vårdnadsöverflyttningar m.m. för år 2019* 18/05156 https://skr.se/tjanster/mer franskr/cirkular/cirkular/2018/ersattningarochvillkorvidfamiljehemsvardavbarnun gaochvuxnavardnadsoverflyttningarmmforar2019.25941.html. Accessed 8 January 2020.
SALAR. 2019b. Recording of Conference at *Familjehem Sverige*, Stockholm 23 October 2019. https://www.uppdragpsykiskhalsa.se/kalender/familjehemsveri ge-3/. Accessed 7 January 2020.
SFS 2001:453 Socialtjänstlagen [Social Services Act].
SHSCI. 2017. *Barns rätt till familjehemsvård av god kvalitet*. https://www.ivo.se/globalassets/dokument/publicerat/rapporter/rapporter-2017/barns-ratt-till-familj ehemsvard-av-god-kvalitet.pdf. Accessed 7 January 2020.
Social Insurance Agency. 2019. Entry on 'Adoptionsbidrag'. https://www.forsakrin gskassan.se/privatpers/foralder/adoptera_barn/adoptionsbidrag.
UN. 1989. *The United Nations Convention on the Rights of the Child*. Geneva: United Nations.
UNICEF. 2013. *Child Well-Being in Rich Countries: A Comparative Overview*. https://time.com/wp-content/uploads/2015/04/rc11_eng.pdf. Accessed 23 July 2020.
Wells, Michael B., and Disa Bergnehr. 2014. "Families and Family Policies in Sweden." In *Handbook of Family Policies Across the Globe*, edited by M. Robila, 91–107. New York, NY: Springer.
Westman, Jack C. 1996. "The Rationale and Feasibility of Licensing Parents." *Society* 34 (1): 46–52.

CHAPTER 22

Towards a 'Parenting Regime': Globalising Tendencies and Localised Variation

Jan Macvarish and Claude Martin

INTRODUCTION

The re-framing of family relationships through the prism of 'parenting' has become a significant area of sociological study (Betz et al. 2017; Daly 2013, 2015; Edwards and Gillies 2011; Edwards et al. 2016; Ellingsæter and Leira 2006; Faircloth et al. 2013; Faircloth and Rosen 2020; Furedi 2001; Lee et al. 2014a; Sihvonen 2020; Welshman 2007). Variations have been identified in the extent to which this new framework for understanding families has been adopted at global and local levels, socio-culturally and within public policy. Scholars have also considered the degree to which it represents a departure from previous ways of understanding family life (Boddy et al. 2009; Commaille and Martin 1998; Lenoir 2003; Martin et al. 2017).

According to one literary scholar (Couchman 1983), use of the word 'parenting' 'exploded' in the United States during the 1970s, having first appeared in the 1950s. The expansion was largely in self-help literature instructing parents how to 'parent' their children. A similar trajectory is evident in other countries: in France, the word 'parentalité' appeared in anthropology and psychoanalysis in the late 1950s (Martin 2003, 2013), entering French public debate in the late 1990s. Sihvonen found that Finnish newspapers' use of the term 'vanhemmuus' (parenting) tripled between 1999 and 2014 (Sihvonen

J. Macvarish
University of Kent, Canterbury, UK

C. Martin (✉)
CNRS, University of Rennes, Rennes, France
e-mail: claude.martin@ehesp.fr; claude.martin@cnrs.fr

2020). The use of 'parenting' and related terms expanded very rapidly in public health campaigns, family intervention programmes, legal innovations, government institutions, and state-trained workforces (ChildONEurope 2007; Clarke 2006; Daly and Bray 2015; European Commission 2012). This was first evident in North America and parts of South America, Australasia, and the UK, at intergovernmental level in the work of organisations such as the United Nations, the World Health Organisation and the Organisation for Economic Co-operation and Development, and has now been studied in the Nordic countries (Finland, Sweden, Denmark), China and Brazil, amongst other places.

The emergence of new words to describe family relations and the raising of children, and the adoption of these words by policy-makers, suggest the development of a new nexus through which families are understood. The 'parenting support' policy frame has been described by Daly as, 'wide-ranging and rather rapid mobilisation of social policy to focus attention on, and effect a change in, parental behaviour and child-rearing competence' (Daly 2015, 597). This chapter does not pretend to offer a systematic survey of the extent to which the 'parenting' frame has come to prominence in different nation states, although this would undoubtedly be of value.[1] As a focus for synthesising existing research and developing theory regarding what 'parenting' is and how it reworks previous assumptions about the parent–child relationship, we pose the question, 'What can social scientists tell us about the significance of the construction of 'parenting' as a public and private problem?'. We hope that this will prove useful for future international comparisons which can identify 'typical historical configurations of social, economic and political issues' through which the 'question familiale' (Lenoir 2003, 20–21) has been re-framed as a question of 'parenting'.

This chapter first outlines the ways in which 'parenting' is discussed primarily as a problem of public and private disorder and then considers how 'parenting' reconceptualises the role and status of parents. The field of 'parenting culture studies' was established in order to bring diverse scholarship into a collective dialogue and both authors have been part of its development. This is reflected in the fact that insights from a wide range of social sciences including sociology, social policy, anthropology, criminology, gender studies, and media and cultural studies are drawn upon to conceptualise this still-emerging phenomenon in as open-ended a way as possible. The authors are aware that there is more published research that is currently beyond their linguistic reach, they therefore draw primarily on scholarship from the Anglosphere, and Western and Northern Europe. The chapter refers in particular detail to literature from the UK, France, and Finland, in the case of the first two, reflecting the authors' home countries and in the case of Finland, resulting from an engagement with the work of Ella Sihvonen, which resonates particularly strongly with the approach taken by the authors.

'Parenting': What Is 'the Problem'?

At its most general, today's problematisation of 'parenting' appears to contain a reworking of the very long-standing perception that modernity has weakened social bonds. The concern that society is no longer able to hold individuals together in a meaningful way is, of course, as old as sociology itself. Today's focus on 'parenting' seems to express the same fear about diminishing social bonds in intergenerational terms: that one generation (parents) is unable to care for, or exert a positive influence over the next (children). More specifically, the central tenet of the 'parenting' frame is that parental behaviour is identified as both the cause of, and the solution to, numerous social and individual problems.

In the dominant political and cultural representations of 'parenting', the positive influence of parents is often cast as very weak, while their negative influence is cast as very strong. This can have a strong class dimension, with middle-class parents portrayed as exerting a positive influence and working-class parents a negative one (Lareau 2011). However, the problematisation does not always follow class lines, as the more recent development of concern about 'over-protective' (middle-class) 'helicopter' parents demonstrates (Lee and Macvarish 2020). The overarching theme in 'parenting culture' is that 'parenting' influences the public and private ordering of the individual and society more than anything else, for good or ill. This view of causation has been termed 'parental determinism' (Furedi 2001; Lee et al. 2014a) and is a development of the longer-standing perspective identified as 'infant determinism', whereby experiences during the early years of life are described as being overwhelmingly determinant of individual personality and life chances (Kagan 1998).

In France and the UK, an important theme in the early politicisation of 'parenting' was that the failure of parents to assert their authority was to blame for social disorder. A particularly explicit example comes from France in 2001, when the Socialist Minister for Family and Children, Segolene Royal declared in the middle of a rightwing campaign about the collapse of parental authority:

> Parents need to exercise authority in response to antisocial behavior and at-risk behavior of young people. We must stop the laissez-faire attitude and the parents' desire to be "best friends" with their children, often because they feel guilty for divorcing. Without rules or limits, young people become immature adults. All fathers and mothers, regardless of their living conditions, need more help in putting their authority in practice. (Martin 2013, 191)

French sociologist Jacques Faget commented at the time:

> 'If political speeches, television or radio shows and newspaper articles are focusing on this issue, it is to stigmatize the collapse of the role of parents in the socialization of children, those children who are seen as "sauvageons" (little savages) and who have not inherited the cultural codes that enable them

to behave themselves in society. Without a doubt, the debate on parenting is a debate on public order' (Faget 2001: 70). (In Martin 2013, 187–188)

Similarly, the UK's New Labour government (1997–2010) partially framed the problem of 'parenting' as stemming from a lack of parental authority, resulting in anti-social behaviour in public places, truanting from school and poor behaviour within school. New legislation in the 1998 Crime and Disorder Act imposed 'Parenting Orders' on parents (usually mothers) judged to have failed to control their children and this was extended in the 2003 Anti-Social Behaviour Act and the 2006 Education and Inspections Act (Peters 2012).

The most obvious cultural expression of the concern about diminished parental authority is the global popularity of the 'Supernanny' 'reality' television programmes, which exposed 'out of control' parenting and subjected it to the intervention of 'parenting experts'. The series began in the UK in 2004, but by 2014 had been adapted for broadcast in 48 countries. In each episode, a family where the parents had requested help to 'regain control' of their children submitted themselves to the scrutiny of the 'parenting expert' dubbed 'Supernanny'. Their 'parenting' failures were exposed in extremis to a national audience and critiqued by the 'expert'. That the parents were loving was rarely in doubt, the problem was usually diagnosed as stemming from the parents' failings as either too 'soft' or too 'hard'. Each episode finished with the children's behaviour much-improved, after the whole family adopted Supernanny's behaviour-management techniques.

Supernanny implicitly framed the 'problem' as the existence of a generalised crisis of authority in contemporary 'parenting', leading to unruly children and unhappy families (Bristow 2009; Jensen 2018). The series was influential in normalising the idiom of 'parenting' as a way of describing family life, identifying 'parenting' as an improvable set of techniques and behaviours and establishing the superior authority of self-styled 'parenting experts' over adults and children alike. This reveals a key aspect of the focus on 'parenting': although a lack of parental authority is identified as the problem, solutions often take a humiliating and infantilising approach to parents, which seems more likely to undermine than restore that authority.

'Supernanny' also popularised the tenets of 'positive parenting': rejecting physical punishment as ineffectual or counter-productive, keeping a close watch on the child for opportunities to praise good behaviour and adopting a parental stance of self-reflection, to the extent of observing one's own 'parenting' through the eyes of a real or imagined third party or camera lens (Council of Europe 2006; Reece 2013). The 'positive parenting' approach, which has become ubiquitous in national and international parenting programmes, seeks to discourage existing forms of behaviour through which parental authority has been exercised and coincides with legislative reforms to outlaw physical chastisement. Parental authority embedded in existing lay knowledge and practices is thus actively delegitimised and substituted with expert or professionally-shaped techniques.

Over time, the more punitive approach to parents appears to have given way to an ostensibly more sympathetic account of 'the problem'. Rather than the weak transmission of parental authority, the diagnostic stick is increasingly bent towards the weak transmission of parental love, not because parents are cruel or distracted, but because they face psychological or emotional barriers to loving their children. In the UK, the portrayal of early parenthood as a period of possibly traumatic adjustment and of vulnerability, especially to depression and anxiety, has achieved a particularly high cultural, political, and institutional profile, promoted by celebrities, members of the royal family, the National Health Service and government ministers. According to an article in the *Journal of Health Visiting*, there is:

> Increasing recognition of the importance of supporting women and men in building healthy relationships with their new babies and in negotiating relationship changes during the transition to parenthood... (Underdown 2013, 77)

This problematisation is not confined to a particular social class but generalised to a universal problem of 'attachment' and 'connection' between parents and children.

Concern with the struggle to achieve love between parent and child is not new. In the 1950s, John Bowlby was highly influential in problematising the lack of 'attachment' between mothers (or the mothering figure) and children. His theory had international reach at a time when states were adjusting to the major disruptions of the post-World War II world (Cassidy and Shaver 2016; Hendrick 2016; Sihvonen 2016). But how do we understand why the problematisation of parent–child love in the twenty-first century has achieved such cultural and political prominence?

In 1995, the influential communitarian sociologist Amitai Etzioni diagnosed a 'parenting deficit', caused, he said, by a lack of parental involvement in children's lives. This he attributed to mothers entering the workplace, and the breakdown of the 'educational coalition' between parents as a result of divorce and single parenthood (Etzioni 1993). But according to Etzioni, the problem was not the move away from traditional gendered roles but 'the dearth of parental involvement of both varieties: mothers and fathers' (Etzioni 1993, 7). Contemporary parents, he argued, had become 'distracted' from loving and raising their children by the twin individualising pulls of consumerism and careerism. Professional daycare, he argued, cannot replicate the kind of quasi-parental care children in previous eras received from grandparents or other family members, and, most crucially, professional childcare workers are unable to inculcate the child with the family's values.

However, while Etzioni was concerned with the transmission of values, he was equally keen to avoid a return to the 'moral authoritarianism' of the past, whereby the state and mediating institutions bolstered 'traditional' family values. The solution was therefore more 'parenting', facilitated by greater investment in what Etzioni called the 'parenting industry'. The idea that parents need to be more 'involved' or more 'engaged' in the child's development formed the basis of new policies addressing the 'parenting deficit'. This implicitly posed 'the problem' as one of physical or psychological distance between parent and child, the solution being strengthening the emotional connection between parent and child.

In contrast, sociologist Frank Furedi argues that 'the problem' is not a lack of physical or psychological proximity between parents and their children but a broader societal problem of a lack of clarity about *which* values parents ought to instil in their children (Furedi 2010). The focus on 'parenting' expresses an evident concern for the relationship between the past, the present, and the future, but diverts away from addressing the more fundamental question of what can society in general agree as the foundation for authority in the twenty-first century (Furedi 2010, 2013) and as a result of this diversion, parental authority is further undermined rather than strengthened. The vacuum created by the avoidance of questions of authority and legitimacy becomes filled by technical or therapeutic solutions at the level of interpersonal behaviour such as the advocacy of 'more parenting' or 'better parenting'.

We will now consider how 'parenting', understood as a framework for understanding and addressing social problems through action at the interpersonal level, has the effect of transforming the status and role of the parent.

Consequences of the 'Parenting' Turn

'Parenting' De-Gendered

The most obvious feature of 'parenting' is that, as a word, it floats free from gendered meanings, moving us away from the cultural weight of the complex meanings carried by the words 'mother' and 'father'. Many sociologists have pointed out that, despite the apparent gender-neutrality of 'parenting', in reality, it is mothers who fall under the spotlight and who bear the burden of responsibilisation through the 'parenting' frame. Another way of looking at this de-gendering is that it not only obscures the reality of a still-gendered division of labour, but moves attention away from the question of who should care for children, to the question of how 'parenting' ought to be done. This takes societal interest in the raising of children further inside the walls of the family home.

'Parenting' also effaces the specific authority that has historically been attached to the status of being either a 'father' or a 'mother', in particular, gendered notions of instinctual inclinations towards love and protection. 'Parenting', Smith argues, particularly 'marginalises motherhood' (2010, 362). This is perhaps because modern mothers have historically been attributed authority in partially naturalised terms as instinctive carers, hormonally and neurologically suited to nurturing infants. Although this of course has trapped women in sex-based, highly-moralised gender roles, much has been written about how mothers gained authority relative to fathers by the creation of a scientised version of 'good mothering', which incorporated external expertise from the sciences of hygiene, medicine, psychology and psychoanalysis into the attributes of mothercraft (Apple 1995, 2006). By separating off 'parenting' from the sexed or gendered aspects of family life, mothers can become detached from the ideologically naturalised authority they previously held.

Policy-makers and practitioners often talk of the need to 'engage fathers' in 'parenting' in order to 'involve' them in family life. This is sometimes argued for in terms of redressing the gender imbalance within the home, but it also contains an implicit assumption that natural paternal affinity with the child is lacking and must, therefore, be cultivated by father-focused 'parenting support'. Both mothers and fathers are therefore reconceptualised by 'parenting' in a de-gendered way, which detaches them from some of the past foundations of their authority.

'Parenting' De-Naturalised

Back in 1983, the US sociologists Brigitte and Peter Berger felt able to write:

> When a child is born into this world, he seems to enter into it in a natural, effortless fashion. This process of growth is a source of never-ending excitement in the child and of joy to his or her parents. (Berger and Berger 1983, 149)

And yet in the subsequent 37 years, bringing children into the world has come to be viewed as anything but 'natural' or 'effortless' and parental experience has become associated as much with anxiety as with joy. Advice often states that 'parents are made, not born', emphasising that parenthood, viewed through the lens of 'parenting', is de-naturalised, disassociated from notions of 'instinct'. The use of 'parenting' tends to separate the status of biological parenthood from acts which constitute 'parenting', and raising children is re-imagined as a collection of acts of 'parenting', each requiring active decision-making from a range of behavioural options. By separating 'parenting' from the naturalised state of parenthood, a contingency is introduced into the parent–child bond. Parental status does not derive from the fact of conception but from social recognition of parental identity, forged through a demonstrable performance of 'parenting', preferably 'good parenting'. This requires external affirmation of the parental identity rather than an internal development of familial feeling and confidence.

'Parenting' Floats Free from Parents

What is notable about verbal nouns such as 'parenting' is that they have no subject. While calling someone 'the parent' defines a person in particular ways, 'parenting' is detached from actual parents, floating more freely from the particular adult subject. Many have observed that 'parenting' transforms the parental role from a state of being to acts of doing (du Bois-Reymond 2017; Ramaekers and Suissa 2012; Suissa 2006; Lee et al. 2014a). In this respect, 'parenting' can be performed by people who need not be parents and, parents may not necessarily be 'parenting' at all times or at any time all. Thus, it has been argued, 'parenting' signifies a de-centring or demoting of the parent as an autonomous subject while focusing attention on monitoring their relationship with their child as the implementation of a series of tasks requiring the acquisition and application of skills and techniques (Gillies 2011; Macvarish et al. 2015; Reece 2013; Waiton 2016).

Picking up on Couchman's research into the origins of the word, Smith describes 'parenting' as being from the outset concerned with techniques and 'what works' (2010), as such, others have argued that 'parenting' represents an 'impoverished' (Suissa 2006) but 'expanded' (Furedi 2001) conceptualisation of the parental role. Although it is still parents who are expected to do 'parenting', abstracting it from them creates a space for third parties to become involved and for external criteria to apply.

'Parenting' as Work

'Parenting' is often described as both 'the most important job in the world' and 'the most difficult job in the world', indicating that raising children has become, in some respects, reconceptualised as 'work'. Hays (1998) was one of the first sociologists to identify the application of workplace criteria to the mothering role, while du Bois-Reymond describes the 'blurring of boundaries' involved in the semi-professionalisation of the parent through 'parenting' (2017, 89). Redefining familial child-rearing as 'work' has the effect of undermining the distinction between public and private life and of exposing the more intimate aspects of family life to the language and criteria of the public domain. This leads to parents becoming appreciated less in their specificity as individuals who love their own child more than anybody else could, but rather flattens them out into rest of the childcare workforce.

'Parenting' Requiring Expertise, Self-Reflection and Scaffolding

As noted above, the 'parenting' concept emerged from expert and 'self-help' knowledge frameworks. While there have long been experts advising parents how to raise their children (Lee et al. 2014a; Hulbert 2011), the 'parenting' frame brings with it a great proliferation in their number. Lee argues that today's parent is called upon not only to listen to experts but also to adopt the stance of an expert themselves, accessing multiple sources of information and performing the role of 'risk-manager' in relation to her/his child (2014a). Many scholars have described how the number of potential physical and psychological harms to be considered has expanded enormously during the rise of 'parenting culture' (Lee et al. 2014a). And in addition to protecting the child from risks from without, the parent must recognise their own potential as a risk to their child's development, modifying their behaviour and emotional disposition, in accordance with expert knowledge, to avoid harming the child or to optimise their future.

To achieve a sufficiently reflective parenting style, the parent must adopt a distanced view of their child and of their own feelings towards him or her. In the Journal of Health Visiting article cited earlier, 'reflective parenting' is said to be essential for the 'optimisation' of the child's development. Becoming 'reflective' requires 'mentalising' by the parent to 'make sense of their own and their child's mental state', but this requires professional support, sometimes described as 'scaffolding':

> ...health visitors and early years workers are ideally placed to explicitly 'scaffold' parents to adopt a reflective stance when trying to make sense of their infant's behaviour...beginning in the prenatal period. (Underdown 2013, 76)

The concept of 'scaffolding' comes from developmental psychology (it is associated with Vygotsky, although was not actually used by him), where it typically describes the adult's role in relation to a child's learning. Its use in the context of 'parenting' support indicates that parents have come to be seen in an infantilised, developmental way as 'works in progress', who require parental-style support from professionals.

'Parenting' as a Reversal of the Parent–Child Relationship

Through 'parenting', parents are reconfigured as 'becomings' rather than 'beings'. The particular form of 'becoming' imagined through 'parenting' is not the self-development of a morally autonomous individual but a process involving external assistance, assessment, and validation. It has been characterised as 'performative parenting' (Faircloth 2013), whereby parental behaviour is oriented towards external validation. Du Bois-Reymond (2017) likens this to Reisman et al.'s (1950) characterisation of 'other-directedness' and explains how this further erodes parental authority.

Much sociological work has described how, despite greater gender equality in the public domain, being a mother has become a fraught process of struggling to meet external expectations (Hays 1998). When considering the highly demanding contemporary ideals of 'mothering', Gillis describes the identity work now central to being a mother as adding:

yet another task to mothers' work; representing herself to herself and to others as something she can never completely be. Never before has this cultural imperative taken up so much space and time in women's lives. Never have mothers been so burdened by motherhood. (Gillis 1996, 178)

Understood through the lens of uncertain identity, the 'burden of motherhood' becomes a psychological one. But the uncertain maternal identity is dependent not only on validation from outside the family, but perhaps even more disturbingly, on validation from the child. In tandem with the parent reconceptualised from a 'being' to a 'becoming', children's rights and childhood studies advocates often stress that children should be reconceptualised from 'becomings' to 'beings'. This indicates a potentially disturbing development of not just a blurring of boundaries but a reversal in the parent–child relationship, with the child re-posed as the more certain pole and the adult conceived of as less fixed and more unstable. Villalobos has written of this adult dependence on the child as 'attachment in reverse' (2014) and Furedi suggests that 'At a time when very few human relations can be taken for granted, the child appears as a unique emotional partner' (2001, 120).

Discussion: Globalising Tendencies and Localised Variation

In his paper 'Total Parenting', Richard Smith explores the significance of the changes which have normalised 'particular language' and a 'particular outlook on being a parent in general and a mother in particular'. He describes this process as 'soft totalitarianism' (Smith 2010, 364). In a similar vein, Furedi refers to 'linguistic engineering' projects which change language in order to change ideas (2016). He suggests that such projects are driven by cultural and political elites who have the power to consolidate and disseminate new frameworks of knowledge. There is evidence to support this view of a conscious political argument being made to effect a cultural shift in understandings of the relationship between families and the state. In the US and the UK, policy advocates associated with the 'parenting' project have argued that the conventional boundary which upholds the privacy and autonomy of the family acts as a barrier to social improvement (Bruer 1999; Macvarish 2016).

A leading charity's contribution to a UK government consultation exercise in the early days of the shift to 'parenting' exemplifies the depth of the reconceptualisation being pursued:

> Traditionally parenting was considered to be a private issue with support coming only from the extended family. Although this is no longer appropriate, due to lifestyle changes, people may often feel that they have failed if they need help with parenting. There must be no stigma in seeking support with parenting. The National Family and Parenting Institute needs to promote support so that it is seen as a responsible and caring option, accessible to all parents. (The Children's

Society, in Supporting Families [Responses to the Consultation] Department of Education 1998)

This statement implicitly problematises the existing model which validated familial self-sufficiency and parental responsibility. Similar arguments for a reframing of the relationship between families and the state are evident in a much later statement by a member of the House of Lords:

> For too long, fear of being criticised for interfering in family life has led politicians and policy makers to shy away from this arena... The early years and particularly what happens in the home are of utmost importance for a child's future... it is time to change our views about parenting: not all parents know how to be a good parent...it is time to end the last great taboo in public policy. (Tyler 2015)

In this, we can see the speaker invoke early years determinism, whereby 'what happens in the home' is dramatised into a position of primary importance and also separate out 'parenting' from parents: not all parents are capable of good 'parenting'. The explicit intention is to open up the family to greater political interference by removing the 'taboo' of family privacy.

In the US, the Harvard Center on the Developing Child worked with public relations experts to 'frame and re-frame' the issue of early years intervention, deploying metaphors from neuroscience to 'trigger(s) the shared and durable cultural models that people use to make sense of their world' (Nisbet 2010). The strategy was designed to challenge the 'dominant cultural model' which treated early childhood as being contained within the 'family bubble' (ibid.), and therefore resistant to political attention and policy intervention. Parental influence was dramatised through this strategy in what can be described as neurobiologised parental determinism or 'neuroparenting' (Macvarish 2016; Vandenbroeck et al. 2017; Wastell and White 2012).

Similar developments have been analysed in other European states, even those with very different histories of state intervention in early childhood (Knijn et al. 2018; Martin 2013, 2014; Martin et al. 2017; Sihvonen 2018a, b; Widding 2018) and neuro-focused 'parenting' support has been disseminated in very diverse national contexts beyond Europe and North America, such as Singapore and West Africa. Scientific authority appears to promise a 'culture-less blueprint' for child-rearing which can be universalised, posing challenges to existing beliefs and practices in apparently non-judgemental, value-neutral terms (Faircloth 2013; Kagan 1998).

While social policy has developed tools for comparing the implementation of 'parenting support' policies across varied welfare state contexts (Daly 2013, 2015; Daly et al. 2012, 2015), the political and cultural dimensions of the 'parenting' frame may require different analytical tools by which we can consider highly complex variables. Work exists which points towards the development of some helpful distinctions, for example, according to Sihvonen, in

Finland there has been a reluctance to impose external expertise on parents, rather, their own expertise is emphasised, with a focus on drawing out parental capacity 'from within', with the intention of 'empowering' the parent. Early intervention 'parenting' support was aimed at encouraging 'active and responsible parental agency' and 'avoiding dependence' (Sihvonen 2016, 8). This, Sihvonen argues, is shaped by Finnish cultural expectations of autonomous personhood. Another distinction is the extent to which 'parent-shaming' has taken place, for example, in France, Sweden, Belgium, and Hungary there has been a greater emphasis on non-hierarchical and peer support which avoids a 'deficit' model (Molinuevo 2013). The novelty of the 'parenting' frame also varies. In Sweden and France (Stolberg 2017; Martin 2014), both countries with a long history of health services 'claiming' child welfare as a national concern, 'parenting' policies do not appear so markedly different from modes of family intervention which existed throughout the twentieth century. In contrast, many scholars attest to the qualitative shift in Britain from 'implicit to explicit' family policy associated with the turn to 'parenting', which reflected a move away from a laissez-faire social framework to a more interventionist one.

Analysis also needs to take account of variation over time. It could be argued that policy-makers in the UK have learned that blaming and shaming parents in certain social groups (such as teenage mothers) provokes resistance to the development of a 'help-seeking' disposition. More recent approaches have therefore been less targeted at 'poor parents' who do 'poor parenting' and instead have been universalised through the prisms of 'mental health' and 'vulnerable transitions'.

Variation in the dominant sources of authority across societies seems particularly significant in shaping the way 'parenting support' is argued for and delivered. For example, the salience of religious institutions or different types of expertise (medical or psychotherapeutic) has influenced the development of policy in France (Martin 2015). Also significant are varying levels of social solidarity and social homogeneity reflecting post-Cold War social arrangements, class politics and migration patterns.

Conclusion: Reposing the Problem of 'Parenting'

The figure of the weakened, over-burdened, and anxious parent is a prevalent theme in the discourse of both the promoters and the critics of 'parenting' culture (Vansieleghem 2010). The French sociologist Robert Castel describes how the therapeutic tendency, which continually draws attention to parental deficiencies and poses external experts as authorities in family life, contributes to 'parental decline' which results in demands not only to 'educate the children' but 'also teach the parents their 'job'' (Castel 1981; Martin 2013, 182). Castel's work echoes that of Christopher Lasch in the US (1979, 1985, 1995) and resonates with that of Furedi in the UK (2001, 2004).

Although family life has often been politicised and long been subject to public policy, this has generally co-existed with the cultural validation of relatively autonomous parental judgement and presumptions that natural or instinctive familial feelings were the norm. The overarching meaning of family life as it has been reconceived through 'parenting' is that the task of raising children has become detached from the distinctiveness of the parental role and the specificities of individual parents. The internal life of the family is also rendered less specific and less special by the fact that it is opened up to judgement by criteria derived from the public domain rather than the private domain. For example, the generalised goals of increasing 'social mobility' or 'child welfare' overwhelm internal values such as lovingness and idiosyncratic family customs. Perhaps 'parenting' can be understood as a flexible concept which unlocks aspects of the private sphere by transforming the parent from a wall around the home to a window into it.

Although the stated aim of 'early intervention' and 'parenting support' is to create individuals 'free' from problems which will lead them to place fewer demands on the state in later life, it does so by encouraging 'help-seeking' behaviour in parents and children and flattening out the distinction between adults and children. This suggests that attempts to deal with 'the problem' of weakened social bonds and weakened adult authority by more direct intervention in the parent–child relationship, as encapsulated by the turn to 'parenting', may well turn out to be counter-productive.

Note

1. For a policy tracing in the French case, see Martin et al. (2017). To achieve a comparison, research would need to be undertaken based on a coherent understanding of what constitutes 'parenting' as a general and distinct phenomenon and employing a method of analysis capable of tracing the process of adoption and adaptation in countries with very different histories and with varying relations with one another. One study developed this perspective for five European countries (UK, Germany, the Netherlands, France, and Sweden) with the support of the Open research area in social sciences (ORA) programme. See the special issue of *Social Policy and Society* (Daly 2015).

Bibliography

Apple, R. D. 1995. "Constructing Mothers: Scientific Motherhood in the Nineteenth and Twentieth Centuries." *Social History of Medicine* 8 (2): 161–178.

Apple, R. D. 2006. *Perfect Motherhood: Science and Childrearing in America*. New Brunswick: Rutgers University Press.

Berger, B., P. L. Berger, and P. L. Berger. 1983. *The War over the Family: Capturing the Middle Ground*. London: Hutchinson.

Betz, T., M. S. Honig, and I. Ostner, eds. 2017. *Parents in the Spotlight: Parenting Practices and Support from a Comparative Perspective*. Berlin: Verlag Barbara Budrich.

Boddy, J., et al. 2009. International Perspectives on Parenting Support: Non-English Language Sources, DCSF Research Report NO DCSF-RR 114, Institute of Education, London. Available at https://www.expoo.be/sites/default/files/kennisdocument/UK_international_perspective_on_parenting_support1.pdf.
Bristow, J. 2009. *Standing up to Supernanny*. Exeter: Societas.
Bruer, J. T. 1999. *The Myth of the First Three Years: A New Understanding of Early Brain Development and Lifelong Learning*. New York: Simon and Schuster.
Cassidy, J., and R. Shaver Phillip, eds. 2016. *Handbook of Attachment. Theory, Research and Clinical Applications*. New York: The Guilford Press.
Castel, R. 1981. *La gestion des risques. De l'anti-psychiatrie à l'après-psychanalyse*. Paris: Les éditions de minuit.
ChildONEurope. 2007. *Survey on the Role of Parents and the Support from the Governments in the European Union*. Florence, Italy: ChildONEurope.
Clarke, K. 2006. "Childhood, Parenting and Early Intervention: A Critical Examination of the Sure Start National Programme." *Critical Social Policy* 26: 699–721.
Commaille, J., and C. Martin. 1998. *Les enjeux politiques de la famille*. Paris: Bayard.
Couchman, Gordon W. 1983. "Parenting: An Informal Survey." *American Speech* 58 (3): 285–288.
Council of Europe. 2006. "Recommendation (2006): 19 Recommendation of the Committee of Ministers to Member States on Policy to Support Positive Parenting." Available at https://wcd.coe.int/wcd/ViewDoc.jsp?id=1073507&Site=CM.
Daly, M. 2013. "Parenting Support Policies in Europe." *Families, Relationships and Societies* 2 (2): 159–174.
Daly, M. 2015. "Parenting Support as Policy Field: An Analytic Framework." *Social Policy and Society* 14 (4): 597–608.
Daly, M., and R. Bray. 2015. "Parenting Support in England: The Bedding Down of a New Policy." *Social Policy and Society* 14 (4): 633–644.
Daly, M., T. Knijn, C. Martin, and I. Ostner. 2012. "Parenting Support in Four European Countries: Element for a Comparison." In 10th Annual ESPAnet Conference, Edinburgh, Scotland.
Daly, M., R. Bray, Z. Bruckauf, J. Byrne, A. Margaria, N. Pec´nik, and M. Samms-Vaughan. 2015. *Family and Parenting Support: Policy and Provision in a Global Context*. Innocenti Insight. Florence: UNICEF Office of Research.
du Bois-Reymond, M. 2017. "Learning Processes in the Transition to Young Parenthood". In *Parents in the Spotlight: Parenting Practices and Support from a Comparative Perspective*, edited by T. Betz, M. S. Honig, and I. Ostner, 81-98. Berlin:Verlag Barbara Budrich.
Edwards, R., and V. Gillies. 2011. "Clients or Customers, Commonplace or Pioneers? Navigating the Contemporary Class Politics of Family, Parenting Skills and Education." *Ethics and Education* 6: 141–154.
Edwards, R., V. Gillies, and N. Horsley. 2016. "Early Intervention and Evidence-Based Policy and Practice: Framing and Taming." *Social Policy and Society* 15: 1–10.
Ellingsæter, A. L., and A. Leira, eds. 2006. *Politicising Parenthood in Scandinavia: Gender Relations in Welfare States*. Bristol: Policy Press.
Etzioni, A. 1993. *The Parenting Deficit*. London: Demos.
Commission, European. 2012. *Parenting Support Policy Brief*. Brussels: Employment, Social Affairs and Inclusion.
Faircloth, C. 2013. *Militant Lactivism?: Attachment Parenting and Intensive Motherhood in the UK and France*, Vol. 24. Berghahn Books.

Faircloth, C., D. M. Hoffman, and L. L. Layne, eds. 2013. *Parenting in Global Perspective: Negotiating Ideologies of Kinship, Self and Politics.* London: Routledge.
Faircloth, C., and R. Rosen. 2020. "Childhood, Parenting Culture, and Adult-Child Relations in Global Perspectives [Whole Issue]." *Families, Relationships and Societies* 9 (1): 3–6.
Furedi, F. 2001. *Paranoid Parenting: Abandon Your Anxieties and Be a Good Parent.* Allen Lane.
Furedi, F. 2004. *Therapy Culture: Cultivating Vulnerability in an Uncertain Age.* London: Routledge.
Furedi, F. 2010. *Wasted: Why Education Isn't Educating.* London: Bloomsbury Publishing.
Furedi, F. 2013. *Authority: A Sociological History.* Cambridge: Cambridge University Press.
Furedi, F. 2016. *What's Happened to the University?: A Sociological Exploration of Its Infantilisation.* London: Routledge.
Gillis, J. R. 1996. *A World of Their Own Making: Myth, Ritual, and the Quest for Family Values.* Cambridge: Harvard University Press.
Gillies, V. 2011. "From Function to Competence: Engaging with the New Politics of Family." Sociological Research Online. 16 (4) http://www.socresonline.org.uk/16/4/11.html.
Hays, S. 1998. *The Cultural Contradictions of Motherhood.* New Haven: Yale University Press.
Hendrick, H. 2016. *Narcissistic Parenting in an Insecure World: A History of Parenting Culture 1920s to Present.* Bristol: Policy Press.
Hulbert, A. 2011. *Raising America: Experts, Parents, and a Century of Advice About Children.* New York: Vintage.
Jensen, T. 2018. *Parenting the Crisis: The Cultural Politics of Parent-Blame.* Bristol: Policy Press.
Kagan, J. 1998. *Three Seductive Ideas.* Cambridge, MA: Harvard University Press.
Knijn, T., C. Martin, and I. Ostner. 2018. "Triggers and Drivers of Change in Framing Parenting Support in North Western Europe." In *Handbook of Family Policy,* edited by G. B. Eydal & T. Rostgaard, 152-166. Cheltenham: Edward Elgar.
Lareau, A. 2011. *Unequal Childhoods: Class, Race, and Family Life.* Berkeley: University of California Press.
Lasch, C. 1995. *Haven in a Heartless World: The Family Besieged.* W. W. Norton.
Lasch, C. 1979. *The Culture of Narcissism: American Life in an Age of Diminishing Expectations.* New York: Warner Books.
Lasch, C. 1985. *The Minimal Self: Psychic Survival in Troubled Times.* W. W: Norton.
Lee, E., and J. Macvarish. 2020. "Le 'parent hélicoptère' et le paradoxe de la parentalité intensive au 21$^\text{è}$ siècle (The 'Helicopter Parent' and the Paradox of Intensive Parenting in the 21st Century)." *Lien social et politiques* (85): 19–42.
Lee, E., J. Bristow, C. Faircloth, and J. Macvarish. 2014a. *Parenting Culture Studies.* Basingstoke: Palgrave Macmillan.
Lee, E., J. Macvarish, and P. Lowe. 2014b. *The Uses and Abuses of Biology: Neuroscience, Parenting and Family Policy in Britain: A 'Key Findings' Report.*
Lenoir, R. 2003. *Généalogie de la morale familiale.* Paris: Seuil.
Macvarish, J. 2016. *Neuroparenting, the Expert Invasion of Family Life.* London: Macmillan.

Martin, C. 2003. *La parentalité en questions. Perspectives sociologiques*. Paris: La Documentation Française. https://www.ladocumentationfrancaise.fr/rapports-publics/034000552/index.shtml.

Martin, C. 2013. "The Invention of a Parenting Policy in the French Context: Elements for a Policy Tracing." In *Sustainability and transformation in European social policy*, edited by J. Garcès and I. Monsonis Paya, 179–197. Oxford: Peter Lang Publishing.

Martin, C. 2014. "Le soutien à la parentalité : une nouvelle politique en Europe." *Politiques sociales et familiales* (118): 9–22.

Martin, C. 2015. "Parenting Support in France: Policy in an Ideological Battlefield." *Social Policy and Society* 14 (4): 609–620.

Martin, C. 2017. "Parenting as a Public Problem in a Neoliberal Era." *Journal of Comparative Family Studies*, special issue on "Families, Citizenship and Human Rights in a Global Era," S. Fogiel-Bijaoui and Zvi Triger as guest editors, vol. XLVIII, no. 3, 303–314.

Martin, C., ed. with, A. Hammouche, M. Modak, G. Neyrand, C. Sellenet, M. Vandenbroeck, C. Zaouche-Gaudron, S. Dauphin, and J. Moeneclaey. 2017. *Accompagner les parents dans leur travail éducatif et de soin*. Paris: La documentation française.

Molinuevo, D. 2013. *Parenting Support in Europe*. Dublin: Eurofound. https://digitalcommons.ilr.cornell.edu/cgi/viewcontent.cgi?article=1247&context=intl.

Nisbet, M. 2010. The Frameworks Institute: Changing the Conversation About Policy Problems. https://bigthink.com/age-of-engagement/the-frameworks-institute-changing-the-conversation-about-policy-problems. Accessed 8 March 2020.

Peters, E. 2012. "'I Blame the Mother': Educating Parents and the Gendered Nature of Parenting Orders." *Gender and Education* 24 (1): 119–130.

Ramaekers, S., and J. Suissa. 2012. *The Claims of Parenting: Reasons, Responsibility and Society*, Dordrecht: Springer Science & Business Media.

Reece, H. 2013. "The Pitfalls of Positive Parenting." *Ethics and Education* 8 (1): 42–54.

Reisman, D., N. Glazer, and R. Denny. 2001. *The Lonely Crowd. A Study of The Changing American Character*. New Haven: Yale University Press.

Sihvonen, E. 2016. Huoli kadonneesta vanhemmuudesta 2000-luvun suomalaisessa yhteiskunnassa: lasten kasvatus ja vastuullinen vanhemmuus. *Kasvatus & Aika* 10 (1) [English translation provided by author].

Sihvonen, E. 2018a. "Early Interventionist Parenting Support: The Case Study of Finland." *Families, Relationships and Societies* 7 (1): 123–139.

Sihvonen, E. 2018b. "Parenting Support Policy in Finland: Responsibility and Competence as Key Attributes of Good Parenting in Parenting Support Projects." *Social Policy and Society* 17 (3): 443–456.

Sihvonen, E. 2020. "From Family Policy to Parenting Support. Parenting-Related Anxiety in Finnish Parenting Support Projects." Dissertation. University of Helsinki.

Smith, R. 2010. "Total Parenting." *Educational Theory* 60 (3): 357–369.

Suissa, J. 2006. "Untangling the mother knot: Some thought on parents, children and philosophers of education." *Ethics and Education* 1 (1): 65–77.

Stolberg, C. 2017. "Converging Interventions? Social Investment Elements in Child Health Strategies in Germany, Sweden, and the United Kingdom." In *Parents in the Spotlight: Parenting Practices and Support from a Comparative Perspective*, edited by T. Betz, M-S. Honig, I. Ostner, 293–312. Berlin: Verlag Barbara Budrich.

Tyler, Baroness of Enfield. 2015. Foreword to The Parliamentary Inquiry into Parenting and Social Mobility Enhancing Parenting Support Across the UK. Family and Daycare Trust, March 5

Underdown, A. 2013. "Parent-Infant Relationships: Supporting Parents to Adopt a Reflective Stance". *Journal of Health Visiting* 1 (2): 76–79.

Vandenbroeck, M., J. De Vos, W. Fias, L.M. Olsson, H. Penn, D. Wastel, and S. White. 2017. *Constructions of Neuroscience in Early Childhood Education*. London: Routledge.

Vansieleghem, N. 2010. "The Residual Parent to Come: On the Need for Parental Expertise and Advice." *Educational Theory* 60 (3): 341–355.

Villalobos, A. 2014. *Motherload: Making It All Better in Insecure Times*. Berkeley: University of California Press.

Waiton, S. 2016. "Third Way Parenting and the Creation of the 'Named Person' in Scotland: The End of Family Privacy and Autonomy?" *SAGE Open*. https://doi.org/10.1177/2158244016629525.

Wastell, D., and S. White. 2012. "Blinded by Neuroscience: Social Policy, the Family and the Infant Brain." *Families, Relationships and Societies* 1: 397–414.

Welshman, J. 2007. *From Transmitted Deprivation to Social Exclusion: Policy, Poverty, and Parenting*. Bristol: Policy Press.

Widding, U. 2018. "Parental Determinism in the Swedish Strategy for Parenting Support." *Social Policy and Society* 17 (3): 481–490.

PART V

Family Lives in Migration: Intergenerational and Transnational Relationships

Edited by Isabella Crespi

CHAPTER 23

Migration and Families in European Society

Laura Zanfrini

In contemporary Europe, the ample presence of families with a migratory background, originating from both EU and non-EU countries, can be understood as an unexpected phenomenon, due to the permanent settlement of migrants initially selected as "guest workers" and to other unplanned processes—from decolonisation to the influx of asylum seekers. Moreover, family reunion has been the main channel to enter Europe for many years, and in several EU States those from migrant parents make up an important share of new births.[1] Given this, this chapter aims to describe some of the processes that have made migrant families a relevant topic in contemporary Europe: an unescapable theme for family scholars, but also a "lens" through which to analyse many topics connected with the present and the future of European societies.

The chapter firstly analyses the transition from a migration of (temporary) workers to a migration of permanent settlers and families, which have completely changed the "meaning" of migration and its long-term impact

---

The original version of this chapter was revised: The affiliation of the author Laura Zanfrini has been changed from "Universita Cattolica, Milan, Italy" to "Fondazione ISMU, Milan, Italy". The correction to this chapter is available at https://doi.org/10.1007/978-3-030-73306-3_33

L. Zanfrini (✉)
Fondazione ISMU, Milan, Italy
e-mail: laura.zanfrini@unicatt.it

© The Author(s), under exclusive license to Springer Nature Switzerland AG 2021, corrected publication 2021
A.-M. Castrén et al. (eds.), *The Palgrave Handbook of Family Sociology in Europe*, https://doi.org/10.1007/978-3-030-73306-3_23

(Section "The Discovery of the Immigrant Family"). Then, it focuses on family reunion, analysing the relationship between the legislative framework and a set of social, cultural, and ethical issues (Section "Family Reunions"). Section "Inequality and Diversity" discusses how migrants are challenging both the sustainability of the European social model and the European way of life, that is the ability to reconciling the principle of equality and the recognition of diversity. As synthetised in the concluding section (Section "Conclusions"), given their quantitative importance—in the demographic scenario of the "old" continent—many reasons contribute to making the immigrant family a relevant topic for the present and the future of Europe.

The Discovery of the Immigrant Family

For many years, since the end of World War II to the early 1970s, several European States were characterised by an approach to migration based on the idea of the *Guest Worker* (Penninx 2005). This approach contained in itself the reasons for (Zanfrini 2019): defining migration as a pure economic phenomenon, akin to the importation of any other productive factor; encouraging the "natural" concentration of foreign workers in the lower layers of the professional hierarchy; cultivating the illusion of the temporary nature of migration, and contrasting the settlement of migrants and their inclusion in the citizens' community. Since migrants were expected to be alone and family reunification was not envisioned, one can understand how the appearance on the public scene of the immigrant family can be viewed as an unexpected—if not unwelcome—phenomenon.

Actually, many European States have not really chosen to become a place of permanent migration and a multi-ethnic society. The large presence of people and families with a migratory background is the outcome of a set of "unintentional" processes occurred in the last few decades. In some ways, it was precisely the block of economic migrations, in the early 1970s, that stimulated the settlement of migrants and the arrival of their family members. More generally, European States' transformation into immigration countries is due to a context of *embedded liberalism* (Cornelius et al. 1994), which strongly influences the decisions on both the volume of arrivals and the treatment imposed to migrants. The normative foundations of a democracy impose serious limits on the governments' ability to restrict immigration and immigrants' rights (Hampshire 2013), not to mention the presence of civil society organisations lobbying in favour of migrants. As a result, European countries had to recognise many of their "guest workers" the right to permanent residence, as well as the possibility of either reuniting with their left-behind family members or creating new families. Similarly, despite the attempts to reduce their volume, the entrances for reasons of protection are difficult to contain, since they call into question fundamental human rights. Particularly in critical phases—such as the Balkan War (1991–2001), the events following the Arab Springs (started in 2010) or the crises in Syria (2011 to now)—EU States have had to manage the arrival of asylum seekers who, in many cases, become permanent settlers. As a result of all these processes, despite the official suspension of policies for the attraction of migrants for a prolonged

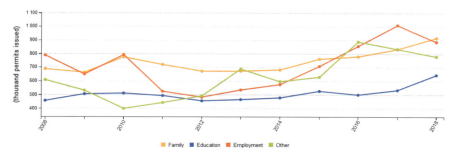

Fig. 23.1 First permits by reason in the EU28

phase of its recent history, Europe has continued to be one of the first destinations in the world. With the new millennium, and the timid reopening of economic migrations (through increasingly selective migration schemes, which often allow the migrants to bring with them their dependent family members—the so-called *accompanying members*), migration for family reasons have continued to constitute the prevailing share of the new entries—besides those for "other" reasons, mainly asylum seekers. Also in the latest year for which data are available (2018), the highest number of first residence permits in the EU-28 was issued for family-related reasons (915,000, or 28.4% of all permits issued), followed by employment-related reasons (886,000; 27.5%), other reasons (781,000; 24.2%) and education-related reasons (644,000; 20%) (Fig. 23.1).

Moreover, thanks to the right of free circulation, awarded in 1992 to the holders of the *European Citizenship*[2]—in its turn conferred to any person holding the nationality of an EU country—millions of people have been freed from the restrictions to immigrate imposed to non-EU citizens. From this moment on, non-nationals from another EU country, formally, are no longer migrants, although they are often perceived as such and sometimes encounter integration difficulties. However, while encouraging intra-EU mobility, the institution of the European Citizenship has formalised the distinction between EU and non-EU foreign residents, making it the most important base of the system of *civic stratification* (Lockwood 1996).

According to this author, the concept of civil stratification refers to the construction of formal devices of inclusion and exclusion with respect to rights: in the EU, only national citizens benefit from the status of full citizen; the nationals of an EU country different from that of residence are granted additional rights as compared to the foreigners coming from a non-EU country (the so-called *Third-Country Nationals*); these latter, on their turn, fall into a variety of subgroups (Morris 2003). For example, the *long-term residents*[3] are a sort of "semi-citizens" (or *denizens*: Hammar 1989), since they benefit from most of the citizen's prerogatives—even if they do not "belong" to the State—differently from the holders of a temporary permit of stay, particularly seasonal workers. Even the migrants for reasons of protection fall into different categories: only a minority of them obtain the *refugee status*, whereas others receive a form of *subsidiary protection*. Furthermore, all the countries register, albeit to different extents, the presence of *irregular migrants*, who are eligible only to few citizenship rights (e.g. a minimum level of health assistance). Finally, millions of migrants have acquired the citizenship of the country of residence (765,000 only in 2017, latest year available), and have consequently "disappeared" from the statistics; many of them have also been allowed a *dual citizenship*, thus benefiting from rights both in their sending country and in the hosting one. As it is easy to understand, the collocation within these different categories influences the life and working opportunities of the migrants and of their offspring, and affects their sense of belonging to the society. This is particularly relevant in the case of children born to migrant parents, despite the protection offered by the legislation of EU States, even in the case of undocumented minors (who, for example, have the right to attend public schools).

In view of our previous considerations, it was in 1970, after the restrictive turn in the possibility of migrants' legal entry, that, for a sort of historical nemesis, European societies acknowledged that they had turned into immigration societies. The emblem of this transformation is exactly the appearance on the public scene of immigrant families. Not by chance, the theories (e.g. Bohning 1984) identifying the different phases of an ideal-typical *migration cycle* and the relative implications for the hosting communities date back to the 1980s. Although today they seem too schematic in describing a multifaceted reality such as immigration, these theories document the awareness of the stable character of the immigrant presence, and of its inevitable consequences. When migration becomes familiar, it radically changes its impact and its meaning for the recipient society, transforming an economic issue—just as the importation of temporary workers—into a political and an identity one. It is precisely through families that migration manifests itself as a phenomenon capable of changing the very constitutive features of a society, affecting the somatic, ethnic, and religious characteristics of the population. This is especially true for the nations involved in deep demographic changes, therefore making the incidence of the population with a migratory background increasingly important (Van Mol and de Valk 2016). And in many countries, family law issues often rank among the most sensitive arguments in the governance of interethnic coexistence.

The familial character of immigration in Europe is amply confirmed by the latest data (OECD 2019): for nearly 95% of married migrants, the spouse is present in the same household in the destination country (ranging from 66% in Lithuania to 98% in the UK), and 44% of married migrants arrived in the host country in the same year as their spouse. Initially, slightly more than half of married migrants live with their children; this share, then, rises steadily over time and reaches a peak with 15–19 years of stay, attaining 75%.

In addition to the new entries, the growth of the residents with a migratory background is due to the births to immigrant parents, which gives life to the so-called *second generations*. Since 2015,[4] in the EU-28, the number of births to foreign-born mothers has been more than 1 million each year. Focusing on 2018 (last available data), in the EU-28 as a whole, births to foreign-born mothers amount to 1,062,797 out of a total of 4,976,628 births, and are particularly numerous in Germany (30% of total births), UK (27.8%), France (23.9%), Italy (22.9%), and Spain (26%). Most of them are from mothers born in a non-EU country, which covers 15.7% of all the births in the EU as a whole, and even 21.6% in Germany and 20.9% in France.

After 1990, migration has become the main driver of population growth (or the main counterweight to its decrease) in many EU countries. Despite also being the least predictable component of population change, its contribution to contain the risk of a demographic decline has been repeatedly acknowledged, even by EU institutions[5]. Migration is expected to have a significant demographic impact also because migrant populations have different levels of fertility and mortality, due to a different age structure and different fertility patterns.[6]

On the one hand, immigration is often referred to as "the" solution to the demographic decline; on the other hand, it is feared to grow to the point of undermining the presumed "original characteristics" of the native population and its cultural and religious identity. Not incidentally, one of the most disputed issues concerns the effects of migration on fertility. In general terms, migrant women register a higher total fertility rate than non-migrant ones; however, the general trend indicates a progressive reduction of this gap, that is a progressive rapprochement of the procreative behaviours of immigrant women with those of the host society (Sobotka 2008). Moreover, fertility levels vary widely from one migrant group to another, a circumstance that affects the perception of social distance towards the immigrant families that most deviate from the average values, particularly when they come from non-EU nations and from Islamic-majority societies. According to available studies, being from an Islamic country tends to be associated with higher levels of fertility, but this does not apply to all national groups and the effect of religion can be strongly offset by other variables, such as the women's levels of education and employment (ibidem). In about half of the European countries, the presence of immigrant women raises fertility rates, whereas in the Baltic countries, Poland, Czechia, Romania, and Bulgaria their numbers are too small to influence these rates; in other cases, their fertility rate is very similar to that of natives (e.g. the Netherlands) and sometimes (Iceland and Denmark) immigrant women even tend to lower national rates (Volant et al. 2019). Finally, immigration can—and in most cases effectively does—offer a positive contribution in contrasting the ageing process affecting Europe, but it cannot be considered the only—and not even the main—solution.

In any case, particularly in countries with a recent immigration history, the foreign population is usually younger than the indigenous one, and concentrated in the reproductive age groups: as a consequence, its contribution to natural growth is comparatively more significant, and the presence of children of immigrant-origin becomes very visible within the school and other public services. This circumstance increases the migrants' "burden" on the welfare system, encouraging the competition with the weaker strata of the indigenous population for access to services and benefits (crèches, subsidised housing, etc.), a risk aggravated by the weak socio-economic condition of immigration in Europe (Section "Inequality and Diversity"). On the other hand, migrants' presence reinforces cultural pluralism—a trait that today often enjoys a positive consideration—and fuels the survival strategies of certain organisations facing the loss of autochthonous clients (e.g. vocational schools); finally, according to some critical observers, it encourages the development of social research and social work applied to the (real or constructed) "problems" of migrants and their descendants. For these and other reasons, in all the European immigration countries, the many issues connected to immigrant families have assumed an increased importance, both in the research agenda and in the political debate.

Family Reunions

The enactment of the legislation on the *right to family reunification* marked the definitive recognition of European societies' transformation into countries of settlement. While economic migrations are freely planned by national governments, those for family and protection reasons are regulated by EU directives that bind member countries. Therefore, with the adoption of the Directive 2003/86—which follows the initiative of many individual States—all the EU countries[7] were obliged to recognise the absolute right to residence to: the sponsor's spouse; the minor children of the sponsor and of his/her spouse, including adopted children; the minor children, including adopted children, of the sponsor when the sponsor has the custody and the children are dependent on him/her. Some EU States have also extended the right beyond these categories, including parents, adult children and, in exceptional circumstances, dependent relatives. Most States also allow same-sex partners (registered or married) to apply for reunification, usually providing them with an equal treatment as that of opposite-sex spouses.

After these legislative developments, family members have become the major components of new entry flows, as confirmed by the most recent data. In the last decade, except for Germany (with arrivals concentrated in the 2015–2018 time-span, following the opening to refugees, many of them have then applied for the arrival of their family members), it is above all the Southern countries—Spain and Italy—that catalyse significant volumes of family reunifications. This is clearly understandable in the light of the migratory history of these countries, which experienced a strong acceleration of arrivals for work reasons between the late 1990s and the beginning of the new millennium. Between 2009 and 2018 (latest available data), in the EU28, nearly 7.5 million first entry permits for family reasons have been issued, mainly by Germany, Spain, and Italy.[8]

Family migrations, due to their typically long—if not permanent—duration, produce powerful consequences on the composition of the population with a migratory background, making it more and more heterogeneous. Migrants of different origin, gender, age, and qualification leave behind countries with different levels of development, different political-institutional contexts, and different socio-cultural, religious, and linguistic landscapes that influence both families' lifestyles (particularly gender models and parent-child relationships) and the relation between immigrant families and the host community. In addition to considerations relating to the economic sustainability of entries for family reasons, it is the "diversity" that migrants bring with them from a cultural and religious point of view that is perceived as a challenging factor. This also emerges from the rules regulating new entrances.

As any other policy, rules on family reunification have a *normative* content, and mirror a "European" idea of family—that is a nuclear family—but not without some ambiguity (Zanfrini 2012). This right is based, firstly, on the *relationship of dependency* between the applicants and the family member they are joining. Among other consequences, this provision compromises the fate of the children when they become of age: if they have not yet reached their parents, they will no longer be able to do so; if they have already entered the immigration country, they may even risk to lose their permit of stay if they lack the prerequisites for obtaining its renewal (e.g. a job-contract or school attendance). In any case, these provisions reflect a legal definition of the family, thus disregarding the concept of kinship according to the cultures of origin, but also the reciprocity bonds reinforced because of the migration (e.g. the caregiver of the children left behind), or even shared in the host country (e.g. children of age who, in most European societies, continue to depend on their parents and still live with them).

Two other criteria make the right to reunification selective. The first is the *status of the applicant*: temporary migrants, permanent migrants, refugees, EU citizens, and naturalised citizens enjoy different opportunities and rights, up to the case of being completely excluded from this possibility. The second criterion concerns the *socio-economic status* of the applicant. All national legislations define requirements that the applicant must possess in order to reunite to his/her family members in terms of accommodation, income, sickness insurance, etc. Furthermore, even family members are sometimes requested to possess given requisites (e.g. a certain level of linguistic competence) before being reunited. In many States, the income threshold is today either equivalent to or higher than the basic income or minimum monthly income (EMN 2017a), thus excluding many low-income migrants (particularly when any public subsidies are omitted from the calculation). This kind of request reflects an interest in preventing families from living in poverty and ensuring that migrants are not benefit-dependent (OECD 2017). Besides, it reflects an interest in encouraging—if not imposing—specific civic values and norms of family and work-life related to gender equality and (women's) individual autonomy (Bech et al. 2017). Significantly, some countries have made it easier for family members of high-skilled migrants to join them, thus amplifying the selective attitude of migration management.

In this regard, co-ethnic marriages are another discussed topic, particularly when they are carried out by recalling a partner from the country of origin, thus configuring the occurrence of an arranged or even a *contracted marriage*. In statistical terms, the endogamy of marital choices is in fact much more frequent in groups from countries where arranged marriages are more widespread (Alba and Foner 2015), albeit its varying diffusion in the different EU countries suggests that the variables involved are manifold. In any case, it is useful to distinguish between consensual and *forced marriages*: the consent of an adult to marriage, in fact, remains such even if it is the result of the psychological pressure, ranging between the emotional blackmail and the request to respect a cultural tradition (Valtolina 2014); furthermore, it can also provide some kind of advantage, such as the opportunity to break free from family control and to enjoy a strong position in the conjugal relationship (Beck-Gernsheim 2007). Contracted marriages can also represent a strategy to circumvent restrictive migration policies, which make endogamic traditions necessarily dependent on the import of a partner from abroad (Alba and Foner 2015).

The phenomenon of arranged and contracted marriages must be analysed in the context of migrants' transnational links.[9] Here we can observe that some States (e.g. Belgium and the Netherlands), basing on the possibility admitted by the Directive 2003/86/EC to contrast forced marriages, have instituted a minimum age above the age of majority, that is higher than the legal marriage age for resident spouses (EPC 2011). Not to mention the rules that, by forcing the imported spouse to stay married for a certain number of years in order to retain the residence permit, amplify the spouse's potential dependence. Since in most cases it is the wife who reunites, this rule produces an opposite outcome than the one envisaged by the gender equity rhetoric, which emphasises women's economic autonomy. It is very complex to find a balance between the protection of individual choices and rights and the risk of imposing rules based on the so-called liberal values, when it comes to identifying a forced marriage from an external perspective, i.e. not that of the spouses. On the one hand, the arranged marriage can have a positive meaning within the parent's culture of origin, thus defining itself as consensual. On the other hand, the processes of acculturation to which the children of migrants are subjected lead many of them to reject this custom and ask for the authorities' help (Valtolina 2014).

Nevertheless, according to many scholars, current rules concerning family migration are in line with a more general tendency to select new arrivals and regulate the eligibility to rights with the aim of both accelerating and rewarding the integration process, through the adoption of a set of measures described as an "integrationist turn" (Joppke 2004; Anderson 2013). In recent years, several countries—Austria, Denmark, Finland, France, Germany, Italy, Luxembourg, the Netherlands, Sweden, and the UK—have decided to subordinate the delivery/renewal of the residence permit to the signing of an *integration agreement/contract*, and monitoring systems have registered a trend to make integration measures compulsory (OECD 2017). For example, new arrivals are often expected to enter different kinds of "integration pathways"—usually represented by language and civic education courses—and to pass a test. Moreover, sometimes migrants have to finance the course and the test on their own—as it happened in the Netherlands, Germany, UK, and Austria. This tendency has also inspired recent developments in the field of naturalisation, where the applicant is sometimes required to demonstrate a good level of linguistic and cultural competence (Guild et al. 2009) or even a given economic status (Seubert and Gaus 2016).

These measures have solicited a critical examination of the historical approaches in these fields, particularly in the countries that are usually depicted as open and inclusive towards migrants. In the Netherlands, integrationist devices are sometimes judged as new versions of the disciplinary policies used in the past to sanction those who do not comply with the normative "standards". According to critics, in Scandinavian countries, new rules in the field of both humanitarian and family migrations have even entailed the risk of a drastic decline in their traditional generosity towards migrants and refugees (Bech et al. 2017). Reflecting an ideological frame which supports an *economic model* of citizen (Seubert and Gaus 2016), these solutions can be understood as a paradigmatic example of a Darwinist drift which the European social model may encounter, to the point of undermining the principle of equality (Zanfrini 2019). In fact, fundamental human rights—such as that to family reunification or to marry a freely-chosen person, even if foreign and residing abroad—are in this way transformed into a filter to discriminate migrants and would-be migrants according to their socio-economic status and level of acculturation, finally forcing them to become "good citizens" (Bech et al. 2017). Significantly, some of the most controversial choices are supported by the political aim to prevent segregation and discrimination, particularly towards the most vulnerable categories, such as women coming from "patriarchal" cultures. All this within a context marked by the "ethnicisation of sexism" (Jäger and Jäger 2007), which, for instance, associates Islam with gender violence and female subordination.

The developments described above directly involve the lives of migrant families. At a practical level, by influencing their opportunities of living together and improving their condition. At a symbolic level, since many of the issues called into question to justify these choices have to do with the gender and the generational relationship within the family (as in the case of arranged marriages). The measures aimed at selecting new arrivals could reflect not only the interest of maximising their (positive) economic impact, but also that of minimising their (negative) cultural impact, since the "wanted" migrants are, in a certain way, less "diverse" than the ordinary ones, made "more diverse" by their low socio-economic status and their deficit in linguistic and civic integration. Finally, the integrationist turn can also be viewed as a reaction towards the migrants' condition of structural disadvantage and its strict relationship with the diversity issues (Section "Inequality and Diversity").

However, the real impact of these provisions is strongly limited, once again, by the context of embedded liberalism that characterises European democracies, which can be seen in the tendency to invoke fundamental individual rights and involve tribunal courts. Because of this, for example, it has become rather impossible to expel a family member just because he/she has not fulfilled the obligations contained in the integration contract. Besides, it is not clear how to deal with the large number of requests for family reunification submitted by recently-arrived refugees: they are often not yet able to support their families, but may however be exempted from income requirements (OECD 2019). Finally, even policies involving migrant families can be considered as an emblematic example of the persistent tension, strongly embedded in the European history, between an economicistic approach—the illusion to select entrants and residents according to the economic gain of the host society—and the principles of equality and solidarity, which has engendered the progressive extension of migrants' prerogatives, claimed by the tradition of respect of human rights (Zanfrini 2019).

Besides all these considerations, one question arises: is family reunification the best solution when the life chances and the wellbeing of all the family members are taken into account?

The link between family presence and the outcomes of migrants' long-term integration is today the object of an increasing, but still not sufficient, attention. One of the first empirical examination provided by the OECD (2019) suggests that delays in reunification affect the integration prospects, particularly for women (e.g. by influencing their level of language proficiency) and for children (long delays strongly affect both their language proficiency and their school outcomes). Finally, evidence on how a delayed family reunification affects the principal migrant is not clear-cut and is difficult to measure, since only successfully integrated migrants are commonly allowed to bring their family members.

The experience of reunited families (and particularly of reunited wives) has often emerged in the public debate as a signal of cultural backwardness and integration difficulties. Moreover, scientific literature has focused also on the reunited children and has provided contradictory findings (for a review: Valtolina, 2013). Separated families represent one of the most dramatic implications of contemporary human mobility (Ehrenreich and Hochschild 2002), particularly when they involve left-behind children, emblematically named "orphans of migration" (see, among others: Paiewonsky 2006; Parreñas 2005). However, the decision to reunite with the family members can produce paradoxical and even negative outcomes, resulting from the intersection between families' strategies and projects, on the one hand, and the legislation on the other. For example, a "strong" status (e.g. that of a EU citizen living in another EU country) may discourage reunification or favour a sort of physical and symbolic commuting with the sending State, which could be detrimental to young children and their school careers (Romanian living in Italy or in Spain are a case in point: Valtolina 2013). More often, migrant parents reunite with their children even if they lack the best conditions and the time for taking care of them, to the point that the difficulties encountered can induce them to send their children back home and let them be raised by their relatives. In many cases, reunification involves children who are about to reach the age of majority (the limit age stated by the law), who frequently encounter difficulties of integration in the new society. Finally, when they lack some of the legal requirements, migrants can realise a de facto-*reunification*, sponsoring the arrival of the spouse or/and the children who will not have a permit of stay, staking a claim on their life chances. In this case, a possible outcome is a *mixed-status family*, whose members enjoy different legal conditions.

Besides, migrant parents' interests and feelings are not always matching with those of their children, even when immigration is apparently steered by the best interest of the latter (Kofman 2004). Reunited children often live in precarious economic and housing conditions—very far from the mythical representation they had before leaving—and suffer from the physical absence of parents (or parent, in cases of single-parent families), strongly absorbed by work. In some sending communities, the institutionalisation of the family divided by migration is an integral part of a deeply rooted "culture of migration"; however, once reunited with their parents, migrants' children start to perceive the separation as a behaviour not compliant with the norm, then changing their attitude towards the parents (Waters 1997). In addition, experts denounce the repercussions of the reunification on the migrants' psychological and emotional equilibrium (Valtolina and Colombo 2012), especially when it involves people who are going through particularly delicate phases of their personal or family life, or when it gives rise to situations of cohabitation among people who were previously not acquainted (i.e. the mother's new partner, or brothers or sisters born after the parents' emigration). Parents also tend to underestimate how kids, even if very young, have their own projects and their own perceptions of what is their well-being, and are unaware of the challenges and the suffering that family migrations or reunifications can imply for their children. Finally, while left-behind children can take advantage of opportunities thanks to the remittances sent by their parents, such as the possibility of attending a high-quality education (e.g.: Zanfrini and Asis 2006), the school careers of reunited children are often marked by interruptions and failures (Section "Inequality and Diversity"). More in detail, cross-country evidence clearly indicates that children who spend their early years in the destination country achieve substantially better integration outcomes compared with those who arrive when they are almost adult; arriving after the critical period for the acquisition of language (i.e. 9 years old) adversely affects the proficiency in the host country's language—which influences both educational and employment outcomes, and wages (OECD 2019).

Inequality and Diversity

In continuity with the Guest Worker model (Section "The Discovery of the Immigrant Family"), many migrants living in the EU are still concentrated in the lower ladders of the occupational hierarchy. Albeit with some differences from one country to another, foreign workers are usually over-represented in some sectors: manufacturing and construction, hotels and restaurants, healthcare and social services, domestic services, care for children and for the elderly. Since much of the demand is concentrated in low-skilled occupations, foreign workers largely hold low-wage and low-status jobs[10] and are over-represented in many types of businesses at high risk of undeclared employment (EMN 2017b). Moreover, since they have a lower reservation wage and tend to accept lower-quality jobs, migrants are often accused of being a cause of *social dumping*, and enter in competition with the weakest components of the native labour force, at least according to a common perception. Particularly during periods of economic crisis, the impression that immigrants "steal jobs" feeds aversion towards them and negatively affects the quality of interethnic relationships, especially in disadvantaged neighbourhoods (OECD 2016). This circumstance engenders a "war among the poor", easily exploitable by xenophobic campaigns, and strongly detrimental for the well-being of migrant families.

Moreover, the model of migrants' economic incorporation has exposed the ones largely employed in low-productivity and mature sectors and profiles to the risk of losing their jobs, thus contributing to increasing migrants' unemployment rate: in most EU countries, foreign workers (particularly if they come from non-EU countries) register a higher rate than the native ones. This negative gap is also largely due to the difficulties encountered by newly-arrived migrants—particularly family members and refugees—in accessing the labour market: it took 5–10 years for most previous generations of family migrants and refugees to be employed in Europe, and as much as 15–20 years for them to reach a level of employment similar to that of the natives, if ever (OECD 2017). Finally, since the current models of economic incorporation are often based on a sort of "complementarity postulate"—which emphasises migrants' adaptability to the jobs refused by native workers—they tend to discourage both the investments in the development and recognition of skills and competences, and the participation in the socio-cultural and political life of the hosting communities (Zanfrini 2015). Sometimes, these patterns of integration have even produced a tendency towards self-segregation, nurturing the perception of social distance and of integration's failure, and hampering the social mobility of migrants and their offspring.

Indeed, not only EU countries continue to attract a "poor" migration, predestined to concentrate in the bottom ranks of the professional hierarchy, earn low salaries and generate disadvantaged families; what's more, the restrictions towards the entries of economic migrants produce the dominance of the arrivals of inactive migrants, especially the dependent family members. Significantly, the low share of migrant women employed is today a critical issue, to the point that increasing their activity and employment rates is a specific goal set by EU institutions. Not only for its economic consequences—in terms of female independence and of the vulnerability characterising single-revenue households—but also because migrant women's (self-)exclusion from active roles exacerbates the perception of social and cultural distance, since it contradicts the normative principle of gender equity. This problem particularly affects women coming from non-EU countries, whose employment rate is 55.2% in the European Union as a whole, compared to 68.6% as for native-born females (and 69.7% for EU-born migrant females), and this negative gap becomes definitively greater in some of the main immigration countries, such as Germany (63.3 vs 79.1% of native-born and 73.4% of EU-born), France (52.1 vs 70.3% and 67.9%), and the Netherlands (58 vs 77.3% and 70.6%).[11]

A consequence of these phenomena is the high exposition of migrants and migrant families to the risk of poverty and social exclusion. According to the latest available data (2018),[12] among people living in the EU, 21% of nationals, 29% of foreign EU citizens, and 45% of non-EU citizens face this kind of risks. The risk of monetary poverty is approximately twice as high for foreign citizens (33%) as it is for nationals (15%) and is particularly concentrated among non-EU citizens (38%). Finally, the incidence of severe material deprivation is approximately twice as high among non-EU residents (13%) as it is among EU citizens (7%) or nationals (6%).

A disadvantaged immigrant population feeds the idea that they are a "burden" for society and for the welfare system: this kind of perception is today a stumbling block for the harmonic cohabitation, to the point of constituting one of the main drivers of contemporary xenophobia and racism. Moreover, it gives birth to second generations who suffer from a weaker starting position in the competition to accede to social resources and opportunities, and sometimes are (or feel they are being) clearly discriminated. If not because of the quantitative importance of migrant offspring, this issue has gained a great attention at both the academic and the political level.

The school career of migrants' offspring is one of the most inquired topics, since educational achievements are strongly predictive of future occupational outcomes. Several factors contribute to explaining the disadvantages affecting migrants' children; however, the ascribed (family) status is tremendously important, since it can either reinforce or counterbalance the influence of other variables. To avoid any prejudices, we should note that scholastic attainments are different for different national groups—as well as for students of the same origin residing in different countries. Sometimes, the results of the children of immigrants are even better than the average, contributing to the creation of a positive stereotype regarding their abnegation to study and the sacrifices of their parents. However, apart from a few exceptions, students with an immigrant background suffer from a systematic disadvantage, in terms of type of school (their presence is higher in the less "noble" courses and in those for underachievers), duration of the educational career, scholastic performance, and failure and dropout rates.

The explanation of this disadvantage involves many variables at the macro-level (in terms of national scholastic policies and immigration policies), the meso-level (pertaining to the relationship between students/students' families and teachers/schools), and the micro-level (regarding the students' family and community backgrounds) (for a comprehensive analysis see: Heckmann 2008). However, many variables have to do with the migrant/minority condition of failing students. Hence, despite sharing the desire for a better future for their children, not all immigrant families are able to support a scholastic career, just as not all immigrant communities appear equally able to produce "successful models" to emulate and to adequately interface with educational institutions. Furthermore, the family's migratory projects can negatively affect the educational careers, as it happens to those students who arrive in the new country in a pre-adolescent or adolescent age, and are often victims of a retrocession both in terms of the classes attended and in terms of the quality and prestige of the study programmes compared to their pre-migration status (Section "Family Reunions").

However, many studies demonstrate that the disadvantages experienced by second-generation immigrants cannot be explained entirely by their educational careers. Evidence from some countries seems to prove the influence of *ethnic penalties* driven by cultural, religious or racial factors, which persist even after considering the differences in schooling, skills, and social origins (Gracia et al. 2016); besides, migrants' offspring are more likely to hold jobs beneath their educational attainment (Istat 2016). Labour statistics too confirm the disadvantage hitting young migrants of both first and second generations, which sometimes turns into exclusion due to early abandonment of the school system, poor credentials, weak social capital, discrimination and—as far as the female component is concerned—the persistence of a traditional pattern of gender roles. It is sufficient to observe that, with the only exception of Cyprus, in all the EU countries for which data are available, foreign-born are over-represented in NEET-*Not in Education, Employment, or Training*. Globally, in the EU, 16.1% of foreigners aged 15–24 fall into this category, compared to 9.7% of their native peers. This gap is even greater in the countries that are most affected by this problem: Italy (25.2% of foreigners vs 17.4% of natives), Greece (22.6 vs 11.9%), Spain (22.3 vs 10.8%), and France (21.9 vs 10.1%). Moreover, it is particularly dramatic for female immigrants, among whom the share of NEET reaches 19.6%, compared to 9.7% of their native peers.[13]

These phenomena, largely documented in most countries—together with some significant exceptions, described by a new wave or studies focused on successful stories and empowering variables (see, e.g., Besozzi et al. 2009; Brinbaum et al. 2012; Crul et al. 2017), eventually based on the exploitation of the specific resources of migrants' children, such as bilingualism and intercultural skills—produce dramatic consequences in terms of both economic and social immigration's long-term impact. Born, grown up and educated in the "equalitarian" European democracies, migrants' offspring frequently suffer from the *paradox of integration*: since they are generally more "integrated" than their parents, and aspire to be fully included in the mainstream society, these youths experience more frustration whenever they feel to be discriminated in the allocation of opportunities. Significantly, middle-class and well-educated second-generation immigrants report higher levels of discrimination than less educated ones (Beaman 2017). Finally, strong equalising efforts on a legislative level have not been sufficient to remove both practical and symbolic borders, which distinguish between who "belongs" and who does not belong to the "community of equals". Significantly, the discrimination issue—and its strict interaction with the diversity connected to a migratory background—has been catapulted at the core of the political agenda exactly thanks to the experience and the initiative of second-generation members.

From many points of view, migrants' children are the archetypes of the youthful condition *tout court*, and solicit a renewed effort in realising the ambition to build a real universalistic and equalitarian society. Once ascribed to specific characters of minority groups (such as their low engagement in educational attainments) or to the intentional discriminatory attitude of the hosting society and its influential actors (such as teachers and employers), migrants' disadvantage is today increasingly being regarded as the consequence of the "normal" functioning of the educational system, the labour market, welfare regimes, and political institutions (Zanfrini 2016). In this perspective, the migration-related minority condition turns out to be emblematic of the mechanisms through which a society generates and reproduces social inequalities and is then able to stimulate remedial policies and mechanisms.

In many cases, migrants' children have not directly experienced international mobility, since they were born and grown up in the country where their parents had decided to immigrate. However, it is the very fact of descending from an immigrant family that leaves them the legacy of the migrant condition which is usually a disadvantageous one. Besides influencing the structure of opportunities to which they will have access to realise their life and work projects, this legacy cannot help but influence their feelings of belonging to the society in which they live. This crucial question has a "private" and psychological declension, represented by individual experiences and sentiments, which lead descendants from immigrant families to position themselves differently along the *continuum* insider/outsider (Berry et al. 2006). From a sociological perspective, it is interesting to observe how self-definitions of identity reverberate—besides being influenced by them—both on the prospects of inclusion and social mobility of the people involved, and on collective attitudes, namely those of minority groups towards the hosting society, and those of the latter towards minority groups (Zanfrini 2019). Not incidentally, particularly after the episodes of religious radicalisation occurred in various European nations, scholars have directed their attention to the aspects that make immigrants' offspring either feel as a part of society or excluded (for a general appraisal see: Alba and Foner 2015): from the migration regimes historically adopted by EU

States to the social marginality of some migrant families; from the characters of citizenship regimes (particularly when they mirror an ethnic conception of the nation) to the social prejudices towards given migrant communities; from the identity choices and strategies developed by some minority communities to the role of religious affiliations and the manner in which they are acknowledged in the different political and institutional contexts. Without deeply entering in this suggestive analysis, it must be stressed that it is the association between the "inequality" suffered by migrant families and their "diversity" from an ethnic, cultural, and religious point of view that largely shapes the relationship between them and European societies.

Conclusions

Finally, it is precisely the fact of having a migratory background that can generate a differential "destiny" for immigrant-origin families and individuals, on both a practical and a symbolic level. Many are the exceptions, of course— namely individual cases of full integration, scholastic success, social mobility and a feeling of being fully "included" in society. But these cases have not been sufficient to neutralise the migrant condition as a variable deeply influencing both family and social life.

To appreciate the relevance of this issue, there is another point to consider, directly related to the demographic situation of the "old" European continent. Given the quantitative importance of the population with a migratory background, migrants and migrant offspring's failures and feelings are no longer a "simple" matter of social justice. In fact, migrants' condition of structural disadvantage and their possible perception of being excluded are crucial issues for both the social cohesion and the economic competitiveness of contemporary and future Europe. This awareness explains the proliferation of policies and initiatives intended to combat discrimination and promote equal opportunities, finally acknowledging and valorising cultural differences inherited from a migration family history: from intercultural education (intended as a basic competence for every European citizen) programmes, to diversity management initiatives within the workplace (intended as an instrument not only to include minority members, but also to improve the organisational performances).

The long-term impact of these efforts will be determined by the ability to "metabolise" Europe's transformation into a multi-ethnic and multicultural society, acknowledging pluralism as a genuine component of its institutional functioning. In this scenario, family is a particularly challenging issue: "imported" models and values make European societies consider different conceptions of this fundamental institution, here intended both as a social construct and a moral order (Grillo 2008). Indeed, migrant households defy the "normal" configuration of family structures and behaviours (Alba and Nee 1997) and make the family's patterns and styles of functioning even more heterogeneous through the appearance of disputable practices (such as polygamous cohabitations), or past practices (such as arranged marriages), but also of new family models that take shape in the context of transnational communities and circuits of migrants (Foner 1997). According to some influential scholars, these models represent new ways of making a family, thus possibly supplanting the traditional family model made up of members who share the same nationality and live under the same roof (Beck and Beck-Gernsheim 2011).

NOTES

1. See the yearly report produced by OECD, *International Migration Outlook*.
2. 2016/C 202/01, *Consolidated versions of the Treaty on European Union and the Treaty on the Functioning of the European Union*.
3. https://ec.europa.eu/home-affairs/what-we-do/policies/legal-migration/long-term-residents_en.
4. https://appsso.eurostat.ec.europa.eu/nui/show.do?dataset=demo_facbc&lang=en.
5. The most influential communication through which the European Commission started to overtly encourage more economic immigration dates to 2000: COM (2000) 757 final, *Communication from the Commission to the Council and the European Parliament on a Community Immigration Policy*.
6. https://ec.europa.eu/eurostat/statistics-explained/pdfscache/41896.pdf.
7. Except Denmark, Ireland, Norway, and the UK.
8. https://appsso.eurostat.ec.europa.eu/nui/show.do?dataset=migr_resfirst&lang=en.
9. See Chapter 24 in this part.
10. See OECD (various years), *International Migration Outlook*. Paris: OECD Publishing.
11. https://appsso.eurostat.ec.europa.eu/nui/show.do?dataset=lfsa_ergan&lang=en.
12. https://ec.europa.eu/eurostat/statistics-explained/index.php?title=Migrant_integration_statistics_-_at_risk_of_poverty_and_social_exclusion.
13. http://appsso.eurostat.ec.europa.eu/nui/show.do?dataset=edat_lfse_23&lang=en.

REFERENCES

Alba, Richard, and Nancy Foner. 2015. *Strangers No More. Immigration and Challenges of Integration in North America and Western Europe*. Princeton and Oxford: Princeton University Press.

Alba, Richard, and Victor Nee. 1997. "Rethinking Assimilation Theory for a New Era of Immigration." *International Migration Review* XXXI (4): 826–874.

Anderson, Bridget. 2013. *Us and Them? The Dangerous Politics of Immigration Control*. Oxford: Oxford University Press.

Beaman, Jean. 2017. *Citizen Outsider: Children of North African Immigrants in France*. Oakland: University of California Press.

Bech, Emily Cochran, Karin Borevi, and Per Mouritsen. 2017. "A 'Civic Turn' in Scandinavian Family Migration Policies? Comparing Denmark, Norway and Sweden." *Comparative Migration Studies* 5 (1): 1–24.
Beck-Gernsheim, Elisabeth. 2007. "Transnational Lives, Transnational Marriages: A Review of Evidence from Migrant Communities in Europe." *Global Networks* 8: 272–88.
Beck, Ulrich, and Elisabeth Beck-Gernsheim. 2011. *Fernliebe. Lebensformen im globalen Zeitalter*. Berlin: Suhrkamp.
Berry, John, Jean Phinney, David Sam, and Paul Vedder, eds. 2006. *Immigrant Youth in Cultural Transition. Acculturation, Identity and Adaptation Across National Context*. Mahwah: Lawrence Erlbaum Associates.
Besozzi, Elena, Maddalena Colombo, and Mariagrazia Santagati. 2009. *Giovani stranieri, nuovi cittadini. Le strategie di una generazione ponte*, Milano: Franco Angeli.
Bohning, Wolf-Rüdiger. 1984. *Studies in International Labour Migration*. London: Macmillan Editor.
Brinbaum, Yaël, Moguérou Laure, and Jean-Luc Primon. 2012. *Les enfants d'immigrés ont des parcours scolaires différenciés selon leur origine migratoire*, 43–59. INSEE.
Cornelius, Wayne A., Philip L. Martin, and James Frank Hollifield. 1994. "Introduction: The Ambivalent Quest for Immigration Control." In *Controlling Immigration: A Global Perspectives*, edited by W. A. Cornelius, P. L. Martin, and J. F. Hollifield, 3–41. Stanford: Stanford University Press.
Crul, Maurice, Elif Keskiner, and France Lelie. 2017. "The Upcoming New Elite Among Children of Immigrants. A Cross-Country and Cross-Sector Comparison." *Ethnic and Racial Studies* 40 (2): 209–229.
Ehrenreich, Barbara, and Arlie Russel Hochschild, eds. 2002. *Global Woman. Nannies, Maids, and Sex Workers in the New Economy*. New York: Henry Holt.
EMN – European Migration Network. 2017a. *Family Reunification of Third-Country Nationals in the EU Plus Norway: National Practices – Synthesis Report*. Brussels: European Migration Network.
EMN – European Migration Network. 2017b. *Illegal Employment of Third-Country Nationals in the European Union – Synthesis Report*. Brussels: European Migration Network.
EPC – European Policy Centre 2011. *Conditions for Family Reunification Under Strain*. Brussels: King Baudouin Foundation – European Policy Centre Odysseus Network.
Foner, Nancy. 1997. "The Immigrant Family: Cultural Legacies and Cultural Changes." *International Migration Review* IV (2): 961–975.
Gracia, Pablo, Lucia Vázquez-Quesada, and Herman G. Van de Werfhorst. 2016. "Ethnic Penalties? The Role of Human Capital and Social Origins in Labour Market Outcomes of Second-Generation Moroccans and Turks in the Netherlands." *Journal of Ethnic and Migration Studies* 42 (1): 69–87.
Grillo, Ralph, ed. 2008. *The Family in Question. Immigrant and Ethnic Minorities in Multicultural Europe*. Amsterdam: Amsterdam University Press.
Guild, Elspeth, Krysha Groenenduk, and Sergio Carrera. 2009. *Illiberal Liberal States: Immigration, Citizenship and Integration in the EU*. Farnham: Ashgate.
Kofman, Eleonore. 2004. "Family-Related Migration: A Crucial Review of European Studies." *Journal of Ethnic and Migration Studies* 21: 243–259.

Hammar, Tomas. 1989. "State, Nation and Dual Citizenship, in Immigration and the Politics of Citizenship in Europe and North America." In *Immigration and the Politics of Citizenship in Europe and North America*, edited by R. Brubaker, 81–95. New York: University Press of America.

Hampshire, James. 2013. *The Politics of Immigration: Contradictions of the Liberal State*. Oxford: Polity Press.

Heckmann, Friedrich. 2008. *Education and Migration. Strategies for Integration Migrant Children in European School and Societies*. Brussels: D.G. Education and Culture.

Istat 2016. *Rapporto annuale 2016. La situazione del paese*. Roma: Istituto nazionale di Statistica.

Jäger, Margarate, and Siegfried Jäger. 2007. *Deutungskämpfe Theorie und Praxis Kritischer Diskursanalyse*. Wiesbaden: VS, Verl. für Socialliwiss.

Joppke, Christian. 2004. "The Retreat of Multiculturalism in the Liberal State." *British Journal of Sociology* 55 (2): 237–257.

Lockwood, David. 1996. "Civic Integration and Class Formation." *British Journal of Sociology* 47: 531–550.

Morris, Lydia. 2003. "Managing Contradiction: Civic Stratification and Migrants' Rights." *International Migration Review* 37 (1): 74–100.

OECD. 2016. *International Migration Outlook 2016*. Paris: OECD Publishing.

OECD. 2017. *International Migration Outlook 2017*. Paris: OECD Publishing.

OECD 2019. *International Migration Outlook 2019*. Paris: OECD Publishing.

Paiewonsky, Donald. 2006. "Gender, Remittances and Development in the Dominican Republic." In *Female Migrants: Bridging the Gaps Throughout the Life Cycle*. New York: Unfpa-Iom Expert Group Meeting. https://www.un.org/en/development/desa/population/migration/events/coordination/5/docs/P02_INSTRAW.pdf.

Parreñas, Rhacel Salazar. 2005. *Children of Global Migration. Transnational Families and Gendered Woes*. Stanford, CA: Stanford University Press.

Penninx, Rinus. 2005. "Integration of Migrants: Economic, Social, Cultural and Political Dimensions." In *The New Demographic Regime. Population Challenges and Policy Responses*, edited by M. Macura, A. L. MacDonald, and W. Haug, 137–152. New York and Geneva: United Nations.

Seubert, Syibille, and Dereck Gaus. 2016. Report: Voter Turn-out and Political Equality in the European Union. bEUcitizen, Deliverable D.8.6. https://www.bEUcitize.er/publications.

Sobotka, Tomas. 2008. "The Rising Importance of Migrants for Childbearing in Europe." In *Demographic Research 19*, Article 9, 225–248. http://www.demogr aphic-research.org/special/7/.

Valtolina, Giovanni G., ed. 2013. *Migrant Children in Europe. The Romanian Case*. Amsterdam: IOS Press.

Valtolina, Giovanni G. 2014. "Processi di acculturazione e matrimoni combinati nelle seconde generazioni." *Studi Emigrazione* XLI (193): 133–142.

Valtolina, Giovanni G., and C. Colombo. 2012. "La ricerca sui ricongiungimenti familiari: una rassegna." *Studi Emigrazione* XLIX (185): 129–143.

Van Mol, Christof, and Helga de Valk. 2016. "Migration and Immigrants in Europe: A Historical and Demographic Perspective." In *Integration Processes and Policies in Europe. Contexts, Levels and Actors*, edited by Garcés-Mascareñas and R. Penninx, 31–56. London: Springer.

Volant, Sabrina, Gilles Pison, and François Héran. 2019. "French Fertility Is the Highest in Europe. Because of Its immigrants?" *Population & Societies* 568 (July–August).
Waters, Mary C. 1997. "Immigrant Families at Risk. Factors that Undermine Chances for Success." In *Immigration and the Family Research and Policy on U.S. Immigrants*, edited by A. Booth, A. C. Crouter, and N. Landale. Mahwah, NJ: Lawrence Erlbaum Associates.
Zanfrini, Laura. 2012. "Family Migration: Fulfilling the Gap between Law and Social Processes." *Societies* 2 (3): 63–74. https://doi.org/10.3390/soc2030063.
Zanfrini, Laura, ed. 2015. *The Diversity Value. How to Reinvent the European Approach to Immigration*. Maidenhead, UK: McGraw-Hill Education.
Zanfrini, Laura. 2016. *Introduzione alla sociologia delle migrazioni*. Roma-Bari: Laterza.
Zanfrini, Laura. 2019. *The Challenge of Migration in a Janus-Faced Europe*. London: Palgrave.
Zanfrini, Laura, ed. 2020. *Migrants and Religion. Paths, Issues and Lenses*. Amsterdam: Brill.
Zanfrini, Laura, and M. Asis, eds. 2006. *Orgoglio e pregiudizio. Una ricerca tra Filippine e Italia sulla transizione all'età attiva dei figli di emigrati e dei figli di immigrati*. Milan: FrancoAngeli.

CHAPTER 24

The Multidimensional Nature of Family Migration: Transnational and Mixed Families in Europe

Dafina Kurti Sinatra and Inga Sabanova

Introduction

This chapter aims to give a brief overview of the main research developments in understanding the dynamics of transnational and mixed families in Europe in the last two decades. To achieve this aim, we review the European literature on family migration that deals with the increased diversification of families,[1] migration trajectories, and family arrangements. Collection of the respective theories and empirical studies in this concise chapter represents a rare opportunity for scholars in the field to gain insights into the recent sociological research on migrant and ethnic minority families in Europe. After the critical review, we note that the research on family migration needs more studies that analyse changes among immigrants and their descendants over their life-courses, studying several transitions rather only one transition at a time. Moreover, future comparative research would include consideration of the structural context, for instance, an analysis of how socio-economic, institutional, and policy settings affect family lives of intact families,[2] single-parent, patchwork families, or divorced migrants and their descendants.

In exploring the literature on family migration dynamics, we concentrate on the life-course event of transnational and mixed unions (marriage, cohabitation). Transnational families, including multicultural partnerships,

D. Kurti Sinatra (✉)
University of Cologne, Cologne, Germany

I. Sabanova
Trinity College Dublin, Dublin, Ireland
e-mail: sabanovi@tcd.ie

represent unique types of family arrangements that offer multiple ways of exploring the migration experience of family members based on individualised and specific circumstances related to culture, ethnicity, religion, gender, or intergenerational differences.

Family migration has been the dominant mode of legal immigration into and within the European Union (Kofman et al. 2011). However, it is only in recent years that academic scholarship began to focus on how changes in marriage, family structure, divorce, love, and intimate relationships intertwine with the migration process (Bryceson 2019; Mai and King 2009; Mazzucato et al. 2015). The migration context makes the family as a social institution highly diverse in terms of structures, trajectories, dynamics, and kinship relationships, rendering it a complex and ambiguous construct to study. To date, there has been a set of theoretical and analytical approaches developed in isolation from different disciplinary standpoints that can unveil the economic, socio-cultural, and emotional challenges of transnational and mixed families (Carling et al. 2012; Mazzucato and Dito 2018).

At the empirical level, social science research into family migration has begun to unravel the fluidity of social ties across geographical borders and the complexity of the decision-making process beyond legal aspects of family reunification and labour migration (Bushin 2009; Ryan and Sales 2011; Shmulyar Gréen and Melander 2018). Many studies have demonstrated well that there are both continuity and change in familial relations in a transnational context, facilitated by modern transport and communications technology (Vertovec 2004; Faist 2010). Moreover, the migratory process can also lead to a reformulation of gender and generational roles within both the productive and reproductive spheres (Kofman et al. 2011).

This chapter is structured as follows. The first part focuses on transnational families by discussing the complexity of decision-making, migratory trajectories and family arrangements. Specifically, we emphasise how the importance of gender and childhood perspectives allow us to observe how different actors negotiate their migration experiences. The second part focuses on mixed families by stressing the cultural or ethnic issues that raise in different periods of transition in the life-course, e.g. in the context of family formation, marriage dissolution, and the birth of the first child. In the conclusion section, we provide an overview of discussed research themes and outline opportunities for further developing research on changing dynamics of migrant families in Europe.

Transnational Families

Definition and Characteristics

A transnational family represents a family whose members are separated spatially from the significant others and relatives as a result of migration from one country to another. The separation between migrants and their families can be temporary or permanent (Hondagneu-Sotelo and Avila 1997; Reisenauer 2018). Bryceson and Vuorela (2002, 3) define transnational families as "families that live some or most of the time separated from each other, yet hold together and create something like a feeling of collective welfare and unity, namely 'familyhood', even across borders".

One of the most important developments in recent decades for family migration scholarship was recognising the relevance of family and community ties: ties that do not dissolve but are maintained despite the geographical distance (Faist 2010; Wimmer and Glick-Schiller 2002). Drawing on examinations of family boundaries outside the nation-state, many scholars began to challenge two key assumptions: firstly, that family co-residence is not a prerequisite for family-making, and secondly, that physical co-presence is not the primary means of showing care and affection (e.g. Faist 2010; Parreñas 2005). Due to the essential role of family ties in a transnational family context, i.e. the evident intergenerational family relations and kinship with extended families, in the present literature review, we apply a definition of transnational family that goes beyond the nuclear family.

Scholars of transnationalism recognise the significance of various ties of migrant family members to their home community, while they became incorporated into the host society beyond the nuclear family. Families might split because of migration, or extended family members might become necessary for childcare support (White 2011). However, the importance of the family ties is observed not only in the way how families decide to migrate but also in strategies they adopt for maintaining family unity regardless of the geographical distance.

Migratory Decisions

Investigating the main reasons and motives that influence people to migrate is one of the oldest themes in migration research. For a long time, studies focused predominantly on identifying economic "push and pull" factors of migration; a theoretical model postulated by Lee (1966).[3] However, research on transnational families has shown that migration decisions are not merely about moving abroad; the choices are far more complex and arise at any time throughout a migration project (COFACE 2012; Zanfrini 2012). Various individual and structural factors, often in combination, influence the migratory decision-making process. Yet every family experiences and approaches migration differently (Bryceson 2019; Datta et al. 2007).

With the increasing recognition of the gender perspective and children's agency in migration research, the intertwined relationship between migratory decisions within families and family migration itself has been well explored to date with qualitative research in the form of case studies and ethnographies. Ryan et al. (2009) by looking at Polish families in the United Kingdom (UK) argue that, while many migrants arrive in Britain alone, they are often involved in complex family networks and relationships both in Britain and back home in Poland. Anne White (2011) also showed that single mothers face complicated situations, involving extended family members who take care of the children before they can join mothers abroad. White conceptualises family migration through a "livelihood strategies" approach, the strategy of family members involved in enhancing opportunities by considering actual and potential resources, such as a second job, social networks, time, health, and skills available to a given household (2011, 3).

Studies from Norway, Ireland, the UK, and the new EU-member states have shown that better opportunities available for children abroad can provide additional incentives for families to migrate (Bushin 2009; Moskal and Tyrrell 2016; Sime et al. 2010; Ryan and Sales 2011). Ryan and Sales (2011) also noted that children play a crucial role, especially when they are of school age, as their schooling may become a key incentive for a stay since parents do not want to interrupt their children's education. However, children who migrate with their parents are young and have little agency in the migratory decision-making process themselves. These and other examples confirm that the family is far from being a harmonious decision-making unit. As Faist (2010, 70) noted, "It would be naive to conceptualise all social units such as households as single-interest decision-making bodies. There is too much evidence on the importance of diverging interests and of power relations within social units such as households, for example, expressed in hierarchical and patriarchal decision-making…". Empirical contributions suggest that different family members negotiate their decisions and experience migration differently based on their gender expectations, family obligations, livelihood strategies, and intergenerational care concerns (Shmulyar Gréen and Melander 2018). In the next two sections, we demonstrate the importance of transnational practices of "doing family" despite the geographical distance, especially when it comes to parenting.

Maintaining Transnational Lives

Family migration is not a straightforward process. Expectations and family involvement, as well as non-family networks, can play a significant role in the migration decision-making process and the relationships between different family members. Many studies revealed that migrant networks such as kinship, personal ties, and a shared community from the same country of origin could all shape families' migratory flows (Esveldt et al. 1995; Massey et al. 1993; Reisenauer 2018). For instance, existing community networks can provide migrants with useful information and assistance about work, housing, or even legal advice to overcome restrictions in the admission policies. In societies with strong ties between immigrants and their communities of origin country—ties that are characterised by family obligation, reciprocal exchange, frequent visits or remittances—migrant networks may have a strong influence on the continuation of migration and associated decision-making (Esveldt et al. 1995). Moreover, a family may play a crucial role in managing the flow of economic remittances coming from family members working abroad (see Fauser and Reisenauer 2013; Fresnoza-Flot and Merla 2018). Social remittances in the form of ideas, social capital, and identities that circulate between migrated families with strong transnational ties and practices and the communities in the emigration country, may also reshape traditional norms and (gender) roles in families, networks, and organisations (Dallemagne 2018; Lacroix et al. 2016; Tolstokorova 2018; Zontini 2010).

Transnational practices are influenced by migration regimes that govern the trajectories of migrants and their families. Banfi and Boccagni (2011) note that in the case of Polish, Ukrainian, and Ecuadorian migrant women in Italy, the intensity of the emotional pain and guilt of being separated from their children is related to their legal status mobility (or immobility). While Polish women could travel to Poland based on their rights under European citizenship, Ukrainian and Ecuadorian mothers rarely returned home until they received residence documents in Italy. The use of new technologies was the primary option for them to deal with physical separation.

Particularly referring to migration within the EU, Bailey and Boyle (2004) argued that a single regional market is inevitably linked to the emergence of the migration regime. The encouraged migration of European citizens within the EU borders, together with affordable travel and new communication technologies, all led to the creation of a new transnational space in which new forms of belonging and identities emerge. According to Galasinska and Kozlowska (2009, 90), family migration within the EU represents "a dynamic, flexible and open space, where the living space of migrants is simply extended rather than replaced". Intra-EU migration provides new forms of transnational relationships and identities, rooted in the notion of European citizenship, and promoted through the range of policy mechanisms across the EU-member states. Nevertheless, there is no reason to assume that all modern migrants are transmigrants[4] (Kivisto 2001). Similarly, Bell and Erdal (2015) argue that in the case of Polish families settled in Norway, transnational practices weaken with time for adult migrants. The lack of physical contact with their friends puts pressure on their relationships, even if both parents and children engage in regular visits back to Poland.

Transnational Parenting

Given the fact that transnational migrants are very likely to maintain a variety of ties between "here" (the host society) and "there" (the sending society) (Vertovec 2001), many transnational mothers, as the primary caregivers for their children, have to endure lengthy and emotionally painful separation to provide for their families. Transnational parenting[5] requires different strategies to cope with the situation of separation from their children. A growing body of literature has been focusing on the use of new technologies as a way to maintain emotional closeness among family members (Fresnoza-Flot 2009; Hondagneu-Sotelo and Avila 1997; Longhurst 2013; Madianou and Miller

2012). Madianou and Miller argue that new ways of communicating allow migrant parents to continue parenting from a distance, but they do not solve the problem of physical separation; they instead transform the whole experience of migration and maintaining familial relationships (2012, 2). Their study of Filipina mothers in the UK showed that frequent contact through messaging with their children left behind allowed these women to "feel like mothers again". Specifically, visual aspects of some communication applications are more preferred by mothers because through visual transmission they could assess their children's well-being (see also Longhurst 2013).

A study by Fresnoza-Flot (2009) showed that migration has not completely emancipated Filipina migrant mothers in France from traditional gender ideology and expectations. Instead, they redefine their motherhood while experiencing challenges in managing life and work in domestic service in France. For many transnational mothers, it is not possible to visit the family frequently because of the high cost of travelling, inconvenient job leave arrangements or the risk of losing steady jobs. Mothers with undocumented status are not able to visit their family back home in general, so they are more likely to suffer emotionally from the separation from their families. Consequently, these mothers are tied to endless negotiation and justification of their physical absence (see also Hondagneu-Sotelo and Avila 1997) and they emphasise their motherhood by more intense phone or Internet communication and donation practices (2009, 260). Vives and Vasquez Silva (2017) argued that the established types of networks, kinship, and family structures in the home country have an essential impact on the mothering strategies. For instance, in Senegal, long-distance mothering is a common practice within collective fostering, i.e. migrant mothers rely on a dense network of care providers in the home country. At the same time, they work in Spain to reach their migration goals (2017, 508). Parreñas describes the paradox that impedes the reconstitution of gender caused by the challenge that mothers in the Philippines face as economic immigrants trying to simultaneously maintain intimate transnational family relations with their children (2005, 334).

Parenting behaviour of transnational fathers is an understudied research topic. The key finding is that migrant fathers are not attributed to the same societal gender expectations as transnational mothers (Parreñas 2005). In transnational fatherhood, the traditional male breadwinner role is connected with financial success and much less with maintaining care obligations, implying that migrant women and men vary in their transnational practices. However, studies have also shown commonalities between migrant mothering and fathering in terms of the challenges faced in work life, parenting, and the various strategies fathers carry out to meet the needs of family members (e.g. Fresnoza-Flot 2014; Kilkey et al. 2013). In the case of maternal migration for economic purposes, fathers may take over caring responsibility for their children and other dependent family members. However, a total role reversal takes place only in exceptional circumstances, and it does not mean that fathers automatically step into their role as primary care providers. Often men continue their co-breadwinning employment while childcare and domestic work responsibilities are delegated to grandmothers or other female family members, friends, or paid caregivers (Hondagneu-Sotelo and Avila 1997; Lutz and Palenga-Möllenbeck 2010; Parreñas 2005). Grandparents are usually the primary family members that are directly involved in transnational parenting practices. They provide support not only by taking care of children left behind and helping migrant women to reconcile work and family life but also by acting as cultural and family values transmitters (Wyss and Nedelcu 2018, 178).

Many studies focused on the experience of children, as important social actors within family migration who often experience various emotional challenges due to family separation, reunification, geographic mobility, or immobility. The emotional difficulties of parents living in separation from their children tend to relate closely to poor parent-child relationship quality, which may be a consequence of migration status or/and economic constraints. Lack of access to the resources needed to maintain a smooth flow of transnational communication may increase the risk of feelings of abandonment and dissatisfaction of children over the "unfulfilled" transnational parenting (Parreñas 2005; see also Haagsman et al. 2015). Children's agency in transnational practices strongly relates to their age. For very young children, the participation, that is the power to negotiate in the family's migration processes, is somewhat limited as they are heavily dependent on their caregivers' decisions. Adult children, on the other hand, tend to be more actively involved in transnational family life decisions, such as reunification and settlement processes (Bonizzoni 2015). Children left by a parent at a very young age and for a very long period are often able to build new intimate relationships with their parent retrospectively when reunited. Nevertheless, in the beginning, most children tend to face a strong need for physical and emotional closeness with their mothers to handle the new settlement situation but also to overcome the sense of loneliness that derives from the separation from the people left at home (2015, 178).

So far, the literature review included research on the dynamics of transnational families. We focused mainly on the analysis of determinants for decisions about migration and the respective family separation, the role of family and kin ties, and parenting practices in transnational settings. In the next section, we concentrate on mixed families and the changes they face during their life-course. The emphasis lies here on cultural or ethnic issues that raise in different periods of transition, e.g. in the context of family formation, marriage dissolution, and the birth of the first child.

Mixed Families

Conceptual Framework

In the last several decades, the rise of international migration inevitably led to the diversification of European societies, with a significant increase in the share of mixed couples and parentage. There is little consensus on the terminology for mixed marriages and families. Different communities and fields in the European family research use different terms to refer to "mixed" partnerships: binational, interethnic, inter-religious, multi- or bilingual, interracial, multicultural, and suchlike (compare Feng et al. 2012; King-O'Riain 2019; Lucassen and Laarman 2009; Osanami Törngren et al. 2019; Rodríguez-García 2006; Song and Aspinall 2012). These attributes—ethnic, racial, religious, national, and lingual—are sub aspects of the culture concept, which play an essential role in the understanding of gendered and ethnic dynamics of mixed unions. When describing the family dynamics in mixed partnerships, we prefer a streamlined definition that accounts for all culture-related differences without emphasising spatial divides or any socially constructed borders. We follow a comprehensive definition of culture by Scott and Marshall (2009, 152) as "all that in human society, which is socially rather than biologically transmitted".

Many quantitative longitudinal case studies and cross-country comparisons in the field of culturally mixed partnerships inform us well about the patterns of fertility (e.g. Andersson 2004; Milewski, 2007), marital formation (e.g. González-Ferrer 2006; Kulu and Hannemann 2019; Lucassen and Laarman 2009; Niedomysl et al. 2010) and divorce (e.g. Dribe and Lundh 2012; Feng et al. 2012; Milewski and Kulu 2013) considering the increasingly individualised trajectories of mixed families in Europe. In the next two sections, we introduce some significant results from qualitative and quantitative research on family dynamics and patterns among immigrants and their descendants, focusing on marital formation and culture transmission from a life-course perspective of mixed unions.

Trajectories from a Life-Course Perspective

In recent years, our understanding of family dynamics among migrants has shifted to life-courses, the observation of the social transformation of family structures and the individual transitions, such as marriage, divorce, entry into the labour force, childbirth, or retirement. In the context of mixed families, the most crucial task has been to examine the role of migrant agency in the societal change, meaning to explore how individuals construct their life-courses as self-monitored actors within the particular opportunities and constraints they face in their social environment (Wingens et al. 2011, 12). The European scholarship focused mainly on analysing the partner choice behaviour and (in)stability trends among migrants considering gender, ethnicity and generational effect of the studied populations (González-Ferrer

2006; Niedomysl et al. 2010; Trilla et al. 2008; van Tubergen and Maas 2007).

Studies about partner choice show that people tend to marry someone similar to themselves in terms of education, values, and religion (e.g. Kalmijn 1998). Moreover, for a migrant choosing a partner can be determined by additional factors such as gender, generation, the opportunity structure of the respective ethnic group, experiences in discrimination, and strong cultural ties with a country of origin (compare Kraler et al. 2011; Lucassen and Laarman 2009; Muttarak and Heath 2010; Nauck 2007; Rodríguez-García 2006). Migrant-native marriages are often seen as a proof of immigrant assimilation and integration (Kalmijn 1998) as they may have significant consequences for the personal integration process as well as for the socialisation of the children resulting from these marriages (Nauck 2007, 36). However, the choice of a partner from another cultural background, also known as an exogamous union, varies considerably between different ethnic and migrant groups and across generations. Concerning this matter, Lucassen and Laarman's (2009) comparative study explored family formation trends among the first and second generation of migrants in Germany, France, England, Belgium, and the Netherlands. It reveals that men are more likely to marry partners from outside their ethnic group than their female counterparts are and that second-generation migrants are proportionally more likely to intermarry than the first generation. In the case of guest workers from Southern Europe and West Indies, intermarriage rates of the second generation are twice as high as that of the first generation. Intermarriage rates of male increased more than that of females. Similarly, a comparative study by Huschek et al. (2012) revealed that the descendants of Turkish immigrants who chose a partner of another ethnic background, i.e. a second-generation partner, the choice by their family values seem to resemble the choice of a native-born partner strongly.

Further research has focused on families whose members are socialised to different cultural and/or religious contexts to determine whether the extent of cultural distance between the two partners has an impact on the probability of divorce. Several research findings have revealed that a European intra-marriage is less likely to experience identity crisis than a mixed marriage between two individuals who are socialised in different social environments, with different value systems and lifestyles, e.g. traditional vs modern, individual vs collective, European vs non-European (compare Dribe and Lundh 2012; Gaspar 2008; van Ham and Tammaru 2011). Kalmijn et al. (2005) found in the case of the Netherlands that marriages between Dutch and other ethnic groups have a higher risk of divorce the more significant the cultural differences between the two groups are. Feng et al. (2012) focused on the comparison of culturally mixed partnerships and co-ethnic marriages in Britain to examine the risk of marriage dissolution. Surprisingly, after controlling for group background characteristics such as age, the initial higher risk of mixed-ethnic marriages to end up in divorce, in comparison with co-ethnic couples, was no longer significant.

In the next section, we will review recent research on negotiation and transmission of cultural values within mixed families, another significant research stream on the family life-course perspective of immigrant and ethnic minorities in Europe.

Negotiation and Transmission of Culture

More recently, research has begun to explore interdisciplinary perspectives of everyday life of mixed families by emphasising the cultural aspects such as motivations, values, and identities of the individuals from various countries and ethnic backgrounds. According to cultural dissimilarity hypothesis (see Milweski and Kulu 2013), the distinct family beliefs, traditions, and different values systems that dominate in multicultural/multiethnic families can become a struggle and lead to conflictual family relationships,[6] especially in matters of parental roles and childrearing (see Appel and Singla 2016; Balaban et al. 2018). Special events in their life-course challenge partners' ability to deal with cultural differences. For example, when the first child is born, these couples are likely to renegotiate issues of the child's upbringing, e.g. values, language, and religious education (Crespi 2016). In his recent study, Amirmoayed (2018) examined intercultural marital practices of Persian/non-Persian partnerships in the UK by analysing negotiations over the main challenges that family members face at the birth of a child.[7] He supported the findings of the study by Smart and Shipman (2004) showing that traditions are subject to constant negotiations, change and adjustment occurring across generations, especially religious practices components, such as child name-giving, infant baptism, and circumcision. Participants in this study were involved in constant negotiation between their intermarried partners and their parents (2018, 102). However, when partners share the same values and beliefs, different religious affiliations are instead perceived as an opportunity rather than a threat to their children's enrichment (Crespi 2016).

In contrast, a recent debate related to migrant families, intergenerational, and gender relations criticises the culturalist explanation for potential interpersonal conflicts (Levitt and Jaworsky 2007). Some scholars argue that when people from two different cultures meet, they tend to develop one new cultural category that is not necessarily identifiable, sometimes referred to as hybridity, while the old cultures break down (Nurse 1999). According to this theory, these unique cultural traditions are a result of delocalisation process, i.e. mixing and adaptation of original traditions to the existing modern and postmodern discourses and practices in the destination society (Canclini et al. 1995; Pang 2018). Rodríguez-García (2006) argues that hybridity and segregation should not be treated as contradictory or exclusive realities. Mixed partnerships and their descendants are likely to socialise in multiple localisations and cultural backgrounds rather than experiencing a "clash between two cultures". However, the hybridity approach is contested in its meanings as a social construct lacking a reflexive and critical assessment of the research.

Unveiling different aspects of mixed families has a direct impact on understanding the identity formation processes and social outcomes of children of mixed families. The new generation of people of mixed parentage was considered as a bridge between cultural, ethnic, and racial divides. Nevertheless, cross-country comparisons prove that children of mixed families may still face some forms of discrimination, isolation, or hostility in the society they are born into (Osanami Törngren et al. 2019, 3; see also Appel and Singla 2016). Identity processes and experiences of mixed individuals are heterogeneous and multifaceted (Rodríguez-García et al. 2019, 4). Physical appearance and social environment play a significant role in shaping the experiences of young multicultural people (Song and Aspinall 2012). Individuals can choose or develop different types of identification related to region, language, religious affiliation, and gender. Rodríguez-García et al. (2019, 14) showed that visible markers that distinguish an ethnic group from the native society, such as phenotype, language, or religious affiliation, are crucial factors effecting identity formation for this group of individuals. Mixed-culture individuals with more visible shared characteristics with the native majority population can develop more advantageous identities than those individuals whose heritage involves negative reputation experience more significant identity mismatch, stigmatisation, racism, and discrimination.

Drawing upon individual-level longitudinal studies and research literature review in this section, we aimed to advance the understanding of the determinants of family dynamics about partner choice, marriage, and divorce among ethnically/culturally mixed unions. However, we did not explicitly assess the current research on the contribution of family changes on the integration of immigrants and their descendants in European countries. Instead, we concentrated on a more recent but still under-researched topic on cultural challenges that partners, as well as children, face in an ethnically mixed family environment. We agree that culture is a controversial issue in the context of mixed partnerships. Therefore, we limited our literature review to relevant contributions to the transmission of cultural values and children's identity formation. In the next section, we will outline opportunities for further developing research on changing dynamics of transnational and mixed families.

Conclusion

In this chapter, we have reviewed the literature on migrant families, focusing on the significant research developments in understanding the dynamics of transnational and mixed families in Europe. The review was limited to specific recent research topics, to provide a concise overview of the diversification of migrant family lives in Europe.

Research on transnational families reveals how different family members continue "doing family" regardless of the geographical distance. The significant role of the family ties is observed not only in the way how families decide to migrate but also in strategies that family members adopt for maintaining unity regardless of the spatial separation. For example, transnational parenting requires different strategies by migrant mothers/fathers to cope with the situation of separation from their children. New ways of communication allow migrant women to redefine their mothering strategies and have more intense contact with the family they left behind (Hondagneu-Sotelo and Avila 1997; Parreñas 2005). However, research on transnational fathers and grandparenting is somewhat limited.

In the last several decades, due to the growing international mobility, a significant increase in the share of culturally/ethnically mixed couples and parentage has been evident. The research on mixed families has demonstrated the strong relationship between migration context, different family arrangement, and trajectories based on cultural aspects such as gender, religion, and ethnicity. There is a growing literature on formation and divorce of mixed marriages in Europe that deals with cultural, gender, and generational factors as well as the social norms and expectations influencing the family dynamics, adaptation and integration processes (e.g. González-Ferrer 2006; Feng et al. 2012; Kalmijn 1998; Lucassen and Laarman 2009; Milewski and Kulu 2013). Moreover, empirical findings regarding mixed families indicate that special events in the life-course, such as first childbirth, challenge partners' ability to deal with cultural differences and, in some cases, renegotiate issues concerning child's upbringing, e.g. values, language and religious education (Crespi 2016).

Driven by the insights offered by the family studies, we note that the sociological research on migrant families in Europe needs more studies with a comparative approach. These would include consideration of various institutional and policy contexts, for instance, an analysis of how socio-economic, institutional, and policy settings affect family lives of families, single-parent, or divorced migrants and their descendants. Notably, for mixed families, it is crucial to investigate how these factors can shape migration decisions, identity formation, family values and parenting behaviour, and the process of social integration into the host society. Understanding cultural diversity among migrants is essential for the development of policies aimed at reducing social inequalities for migrants of both the first and second generations. Moreover, we are convinced that individual trajectories should not be ignored when it comes to exploration of family migration and its changing dynamics, structure, and normative behaviour. More studies should analyse changes among migrants and their descendants over their life-courses, studying several transitions rather only one transition at a time.

NOTES

1. In the present chapter, we use the definition of the family in the traditional context, i.e. the nuclear family with heterosexual parents and the accompanying children.
2. The definition of an intact family is "… used to describe a family as one in which there was never dissolution of the marriage either through death or divorce" (Feigon 1975, 2).
3. In the context of family migration, push factors are those that prompt people to decide to leave their home country. These factors include, in particular, a lack of economic opportunities and unemployment, social or political hardship such as lack of political/religious freedom, discrimination, war and conflict, loss of wealth, and lack of health and education facilities in the home country. Pull factors, on the other hand, represent living conditions that attract people to migrate to a particular country, for example, higher wages, better economic opportunities, political and religious freedom, good health or education infrastructure and others (compare European Communities 2000; Massey et al. 1993). The general criticism of these models of the migratory decision-making process is that they do not explain the direction of migration flows and also why some migrant families move whereas other families decide to stay.
4. Transmigrants are migrants whose daily lives depend on multiple and constant interconnections across international borders and whose public identities are configured in relationship to more than one nation-state (Glick-Schiller et al. 1995).
5. Transnational parenting, that is motherhood and fatherhood in the context of transnational migration, is understood here as the thoughts and various nurturing and caring practices that parents carry out for their children from a distance.
6. Milewski and Kulu (2013) mention different aspects of cultural dissimilarity that may influence negatively the relationships of exogamous, i.e. inter-ethnic partnerships comparing to endogamous couples.
7. Amirmoayed confirmed the previous results of the Smart and Shipman's (2004) study on the parental and marital obligations and practices within the immigrant Irish, Indian, and Pakistani communities in the UK, by showing that the traditional values of immigrant families go through a standardised procedure of negotiation and change across cohorts, which is driven by the close inter-generational relationships.

REFERENCES

Amirmoayed, Ali. 2018. "Intercultural Negotiations over a Newborn: The Case of Persians in the United Kingdom." In *Making Multicultural Families in Europe. Gender and Intergenerational Relations*, edited by Isabella Crespi, Stefanie Giada Meda, and Laura Merla, 91–106. Cham: Palgrave Macmillan.

Andersson, Gunnar. 2004. "Childbearing After Migration: Fertility Patterns of Foreign-Born Women in Sweden." *International Migration Review* 38 (2): 747–774. https://doi.org/10.1111/j.1747-7379.2004.tb00216.x.

Appel, Helene Bang, and Rashmi Singla. 2016. "Mixed Parentage: Negotiating Identity in Denmark." In *Contested Childhoods: Growing Up in Migrancy*, edited by

Marie Louise Seeberg and Elżbieta M. Goździak, 139–158. IMISCOE Research Series. Cham: Springer.

Bailey, Adrian, and Paul Boyle. 2004. "Untying and Retying Family Migration in the New Europe." *Journal of Ethnic and Migration Studies* 30 (2): 229–241. https://doi.org/10.1080/1369183042000200678.

Balaban, Ebru, Dafina Kurti, and Jara Kampmann. 2018. "Comparing Sibling Ties in Inter-Ethnic and Intra-Ethnic Families in Germany." In *Making Multicultural Families in Europe. Gender and Intergenerational Relations*, edited by Isabella Crespi, Stefanie Giada Meda, and Laura Merla, 71–89. Cham: Palgrave Macmillan.

Banfi, Ludovica, and Paolo Boccagni. 2011. "Transnational Family Life and Female Migration in Italy: One or Multiple Patterns?" In *Gender, Generations and the Family in International Migration*, edited by Kraler Albert, Kofman Eleonore, Kohli Martin, and Schmoll Camille, 287–312. Amsterdam: Amsterdam University Press.

Bell, Justyna, and Marta Bivand Erdal. 2015. "Limited but Enduring Transnational Ties? Transnational Family Life Among Polish Migrants in Norway." *Studia Migracyjne – Przegląd Polonijny* 3 (157): 77–98. http://www.kbnm.pan.pl/images/pdf/SM_PP_3_2015/St_Migr_3_15_5_J.BellM.Bivand_Erdal.pdf.

Bonizzoni, Paola. 2015. "Here or There? Shifting Meanings and Practices in Mother–Child Relationships Across Time and Space." *International Migration* 53 (6) (December): 166–182. https://doi.org/10.1111/imig.12028.

Bryceson, Deborah Fahy, and Ulla Vuorela. 2002. "Transnational Families in the 21st Century." In *The Transnational Family: New European Frontiers and Global Networks*, edited by Deborah Fahy Bryceson and Ulla Vuorela, 3–30. Oxford: Berg Publishers. https://www.academia.edu/36353367/Transnational_Families_in_the_21st_Century. Accessed May 12, 2020.

Bryceson, Deborah Fahy. 2019. "Transnational Families Negotiating Migration and Care Life Cycles Across Nation-State Borders." *Journal of Ethnic and Migration Studies* 45 (16): 3042–3064. https://doi.org/10.1080/1369183X.2018.1547017.

Bushin, Naomi. 2009. "Researching Family Migration Decision-Making: A Children-in-Families Approach." *Population, Space and Place* 15 (5): 429–443. https://doi.org/10.1002/psp.522.

Canclini, Néstor García, Renato Rosaldo, Christopher L. Chiappari, and Silvia L. López. 1995. "Hybrid Cultures: Strategies for Entering and Leaving Modernity." University of Minnesota Press. www.jstor.org/stable/10.5749/j.cttts9sz.

Carling, Jørgen, Cecilia Menjívar, and Leah Schmalzbauer. 2012. "Central Themes in the Study of Transnational Parenthood." *Journal of Ethnic and Migration Studies* 38 (2): 191–217. https://doi.org/10.1080/1369183X.2012.646417.

COFACE. 2012. *Transnational Families and the Impact of Economic Migration on Families*. Brussels: The Confederation of Family Organisations in the European Union. http://www.coface-eu.org/wp-content/uploads/2017/09/Migration-2012-COFACE-position-on-Transnational-Families-en.pdf. Accessed December 8, 2019.

Crespi, Isabella. 2016. "Living in Multicultural Families: Education, Values and Relationships in a Globalized Society." In *Trust and Conflict in Intercultural Processes. Experiences, Practices and Reflections*, edited by and Flavia Stara and Rosita Deluigi, 137–152. Macerata: EUM. https://u-pad.unimc.it/retrieve/handle/11393/222342/69911/2016%20CRESPI%20in%20Stara_Deluigi_Trust%20and%20conflict.pdf. Accessed December 2, 2019.

Dallemagne, Grégory. 2018. "Intimacies of Power in the Circulation of Care: Making Gender Across Generations. Transnational Andean Families in Quito and Madrid." In *Making Multicultural Families in Europe. Gender and Intergenerational Relations*, edited by Isabella Crespi, Stefanie Giada Meda, and Laura Merla, 127–143. Cham: Palgrave Macmillan.

Datta, Kavita, Cathy McIlwaine, Jane Wills, Yara Evans, Joanna Herbert, and Jon May. 2007. "The New Development Finance of Exploiting Migrant Labour? Remittance Sending Among Low-Paid Migrant Workers in London." *International Development Planning* 29 (1): 43–67. https://doi.org/10.3828/idpr.29.1.3.

Dribe, Martin, and Christer Lundh. 2012. "Intermarriage, Value Context and Union Dissolution: Sweden 1990–2005." *European Journal of Population* 28: 139–158. https://doi.org/10.1007/s10680-011-9253-y.

Esveldt, Ingrid, Isik Kulu-Glasgow, Jeroen M. Schoorl, and Hanna van Solinge. 1995. "*Migratiemotieven, migratienetwerken en partnerkeuze van Turken en Marokkanen in Nederland*." The Hague: Netherlands Interdisciplinary Demographic Institute (NIDI). https://doi.org/10.17026/dans-zwv-f88x.

European Communities. 2000. *Push and Pull Factors of International Migration. A Comparative Report*. Luxembourg: Office for Official Publications of the European Communities. https://www.nidi.nl/shared/content/output/2000/eurostat-2000-theme1-pushpull.pdf.

Faist, Thomas. 2010. "Transnationalisation: Its Conceptual and Empirical Relevance." In *Migration in a Globalised World: New Research Issues and Prospects*, edited by Cédric Audebert and Mohamed Kamel Doraï, 79–106. Amsterdam: Amsterdam University Press. www.jstor.org/stable/j.ctt46mwxq.7.

Fauser, Margit, and Eveline Reisenauer. 2013. "Diversität und Dynamik transnationaler persönlicher Beziehungen türkischer MigrantInnen in Deutschland." In *Transnationale Migration am Beispiel Deutschland und Türkei*, edited by Barbara Pusch, 171–185. Wiesbaden: Springer VS.

Feigon, Jackie S. 1975. *Academic Achievement in Intact and Non-Intact Households*. Master's Thesis, 2777. https://ecommons.luc.edu/luc_theses/2777. Accessed March 13, 2020.

Feng, Zhiqiang, Paul Boyle, Maarten van Ham, and Gillian M. Raab. 2012. "Are Mixed-Ethnic Unions More Likely to Dissolve Than Co-Ethnic Unions? New Evidence from Britain." *European Journal of Population* 28: 159–176. https://doi.org/10.1007/s10680-012-9259-0.

Fresnoza-Flot, Asuncion. 2009. "Migration Status and Transnational Mothering: the Case of Filipino Migrants in France." *Global Networks* 9 (2) (April): 252–270. https://doi.org/10.1111/j.1471-0374.2009.00253.x.

Fresnoza-Flot, Asuncion. 2014. "Men's caregiving practices in Filipino transnational families." In *Transnational Families, Migration and the Circulation Of Care: Understanding Mobility and Absence in Family Life*, edited by Loretta Baldassar and Laura Merla, 170–184. Abingdon, UK: Routledge.

Fresnoza-Flot, Asuncion, and Laura Merla. 2018. "Global Householding' in Mixed Families: The Case of Thai Migrant Women in Belgium." In *Making Multicultural Families in Europe. Gender and Intergenerational Relations*, edited by Isabella Crespi, Stefanie Giada Meda, and Laura Merla, 23–37. Cham: Palgrave Macmillan.

Galasinska, Aleksandra, and Olga Kozlowska. 2009. "Discourses of Normal Life Among Post-Accession Migrants from Poland to Britain." In *Polish Migration to the UK in the 'New' European Union After 2004*, edited by Kathy Burrell, 85–105.

Farnham: Ashgate. https://www.researchgate.net/publication/286956168_Discourses_of_a_'normal_life'_among_post-accession_migrants_from_Poland_to_Britain. Accessed May 18, 2020.

Gaspar, Sofia. 2008. "Towards a Definition of European Intra-Marriage as a New Social Phenomenon." CIES e-WORKING PAPER No. 46/2008. http://hdl.handle.net/10071/725. Accessed January 19, 2020.

Glick-Schiller, Nina, Linda Basch, and Cristina Szanton Blanc. 1995. "From Immigrant to Transmigrant: Theorizing Transnational Migration." *Anthropological Quarterly* 68 (1): 48–63. https://doi.org/10.2307/3317464.

González-Ferrer, Amparo. 2006. "Who Do Immigrants Marry? Partner Choice Among Single Immigrants in Germany." *European Sociological Review* 22 (2): 171–185. https://doi.org/10.1093/esr/jci050.

Haagsman, Karlijn, Valentina Mazzucato, and Bilisuma B. Dito. 2015. "Transnational Families and the Subjective Wellbeing of Migrant Parents: Angolan and Nigerian Parents in the Netherlands." *Ethnic and Racial Studies* 38 (15): 1–20. https://doi.org/10.1080/01419870.2015.1037783.

Hondagneu-Sotelo, Pierrette, and Ernestine Avila. 1997. "'I'm Here, but I'm There': The Meanings of Latina Transnational Motherhood." *Gender and Society* 11 (5): 548–571. https://www.jstor.org/stable/190339.

Huschek, Doreen, Helga A. G. de Valk, and Aart C. Liefbroer. 2012. "Partner Choice Patterns Among the Descendants of Turkish Immigrants in Europe." *European Journal of Population* 28: 241–268. https://doi.org/10.1007/s10680-012-9265-2.

Kalmijn, Matthijs. 1998. "Intermarriage and Homogamy: Causes, Patterns, Trends." *Annual Review of Sociology* 24: 395–421. www.jstor.org/stable/223487.

Kalmijn, Matthijs, Paul M. de Graaf, and Jacques P. G. Janssen. 2005. "Intermarriage and the Risk of Divorce in the Netherlands: The Effects of Differences in Religion and in Nationality, 1974–94." *Population Studies* 59 (1): 71–85. https://doi.org/10.1080/0032472052000332719.

Kilkey, Majella, Ania Plomien, and Diane Perrons. 2013. "Migrant Men's Fathering Narratives, Practices and Projects in National and Transnational Spaces: Recent Polish Male Migrants to London." *International Migration* 52 (1): 178–191. https://doi.org/10.1111/imig.12046.

Kivisto, Peter. 2001. "Theorizing Transnational Immigration: A Critical Review of Current Efforts." *Ethnic and Racial Studies* 24 (4): 549–577. https://doi.org/10.1080/01419870120049789.

Kofman, Eleonore, Albert Kraler, Martin Kohli, and Camille Schmoll. 2011. "Introduction: Issues and Debates on Family-Related Migration and the Migrant Family: A European Perspective." In *Gender, Generations and the Family in International Migration*, edited by Albert Kraler, Eleonore Kofman, Martin Kohli, and Camille Schmoll, 13–54. Amsterdam: Amsterdam University Press. www.jstor.org/stable/j.ctt46n1jm.4.

Kraler, Albert, Eleonore Kofman, Martin Kohli, and Camille Schmoll. 2011. *Gender, Generations and the Family in International Migration*. Amsterdam: Amsterdam University Press. IMISCOE Research. https://www.jstor.org/stable/j.ctt46n1jm.

King-O'Riain, Rebecca Chiyoko. 2019. "How the Irish Became More Than White: Mixed-Race Irishness in Historical and Contemporary Contexts." *Journal of Ethnic and Migration Studies*. https://doi.org/10.1080/1369183x.2019.1654156.

Kulu, Hill, and Tina Hannemann. 2019. "Mixed Marriage Among Immigrants and Their Descendants in the United Kingdom: Analysis of Longitudinal Data with Missing Information." *Population Studies* 73 (2): 179–196. https://doi.org/10.1080/00324728.2018.1493136.

Lacroix, Thomas, Peggy Levitt, and Ilka Vari-Lavoisier. 2016. "Social Remittances and the Changing Transnational Political Landscape." *Comparative Migration Studies* 4 (16): 1–5. https://doi.org/10.1186/s40878-016-0032-0.

Lee, Everett S. 1966. A Theory of Migration. *Demography* 3 (1): 47–57. https://doi.org/10.2307/2060063.

Levitt, Peggy, and Nadya B. Jaworsky. 2007. "Transnational Migration Studies: Past Developments and Future Trends." *Annual Review of Sociology* 33 (1): 129–156. https://doi.org/10.1146/annurev.soc.33.040406.131816.

Longhurst, Robyn. 2013. "Using Skype to Mother: Bodies, Emotions, Visuality, and Screens." *Environment and Planning D: Society and Space* 31 (4): 664–679. https://doi.org/10.1068/d20111.

Lucassen, Leo, and Charlotte Laarman. 2009. "Immigration, Intermarriage and the Changing Face of Europe in the Post War Period." *The History of the Family* 14 (1) (January): 52–68. https://doi.org/10.1016/j.hisfam.2008.12.001.

Lutz, Helma, and Ewa Palenga-Möllenbeck. 2010. "Care Work Migration in Germany: Semi-Compliance and Complicity." *Social Policy and Society* 9 (3): 419–430. https://doi.org/10.1017/S1474746410000138.

Madianou, Mirca, and Daniel Miller. 2012. *Migration and New Media. Transnational Families and Polymedia*. London: Routledge. https://doi.org/10.4324/9780203154236.

Mai, Nicola, and Russel King. 2009. "Love, Sexuality and Migration: Mapping the Issue(s)." *Mobilities* 4 (3) (December): 295–307. https://doi.org/10.1080/17450100903195318.

Massey, Douglas S., Joaquin Arango, Graeme Hugo, Ali Kouaouci, Adela Pellegrino, and J. Edward Taylor. 1993. "Theories of International Migration: A Review and Appraisal." *Population and Development Review* 19 (3) (September): 431–466. https://doi.org/10.2307/2938462.

Mazzucato, Valentina, Djamila Schans, Kim Caarls, and Cris Beauchemin. 2015. "Transnational Families Between Africa and Europe." *International Migration Review* 49 (1): 142–172. https://doi.org/10.1111/imre.12153.

Mazzucato, Valentina, and Bilisuma B. Dito. 2018. "Transnational Families: Cross-Country Comparative PERSPECTIVES." *Population, Space and Place* 24 (7): 1–7. https://doi.org/10.1002/psp.2165.

Milewski, Nadja. 2007. "First Child of Immigrant Workers and Their Descendants in West Germany: Interrelation of Events, Disruption, or Adaptation?" *Demographic Research* 17 (29): 859–895. https://doi.org/10.4054/DemRes.2007.17.29.

Milewski, Nadja, and Hill Kulu. (2013). "Mixed Marriages in Germany: A High Risk of Divorce for Immigrant–Native Couples." *European Journal of Population* 30 (1): 89–113. https://doi.org/10.1007/s10680-013-9298-1.

Moskal, Marta, and Naomi Tyrell. 2016. "Family Migration Decision-Making, Stepmigration and Separation: Children's Experiences in European Migrant Worker Family." *Children's Geographies* 14 (4): 453–467. https://doi.org/10.1080/14733285.2015.1116683.

Muttarak, Raya, and Anthony Heath. 2010. "Who Intermarries in Britain: Explaining Ethnic Diversity in Intermarriage Patterns." *The British Journal of Sociology* 61 (2) (June): 275–305. https://doi.org/10.1111/j.1468-4446.2010.01313.x.

Nauck, Bernhard. 2007. "Immigrant Families in Germany: Family Change Between Situational Adaptation, Acculturation, Segregation and Remigration." *Zeitschrift für Familienforschung* 19 (1): 34–54. https://www.ssoar.info/ssoar/handle/document/5804.

Niedomysl, Thomas, John Östh, and Maarten van Ham. 2010. "The Globalisation of Marriage Fields: The Swedish Case." *Journal of Ethnic and Migration Studies* 36 (7): 1119–1138. https://doi.org/10.1080/13691830903488184.

Nurse, Keith. 1999. "Globalization and Trinidad Carnival: Diaspora, Hybridity and Identity in Global Culture." *Cultural Studies* 13 (4): 661–690. https://doi.org/10.1080/095023899335095.

Osanami Törngren, Sayaka, Nahikari Irastorza, and Dan Rodríguez-García. 2019: "Understanding Multiethnic and Multiracial Experiences Globally: Towards a Conceptual Framework of Mixedness." *Journal of Ethnic and Migration Studies*. https://doi.org/10.1080/1369183X.2019.1654150.

Pang, Mengxi. 2018. "Negotiating the (Non) Negotiable: Connecting 'Mixed-Race' Identities to 'Mixed-Race' Families." *Journal of Intercultural Studies* 39 (4): 414–428. https://doi.org/10.1080/07256868.2018.1486292.

Parreñas, Rhacel. 2005. "Long Distance Intimacy: Class, Gender and Intergenerational Relations Between Mothers and Children in Filipino Transnational Families." *Global Networks* 5 (4) (October): 317–336. https://doi.org/10.1111/j.1471-0374.2005.00122.x.

Reisenauer, Eveline. 2018. "Distant Relationships in Transnational Families and Kinship Networks: The Case of Turkish Migrants in Germany." In *Making Multicultural Families in Europe. Gender and Intergenerational Relations*, edited by Isabella Crespi, Stefanie Giada Meda, and Laura Merla, 109–126. Cham: Palgrave Macmillan.

Rodríguez-García, Dan. 2006. "Mixed Marriages and Transnational Families in the Intercultural Context: A Case Study of African-Spanish Couples in Catalonia." *Journal of Ethnic and Migration Studies* 32 (3): 403–433. https://doi.org/10.1080/13691830600555186.

Rodríguez-García, Dan, Miguel Solana, Anna Ortiz, and Beatriz Ballestín. 2019. "Blurring of Colour Lines? Ethnoracially Mixed Youth in Spain Navigating Identity." *Journal of Ethnic and Migration Studies*. https://doi.org/10.1080/1369183x.2019.1654157.

Ryan, Loise, Rosemary Sales, Mary Tilki, and Bernadetta Siara. 2009. "Family Strategies and Transnational Migration: Recent Polish Migrants in London." *Journal of Ethnic and Migration Studies* 35 (1): 61–77. https://doi.org/10.1080/13691830802489176.

Ryan, Loise, and Rosemary Sales. 2011. "Family Migration: The Role of Children and Education in Family Decision-Making Strategies of Polish Migrants in London." *International Migration* 51 (2) (April): 90–103. https://doi.org/10.1111/j.1468-2435.2010.00652.x.

Scott, John, and Gordon Marshall. 2009. *A Dictionary of Sociology*, 3rd rev. ed. Oxford: Oxford University Press. https://doi.org/10.1093/acref/9780199533008.001.0001.

Shmulyar Gréen, Oksana, and Charlotte Melander. 2018. "Family Obligations Across European Borders: Negotiating Migration Decisions Within the Families of Post-Accession Migrants in Sweden." *Palgrave Communications* 4 (28): 1–13. https://doi.org/10.1057/s41599-018-0084-x.

Sime, Daniela, Rachel Fox, and Emilia Pietka. 2010. "At Home Abroad: The Life Experiences of Eastern European Migrant Children in Scotland." ESRC Report. Glasgow: University of Strathclyde. https://www.researchgate.net/publication/263375909_At_Home_Abroad_The_life_experiences_of_Eastern_European_migrant_children_in_Scotland_Report_for_practitioners_and_policy_makers. Accessed April 6, 2020.

Smart, Carol, and Beccy Shipman. 2004. "Visions in Monochrome: Marriage and the Individualization Thesis." *Sociology* 55 (4) (December): 491–509. https://doi.org/10.1111/j.1468-4446.2004.00034.x.

Song, Miri, and Peter Aspinall. 2012. "Is Racial Mismatch a Problem for Young "Mixed Race" People in Britain? The Findings of Qualitative Research." *Ethnicities* 12 (6): 730–753. https://doi.org/10.1177/1468796811434912.

Tolstokorova, Alissa. 2018. "'And They Shall Be One Flesh...': Gender Convergence of Family Roles in Transnational Families of Ukrainian Migrant Women." In *Making Multicultural Families in Europe. Gender and Intergenerational Relations*, edited by Isabella Crespi, Stefanie Giada Meda, and Laura Merla, 145–159. Cham: Palgrave Macmillan.

Trilla, Clara Cortina, Albert Esteve, and Andreu Domingo. 2008. "Marriage Patterns of the Foreign Born Population in a New Country of Immigration: The Case of Spain." *International Migration Review* 42 (4) (Winter): 877–902. www.jstor.org/stable/27645283.

van Ham, Maarten, and Tiit Tammaru. 2011. "Ethnic Minority–Majority Unions in Estonia." *European Journal of Population* 27 (May): 313–335. https://doi.org/10.1007/s10680-011-9236-z.

van Tubergen, Frank, and Ineke Maas. 2007. "Ethnic Intermarriage Among Immigrants in the Netherlands: An Analysis of Population Data." *Social Science Research* 36 (3) (September): 1065–1086. https://doi.org/10.1016/j.ssresearch.2006.09.003.

Vertovec, Steven. 2001. "Transnationalism and Identity." *Journal of Ethnic and Migration Studies* 27 (4) (August): 573–582. https://doi.org/10.1080/13691830120090386.

Vertovec, Steven. 2004. "Cheap Calls: The Social Glue of Migrant Transnationalism." *Global Networks* 4 (2) (April): 219–224. https://doi.org/10.1111/j.1471-0374.2004.00088.x.

Vives Luna, and Iria Vazquez Silva. 2017. "Senegalese Migration to Spain: transnational Mothering Practices." *Journal of Ethnic and Migration Studies* 43 (3) (May): 495–512. https://doi.org/10.1080/1369183X.2016.1186531.

Wimmer, Andreas, and Nina Glick-Schiller. 2002. "Methodological Nationalism and Beyond: Nation–State Building, Migration and the Social Sciences." *Global Networks* 2 (4) (October): 301–334. https://doi.org/10.1111/1471-0374.00043.

Wingens, Matthias, Helga de Valk, Michael Windzio, and Can Aybek. 2011. *A Life-Course Perspective on Migration and Integration*. Dordrecht: Springer.

White, Anne. 2011. *Polish Families and Migration Since EU Accession*. Bristol, UK: Bristol University Press. www.jstor.org/stable/j.ctt9qgmsz.

Wyss, Malika, and Mihaela Nedelcu. 2018. "Zero Generation Grandparents Caring for Their Grandchildren in Switzerland. The Diversity of Transnational Care Arrangements among EU and Non-EU Migrant Families." In *Childhood and Parenting in Transnational Settings*, edited by Viorela Ducu, Mihaela Nedelcu, and Aron Telegdi-Csetri, 175–190. Cham: Springer.

Zanfrini, Laura. 2012. "Family Migration: Fulfilling the Gap Between Law and Social Processes." *Societies* 2 (3): 63–74. https://doi.org/10.3390/soc2030063.

Zontini, Elisabetta. 2010. *Transnational Families, Migration and Gender: Moroccan and Filipino Women in Bologna and Barcelona*. Berghahn Books. www.jstor.org/stable/j.ctt9qcpt3.

CHAPTER 25

Intergenerational Relations in the Context of Migration: Gender Roles in Family Relationships

Mihaela Hărăguș, Viorela Ducu, and Ionuț Földes

INTRODUCTION

In this chapter, we provide a state of the art on the relations and transfers that take place during adulthood between family generations affected by migration, within Europe. By discussing who initiates intergenerational transfers and towards whom, we focus on the gendered characteristics of such relationships, by positing each gender reconfiguration and gender reaffirmation among families experiencing migration.

We mainly focus on the transfers between parents and adult children. We combine the literature on intergenerational solidarity, which often guides the research into the dyad parents—adult children, with the literature on transnational families (Hărăguș and Telegdi-Csetri 2018). The intergenerational solidarity paradigm sees several dimensions of parent-(adult) child

---

M. Hărăguș (✉)
Centre for Population Studies, Babeș-Bolyai University, Cluj-Napoca, Romania
e-mail: mihaela.haragus@ubbcluj.ro

V. Ducu
Faculty of Political, Administrative and Communication Sciences, Babeș-Bolyai University, Cluj-Napoca, Romania
e-mail: viorela.telegdi@ubbcluj.ro

I. Földes
Faculty of Sociology and Social Work, Babeș-Bolyai University, Cluj-Napoca, Romania
e-mail: ionut.foldes@ubbcluj.ro

© The Author(s), under exclusive license to Springer Nature Switzerland AG 2021
A.-M. Castrén et al. (eds.), *The Palgrave Handbook of Family Sociology in Europe*, https://doi.org/10.1007/978-3-030-73306-3_25

interactions, shaped by geographical proximity as a potential for intergenerational relations. Events and transitions, such as migration, in the life course of members of different generations have profound implications for the evolution of intergenerational relations. The new geographical distance produces certain mutations, and communication and travel technologies become of crucial importance for mediating intergenerational transfers. In the case of generations of migrants, which reside in same destination countries, the geographical proximity is regained, and intergenerational solidarity is reconfigured in other ways: it takes place in different institutional (welfare regime) and cultural contexts.

Research on intergenerational linkages in the family shows that care and emotional support are gendered activities, daughters being more likely to offer such forms of care (Karpinska et al. 2016). The feminisation of international migration, linked with the spread of live-in domestic work and care of older persons as an employment sector for migrant women in many European countries, created the premises for different roles of men and women in families affected by migration. The requirement for recognising the "gendered geographies of power" (Pessar and Mahler 2003) within studies addressing migration has led to the recognition of the "increased agency and independence of women in migration flows and systems" (King et al. 2006, 250).

Some of the first concepts have given attention to transnational motherhood, and concurrently, transnational families. From mainly addressing topics related to the nuclear family, such as transnational parenthood, studies on transnational families brought new actors within the family web, such as children and older parents of the migrants (Ducu 2018b). By expanding the focus from the nuclear family to intergenerational relations, children of migrant and older parents are not to be considered just passive recipients of transnational care, but as active agents in maintaining transnational families (Ducu 2018b). Through methodological and conceptual repositioning, a gendered perspective has become a priority in transnational family research (Ducu 2018b). However, much of the research regards children and spouses who remained in the home country and less approaches the intergenerational relations in adulthood.

Considering Europe as the destination for migration, it is important to distinguish the so-called "old migrants" (such as migrants from former colonies or guest workers) and "new migrants" (from Eastern and Central European countries). They differ on various issues, such as legal restrictions for migration (including mobility of relatives), the geographical distance to the (European) destination country and consequently the accessibility of international transportation, the welfare regimes in home countries (that shape the need of intergenerational transfers of care), the family culture (including norms of intergenerational obligations), and gender roles in origin countries. These are important factors that shape the frequency and intensity of intergenerational relations, as well as the gender roles in ensuring intergenerational solidarity in the migration context. The experience of migration and the contact with different cultural, economic, or institutional contexts, and the ongoing intergenerational relations, reconfigure or reaffirm gender roles in family, in both sending and receiving communities.

In the following sections, we offer an overview of research on different forms of intergenerational relations, performed in families experiencing migration, with or without transnational practices, by emphasising gender differences. Much of our overview addresses the functional intergenerational solidarity (transfers of resources and support) or transfers of care (as in the transnational family literature), but other forms are acknowledged, too.

Intergenerational Relations in Migration Context

Much of the research on intergenerational relations in adulthood relies on the theoretical construct of intergenerational solidarity. It is used "as a means to characterize the behavioural and emotional dimensions of interaction, cohesion, sentiment and support between parents and children, grandparents and grandchildren, over the course of long-term relationships" (Bengtson 2001, 8). It consists of several dimensions of child-parent interaction: affectual (emotional closeness), consensual (similarity or agreement in beliefs and values), functional (resource sharing and exchange of support in various forms), associational (contact and common activities), normative (perceptions of obligations and expectations about intergenerational connections), and structural (opportunities for exchanges, with geographic proximity as the main instance) (Bengtson 2001).

Each of these dimensions may include positive or negative interactions. For a long time, solidarity and conflict have been studied separately, and consequently, intergenerational relations were described either harmonious or conflictual. More recently, the concept of ambivalence (Connidis and McMullin 2002) was described in terms of contrasting behaviours (solidarity and conflict) between parents and their adult children (Van Gaalen and Dykstra 2006). Multidimensional character of intergenerational relations and the co-occurrence of solidarity and conflict allow the construction of typologies of parent-child relations, showing a complex configuration of these relationships.

Lives of members of different generations are linked throughout their life courses (Elder 1994) and events and transitions, such as migration, have profound implications for the evolution of intergenerational solidarity. Geographical distance adds complexity to intergenerational relations but, although they suffer certain mutations, they remain mutual and multidimensional.

Communication and travel technologies play a critical role for (associational) intergenerational solidarity across borders (Merla 2015). Contacts between family members are transnational practices themselves, and also the means for exchanging care across borders (Merla 2015). The lack of spatial proximity is compensated by as much communication and contact as possible to ensure a line of emotional support and a sense of participating in each other's lives. Through digital technologies, migrants develop a sense of co-presence from a distance (Baldassar et al. 2016) or ordinary co-presence routines (Nedelcu and Wyss 2016), and new forms of intimacy emerge (Brown 2016), such as spending special moments together, despite huge physical distances. The older migrants' accessibility to digital technology helps them, not only in maintaining social connections, but also in regaining a sense of cultural identity and protection of their social identity, developing diverse digital kinning practices (Baldassar and Wilding 2020), both with the more distant family members as well as with other significant persons in their lives.

However, through this possibility of permanently staying in touch, these new communication technologies sometimes have "a paradoxical effect of reinforcing the burden of family obligations by giving the illusion of a permanent and almost immediate availability of the migrant" (Degavre and Merla 2016, 294).

Referring to the intergenerational exchange of resources and support (functional solidarity), the literature on transnational families acknowledges its multidimensional character, broadly given the term "care": physical or "hands-on" care, financial, practical and emotional support, and accommodation (Baldassar and Merla 2014). The focus is on the reconfigurations imposed by the absence of geographical proximity. Key characteristics include the distinction between support with co-presence and support from a distance and the emergence of a new way in which support is provided, which is through coordination and delegation to a third person (Kilkey and Merla 2014). The focus on the circulation of care inside the family network rather than on a unidirectional flow from the migrant to those at home allows to identify all actors involved in social relations that manage the care of the family members in a transnational context (Baldassar and Merla 2014).

However, intergenerational solidarity is not always present in local or transnational families. Sometimes autonomy of adult children and parents is maintained, in which cases practical or material support is scarce. Several studies on large samples of immigrants (Baykara-Krumme and Fokkema 2019 for Turks in Germany; Karpinska and Dykstra 2019 for Polish in the Netherlands) describe different typologies of intergenerational relations in migration context and find consistent shares of their samples characterised as having detached or autonomous relationships with their parents. This is not a result of disruption of family relations after migration, but rather of ambivalence or a desire for autonomy of the adult child in respect to his or her parents. In transnational context, given the geographical distance, family relations are reconfigured, and the predominant types involve mainly communication, exchange of advice, or emotional support (Baykara-Krumme and Fokkema 2019; Karpinska and Dykstra 2019).

One notable reconfiguration of functional intergenerational solidarity in a transnational context is that upward transfers from migrant adult children to (older) parents in the home country become the predominant pattern (Attias-Donfut and Cook 2017). In national contexts, research has shown that the downward direction of transfers (from parents to adult children) is generalised, no matter the level of generosity of the welfare state (Attias-Donfut and Cook 2017). Adult children living abroad are more likely to support older parents with financial assistance while native adult children are usually taking on responsibilities such as personal care (König, Isengard, and Szydlik 2018). However, older parents in the home country have an active role in transnational family relations, too, becoming providers of support from a distance or by being geographically mobile (e.g. prolonged visits to their migrant adult children) (Hărăguș, Földes, and Savu 2018; King et al. 2014; King et al. 2016; Nedelcu 2017; Nedelcu and Wyss 2020; Zickgraf 2017). One of the main forms of downward intergenerational care performed within transnational families, both in migration country or the homeland, is grandparenting.

Common values, attitudes, and beliefs among family members (in other words, consensual intergenerational solidarity) do not cease to exist. However, those departed influence those at home, in terms of ideas, norms, lifestyles, behavioural practices, and social capital, a phenomenon captured through the term social remittances. During the last few years, there has been a growing interest to overcome the dual paradigm between those who departed and those who stayed (Ducu 2018a) and to see these families in a relationship of active co-presence. Thus, in the case of social remittance, this double influence (between those who departed and those who stayed) has come to the forefront (Levitt and Lamba-Nieves 2011) and researchers have introduced "the concept of the remittances circulation—a concept which includes reciprocal exchange, the negotiation of the meaning and value of obligation and of remittance, as well as the transformation of remitting and of what is remitted due to both the context of origin and that of the remittance's potential destination" (Nowicka and Šerbedžija, 2016, 15). Studies have begun to take into account this double influence of social remittances within transnational families in what concerns gender relations (Brown 2016), especially between the partners in these families, while a large demand for analysis of social remittance circulation between the older parents and children within these families still stands.

Upward Transfers—Actors Involved and Impact on Gender Roles in the Family

There is a large body of research that documents the flows of different forms of care from migrants towards (adult) family members in origin countries. Among non-European migrants, the legal restrictions for migration and the geographical distance between the origin and destination countries limit the frequency of cross-border travel and physical interactions between family members. In response, transnational intergenerational care in form of financial remittances is more likely to occur. The free movement within European Union borders provides families experiencing migration better opportunities to get in touch and to care for each other.

Studies found that women (daughters) are most often the providers of transnational care, especially when parents suffer serious medical conditions, and hands-on care during visits (Hărăguș and Telegdi-Csetri 2018; Krzyżowski and Mucha 2014; Zickgraf 2017). When the health of the non-migrant parents is not critical (routine activities and medical conditions), coordination and delegation of care are enough for maintaining their well-being. When the parents' health condition becomes worse, co-presence and direct provision of care from the migrant children become necessary. Women take time off work or even temporarily interrupt migration to offer physical care at home (Hărăguș and Telegdi-Csetri 2018, for Romanian migrants). Direct hands-on care may be provided in the destination country, too, making use of more inclusive healthcare systems in Europe (Diaz Gorfinkiel and Escriva 2012, for Peruvians in Spain; Hărăguș and Telegdi-Csetri 2018, for Romanian migrants; King et al. 2014, for Albanian migrants; Zickgraf 2017, for Moroccans in Belgium). Some European countries, such as Spain, offer quasi-universal health care that includes access to medical treatment for non-nationals and non-contributors to the social security system. However, care arrangements from a distance are preferred, migrants acknowledging the shortcomings for a frail older person to migrate—isolation, loneliness, not knowing the language.

Women are the main keepers of emotional closeness, too: daughters are more likely to be in harmonious relationships (frequent contact and emotional exchange, moderate financial support and low practical support) than sons, mothers are also more likely than fathers to have this type of ties, while the mother-daughter dyads are more likely to belong to the harmonious type than are all other dyad configurations (Karpinska and Dykstra 2019, for Polish migrants).

Financial remittances, more frequent among transnational households than among reunited families in the destination country (Holst, Schäfer, and Schrooten 2012; Toth 2009), picture a multidirectional family practice, as both migrants and beneficiaries of financial support are involved to ensure that remit transfers take place (Carling 2014). Migrants are mainly givers; they provide financial support to their parents (in the origin or destination country) more often and in higher amounts than they receive (Attias-Donfut and Cook 2017, about immigrants in France). Most of the literature on remittances suggests that money from abroad is used by family members to escape financial hardship and to improve the well-being of those left in the homeland. Maintaining the consumption level of young children, older members of the family, caregivers, and others who remain in the homeland is a primary function of remittances (Herrera 2012; Toth 2009). "The level of social welfare in the country of origin directly impacts the financial behaviour of migrants" (Attias-Donfut and Cook 2017, 123) and since most of the non-European origin countries do not have pension systems, financial support and other forms of care from migrant adults to their parents back home become insurance for old age.

Sometimes "spatially separated parallel power centres" (Tolstokorova 2012, 6) appear within transnational families. On the one hand, the migrant woman is the income provider from a distance and, on the other hand, another person living back home (usually the mother or the spouse) manages the money received from abroad.

Intensive research on remittances and gender has been made for the case of Albanian migrants in Europe. In Albania, gender roles and remitting practices are highly shaped by the patriarchal norms (King, Dalipaj, and Mai 2006; King, Castaldo, and Vullnetari 2011; Smith 2009), which are reproduced also in the context of migration. The husband is the only decision-maker of the family and he is the only one who decides where remittances go and the amount of remittances (King, Dalipaj, and Mai 2006; King, Castaldo, and Vullnetari 2011; Smith 2009). Also, the father of the migrant son is the person who receives and manages the remittances (King, Dalipaj, and Mai 2006). Even if employed, women were rarely the main remitters for their non-migrant parents (King, Castaldo, and Vullnetari 2011; Smith 2009). However, in-depth interviews showed that women remitting practices exist and are rather hidden from the knowledge of the male members of the family, so-called unofficial remittances (King, Dalipaj, and Mai 2006; King, Castaldo, and Vullnetari 2011; Smith 2009). To be able to give money to her parents, the wife needs permission from the spouse, whom himself will hand on the money to the wife's father (Smith 2009).

Beyond the strong patriarchal structure of the Albanian case, research has shown that women play a leading role in remitting, as both the sender and the recipient and manager of remittances. Research reviewed by Tolstokorova (2012) shows that women are found to be more reliable as senders and as managers of remittances than men in the case of various migration backgrounds, European and non-European alike: they remit more regularly than men, are more prone to invest remittances in productive enterprises, while men may manage remittances more ineffectively.

Sometimes the geographical distance is too large and the travelling costs too high, and financial support has become a socially condoned substitute for hands-on care (Attias-Donfut and Cook 2017; Krzyżowski and Mucha 2014, for Polish migrants), both mainly performed by women migrants (Zickgraf 2017). For the migrants (women, in particular), remittances compensate for the lack of their direct, physical presence, of help in personal care and/or doing household chores in the origin countries. When only the woman emigrates, her role is more complex, being responsible for both (hands-on) care and financial support. The important financial support that women provide towards the family members in the origin country and their increased economic role does not confer more power within the transnational family. Even if Polish female migrants financially support their parents more often than their male counterparts (Krzyżowski and Mucha 2014), they have to deal with both financial and hands-on care of their older parents at home (shown by Basa, Harcourt, and Zarro 2011, for Filipina migrants in Italy, too). Consequently, sometimes women are in conflicting situations, combining care for family members in the destination countries (young children) and in the origin country (older parents), in their attempt to fulfil traditional gender and family roles as daughters, wives, and mothers in transnational settings (Krzyżowski and Mucha 2014; Zickgraf 2017). Bahna and Sekulova (2019), referring to Slovak circular migrant women in Austria, argue that migrant women's perspective on their role in the family varies by life stage and, consequently, older migrant women are more likely to experience a new feeling of freedom and self-esteem through migration than women with young children.

Negotiated care arrangements in the home country are also gendered. Migrant children generally acquire the responsibility for monetary support, while those children remaining in the country of origin take charge of the practical tasks (Diaz Gorfinkiel and Escriva 2012; Krzyżowski 2014). When daughters migrate, gender conflicts may appear in the home country regarding who takes over caring responsibilities. Usually, other women become responsible, such as the daughter-in-law, if the daughter emigrates (Krzyżowski 2014, for Poland) or the daughter if the son (and daughter-in-law) emigrates (Vullnetari and King 2016, for Albania, where the son's wife has to care for older parents). When there are sisters in the homeland, the migrant is more likely to have a detached relationship with parents in the origin country (Karpinska and Dykstra 2019, for Poland), as other daughter(s) take over the care duties. Sometimes, older fathers take care of their ailing wives, while migrant children help them with money and emotional support (Hărăguș and Telegdi-Csetri 2018).

Cultural intergenerational transfers are multidirectional and different actors are involved. Especially in the context of studies that address return migration and consequences upon the family, there is a special emphasis on the redefinition of gender relations between partners (Vlase 2013), but also the effect these social remittances play in the gender emancipation of future generations, especially in the case of girls, by "transmitting new ideas about gender equality and independence to their daughters" (Vlase 2013, 88).

Downward Transfers—Actors Involved and Impact on Gender Roles in the Family

Not only migrants continue to fulfil their filial obligations providing care to their parents left in the origin country, but the parents continue to be a resource for their migrant children and their families, providing practical, personal, and even financial support, from a distance or during visits. The main form of downward support is grandparenting, in the destination or origin country.

When older members of transnational families get involved in international mobility to care for their grandchildren, they become the "zero generation of migration" (Nedelcu 2017). Studies show that, in particular, grandmothers are involved in transnational downward care, as childcare providers (Hărăguş, Földes, and Savu 2018; King et al. 2014; Zickgraf 2017). Through the international mobility of the zero generation, they regain the grandparenting role, which is crucial for their emotional well-being (King et al. 2014). The instance of "flying grandmothers" (Baldassar and Wilding 2014) is characteristic especially in the case of grandchildren born after migration took place (King et al. 2014).

Grandparenting in migration countries happens to free the younger generation to participate in the labour market (Hărăguş, Földes, and Savu 2018, for Romanians in Europe; King et al. 2014, for Albanians in Italy and Greece). When women in migrant families do not work, the role of grandparents is rather symbolic (Barglowski, Krzyżowski, and Świątek 2015): they fulfil the expectations of care for their grandchildren from a distance, for example, by sending goods. During visits, grandmothers are involved in many tasks, such as shopping and cooking, as well as caring for the children, sometimes taking over the role of household manager usually fulfilled by the mother (Barglowski, Krzyżowski, and Świątek 2015).

The mobility of older mothers dominates the process of transnational grandparenting and "gender inequalities are produced and reproduced transnationally" in this process, while "their role as female caregivers within transnational families remains largely unrecognized" (Wyss and Nedelcu 2020, 358). The international mobility of grandmothers is restricted by their care responsibilities in home countries (Zickgraf 2017) and, once abroad, they are usually dependent on their migrant children in terms of finance, housing, and social life (King et al. 2014). Women without husbands spend more time on these visits to the migration country (Zickgraf 2017). During these visits, husbands in origin countries (such as Moroccans) were taken care of by non-migrant daughters or other female relatives, so gender roles were preserved. King et al. (2014) show that, for Albanian families, this process is highly gendered and the patrilineality of Albanian family organisation is preserved with migration: the older-generation parents follow their sons, not their daughters. However, migrant women's participation in the labour market has strengthened their empowerment in the (migrant) family and frail, older parents lose the pivotal role they had in the patriarchal families before migration (King et al. 2014, for Albanian migrants). Sometimes, the mobility of older family members, themselves in precarious working arrangements at home, aims to reconstitute the care support network in the destination country, at the cost of losing social citizenship entitlements in the origin country, while not gaining anything institutionally in the destination country, since they do not engage in paid work (Deneva 2012, on Bulgarian Muslims in Spain).

Grandmothers play an important care role in the origin country, too, for children of migrant mothers, acting like foster mothers (Ducu 2014, for Romania). Grandmothers often look after fathers who, to a large extent, leave or delegate childcare to female relatives, particularly to grandmothers (Lutz and Möllenbeck 2012, about Ukrainian migrants in Poland).

Although grandparenting dominates the downward intergenerational care in the transnational context, there are also other instances: Latvian older women are involved in downward care towards their adult children's family but from the position of the migrant (in the United Kingdom, engaged in wage labour). Migrating to free themselves from the social construct of old women as valueless, these women send remittances and gifts to (adult) children and grandchildren at home, to prevent them migrating (King et al. 2016), an instance of gender role reconfiguration.

Older men play an active role in downward transnational care, too, mainly through direct support from a distance, such as financial (middle-class Moroccan elderly fathers, Zickgraf 2017) or supervising the building of their migrant child's house, developing a small business for their migrant children's family (Hărăguș and Telegdi-Csetri 2018). They also assume the responsibility for communication with migrant members of the family (a traditionally female duty within Romanian families) due to their skill in ITC use (Ducu 2018a). Sometimes, men fly together with their wives to periodically take care of their grandchildren, particularly for cross-continental destinations (Hărăguș and Telegdi-Csetri 2018; Hărăguș, Földes, and Savu 2018, for Romania). An active role of grandfathers in childcare is uncovered for first-generation Portuguese migrants in Luxembourg, who have become grandparents (Ramos and Rodrigues Martins 2020): their position as guest workers, the long work shifts and demanding jobs entitled them to early retirement and becoming involved in caring for grandchildren earlier than their wives.

Through their mobility, besides practical support, grandparents are agents of cultural transmission for their grandchildren (King et al. 2014; Nedelcu and Wyss 2020; Zickgraf 2017), teaching them the home language, traditions, and religious beliefs. Traditional values circulate from adult generations (parents and grandparents) to create "a younger generation's sense of belonging to a homeland" (Wray and Ali 2014, 470).

This cultural role of the older generation is also performed during visits by the grandchildren to the origin country or using digital technologies (Ducu 2020; Krzyżowski and Mucha 2014). Especially in the case of non-European origin countries, grandparents are concerned about the domination of a western upbringing of their grandchildren and, during their visits, they provide in-person moral, religious and social instruction (Tezcan 2019, about first-generation Turkish migrants in Germany, now circular migrants between the two countries; Zickgraf 2017, about Moroccan immigrants in Belgium), and linguistic tutelage (King et al. 2016). Older women also support (migrant) mothers in performing traditional motherhood roles, "mothering the mother", as Wyss and Nedelcu (2020, 350) refer to as the transmission of the traditional postpartum beliefs, rituals, and practices. These reverse social remittances (Zickgraf 2017) contribute to the reinforcement of traditional gender roles in the family. However, gender relations and expectations vary in the same destination country depending on the sending country: among Filipinos in Italy, daughters are favoured over sons in pursuing higher education rather than employment, while the opposite gender bias applies to both Maghrebis and Chinese (Albertini, Gasperoni, and Mantovani 2019).

For the children of migrant parents, it is sometimes very difficult to accept and adopt the cultural specificities of their sending community, given that they are socialised within the receiving country. In a transnational context, the conflict between generations is more pronounced than in any other setting for intergenerational transmission of accepted cultural values and norms. Studies on arranged marriages or the role of young girls within migrant families, especially originating from traditional and religious societies, show conflictual gender expectations between the older and younger generations (Tezcan 2019, for first-generation circular Turkish migrants in Germany; Vathi 2015, for Albanians in the United Kingdom, Italy, and Greece). Transnational families sometimes experience an "intergenerational ambivalence (…) that parents felt in relation to their children's acculturation, wanting them to succeed in their adaptation, but also to maintain the traditional values and identity" (Sime and Pietka-Nykaza 2015, 219, for Polish in UK), even if they are more rooted in the host country (Ducu 2018a).

Although both grandmothers and grandfathers are involved in these relations, nonetheless, grandmothers assume the role of agents of intergenerational transnational cultural transmission more readily. Grandfathers in transnational families are more active on the transmission of a strong work ethic (Brannen 2015, for Irish and Polish grandfathers in the United Kingdom; Ramos and Rodrigues Martins 2020, for Portuguese grandfathers in Luxembourg).

Discussion

Intergenerational relations play a major role in shaping individual life courses and chances for people in a migration context (Albertini, Mantovani, and Gasperoni 2019): for second-generation migrants, family support is highly important for the socio-economic integration in the destination country, while the availability of family care is a decisive factor for the well-being of older people, both in origin and destination countries or for the enabling of (migrant) women to be involved in paid work.

The overview provided showed that migrants and their relatives are involved in a large array of intergenerational transfers: financial remittances, hands-on care, and cultural transfers. Although the chapter focused on ascendant and descendant transfers between parents and adult children, the approach of care circulation (Baldassar and Merla 2014) has shown that other actors are also involved in the management of care in transnational families. When transnational practices are involved, the ways in which these transfers take place diversify, against the background of the increasing importance of digital technology. Sometimes coordination and delegation of care towards a third person are enough for ensuring the well-being of older parents in the home country, sometimes visits to the home country are required for hands-on care or even bringing the older relatives to the destination country for better health services. Intergenerational transfers are not only upward, from migrant to older parents in the home country, but also downward, from older parents to migrant children, with grandparenting as the main form. Being shaped by legal restrictions on migration or free movement and the geographical distance between the origin and destination countries, intergenerational transfers in the migration context are more diverse for European origin migrants than for non-European, which often limit to financial remittances.

Women appear to be the main actors performing intergenerational transfers in the migration context. Referring to non-European migrant women and their wage-earning, some researchers point out their success in escaping patriarchal structures (Attias-Donfut and Cooke 2017; see King et al. 2006). However, other researchers argue that women's migration does not initiate a complete shift in gender practices, as they "contest the myth of the male breadwinner but retain the myth of the female homemaker" (Parreñas 2005, 334, on Filipino migrant women).

The emancipatory potential of migration in the case of non-European migrant women must be analysed in connection with the access to European social policy (Degavre and Merla 2016). Most (women) migrants originate from familialistic societies and experience high pressure to provide transnational care when the migration had economic reasons. Often, both non-European and European migrants have precarious working arrangements (domestic work), with low wages, unstable or irregular contracts, long working hours, and do not qualify for the receiving country's social policy measures (childcare services, help to combine paid work and childcare). It is a paradox here: (different degrees of) defamilialisation policies exist in destination countries, but these migrants do not qualify and their role as caregiver is reinforced instead (Degavre and Merla 2016).

The situation is not much different for migrants from Eastern and Central Europe. They come from former socialist countries, with women's participation in the labour market having a long history, and where the caring responsibility has been shifted back to the families after the demise of socialist regimes. These are societies with strong family ties and a "familialism by default" type of intergenerational solidarity regime[1] (Saraceno and Keck 2010), meaning that family members are responsible for the well-being of vulnerable people, such as children and older persons. Consequently, migrant women continue to perform the culturally ascribed role of caregiver for older parents in the home country (Hărăguș and Telegdi-Csetri 2018, for Romania; Krzyżowski and Mucha 2014, for Poland). Gender roles in the family are reaffirmed; women remain responsible for ensuring transnational care.

Through migration, women become less dependent on their relatives' incomes while their economic role, and thus their agency in the family, becomes more important; at the same time, as carers, they continue to play a crucial role for their family members that remains in the origin country (Degavre and Merla 2016). However, reorganisation of family practices within transnational families shows that gender roles are increasingly being reconfigured among agents in these families (Erdal and Pawlak 2017; Telegdi-Csetri 2018; Telegdi-Csetri and Ducu 2016), especially when minor children exist in the origin country (Ducu 2014).

Results of research on intergenerational relations in families affected by migration and the reconfiguration or reaffirmation of gender roles suffer from some methodological shortcomings. Relying mainly on a qualitative methodology and being focused on a specific origin country, the results have limited generalisability and a comparative dimension is missing. The existing large comparative surveys in Europe that investigate intergenerational relations (such as Survey on Health, Ageing and Retirement in Europe or Generations and Gender Survey) do not succeed in filling this gap because the migration background of residents of a European country is just a variable among others in the attempt to explain the variation in the frequency and intensity of intergenerational solidarity, and transnational relations are not considered.

There are some recent efforts to conduct quantitative surveys to investigate intergenerational relations in the migration context specifically, adopting either the migrants' or their parents' in home country views, addressing temporary migrants and transnational relations, as well as permanent migrants (Attias-Donfut and Cook 2017, for immigrants in France; Baykara-Krumme and Fokkema 2019, for Turkish immigrants in Germany; Hărăguș, Földes, and Savu 2018, for Romanian migrants; Karpinska and Dykstra 2019, for Polish migrants in the Netherlands; Krzyżowski 2014, for Poles in Iceland and Austria). These recent data allow the investigation of the multidimensional character of intergenerational solidarity, extended comparisons (such as stayers/transnationals/(generations of) migrants) and (different degrees of) generalisation of the results. However, for capturing the underlying microlevel causal processes, interviews are necessary, and new developments in the methodological approach are recommended for transnational families' research, as well as developing mixed quantitative and qualitative approaches in cross-country comparisons, and "the inclusion of units that are larger than the nuclear family [so as to] study a matched sample of people at the same time" (Mazzucato and Schans 2011, 710).

Acknowledgements For the work of Viorela Ducu, the research leading to these results has received funding from the EEA Grants 2014–2021, under the Project contract no. 11, EEA-RO-NO-2018-0586.

Note

1. Intergenerational responsibilities are divided between the state and the family, which, in connection with the typology of welfare regimes, leads to different regimes of intergenerational solidarity (Saraceno and Keck 2010). On the continuum of familialism - defamilialisation, the proposed typology distinguishes between (1) familialism by default (where the care of the frail older persons is entirely the family's responsibility, with no financial support for family care or publicly provided alternatives); (2) supported familialism (where families are financially compensated for caring responsibilities); (3) defamilialisation (that reduces family responsibilities and dependencies), and (4) optional familialism (an option between supported familialism and de-familialisation).

References

Albertini, Marco, Debora Mantovani, and Giancarlo Gasperoni. 2019. "Intergenerational Relations Among Immigrants in Europe: The Role of Ethnic Differences, Migration And Acculturation." *Journal of Ethnic and Migration Studies* 45 (10): 1693–1706.

Albertini, Marco, Giancarlo Gasperoni, and Debora Mantovani. 2019. "Whom to Help and Why? Family Norms on Financial Support for Adult Children Among Immigrants." *Journal of Ethnic and Migration Studies* 45 (10): 1769–1789.

Attias-Donfut, Claudine, and Joanne Cook. 2017. "Intergenerational Relationships in Migrant Families. Theoretical and Methodological Issues." In *Situating Children of Migrants across Borders and Origins*, edited by Bolzman, Claudio, Laura Bernardi, and Jean-Marie LeGoff, 115–133. Springer.

Bahna, Miloslav, and Martina Sekulová. 2019. *Crossborder Care. Lessons from Central Europe*. Cham: Palgrave Macmillan.

Baldassar, Loretta, and Laura Merla. 2014. "Locating Transnational Care Circulation in Migration and Family Studies." In *Transnational Families, Migration and the Circulation of Care: Understanding Mobility and Absence in Family Life*, edited by Loretta Baldassar, and Laura Merla, 25–61. New York & Abingdon: Routledge.

Baldassar, Loretta, Mihaela Nedelcu, Laura Merla, and Raelene Wilding. 2016. "ICT-Based Co-Presence in Transnational Families and Communities: Challenging the Premise of Face-to-Face Proximity in Sustaining Relationships." *Global Networks* 16 (2): 133–144.

Baldassar, Loretta, and Raelene Wilding. 2014. "Middle Class Transnational Caregiving: The Circulation of Care between Family and Extended Kin Networks in the Global North." In *Transnational Families, Migration and the Circulation of Care: Understanding Mobility and Absence in Family Life*, edited by Loretta Baldassar, and Laura Merla, 235–253. New York & Abingdon: Routledge.

Baldassar, Loretta, and Raelene Wilding. 2020. "Migration, Aging, and Digital Kinning: The Role of Distant Care Support Networks in Experiences of Aging Well." *Gerontologist* 60 (2): 313–321.

Barglowski, Karolina, Łukasz Krzyżowski, and Paulina Świątek. 2015. "Caregiving in Polish-German Transnational Social Space: Circulating Narratives and Intersecting Heterogeneities." *Population, Space and Place* 21 (3): 257–269.

Basa, Charito, Wendy Harcourt, and Angela Zarro. 2011. "Remittances and Transnational Families in Italy and The Philippines: Breaking the Global Care Chain." *Gender & Development* 19 (1): 11–22.
Baykara-Krumme, Helen, and Tineke Fokkema. 2019. "The Impact of Migration on Intergenerational Solidarity Types." *Journal of Ethnic and Migration Studies* 45 (10): 1707–1727.
Bengtson, Vern L. 2001. "Beyond the Nuclear Family: The Increasing Importance of Multigenerational Bonds." *Journal of Marriage and Family* 63 (1): 1–16.
Brannen, Julia. 2015. *Fathers and Sons. Generations, Families and Migration.* London: Palgrave Macmillan.
Brown, Panitee Suksomboon. 2016. "Circulating Remittances: Cross-Border Negotiation of Family Values Among Thai Migrant Women and Their Dutch Husbands." In *Migration and Social Remittances in a Global Europe. Europe in a Global Context*, edited by Nowicka, Magdalena, and Vojin Šerbedžija, 169–189. London: Palgrave Macmillan.
Carling, Jørgen. 2014. "Scripting Remittances: Making Sense of Money Transfers in Transnational Relationships." *International Migration Review* 48 (S1): S218–S262.
Connidis, Ingrid Arnet, and Julie Ann McMullin. 2002. "Sociological Ambivalence and Family Ties: A Critical Perspective." *Journal of Marriage and Family* 64 (3): 558–567.
Degavre, Florence, and Laura Merla. 2016. "Defamilialization of Whom? Re-Thinking Defamilialization in the Light of Global Care Chains and the Transnational Circulation of Care." In *Family Life in an Age of Migration and Mobility*, edited by Kilkey, Majella, and Ewa Palenga-Möllenbeck, 287–311. London: Palgrave Macmillan.
Deneva, Neda. 2012. "Transnational Aging Carers: On Transformation of Kinship and Citizenship in the Context of Migration Among Bulgarian Muslims in Spain." *Social Politics* 19 (1): 105–128.
Diaz Gorfinkiel, Magdalena, and Angeles Escriva. 2012. "Care of Older People in Migration Contexts: Local and Transnational Arrangements Between Peru and Spain." *Social Politics* 19 (1): 129–141.
Ducu, Viorela. 2014. "Transnational Mothers from Romania." *Romanian Journal of Population Studies* VIII (1): 117–141.
Ducu, Viorela. 2018a. *Romanian Transnational Families: Gender, Family Practices and Difference.* Cham: Palgrave Macmillan.
Ducu, Viorela. 2018b. "Afterword: Gender Practices in Transnational Families." In *Childhood and Parenting in Transnational Settings*, edited by Ducu, Viorela, Mihaela Nedelcu, and Aron Telegdi-Csetri, 191–204. Cham: Springer.
Ducu, Viorela. 2020. "Displaying Grandparenting Within Romanian Transnational Families." *Global Networks* 20 (2): 380–395.
Elder, Glenn H. Jr. 1994. "Time, Human Agency, and Social Change: Perspectives on the Life Course." *Social Psychology Quarterly* 57 (1): 4–15.
Erdal, Marta Bivand, and Marek Pawlak. 2017. "Reproducing, Transforming and Contesting Gender Relations and Identities Through Migration and Transnational Ties." *Gender, Place and Culture* 25 (6): 882–898.
Hărăguș, Mihaela, Ionuț Földes, and Veronica Savu. 2018. "Older Parents in Romania as a Resource for Their Migrant Adult Children." In *Childhood and Parenting in Transnational Settings*, edited by Ducu, Viorela, Mihaela Nedelcu, and Aron Telegdi-Csetri, 155–173. Cham: Springer.

Hărăguş, Mihaela, and Viorela Telegdi-Csetri. 2018. "Intergenerational Solidarity in Romanian Transnational Families." In *Making Multicultural Families in Europe: Gender and Generational Relations*, edited by Crespi, Isabella, Stefania Giada Meda, and Laura Merla, 161–177. London: Palgrave Macmillan.

Herrera, Gioconda. 2012. "Starting Over Again? Crisis, Gender, and Social Reproduction among Ecuadorian Migrants in Spain." *Feminist Economics* 18 (2): 125–148.

Holst, Elke, Andrea Schäfer, and Mechthild Schrooten. 2012. "Gender and Remittances: Evidence from Germany". *Feminist Economics* 18 (2): 201–229.

Karpinska, Kasia, and Pearl A. Dykstra. 2019. "Intergenerational Ties Across Borders: A Typology of the Relationships Between Polish Migrants in the Netherlands And Their Ageing Parents." *Journal of Ethnic and Migration Studies* 45 (10): 1728–1745.

Karpinska, Kasia, Pearl A. Dykstra, Thijs van den Broek, Maja Djundeva, Anita Abramowska-Kmon, Irena I. Kotowska, Mihaela Hărăguş, Paul-Teodor Hărăguş, Cornelia Mureşan, and Pau Marí-Klose. 2016. "Intergenerational Linkages in the Family: The Organization of Caring and Financial Responsibilities: Summary of Results." *Families and Societies Working Papers Series* 61.

Kilkey, Majella, and Laura Merla. 2014. "Situating Transnational Families' Care-Giving Arrangements: The Role of Institutional Contexts." *Global Networks* 14 (2): 210–229.

King, Russell, Adriana Castaldo, and Julie Vullnetari. 2011. "Gendered Relations and Filial Duties Along the Greek-Albanian Remittance Corridor." *Economic Geography* 87 (4): 393–419.

King, Rusell, Eralba Cela, Tineke Fokkema, and Julie Vullnetari. 2014. "The Migration and Well-Being of the Zero Generation." *Population, Space and Place* 20 (8): 728–738.

King, Russell, Mirela Dalipaj, and Nicola Mai. 2006. "Gendering Migration and Remittances: Evidence from London and Northern Albania". *Population, Space and Place* 12 (6): 409–434.

King, Russell, Mark Thomson, Tony Fielding, and Tony Warnes. 2006. "Time, Generations and Gender in Migration and Settlement." In *The Dynamics of International Migration and Settlement in Europe*, edited by Penninx, Rinux, Maria Berger, and Karen Kraal, 233–267. Amsterdam: Amsterdam University Press.

King, Russell, Julie Vullnetari, Aija Lulle, and Eralba Cela. 2016. "Contrasts in Ageing and Agency in Family Migratory Contexts: A Comparison of Albanian and Latvian Older Migrants." In *Family Life in an Age of Migration and*, edited by Kilkey, Majella, and Ewa Palenga-Möllenbeck, 261–286. London: Palgrave Macmillan.

König, Ronny, Bettina Isengard, and Mark Szydlik. 2018. "Migration Matters: Insights into Intergenerational Solidarity Patterns in Europe." In *Making Multicultural Families in Europe: Gender and Generational Relations*, edited by Crespi, Isabella, Stefania Giada Meda and, Laura Merla, 233–244. London: Palgrave Macmillan.

Krzyżowski, Łukasz. 2014. "(Trans)National Intergenerational Care Contract. Attitudes and Practices of Transnational Families Toward Elderly Care." *Studia Humanistyczne Agh* 13 (2): 103–117.

Krzyżowski, Łukasz, and Janusz Mucha. 2014. "Transnational Caregiving in Turbulent Times: Polish Migrants in Iceland and Their Elderly Parents in Poland." *International Sociology* 29 (1): 22–37.

Levitt, Peggy, and Deepak Lamba-Nieves. 2011. "Social Remittances Revisited." *Journal of Ethnic and Migration Studies* 37 (1): 1–22.
Lutz, Helma, and Ewa Palenga- Möllenbeck. 2012. "Care Workers, Care Drain, and Care Chains: Reflections on Care, Migration, and Citizenship." *Social Politics* 19 (1): 15–37.
Mazzucato, Valentina, and Djamila Schans. 2011. "Transnational Families and the Well-Being of Children: Conceptual and Methodological Challenges." *Journal of Marriage and Family* 73 (4): 704–712.
Merla, Laura. 2015. "Salvadoran Migrants in Australia: An Analysis of Transnational Families' Capability to Care across Borders." *International Migration* 53 (6): 153–165.
Nedelcu, Mihaela. 2017. "Transnational Grandparenting in the Digital Age: Mediated Co-Presence and Childcare in the Case of Romanian Migrants in Switzerland and Canada." *European Journal of Ageing* 14 (4): 375–383.
Nedelcu, Mihaela, and Malika Wyss. 2016. "'Doing Family' Through ICT-Mediated Ordinary Co-Presence Routines: Transnational Communication Practices of Romanian Migrants in Switzerland." *Global Networks* 16 (2): 202–218.
Nedelcu, Mihaela, and Malika Wyss. 2020. "Transnational Grandparenting: An Introduction." *Global Networks* 20 (2): 292–307.
Nowicka, Magdalena, and Vojin Šerbedžija. 2016. "Migration and Remittances in a Global Europe." In *Migration and Social Remittances in a Global Europe. Europe in a Global Context,* edited by Nowicka, Magdalena, and Vojin Šerbedžija, 1–20. London: Palgrave Macmillan.
Parreñas, Rhacel. 2005. "Long Distance Intimacy: Class, Gender and Intergenerational Relations Between Mothers and Children in Filipino Transnational Families." *Global Networks* 5 (4): 317–336.
Pessar, Patricia R., and Sarah J. Mahler. 2003. "Transnational Migration: Bringing Gender In." *International Migration Review* 37 (3): 812–846.
Ramos, Anne Carolina, and Heidi Rodrigues Martins. 2020. "First-Generation Migrants Become Grandparents: How Migration Backgrounds Affect Intergenerational Relationships." *Global Networks* 20 (2): 325–342.
Saraceno, Chiara, and Wolfgang Keck. 2010. "Can We Identify Intergenerational Policy Regimes Europe?" *European Societies* 12 (5): 675–96.
Sime, Daniela, and Emilia Pietka-Nykaza. 2015. "Transnational Intergenerationalities: Cultural Learning in Polish Migrant Families and its Implications For Pedagogy." *Language and Intercultural Communication* 15 (2): 208–223.
Smith, Erin. 2009. "'Gap-Fillers' or 'Clan-Destroyers': Transnational Female Solidarity Towards Kin in the Region of Fier." *Southeast European and Black Sea Studies* 9 (4): 555–573.
Telegdi-Csetri, Áron. 2018. "Overview: Transnational Times in Global Spaces – Childhood and Parenting in the Age of Movement." In *Childhood and Parenting in Transnational Settings* edited by Ducu,Viorela, Mihaela Nedelcu, and Áron Telegdi-Csetri, 1–8. Cham: Springer International.
Telegdi-Csetri, Áron, and Viorela Ducu. 2016. "Transnational Difference – Cosmopolitan Meaning." In *Managing Difference in Eastern-European Transnational Families,* edited by Ducu, Viorela and Áron Telegdi-Csetri, 13–23. Frankfurt am Main: Peter Lang.

Tezcan, Tolga. 2019. "First-Generation Circular Migrants Involved in the Upbringing of Their Grandchildren: The Case of Turkish Immigrants in Germany." *Ageing & Society*. http://doi.org/10.1017/S0144686X19000953.

Tolstokorova, Alissa V. 2012. "The Woman and Sixpence: Gendered Impact of Remittances on Social Sustainability of Ukrainian Transnational Households." *Analytical Journal* 9: 74–97.

Toth, Georgiana. 2009. "Remiterile de bani ale migranților români din regiunea Madrid și paternurile de utilizare a acestora [Remittances Sent Home by Romanian Migrants in the Madrid Region and Patterns of Their Usage]." In *Comunități românești în Spania [Romanian communities in Spain]*, edited by Sandu, Dumitru, 129–141. București: Fundația Soros România.

Van Gaalen, Ruben, and Pearl A. Dykstra. 2006. "Solidarity and Conflict between Adult Children and Parents: A Latent Class Analysis." *Journal of Marriage and Family* 68 (4): 947–960.

Vathi, Zana. 2015. *Migrating and Settling in a Mobile World. Albanian Migrants and Their Children in Europe*. Cham: Springer.

Vlase, Ionela. 2013. "Women's Social Remittances and Their Implications at Household Level: A case study of Romanian migration to Italy." *Migration Letters* 10 (1): 81–90.

Vullnetari, Julie, and Russell King. 2016. "'Washing Men's Feet': Gender, Care and Migration in Albania During and After Communism." *Gender, Place & Culture: A Journal of Feminist Geography* 23 (2): 198–215.

Wray, Sharon, and Nafhesa Ali. 2014. "Understanding Generation Through the Lens of Ethnic and Cultural Diversity." *Families, Relationships and Societies* 3 (3): 469–473.

Wyss, Malika, and Mihaela Nedelcu. 2020. "Grandparents on the Move: A Multilevel Framework Analysis to Understand Diversity in Zero-Generation Care Arrangements in Switzerland." *Global Networks* 20 (2): 343–361.

Zickgraf, Caroline. 2017. "Transnational Ageing and the 'Zero Generation': The Role of Moroccan Migrants' Parents in Care Circulation." *Journal of Ethnic and Migration Studies* 43 (2): 321–337.

Despite the Distance? Intergenerational Contact in Times of Migration

Ronny König, Bettina Isengard, and Marc Szydlik

INTRODUCTION

Previous empirical analyses have shown that adult family generations are connected by various forms of cohesion, such as strong emotional closeness, contact, and shared activities, as well as transfers of space, money, and time (for an overview, see Szydlik 2016). However, European findings suggest that the level of support and cohesion is stronger in some countries than in others. This may be because strong welfare states take some pressure off families, thus leading to less intense family support. Besides financial support, help, and care for or support of grandchildren, another important form of intergenerational solidarity is contact between adult generations (parents and children). The different kinds of familial contacts and their frequency generally strongly depend on geographic proximity. Nowadays, in times of modernisation characterised by increasing social and geographical mobility, globalisation, and new technologies, families use various communication opportunities to face the challenges of greater geographical distances and time restrictions.

R. König (✉) · B. Isengard · M. Szydlik
Department of Sociology, University of Zurich, Zurich, Switzerland
e-mail: koenig@soziologie.uzh.ch

B. Isengard
e-mail: isengard@soziologie.uzh.ch

M. Szydlik
e-mail: szydlik@soziologie.uzh.ch

Although contact between parents and their offspring is not only relevant for the individuals themselves but also reflects the importance of families and cohesion in society, little is known about the determinants, country-specific differences, and especially the population-specific patterns of intergenerational contact. Whereas previous studies have mainly addressed the causes and consequences of family support within the native population, the population of foreign origin has often been neglected or limited to a specific (ethnic) population from a single country. Since intergenerational contact can be seen as a relevant precondition for other forms of (functional) solidarity on the one hand and as a direct part of associational solidarity and exchange on the other, this chapter addresses contact frequencies from a multigenerational European perspective.

Intergenerational Solidarity and Contact

Despite the consequences of social and demographic change in recent decades, the relations and bonds between parents and their (adult) children remain impressively strong (Szydlik 2016; Bengtson 2001). Families are connected through various forms of solidarity, such as strong emotional closeness (affectual solidarity; see, e.g., Berger and Fend 2005; Bertogg and Szydlik 2016), transfers of money, time, and space (functional solidarity; see, e.g., Brandt and Deindl 2013; Igel and Szydlik 2011; Isengard et al. 2018; König et al. 2019; Isengard et al. 2019; Albertini et al. 2007), and contact and shared activities (associational solidarity; see, e.g., König 2016; Hank 2007; Sarkisian and Gerstel 2008).

The question as to why some generations are more closely connected than others in terms of emotional attachment and contact can be explained by the theoretical assumptions made by Szydlik (2008, 2016). In general, intergenerational solidarity can be understood as a complex and multi-layered construct composed of the three dimensions of solidarity, namely affectual, associational, and functional solidarity. According to the assumptions of this theoretical framework, intergenerational solidarity in general and parent-child contact in particular can be explained by several relevant determinants at different levels: Opportunities, Needs, Family, and Context (ONFC).

According to the model, intergenerational support can be influenced at the micro-level by individual opportunities and needs on both sides of the relationship. Opportunity structures reflect individual resources that promote, enable, hinder, or even prevent social interaction. Need structures indicate the need for social interaction. They also include the desires, goals, interests, motives, wants, and wishes of individuals for themselves or for their significant others. The relationships between parents and children are furthermore embedded in family structures at the so-called meso-level. They include, for example, family size and composition, prior events in the family history, and family roles and norms. In this context, families are important networks which provide social capital and support. Country-specific differences in general can be traced back to cultural-contextual structures representing societal conditions in which intergenerational relations develop. These include, for instance, economic, cultural, political, and social conditions as well as rules and norms of institutions and groups (Szydlik 2016, 21ff.).

Previous research revealed that family generations are often closely connected by frequent contact (Bordone 2009; Bucx et al. 2008; Dewit et al. 1988; Rossi and Rossi 1990; Hank 2007; Steinbach and Kopp 2008; Tomassini et al. 2004). Although recent studies have identified similar characteristics in single countries at the micro- and meso-levels, they also highlight the prevalence of country-specific differences in contact frequency. From a European perspective, contact between generations is generally more pronounced in Southern and Eastern Europe than in western and northern parts of the continent (e.g. Tomassini et al. 2004; Bordone 2009; Hank 2007; Szydlik 2016). Besides social norms, different welfare state arrangements can be especially significant in terms of country differences (Ganjour and Widmer 2016). This is because welfare benefits directly affect different societal aspects that are important for solidarity, such as poverty, inequality, and (regional) unemployment, and thereby also affect the necessity of relocating or utilising the family as a support network. For example, higher poverty rates in countries or regions can increase the necessity for family members to support each other, especially if state interventions and public transfers are comparatively low.

INTERGENERATIONAL CONTACT AND MIGRATION

Theoretical concepts and previous research have postulated various causes and consequences for intergenerational solidarity of migrants. Overall, there are two contrasting views about the relationship between migration and solidarity (see McDonald 2011; Baykara-Krumme 2008; Nauck 2007). The first approach, the so-called solidarity thesis, assumes a higher level of cohesion and contact in migrated families because differences in family norms are supposed to cause closer connections and stronger dependency within migrated families (see Dumon 1989). According to this view, more intense mutual family support in general and contact frequency in particular should compensate for the loss of contact with former friends, neighbours, and other relatives from the country of origin or for a lack of relationships in the host country. Families should act as a safe haven in times of insecurity and instability due to the situation of being in a foreign country (see Szydlik 2016). The second approach, the cultural-conflict thesis, instead assumes that relationships in migrant families are weakened by the experience of migration and the subsequent situation in the host country (see Park 1964; Portes and Zhou 2005). Migrant families are assumed to have a greater risk of experiencing intergenerational and intercultural conflict (Merz et al. 2009), which affects family relations and reduces contact frequency due to ongoing tensions and conflicts. It seems, against this background, that the generations are assumed to be drifting apart due to the experience of migration.

Research on single countries and specific groups of migrants suggests that intergenerational cohesion does not differ strongly among migrant families and compared to the native population (see, e.g., Baykara-Krumme 2008; Schimany et al. 2012). Overall, empirical research is still scarce and has yielded quite mixed results (de Valk and Schans 2008; Nauck 2007; Nosaka and Chasiotis 2005). However, there is some evidence of differences between the native and migrant population. A relatively recent study by Bordone and de Valk (2016), focused on intergenerational support between natives and migrants in contemporary Europe, has shown, for example, more frequent contact within migrated families. Moreover, previous research on functional solidarity in European families highlighted that monetary and space transfers differ not only between natives and migrants but between the different groups of migrants depending on the type of transfer and direction (König et al. 2018).

Potential differences within the migrant population may depend on their geographical origin and specific cultural family norms (see Kağıtçıbaşı 1996). According to different family regime typologies (see, e.g., Gauthier 1996), countries differ with respect to monetary and non-monetary state interventions for families. This is strongly connected to normative aspects in terms of existing family norms and obligations (see Leitner 2003). Regarding the latter, Dutch studies have indicated stronger attitudes towards filial obligations among different groups of migrants, although their actual intergenerational support was not necessarily stronger (Schans and de Valk 2012). Therefore, migrated generations from countries with more pronounced family norms like the Southern and catholic Eastern European countries should be in touch with each other more often than the generations with more liberal and modern family norms and obligations. Northern countries like Denmark or Sweden belong to this group.

Many studies have pointed to geographical distance as an important determinant of intergenerational support. Living nearby increases the amount of mutual support provided (see, e.g., Knijn and Liefbroer 2006; Tomassini et al. 2003). Thus, geographical proximity is important for many forms of intergenerational solidarity, and the potential differences between natives and migrants can be caused by differences in geographical distance. Therefore, ethnic origin can also explain the geographical proximity or distance between the generations themselves. Two contrary trends are possible. On the one hand, generations might live further apart because they live in different countries; on the other hand, a migration background can lead generations to stay close because they often take advantage of a support network of relatives and friends from their country of origin, which is settled close together (Aslund 2005). Mulder (2007) presented empirical evidence that parents and children with migration backgrounds live closer together in the Netherlands. In contrast, Isengard (2013) found that in other European countries generations live much farther apart when they have a migration background (see also Aquilino 1990, for the US).

Analytical Approach

The empirical analyses were based on the data pooled from the fifth and sixth wave of the Survey of Health, Ageing and Retirement in Europe (SHARE). The data were gathered in 2013 and 2015, respectively, and provided standardised information on respondents aged 50 years and older as well as on their parents and (grand)children in Europe. For the respondents who had participated in both waves, we included their interview from the fifth wave. The dataset contained information on a wide range of topics, such as demography, income, health, accommodation, education, occupation, social support, activities, and expectations. For more information on the data used, please refer to Börsch-Supan (2019a, b). The 18 countries included in the survey were Austria, Belgium, Croatia, the Czech Republic, Denmark, Estonia, France, Germany, Greece, Italy, Luxembourg, the Netherlands, Poland, Portugal, Slovenia, Spain, Sweden, and Switzerland.

For the purpose of our study, we used two subsamples. To account for bottom-up contact, defined as contact from respondents to their parent(s), we used information of all respondents with at least one living parent. To measure the extent of so-called top-down contact, meaning contact from respondents to their child(ren), we further used the information of the family respondents as they only provided the necessary information on their offspring, including their frequency of contact. To evaluate associational solidarity between parents and adult children, we further restricted the second subsample to respondents' children who were at least 18 years old. As we were interested in active established contact, we further restricted both subsamples only to parent-respondent and child-respondent dyads, respectively, using information of dyads in separate house(hold)s. The first subsample resulted in 22,165 observations based on 17,642 respondents with complete, reliable information on intergenerational contact between them and their parents. Dealing with associational solidarity between respondents and their adult offspring, the second subsample included 76,703 observations reported by 37,894 respondents.

The dependent variable for both directions (contact to respondents' parents and children) was constructed on the basis of the following question: During the past twelve months, how often did you have contact with [your mother], [your father], [child X], either in person, by phone, mail, email or any other electronic means? Here, respondents were given seven categories to choose from describing their individual contact frequency to each of their parent and to each child: (1) "daily," (2) "several times a week," (3) "about once a week," (4) "about every two weeks," (5) "about once a month," (6) "less than once a month," and (7) "never." We recoded the related answers for the descriptive part of our study into four distinctive categories in reverse order: (1) "rarely/never," (2) "monthly," (3) "weekly," and (4) "daily."

For our analyses, we defined individual migration as having been born in a different country and/or not possessing citizenship of the country in which the person currently lives. Moreover, to capture the complexity of migration, it was necessary to consider several additional approaches that go beyond simply establishing the fact of migration. This includes the distinction whether a foreign-born person is naturalised in the host country or still possesses foreign citizenship. The comparatively few respondents with foreign citizenship who were born in the host country (0.35%) were excluded as the data did not allow identifying the country in which these persons were socialised. We also considered the duration of the stay in the host country by capturing the age at which the person migrated measured by three categories: childhood (under the age of 18), early adulthood (18–35 years), and later adulthood (over 35 years). In addition, we also included the country of origin for all migrants on the basis of (a) membership of the European Union (EU) or the European Free Trade Association (EFTA) or (b) no membership. To consider the different cultural, historical, political, and economic backgrounds within Europe, we used different measurements of such membership, namely (a) EU-15 and EFTA and (b) EU-28 and EFTA. Moreover, considering the previous findings that highlight country-specific differences regarding a North/West versus South/East divide for intergenerational contact within Europe, we further differentiated the EU-28/EFTA membership based on the geographic region of the respective country. The first subcategory included all EU-28 or EFTA countries of Northern and Western Europe: Austria, Belgium, Denmark, Finland, France, Germany, Iceland, Ireland, Luxembourg, Netherlands, Norway, Sweden, Switzerland, and the United Kingdom. All remaining countries of the EU-28 (Bulgaria, Croatia, Cyprus, the Czech Republic, Estonia, Greece, Hungary, Italy, Latvia, Lithuania, Poland, Portugal, Romania, Slovakia, Slovenia, and Spain) were assigned to the second category, that of Southern or Eastern Europe. To explain country-specific differences, we finally included the distribution of foreigners as a percentage of the entire population. This indicator consisted of people who were born in a country other than the country they were currently living in the year before the used SHARE waves were conducted (2012 respectively 2014), and was drawn from Eurostat (2019).

Given the non-independence between observations, the hierarchical data structure of SHARE violates basic regression assumptions and might lead to inaccurate significance values and biased standard errors. In order to analyse contact frequency based on the initial seven outcomes (in reverse order, ranging from (1) "never" to (7) "daily"), we estimated multilevel linear regression models involving three levels: parents/children nested in respondents nested in countries (Hox 2002; Rabe-Hesketh and Skrondal 2008; Snijders and Bosker 2012).

Parent-Child-Contact in European Families

At first glance, European family generations often appear to be in touch with each other on a regular basis (see Fig. 26.1). Moreover, contact frequencies from older Europeans to their parents and to their adult children seem to

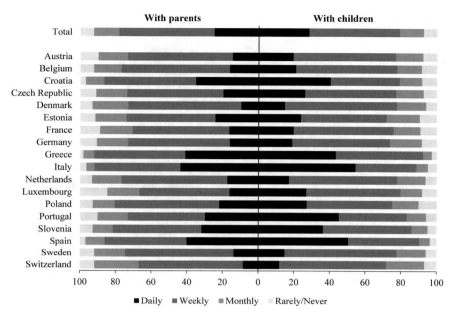

Fig. 26.1 Intergenerational Contact and Countries (Proportion) (*Source* SHARE, wave five [2013] and wave six [2015], release 7.0.0, n = 22,165 for parents and 76,703 for children, countries sorted in alphabetical order, weighted, own calculations)

be quite similar. Here, at least one quarter see or hear each other every day, and a further 50% do so at least on a weekly basis. Only seven per cent of respondents are rarely or never in contact with their parents and children.

However, as expected, the situation varies widely across Europe. The results underpin that variations in the extent of (daily) contact depend strongly on a country's cultural context. While daily contact occurs very often in Southern and Eastern Europe, the rates of daily contact are relatively low in Western and Northern European welfare states. In Portugal, Slovenia, Croatia, Greece, and Italy, 30–44% of the respondents are in contact with their parents on a daily basis, and 36–54% with their children. Conversely, this frequency is particularly low (less than 20%) in both directions in Western and Northern Europe such as in Austria, Denmark, France, Germany, the Netherlands, Sweden, and Switzerland.

Migration and Intergenerational Contact in Europe

In addition to the differences between countries, our results also highlight different patterns for natives and individuals with a migration background living in these European countries (see Fig. 26.2). While 80% of all older native Europeans aged 50+ are in contact with their parents at least weekly,

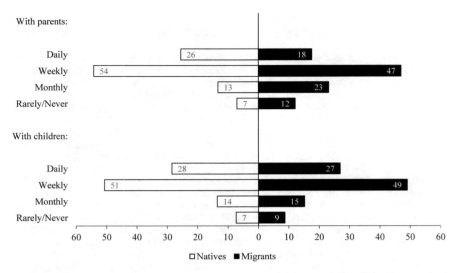

Fig. 26.2 Intergenerational Contact in Native and Migrated Families (Proportion) (*Source* SHARE, wave 5 [2013] and wave 6 [2015], release 7.0.0, n = 22,165 for parents and 76,703 for children, weighted, own calculations)

migrated respondents less often reported at least weekly contact with their parents (65%). Moreover, daily contact can be observed more often for the native population in European countries compared to the population with a migration background, at 26% versus 18%, respectively. Instead, migrants are more often in monthly contact with their parents than the native population (23% vs. 13%) or rarely/never (12% vs. 7%).

Regarding top-down contact, the relations between respondents and their adult children who do not live in the same house(hold) are more balanced between the native and the migrated population. More than three quarters of such parents are at least in weekly contact with their offspring, regardless of their ethnic background. Overall, around 50% are in touch weekly, and about one quarter (28% of the native population and 27% of the migrants) daily. Monthly or rarer contact between parents and children is also less frequent when focusing on top-down contact and differentiating between natives and migrants. Here, only 14 and 15%, respectively, are in contact with their adult children at least monthly, and only 7 and 8%, respectively, report rarer contact or a loss of contact.

As previous research indicates, geographical proximity is an important precondition for many forms of intergenerational solidarity including contact frequency. Figure 26.3 summarises the geographical distances between respondents and their parents and adult children in native and migrated families in Europe. The results show huge differences between natives and migrants with respect to geographical proximity for the generation 50 + and their parents, which may explain the difference in bottom-up contact. While two-thirds of

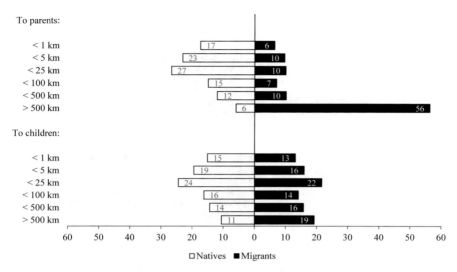

Fig. 26.3 Intergenerational Distance in Native and Migrated Families (Proportion) (*Source* SHARE, wave 5 [2013] and wave 6 [2015], release 7.0.0, n = 22,165 for parents and 76,703 for children, weighted, own calculations)

the native respondents in Europe live no more than 25 km away from their parents, only around one quarter of individuals with a migration background have parents within the same distance. By contrast, 56% of all migrated respondents in Europe report that their parents live more than 500 km away, which is true for only 6% of the native population. Conversely, closer residential proximity (less than 1 km) is more frequent among natives (17%) than migrants (6%).

The picture of geographical distance between the respondents and their adult children is much more balanced among ethnic groups, suggesting that most children of migrants were born after their parents' migration to the host country. Nevertheless, we again observe that, overall, native Europeans live closer together than generations with a migration background. While 59% of native parents and adult children live less than 25 km apart, fewer migrated parents live so close to their adult children (51%). The opposite tendency can be observed for greater distances: 11% of native respondents and 19% of migrated respondents have children who live more than 500 km away. In general, the differences are much lower compared to the bottom-up distances between respondents and their parents.

Regarding the question of the influence of geographical distance on the frequency of intergenerational contact, further analyses highlighted that contact frequency varies with geographic proximity (see Fig. 26.4). In general, daily or frequent contact depends directly on geographical distance. With increasing geographical distance between generations, frequent contact occurs less often in both directions (bottom-up and top-down contact). Frequent

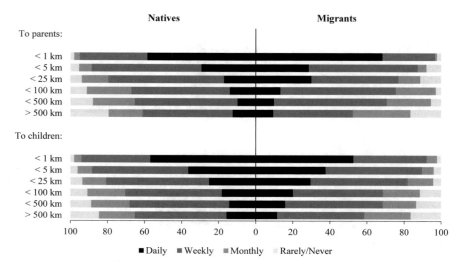

Fig. 26.4 Intergenerational Contact and Distance for Native and Migrated Families (Proportion) (*Source* SHARE, wave 5 [2013] and wave 6 [2015], release 7.0.0, n = 22,165 for parents and for 76,703 children, weighted, own calculations)

contact declines almost linearly with increasing geographical distance, which appears to be true for both native and migrated families. However, when comparing older Europeans based on their ethnic origin, differences between natives and migrants do emerge. If migrants live near their parents (less than 1 km away), they are more often in daily contact with them compared to the native population (68% vs. 59%). In contrast, native respondents are more often in touch with their parents at least weekly (61% vs. 52%) compared to the migrated population (61% vs. 52%), even when they live far apart (more than 500 km).

The picture is somewhat different for top-down contact between respondents and their adult children. Here, native parents are slightly more often in daily contact with their adult children who live outside the house(hold) but nearby (less than 1 km away) than parents with a migration background (57% vs. 53%). But overall, contact frequencies are very high for generations living very close: 94% of native families and 92% of migrants are at least in weekly contact with their adult children when they live less than one kilometre apart. With increasing distance, contact frequency decreases, as was the case with bottom-up contact. However, with increasing geographical distance respondents are generally more often in touch with their adult children than with their own parents.

Explaining Intergenerational Contact in European Families

In order to analyse intergenerational contact frequencies for natives and migrants in Europe, we first estimated multilevel linear regression models for bottom-up and top-down contact, taking general individual and familial indicators into account. For the next step, we focused on the differences between the native population and migrants, using different measurements to capture the complexity of migration. Finally, we examined the potential of information and communications technologies (ICT) such as the Internet to reduce barriers for intergenerational bottom-up and top-down contact within native and migrated families living far apart.

The results in Table 26.1 confirm previous findings about the determinants of intergenerational contact based on linear regressions. Here, a coefficient above zero indicates a positive relation regarding more frequent contact, while a value below zero implies a negative effect and thus less frequent contact within families. Overall, it can be shown that both individual need and opportunity structures and family structures at the meso-level matter for explaining intergenerational contact frequencies. At first glance, we can observe that intergenerational contact occurs more often within higher-class families with higher educational credentials and fewer financial restrictions. Moreover, the results concerning children's occupational situation show that children who are currently in (higher) education—which is often the case in well-educated families—are in more frequent contact with their parents as they have probably recently moved out of their parents' home and thus still depend on them. Regarding the older generation's health status and need for support, the findings show that parents (respondents as well as respondents' parents) in poor physical condition have less contact with the younger generation. Moreover, the analyses show that larger family size results in less intergenerational contact. This applies especially to the presence of siblings, suggesting that parent-child contact will, can, or has to be shared among siblings.

While non-biological children generally have less frequent contact with their stepparents, the gender-specific and structural characteristics of the dyad are important for intergenerational contact in both directions. Mothers and daughters are most often in touch with each other, whereas fathers and sons rarely communicate. As expected, geographical distances matter for both bottom-up and top-down contact. The closer generations live to each other, the more often they are in contact. In other words, living farther apart hampers contact between parents and children. However, the empirical results also show that the use of modern technology, such as the Internet, significantly affects the frequency of intergenerational contact in European families. Without knowing whether the Internet is used for communication between family members, it is evident that contact is more frequent in families that use the Internet.

Table 26.1 Determinants of Intergenerational Contact in Europe

	With parents	With children
Respondents' characteristics		
Age	0.01	−0.01
Education *(Ref.: Low)*		
Medium	0.10**	0.06***
High	0.22***	0.06***
Income *(Ref.: With great difficulty)*		
With some difficulty	0.13***	0.13***
Fairly easily	0.16***	0.16***
Easily	0.21***	0.17***
Occupation *(Ref.: Employed)*		
Unemployed	0.05	
Retired	0.04	
Not employed	−0.01	
Health *(Ref.: Excellent)*		
Very good		0.08***
Good		0.04***
Fair		−0.01
Poor		−0.15***
Partner	0.04	0.28***
Children *(Ref.: None)*		
One	0.02	
Two	0.03	
Three and more	−0.05	
Siblings *(Ref.: None)*		
One	−0.03	
Two	−0.14***	
Three and more	−0.37***	
Internet use (past seven days)	0.11***	0.10***
Interview: 6th wave (2015)	−0.05	-0.06
Parents' characteristics		
2nd parent alive	−0.11***	
Health *(Ref.: Good)*		
Excellent	0.15***	
Very good	0.09**	
Fair	−0.05**	
Poor	−0.17***	

(continued)

Table 26.1 (continued)

	With parents	With children
Children's characteristics		
Natural child		0.82***
Occupation *(Ref.: Employed)*		
Unemployed		−0.01
In education		0.17***
Not employed		−0.07***
Partner		−0.01
Children *(Ref.: None)*		
One		0.04***
Two		−0.01
Three and more		−0.07***
Siblings *(Ref.: None)*		
One		−0.13***
Two		−0.32***
Three and more		−0.62***
Dyads' characteristics		
Relationship *(Ref.: Mother-daughter)*		
Mother-son	−0.46***	−0.40***
Father-daughter	−0.32***	−0.36***
Father-son	−0.62***	−0.60***
Residential distance *(Ref.: < 1 km)*		
≤ 5 km	−0.50***	−0.40***
≤ 25 km	−0.86***	−0.70***
≤ 100 km	−1.27***	−1.05***
≤ 500 km	−1.51***	−1.27***
> 500 km	−1.84***	−1.52***
n (parents/children)	22,165	76,703
n (respondents)	17,642	37,894
n (countries)	18	18

Source SHARE, wave 6 (2015), release 7.0.0, multilevel linear regressions, robust standard errors, all independent metric variables standardized, own calculations. Significance levels: *** ≤ 0.01, ** ≤ 0.05, * ≤ 0.10

Explaining Intergenerational Contact in the Light of Migration

Because geographical distance between generations is important for contact frequency and migrants live farther apart, especially from their parents (see Fig. 26.2), it is important to take a closer look at the influence of migration on intergenerational contact. In this respect, the analyses presented in Table 26.2 consider the complexity of migration on intergenerational bottom-up and

Table 26.2 Migration and Intergenerational Contact in Europe

	With parents	With children
Migration		
Migrant	0.22***	0.13***
Migration status *(Ref.: Native)*		
Citizen, foreign birth	0.18***	0.12***
Not citizen, foreign birth	0.31**	0.16***
Migration country *(Ref.: Native)*		
EU-15/EFTA	0.29***	0.09
Non-EU-15/EFTA	0.19*	0.15***
Migration country *(Ref.: Native)*		
EU-28/EFTA	0.27***	0.07
Non-EU-28/EFTA	0.18*	0.19***
Migration country *(Ref.: Native)*		
EU-28/EFTA: North/West	0.08	−0.05**
EU-28/EFTA: South/East	0.46***	0.19**
Non-EU-28/EFTA	0.19*	0.20***
Migration time *(Ref.: Native)*		
Childhood	0.30***	0.09***
Early adulthood	0.16	0.17***
Later adulthood	0.20	0.10
% foreign population	−0.05	−0.05
n (parents/children)	22,165	76.703
n (respondents)	17,642	37,894
n (countries)	18	18

Source SHARE, wave 6 (2015), release 7.0.0, Eurostat (2019), multilevel linear regressions (models under control of all variables mentioned in Table 4.1), robust standard errors, all independent metric variables standardized, own calculations. Significance levels: *** ≤ 0.01, ** ≤ 0.05, * ≤ 0.10

top-down contact. Each indicator, capturing some dimension of migration, is estimated separately under control of the variables mentioned in Table 26.1. In general, we observe that migration matters for explaining intergenerational contact with elderly parents and with adult children. Here, respondents with a migration background are more often in touch with their family members than natives. This picture can be observed for bottom-up contact to parents as well as for top-down contact to adult children.

Moreover, the results point out similarities and differences among various groups of migrants. First, regarding foreign-born respondents regardless of citizenship, the results again show that a migration background matters. Foreign-born individuals are more often in contact with their parents and children compared to the native population, independent of citizenship. However, the geographical and cultural region of origin affects the differences in intergenerational contact among migrated families. While migrants, regardless of origin, have more frequent contact with their elderly parents, respondents not born in a member country of the EU or EFTA are more frequently in contact with their children. This pattern remains true when considering the different definitions of EU-membership, namely EU-15 or EU-28. However, when differentiating among migrants born within the EU, the results further show that those who were born in Southern or Eastern Europe have more frequent bottom-up and top-down contact, while those from Northern and Western Europe either do not differ (bottom-up) or have less (top-down) contact than natives.

In addition to the country of origin and host country citizenship, the life course–specific timing of migration, and thus the amount of time spent in the host country, has a lasting effect on intergenerational contact. For bottom-up contact, we observe that respondents who migrated in childhood and probably together with their parents have more frequent contact. The situation is partly similar for top-down contact, whereby respondents who migrated as in childhood or younger adults and therefore probably without their parents have more frequent contact with their children (born in the host country).

While individual circumstances of migration have a lasting effect on intergenerational contact, on an aggregated level the cultural differences associated with migration are not important for explaining different intergenerational contact patterns across Europe. The results show that the percentage of the foreign population in European countries does not significantly affect the frequency of intergenerational bottom-up and top-down contact. However, this is not surprising considering that the proportion of migrants is comparatively low in the majority of the Eastern and Southern European countries, whose residents simultaneously have more intergenerational contact. Conversely, as migrant families are generally in contact more often, this means that the frequency of intergenerational contact would be even lower in Western and Northern Europe if one only looked at the native population.

Finally, we focus on the impact of Internet use, residential distance, and migration on intergenerational contact by including interaction terms (see Table 26.3). Overall, the results emphasise that Internet use in general facilitates contact, especially with greater geographical distances between parents and children. However, this is true regardless of cultural or geographical background and allows both native and migrated families to stay in contact over long distances.

Table 26.3 Internet Use, Residential Distance, and Migration

	With parents				With children			
Internet use	−0.04	0.11***	0.11***	−0.04	−0.03	0.10***	0.10***	−0.03
Residential distance (Ref.: < 1 km)								
≤ 5 km	−0.57***	−0.50***	−0.51***	−0.58***	−0.41***	−0.40***	−0.41***	−0.42***
≤ 25 km	−0.98***	−0.86***	−0.86***	−0.98***	−0.73***	−0.70***	−0.71***	−0.74***
≤ 100 km	−1.42***	−1.27***	−1.28***	−1.42***	−1.12***	−1.05***	−1.05***	−1.12***
≤ 500 km	−1.66***	−1.53***	−1.52***	−1.66***	−1.37***	−1.27***	−1.27***	−1.37***
> 500 km	−2.24***	−1.96***	−1.89***	−2.23***	−1.70***	−1.53***	−1.52***	−1.69***
Migrant	0.23***	0.17*	0.22	0.31*	0.13***	0.12***	0.08	0.08
Interactions:								
Internet use*Residential distance								
Internet use* ≤ 5 km	0.11*			0.11*	0.06			0.06
Internet use* ≤ 25 km	0.18***			0.18***	0.10**			0.10**
Internet use* ≤ 100 km	0.21**			0.22**	0.18***			0.18***
Internet use* ≤ 500 km	0.19			0.20	0.24***			0.23***
Internet use* > 500 km	0.40***			0.48***	0.36***			0.36***
Migrant*Internet use		0.07		−0.13		0.02		0.01
Migrant*Residential distance								
Migrant* < 5 km			0.19	0.20			0.13	0.13

	With parents			With children	
Migrant* < 25 km		0.10	0.11		0.12**	0.11*
Migrant* < 100 km		0.06	0.08		0.05	0.05
Migrant* < 500 km		−0.07	−0.06		−0.05	−0.04
Migrant* > 500 km		−0.11	−0.09		−0.03	−0.03
n (parents/children)	22,165	22,165	22,165	76.703	76.703	76.703
n (respondents)	17,642	17,642	17,642	37,894	37,894	37,894
n (countries)	18	18	18	18	18	18

Source SHARE, wave 6 (2015), release 7.0.0, multilevel linear regressions (models under control of all the variables mentioned in Table 4.1), robust standard errors, all independent metric variables standardized, own calculations. Significance levels: *** ≤ 0.01, ** ≤ 0.05, * ≤ 0.10

Conclusions

Support and lifelong exchange between generations are important characteristics of family relationships. Besides the relatively well-studied functional solidarity, contact between parents and their adult children is another important form of solidarity that has so far been under-researched, especially with regard to population-specific patterns.

The chapter addresses contact frequency with a special focus on the differences due to geographical and cultural distance. Overall, the empirical analyses indicate that European families are generally characterised by strong and frequent contact regardless of spatial distance and ethnic origin. In addition to country-specific differences, such as more frequent intergenerational contact in Southern and Eastern Europe, distance and migration also matter. Aside from general findings for individual and familial variations, we can also detect differences due to residential distance as well as between natives and migrants. If we control for individual indicators, family structures, and geographical distance, migrants are more frequently in contact with their family than the native population (solidarity thesis). In addition, the analyses also highlight specific patterns among migrants depending on naturalisation, country of origin, and duration of stay. Differences between natives and migrants in Europe are observable for those born outside the EU/EFTA. While they are, despite longer distances, more often in touch with their offspring (safe-haven thesis), the opposite is generally true for migrants from EU-member states in their contact with their parents (drift thesis). However, the analyses show that this increased contact among migrants born within the EU is prevalent mainly among those born in Southern or Eastern Europe. Migrants from these countries are more often in touch with their own older parents (bottom-up) and with their adult children outside the household (top-down). In the light of the theoretical assumptions and previous (own) research it can be assumed that these differences within the EU and between EU and non-EU countries of origin are caused by varying family norms and attitudes which are stronger in Southern and Eastern Europe, as well as isolation in the host country and different historical migrations flows such as the recruitment of guest workers in 1970s for example.

Although migrants in Europe have to bridge greater distances to keep in touch with their families, especially if they originate from outside the EU, their contact frequencies are higher compared to natives. This is not least due to stronger family bonds and obligations, especially for migrants from the more family-oriented countries. Previous research noted that, according to the solidarity and the safe-haven theses, migrants are more likely to maintain stronger family bonds than natives. Cultural differences as well as economic and linguistic uncertainties may cause migrants to have a greater need for close family networks (safe havens) in a largely unknown environment. Therefore, it is important for them to keep in touch with their family members, even across great distances.

Overall, the findings confirm that both native and migrated generations in Europe are often in touch with each other and that large geographical distances can be bridged by modern communication technology. Furthermore, migrants are not isolated in their host country. On the contrary, they are more often connected with their families, parents, and adult children than natives, even though they often live farther apart. The drift hypothesis, which assumes that family generations drift apart to some degree due to spatial mobility and migration, thus does not seem to be true. Although the present contribution clearly shows that families are in frequent contact despite geographical distances, we have to bear in mind that some forms of solidarity and support are less probable across great distances. In this vein, future research should take qualitative aspects into account to understand in more detail how cultural differences among migrants affect their intergenerational solidarity. As the data used in this study is limited to only a specific population (50+) in Europe, the perspectives of younger generations should be considered in future research as well, in order to determine mutual contact behaviour within families.

Note Researchers using SHARE data are asked to issue the following declaration: "This paper uses data from SHARE Waves 5 and 6 (https://doi.org/10.6103/share.w.700, https://doi.org/10.6103/share.w6.700), see Börsch-Supan et al. (2013) for methodological details. The SHARE data collection has been funded by the European Commission through FP5 (QLK6-CT-2001-00360), FP6 (SHARE-I3: RII-CT-2006-062193, COMPARE: CIT5-CT-2005-028857, SHARELIFE: CIT4-CT-2006-028812), FP7 (SHARE-PREP: GA No. 211909, SHARE-LEAP: GA No. 227822, SHARE M4: GA No. 261982) and Horizon 2020 (SHARE-DEV3: GA No. 676536, SERISS: GA No. 654221) and by DG Employment, Social Affairs and Inclusion. Additional funding from the German Ministry of Education and Research, the Max Planck Society for the Advancement of Science, the U.S. National Institute on Aging (U01_AG09740-13S2, P01_AG005842, P01_AG08291, P30_AG12815, R21_AG025169, Y1-AG-4553-01, IAG_BSR06-11, OGHA_04-064, HHSN271201300071C) and from various national funding sources is gratefully acknowledged (see www.share-project.org)." The data were adjusted for this investigation, and extensive consistency checks were made.

References

Albertini, Marco, Martin Kohli, and Claudia Vogel. 2007. "Intergenerational Transfers of Time and Money in European Families: Common Patterns Different Regimes?" *Journal of European Social Policy* 17 (4): 319–334. https://doi.org/10.1177/0958928707081068.

Aquilino, William S. 1990. "The Likelihood of Parent-Adult Child Coresidence: Effects of Family Structure and Parental Characteristics." *Journal of Marriage and Family* 52 (2): 405–419. https://doi.org/10.2307/353035.

Aslund, Olof. 2005. "Now and Forever? Initial and Subsequent Location Choices of Immigrants." *Regional Science and Urban Economics* 35 (2): 141–165.

Baykara-Krumme, Helen. 2008. *Immigrant Families in Germany: Intergenerational Solidarity in Later Life*. Berlin: Weissensee Verlag.

Bengtson, Vern L. 2001. "Beyond the Nuclear Family: The Increasing Importance of Multigenerational Bonds." *Journal of Marriage and Family* 63 (1): 1–16. https://doi.org/10.1111/j.1741-3737.2001.00001.x.

Berger, Fred, and Helmut Fend. 2005. "Kontinuität Und Wandel in Der Affektiven Beziehung Zwischen Eltern Und Kindern Vom Jugend-Bis Ins Erwachsenenalter." *Zeitschrift für Soziologie der Erziehung und Sozialisation* 25 (1): 8–31.

Bertogg, Ariane, and Marc Szydlik. 2016. "The Closeness of Young Adults' Relationships with Their Parents." *Swiss Journal of Sociology* 42 (1): 41–59.

Bordone, Valeria. 2009. "Contact and Proximity of Older People to Their Adult Children: A Comparison Between Italy and Sweden." *Population, Space Place* 15 (4): 359–380. https://doi.org/10.1002/psp.559.

Bordone, Valeria, and Helga A. G. de Valk. 2016. "Intergenerational Support Among Migrant Families in Europe." *European Journal of Ageing* 13 (3): 259–270. https://doi.org/10.1007/s10433-016-0363-6.

Börsch-Supan, Axel. 2019a. "Survey of Health, Ageing and Retirement in Europe (SHARE) Wave 5. Release Version: 7.1.0. SHARE-ERIC. Data Set.".

Börsch-Supan, Axel. 2019b. "Survey of Health, Ageing and Retirement in Europe (SHARE) Wave 6. Release Version: 7.1.0. SHARE-ERIC. Data Set.".

Börsch-Supan, Axel, Martina Brandt, Christian Hunkler, Thorsten Kneip, Julie Korbmacher, Frederic Malter, Barbara Schaan, Stephanie Stuck, and Sabrina Zuber. 2013. "Data Resource Profile: The Survey of Health, Ageing and Retirement in Europe (SHARE)." *International Journal of Epidemiology* 42 (4): 992–1001. https://doi.org/10.1093/ije/dyt088.

Brandt, Martina, and Christian Deindl. 2013. "Intergenerational Transfers to Adult Children in Europe: Do Social Policies Matter?" *Journal of Marriage and Family* 75 (1): 235–251. https://doi.org/10.1111/j.1741-3737.2012.01028.x.

Bucx, Freek, Frits van Wel, Trudie C. M. Knijn, and Louk Hagendoorn. 2008. "Intergenerational Contact and the Life Course Status of Young Adult Children." *Journal of Marriage and Family* 70 (1): 144–156. https://doi.org/10.1111/j.1741-3737.2007.00467.x.

Cesnuityte, Vida, and Gerardo Meil, eds. 2019. *Families in Economically Hard Times: Experiences and Coping Strategies in Europe*. Bingley: Emerald Publishing Limited.

de Valk, Helga A. G., and Djamila Schans. 2008. "'They Ought to Do This for Their Parents': Perceptions of Filial Obligations Among Immigrant and Dutch Older People." *Ageing and Society* 28 (1): 49–66. https://doi.org/10.1017/S0144686X07006307.

Dewit, D. J., A. V. Wister, and T. K. Burch. 1988. "Physical Distance and Social Contact Between Elders and Their Adult Children." *Res Aging* 10 (1): 56–80. https://doi.org/10.1177/0164027588101003.

Dumon, Wilfried A. 1989. "Family and Migration." *International Migration* 27 (2): 251–270.

Eurostat. 2019. "Population on 1 January by Age Group, Sex and Country of Birth [Migr_pop3ctb]." Accessed December 02, 2019. https://appsso.eurostat.ec.europa.eu/nui/show.do?dataset=migr_pop3ctb&lang=en.

Ganjour, Olga, and Eric D. Widmer. 2016. "Patterns of Family Salience and Welfare State Regimes: Sociability Practices and Support Norms in a Comparative Perspective." *European Societies* 18 (3): 201–220. https://doi.org/10.1080/14616696.2016.1158846.

Gauthier, Anne Hélène. 1996. "The State and the Family: A Comparative Analysis of Family Policies in Industrialized Countries." Oxford: Clarendon Press. http://www.loc.gov/catdir/enhancements/fy0640/96228150-d.html.

Hank, Karsten. 2007. "Proximity and Contacts Between Older Parents and Their Children: A European Comparison." *Journal of Marriage and Family* 69 (1): 157–173. https://doi.org/10.1111/j.1741-3737.2006.00351.x.

Hox, Joop J. 2002. "Multilevel Analysis: Techniques and Applications." *Quantitative methodology series*. Mahwah, NJ: Lawrence Erlbaum Associates.

Igel, Corinne, and Marc Szydlik. 2011. "Grandchild Care and Welfare State Arrangements in Europe." *Journal of European Social Policy* 21 (3): 210–224. https://doi.org/10.1177/0958928711401766.

Isengard, Bettina. 2013. "'The Apple Doesn't Live Far from the Tree': Living Distances Between Parents and Their Adult Children in Europe." *Comparative Population Studies – Zeitschrift für Bevölkerungswissenschaft* 38 (2): 263–90.

Isengard, Bettina, Ronny König, and Marc Szydlik. 2018. "Money or Space? Intergenerational Transfers in a Comparative Perspective." *Housing Studies* 33 (2): 178–200. https://doi.org/10.1080/02673037.2017.1365823.

Isengard, Bettina, Ronny König, and Marc Szydlik. 2019. "Here to Stay? Intergenerational Spatial Proximity in Europe." In Cesnuityte and Meil 2019, 145–166.

Kağıtçıbaşı, Çiğdem. 1996. *Family and Human Development Across Cultures: A View from the Other Side*. Mahwah, NJ: Lawrence Erlbaum Associates.

Knijn, Trudie C. M., and Aart C. Liefbroer. 2006. "More Kin Than Kind: Instrumental Support in Families." In *Family Solidarity in the Netherlands*, edited by Pearl A. Dykstra, Matthijs Kalmijn, Trudie C. M. Knijn, Aafke E. Komter, Aart C. Liefbroer, and Clara H. Mulder, 89–105. Amsterdam: Dutch University Press.

König, Ronny. 2016. *Bildung, Schicht Und Generationensolidarität in Europa*. Wiesbaden: Springer VS.

König, Ronny, Bettina Isengard, and Marc Szydlik. 2018. "Migration Matters: Insights into Intergenerational Solidarity Patterns in Europe." In *Making Multicultural Families in Europe: Gender and Generational Relations*, edited by Isabella Crespi, Stefania G. Meda, and Laura Merla, 233–253: Palgrave Macmillan.

König, Ronny, Bettina Isengard, and Marc Szydlik. 2019. "Social Inequality and Intergenerational Solidarity in European Welfare States." In Cesnuityte and Meil 2019, 31–52.

Leitner, Sigrid. 2003. "Varieties of Familialism: The Caring Function of the Family in Comparative Perspective." *European Societies* 5 (4): 353–375. https://doi.org/10.1080/1461669032000127642.

McDonald, Lynn. 2011. "Theorising About Ageing, Family and Immigration." *Ageing and Society* 31 (07): 1180–1201. https://doi.org/10.1017/S0144686X1100 0511.

Merz, Eva-Maria, Ezgi Özeke-Kocabas, Frans J. Oort, and Carlo Schuengel. 2009. "Intergenerational Family Solidarity: Value Differences Between Immigrant Groups and Generations." *Journal of Family Psychology* 23 (3): 291–300. https://doi.org/10.1037/a0015819.

Mulder, Clara H. 2007. "The Family Context and Residential Choice: A Challenge for New Research." *Population, Space Place* 13 (4): 265–278. https://doi.org/10.1002/psp.456.

Nauck, Bernhard. 2007. "Immigrant Families in Germany: Family Change Between Situational Adaptation, Acculturation, Segregation and Remigration." *Zeitschrift für Familienforschung* 19 (1): 34–54.

Nosaka, Akiko, and Athanasios Chasiotis. 2005. "Exploring the Variation in Intergenerational Relationships Among Germans and Turkish Immigrants: An Evolutionary Perspective on Behaviour in a Modern Social Setting." In *Grandmotherhood: The Evolutionary Significance of the Second Half of Female Life*, edited by Eckart Voland, Athanasios Chasiotis, and Wulf Schiefenhovel, 256–276. New Brunswick, NJ: Rutgers University Press.

Park, Robert Ezra. 1964. *Race and Culture*. Pbk. Ed. Glencoe: The Free Press of Glencoe.

Portes, Alejandro, and Min Zhou. 2005. "The New Second Generation: Segmented Assimilation and Its Variants." In *The New Immigration: An Interdisciplinary Reader*, edited by Marcelo M. Suárez-Orozco, Carola Suárez-Orozco, and Desirée Qin-Hilliard, 85–103. New York: Routledge.

Rabe-Hesketh, Sophia, and Anders Skrondal. 2008. *Multilevel and Longitudinal Modeling Using Stata*. College Station. Texas: Stata Press.

Rossi, Alice S., and Peter Henry Rossi. 1990. *Of Human Bonding: Parent-Child Relations Across the Life Course*. New York: Aldine de Gruyter.

Sarkisian, Natalia, and Naomi Gerstel. 2008. "Till Marriage Do Us Part: Adult Children's Relationships with Their Parents." *Family Relations* 70 (2): 360–376. https://doi.org/10.1111/j.1741-3737.2008.00487.x.

Schans, Djamila, and Helga A. G. de Valk. 2012. "Filial Obligations Among Migrants and Dutch: A Comparison of Perceptions and Behaviour Among Ethnic Groups and Generations." In *Gender, Generations and the Family in International Migration*, edited by Albert Kraler, Eleonore Kofman, Martin Kohli, and Camille Schmoll, 99–120. Amsterdam: Amsterdam University Press.

Schimany, Peter, Stefan Rühl, and Martin Kohls. 2012. Ältere Migrantinnen Und Migranten: Entwicklungen, Lebenslagen, Perspektiven 18. Nürnberg: Bundesamt für Migration und Flüchtlinge.

Snijders, Tom A.B., and Roel J. Bosker. 2012. *Multilevel Analysis: An Introduction to Basic and Advanced Multilevel Modeling*. 2nd ed. Los Angeles: Sage.

Steinbach, Anja, and Johannes Kopp. 2008. "'When Will I See You Again?' Intergenerational Contacts in Germany." In *Families, Ageing and Social Policy: Intergenerational Solidarity in European Welfare States*, edited by Chiara Saraceno, 88–104. Cheltenham: Edward Elgar Publishing.

Szydlik, Marc. 2008. "Intergenerational Solidarity and Conflict." *Journal of Comparative Family Studies* 39 (1): 97–114. https://doi.org/10.2307/41604202.

Szydlik, Marc. 2016. *Sharing Lives—Adult Children and Parents*. London, New York: Routledge.

Tomassini, Cecilia, Stamatis Kalogirou, Emily Grundy, Tineke Fokkema, Pekka Martikainen, Marjolein Broese van Groenou, and Antti Karisto. 2004. "Contacts Between Elderly Parents and Their Children in Four European Countries: Current Patterns and Future Prospects." *European Journal of Ageing* 1 (1): 54–63. https://doi.org/10.1007/s10433-004-0003-4.

Tomassini, Cecilia, Douglas A. Wolf, and Alessandro Rosina. 2003. "Parental Housing Assistance and Parent-Child Proximity in Italy." *Journal of Marriage and Family* 65 (3): 700–715. https://doi.org/10.2307/3600033.

CHAPTER 27

Parenting and Caring Across Borders in Refugee Contexts

Lena Näre

INTRODUCTION

A humanitarian crisis has been unfolding for decades at the European borders. Since 2014, over 21,000 migrants have died in Europe, in the Mediterranean, and in the Middle East while trying to reach Europe (IOM 2020). Those who arrive in Europe are met with increasingly hostile environments. Especially after the asylum crisis of 2015, during which 1.2 million refugees arrived in the EU, migrants are confronted with rapidly changing laws and policies affecting their right to asylum (Näre 2020a) and limitations to their possibilities for family reunification (Näre 2020b). Thus, the right to family, a principle guaranteed by international conventions and national legislations, is being curtailed through restrictions to family reunification policies in European migrant destination countries (OECD 2019). For refugees and irregular migrants in EU countries, family life is characteristically transnational but existing research on transnational families has largely overlooked their experiences.

In this chapter, I examine how refugee men carry out transnational parenting and caregiving across borders within the context of restrictive migration regimes. I discuss how transnational care is shaped by migration and gender regimes but also by other structural conditions in both the contexts of origin and settlement. I argue that care for their family members, especially children and parents, is a central motivation for male refugees' migratory mobility. I demonstrate that men with refugee backgrounds continue to

---

L. Näre (✉)
Faculty of Social Sciences, University of Helsinki, Helsinki, Finland
e-mail: lena.nare@helsinki.fi

© The Author(s), under exclusive license to Springer Nature Switzerland AG 2021
A.-M. Castrén et al. (eds.), *The Palgrave Handbook of Family Sociology in Europe*, https://doi.org/10.1007/978-3-030-73306-3_27

provide care as fathers and adult sons for their family members back home after fleeing the conditions in their countries of origin. They face difficult structural conditions that they need to encounter: war, violence, insecurity, and discrimination in their countries of origin and the hostile environments in the countries of settlement in which they are racialised, discriminated against and where they have to struggle for a right to asylum.

This chapter is based on data collected during a multi-sited ethnographic project among Iraqi and Afghan refugees in Finland, Greece, Turkey, and Iran (2017–2020). This multi-sited fieldwork has provided me a manifold perspective to the practices and limits of transnational care and parenting in refugee contexts and the role that male refugees have in their families. In what follows, I use insights and examples from my fieldwork to illustrate how transnational parenting and care across borders looks like in practice. Before discussing the practices of transnational care and parenting, I shortly present the data this chapter draws on.

Data and Methods

During the project, I interviewed 43 Afghan, Iraqi, and Pakistani refugees in Finland at various sites, including a protest organised by the refugees in the centre of Helsinki (see Näre 2020a), reception and detention centres, and private homes. Of the research participants, 31 were men and 12 were women, aged between 20 and 55 years. In addition to the qualitative interviews, I also conducted ethnographic interviews on specific topics. I spoke to 37 other research participants (30 men and seven women) during my fieldwork. The families of the research participants varied. Most of the interviewed men (20) were unmarried, and of those who had their own family, only two had travelled with their family. Of the 30 other men I spoke to during the fieldwork, most had left their families behind. For most families, the strategy had been, if possible, for the men to make the dangerous journey alone with the hope of applying for family reunification after receiving their residence permit in Europe. Most of the interviews were conducted face-to-face in English. In six of the interviews, a friend of the research participant who spoke English well acted as an interpreter, and four interviews were conducted in Farsi or Arabic with the help of a Finnish-speaking translator. Two interviews with Afghans were conducted in Finnish, as these interviewees had learnt to speak Finnish fluently. I conducted follow-up interviews on specific themes in the spring of 2019. These interviews focused on experiences of family separation and reunification.

In addition to the main fieldwork in Finland, I conducted shorter research visits to Tehran, Athens, and Istanbul in 2019. In Tehran, I interviewed six Afghans (four men and two women) who had been deported from northern Europe to Afghanistan or from the Turkish border back to Iran. Of these research participants, two men were unmarried and the others were married with children. In May 2019, I conducted participant observations in a refugee camp in Athens and interviewed eight Afghan refugees (six men and two women) who all had families of their own either in the camp, back home, or in other European countries. In October 2019, I conducted fieldwork in Istanbul and interviewed nine Afghan families, in total 16 adults and 21 children, most of whom were waiting for smugglers to take them to Lesbos, Greece. I conducted these interviews with a research assistant who translated from Farsi to Finnish. All the mentioned names are pseudonyms and the examples are carefully chosen as representative of the larger data set.

REFUGEE MEN'S PRACTICES OF TRANSNATIONAL PARENTING AND CARE ACROSS BORDERS

Yasin was 40 years old when I first met him in the spring of 2017. He had come to Finland in the autumn of 2015 from Baghdad, Iraq where he was working as a driver, construction worker, and tailor. In 2015, he decided to leave Iraq in order to provide a better future for his children. As for so many migrants, the hope for a better and safer future for family members (Näre 2012; Coe 2015) is what drove Yasin to come to Europe during the so-called Long Summer of Migration (Kasparek and Speer 2015). Yasin left his wife, four under 15-year-old children, and his 80-year-old mother in Baghdad, Iraq. He had applied for asylum in Finland but was working while waiting for the decision when I first met him. He explains:

> I take care of [my mother], absolutely because she is my mother and this is not like I make a favour or anything. [...] My mother, my wife and four kids, [it] is a big responsibility, I should work many, many hours to bring everything for medicine, medical things, food, clothes, for living, everything you know.

Yasin, as most of the refugee men I met during my fieldwork were providing transnational care for their children and ageing parents. Before migrating Yasin was responsible for over-seeing his children's schooling, but after Yasin migrated, his wife has the main responsibility for childcare. Still, Yasin continues to provide for them: 'my wife now takes care of buying everything and teaching them for school, all of them in school and she takes care of my family'. His wife is not working, so the family depends on the money Yasin sends them. His family is the reason he needs to work hard in Finland, he tells me. Although Yasin provides resources for caring, the person providing the daily care is not Yasin, but his wife. Yasin is the facilitator of care as he sends the money that enables her hands-on care. Yasin, in this case, could be described, as Kilkey and Merla (2014) have done, as the manager of care by distance and the transnational care arrangement in Yasin's case as personal care by proxy. His mother is helping Yasin's wife with childcare and Yasin is providing care for his ageing mother who is dependent on regular medication.

Since the 1990s, transnational families have attracted scholarly attention (Baldassar et al. 2014; Bryceson and Vuorela 2002; Glick Shiller et al. 1992,

1995; Skrbiš 2008). While this research has been important in demonstrating that individuals have innovative ways to continue to 'do' family (Morgan 2011) despite physical separation, the continuing impact that nation-state borders and increasingly restrictive migration regimes have on the lives of transnational families has been somewhat side-lined in this research. Unlike most research on transnational families, Yasin does not fit the celebrated protagonist of the 'mobility turn' in social sciences (Sheller and Urry 2006). He is a refugee whose border crossing means risking his life and an asylum seeker who was forced to immobility during a long waiting period during which his case was assessed. If he would have been granted refugee status, it would have signified a situation that bears little resemblance to the labour migrants who can go back and visit their families back home. Going back would have endangered his refugee status.

In addition to the literature on transnational families, a great deal has been written since the classic article by Hondagneu-Sotelo and Avila (1997) on transnational motherhood. The existing research has focused mostly on how mothers negotiate separation and notions of good motherhood in terms of emotional closeness despite physical separation after migration (Åkesson et al. 2012; Chamberlain 1999; Erel 2016; Hondagneu-Sotelo and Avila 1997; Leinaweaver 2010; Zontini 2004). This research has examined how women's labour migration challenges gendered divisions of labour between a male breadwinner and a female carer (Dreby 2006; Hondagneu-Sotelo and Avila 1997; Lutz 2011; Parreñas 2005). The researchers have argued that women's migration disrupts ideologies that stress physical and emotional closeness in mother-child relationships (Dreby 2006; Horton 2009; Parreñas 2001a) and the risks that migration and family separation hold for their children (e.g. Boehm 2008, 2012; Mazzucato and Shans 2011; Suárez-Orozco et al. 2002).

In a great deal of literature on transnational families, men's roles are not discussed at all or men are given the role of the deviant other through either abandoning the family upon migration or as being incapable of taking over caring roles after mothers' migration (see Sørensen and Vammen 2014 for discussion). Research from the Philippines indicates that, at least at the time of maternal migration, some fathers do step in and get more involved in domestic and child caring tasks (Asis 2006; Pingol 2001). While transnational fathering is a less explored area in the research literature, some authors have focused on the role of fathers in transnational families as well as on their transnational caregiving duties (Fresnoza-Flot 2014; Parreñas 2008; Pingol 2001).

My research with Afghan and Iraqi men contributes to this emerging research on men's role as transnational caregivers. The men I met during my fieldwork were providing care for their ageing parents and if they had their own children, they had double caring roles, as adult sons and as fathers. Hence, my research questions a common assumption found in research, namely that migrating fathers abandon their families after migrating—an assumption that is also criticised in the emerging literature on transnational fatherhood (see, e.g., Datta et al. 2009; Nobles 2011).

Yasin is forced to return to Baghdad in 2017 because his asylum application is rejected. Although Yasin works 40 hours per week, he has a zero-hour work contract with no guaranteed working hours which is not accepted as the basis of a work-based residence permit application—that would require a full-time work contract. Thus, later in the year, Yasin 'deports himself' to Baghdad, as he describes his decision to opt for a 'voluntary return' to Iraq. A short time before returning to Iraq, Yasin met a Finnish woman with whom he had an affair. Although Yasin returned to Iraq in order to continue married life, his marriage did not survive the infidelity and the long, almost two-year separation. Yasin and his wife ended up divorcing. A year later, Yasin married his Finnish girlfriend and returned back to Finland. From Finland he continues to care for his children and his mother by sending remittances to his family. He tells me that one day he hopes to get custody of his children and bring them to live with him in Finland. Although Yasin's marriage did not survive the long separation, his role as a caregiver for his children and ageing mother did not end with the divorce. The restrictive migration regime transformed Yasin's family relationships in profound and complex ways. He can continue to provide care to his children transnationally. But now, with a marriage-based residence permit, he can travel back to Iraq and visit his children and his mother.

Migration mobilities, migration regimes and policies affect the gendered redistribution of parenting responsibilities and practices (Herrera 2013; Kofman 2013). During my fieldwork in the refugee camp in Athens, I realised that the asylum policies that are created to protect individuals who are constructed as 'the most vulnerable' encouraged practices of sending mothers alone to seek asylum in another EU country; sometimes underage children were sent. Hence, many Afghan families who had travelled together to Greece had decided to separate in order to strategise on who would be most likely to receive asylum in Germany or Switzerland and then able to apply for family reunification for the rest of the family. In these situations, men were left to care alone for the children in the refugee camp.

Migration does not only transform parenting responsibilities but can also transform grandparents' parenting roles. As Åkesson et al. (2012) remind us, individuals remain children of their parents also when they are adults and transnational parenthood can also exist between adults. In fact, a lot of recent research has examined how migration changes the roles of grandparents who either take roles caring for their grandchildren in the country of origin (Åkesson et al. 2012) or who migrate or travel back and forth in order to help their children with their care duties (Goulbourne et al. 2010; King et al. 2014; Zontini 2010, see also Walsh and Näre 2017). Taking care of grandchildren can be understood as one dimension of transnational care that grandparents provide to their adult children in addition to the actual care duties that they have towards their grandchildren.

Marchetti-Mercer's (2012) research on South African migrating families emphasises the sense of loss among grandparents whose children and grandchildren have migrated. In a similar way, my research revealed that migration impacted profoundly the lives of refugees' parents who stayed behind. In some cases, the threats that individuals had faced in their home countries were extended to the family members of the refugees.

Adil was a young Iraqi man whom I met regularly during my fieldwork in the protest camp that asylum seekers had organised in the centre of Helsinki in 2017. Adil had escaped Iraq because of the threats he started receiving for his work as a journalist and for his atheism. His family members, except his mother, had severed ties with him. While waiting for his asylum application to be processed, Adil discovered that his mother had received threats because of him. Adil was so worried for his mother's safety that he often contemplated opting for voluntary return even though he knew his life would be in danger in Iraq. His friends in Finland were able to talk him out of leaving Finland and Adil, in turn, managed to organise his mother to a safer place in Iraq. In 2018, after a three-year wait for a decision, Adil was granted asylum in Finland. Like Adil, the young men I met during my fieldwork were in constant contact with their parents and the well-being of their distant parents directly affected their own well-being.

My research on Afghan and Iraqi refugees demonstrates that adult sons and fathers do not abandon their families; on the contrary, they continue to provide various forms of care and provision across borders as fathers and adult sons. It also reveals the profound ways in which increasingly restrictive migration regimes mould family and caregiving practices in refugee families. The examples I have discussed all demonstrate the complexities of caring and parenting across borders and raise questions about what we mean by transnational care and family life.

What Is Transnational Care?

Researchers on transnational care have proposed the notion of 'care circulations' as a theoretical approach for studying care at the crossroads of family studies and migration (Baldassar and Merla 2014). Baldassar and Merla (2014, 25) define 'care circulation' as 'the reciprocal, multidirectional and asymmetrical exchange of care that fluctuates over the life course within transnational family networks subject to the political, economic, cultural and social contexts of both sending and receiving societies'. While care circulation is a useful concept in paying attention to potential changes across the life course and in emphasising the dyadic back-and-forth of care transactions as depending on the social contexts in both sending and receiving countries, it does seem to denote an idea of care as somewhat dis-embodied and free-flowing. Thus, even though researchers have emphasised the importance of the institutional context, state policies, and migration and asylum regimes in enabling or disabling transnational care and family relations across borders (Kilkey and

Merla 2014), I argue that the embodied, situated, and temporal nature of care warrants more attention. The case of Dawood, a young Afghan I met in Tehran, is an illustrative case of how the situated need for care shapes migratory mobilities.

Dawood, a young Afghan refugee in his twenties living irregularly with his family near Tehran, had made the dangerous journey from Iran to Turkey and across Europe to Sweden in 27 days in 2015. He had applied for asylum and started studying in Sweden. Although he had a chance of being granted asylum, he decided to 'deport himself, i.e., opt for voluntary return, 'due to problems in the family':

> I received a negative decision to my asylum application but I appealed. Sweden had passed a new piece of legislation, the 'high-school law' that allowed asylum seekers to get a temporary residence permit for their high-school studies. I had a good chance of getting asylum but I decided to return because my mother was very ill and there was a bad situation in the family. (Dawood's interview in Tehran, July, 2019)

For Dawood, the situated and temporal need for care of his mother could not wait for the long asylum process and he decided to return to respond to this need for care even though he had a chance of getting asylum in Sweden.

Transnational care is often defined so broadly that it encompasses everything from sending remittances to keeping in touch or even worrying about family members. In my fieldwork, my research participants were in constant contact with their family members through smartphones using text messages, instant messages, and calls through voice over Internet protocol (VOIP) in Finland, in Athens, in Istanbul, and even in Tehran—although there restrictions to Internet access had to be mediated by establishing vpn—(virtual private network) connections. Through various mobile devices, that Madianou and Miller (2013) call polymedia, refugees are able to stay in touch with their family members on a daily basis.

The regular contact can vary from phatic communication (Licoppe and Smoreda 2005)—which has the main function of keeping the communicative interaction 'open', where contact is more important than content—to care-related communication used for the organisation of practical care or for emotional support. Hence, not all staying in touch through ICTs is necessarily about transnational care. Can conflicts and fighting over Skype be considered as part of transnational care? During my fieldwork I heard of countless cases in which the partner in the country of origin was so tired of the separation and the state of limbo involved in the long waiting for the asylum decision and the possibility of family reunification that they refused to talk to their partners (Näre 2020b). The cases of Adil and Dawood demonstrate that care and worry are often inseparable. Both Dawood and Adil empathise so vividly with the sickness, troubles, and dangers their family members encounter that their own health is jeopardised and that they can even give up on their individual migration projects in order to return to care for their family members, as Dawood did.

The complexity of what counts as transnational care is also well exemplified by the case of remittances. Sending money back home is a universal practice of migrancy. Global remittances, including monetary transfers to low and high-income countries, reached a record high in 2018 when the amount of formal remittances reached $689 billion (World Bank 2019). In order to know whether these monetary flows relate to transnational care would require us to know what the money is used for. If it is used to sustain a migrant's family members, as in Yasin's case, we can easily speak of transnational care, but if remittances are used for business investments or for building a house to signal increased social status through successful migration, an almost universal practice of migrancy (Dalakoglou 2017; Näre 2012, 2013), it would be difficult to consider it transnational care. However, if an individual is sending money so that his or her members of kin can move from a rundown, unhealthy, or unsafe accommodation to a safer and healthier home, as was the case with Adil's mother, it is clear that accommodation can be considered an important dimension of transnational care, as also argued by Baldassar, Baldock, and Wilding (2006).

Thus, what constitutes transnational care cannot be discerned from the practice itself, but rather, whether it responds to a *situated need for care*. From here, we can move to define *transnational care as those activities that meet the physical, social, psychological and emotional needs and requirements of the individual and that take place cross nation-state borders*. Migration, gender regimes, and other structural conditions in the country of destination and the country of origin shape transnational care.

Needs for care are situational and temporal. They can vary even when individuals have the same condition and age, and they might vary for the same person at different times (Mol 2008). The need for care also calls for a response and creates a care relation (Tronto and Fisher 1990). We can think that failing to respond to the need for care is also a response (Hoppania et al. 2016). Following this definition, we can agree that remittances and organising accommodation can indeed be part of transnational care if such activities respond to a situated and individual need for care. Similarly, staying in touch with family or kin members can constitute transnational care if there is a need for emotional support or if communication meets a care need in that communication is used to organise care. The relationality of care allows for an investigation into potential ambivalences that might exist around transnational care.

Care can thus be understood as a process of practices accompanied by different skills and values (Tronto and Fisher 1990). From this definition, it is evident that care can come in various forms and it does not have to be limited to informal care provided by family members. Thus, this definition is broader than that in most research that focuses on transnational care as part of kin or family networks (Baldassar and Merla 2014; Madianou and Miller 2012). Although transnational care is commonly based on generalised asymmetrical, reciprocal exchange obligations that characterise families and kin networks (Baldassar and Merla 2014), caregiving does not need to be provided by members of kin or family. In fact, transnational care often involves various caregivers, including family and kin members but also foster parents, paid domestic and care workers as well as formal care workers in institutional care settings.

Migration hence can create new forms of kin relations that can be referred to as practices of kinning. Howell (2003, 465) defines kinning as processes through which biological non-kin, or any previously unconnected person, 'is brought into a significant and permanent relationship that is expressed in a kin idiom'. Kinning can thus be a useful concept to refer to the ways in which significant relations expressed by kin idiom are created and maintained in transnational migration contexts. Most of the Iraqi and Afghan asylum seekers I met in Helsinki had Finnish 'sisters', 'mothers', and/or 'brothers', i.e. Finnish friends who helped them with their asylum processes and finding accommodation or work. Yasin, for instance, had a Finnish brother who had organised work for him, with whom he was sharing a flat and who was helping him to apply for a work-based residence permit.

Migration of an individual with care responsibilities always demands that care has to be redistributed and reconfigured anew locally and across borders. This has been examined thoroughly in the literature on transnational child care since the pioneering work of Colen (1995), who was one of the first scholars to discuss the global hierarchies of reproduction or what she termed 'stratified reproduction' presented by the case of West Indian domestic workers in the USA. Later Parreñas (2001b) examined the case of Filipino domestic workers in the USA and Italy. Based on her work, Hochshild (2000) coined the notion of global care chains to exemplify how care is commodified globally, resonating with the concept of global commodity chains. Clearly, global care chains are not only created around child care, but exist around all forms of care, including elder care and nursing, as discussed by Yeates (2009a, b) and by researchers studying labour migrations for domestic and care work in Europe (e.g. Isaksen 2010; Isaksen and Näre 2019; Lutz 2008; Marchetti and Venturini 2014; Näre 2012; Wrede and Näre 2013).

From the perspective of the country of origin, the need for care does not disappear with the person who has previously provided care. The migration of a family or kin member usually signifies a redistribution and reorganisation of both child-care and elder-care responsibilities. Leinaweaver (2010) discusses how the practice of child fostering enables Peruvian migrants to ensure care for their children and company for their parents in a situation in which migration has left what she terms a *care slot* that needs to be filled. Increasingly, the care slot, especially in relation to care of ageing parents, is filled by institutionalised care in middle-income countries such as Ghana (Coe 2017) and India (Lamb 2009).

The institutionalisation of elder care in Ghana and India is a phenomenon partly driven by migration and remittances. Social remittances, i.e. values and cultural norms that are transmitted by migrants to their countries of origin, are transforming ideas about what constitutes culturally acceptable and valuable care (Levitt and Lamba-Nieves 2011). Economic remittances, on the other hand, contribute financially to the establishment of institutions for old-age care and enable migrants to pay for formal care. Migration thus transforms both care cultures as well as everyday practices of care in complex ways (Näre et al. 2017). While in the country of origin, the migration of an individual with care responsibilities results in a situation in which the situated need for care needs to be organised locally—the organisation that can take place also at a distance—in the country of migration, individuals strive to provide care across borders at a distance. I will next discuss the different ways in which transnational care can be practiced.

Practices of Transnational Care and ICT-Mediated Transnational Care

Important work by Baldassar, Baldock, and Wilding (2006) explored in detail Australia-based transnational families and their caregiving relationships. Their research indicates that transnational families provide the five types of care that Finch and Mason (1993) identified in proximate families: financial support (e.g. remittances), practical support (e.g. availability to assist with daily household activities), personal support (intimate or manual care), accommodation (shelter), and emotional or moral support. Baldassar et al. (2014) distinguish five dimensions of care—namely, financial and material (e.g. remittances or goods), practical (exchanging advice and assisting with tasks), personal (like feeding and bathing), accommodation (providing shelter and security), and emotional or moral support. Similarly, Kilkey and Merla (2014) present a typology of transnational care that includes direct provision with physical co-presence, coordination, delegation of support, and/or direct provision from a distance. Transnational caregiving is hence mainly provided through the coordination and delegation of direct provision and distanced support and through the use of information and communication technologies (ICTs), especially through regular contact via smartphones but also through other technological means such as surveillance cameras and electronic monitoring systems. Madianou and Miller's (2013) multi-sited ethnographic research on the role of polymedia in transnational families' daily lives, shows how the proliferation of communicative opportunities transforms the cross-border relationships, as 'they can make the absent other "tangible"' (Madianou and Miller 2012, 144). ICTs can allow for new forms of intimacy and 'co-presence' in transnational families (Baldassar et al. 2016; Nedelcu and Wyss 2016).

For instance, the research by Madianou (2016) on Filipina mothers examines how the use of polymedia, various ICTs, enables intensive mothering across nation-state borders. The visuality of Skype enables mothers to watch their children develop and prevents a situation in which children would no longer recognise their mothers upon return. Instant messaging is used by mothers and children to help with homework, while mothers can seek to micromanage their households through the use of social media. Being constantly online through smartphones enables mothers to create a peripheral awareness of life back home, or what Madianou terms 'ambient co-presence'. Similarly, Nedelcu and Wyss (2016) discuss various forms of polymedia interactions in Romanian families living in Switzerland, including ritual interaction, i.e. short regular communications; omnipresent interaction involving the creation of a shared virtual space of doing family and reinforced co-presence relating to the organisation of care for the elderly and being digitally present during emergency situations. Also, during important family rituals, such as weddings, smartphones allow for an online presence as a substitute for physical presence. Nedelcu and Wyss also argue that ICT-mediated routines of co-presence involve ambivalent effects and emotions ranging from positive well-being to feelings of constraint and guilt. These examples of existing research question the celebratory arguments according to which ICTs could radically transform our relationships and sociality by blurring presence and absence (Licoppe 2004).

Instead of ICT's transforming practices, existing forms of sociality and relationship rituals are adapted to the online space. In Tehran I attended a wedding party of an Afghan couple in which the bride was living with the groom's family in Tehran but the groom was living in Finland. Both families were truly transnational, extending to Australia, different European countries, and Canada. Those who could not attend the wedding because of lacking travel documents were able to participate in the event via smartphone calls. Those present in Tehran would call a family member abroad from the living room of the bride and her family where wedding preparations were taking place. The smartphones would then be passed around the room so that the non-present family member could not only congratulate the bride and groom and their families but also 'meet' those more distant family members who had arrived at the event. They could send their wedding gifts to the couple through those family members who had travelled to the wedding, as transferring money to Iran is impossible because of the economic sanctions. Hence, celebratory customs and rituals were reproduced online as closely as possible to traditional, offline practices, rather than being radically transformed by ICTs.

While for migrant parents the availability of ICTs can even justify the prolongation of absence, for left-behind children, ICT-mediated communication is a more ambivalent experience (Madianou and Miller 2011). While some left-behind children in Madianou's and Miller's (2011) research on Filipino transnational families felt that ICT-mediated communication could allow for more open expressions of emotions than face-to-face communication, for others meaningful relationships were difficult to maintain over ICT-mediated distance. Several factors are key here: whether family members had already been using mobile technologies before migrating, the age of the children at the time of migrating and the quality of the relationship prior to migrating are all important aspects that affect practices of transnational care. As discussed by Wilding (2006), virtual communication does not displace or eliminate the emotional effects of distance, on the contrary, the disjuncture between imagined co-presence and physical separation can in some cases enforce conflict. Also, in the refugee camp in Athens, Afghan fathers told me that smaller children often refused to speak with their mothers on the smartphone because seeing and hearing their mothers without being able to touch them was clearly too much to bear.

Thus, transnational care activities are 'processual and fluctuating' and mediated by time, distance, history (including available technologies), the migration stage, family life-cycle, and the more tenuous 'bonds of kinship' (Baldassar 2007, 294). Moreover, the use of ICTs depends on the possibilities and physical abilities to access technological devices that can be hampered by the digital divide (Benítez 2006), illness, or ageing. In the case of asylum seekers and refugees, using ICTs can have ambivalent consequences, deriving from the vulnerable position that they hold. Key conflicts and disjunctures that emerge from my research are caused by the discrepancies between family members who continue to live in conflict and war zones, and the refugees who continue to live these conflicts and dangers by being in contact with their family members.

Conclusions

Research on transnational families, care, and parenting has been important in challenging the methodological nationalism that continues to haunt the ways in which researchers and policymakers perceive the world and its inhabitants bounded by nation-state containers (Wimmer and Glick Schiller 2002). By emphasising the importance of family and kin relations, this research tradition has also challenged the individual-centred epistemology of mainstream migration research. Yet, a great deal of research continues to focus on one ethnic or migrant group. This overlooks the complexities that go beyond ethnic boundaries and transformations that change over the life course. Moreover, current and future research should aim to strike a balance between the celebration of cross-border activities and the continued significance and violence of current border and asylum regimes (Näre 2020a). Migration regimes and policies, gender regimes and other structural conditions both in the countries of origin and in host countries shape transnational care and parenting practices in profound ways. While ICTs enable migrant families to be in touch via smartphones on a regular basis, researchers should be wary of celebrating ICTs for solving problems of distance or radically transforming social practices and rituals. Moreover, for asylum seekers and refugees, using ICTs can have ambivalent consequences, deriving from the vulnerable position that they and their family members hold.

I have suggested that one important way forward is to start from a stricter notion of care as activities that respond to physical, social, psychological, and emotional needs and requirements of individuals. The need for care is individual and changing. Hence an activity that can satisfy an individual's need for care today might not be sufficient tomorrow due to sudden illness or the effects of ageing. To account for these transformations, research designs that would follow kin and family networks over time and across multiple spaces and locations would be much welcomed.

REFERENCES

Åkesson, Lisa, Jørgen Carling, and Heike Drotbohm. 2012. "Mobility, Moralities and Motherhood: Navigating the Contingencies of Cape Verdean Lives." *Journal of Ethnic and Migration Studies* 38 (2): 237–260.

Asis, Maruja M. B. 2006. "Living with Migration: Experiences of Left-Behind Children in the Philippines." *Asian Population Studies* 2 (1): 45–67.

Baldassar, Loretta. 2007. "Transnational Families and Aged Care: The Mobility of Care and the Migrancy of Ageing." *Journal of Ethnic and Migration Studies* 33 (2): 275–297.

Baldassar, Loretta, Cora Baldock, and Raelene Wilding. 2006. *Families Caring Across Borders: Migration, Ageing and Transnational Caregiving*. Houndmills: Palgrave Macmillan.

Baldassar, Loretta, Majella Kilkey, Laura Merla, and Raelene Wilding. 2014. "Transnational Families." In *The Wiley-Blackwell Companion to the Sociology of Families*, edited by Judith Treas, Jacqueline Scott and Martin Richards, 155–175. Hoboken, NJ: Wiley.

Baldassar, Loretta and Laura Merla. 2014. "Introduction: Transnational Family Caregiving Through the Lens of Circulation." In *Transnational Families, Migration and the Circulation of Care: Understanding Mobility and Absence in Family Life*, edited by Loretta Baldassar and Laura Merla, 3–24, New York: Routledge.

Baldassar, Loretta, Mihaela Nedelcu, Laura Merla, and Raelene Wilding. 2016. "ICT-based Co-presence in Transnational Families and Communities: Challenging the Premise of Face-to-face Proximity in Sustaining Relationships." *Global Networks* 16 (2): 133–144.

Benítez, Jose Luis. 2006. "Transnational Dimensions of the Digital Divide Among Salvadoran Immigrants in the Washington DC Metropolitan Area." *Global Networks* 6 (2): 181–199.

Boehm, Deborah A. 2008. "'For My Children': Constructing Family and Navigating the State in the US-Mexico Transnation." *Anthropological quarterly* 81 (4): 777–802.

Boehm, Deborah A. 2012. *Intimate Migrations: Gender, Family, and Illegality among Transnational Mexicans*. New York: NYU Press.

Bryceson, Deborah Fahy and Ulla Vuorela, eds. 2002. *The Transnational Family: New European Frontiers and Global Networks*. Oxford: Berg.

Chamberlain, Mary. 1999. "The Family as Model and Metaphor in Caribbean Migration to Britain." *Journal of Ethnic and Migration Studies* 25 (2): 251–266.

Coe, Cati. 2015. "The Temporality of Care: Gender, Migration, and the Entrainment of Life-courses." In *Anthropological Perspectives on Care. Work, Kinship, and the*

Life-Course, edited by Erdmute Alber and Heike Drotbohm, 181–205. New York: Palgrave Macmillan.

Coe, Cati. 2017. "Transnational Migration and the Commodification of Eldercare in Urban Ghana." *Identities* 24 (5): 542–556.

Colen, Shellee. 1995. "Like a Mother to Them: Stratified Reproduction and West Indian Childcare Workers and Employers in New York." In *Conceiving the New World Order*, edited by Faye D. Ginsburg and Rayna Rapp, 78–102. Berkeley: University of California Press.

Dalakoglou, Dimitri. 2017. *The Road: An Ethnography of (Im)Mobility, Space, and Cross-Border Infrastructures in the Balkans*. Manchester: Manchester University Press.

Datta, Kavita, Cathy McIlwaine, Joanna Herbert, Yara Evans, Jon May, and Jane Wills. 2009. "Men on the Move: Narratives of Migration and Work Among Low Paid Migrant Men in London." *Social and Cultural Geography* 10 (8): 853–873.

Dreby, Joanna 2006. "Honor and Virtue: Mexican Parenting in the Transnational Context." *Gender and Society* 20 (1): 32–59.

Erel, Umut. 2016. *Migrant Women Transforming Citizenship: Life-Stories from Britain and Germany*. London: Routledge.

Finch, Janet, and Jennifer Mason. 1993. *Negotiating Family Responsibilities*. London: Tavistock/Routledge.

Fresnoza-Flot, Asuncion. 2014. "Men's Caregiving Practices in Filipino Transnational Families." In *Transnational Families, Migration and the Circulation of Care. Understanding Mobility and Absence in Family Life*, edited by Loretta Baldassar and Laura Merla, 170–184. London: Routledge.

Glick Schiller, Nina, Linda Basch, and Cristina Szanton-Blanc. 1992. *Towards a Transnational Perspective on Migration*. New York: New York Academy of Sciences.

Glick Schiller, Nina, Linda Basch, and Cristina Szanton-Blanc. 1995. "From Immigrant to Transmigrant: Theorizing Transnational Migration." *Anthropological Quarterly* 68 (1): 48–63.

Goulbourne, Harry, Tracey Reynolds, John Solomos, and Elisabetta Zontini. 2010. *Transnational Families: Ethnicities, Identities and Social Capital*. London: Routledge.

Herrera, Gioconda. 2013. "Gender and International Migration: Contributions and Cross-fertilizations." *Annual Review of Sociology* 39: 471–489.

Hochschild, Arlie Russell. 2000. "Global Care Chains and Emotional Surplus Value." In *On the Edge. Living with Global Capitalism*, edited by Will Hutton and Anthony Giddens, 130–146. London: Jonathan Cape.

Hondagneu-Sotelo, Pierrette, and Ernestine Avila. 1997. "'I'm Here, But I'm There' the Meanings of Latina Transnational Motherhood." *Gender and Society* 11 (5): 548–571.

Hoppania, Hanna-Kaisa, Olli Karsio, Lena Näre, Antero Olakivi, Liina Sointu, Tiina Vaittinen, and Minna Zechner. 2016. *Hoivan arvoiset: Vaiva yhteiskunnan ytimessä* [Worthy of Care: Ailment in the Society]. Helsinki: Gaudeamus.

Horton, Sarah 2009. "A Mother's Heart Is Weighed Down with Stones: A Phenomenological Approach to the Experience of Transnational Motherhood." *Culture, Medicine and Psychiatry* 33 (1):21–40.

Howell, Signe. 2003. "Kinning: The Creation of Life Trajectories in Transnational Adoptive Families." *Journal of the Royal Anthropological Institute* 9 (3): 465–484.

IOM. 2020. "Missing Migrants. Tracking Deaths Along Migratory Routes." https://missingmigrants.iom.int/. Accessed 26 June 2020.

Isaksen, Lise, ed. 2010. *Global Care Work: Gender and Migration in Nordic Societies*. Oslo: Nordic Academic Press.

Isaksen, Lise, and Lena Näre. 2019. "Local Loops and Micro-mobilities of Care: Rethinking Care in Egalitarian Contexts." *Journal of European Social Policy* 29 (5): 593–599.

Kasparek, Bernd, and Marc Speer. 2015. "Of Hope. Hungary and the Long Summer of Migration." *Bordermonitoring.eu*. September 9, 2015. http://bordermonitoring.eu/ungarn/2015/09/ofhope-en/.

Kilkey, Marjella, and Laura Merla. 2014. "Situating Transnational Families' Caregiving Arrangements: The Role of Institutional Contexts." *Global Networks* 14 (2): 210–229.

King, Russell, Eralba Cela, Tine Fokkema, and Julie Vullnetari. 2014. "The Migration and Well-being of the Zero Generation: Transgenerational Care, Grandparenting, and Loneliness amongst Albanian Older People." *Population, Space and Place* 20 (8): 728–738.

Kofman, Eleonore. 2013. "Gendered Labour Migrations in Europe and Emblematic Migratory Figures." *Journal of Ethnic and Migration Studies* 39 (4): 579–600.

Lamb, Sarah E. 2009. *Aging and the Indian Diaspora: Cosmopolitan Families in India and Abroad*. Bloomington: Indiana University Press.

Leinaweaver, Jessaca B. 2010. "Outsourcing Care: How Peruvian Migrants Meet Transnational Family Obligations." *Latin American Perspectives* 37 (5): 67–87.

Levitt, Peggy, and Deepak Lamba-Nieves. 2011. "Social Remittances Revisited." *Journal of Ethnic and Migration Studies* 37 (1): 1–22.

Licoppe, Christian. 2004. "'Connected' Presence: The Emergence of a New Repertoire for Managing Social Relationships in a Changing Communication Technoscape." *Environment and Planning D: Society and Space* 22 (1): 135–156.

Licoppe, Christian, and Zbigniew Smoreda. 2005. "Are Social Networks Technologically Embedded?" *Social Networks* 27 (4): 317–335.

Lutz, Helma, ed. 2008. *Migration and Domestic Work. A European Perspective on a Global Theme*. London: Routledge.

Lutz, Helma. 2011. *The New Maids: Transnational Women and the Care Economy*. London: Zed Books.

Madianou, Mirca. 2016. "Ambient Co-Presence: Transnational Family Practices in Polymedia Environments." *Global Networks* 16 (2): 183–201.

Madianou, Mirca, and Daniel Miller. 2012. *Migration and New Media: Transnational Families and Polymedia*. London: Routledge.

Madianou, Mirca, and Daniel Miller. 2011. "Mobile Phone Parenting: Reconfiguring Relationships Between Filipina Migrant Mothers and Their Left-Behind Children." *New Media and Society* 13 (3): 457–470.

Madianou, Mirca, and Daniel Miller. 2013. "Polymedia: Towards a New Theory of Digital Media in Interpersonal Communication." *International Journal of Cultural Studies* 16 (2): 169–187.

Marchetti, Sabrina, and Alessandra Venturini. 2014. "Mothers and Grandmothers on the Move: Labour Mobility and the Household Strategies of Moldovan and Ukrainian Migrant Women in Italy." *International Migration* 52 (5): 111–126.

Marchetti-Mercer, Maria C. 2012. "Those Easily Forgotten: The Impact of Emigration on Those Left Behind." *Family Process* 51 (3): 376–390.

Mazzucato, Valentina, and Djamila Schans. 2011. "Transnational Families and the Well-Being of Children: Conceptual and Methodological Challenges." *Journal of Marriage and Family* 72 (3): 704–712.

Mol, Annemarie. 2008. *The Logic of Care: Health and the Problem of Patient Choice.* London: Routledge.

Morgan, David. 2011. *Rethinking Family Practices.* Houndsmills, Basingstoke: Palgrave Macmillan.

Näre, Lena. 2012. *Moral Economies of Reproductive Labour. An Ethnography of Migrant Domestic and Care Labour in Naples, Italy.* Helsinki: University of Helsinki Press.

Näre, Lena. 2013. "Migrancy, Gender and Social Class in Domestic and Social Care Labour in Italy—An Intersectional Analysis of Demand." *Journal of Ethnic and Migration Studies* 39 (4): 601–623.

Näre, Lena. 2020a. "'Finland Kills with a Pen'—Asylum Seekers' Protest Against Bureaucratic Violence as Politics of Human Rights." *Citizenship Studies* 24 (8): 979–993.

Näre, Lena. 2020b. "Family Lives on Hold: Bureaucratic Bordering in Male Refugees' Struggle for Transnational Care." *Journal of Family Research*. https://doi.org/10.20377/jfr-353.

Näre Lena, Katie Walsh, and Loretta Baldassar. 2017. "Ageing in Transnational Contexts: Transforming Everyday Practices and Identities in Later Life." *Identities* 24 (5): 515–523.

Nedelcu, Mihaela, and Malika Wyss. 2016. "'Doing Family' through ICT-mediated Ordinary Co-presence: Transnational Communication Practices of Romanian Migrants in Switzerland." *Global Networks* 16 (2): 202–218.

Nobles, Jenna. 2011. "Parenting from Abroad: Migration, Nonresident Father Involvement, and Children's Education in Mexico." *Journal of Marriage and Family* 73 (4): 729–746.

OECD. 2019. *International Migration Outlook 2019.* Paris: OECD Publishing.

Parreñas, Rhacel Salazar. 2001a. "Mothering from a Distance: Emotions, Gender, and Intergenerational Relations in Filipino Transnational Families." *Feminist Studies* 27(2): 361–390.

Parreñas, Rhacel Salazar. 2001b. *Servants of Globalization: Women, Migration and Domestic Work.* Stanford, CA: Stanford University Press.

Parreñas, Rhacel Salazar. 2005. *Children of Global Migration: Transnational Families and Gendered Woes.* Stanford, CA: Stanford University Press.

Parreñas, Rhacel Salazar. 2008. "Transnational Fathering: Gendered Conflicts, Distant Disciplining and Emotional Gaps." *Journal of Ethnic and Migration Studies* 34 (7): 1057–1072.

Pingol, Alicia. 2001. *Remaking Masculinities: Identity, Power, and Gender Dynamics in Families with Migrant Wives and Househusbands.* Quezon City: University Center for Women's Studies.

Sheller, Mimi, and John Urry. 2006. "The New Mobilities Paradigm." *Environment and planning A* 38(2): 207–226.

Skrbiš, Zlatko. 2008. "Transnational Families: Theorising Migration, Emotions and Belonging." *Journal of Intercultural studies* 29 (3): 231–246.

Sørensen, Ninna Nyberg, and Ida Marie Vammen. 2014. "Who Cares? Transnational Families in Debates on Migration and Development." *New Diversities* 16 (2): 89–108.

Suárez-Orozco, Cerola, Irina LG Todorova and Josephine Louie. 2002. "Making up for Lost Time: The Experience of Separation and Reunification Among Immigrant Families." *Family process* 41 (4): 625–643.

Tronto, Joan C., and Berenice Fisher. 1990. "Toward a Feminist Theory of Caring." In *Circles of Care: Work and Identity in Women's Lives*, edited by Emily K. Abel and Margaret K. Nelson, 35–62: Albany, NY: SUNY Press.

Walsh, Katie, and Lena Näre, eds. 2016. *Transnational Migration and Home in Older Age*. London: Routledge.

Wilding, Raelene. 2006. "'Virtual' Intimacies? Families Communicating Across Transnational Contexts." *Global networks* 6 (2): 125–142.

Wimmer, Andreas, and Nina Glick Schiller. 2002. "Methodological Nationalism and Beyond: Nation–state Building, Migration and the Social Sciences." *Global Networks* 2 (4): 301–334.

World Bank 2019. "Migration and Remittances. Recent Developments and Outlook." Migration and development brief 31. https://www.knomad.org/publication/migration-and-development-brief-31. Accessed 26 June 2020.

Wrede, Sirpa, and Lena Näre. 2013. "Glocalising Care in the Nordic Countries." *Nordic Journal of Migration Research* 3 (2): 57–62.

Yeates, Nicola. 2009a. *Globalizing Care Economies and Migrant Workers: Explorations in Global Care Chains*. Houndsmills, Basingstoke: Palgrave Macmillan.

Yeates, Nicola. 2009b. *Globalizing Care Economies and Migrant Workers: Explorations in Global Care Chains*. Houndsmills, Basingstoke: Palgrave Macmillan.

Zontini, Elisabetta. 2004. "Immigrant Women in Barcelona: Coping with the Consequences of Transnational Lives." *Journal of Ethnic and Migration Studies* 30 (6): 1113–1144.

Zontini, Elisabetta. 2010. *Transnational Families, Migration and Gender: Moroccan and Filipino Women in Bologna and Barcelona*. Oxford: Berghahn Books.

PART VI

Family Trajectories: (Un)Linking Lives Over Time and Place

Edited by Jacques-Antoine Gauthier and Rita Gouveia

CHAPTER 28

The Contribution of the Life-Course Perspective to the Study of Family Relationships: Advances, Challenges, and Limitations

Gaëlle Aeby and Jacques-Antoine Gauthier

INTRODUCTION

Changes in family roles over time have long been studied with explanatory models based on a developmental view of the family, stemming from the early contributions of Havighurst (1949) and the more integrative work of Hill and his colleagues (Hill and Rodgers 1964). One of the most prominent developmental models is the *family life cycle* (FLC), which centres on the presence and age of children in the household. From a systemic perspective, it postulates a normal, ordered, and quasi-universal pathway through various family roles, each corresponding to a specific functional prerequisite associated with a developmental task (Aldous 1996). The FLC model has undisputed conceptual and heuristic strengths but is not without limitations, especially regarding empirical utility, due to operationalisation issues (Nock 1979; Spanier et al. 1979). First, the long-term popularity of family developmental models is partly explained by its broadened and efficient use in psycho- and family therapy (Rice 1994). Second, according to Smith (1993), the FLC model implicitly reflects the strong historical structuring process converging

---

G. Aeby (✉)
Institute of Sociological Research, Swiss National Centre of Competence in Research LIVES, University of Geneva, Geneva, Switzerland
e-mail: gaelle.aeby@unige.ch

J.-A. Gauthier
Life Course and Inequality Research Centre, Swiss National Centre of Competence in Research LIVES, University of Lausanne, Lausanne, Switzerland
e-mail: Jacques-Antoine.Gauthier@unil.ch

in the 1950s towards an idealised historical representation of "the" Western family, described, for instance, in the research of Parsons and Bales (1955) on role complementarity. Third, despite the many attempts to adapt such developmental models to family disruption and recomposition in particular, they have been criticised for their static nature and their inability to deal adequately with the increasing complexity of household structures starting in the late 1950s (Bengtson and Allen 1993). In this perspective, the spread of singlehood, childlessness, divorce, and remarriage progressively challenged the idea of a hierarchical quasi-universal order of family stages associated with fixed functional prerequisites (Widmer and Gauthier 2013). This was evidenced by Laszloffy (2002), for instance, who showed that the variance of age at each family transition is increasing, which indicates a progressive deviation from the FLC model over the course of life. Finally, the fact that the FLC model centres on household composition rather than on inter-individual relationships (Widmer 2010) contradicts the postulate of Burgess and Locke (1960), according to which the family should not be defined by a legal conception or a formal contract but always by the interactions between its members, independently of their co-residential setting.

In this context, the life-course perspective has brought new conceptual and methodological developments to account for changes over time, by doing so, it offers a rich source of inquiries for the sociology of family. In their seminal work *The life-course perspective Applied to Families over Time* published in 1993, Bengtson and Allen traced the interdisciplinary history of the life-course perspective as relevant to family research, starting at the beginning of the twentieth century, and concluded that the life-course perspective is a new, promising paradigm that "offers the missing conceptual links of 'lineage' and 'generational time' to analyses of family behavior"(1993, 479). This chapter starts with the formal conceptualisation of the life-course perspective in the 1960s. We present its key principles and dimensions, as applied to family research, and a method of empirically operationalising family trajectories. In the second part, we tackle three topics of interest for the sociology of family: the diversity of family forms, gender roles, and family configurations. In conclusion, we return to the global contributions of the life-course perspective to the study of changes in family relationships over time and its application to other significant relationships outside the family.

The Emergence and Expansion of the Life-course Perspective

The life-course perspective emerged in the second half of the twentieth century and crystallised during the 1960s (Lalive d'Epinay et al. 2005; Marshall and Mueller 2003). It is inherently interdisciplinary (Mortimer and Shanahan 2003; Levy et al. 2005) because it stands at the crossroads of life histories, longitudinal studies, historical demography, psychology and sociology of ageing (Giele and Elder 1998), which allows one to apprehend individual trajectories as resulting from macro-, meso-, and micro-levels determinants. The life-course perspective has progressively reached high formalisation through the systematic formulation of an integrative definition and key principles (Elder 1985, 1994, Elder et al. 2003). Elder and his colleagues proposed the following definition of the life-course: "as consisting of age-graded patterns that are embedded in social institutions and history. This view is grounded in a contextualist perspective and emphasises the implications of social pathways in historical time and place for human development and ageing" (Elder et al. 2003, 4). According to them, five principles are at the core of the life-course perspective: linked lives, timing, time and place, life span development, and agency. *Linked lives* stresses that individual lives are interdependent and mutually constructed over time. *Timing* refers to the fact that individuals are influenced by biographical or personal time and can be used to differentiate the meaning and effects of events according to the moment when they occur in one's lifetime. *Time and place* indicates that the socio-historical context as well as the cultural and economic environment helps to give sense to the events experienced by individuals. *Life-span development* supports the idea that a life course is an ongoing process from birth to death, shaped by both cumulative and compensatory effects. *Agency* highlights individuals' ability to make choices within a web of constraints and opportunities. Taken together, these five principles allow one to apprehend the multidimensionality of contemporary life courses.

Applied to the sociology of family, these five principles contribute to highlighting different family processes unfolding over time. *Linked lives* reveals that family members provide reciprocal, synchronic influences, such as in a couple's family trajectories when one spouse has to follow the other abroad for a job opportunity, but also diachronic influences, such as when a parental divorce influences children's later conjugal behaviours (Diekmann and Engelhardt 1999; Wolfinger 2005). *Timing* points out, for instance, that parental divorce does not have the same impacts on young versus adult children. Similarly, the conditions for the transition to parenthood will vary significantly if it is experienced at age 22 versus age 42, as age is notably associated with resource availability (Hofferth and Goldscheider 2010). Regarding *time and place*, for instance, marriage—once a sacred heterosexual institution—is becoming more inclusive of same-sex couples in many Western societies (Paternotte and Kollman 2013). Similarly, the context and dynamics of residential (im)mobility from one cohort to another helps to explain couple and family formation and dissolution (Falkingham et al. 2016). *Lifespan development* illustrates the fact that family trajectories are not fully predictable but are continuously influenced by internal and external forces, which may accumulate and/or compensate for existing social (dis)advantages (Dannefer 2003). For instance, a painful divorce may be followed by a stable union and then a second separation (Zartler et al. 2015), or a loner may enter a conjugal relationship at a later age (Ammar et al. 2014). Finally, the use of the word "childfree" instead of "childless" by people who express their willingness to embrace life outside child-rearing is a striking example of an emphasis being put on *agency* rather than on social norms.

More recently, in the context of the expansion of life-course research to a variety of disciplines, Bernardi, Huinink, and Settersten (2019) proposed a new systematised approach to life-course theory by developing a tool for studying lives—the *life-course cube*—to provide a common conceptual foundation across disciplines. This *life-course cube* graphically defines and illustrates three axes of interdependencies (time, domains, and levels) and their multiple interactions, which characterise the dynamics of individual life courses. For these authors, the life course can be conceptualised as a multidimensional behavioural process characterised by interdependencies across time, life domains and three levels of analysis (inner-individual, individual, and supra-individual). Interdependence between life domains means, for instance, that individuals' goals, resources, and behaviours in their family are interrelated with goals, resources, and behaviours in work or leisure.

The Life Course: Key Dimensions

Life-course sociologists have stressed the importance of considering individual lives as comprehensive wholes made up of interdependent sequences of social participation (Levy 2013). Indeed, individuals hold statuses and roles related to their social participation in different life domains (Bernardi et al. 2019) or social *fields*. According to Levy (2013), the notion of field combines three dimensions: participation, position, and role. Participation in a field and holding a position go together with enacting the corresponding roles to handle the related rights and duties. At each moment of their lives, individuals are simultaneously active in several social fields and therefore hold several statuses and roles, which define the profile of their social participation at that time. A woman may be a mother to her children, a daughter to her own mother, a teacher in her occupation, and the treasurer of the neighbourhood association. Throughout their life course, individuals' statuses and roles are subject to change in accordance with experienced transitions and events (Sapin et al. 2007). For instance, the woman we just mentioned may become a grandmother, retired, widowed, president of the association, and so on. In this perspective, an individual's life course can be defined as a chronological sequence of participation profiles (Levy 2013). This definition accounts for micro-, meso- and macro-levels of participation since social fields are components of larger social structures such as welfare states.

Abbott (1992, 2001) suggested expressing life courses as what he calls *narratives*, characterised by three properties—enchainment, order, and convergence—that make it possible to elaborate processual (diachronic) rather than causal (often synchronic) explanations. According to Levy and colleagues (2005), most sequential processes may be formally described using four formal aspects: trajectory, stage, event, and transition. The *trajectory* may be seen as a "model of stability and long term change" (George 1993) corresponding to the sequence of participation profiles (Levy 2013) described above. It is used to describe the movements or developments occurring throughout the whole or a significant part of the life course. *Stage* points to a life period of relative structural or functional stability (e.g. family life stages or Eriksson's (1950) stages of psychosocial development). An *event* is something that happens at a given time in a specific place and is meaningful for the individuals concerned. Events can be normative (birth, marriage) or non-normative (divorce, death of a child) and are often associated with a transition. A *transition* describes the changes in one's role structure when passing from one life stage to another, such as those associated with the transition to parenthood. These four concepts are useful to describe the structure of many sequential processes in family life.

Operationalising the Life-Course and Creating a Family Trajectory Typology

Using a life-course perspective to study family relationships can rely on both quantitative and qualitative approaches or an integrated mixed-methods approach (Giele and Elder 1998). For instance, qualitative research encompasses biographies, personal narratives, and life stories collected through interviews or archives. In this chapter, we mainly focus on contributions stemming from quantitative research. Capturing the life-courses dimensions described above at an individual level without aggregating the longitudinal level is a challenge that only a few methods can meet. Historically, survival analysis, or event history analysis, is the foremost method of studying the occurrence of particular events over time (Viry and Gauthier 2019). Survival analysis is based on only two temporal benchmarks and describes the probability of an event, based on another event or time point. For instance, it may estimate the age at first marriage given the age when one leaves his or her parental home. This method is therefore not necessarily adequate for capturing the fluctuations of family life in contemporary societies.

In contrast, sequence analysis allows a longitudinal perspective to be adopted that considers individual variations over time in one or more life domains or social fields (Blanchard et al. 2014; Gauthier 2013). By considering the life course as a chronological sequence of participation profiles (Levy 2013), one can build a life trajectory based on the series of *statuses* an individual holds in one or several social field(s) over time. Choosing a meaningful number of statuses representing the *universum* of that field has theoretical and methodological implications. For instance, when modelling family trajectories, one can distinguish between living in a one-parent versus a two-parent household, with or without considering the presence of siblings in the household. Depending on the research question (e.g., types of family structures or sibling relationships), the definition of the *universum* will differ and may logically influence the results.

When modelling data through this approach, individual life courses can be systematically compared and grouped by (dis)similarity, producing an empirical typology. The main idea of sequence comparison is to univocally quantify the differences between two sequences (Gabadinho et al. 2011; Kruskal 1983; Levenshtein 1966). The results of the sequence analysis are a matrix of distances, on which cluster analysis can be performed to determine the best number of groups for a typology of trajectories (Gauthier 2013). Creating typologies of life trajectories is an efficient and revealing way to capture the diversity of individual lives, as summarised in a few meaningful patterns. It is also possible to study two kinds of life trajectories simultaneously, such as family and occupation (Gauthier et al. 2010).

The following empirical example of a typology of family trajectories comes from the international survey *Life Trajectories and Social Networks*, conducted in three countries (Portugal, Switzerland, and Lithuania) (Wall et al. 2018). This typology is based on co-residence changes over the 20-year period preceding the date of the interviews (1990–2010) for people born between 1950–1955 and 1970–1975 (n = 2852). Nine types of family trajectories were uncovered and named according to their main trend, either a lasting stage or a key transition: *parenthood* (35%), *transition to parenthood* (16%), *transition to empty nest* (11%), *conjugality* (10%), *solo* (8%), *leaving one's parental home* (8%), *transition to lone parenthood* (5%), *alternatives* (4%), and *nesting one parent* (3%) (Gauthier et al. 2018). In Fig. 28.1, we present the two first most common types. Each line represents an individual, and the colour of the line indicates which of the ten possible statuses he or she holds at a given time. The *parenthood* type shows a long stage of family life characterised by living with one's partner and children. The *transition to parenthood* type shows a first stage spent in a parental home, followed by a stage of family life after a short transition period of mainly living solo or with a partner. Despite clear

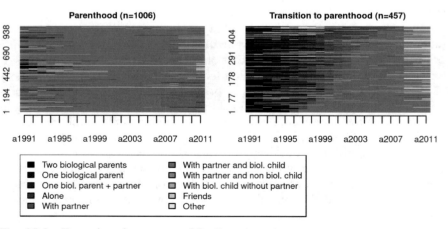

Fig. 28.1 Examples of two types of family trajectories

inter-individual differences, principally in terms of timing and sequencing, the heuristic value of both types is clearly identifiable. Once created, the resulting typology may be used as a categorical variable in any kind of quantitative and qualitative analysis. For instance, results have shown that the *parenthood* type was the most frequent family trajectory in all three countries and that it was more representative of individuals of the 1950–1955 birth cohort, while the *transition to parenthood* type was more representative of individuals of the 1970–1975 birth cohort.

Note that sequence-analysis techniques are constantly developing as well as enriching life-course research (Aisenbrey and Fasang 2010; Blanchard et al. 2014; Gabadinho et al. 2011). In summary, in contrast to developmental models such as the FLC presented in the introduction, the life-course perspective relies on a set of principles and formal concepts that increase the flexibility in how human lives may be modelled, particularly by accounting for variation and back-and-forth movements between stages. Moreover, it can identify personal life course accidents concisely without theoretical preconceptions concerning the data structure. After this brief overview of some of life-course perspective's theoretical and methodological advances, we will show in greater detail the life-course perspective's contributions to the study of family by addressing some of the current debates concerning family relationships.

Understanding Diversity in Family Forms: Standardisation and Individualisation Processes of the Life Course

In the sociology of family, the prevalent model had long been the so-called nuclear family, based on early, uninterrupted heterosexual marriage, with children in a common household (Parsons and Bales 1955). The last quarter of the twentieth century has featured increases in non-marital unions (cohabitation) preceding or replacing marriage, childbirth outside wedlock, the rise of divorce, the (partial) opening-up of marriage to same-sex couples, and the development of assisted reproductive technologies (Amato 2010; Cherlin 2009). This has led to a diversity of more or less institutionalised alternative family forms, such as one-parent families, stepfamilies, same-sex families, and together but living apart families (Sweeney 2010). This greater diversity has been explained by an individualisation process, according to which individuals are gaining greater control over their lives and pursuing self-realisation goals (Beck and Beck-Gernsheim 1995; Giddens 1992). The life-course perspective provides an insightful framework with which to apprehend how those major transformations create new family forms over time with the concepts of *institutionalisation* and *(de-)standardisation*.

The institutionalisation of life courses refers to the processes by which human lives are socially and temporally organised and framed by welfare state institutions through normative, legal, and organisational rules (Brückner and

Mayer 2005). The seminal article of Kohli (1989) on life-course institutionalisation reveals the existence of a standardisation process for the occupational life course, which ended up having three distinct and integrated phases in the 1960s: education, paid work, and retirement. The standardisation of life courses refers to an increasing universality of life events, transitions, and phases and their sequencing as well as the increasing uniformity of their timing for given populations (Brückner and Mayer 2005, 32). Thus, the progressive institutionalisation of the life course has contributed to standardising human lives. A straightforward example is compulsory education, which is institutionally organised and leads to this period of life being standardised for all children and for their family members who also have to adapt their routines to the school schedule. For family trajectories, this translated into a standardised sequence of transitions (e.g., departure from the parental home coinciding with marriage and rapidly being followed by the arrival of children) and a standardised timing of the transitions (e.g., low variation in the age at marriage and first child). While the very beginning of the standardisation process itself can be traced back to the late eighteenth century, the high point of the life course's standardisation and the emergence of distinct life phases happened during the "Glorious Thirty" in the second half of the twentieth century, a period of political stability and economic growth in many (but not all) of the Western countries. Hence, Mayer (2001) stresses that the peak of standardisation corresponds to a fairly short and exceptional historical period.

Indeed, around the 1960s, some scholars observed an "increasing de-standardisation across the lifetime and increasing differentiation and heterogeneity across the population" (Mayer 2001, 7; Kohli 2007; Levy and Widmer 2013). In this context, some life phases or events either are experienced by a smaller part of given populations or occur at more dispersed ages and with uneven durations (Brückner and Mayer 2005). For instance, the age at departure from one's parental home among young adults in Europe is becoming more flexible through the de-synchronisation and reversibility of transitions (e.g. return to the parental home) (Buchmann and Kriesi 2011). This perspective also implies that fewer contextual influences are at play and that people would be freer to choose how they want to "navigate" between positions and therefore to build their "own" trajectories. Despite the passionate debates, empirical evidence supporting the de-standardisation hypothesis is lacking (Brückner and Mayer 2005).

Looking simultaneously at family and occupational trajectories, several studies conducted in Switzerland investigated the extent to which individuals' life courses can be described in terms of standardisation or individualisation (Aeby et al. 2019; Levy and Widmer 2013; Widmer and Gauthier 2013). The majority of men's trajectories proved to be quite standardised, as most of them followed full-time occupational trajectories, while family formation and development did not alter their career. The presence of a prevailing pattern for men confirms the existence of a standardisation process leading to generalised transitions following similar timings. In that regard, women's occupational trajectories were found to be less standardised because there was more diversity among them, mainly explained by family events such as marriage and parenthood. This further indicates the existence of two gendered life-course models: standardisation for men and limited pluralisation for women. Finally, some non-standardised men's trajectories existed that were difficult to encompass in specific patterns, indicating that the individualisation thesis also had some validity. The prevalence of those different models varies among countries, as the next section will show.

Understanding Family Roles: Institutional Gendering of the Life Course

The sociology of family has paid significant attention to family roles, the unequal division of domestic work among men and women, and the "work–family conflict" resulting from difficulties in reconciling work and family duties (Grönlund and Öun 2010). The concept of "master status" postulates that an institutional and normative framing of gender relationships exists in the division of paid work and family, with men being assigned the former as a priority and women being led to prioritise the latter (Krüger and Levy 2001). Consequently, although most women participate in paid work to some extent, in terms of structuring power, this participation does not significantly contribute to their identity formation. This division is institutionally crystallised in the "complementary" model of a male breadwinner and a female home carer and caregiver.

How life courses are institutionally structured vary from one political state to another. An in-depth study of social policies should allow a better understanding of how life courses are apprehended in a given society. The relationships among the state, the market, and the family are key elements in building ideal types of welfare states (Esping-Andersen 1990; Arts and Gelissen 2002), such as the *liberal, conservative, social-democratic, Mediterranean*, and *post-communist*. Each type of welfare state has specific ways of connecting different life phases (e.g. education and employment) and of filling the unexpected "holes" in the individual trajectories (e.g. accidents, disease, unemployment, or maternity) through social and family policies (Korpi and Palme 1998; Levy 2013). Following their types and modalities of application, these particular policies have differing influences on the individual life course (Mayer and Schoepflin 1989; Mayer 2001). Generalising such observations, the life-course perspective sheds light on how the so-called life course *regimes* regulate gender inequalities in individuals' family trajectories, and it explains how gender identities are institutionally shaped from birth to old age (Möhring 2016).

A good example is the diversity of maternity leave arrangements across Europe. They reflect different family norms and have strong impacts on the experience of motherhood and fatherhood in individual life courses (Wall and

Escobedo 2009). Another example is women's integration into the employment market and the institutional forces at play in the gendered attributions of the roles related to family and paid work. Overall, women's increased participation in the educational system and in the labour force has led to a relative homogenisation of women's and men's life courses (Brückner and Mayer 2005), but in many European countries, part-time employment is mainly left to women. The life-course perspective proposes a triple-institutional mechanism of sequential, simultaneous, and adjacent institutionalisations (Krüger and Levy 2001). First, sequential institutionalisation—which encompasses educational and vocational training processes—prepares the futures of girls and boys in a differentiated way. The latter are expected to enter occupations conceived as uninterrupted full-time activities, whereas the former are prepared for jobs that one can more easily stop, interrupt, or practice on a part-time basis and, hence, to anticipate a "home carer career" with low transition costs (Guilley et al. 2019). Second, simultaneous institutionalisation refers to the quasi-obligation to take part in, at least for some time, the two fields of participation: paid work and the family. Third, adjacent institutionalisation is the constraints exerted by the institutional environment (school, administration, stores, etc.), the schedules of which are loosely or not at all compatible for dual-earner parents with a full-time occupational activity. Thus, simultaneous institutionalisation uses women's greater availability—supported by sequential institutionalisation—to socialise them as spouses, mothers, and housewives, whereas adjacent institutionalisation contributes to maintaining them in this situation (Krüger and Levy 2001). This mechanism is particularly salient in *conservative* regimes such as Germany, Austria, and Switzerland (*liberal-conservative*), which are characterised by strongly gendered pathways and strong institutional school-to-work transitions, and are less visible in the *social-democratic* regimes prevalent in Scandinavian countries.

Understanding Family Configurations and Beyond: The Interplay Between Family Stages and Transitions

The sociology of family has extensively investigated family relationships, paying special attention to parent–child relationships, intergenerational solidarity, and spousal support (Bonvalet and Ogg 2007). The configurational perspective, when applied to families, suggests starting with individuals' own subjective family definition rather than focusing on genetic ties, legal definitions, or household structures (Widmer 2010). The unfolding of life trajectories and the development of family configurations are dynamic and intertwined processes. The boundaries of a family configuration change with events and transitions occurring in the life course (Antonucci et al. 2010; Bidart et al. 2011; McDonald and Mair 2010; Pahl and Pevalin 2005). While some transitions, such as becoming a parent, may put the focus on the family of procreation (partners and children), other transitions, such as leaving the parental nest, may represent a shift away from the family of orientation (parents and siblings). This indicates that the development of relationships depends on individuals' changing statuses and roles or, in other words, on the sequence of their participation profiles (Levy 2013). Nevertheless, the duration of specific life stages is also an important dimension in creating strong ties (Granovetter 1973), along with the timing of the transitions leading to them (Aeby et al. 2019). For instance, individuals with an earlier transition to parenthood who have spent more time in a stage of family life (living with a partner and children) are more family-focused in their relationships (Aeby et al. 2019). Thus, family trajectories, such as those characterised by the experience of growing up in a one- or two-parent household, leaving the parental nest early or late, cohabiting with a partner, living alone, becoming a parent, divorcing, etc., will differentially influence the development of one's relationships and the composition of one's family configurations. Moreover, as family relationships evolve throughout the life course, the strength and quality of the ties between different family members may vary depending on previous life events and transitions associated with different statuses and roles.

Interest in significant relationships further led to a more inclusive approach going beyond family boundaries to include all significant relationships in an individual's personal life (Smart 2010). Some authors state that a suffusion process exists between friendship and family roles (Wall and Gouveia 2014; Pahl and Spencer 2004), while others believe that different principles still sustain them (Allan 2008). In the previously mentioned *Life Trajectories and Social Networks* survey across three types of welfare states (Portugal/*Mediterranean*, Switzerland/*liberal-conservative*, and Lithuania/*post-communist*) (Wall et al. 2018), significant differences were found regarding the share of kin and non-kin in personal networks. About 83% of Lithuanian respondents included only kin ties in their networks, followed by Portugal (65%), and Switzerland (46%), where mixed networks were more frequent due to higher proportions of friendship ties (Aeby et al. 2018). In addition to different friendship and family cultural norms, the different types of family trajectories across the transition to adulthood provided complementary explanations. Indeed, the greater diversity of personal networks was accounted for by trajectories deviating from the most common type of trajectory, characterised by a transition to parenthood followed by a long stage spent in a household composed of a couple with children (Aeby et al. 2017; Wall et al. 2018). In this debate on the prevalence of family solidarity, the life-course perspective can offer a dynamic view by highlighting, for instance, that the shares of kin and non-kin in personal networks can vary over time depending on the past sequence of participation profiles and on other key life course dimensions.

CONCLUSION

The life-course perspective suggests new and innovative ways to look at individuals and their family life within societies. The use of a common terminology (Elder 1985, 1994; Elder et al. 2003) and the development of longitudinal studies and associated methodologies (Aisenbrey and Fasang 2010; Blanchard et al. 2014; Gabadinho et al. 2011; Gauthier et al. 2010) have proved especially fruitful for creating theoretical linkages between neighbouring disciplines and for bringing social, biographical, and subjective dimensions closer together. When applied to family research, the life-course perspective has put a renewed focus on family relationships over time.

In this chapter, we specifically discussed the contributions of the life-course perspective to existing developmental models such as the FLC and to three long-standing topics of interest for the sociology of family: the diversity of family forms, gender roles, and family configurations. We introduced different concepts stemming from the life-course perspective, such as the institutionalisation and (de-)standardisation of the life course (Kohli 1989, 2007; Mayer 2001; Brückner and Mayer 2005), life-course regimes (Mayer 2001; Möhring 2016), and participation profiles (Levy 2013). For instance, we highlighted the persistent gendering of the occupational trajectories associated with family transitions and events at the micro-level (Levy and Widmer 2013) and the emergence of new family forms at the macro-level. Thinking in terms of life course also means considering the unfolding of human lives within a global socio-historical context, characterised by a specific (welfare) state organisation and cultural norms that significantly frame life trajectories.

The sociology of family has always paid attention to other life domains interacting with family life, especially work through work-family conflict (Grönlund and Öun 2010). In this matter, the life-course perspective helps to re-enforce this idea by stating that the interconnectedness between these life domains requires a certain time frame and may vary over time. Indeed, life courses are multidimensional because they comprise a series of trajectories, such as family, co-residence, partnership, occupation, spatial mobility, and health trajectories. Thus, family trajectories have to be understood holistically, in the light of other trajectories; events happening in one life domain (such as geographic mobility) have lasting spill-over effects in the others (Bernardi et al. 2019; Spini et al. 2017). Thus, this life-course perspective helps to bring the sociology of family and the sociology of work closer together. Furthermore, spill-over effects and this (often unseen) interconnectedness are an important area needing further investigation because they are sources of gender and other social inequalities.

This idea of interconnectedness is important for intergenerational relationships, which are a key topic in the sociology of family, and it consistently echoes the principle of linked lives. The development of family configurations and the unfolding of life trajectories are dynamic and intertwined processes. Family trajectories, stages, events, and transitions explain the salience of some types of relationships, the shares of kin and non-kin in personal networks, and the differentiated social integration among individuals. More generally, this perspective brings to light the relational dynamics at play during most major family transitions, and it adopts a holistic approach integrating whole multidimensional trajectories, rather than focusing on single family transitions. The link between the life course and personal networks would also benefit from further investigation, in the light of other interdependent dimensions such as sex, cohort, and position in the social structure and local policies.

The life-course perspective also has its limitations; because of the expansion of life course research, a variety of disciplines use it in different ways, which therefore creates a renewed need for a common conceptual foundation (Bernardi et al. 2019; Levy and Bühlmann 2016). The life-course perspective also often relies on longitudinal data, which are complex to handle despite the methodological advances described earlier, as well as time-consuming and expensive to collect. Finally, our own approach also has limitations, especially because of our primary focus on quantitative research and on Swiss empirical data. We also had to make drastic choices on what to include in this chapter, and we left out other topics. Nevertheless, we believe that this chapter convincingly shows that the life-course perspective efficiently accounts for the increased variability in the order and duration of life stages, as well as the timing of events. The life-course perspective also sheds new light on changes in family relationships and beyond, both over socio-historical time and in individuals' life courses. As the life-course perspective is constantly evolving through new concepts being developed in a variety of disciplines and new attempts to integrate them, it offers a rich source of inquiries for family sociologists.

Acknowledgements This publication benefited from the support of the Swiss National Science Foundation (grant number: 100017_130343/1), and of the Swiss National Centre of Competence in Research LIVES – Overcoming vulnerability: Life course perspectives (NCCR LIVES), which is financed by the Swiss National Science Foundation (grant number: 51NF40-160590). The authors are grateful to the Swiss National Science Foundation for its financial assistance.

References

Abbott, Andrew. 1992. "From Causes to Events: Notes on Narrative Positivism." *Sociological Methods & Research* 20 (4).
Abbott, Andrew. 2001. *Time Matters: On Theory and Method*. Chicago: University of Chicago Press.
Aeby, Gaëlle, Jacques-Antoine Gauthier, and Eric D. Widmer. 2019. "Beyond the Nuclear Family: Personal Networks in Light of Work-Family Trajectories." *Advances in Life Course Research* 39: 51–60.
Aeby, Gaëlle, Gauthier, Jacques-Antoine, Gouveia, Rita, Ramos, Vasco, Wall, Karin, et Česnuitytė, Vida. 2017. "The impact of co-residence trajectories on the transition to adulthood: a comparative perspective." In *Family Continuity and Change:*

Contemporary European Perspectives, edited by V. Česnuitytė, E. D. Widmer, and D. Lück, 211–242. London: Palgrave Macmillan.

Aeby, Gaëlle, Eric D. Widmer, Vida Česnuitytė, and Rita Gouveia. 2018. "Mapping the Plurality of Personal Configurations." In *Families and Personal Networks: An International Comparative Perspective*, edited by Karin Wall, Eric D Widmer, Jacques-Antoine Gauthier, Vida Česnuitytė, and Rita Gouveia, 131–166. London: Palgrave Macmillan.

Aisenbrey, Silke, and Anette Eva Fasang. 2010. "New Life for Old Ideas: The 'Second Wave' of Sequence Analysis Bringing the 'Course' Back into the Life Course." *Sociological Methods & Research* 38 (3): 420–462.

Aldous, Joan. 1996. *Family Careers: Rethinking the Developmental Perspective*. Thousand Oaks, CA: Sage.

Allan, Graham. 2008. "Flexibility, Friendship, and Family." *Personal Relationships* 15 (1): 1–16.

Amato, Paul R. 2010. "Research on Divorce: Continuing Trends and New Developments." *Journal of Marriage and Family* 72 (3): 650–666.

Ammar, Nadia, Jacques-Antoine Gauthier, and Eric D. Widmer. 2014. "Trajectories of Intimate Partnerships, Sexual Attitudes, Desire and Satisfaction." *Advances in Life Course Research* 22: 62–72.

Antonucci, Toni C., Katherine L. Fiori, Kira Birditt, and Lisa M. H. Jackey. 2010. "Convoys of Social Relations: Integrating Life-Span and Life-Course Perspectives." In *The Handbook of Life-Span Development*, edited by Richard M. Lerner and Willis F. Overton. John Wiley & Sons, Inc.

Arts, Wil, and John Gelissen. 2002. "Three Worlds of Welfare Capitalism or More? A State-of-the-Art Report." *Journal of European Social Policy* 12 (2): 137–158.

Beck, Ulrich, and Elisabeth Beck-Gernsheim. 1995. *The Normal Chaos of Love*. Cambridge: Wiley-Blackwell.

Bengtson, Vern L., and Katherine R. Allen. 1993. "The Life Course Perspective Applied to Families over Time." In *Sourcebook of Family Theories and Methods*, edited by Pauline Boss, William J. Doherty, Ralph LaRossa, Walter R. Schumm, and Suzanne K. Steinmetz, 469–504. USA: Springer.

Bernardi, Laura, Johannes Huinink, and Richard A. Settersten. 2019. "The Life Course Cube: A Tool for Studying Lives". *Advances in Life Course Research, Theoretical and Methodological Frontiers in Life Course Research* 41: 100258.

Bidart, Claire, Alain Degenne, and Michel Grossetti. 2011. *La vie en réseau : dynamique des relation sociales. Le lien social*. Paris: PUF.

Blanchard, Philippe, Felix Bühlmann, and Jacques-Antoine. Gauthier, eds. 2014. *Advances in Sequence Analysis: Theory, Method, Applications. Life course research and social policies* 2. New York: Springer.

Bonvalet, Catherine, and Jim Ogg, eds. 2007. *Measuring Family Support in Europe*. London: Southern Universities Press.

Brückner, Hannah, and Karl Ulrich Mayer. 2005. "De-standardization of the Life Course: What It Might Mean? And If It Means Anything, Whether It Actually Took Place?" *Advances in Life Course Research* 9: 27–53.

Buchmann, Marlis C., and Irene Kriesi. 2011. "Transition to Adulthood in Europe." *Annual Review of Sociology* 37 (1): 481–503.

Burgess, Ernest Watson, and Harvey J. Locke. 1960. *The Family: From Institution to Companionship*. 2nd ed. American sociology series. New York: American Book.

Cherlin, Andrew J. 2009. *The Marriage-Go-Round: The State of Marriage and the Family in America Today*. New York: Alfred A. Knopf.
d'Epinay, Lalive, Jean-François Bickel. Christian, Stefano Cavalli, and Dario Spini. 2005. "Le parcours de vie : émergence d'un paradigme interdisciplinaire." In *Parcours de vie: regards croisés sur la construction des biographies contemporaines*, edited by Jean-François, Guillaume, 187–210. Liège: Les Éditions de l'Université de Liège.
Dannefer, Dale. 2003. "Cumulative Advantage/Disadvantage and the Life Course: Cross-Fertilizing Age and Social Science Theory." *The Journals of Gerontology Series B: Psychological Sciences and Social Sciences* 58 (6): S327–S337.
Diekmann, Andreas, and Henriette Engelhardt. 1999. "The Social Inheritence of Divorce: Effects of Parent's Family Type in Postwar Germany." *American Sociological Review* 64 (6): 783.
Elder, Glen H. 1985. "Perspectives on the Life Course". In *Life Course Dynamics: Tajectories and Transitions, 1968–1980*, edited by Glen H Elder, 23–49. Ithaca: Cornell University Press.
Elder, Glen H. 1994. "Time, Human Agency, and Social Change: Perspectives on the Life Course". *Social Psychology Quarterly* 57 (1): 4–15.
Elder, Glen H., Monica Kirkpatrick Johnson, and Robert Crosnoe. 2003. "The Emergence and Development of Life Course Theory". In *Handbook of the Life Course*, edited by Jeylan T. Mortimer and Michael J. Shanahan, 3–19. Handbooks of sociology and social research. New York: Kluwer Academic / Plenum Publishers.
Erikson, Erik H. 1950. *Childhood and Society*. New York: Norton.
Esping-Andersen, Gøsta. 1990. *The Three Worlds of Welfare Capitalism*. Cambridge: Polity Press.
Falkingham, Jane, Jo Sage, Juliet Stone, and Athina Vlachantoni. 2016. "Residential Mobility Across the Life Course: Continuity and Change Across Three Cohorts in Britain". *Advances in Life Course Research* 30: 111–123.
Gabadinho, Alexis, Gilbert Ritschard, Nicolas Séverin. Müller, and Matthias Studer. 2011. "Analyzing and Visualizing State Sequences in R with TraMineR. *Journal of Statistical Software* 40 (4): 1–37.
Gauthier, Jacques-Antoine. 2013. "Optimal Matching, a Tool for Comparing Lifecourse Sequences". In *Gendered Life Courses Between Standardization and Individualization: A European Approach Applied to Switzerland*, edited by René Levy and Eric D. Widmer, 37–49. Wien: LIT Verlag.
Gauthier, Jacques-Antoine, Gaëlle Aeby, Vasco Ramos, and Vida Česnuitytė. 2018. "Linking Family Trajectories and Personal Networks". In *Families and Personal Networks An International Comparative Perspective*, edited by Karin Wall, Eric D. Widmer, Jacques-Antoine Gauthier, Vida Česnuitytė, and Rita Gouveia, 187–224. London: Palgrave Macmillan.
Gauthier, Jacques-Antoine., Eric D. Widmer, Philipp Bucher, and Cédric. Notredame. 2010. "Multichannel Sequence Analysis Applied to Social Science Data." *Sociological Methodology* 40 (1): 1–38.
George, Linda K. 1993. "Sociological Perspectives on Life Transitions." *Annual Review of Sociology* 19 (1): 353–373.
Giddens, Anthony. 1992. *The Transformation of Intimacy: Sexuality, Love and Eroticism in Modern Societies*. Cambridge: Polity Press.
Giele, Janet, and Glen Elder. 1998. *Methods of Life Course Research: Qualitative and Quantitative Approaches*. Thousand Oaks, CA: SAGE Publications, Inc.

Goldscheider, Frances K. 2016. "The Aging of the Gender Revolution: What Do We Know and What Do We Need to Know?" *Research on Aging* 12 (4): 531–545.

Granovetter, Mark S. 1973. "The Strength of Weak Ties." *American Journal of Sociology* 78 (6): 1360–1380.

Grönlund, Anne, and Ida Öun. 2010. "Rethinking Work-Family Conflict: Dual-Earner Policies, Role Conflict and Role Expansion in Western Europe." *Journal of European Social Policy* 20 (3): 179–195.

Guilley, Edith, Carolina Carvalho Arruda, Jacques-Antoine Gauthier, Lavinia Gianettoni, Dinah Gross, Dominique Joye, Elisabeth Issaieva Moubarak Nahra, and Karin Müller. 2019. *À l'école du genre. Projets professionnels de jeunes en Suisse*. Genève: Éditions Seismo.

Havighurst, Robert J. 1949. *Developmental Tasks and Education*. Chicago: University of Chicago Press.

Hill, Reuben, and Roy H. Rodgers. 1964. "The Developmental Approach." In *Handbook of Marriage and the Family*, edited by H. T. Christensen, 171–211. Chicago: RandMcNally.

Hofferth, Sandra L., and Frances Goldscheider. 2010. Family Structure and the Transition to Early Parenthood. *Demography* 47: 415–437.

Kohli, Martin. 1989. "Le cours de vie comme institution sociale". *Enquête* 5. https://doi.org/10.4000/enquete.78.

Kohli, Martin. 2007. "The Institutionalization of the Life Course: Looking Back to Look Ahead". *Research in Human Development* 4 (3–4): 253–271.

Korpi, Walter, and Joakim Palme. 1998. "The Paradox of Redistribution and Strategies of Equality: Welfare State Institutions, Inequality, and Poverty in the Western Countries." *American Sociological Review* 63 (5): 661.

Krüger, Helga, and René Levy. 2001. "Linking Life Courses, Work, and the Family: Theorizing a Not So Visible Nexus Between Women and Men." *The Canadian Journal of Sociology / Cahiers canadiens de sociologie* 26 (2): 145–166.

Kruskal, Joseph B. 1983. "An Overview of Sequence Comparison: Time Warps, String Edits, and Macromolecules." *SIAM Review* 25 (2): 201–237.

Laszloffy, Tracey A. 2002. "Rethinking Family Development Theory: Teaching With the Systemic Family Development (SFD) Model." *Family Relations* 51 (3): 206–214.

Levenshtein, Vladimir I. 1966. "Binary Codes Capable of Correcting Deletions, Insertions and Reversals." *Cybernetic Control Theory* 10 (8): 707–710.

Levy, René. 2005. "Why Look at Life Courses in an Interdisciplinary Perspective?". In *Advances in Life Course Research* 10 (Towards an Interdisciplinary Perspective on the Life Course), edited by René Levy, Paolo Ghisletta, Jean-Marie Le Goff, Dario Spini, and Eric D. Widmer, 3–32.

Levy, René. 2013. "Analysis of Life Courses—A Theoretical Sketch". In *Gendered Life Courses Between Standardization and Individualization: A European Approach Applied to Switzerland*, edited by René Levy and Eric D Widmer, 13–36. Wien: LIT Verlag.

Levy, René, and Felix Bühlmann. 2016. "Towards a Socio-structural Framework for Life Course Analysis." *Advances in Life Course Research* 30: 30–42.

Levy, René, Paolo Ghisletta, Jean-Marie. Le Goff, Dario Spini, and Eric D. Widmer, eds. 2005. *Towards an Interdisciplinary Perspective on the Life Course. Advances in Life Course Research* vol. 10. Amsterdam: Elsevier JAI Press.

Levy, René, and Eric D. Widmer, eds. 2013. *Gendered Life Courses Between Standardization and Individualization: A European Approach Applied to Switzerland.* Wien: LIT Verlag.

Marshall, Victor W., and Margaret M. Mueller. 2003. "Theoretical Roots of the Life-Course Perspective". In *Social Dynamics of the Life Course: Transitions, Institutions, and Interrelations*, edited by Walter R. Heinz and Victor W Marshall. New York: Aldine de Gruyter.

Mayer, Karl Ulrich. 2001. "The Paradox of Global Social Change and National Path Dependencies: Life Course Patterns in Advanced Societies". In *Inclusions and Exclusions in European Societies*, edited by Alison E. Woodward and Martin Kohli, 89–110. Routledge/ European sociological association studies in European societies 5. London: Routledge.

Mayer, Karl Ulrich, and Urs Schoepflin. 1989. "The State and the Life Course." *Annual Review of Sociology* 15 (1): 187–209.

McDonald, Steve, and Christine A. Mair. 2010. "Social Capital Across the Life Course: Age and Gendered Patterns of Network Resources." *Sociological Forum* 25 (2): 335–359.

Möhring, Katja. 2016. "Life Course Regimes in Europe: Individual Employment Histories in Comparative and Historical Perspective. *Journal of European Social Policy* 26 (2): 124–139.

Mortimer, Jeylan T., and Michael J. Shanahan, eds. 2003. *Handbook of the Life Course*. Handbooks of Sociology and Social Research. USA: Springer.

Nock, Steven L. 1979. "The Family Life Cycle: Empirical or Conceptual Tool?" *Journal of Marriage and the Family* 41 (1): 15–26.

Oppenheimer, Valerie Kincade, and Alisa Lewin. 1997. "Career Development and Marriage Formation in a Period of Rising Inequality: Who Is at Risk? What Are Their Prospects?". In *Transitions to Adulthood in a Changing Economy: No Work, No Family, No Future?*, edited by Alan Booth, Ann C. Crouter, et Michael J. Shanahan, 187–225. Westport, CT: Praeger.

Pahl, Ray, and David J. Pevalin. 2005. "Between Family and Friends: A Longitudinal Study of Friendship Choice." *The British Journal of Sociology* 56 (3): 433–450.

Pahl, Ray, and Liz Spencer. 2004. "Personal Communities: Not Simply Families of 'Fate' or 'Choice.'" *Current Sociology* 52 (2): 199–221.

Parsons, Talcott, and Robert Freed Bales. 1955. *Family: Socialization and Interaction Process.* New York : London: The Free Press; Collir-Macmillan.

Paternotte, David, and Kelly Kollman. 2013. "Regulating Intimate Relationships in the European Polity: Same-Sex Unions and Policy Convergence." *Social Politics: International Studies in Gender, State & Society* 20 (4): 510–533.

Rice, Joy K. 1994. "Reconsidering Research on Divorce, Family Life Cycle, and the Meaning of Family." *Psychology of Women Quarterly* 18 (4): 559–584.

Sapin, Marlène, Dario Spini, and Eric D Widmer. 2007. *Les parcours de vie: de l'adolescence au grand âge*. Le savoir suisse Société 39. Lausanne: Presses polytechniques et universitaires romandes.

Smart, Carol. 2010. *Personal Life: New Directions in Sociological Thinking*. Cambridge: Polity.

Smith, Dorothy E. 1993. "The Standard North American Family: SNAF as an Ideological Code." *Journal of Family Issues* 14 (1): 50–65.

Spanier, Graham B., William Sauer, and Robert Larzelere. 1979. "An Empirical Evaluation of the Family Life Cycle." *Journal of Marriage and Family* 41 (1): 27–38.

Spini, Dario, Laura Bernardi, and Michel Oris. 2017. "Toward a Life Course Framework for Studying Vulnerability." *Research in Human Development* 14 (1): 5–25.

Sweeney, Megan M. 2010. "Remarriage and Stepfamilies: Strategic Sites for Family Scholarship in the 21st Century." *Journal of Marriage and Family* 72 (3): 667–684.

Viry, Gil, and Jacques-Antoine Gauthier. 2019. "L'analyse de séquence pour étudier les comportements de mobilité spatiale dans le parcours de vie." *Recherche Transports Sécurité*.

Wall, Karin, and Rita Gouveia. 2014. "Changing Meanings of Family in Personal Relationships." *Current Sociology* 62 (3): 352–373.

Wall, Karin, and Anna Escobedo. 2009. "Portugal and Spain: Two Pathways in Southern Europe." In *The Politics of Parental Leave Policies: Children, Parenting, Gender and the Labour Market*, edited by Sheila B. Kamerman and Peter Moss, 207–226. Bristol: Policy Press.

Wall, Karin, Eric D. Widmer, Jacques-Antoine. Gauthier, Vida Česnuitytė, and Rita Gouveia. 2018. *Families and Personal Networks An International Comparative Perspective*. London: Palgrave Macmillan.

Widmer, Eric D. 2006. "Who Are My Family Members? Bridging and Binding Social Capital in Family Configurations." *Journal of Social and Personal Relationships* 23 (6): 979–998.

Widmer, Eric D., and Jacques-Antoine Gauthier. 2013. "Cohabitational Trajectories". In *Gendered Life Courses Between Standardization and Individualization: A European Approach Applied to Switzerland*, edited by René Levy and Eric D. Widmer, 53–69. Wien: LIT Verlag.

Wolfinger, Nicholas H. 2005. *Understanding the Divorce Cycle: The Children of Divorce in Their Own Marriages*. Cambridge: Cambridge University Press.

Zartler, Ulrike, Valeri Heintz-Martin, and Oliver Arrán Becker. 2015. *Family Dynamics After Separation : A Life Course Perspective on Post-Divorce Families*. Opladen: Verlag Barbara Budrich.

CHAPTER 29

Varieties of Youth Transitions? A Review of the Comparative Literature on the Entry to Adulthood

Tom Chevalier

INTRODUCTION

The transition to adulthood has long been analysed, and the literature dealing with such an issue is plethoric. Its forms and transformation have been analysed from a range of perspectives and within several disciplines. Although sociology is one of the main disciplines represented, and more specifically the sociology of youth (within the so-called Youth Studies) and of the family, many other analyses of the entry into adulthood have also been proposed—in the fields of history, demography, psychology, economics, and more recently, political science.

Many literature reviews (Buchmann and Kriesi 2011; Hogan and Astone 1986; Shanahan 2000) and handbooks (Furlong 2017; Jones 2009) thus already exist in the literature. Alongside an updated general description of the state of play in the transition to adulthood, in this chapter I present this literature from a dual perspective. Firstly, since the various approaches and disciplines that have analysed young people and the transition to adulthood rarely communicate with one another, I present an overview of these approaches and disciplines.

Secondly, I focus on the issue of cross-national variation, presenting comparative works. One of the biggest controversies has been to determine whether we are seeing convergence towards a new pattern of entry to adulthood (Sect. 1) or a persistence of cross-national diversity (Sect. 2). I will

---

T. Chevalier (✉)
CNRS/Arènes, Rennes, France
e-mail: tom.chevalier@sciencespo.fr

© The Author(s), under exclusive license to Springer Nature Switzerland AG 2021
A.-M. Castrén et al. (eds.), *The Palgrave Handbook of Family Sociology in Europe*, https://doi.org/10.1007/978-3-030-73306-3_29

therefore stress the importance of institutional arrangements in explaining such diversity—not only with regard to youth transitions in general, but also to youth unemployment (Sect. 3) and youth poverty (Sect. 4).

Transformation of the Transition to Adulthood: The Rise of a New Pattern?

The commonality between all youth transitions studies is an acknowledgement that the life course in general, and the transition to adulthood in particular, has undergone significant and structural change since the 1970s. In contrast to the preindustrial period (Gillis 1981), the industrial period saw the progressive "institutionalization" and "standardization" of the life course as a result of the new organisation of work (Kohli 1986) and the growing role of the state (Mayer and Schoepflin 1989). This led to a "tripartition" of the life course, meaning a distinction was made between three phases in life: childhood (the phase of full-time education, i.e. preparation for work), adulthood (the phase of work), and old age (the phase of retirement from work). From this perspective, the transition from childhood to adulthood (defined as the negotiation of several markers, namely: leaving parental home, getting married, having a child, completing education, getting a job) is fairly smooth and quick: children directly become adults, leaving no space for "youth". And the reason why this is the case is precisely because the life course is highly standardized: the transition is *"early, contracted, and simple"* (Billari and Liefbroer 2010, 60).

In the 1970s, such a pattern of transition was altered by the transformation of the economy and the rise of both youth unemployment and levels of education, alongside the evolution of the cultural norms of adulthood. Scholars identified this trend as early as in the late 1970s, especially when looking at the American case (Modell et al. 1976). The first literature review on the topic dates from (Hogan and Astone 1986). One of the most important works of that time was by Buchmann (1989), who argued that the transformation of the context had led, on the contrary, to a process of "destandardization", more generally reflecting a trend of "individualization" of the life course.

Many works have indeed shown that a process of destandardisation has taken place, transforming entry to adulthood and ultimately creating "youth" as a specific period in life (Cavalli and Galland 1995). The timing of transitions has changed: the age at which transitions happen has been gradually postponed. Moreover, these transitions have been desynchronised; they no longer happen at the same pace or at the same moment in time. They have also become "reversible", allowing for back-and-forth movement that has led to what has been referred to as "yo-yo transition" (Walther et al. 2002). Billari and Liefbroer (2010) have argued that this new "ideal-typical pattern" means a transition that is now *"late, protracted, and complex"*.

This long-term trend, as scholars have stressed, is embedded into the overall transformation of society. On the one hand, they have underlined the fact that this "destandardization" of the life course echoes the "individualisation" process taking place in modern societies, which has been analysed by both Giddens (1991) and Beck (1992). On the other, Lesthaeghe (1995) has theorised a "second demographic transition" reflecting this change of behaviours. This transition stems from Nordic countries before spreading to other countries—for example, a preference for postponing demographic choices in favour of independent living, unmarried cohabitation, and extramarital childbearing.[1]

From a different perspective, other scholars have analysed what has been called "emerging adulthood" (Arnett 2000). This concept comes from Developmental Psychology and is intended to supplant the notion of "youth" that used to cover young people aged 10 to 25. Because of structural transformations to the life course, Arnett considers that we now need to distinguish between the periods of "adolescence" (10–17) and the period of "emerging adulthood" (18–25). Conceptually close to the studies presented above, this approach focuses on subjective aspects of such new periods of life (including young people's need to try out diverse pathways with an increasing level of reflexivity on their own choices), in contrast to studies in demography, which generally stick to objective behaviour indicators (markers of transitions).

These long-term transformations are seen as structural changes of modern societies and thus suppose a progressive convergence of transitions across individuals and countries. Billari and Liefbroer (2010) have however shown that, despite similar trends across Europe, in terms of both the timing and the rise of new behaviours (such as living alone, unmarried cohabitation, or out-of-wedlock births), there is no convergence across countries. If anything, there is even more divergence in terms of increased variance for many behaviours. Lesnard et al. (2016) have also tested this convergence hypothesis, and they did so using the identical 2006 European Social Survey module (on the timing of life events) as did Billari and Liefbroer (2010). Having identified a range of 14 pathways to adulthood, Lesnard et al. show that there is indeed a convergence between male and female patterns. However, on the other hand, they underline the fact that, despite some convergence, important cross-national variation persists, depending on historical family systems. In Nordic countries, for instance, there is a historical tendency to leave home early, unlike Southern countries having strong family ties.

The proponents of the "modernity argument" presented above (Shanahan 2000, 668) have therefore been able to identify the new challenges of the transition to adulthood as well as the forms taken by its transformation. This was supposed to lead into two trends: the growing *individualization* of transitions and their following *convergence* across countries. In other words, the rise of *agency* over *structures*. Yet the resilience of the diversity of trajectories has called this argument into question by stressing the longevity of structures, and this has led to several controversies in the literature. Bynner (2005) has, for instance, defended the importance of structures against the "emerging adulthood" argument of Arnett (2006), who in turn defended the focus on agency—and hence in support of the individualisation argument (though some scholars have emphasised the diversity of emerging adulthood pathways, see Buhl and Lanz 2007). This debate resurfaced some years later in relation to the use of Ulrich Beck's argument (also focused on the process of individualisation) in Youth Studies (Roberts 2012, 2010; Threadgold 2011). Ken Roberts (2009) has continuously argued in favour of the concept of "opportunity structures" to explain youth transitions, i.e. the fact that young people's choices remain in context (especially in terms of family, education, and the labour market), whereas change would be related more to the transformation of such contexts than to their own choices.

The Resilience of Cross-National Diversity

Since the beginning of the 2000s scholars have focused on cross-national diversity, stressing the importance of structures. Studies have shown that there was no convergence towards destandardisation of the life course, and cross-national diversity has remained significant. This has been shown not only through quantitative analyses of many countries (Billari and Wilson 2001; Liu and Esteve 2020; Nico 2014), but also using more case-oriented research, comparing a smaller set of countries (Corijn and Klijzing 2001; Van de Velde 2008). The question is, then—what are the macro determinants of such cross-national diversity?

Billari (2004) has identified and presented two major factors found in the literature: long-term "cultural" factors, and "institutional" factors. Hajnal (1965) argued that a line drawn from Trieste to St-Petersburg divides Europe into two parts that are distinguished by different family systems (the so-called Hajnal line). To the west of this line, there is neo-local nuclear family, late marriage, and a high proportion of people who do not get married. To its east, there is early and universal marriage, while the family is extended. Reher (1998) has further analysed this hypothesis by focusing on countries situated to the west of the line, especially Southern European countries in which both the late Roman Empire and Muslims were influential in the Middle Ages. Van de Velde (2008) also emphasised the role of cultural representations of family (among other factors), though without using such a theoretical framework. However, Aassve et al. (2013) have shown that preferences—namely subjective age norms for leaving the parental home—ultimately depend on institutional macro-factors.

In fact, most of the studies are more insistent on institutional factors in their explanations of cross-national diversity. Usually, they rely on the seminal typology of welfare regimes (Esping-Andersen 1990; Gallie and Paugam 2000) distinguishing Nordic countries, Continental Europe, the Mediterranean, and the English-speaking world. Both Breen and Buchmann (2002) and Cook and Furstenberg (2002) have stressed the role of institutional arrangements and welfare states in explaining the situation of young people, while Mayer (2001) first used this typology in an attempt to explain variation in transition patterns. Other works in Youth Studies have since tried to better understand the role played by welfare institutions in the transition to adulthood.

Walther (2006) and Walther et al. (2003) have proposed a typology of "youth transition regimes" that is largely reliant on Esping-Andersen (1990, 1999), in which four regimes are identified: the "universalistic" regime (Nordic countries), the "employment-centred" regime (Continental European countries), the "liberal" regime ("English-speaking" countries), and the "sub-protective" regime (Mediterranean countries). Van de Velde's work (2008) also confirms this typology by comparing Denmark, the UK, France, and Spain; she shows that entry into adulthood is very different in the four countries, reflecting different combinations of culture, welfare regimes, and education systems. The Mediterranean model, illustrated by Spain in her study, presents a "logic of family affiliation", whose objective is to set up their own home ("*s'installer*")—that is, to leave the parental home solely in order to establish one's own household. Parental decohabitation is directly related to entry to the labour market, marriage, and a first child. It is characterised by familialised policies that offer young people virtually no direct help from the state, leaving it up to families to care for them. The Liberal model, illustrated by the UK, presents a "logic of individual emancipation", with the objective of "taking personal responsibility" ("*s'assumer*"). The possibility of entering the labour market relatively early, coupled with an individualistic norm, allows young people to have relatively early access to autonomy through the market.

The Social-Democratic model, represented by Denmark, promotes a "logic of personal development", whose purpose is "to find oneself" ("*se trouver*"). In this model, the state, with its generous benefits system, is responsible for ensuring that young people have sufficient resources—both to live, and to multiply experiences in a fairly flexible way. Here, access to autonomy comes very early on, and is coupled with lengthy studies, unlike the UK. Lastly, the Continental model, illustrated by France, offers a logic of "social integration" whose purpose is to "find one's place" ("*s'insérer*"), using a hybrid set of public policies that borrow from both the familialism of Mediterranean countries (with minimum income benefits unavailable to under-25s, for instance), and the pro-autonomy approach of Scandinavian countries (with individualised housing benefits).

In a bid to better understand how these institutional features interact, Chevalier (2016) has drawn up a two-dimension typology of "youth welfare citizenship" regimes. In line with these studies, it is possible to identify two types of public intervention aimed at promoting young people's autonomy (or "youth welfare citizenship"). On the one hand, the state can build "economic citizenship" through the use of education and employment policies to address the school-to-work transition, and on the other, it can build "social citizenship" by delivering benefits to young people (family benefit, unemployment benefit, housing benefit, and student support).

Two models of "social citizenship" for young people can be discerned. First, it can be "familialised"; youth is considered an extension of childhood, so that young people are treated, institutionally, as children (importance of family policies, age limit of around 25, etc.). Second, it can be "individualised". Young people are thus considered adults when they reach civil majority (no role for family policies to support young people and age limit of around 18). Two strategies can also be distinguished in terms of "economic citizenship". The first is "inclusive", in that its objective is to ensure that every young person attains a minimum level of skills that permits access to employment. In order to help young people get a job, emphasis is put on education and training above all, in a "learn-first" perspective (OECD 2010). The second strategy is "selective" in that its objective is to provide skills only to the "best": the objective is to rank students in order to produce an élite, rather than to guarantee a minimum level of education to all. The education system is elitist and results in significant educational inequalities among young people—as well as high dropout rates.

By interweaving these two dimensions, the typology distinguishes four regimes of youth welfare citizenship: the "enabling citizenship" (individualisation and inclusive strategy) of Nordic countries (Sweden, Finland, Denmark, the Netherlands); the "monitored citizenship" (familialisation and inclusive strategy) of Continental European countries with an apprenticeship-based education system (Germany, Austria); the "denied citizenship" (familialisation and selective strategy) of Mediterranean countries (Spain, Portugal, Greece, Italy, France but also Belgium and Luxembourg); and the "second-class citizenship" (individualisation and selective strategy) of "English-speaking" countries (the UK and Ireland).

Youth Unemployment and the School-to-Work Transition

Because the transition to adulthood is composed of many transitions, it is multidimensional. Despite its focus on family formation, the literature presented above tries to take account of all the various markers of transitions. However, a different stream of literature has conducted more in-depth analysis of another transition, namely the "school-to-work transition", that describes the ending of education and entry to the labour market. Because such literature issues more from the sociology of education and work and the economics of youth unemployment, it is quite different from that which is based in demographics and the sociology of youth.

In economics, the significance of the economic cycle has been shown to have an effect on youth unemployment, since young people are more vulnerable in the labour market than their older counterparts (Bell and Blanchflower 2011; Blanchflower and Freeman 2000; Dietrich 2013). Blossfeld et al. (2005) have also shown that globalisation has increased uncertainty and destandardised entry into adulthood (both in general, and in the labour market in particular)—though this trend is mediated by national institutional arrangements. Demographic factors and labour market institutions are also important, but vocational education and training (VET) seems the most important factor in explaining youth unemployment (Biavaschi et al. 2012).

In 1982, Marc Maurice, François Sellier, and Jean-Jacques Silvestre published an analysis of the links between the training system and the industrial organisation, comparing France and Germany (Maurice et al. 1982). They showed that the two institutional areas are complementary to one another because of distinct "societal coherences" in both countries. In Germany, VET has a central place in the education system, since it concerns almost half of any given cohort. It illustrates the presence of the world of production in the educational system, since both employers and trade unions are important players in the system, and they consider VET very important. In France, on the other hand, the education system is completely separated from the world of production, and as a result only a very small proportion of students are in VET, which is integrated to the academic system. It is this difference between France and Germany that was then to be taken up by the works on the subject.

A few years later, Paul Ryan and Paolo Garonna (Garonna and Ryan 1989; Ryan et al. 1991) proposed a typology of "youth regulation" systems, echoing this first study comparing France and Germany. Based on the distinction between the "internal labour market" and the "professional labour market" (Marsden 1990), to which a third "external labour market" was subsequently added, they distinguished three systems of youth regulation: "regulated integration" represented by the German case (access to a job guaranteed by the highly regulated system of apprenticeship), "selective exclusion" illustrated by the French case (access to jobs on the secondary labour market after education in order to get the specific skills required to get a permanent job on the primary labour market later on), and "competitive regulation", represented in Europe by the UK (low labour market regulation so that access to jobs is based on competition among workers). Three elements are important here: types of skills ("specific" and non-transferable across firms or sectors, or "general" and transferable); types of labour market (in relation to the types of skill), and the state's role in regulation (whether by market or state).

These works have inspired a very rich literature analysing the impact of education systems on young people's entry to the labour market (Raffe 2003). Lessons can be learned from this literature; types of skills (and their relation to the labour market) are key to understanding the school-to-work transition, yet complementarities and coherences exist between the institutional realms of education, the labour market, and social policy. And these complementarities lead to distinct systems (or models) of school-to-work transition (Gangl 2001; Müller and Gangl 2003).

In her seminal article, Jutta Allmendinger (1989) provided an alternative analysis of the school-to-work transition, accounting not only for types of skills, but also for their distribution. She maintains that education systems should be considered in terms of the two dimensions of "standardization" (issuance of standard certificates that are nationally recognised - or not) and "stratification" (the presence of selection in the education system). She shows that, depending on the variation in these dimensions, the effects on young people's access to employment are different. The more "standardized" the education system, the more employers know what young people's qualifications actually attest to, so that the school-to-work transition is more fluid. In a "stratified" system, the transition is also smoother, because of the more pronounced link between education and the labour market.

By distinguishing between their "commodification" and their "social stratification", Busemeyer (2015) made a valiant attempt at drawing up a typology of skill formation systems, both explaining their development and evaluating their effects on youth unemployment, among other outcomes. He revealed a trade-off between youth unemployment and inequality—education systems reliant on apprenticeship do decrease youth unemployment but at the same time, they also increase overall inequality. The significance of VET has long been demonstrated in the literature (as well as in economics, see Caroleo et al. 2010), but its combination with other institutions has been under discussion. Breen (2005) has argued, for instance, that low youth unemployment can be achieved either through VET or through a flexible labour market that allows employers to dismiss workers easily. However, Brzinsky-Fay (2017) has emphasised the fact that the interplay between different institutions must be taken into account: it is not the regulation of the labour market or VET in itself that has an effect on youth unemployment, but the combination of the two[2]. For instance, a high level of employment protection can lead to high relative youth unemployment—but only where there is also low development of VET (in Belgium, for instance). Where VET does exist, only a low level VET would lead to such an outcome (Greece, Korea, or Italy). Lastly, O'Reilly et al. (2019) have recently published a comprehensive overview on the issue of youth labour[3] and young people's access to employment.

Youth Poverty and Social Exclusion

Rising youth unemployment has led to rising inequalities and the development of youth poverty and social exclusion (Hammer 2003; Kieselbach 2000). Kangas and Palme (2000) have stressed the fact that "the young have replaced the old as the lowest income group" (Kangas and Palme 2000, 349) as a result of the expansion of higher education, greater difficulties entering the labour market and a lack of appropriate social protection. Inter-generational inequalities are thus often at the expense of the young, leading to low levels of life satisfaction (Schels 2020) and the rise of a "precarious generation" (Bessant et al. 2017).

This explains why the literature on the welfare state has claimed that young people face a "new social risk" (NSR) (see Knijn 2012). In fact, many authors have argued that young people represent a segment of the population that is more likely to display an NSR (as are women and immigrants, for instance), especially given their higher rate of unemployment (Bonoli 2005). Although these authors describe this as a common trend occurring in most countries, Ferragina, Seeleib-Kaiser, and Spreckelsen (2015) have tried to underline the cross-national variation of NSR levels, using youth poverty rates as an indicator (among others): their results largely confirm the typology of welfare regimes, showing NSRs to be higher in Mediterranean countries, for example. However, they also stress the fact that this does not really hold true for youth poverty, which is higher in Nordic countries because of the measurement effect of calculating poverty at household level (Ferragina et al. 2015, 6–8).

To solve these problems, it is necessary to look at intra-generational inequalities and the individual determinants of youth poverty from a comparative perspective. First, labour market factors are crucial, since unemployment or low pay can lead to situations of income poverty among young people (Aassve et al. 2005, 2006). Second, the key role of education has been underlined, since low-educated young people struggle more to get a job, and when they do, are often trapped in low-paid work. Third, living arrangements are central. Not living with the family of origin, living in a household in which the head is female, young or a single parent increase the chances of being poor. Above all, leaving the parental home is a strong predictor of poverty among young people, as the income of the whole household is no longer taken into account. This is why we find high levels of youth poverty in Nordic countries, where young people leave home fairly early, increasing the proportion of young people for whom only their own income is taken into account (Aassve et al. 2007; Ayllon 2015): it is a sort of statistical artefact. This also explains the fact that students can also be at risk of poverty, especially in Nordic countries: since they neither have income from full-time work nor continue living with their parents, their households show lower levels of income.

Because of the limitations of income levels (usually below 60% of median net equivalised household income) as an indirect measure of poverty, several scholars have looked to use other indicators as well, in order to get a more comprehensive overview of youth vulnerability. Mendola et al. (2009) have, for instance, shown that it is also important to take into account the *permanence* of poverty; while poverty rates are quite high in Nordic countries, the permanence of poverty among young people remains fairly low in these countries. Fahmy (2014) has systematically compared income poverty with two other direct measures of poverty, namely material deprivation (an additive index of necessities of life) and subjective poverty (ability to "make ends meet"), and has shown that these indicators barely overlap. Their levels do not correlate: for example, in Nordic countries, though income poverty is high, deprivation and subjective poverty are very low. Neither do they correlate in terms of difference between young and old; young people do seem poorer in terms of income, in comparison with other age groups, but this does not seem to be the case in terms of deprivation.

These results highlight the high cross-national variation at work, confirming Vogel's argument (2001) on the decisive effect of transition pattern variations across countries on youth vulnerability. Yet although these studies do distinguish between countries on the basis of welfare regime (Antonucci et al., 2014) they do not precisely identify the macro-determinants of such cross-national variation. Rovny (2014) has tried to analyse the effects of social policies in order to evaluate their effects on NSR. Using multilevel modelling, she has shown that neither social spending nor family policies have any effect on low-skilled young women and men (who are most at risk of poverty). On the contrary, active labour market policies (ALMP) are the most important predictor of a fall in poverty levels among this population, followed by passive labour market policies.

Guillén and Pavolini (2012) have also provided a detailed analysis of the effect of social policies on youth poverty in a comparative perspective. They show that though generous social assistance and unemployment benefits do have a negative effect on youth poverty, so too do "indirect" social policies, that is, social policies not aimed primarily at poverty reduction, such as family policies. However, their sample remains fairly limited, given that it focuses on just eight countries, none of which are Nordic. Although Brady, Fullerton, and Cross (2009) have shown that welfare generosity does reduce poverty levels in households headed by a person under 30, they then continued looking at income poverty alone. Lastly, Antonucci (2016) has shown, in line with these studies, the extent to which "welfare mixes" (the diverse combinations of state policies, market income, and family support) structure the experience of students and their access to resources and welfare. Nevertheless, in comparison with other youth transition issues, systematic analyses of the macro-determinants of youth poverty are lacking, thus far.

Cross-national diversity is certainly crucial as far as youth poverty is concerned, though temporal variation matters too: Aassve et al. (2013) have demonstrated the extent to which the economic crisis has increased youth vulnerability, resulting in more young people remaining with their parents as a coping strategy. The crisis has also increased income poverty among young people no longer living with parents. The subjective measure of poverty has steeply increased among young people in general, in almost every country.

Conclusion

In this chapter, I have shown that the transition to adulthood, while transformed, still takes a variety of forms: most literature stresses the importance of cross-national variation and underlines the importance of institutional arrangements. Youth transitions (i.e. the different patterns of transitions to adulthood) do seem to be structured by welfare regimes. However, insofar as the school-to-work transition is concerned, the education system, together with labour market regulation, seems to better explain the varying patterns of access to employment. Lastly, studies on youth poverty are less numerous; though cross-national diversity is put forward, systematic analyses of precise macro-determinants of such variation are still missing. Further research should engage in this direction, since the 2007 economic crisis and the subsequent boom of youth unemployment seem to have increased youth poverty. The new crisis that will follow the COVID-19 pandemic will also put the issue of youth poverty at the heart of the social agenda, stressing the need for more research on the topic.

Notes

1. Mitchell's book on *The Boomerang Age* (2006) provides a detailed (historical and comparative) overview of family issues. She stresses the role of the family and its network of relations in the support of young people and their "boomerang" transitions.
2. Other policies can also have an effect on youth unemployment, such as active labour market policies (Caliendo et al. 2011), although their effect seems to be lower compared to the education system and the regulation of the labour market.
3. See also Petersen and Mortimer (2006) and the recent special issue on "Youth Employment in Europe: Coordination as a Crucial Dimension" edited by Tosun J., Hörisch F., and Marques P., *International Journal of Social Welfare* 28 (4), 2019.

References

Aassve, A., Arpino, B., and Billari, F. C. 2013. "Age Norms on Leaving Home: Multi-level Evidence from the European Social Survey." *Environment and Planning A* (45): 383–401.

Aassve, A., Cottini, E., and Vitali, A. 2013. "Youth Vulnerability in Europe During the Great Recession." *Dondena Working Papers*.

Aassve, A., Davia, M. A., Iacovou, M., and Mazzuco, S. 2007. "Does Leaving Home Make You Poor? Evidence from 13 European Countries: Quitter la maison rend-il pauvre? Une analyse des données de 13 pays européens." *European Journal of Population / Revue européenne de Démographie* (23): 315–338.

Aassve, A., Iacovou, M., and Mencarini, L. 2006. "Youth Poverty and Transition to Adulthood in Europe." *Demographic Research* (15): 21–50.

Aassve, A., Iacovou, M., and Mencarini, L. 2005. "Youth Poverty in Europe: What Do We Know?" *ISER Working Papers*. Institute for Social and Economic Research.

Allmendinger, J. 1989. "Educational Systems and Labour Market Outcomes." *European Sociological Review* (5): 231–250.

Antonucci, L. 2016. *Student Lives in Crisis. Deepening Inequality in Times of Austerity*. Bristol: Policy Press.

Antonucci, L., Hamilton, M., and Roberts, S., eds. 2014. *Young People and Social Policy in Europe. Dealing with Risk, Inequality, and Precarity in Times of Crisis*. Basingstoke: Palgrave Macmillan.

Arnett, J. J. 2006. "Emerging Adulthood in Europe: A Response to Bynner." *Journal of Youth Studies* (9): 111–123.

Arnett, J. J. 2000. "Emerging Adulthood: A Theory of Development from the Late Teens Through the Twenties." *American Psychologist*: 469–480.

Ayllon, S. 2015. "Youth Poverty, Employment, and Leaving the Parental Home in Europe." *The Review of Income and Wealth* (61): 651–676.
Beck, U. 1992. *Risk Society: Towards a New Modernity*. London: Sage.
Bell, D., and Blanchflower, D. 2011. "Youth Unemployment in Europe and the United States." *IZA Discussion Paper*.
Bessant, J., Farthing, R., and Watts, R. 2017. *The Precarious Generation: A Political Economy of Young People*. London: Routledge.
Biavaschi, C., Eichhorst, W., Giulietti, C., Kendzia, M. J., Muravyev, A., Pieters, J., Rodriguez Planas, N., Schmidl, R., and Zimmermann, K. F. 2012. "Youth Unemployment and Vocational Training." *IZA Discussion Paper*.
Billari, F. 2004. "Becoming an Adult in Europe: A Macro(/Micro)-Demographic Perspective." *Demographic Research Special* (3): 15–44.
Billari, F. C., and Liefbroer, A. C. 2010. "Towards a New Pattern of Transition to Adulthood?" *Advances in Life Course Research* (15): 59–75.
Billari, F. C., and Wilson, C. 2001. "Convergence Towards Diversity? Cohort Dynamics in the Transition to Adulthood in Contemporary Western Europe." *Max Planck Institute for Demographic Research, Working Paper* WP2001-039.
Blanchflower, D., and Freeman, R. B., eds. 2000. *Youth Employment and Joblessness in Advanced Countries*. Chicago: University of Chicago Press.
Blossfeld, H.-P., Klijzing, E., Mills, M., and Kurz, K., eds. 2005. *Globalization, Uncertainty and Youth in Society*. London: Routledge.
Bonoli, G. 2005. "The Politics of the New Social Policies: Providing Coverage Against New Social Risks in Mature Welfare States." *Policy & politics* (33): 431–449.
Brady, D., Fullerton, A. S., Cross, J. M. 2009. "Putting Poverty in Political Context: A Multi-Level Analysis of Adult Poverty Across 18 Affluent Democracies." *Social Forces* (88): 271–299.
Breen, R. 2005. "Explaining Cross National Variation in Youth Unemployment. Market and Institutional Factors." *European Sociological Review* (21): 125–134.
Breen, R., and Buchmann, M. 2002. "Institutional Variation and the Position of Young People: A Comparative Perspective." *The Annals of the American Academy of Political and Social Science* (580): 288–305.
Brzinsky-Fay, C. 2017. "The Interplay of Educational and Labour Market Institutions and Links to Relative Youth Unemployment." *Journal of European Social Policy* (27): 346–359.
Buchmann, M. 1989. *The Script of Life in Modern Society: Entry into Adulthood in a Changing World*. Chicago: University of Chicago Press.
Buchmann, M. C., and Kriesi, I. 2011. "Transition to Adulthood in Europe." *Annual Review of Sociology* (37): 481–503.
Buhl, H. M., and Lanz, M. 2007. "Emerging Adulthood in Europe: Common Traits and Variability Across Five European Countries." *Journal of Adolescent Research* (22): 439–443.
Busemeyer, M. R. 2015. *Skills and Inequality. Partisan Politics and the Political Economy of Education Reforms in Western Welfare States*. Cambridge: Cambridge University Press.
Bynner, J. 2005. "Rethinking the Youth Phase of the Life-course: The Case for Emerging Adulthood?" *Journal of Youth Studies* (8): 367–384.
Caliendo, M., Künn, S., and Schmidl, R. 2011. "Fighting Youth Unemployment: The Effects of Active Labour Market Policies." *IZA Discussion Paper*.

Caroleo, F. E., Ciociano, E., and Destefanis, S. 2010. "Youth Labour Market Performance, Institutions and Vet Systems: A Cross-Country Analysis." *Italian Economic Journal* (38): 119–148.
Cavalli, A., and Galland, O. 1995. *Youth in Europe*. London: Pinter.
Chevalier, T. 2016. "Varieties of Youth Welfare Citizenship. Towards a Two-dimension Typology." *Journal of European Social Policy* (1): 3–19.
Cook, T. D., and Furstenberg, F. F. 2002. "Explaining Aspects of the Transition to Adulthood in Italy, Sweden, Germany, and the United States: A Cross-disciplinary, Case Synthesis Approach." *The Annals of the American Academy of Political and Social Science* (580): 257–287.
Corijn, M., and Klijzing, E., eds. 2001. *Transitions to Adulthood in Europe, European Studies of Population*. Springer: The Netherlands.
Dietrich, H. 2013. "Youth Unemployment in the Period 2001–2010 and the European Crisis—Looking at the Empirical Evidence." *European Review of Labour and Research* (19): 305–324.
Esping-Andersen, G. 1990. *The Three Worlds of Welfare Capitalism*. Princeton: Princeton University Press.
Esping-Andersen, G. 1999. *Social Foundations of Postindustrial Economies*. Oxford: Oxford University Press.
Fahmy, E. 2014. "The Complex Nature of Youth Poverty and Deprivation in Europe." In *Young People and Social Policy in Europe. Dealing with Risks, Inequality and Precarity in Times of Crisis*, edited by Antonucci, L., Hamilton, M., Roberts, S, 37–61. Basingstoke: Palgrave Macmillan.
Ferragina, E., Seeleib-Kaiser, M., and Spreckelsen, T. 2015. "The Four Worlds of "Welfare Reality"—Social Risks and Outcomes in Europe." *Social policy and Society* (14): 287–307.
Furlong, A. 2017. *Handbook of Youth and Young Adulthood: New Perspectives and Agendas*. London: Routledge.
Gallie, D., and Paugam, S., eds. 2000. *Welfare Regimes and the Experience of Unemployment in Europe*. Oxford: Oxford University Press.
Gangl, M. 2001. "European Patterns of Labour Market Entry. A Dichotomy of Occupationalized vs. Non-occupationalized Systems?" *European Societies* (3): 471–494.
Garonna, P., and Ryan, P. 1989. "Le travail des jeunes, les relations professionnelles et les politiques sociales dans les économies avancées." *Formation Emploi*: 78–90.
Giddens, A. 1991. *Modernity and Self-Identity: Self and Society in the Late Modern Age*. Stanford: Stanford University Press.
Gillis, J. R. 1981. *Youth and History: Tradition and Change in European Age Relations, 1770-Present*. London: Academic Press.
Guillén, A. M., and Pavolini, E. 2012. "Young Adults, Poverty and the Role of Social Policies." In *Work, Family Policies and Transitions to Adulthood in Europe*, edited by Knijn, T., 155–179. Basingstoke: Palgrave Macmillan.
Hajnal, J. 1965. "European Marriage Patterns in Perspective." In *Population in History: Essays in Historical Demography*, edited by Glass, D., Eversley, D, 101–143. London: Edward Arnold.
Hammer, T. 2003. *Youth Unemployment and Social Exclusion in Europe: A Comparative Study*. Bristol: Policy Press.
Hogan, D. P., and Astone, N. M. 1986. "The Transition to Adulthood." *Annual review of sociology* (12): 109–130.

Jones, G. 2009. *Youth*. Cambridge: Polity.
Kangas, O., and Palme, J. 2000. "Does Social Policy Matter? Poverty Cycles in OECD Countries." *International Journal of Health Services* (30): 335–352.
Kieselbach, T., ed. 2000. *Youth Unemployment and Social Exclusion: Comparison of Six European Countries*. VS Verlag für: Sozialwissenschaften.
Knijn, T., ed. 2012. *Work, Family Policies and Transitions to Adulthood in Europe*. Basingstoke: Palgrave Macmillan.
Kohli, M. 1986. "The World We Forgot: A Historical Review of the Life Course." In *Later Life: The Social Psychology of Ageing*, edited by Marshall, V. W, 271–303. Beverly Hills: Sage.
Lesnard, L., Cousteaux, A.-S., Chanvril, F., and Le Hay, V. 2016. "Do Transitions to Adulthood Converge in Europe? An Optimal Matching Analysis of Work–Family Trajectories of Men and Women from 20 European Countries." *European Sociological Review* (32): 355–369.
Lesthaeghe, R. 1995. "The Second Demographic Transition in Western Societies. An Interpretation." In *Gender and Family Change in Industrialized Countries*, edited by Oppenheim Mason, K., Jensen, A.-M, 17–62. Oxford: Clarendon Press.
Liu, C., and Esteve, A. 2020. "Living Arrangements Across Households in Europe". *Max Planck Institute for Demographic Research*, No. WP-2020-002, Rostock.
Marsden, D. 1990. "Institutions and Labour Mobility: Occupational and Internal Labour Markets in Britain, France, Italy and West Germany." In *Labour Relations and Economic Performance*, edited by Brunetta, R., Dell'Aringa, C, 414–438. Basingstoke: Macmillan.
Maurice, M., Sellier, F., and Silvestre, J.-J. 1982. *Politique d'éducation et organisation industrielle en France et en Allemagne*. Paris: PUF.
Mayer, K. U. 2001. "The Paradox of Global Social Change and National Path Dependencies: Life Course Patterns in Advanced Societies." In *Inclusions-Exclusions*, edited by Woodward, A. E., Kohli, M, 89–110. London: Routledge.
Mayer, K. U., and Schoepflin, U. 1989. "The State and the Life Course." *Annual Review of Sociology* (15): 187–209.
Mendola, D., Busetta, A., and Aassve, A. 2009. "What Keeps Young Adults in Permanent Poverty? A Comparative Analysis Using ECHP." *Social Science Research* (38): 840–857.
Mitchell, B. 2006. *The Boomerang Age. Transitions to Adulthood in Families*. London: Routledge.
Modell, J., Furstenberg, F. F., and Hershberg, T. 1976. "Social Change and Transitions to Adulthood in Historical Perspective." *Journal of Family History* (1): 7–32.
Müller, W., and Gangl, M., eds. 2003. *Transitions from Education to Work in Europe: The Integration of Youth into EU Labour Markets*. Oxford: Oxford University Press.
Nico, M. 2014. "Variability in the Transitions to Adulthood in Europe: A Critical Approach to De-standardization of the Life Course." *Journal of Youth Studies* (17): 166–182.
OECD. 2010. *Off to a Good Start? Jobs for Youth*. Paris: OECD.
O'Reilly, J., Leschke, J., Ortlieb, R., Seeleib-Kaiser, Martin, M., and Villa, P., eds. 2019. *Youth Labour in Transition. Inequalities, Mobility, and Policies in Europe*. Oxford: Oxford University Press.
Petersen, A. C., and Mortimer, J. T., eds. 2006. *Youth Unemployment and Society*. New York: Cambridge University Press.

Raffe, D. 2003. "Pathways Linking Education and Work: A Review of Concepts, Research, and Policy Debates." *Journal of Youth Studies* (6): 3–19.

Reher, D. S. 1998. "Family Ties in Western Europe: Persistent Contrasts." *Population and Development Review* (24): 203–234.

Roberts, S. 2012. "One Step Forward, One Step Beck: A Contribution to the Ongoing Conceptual Debate in Youth Studies." *Journal of Youth Studies* (15): 389–401.

Roberts, S. 2010. "Misrepresenting 'Choice Biographies'?: A Reply to Woodman." *Journal of Youth Studies* (13): 137–149.

Roberts, S. 2009. "Opportunity Structures Then and Now." *Journal of Education and Work* 22 (5): 355–368.

Rovny, A. E. 2014. "The Capacity of Social Policies to Combat Poverty Among New Social Risk Groups." *Journal of European Social Policy*.

Ryan, P., Garonna, P., and Edwards, R. C., eds. 1991. *The Problem of Youth: The Regulation of Youth Employment and Training in Advanced Economies*. London: Macmillan Academic and Professional, Limited.

Schels, B. 2020. "When Poverty Becomes Detrimental to life Satisfaction in the Transition to Adulthood." *Longitudinal and Life Course Studies*.

Shanahan, M. J. 2000. "Pathways to Adulthood in Changing Societies: Variability and Mechanisms in Life Course Perspective." *Annual Review of Sociology* (26): 667–692.

Threadgold, S. 2011. "Should I Pitch My Tent in the Middle Ground? On 'Middling Tendency', Beck and Inequality in Youth Sociology." *Journal of Youth Studies* (14): 381–393.

Van de Velde, C. 2008. *Devenir Adulte : Sociologie comparée de la jeunesse en Europe*. Paris: PUF.

Vogel, J. 2001. "European Welfare Regimes and the Transition to Adulthood: A Comparative and Longitudinal Perspective." In *Family Forms and the Young Generation in Europe*, edited by Chisholm, L., de Lillo, A., Leccardi, C., Richter, R, 125–142. Milan: European observatory on the social situation, Demography and family.

Walther, A. 2006. "Regimes of Youth Transitions: Choice, Flexibility and Security in Young People's Experiences Across Different European Contexts." *Young* (14): 119–139.

Walther, A., Blasco, A. L., McNeish, W. 2003. *Young People and Contradictions of Inclusion: Towards Integrated Transition Policies in Europe*. Bristol: Policy Press.

Walther, A., Stauber, B., Biggart, A., du Bois-Reymond, M., Furlong, A., Lopez Blasco, A., Morch, S., Pais, J. M., eds. 2002. *Misleading Trajectories—Integration Policies for Young People in Europe?* Opladen: Leske + Budrich.

CHAPTER 30

Transitions in Later Life and the Re-configuration of Family Relationships in the Third Age: The Case of the Baby Boomers

Catherine Bonvalet, Rémi Gallou, and Jim Ogg

INTRODUCTION: BABY BOOMERS AND THE THIRD AGE

During the past 50 years Europe and other post-industrial countries have witnessed the arrival of the second demographic transition driven by declines in fertility, child mortality, and late-life mortality together with a diversity of union and family type (Avdeev et al. 2011). In addition, the cohort of the baby-boomer generation, large in numbers, has also contributed towards the changing composition of age structures within society (Monnier 2007). These trends have led to ageing populations with major consequences for family life and intergenerational personal relationships (Fingerman and Birditt 2011). Individuals who are currently reaching the age of retirement or the 'third age' are witnessing the gains of longevity of their parents, although this increase in life expectancy is frequently accompanied by a need for social care (Bonvalet et al. 2015). This demographic trend is in marked contrast to the cohorts born between 1915 and 1930, who mostly did not have a parent alive when they approached the age of retirement. Moreover, their children—the baby-boomer

---

C. Bonvalet
Institut national d'études démographiques, Aubervilliers Cedex, France
e-mail: bonvalet@ined.fr

R. Gallou · J. Ogg (✉)
Unité de recherche sur le vieillissement, Paris, France
e-mail: jim.ogg@wanadoo.fr

R. Gallou
e-mail: remi.gallou@cnav.fr

generations—gained their independence at an early age, as by the 1970s, the post-war housing shortage experienced in many countries had finally started to ebb. Low rates of unemployment enabled the baby boomer generation to become independent from their parents at a relatively young age.

In order to understand the individual, conjugal, and family behaviour of young retirees today it is necessary to review the arguments for and against the conceptualisation of the baby boomers as a generation that shared a distinctive formative experience. The concepts of the 'third' and 'fourth' age (Phillipson 2015) are also presented as an important theoretical framework to explain family relationships in later life. Family relationships in later life can also be understood within the framework of intergenerational solidarity and the concepts of conflict and ambivalence provide a useful theoretical tool to study ageing baby boomers (Lüscher and Pillimer 1998), and these concepts are presented as being integral to the reconfiguration of family relationships in later life and old age.

In the social sciences, the baby boomer generation has received considerable attention by demographers (Van Bavel and Reher 2013), historians (Owram 1996), and sociologists (Phillipson et al. 2008). The concept of 'a generation' (Mannheim 1928) is derived from the assumption that members of a birth cohort share a distinctive formative experience that can be studied empirically. This formative experience can be referred to as a 'cohort effect', defined as 'the impact of historical events and processes on individual lives, particularly during the formative years' (Alwin et al. 2004, 4). The baby boomer generation of individuals born immediately after the Second World War have been particular associated with this cohort effect (Chauvel 2013). If the first generations of the cohorts born between 1946 and 1954 experienced harsh post-war social and economic conditions in their early childhood, growing economic growth and prosperity during the 'Thirty Golden Years' (1945–1975) quickly resulted in a better quality of life and social mobility. The 1960s witnessed a massive increase in consumerism, fuelled in part by full employment. In addition, home ownership rates increased in many European countries, allowing children to live apart from their parents (Angelini et al. 2013). These conditions led to a rise in individual aspirations and opportunities for personal choice that was increasingly accessible as consumer societies evolved. Alongside these economic transformations, the baby boomers challenged what was perceived as traditional ways of family life, and many rejected the conventions of the old social order (Gilleard and Higgs 2007; Bonvalet et al. 2015). Women were no longer confined to the domestic sphere of family life and new family forms began to arise, such as one parent families and 'recomposed' families following separation and divorce (Allan 2001). Gender roles began to be redefined, especially within the couple (Amato and Booth 1995; Hakim 1996). The baby boomer generation has therefore lived through a unique and defining moment, which could be studied through the lens of a 'cohort effect' (Gilleard and Higgs 2007; Leach et al. 2013). This cohort effect has often been caricatured by presenting the baby boomer generation as a homogenous group of active seniors and avid consumers of leisure. Baby boomers have also been pejoratively depicted in certain scientific and media discourse as a 'spoilt', 'golden', 'selfish', or 'parasite' generation. However, as research has shown, particularly in Quebec, not all individuals born between 1946 and 1954 are 'baby boomers' in the sociological sense of the term (Biggs et al. 2007; Olazabal 2009) and some researchers question the usefulness of the term 'baby boomer' to describe a homogenous group (Bonvalet et al. 2015). The reality is more complex.

In fact, as the baby boomer generation moved through the life course, it became increasingly apparent that the concept of a cohort effect fell short of explaining the growing heterogeneity of the baby boomer generation (George 1993). Social and economic transformations in the 1970s and 1980s meant that increasing numbers of baby-boomers experienced unemployment and housing shortages in the 1980s and 1990s at a time when their family responsibilities as young parents were numerous. Social inequalities within and between generations became more common. Moreover, although the virtues of personal choice, self-identity, and autonomy had been represented as a liberating experience, the rise of individualism that was characteristic of the baby boomers was also been portrayed as threatening the fabric of society and in particular family solidarity. For example, American sociologists, such as Etzioni (1995) and Putnam (2000), associate a rise in individualism with a decline in civic engagement and more traditional forms of sociability. In the UK and France, some commentators have portrayed baby boomers as a selfish generation that has attained a privileged social, cultural and economic status at the expense of their children (Chauvel 1998; Willetts 2010.) At the same time, other authors such as de Singly in France (2009) and Giddens (1991) in the UK have been more positive about the possibilities of reconciling individualism with social responsibilities. These authors maintain that individualism can lead to the creation of new forms of social ties that are not constrained to the traditional and restrictive roles of the family whilst at the same time maintaining intergenerational solidarity. Questions relating to the emergence of weakening family ties or the re-negotiation of relations that have taken place among the baby boomer and succeeding generations have been the subject of much debate and research, but the consensus seems to be, at least for the baby boomer generation, that family solidarity has been transformed but did not disappear (Arber and Attias-Donfut 2002; Olazabal 2009; Bonvalet et al. 2015).

The theoretical and empirical literature points to a re-configuration of family relations that has taken place over the past 50 years. In line with this literature, we suggest that the intersection of demographic, economic, and social trends has compelled the baby boomers and other third agers that follow them into later life to reconcile individual aspirations of activities associated with self-fulfilment and leisure with family obligations and responsibilities. The situational characteristics of the current generation of young retirees, as the children of sometimes frail elderly parents and the parents of adult children, is made all the more difficult by the fact that norms of independence between the generations and individualism continue to prevail, often placing the baby boomer generation in a situation of tension relating to their family relationships (Bonvalet et al. 2015). Gender issues are at the forefront of these tensions between self-fulfilment and family obligations (Arber et al. 2007). Women of the baby boomer and subsequent generations who are entering the third age have moved away from the housewife model of their mothers and grandmothers. They have gained financial independence by entering the labour market on a massive scale and have had to reconcile family and working life during their working lives. They are faced with a new dilemma of reconciling caring responsibilities within the family with paid work in the context of legal retirement ages being pushed back (Bonvalet et al. 2015). We also suggest that in order to understand how these transformations are affecting the re-configuration of family relationships that men and women experience in later life, it is necessary on the one hand to place them in the context of the life course perspective (Hareven and Adams 1978) and the changes associated with the baby boomer generation and on the other hand to re-locate these changes in the contemporary experience of a rise in social inequalities (Peugny and Van de Velde 2013).

With the advancing age of the baby boom generation and the third agers who follow them, many questions arise. How are the post-war generations that transformed the stages of family life by initiating cohabitation outside marriage, separation and divorce, recomposed families, solo living, and changing gender roles within the couple, experiencing the third age? How has the baby boom generation, which finds itself demographically confronted with an unprecedented situation by being 'sandwiched' between an elderly parent and children who often need support to establish themselves in adult life, responded to family demands and obligations without abandoning the values of modern societies such as autonomy and personal fulfilment? Finally, as the first baby boomers approach the fourth age, how will they experience the increased gains in longevity in the knowledge that these gains risk being compromised by frailty and disability and thus the need for care and support?

The objective of this chapter is to examine from a theoretical perspective how the baby boomer generations have transformed the third age by remaining active in cultural activities and consumerism, whilst reconciling new family solidarities with independence. The chapter presents both theoretical and empirical studies that have examined the contemporary relations between the baby boomer generation, their ageing parents, and their adult children. The first section deals with retirement as a life course transition that implies a reorganisation of time both at an individual level and in the context of life within a couple. The second section examines the help and support that is directed towards ascending and descending generations.

The Transition to Retirement: Conjugal Projects

Increased life expectancy has opened up 'a new period of life after work', offering individuals who have adequate resources the ability to pursue leisure or other activities for many years after retirement from paid work. Retirement from paid work is no longer a period of a short number of years in good health before the onset of illness or disability, but a significant length of time spanning from 20 to 30 years for many individuals. In the 1960s, as the word itself signifies, 'retirement' meant a complete disengagement from paid work and even civil society. Considered as a form of 'social death' (Guillemard 1972; Townsend 1981), retirement was a period of the life course in which family activities and the home became the central preoccupation in anticipation of only a short number of years before the end of life (Roussel and Bourguignon 1978). Actually, retirement is no longer a final stage in the life course, but an opportunity for individuals to take on new projects, whether they be family orientated or in the context of civic engagement (Van den Bogaard 2014) and even paid work (Platts et al. 2019). This transformation of the third age, made possible in large part by medical progress (particularly preventive medicine), higher pensions, and improvements in life quality compared to earlier generations, has modified the behaviour of current retirees. As we have seen, they are advancing in age in the context of having their parents alive, their children beginning adult life, and the new challenges for intergenerational solidarity that results from these transformations (Fingerman and Birditt 2011; Phillipson 2015). In order to understand these challenges, it is necessary to begin by examining the gendered experience of couples entering the third age.

It is important to stress that for the baby boomer generations who entered retirement, as well as the third agers who are following them, living together as a couple is the most common form of household composition (Delbès and Gaymu 2003; Gaymu and Springer 2012). Data from Wave 7 of the SHARE survey (2017), when the baby boomer birth cohort of Europeans born between 1946 and 1950 were aged between 67 and 74, show that despite this cohort having experienced a rise in separation and divorce, approximately 7 out of 10 individuals were married and living together as a couple (authors' analysis).[1] As this birth cohort ages, widowhood becomes more common and women are much less likely than men to share a household with a partner as they advance in age, but living in a couple is still the norm for the majority of European baby boomers and other third agers.[2] This is the reason why we focus in this section mainly on couples and the negotiations undertaken between men and women at the time of retirement together with the life choices that are made in the third age.

Retirement Timing in Couples

The transition from work to retirement can have a significant effect on relationships within a couple. Women of the baby boomer generation have for the most part participated in the labour market, either full-time or part-time and many continue to be in paid employment at the age of 60 years (Hakim 2000). Retirement timing and projects no longer depend solely on the decision of men. Age differences between partners can affect retirement timing, not only with regard to the legal retirement age but also where women have to extend their working life to build up contributions to their pension that are missing due mostly to earlier child-rearing career breaks (Ogg et al. 2013). Retirement timing within couples is increasingly planned, anticipated, and negotiated (Ogg et al. 2012). Several factors need to be taken into account, not least the evolution of respective careers over the life course (periods of unemployment, quality of workplace conditions) and respective incomes and rights to a pension (Eismann et al. 2017). Given the increasing participation of women in the labour market, the negotiating 'force' of women within couples has become stronger, especially where women have been upwardly mobile in their career or where their partner has experienced unemployment and is no longer able to maintain his 'breadwinner' status (Bertaux-Wiame 2006). It is not uncommon therefore to find situations where men are retired and women continue to work and where traditional gender roles are inverted at this stage of the life course (Ogg et al. 2012).

In addition, health factors, family responsibilities, and respective choices regarding the work-life balance are important factors that influence the reorganisation of the domestic sphere of third agers living in a couple (Auger 2016). Moreover, even though most couples moving into retirement are composed of unions that have lasted many years, the increase in the number of recomposed families can widen the age gap between spouses of a new union (Bergström 2018). The birth of a child in a recomposed family where age differences are large between partners can have an important impact on respective retirement decisions within a couple.

Gender differences in labour force participation over the life course also play an important role in retirement timing. In many countries strong normative expectations concerning gender roles result in women combining paid and unpaid (family) work with the consequence that their earnings and later-life financial security are disadvantaged compared to men. Traditional gender roles within couples—men as 'bread-winners', women as 'home makers'—influence patterns of retirement timing. In countries where childcare continues to be predominately undertaken by women, gender pension gaps are large. Women have a lower probability of achieving the requisite minimum contributions that give them the right to receive a pension. Consequently, their retirement timing is more conditioned by their husband's retirement or is forced upon them for family reasons, including the need to care for family members in poor health.

In some cases, women have no access to pensions in their own right, relying instead on derived rights from their husband (OECD 2018).

Retirement: A New Stage in the Life Course of Couples

Several studies have pointed to the process of renegotiation of roles that takes place within couples following the transition to retirement. Once both partners have retired, couples seek to organise the time previously consecrated to work. Given sufficient income and wealth, life projects can be realised and new activities envisaged. The passage to retirement can therefore bring about a questioning for respective partners concerning their role in a couple and the realisation of personal projects. Couple dynamics and gender roles can change and a new equilibrium is sometimes sought (Caradec 2004). This process often becomes apparent through residential mobility choices and strategies related to the accumulation of wealth, both of which in the past may have been influenced by the career patterns of men. Today, women in a couple increasingly take part in the planning of projects and the decisions that accompany them (Bertaux-Wiame 2006).

For some couples, retirement also entails readjusting to respective needs and wishes, often brought to the fore by the increased amount of time spent together within the household (Segalen and Martial 2019). Indeed, the passage to retirement can be a time to reassess the suitability of the home and the immediate environment. Home improvements or adaptations can be undertaken as well as a residential move envisaged. Anticipating the future and the arrival of advanced old age can present challenges or even in some case a denial of the possibility of ill health rendering the home and its immediate environment unsuitable (Auger 2016). Young retirees can consider themselves to be 'ageing' but not 'old' and they want to live for the moment rather than plan for advanced old age. Thus personal projects related to immediate improvements in life quality are privileged.

Residential mobility can become part of a life-style project. For couples, choices can often entail difficult negotiations, with divergent wishes. Research has shown that women tend to prefer towns and cities to the countryside as places to retire, whereas men prefer detached homes and the availability of a garden (Bonvalet and Ogg 2009). Compromises are often needed on the choice of location, although for the middle and higher classes the possession of a second home simplifies location choices. In previous research on the residential mobility of persons approaching retirement and living in London and Paris (Bonvalet and Ogg 2009), the possession of two homes allowed couples to move between the city with its access to services and culture and the countryside or coastal locations (Pickering et al. 2019). Moving between homes is not only confined to higher social class groups, but also practised by migrant retirees who spent periods of the year both in the host and home country. In France, among the Portuguese, Maghrebin, and Turkish populations, retired men often prefer to live in the home they have built in their home country, whilst their partners prefer to keep a foothold in the host country and to move between the two countries, thus sometimes leading to tensions in the couple (Attias-Donfut 2006).

In some cases, compromise in the couple regarding retirement decisions and planning is not possible and the passage to retirement triggers latent relationship difficulties within the couple and an identity reconstruction leading finally to a separation (Caradec 2004). In this respect, the baby boomer generation and third agers retain certain characteristics of their formative years by privileging individual fulfilment over an unsatisfactory life in a couple. Many countries are experiencing a rise in divorce after the age of 60 (Brown and Wright 2017) as well as the formation of new affective relationships (Bonvalet and Ogg 2009). Finally, the passage in retirement for couples often occurs at the moment when children finally leave the parental home, since many children of third agers are delaying leaving home on account of difficulties in finding employment and housing. When these two life events occur, family dynamics change and evolve, with couples experiencing the 'empty nest' phase of parenting and the reorganisation of time and mobility that occurs with passage to retirement.

FAMILY RELATIONSHIPS FROM THE PERSPECTIVE OF THE THIRD AGE

The rise of individualism and the desire to 'become oneself' can be at odds with family norms of responsibility and obligation, which according to some authors remain strong in Europe (Lowenstein and Daatland 2006). Today, family obligations are enshrined with a series of principles and practices that place constraints on individual freedom whilst at the same time emphasising the need 'for each individual to fulfil their own needs and to be unique' (Déchaux 2010, 107).

Retirees Faced with the Ageing of Their Parents

Family relations in later life and old age depend on a number of factors. At the micro-level, the availability of kinship ties, the distance separating family members, and the quality of relationships are important determinants. With advancing age, a certain number of older people prefer to maintain close geographical proximity with their family (Bonvalet 2003), and sometimes move home to be nearer to family members (children, siblings, nephews, or nieces). This form of close family solidarity is particularly observed among lower social class group.

Research has shown the diversity of family functioning according to these different criteria (emotional proximity, geographical proximity, mutual aid, and frequency of contact). Several types of families can be distinguished: the local family-centre, which functions as a supportive group living in the same city and more often found among the working classes; the dispersed family-centre, whose solidarity does not depend on geographical scale, typical of the upper classes; and the attenuated family, where ties with the family are distended or even non-existent and are the result of family history (Bonvalet 2003).

At the macro-level, institutional and legal frameworks that place responsibilities and obligations relating to different family members shape normative patterns of behaviour. The gains in life expectancy that have been a major trend of ageing populations do not match gains in health life expectancy and the parents of the baby boomer generation and third agers increasingly experience a loss of autonomy that is accompanied by a need for social care (Cambois and Robine 2017). As we have noted, research undertaken in the past 30 years on the family relationships of the baby boomer generation has largely determined that intergenerational solidarity has been transformed but not disappeared (Arber and Attias-Donfut 2002). In a study of Europeans baby boomers' role in supporting their parents, it was found that they are regularly involved in helping their parents when they live close by, when they are not working and when the health status of the parents suggests that help is needed (Ogg and Renaut 2006). This is the case for all European countries, but the two factors of closer geographical proximity and less developed welfare systems in southern European countries means that baby boomers there are more implicated in the lives of their parents than in continental and northern Europe, although even in southern European countries there is diversity in family modes of organisation (Wall et al. 2001).

Central to this transformation is the encounter between individual aspirations and new family obligations resulting from demographic, social, and economic trends which place constraints and limits to personal projects in the third age. Baby boomers and other third agers are therefore confronted with the need to reconcile their own personal or conjugal projects with the new and often unexpected social and economic circumstances of their wider family as for example in the case of 'boomerang' children who return to live with their parents after having left home (Mitchell 2006).

A useful theoretical framework to understand this encounter has been developed by several authors, whereby the concepts of conflict and ambivalence are employed as adjuncts to the prevailing notion of solidarity (Lüscher and Pillemer 1998; Lüscher 2002; Connidis and McMullin 2002). The term 'intergenerational ambivalence' refers to the contradictions in intergenerational family relationships that exist on two dimensions: contradictions at the macro-social structure in roles and norms, particularly in relation to gender roles; and contradictions at the psychological-subjective level, in terms of cognition, emotions, and motivation. The concepts of conflict and ambivalence in family relations from the perspective of the baby boomer generation and their ageing parents have been empirically investigated by the OASIS (Old Age and Autonomy: the role of service systems and intergenerational autonomy) study undertaken in 2001 in Norway, England, Germany, Spain, and Israel (Daatland and Herlofson 2003). This research found that overt conflict between older parents and their children is rare. However, the findings also showed that low levels of conflict between parents and their adult children can co-exist with harmonious and positive affective family relations. Ambivalence about roles can be a 'normal' state as parents and adult children struggle to negotiate a path between autonomy and dependence. For the baby boomer generation, many women in their youth had to contend with conflicts arising from the differences in values and norms between children and parents, often manifested in the issue of whether young mothers should participate in the labour market (Badinter 2010). The resolution of this conflict was manifestly in the favour of the baby boomer generation women, who entered the labour market in large numbers. Once in the third age, they faced a new dilemma of whether to continue working or to look after their ageing parents and parents-in-law. The needs of ageing parents therefore present new demands that can force women to cut down on their professional or leisure activities or even curtail them altogether (Ní Léime et al. 2020).

Although the tension between work and motherhood has been extensively examined in recent years, there is less research on how women combine looking after frail and elderly relatives with full-time employment. Daughters can be expected to 'be present on all fronts - family, personal and professional' (Le Bihan-Youinou and Martin 2006). The way in which women negotiate these demands is strongly associated with social class, with women in manual or service related employment often having to resort to part-time work and unsociable hours in order to combine paid employment with family obligations. The availability of services also plays a strong part in providing opportunities or constraints for older working women to combine paid employment with family obligations. In Denmark, for example, 'routine access to high quality child and eldercare institutions means that women can participate in paid employment rather than provide unpaid care to grandchildren or frail elder parents or partners' (Jensen 2020, 229–230).

The parent-child relationship is not the only one affected by ageing, since the lengthening of the lives of older people can result in changes in the relationships between siblings and a redistribution of roles (Bonvalet et al. 2015). Studies have repeatedly shown that caregiving to older parents is concentrated on one sibling, and that this sibling is more likely to be the youngest child (Lin and Wolf 2019). Where caring for an elderly parent is shared between siblings, research suggests that younger siblings are likely to act independently of older siblings and provide an amount of care dependent on their own family circumstances and the needs of their parents (Roquebert et al. 2018). The involvement of older siblings in caregiving to a parent is more dependent on the younger sibling's behaviour and the older sibling is more likely to give support if the younger sibling is a caregiver (ibid.). These trends seem to act independently of a 'cohort effect' associated with baby boomer and subsequence generations.

Qualitative research has shown that the implication of siblings in the care of their older parents can also depend on the quality of parent/child relationships (Bonvalet et al. 2015). Faced with their parent's loss of autonomy, some children remained 'impassive' to family obligations because relationships with their parents had been distant for many years. Others assumed the role of 'passive caregivers', in the sense that they did not provide 'hands-on' care either because geographical distance rendered daily help impossible, or because a 'preferred' or more available sibling provided care. Unlike *active* helpers, who are at the centre of a comprehensive support system, the passive helpers, delegate to a brother or, more generally, a sister. Others played a central role in help and support to their elderly parents. Gender roles were apparent, since men tended to rely upon their wife, sister, or sister-in-law. It should also be noted that elderly parents themselves can be active in determining the respective roles of their children when help and support is needed. The quality of parent/child relations is an important factor and daughters seem to be preferred over sons (Gallou et al. 2019). Again, these findings suggest that a strong cohort effect is not present, with caregiving to elderly parents still being seen as the responsibility of daughters irrespective of the cohort. At the same time, the baby boomer generation and other third agers are reluctant to substitute their place as children for that of carers and to reduce their role to that of mere service provider. Adult child carers are thus confronted with a new situation in which they seek to preserve the autonomy of their parents whilst providing support (Van Pevenage 2015). Moreover, the dynamics of intergenerational support takes place in the context of ambivalence over respective roles, both within families and between third agers and the wider professional support services.

Relations with Children and Grandchildren

As we have seen, the baby boomer generation and other third agers occupy a 'pivotal' position in family life, since they are placed within ascending and descending generations (Grundy and Shelton 2001; Grundy and Henretta 2006; Fingerman and Dolbin-MacNab 2006). The compromises that are sought between self-aspiration and intergenerational family solidarity which is a defining attribute of this 'pivot' generation can also be clearly seen in relations with children and grandchildren. The rise in unemployment and precarious jobs that has been a feature of all Europeans societies, coupled with shortages in the housing market and economic barriers for young adults to become home-owners and leave the parental home, has resulted in increased or prolonged periods of support provided by the baby-boomer generation to their children. This support can be provided by financial transfers, intergenerational cohabitation, and care for grandchildren. Empirical studies have long confirmed that the baby-boomer generation has been active in these areas of support for their children whilst at the same time pursuing an active lifestyle in later life (Attias-Donfut 1995; Bonvalet et al. 2015; Siren and Casier 2019).

The baby-boomer generation has also formed affective relations with their adult children which are qualitatively different from those that they experienced with their own parents. Leisure pursuits are often shared together and lifestyles can be convergent. Parents who financially support children in their passage to adulthood and beyond have lower margins to save for retirement.

The intersection of family obligations with individual aspirations and the tensions that result can be clearly seen in the case of grandchildren. On the one hand, the attitudes and behaviour of the baby boomer generation of grandparents can be seen as a continuity of family values and obligations (Bonvalet et al. 2015). By transmitting family memoires, grandparents act as a bridge between the generations and they play an important role in fulfilling the 'need to know roots and origins' (Attias-Donfut et al. 2012; Gourdon 2001; Bonvalet and Lelièvre 2016). Several studies have shown that grandparenting continues to be an important role assumed by the baby-boomer generation and that furthermore, the affective relations forged with children are manifest in relations with grandchildren. As far as patterns of grandparenting in Europe are concerned, differences exist between northern and southern Europe. The intervention of grandparents is crucial in southern European countries on account of a low level of investment in childcare provision outside of the family. In Spain, the mothers of young children often cannot participate in paid work were it not for their help of their parents (Tobio 2001), and a similar situation exists in Italy (Gattai and Musatti 1999). Grandparents also play an important role in the advent of their grandchildren's parental separation by offering support in times of difficulty, a role adding to routine grandchildren tasks. With the rise of individualism it may have been expected that the baby boomer generation would give priority to their professional and friendship network to the detriment of family relations. The modernity of the baby boomer generation grandparents is less the fact that they continue to play an important role in grandparenting than the fact they do so whilst combining their own needs for autonomy and individual desires. On the other hand, elements of conflict and ambivalence can arise if grandparents are expected to do 'too much' in terms of child-care and other supportive activities. Several studies have found that providing long hours of care for young grandchildren can affect the health and well-being of grandparents (Dench and Ogg 2002; Statham 2011). Contemporary grandparents are prepared to look after their grandchildren and to develop strong bonds with them, but they do not wish to over invest and to relinquish their own activities.

The majority of older people are parents with adult children alive. But childless older people represent approximately ten per cent of the population and their position within family life and their access to family support is also an important component of the inclusion of elders in family life. According to Albertini and Kohli (2009) childless older people have been treated as a problematic group and several studies have found an association between childlessness and isolation (Koropeckyj-Cox 1998; Zhang and Hayward 2001). Often assigned a strong social stigma, childlessness is commonly assumed to be a cause of social isolation. Although some patterns observed among older childless groups, such as their over-representation in residential care homes (Renaut 2001) or lower levels of social support (Gray 2009), suggest that there may be an 'at-risk' group, much of the research evidence is equivocal. Several authors have challenged the notion of older childless persons as a group 'at-risk' of social exclusion by refocusing on what they give to their families, friends, and wider society rather than what they receive (Albertini and Kohli 2009). Often childless older people maintain close relations with their siblings, nieces, and nephews (Bonvalet et al. 2015)

The importance of non-immediate family members (*i.e.* other than spouses, children, grandchildren, parents, or siblings) as well as the role of non-family members has been explored through the development of social network studies (Phillipson et al. 1998; Nocon and Pearson 2000; Girardin and Widmer 2015). These studies have shown the importance of social support that exists outside the immediate family members, although there appear to be limits to the types of tasks, regularity, and volume of support that non-family members give to older people. Some commentators see a change taking place from the predominance of 'family groups to personal communities', where both families and other social ties form a spectrum of relations that are 'part of the more fluid social world of late modernity' (Phillipson 2001). The importance of friendship as a form of 'hidden solidarity', where friends take on roles more traditionally associated with families (as well as family members becoming more 'friend-like'), has been the subject of several studies (Pahl 2000; Pahl and Spencer 2006; Stevens and Van Tilburg 2011). Friendships as a source of social support in later life are clearly important for childless older people. But friendship may also be an important source of social capital for separated and divorced persons in later life, the numbers of which are growing.

Conclusion

The baby-boom generation, which has been the main actor of family transformations over the last fifty years, has also reshaped the third age. Retirement no longer appears as a retreat into the private sphere as it used to be for the parents of baby boomers, but as a stage that is increasingly negotiated within the couple, whether regarding decisions concerning the end of working life or for life choices during retirement. The financial autonomy acquired by women since the 1960s through massive access to the labour market enables them to manage their retirement better and according to their aspirations and desires. Like men, women have contributed to changing the image of retirees. They are active in civil society, want to continue to 'stay young', to consume, to travel, to pursue professional or voluntary activities while enjoying looking after their grandchildren. It can be concluded that their desire for autonomy and mobility has not been realised—as some may have feared—to the detriment of family solidarity, both with regard to ascending and descending generations.

However, in examining these later life transformations within the couple and the family it can be seen that the individualistic lifestyle associated with the baby boomer generation should be nuanced because of the heterogeneity of this generation and the persistence of inequalities. First of all, gender inequalities persist, with individualisation having paradoxical effects for women. Autonomy remains precarious, with higher expectations placed on women to meet family obligations than for men. There are social class inequalities, since not all baby boomers are healthy 'young retirees', or consumers of leisure and travel. Differences between social classes continue throughout retirement, pitting higher social classes with longer life expectancy, comfortable resources accumulated throughout life, often with a second home and an appetite for new technologies, against lower social class groups who experience health problems more quickly, sometimes face financial difficulties, are less able to cope with the digital revolution and are sometimes forced to continue working beyond retirement. It is among them that we find the most isolated and socially excluded people. Finally, there are inequalities between countries due to different social protection systems, which may or may not alleviate or accentuate family obligations.

As they age the baby boomer generation that adopted the values of freedom and mobility and who 'refused to grow old', have found themselves confronted with the harsh reality of their advanced age and the fragilities associated with it. From 'young retirees', they are moving into a life stage associated with increased risks to their health. The question is to what extent and with what intensity (depending on European contexts), will this last stage of life be marked by a generation effect that significantly adds to the period effect (as for example the current COVID-19 crisis), modifying the relationship to old age and the response to it through private and public forms of solidarity.

Notes

1. This paper uses data from SHARE Wave 7 (https://doi.org/10.6103/share.w7.700), see Börsch-Supan et al. (2013) for methodological details. The SHARE data collection has been funded by the European Commission through FP5 (QLK6-CT-2001-00360), FP6 (SHARE-I3: RII-CT-2006-062193, COMPARE: CIT5-CT-2005-028857, SHARELIFE: CIT4-CT-2006-028812), FP7 (SHARE-PREP: GA NO. 211909, SHARE-LEAP: GA NO. 227822, SHARE M4: GA NO. 261982) and Horizon 2020 (SHARE-DEV3: GA NO. 676536, SERISS: GA NO. 654221) and by DG Employment, Social Affairs & Inclusion. Additional funding from the German Ministry of Education and Research, the Max Planck Society for the Advancement of Science, the U.S. National Institute on Aging (U01_AG09740-13S2, P01_AG005842, P01_AG08291, P30_AG12815, R21_AG025169, Y1-AG-4553-01, IAG_BSR06-11, OGHA_04-064, HHSN271201300071C) and from various national funding sources is gratefully acknowledged(see www.share-project.org).

2. In 2017, almost three fifths (58.5%) of all men aged 65 years or more living in the EU-28 shared their household with a partner (but no other persons in the household); the corresponding share for women of the same age was much lower, at 39.6%). https://ec.europa.eu/eurostat/statistics-explained/index.php?title=Ageing_Europe_-_statistics_on_housing_and_living_conditions#Household_composition_among_older_people. Accessed on 1 November 2020.

References

Albertini, M., and Kohli, M. 2009. "What Childless Older People Give: Is the Generational Link Broken?" *Ageing & Society* 29 (8): 1261–1274.

Allan, G. 2001. "Personal Relationships in Late Modernity." *Personal Relationships* 8 (3): 325–339.

Alwin, D. F., McCammon, R. J., and Hofer, S. M. (2004). "Studying Baby Boom Cohorts Within a Demographic and Developmental Context: Conceptual and Methodological Issues." In *The Baby Boomers at Midlife: Contemporary Perspectives on Middle Age*, edited by Krauss Whitbourne, S. and Willis, S. L. Mahwah, NJ: Lawrence Erlbaum Associates Inc.

Amato, P., and Booth, A. 1995. "Changes in Gender ROLE Attitudes and Perceived Marital Quality." *American Sociological Review* 60 (1): 58–66.

Angelini, V., Laferrère, A., and Weber, G. 2013. "Home-ownership in Europe: How Did It Happen?" *Advances in Life Course Research* 18 (1): 83–90.

Arber, S., Andersson, L., and Hoff, A. 2007. "Changing Approaches to Gender and Ageing: Introduction." *Current Sociology* 55 (2): 147–153.

Arber, S., and Attias-Donfut, C. 2002. *The Myth of Intergenerational Conflict: The Family and State in Ageing Societies*. London: Routledge.

Attias-Donfut, C., ed. 1995. *Les solidarités entre générations. Vieillesse, Familles, État*. Paris: Nathan.

Attias-Donfut C., ed. 2006. *L'enracinement*. Paris: Armand Colin.

Attias-Donfut C., Cook J., Hoffman J., and Waite L. 2012. *Citizenship, Belonging and Intergenerational Relations in African Migration*. London: Palgrave Macmillan.

Auger, F. 2016. *L'aménagement de l'habitat chez des couples de nouveaux retraités Baby-Boomers : vivre le présent, anticiper l'avenir ?* (The Development of Housing by Newly Retired Couples of Baby-Boomers : Living the Present, Anticipating the Future ?) Sociologie. Université Charles de Gaulle—Lille III, Français. Available at https://tel.archives-ouvertes.fr/tel-01469229/ Accessed 1 November 2020.

Avdeev, A., Eremenko, T., Festy, P., Gaymu, J., Le Bouteillec, N., and Springer, S. 2011. "Populations et tendances démographiques des pays européens (1980–2010)." *Population* 66 (1): 9–129. https://doi.org/10.3917/popu.1101.0009.

Badinter, E. 2010. *Le conflit. La femme et la mère*. Paris: Flammarion.

Bergström, M. 2018. "De quoi l'écart d'âge est-il le nombre ? L'apport des big data à l'étude de la différence d'âge au sein des couples." *Revue française de sociologie* 59 (3): 395–422.

Bertaux-Wiame, I. 2006. "Conjugalité et mobilité professionnelle : le dilemme de l'égalité." *Cahiers du Genre* 41 (2): 49–73.

Biggs, S., Phillipson, C., Money, A. M., and Leach, R. 2007. "Baby Boomers and Adult Ageing: Issues for Social and Public Policy." *Quality in Ageing and Older Adults* 8 (3).

Bonvalet C. 2003. "The Local Family Circle." *Population (English Edition)* 58 (1): 9-42.
Bonvalet, C., and Ogg, J. 2009. *The Baby-Boomers: A Mobile Generation*. Oxford: The Bardwell Press.
Bonvalet, C., Clément, C., and Ogg, J. 2015. *Renewing the Family. : A History of the Baby Boomers*. Series: INED Population Studies, Vol. 4. New York: Springer.
Bonvalet C., and Lelièvre E. 2016. "Grandparents : From Neglect to Idolization." In *Family Beyond Household and Kin : Life Event Histories and Entourage, a French Survey*, INED population studies 6, 133-149. Cham: Springer.
Brown, S. L., and Wright, M. R. 2017. "Marriage, Cohabitation, and Divorce in Later Life."*Innovation in Aging* 1 (2): igx015. https://doi.org/10.1093/geroni/igx015.
Cambois, E., and Robine, J-M. 2017. "L'allongement de l'espérance de vie en Europe: Quelles conséquences pour l'état de santé." *Revue européenne des sciences sociales* 55-1: 41–67.
Caradec, V. 2004. *Vieillir après la retraite. Approche sociologique du vieillissement*. Paris: Presses Universitaires de France.
Chauvel, L. 1998. *Le destin des générations. Structure sociale et cohortes en France au XXe siècle*. Paris: Presses Universitaires de France.
Chauvel, L. 2013. "Specificity and Consistency of Cohort Effects: The APCD Model Applied to Generational Inequalities, France, United States, 1985–2010." *Revue française de sociologie* 54: 665–705.
Connidis, I., and McMullin, J. 2002. "Sociological Ambivalence and Family Ties: A Critical Perspective." *Journal of Marriage and the Family* 64 (3): 558–567.
Daatland, S. O., and Herlofson, K. 2003. "'Lost Solidarity' or 'Changed Solidarity': A Comparative European View of Normative Family Solidarity." *Ageing and Society* 23 (5): 537–560.
Déchaux, J. H. 2010. *Sociologie de la famille*. Paris: Repères.
Delbès, C., and Gaymu, J. 2003. "Passé 60 ans : de plus en plus souvent en couple?" *Population et sociétés*, Num 389, 4 p.
Dench, G., and Ogg, J. 2002. *Grandparenting in Britain*. London: Institute of Community Studies.
De Singly, F. 2009. *Sociologie de la famille contemporaine*. Paris: Armand Colin.
Eismann, M., Henkens, K., and Kalmijn, M. 2017. "Spousal Preferences for Joint Retirement: Evidence from a Multiactor Survey Among Older Dual-earner Couples." *Psychology and Aging* 32 (8): 689–697.
Etzioni, A. 1995. *The Responsive Community: A Communitarian Perspective*. Presidential Address, American Sociological Association, (August 20).
Fingerman, K. L., and Dolbin-MacNab, M. 2006. "The Baby Boomers and Their Parents: Cohort Influences and Intergenerational Ties." In *The Baby Boomers Grow Up: Contemporary Perspectives on Midlife*, edited by S. K. Whitbourne and S. L Willis, 237–259. Mahwah, NJ: Lawrence Erlbaum Associates.
Fingerman, K. L., and Birditt, K. S. 2011. "Adult Children and Aging Parents." In *Handbook of the Psychology of Aging*, edited by K. W. Schaie and S. L. Willis, 7th ed., 219–232. New York: Elsevier.
Gallou, R. et al. 2019. *Vers de nouvelles dynamiques de mobilité résidentielle ? L'enquête Amare (Ancrage et Mobilité résidentielle à la Retraite)*, Les cahiers de la Cnav, juillet 2019, no. 13.

Gattai, F. B., and Musatti, T. 1999. "Grandmothers' Involvement in Grandchildren's Care: Attitudes, Feelings, and Emotions." *Family Relations* 48 (1): 35–42.

Gaymu, J., and Springer, S. 2012. "How Does Living Alone or With a Partner Influence Life Satisfaction Among Older Men and Women in Europe?" *Population* (English edition) 67: 43–69.

George, L. K. 1993. "Sociological Perspectives on Life Transitions." *Annual Review of Sociology* 19 (1): 353–373.

Giddens, A. 1991. *Modernity and Self-Identity:. Self and Society in the Late Modern Age*. Cambridge: Polity Press.

Gilleard, C., and Higgs, P. 2007. "The Third Age and the Baby Boomers." *International Journal of Ageing and Later Life* 2 (2): 13–30.

Girardin, M., and Widmer, E. D. 2015. "Lay Definitions of Family and Social Capital in Later Life." *Personal* Relationships 22: 712–737.

Gourdon, V. 2001. *Histoire des grands-parents*. Paris: Plon.

Gray, A. 2009. "The Social Capital of Older People." *Ageing &* Society 29 (1): 5–31.

Grundy, E., and Shelton, N. 2001. "Contact Between Adult Children and Their Parents in Great Britain 1986–99." *Environment and Planning A: Economy and Space* 33 (4): 685–697.

Grundy, E., and Henretta, J. C. 2006. "Between Elderly Parents and Adult Children: A New Look at the Intergenerational Care Provided by "the Sandwich Generation". *Ageing and Society* 26: 707–722.

Guillemard, A.-M. 1972. *La retraite, une mort sociale*. Paris/La Haye: Mouton.

Hareven, T., and Adams, K. J., eds. 1978. *Ageing, and Life Course Transitions*. New York: Tavistock.

Hakim, C. 1996. "The Sexual Division of Labour and Women's Heterogeneity." *The British Journal of Sociology* 47 (1): 178–188.

Hakim C. 2000. *Work Lifestyle Choices in the 2st Century: Preference Theory*. Oxford: Oxford University Press.

Jensen, P. 2020. "Denmark." In *Extended Working Life Policies: International Gender and Health Perspectives*, edited by Léime, Aine, Ogg, Jim Rasticova, Martina, Street, Debra, Krekula, Clary, Bédiovà, Monika, and Madero-Cabib, Ignacio. New York: Springer.

Koropeckyj-Cox, T. 1998. "Loneliness and Depression in Middle and Old Age: Are the Childless More Vulnerable?" *Journal of Gerontology: Social Sciences* 53B (6): S303–S312.

Leach, R., Phillipson, C., Biggs, S., and Money, A. 2013. "Baby Boomers, Consumption and Social Change: The Bridging Generation?" *International Review of Sociology: Revue Internationale de Sociologie* 23 (1): 104–122.

Le Bihan-Youinou, B., and Martin, C. 2006. "Travailler et prendre soin d'un parent âgé dépendant." *Travail, genre et sociétés* 16 (2): 77–96.

Lin, I. F., and Wolf, D. A. 2019. "Division of Parent Care Among Adult Children." *The Journals of Gerontology: Series B,* gbz162, https://doi.org/10.1093/geronb/gbz162.

Lowenstein, A., and Daatland, S. O. 2006. "Filial Norms and Family Support in a Comparative Cross-National Context: Evidence from the OASIS Study." *Ageing amp; Society* 26: 203–223.

Lüscher, K., and Pillemer, K. A. 1998. Inter-generational Ambivalence: A New Approach to the Study of Parent-Child Relations in Later Life. *Journal of Marriage and the Family* 60: 413–425.

Lüscher, K. 2002. "Intergenerational Ambivalence: Further Steps in Theory and Research." *Journal of Marriage and Family* 64 (3): 585–593.
Mannheim, K. 1928. "Das Problem der Generationen." *Kölner Vierteljahres Hefte für* Soziologie 7: 157–185, 309–330; 1952, The Problem of Generations. In *Essays on the Sociology of Knowledge*. London: Routledge and Kegan Paul, 276–320; 2011.
Mitchell, B. 2006. *The Boomerang Age. Transitions to Adulthood in Families*. London: Adline Transaction.
Monnier, A. 2007. "Baby Boomers: Towards the End of an Era."*Population & Societies*: 1–4.
Ní Léime, A., Ogg, J., Rasticova, M., Street, D., Krekula, C., Bédiovâ, M., and Madero-Cabib, I., eds. 2020. *Extended Working Life Policies: International Gender and Health Perspectives*. New York: Springer.
Nocon, A., and Pearson, M. 2000. "The Roles of Friends and Neighbours in Providing Support for Older People." *Ageing & Society* 20 (3): 341–367.
OECD. 2018. "Are Survivor's Pensions Still Needed?" In *OECD Pensions Outlook*, 2018. Available at https://www.oecd-ilibrary.org/sites/pens_outlook-2018-10-en/index.html?itemId=/content/component/pens_outlook-2018-10-en. Accessed 1 November 2020.
Ogg, J., and Renaut, S. 2006. "The Support of Parents in Old Age by Those Born During 1945–1954: A European Perspective." *Ageing & Society* 26 (5): 723–743.
Ogg, J., Bonvalet, C., and Gallou, R. 2012. "Patrimoine immobilier et retraite: regard sur les couples." *Retraite et société* 62 (1): 59–78.
Ogg, J., Gallou R., and Bonvalet, C. La fin de carrière professionnelle : une affaire de couple (The End of Working Life: A Joint Decision). *Espace populations sociétés* [Online, 2013/3 | 2013, last accessed 9 September 2020, http://journals.opened ition.org/eps/5570; DOI: https://doi.org/10.4000/eps.5570.
Olazabal, I., ed. 2009. *Que sont les baby-boomers devenus ? Aspects sociaux d'une génération vieillissante*. Québec: Éditions Nota Bene.
Owram, D. 1996. *Born at the Right Time: A History of the Baby Boom Generation*. Toronto: University of Toronto Press.
Pahl, R. 2000. *On Friendship*. Oxford: Polity Press.
Pahl, R., and Spencer, L. 2006. *Rethinking Friendship: Hidden Solidarities Today*. Princeton University Press.
Peugny, C., and Van de Velde, C. 2013. "Rethinking Inter-generational Inequality." *Revue française de sociologie* 54: 641–662.
Phillipson, C., Bernard, M., Phillips, J., and Ogg, J. 1998. "The Family and Community Life of Older People: Household Composition and Social Networks in Three Urban Areas." *Ageing & Society* 18 (3): 259–289.
Phillipson, C. 2001. "Change in the Family Life of Older People." In *International Perspectives on Families, Aging and Social support*, edited by V. Bengtson and A. Lowenstein. New York: Aldine de Gruyter.
Phillipson, C., Leach, R., Money, A., and Biggs, S. 2008. "Social and Cultural Constructions of Ageing: The Case of the Baby Boomers." *Sociological Research* 13 (3): 1–14.
Phillipson, C. 2015. "The Political Economy of Longevity: Developing New Forms of Solidarity for Later Life." *The Sociological Quarterly* 56 (1): 80–100.
Platts, L., Corna, L., Worts, D., McDonough, P., Price, D., and Glaser, K. 2019. "Returns to Work After Retirement: A Prospective Study of Unretirement in the United Kingdom." *Ageing and Society* 39 (3): 439–464.

Pickering, J., Crooks, V. A., Snyder, J., and Morgan, J. 2019. "What Is Known About the Factors Motivating Short-term International Retirement Migration? A Scoping Review." *Journal of Population Ageing* 12 (3): 379–395.

Putnam Rt., D. 2000. *Bowling Alone: The Collapse and Revival of American Community*. New York: Simon & Schuster.

Renaut, S. 2001. L'entraide familiale dans un environnement multigénérationnel: Familles, vieillissement et générations' [Counting on the Family in a Multigenerational Environment : Families, Aging and Generations]. *Recherches et Prévisions* 71: 21–44.

Roquebert, Q., Fontaine, R., and Gramain, A. 2018. "Caring for a Dependent Elderly Parent: Care Arrangements and Sibling Interactions in France." *Population* 73: 307–332.

Roussel, L., and Bourguignon, O. 1978. *Générations nouvelles et mariage traditionnel*. Paris: Presse Universitaires de France.

Segalen, M., and Martial, A. 2019. *Sociologie de la famille*. Paris: Armand Colin.

Siren, A., and Casier, F. 2019. "Socio-Economic and Lifestyle Determinants of Giving Practical Support to Adult Children in the Era of Changing Late Life." *Ageing & Society* 39 (9): 1933–1950.

Statham, J. 2011. *Grandparents Providing Child Care. Briefing Paper*. London: Child Wellbeing Research Centre.

Stevens, N. L., and Van Tilburg, T. G. 2011. "Cohort Differences in Having and Retaining Friends in Personal Networks in Later Life." *Journal of Social and Personal Relationships* 28 (1): 24–43.

Townsend, P. 1981. "The Structured Dependency of the Elderly: A Creation of Social Policy in the Twentieth Century." *Ageing & Society* 1 (1): 5–28.

Tobio, Constanza. 2001. "Working Grandmothers in Spain." *European Societies* 3 (3).

Van Bavel, J., and Reher, D. S. 2013. "The Baby Boom and Its Causes: What We Know and What We Need to Know." *Population and Development Review* 39 (2): 257–288.

Van Pevenage, I. (2015). "Les sens de l'autonomie. Regards d'enfants du baby-boom sur leurs mères âgées." In *Les baby-boomers, une histoire de familles. Une comparaison Québec-France*, edited by Bonvalet, C., Olazabal, I., and Oris, M. Presses Universitaires du Québec, 145–175.

Van den Bogaard, L., Henkens, K., and Kalmijn, M. 2014. "So Now What? Effects of Retirement on Civic Engagement." *Ageing & Society* 34 (7): 1170–1192.

Wall, K., Aboim, S., and Cunha, V. 2001. "Families and Informal Support Networks in Portugal: The Reproduction of Inequality." *Journal of European Social Policy* 11 (3): 213–233.

Willetts, D. (2010). *The Pinch: How the Baby Boomers Took Their Children's Future-and Why They Should Give It Back*. London: Atlantic Books Ltd.

Zaidi, B., and Philip Morgan, S. 2017. "The Second Demographic Transition Theory: A Review and Appraisal." *Annual Review of Sociology* 43: 473–492.

Zhang, Z., and Hayward, M. D. 2001. "Childlessness and the Psychological Wellbeing of Older Persons." *Journals of Gerontology: Social Sciences* 56B (5): S311–S320.

CHAPTER 31

From *Taken for Granted* to *Taken Seriously*: The *Linked Lives* Life Course Principle Under Literature Analysis

Magda Nico, Diana Carvalho, Helena Carvalho, and Maria Silva

INTRODUCTION

The life course perspective in based on well-established theoretical principles that may be understood as corresponding to different analytical levels of interest to the social sciences, particularly to sociology. From a macro to a micro lens, the life course principles are the following. Historical and cultural location, also denominated the principle of time and place, holds that "the life course of individuals is embedded and shaped by the historical times and

---

This research was funded by the Portuguese Foundation for Science and Technology (FCT), through the project "Linked lives: A Longitudinal Multi-level and Mixed Approach to Family Life Course" (Reference: PTDC/SOC-SOC/29132/2017).

M. Nico (✉) · D. Carvalho · H. Carvalho · M. Silva
Instituto Universitário de Lisboa (ISCTE-IUL), Centro de Investigação E Estudos de Sociologia (CIES-IUL), Lisbon, Portugal
e-mail: magda.nico@iscte-iul.pt

D. Carvalho
e-mail: dianadiascarvalho@gmail.com

H. Carvalho
e-mail: helena.carvalho@iscte-iul.pt

M. Silva
e-mail: maria.gilvania@iscte-iul.pt

© The Author(s), under exclusive license to Springer Nature Switzerland AG 2021
A.-M. Castrén et al. (eds.), *The Palgrave Handbook of Family Sociology in Europe*, https://doi.org/10.1007/978-3-030-73306-3_31

places they experience over their lifetime" (Elder et al. 2003, 12). This principle emphasises the historical meaning of age as year of birth, in the sense that people that are born in a particular year and place have a specific historical experience (Elder and Giele 2009), and so, are associated to social change that can be recognised through the idea of generations. The principle of timing of lives stresses that people's lives are shaped by the timing, but also, the sequencing of life events (Scott and Alwin 1998), being related to articulation with social times, i.e. to the expectations or values of the age and its social roles (Elder 1994). Linked lives, for now, in a nutshell, focuses on the social embeddedness of individuals, recognising their interdependence and the interconnections of trajectories, in a context of social networks, crucial for understanding family and intergenerational relations. And finally, agency, also known as strategic adaptation. Agency is a principle based on the idea that "individuals construct their own life course through the choices and actions they take within the opportunities and constrains of history and social circumstances" (Elder et al. 2003, 11).

These principles contribute, together with linked lives, to the notable and solid foundations of the life course theory and perspective (Elder 1974). The relevance of this theoretical principle, and its underlying research, is indisputable, not only in regard to life course research but in regard to social sciences. The idea that, even more so within the family, individual lives are linked by threads that connect people's work, health, interpersonal relations, education, and housing spheres, is quite familiar and consensual in academia. In a pandemic era, the importance of these invisible threads between individuals, the intergenerational consequences of individual events, and the intertwinement of trajectories are enhanced, and we suspect the field of linked lives research will undergo significant changes and developments in the coming years.

The importance of this life course principle is indeed so indisputable that it is found to currently perform a "mantra" discourse in life course research, displaying itself as a hollow concept lacking substance and meaning (Settersten 2015, 2018). As such, it is *taken for granted*, its potential to perform empirical hypothesis purposes is relatively wasted, and its agenda-setting ability falls short. Albeit there is such a consensual importance attributed to the linked lives principle–either as a relevant theoretical principle of the life course perspective, as an observatory to comprehend and explain social interactions, or as a basic premise of sociological understanding of individuals in society in a general manner–this consensus is diffuse. As such, presently, little is known on how the research agendas, thematic interests, methodological advances, and empirical results on linked lives are being developed and evolving. Our systematic review of such publications aims at providing a panoramic view on this field of research, while acknowledging advances, trends, and profiles, on the one hand, and research gaps and future avenues, on the other. This comprehensive knowledge of how this life course principle is being developed, in the context of the life course perspective, and with family as the key observatory of these interdependencies of events and trajectories, is lacking. This lacuna is particularly felt by family sociologists and life course researchers, to whom this chapter might be of most use. In fact, "the principle of 'linked lives' – that the lives of individuals affect and are affected by the lives of others – is ritually repeated as a mantra in life course literature (...). And yet this stands in direct contrast to the state of research, which largely treats individuals as if they exist in isolation of others. To say that lives are 'linked' says nothing about their nature, length, purposes, or consequences" (Settersten 2015, 217). As such, we need to know more.

This chapter is a modest contribution in this regard. It presents a selection of a larger set of findings of a bibliometric analysis on how linked lives are addressed and studied in the sociological (mainly sociology of family) and the life course perspective research arenas–themselves *linked* at the very core of the emergence and development of life course research (Billari 2009). We use published research as proxy of the research field itself. The goals of this chapter are to contribute to a panoramic knowledge of the field of linked lives; identifying its blind spots (as to certain generations, topics, impacts) and its biases (towards certain methodologies, theories or purposes); and consequently, contribute to setting the scenario for a new lead and agenda of linked lives research. For this purpose, the chapter is framed by three sets of discussions on "linked lives" (epistemological, theoretical and analytical). Each one of these sets follows specific analytical strategies, all under the umbrella of a bibliometric literature analysis.

A transversal objective of this chapter is, in a way, epistemological. One of the reasons for this analysis is the need to revisit, and specially, restore the founding *rationale* of the life course theory. It has been argued that the life course should be understood primarily as a "theoretical orientation", and not as an observable "construct" (Elder et al. 2003, 4). Notwithstanding the validity of this dichotomy, it may also be true that a multiple approach–both as orientation and construct, could be theoretically fruitful, as each one of the theoretical principles can also be understood as empirical observatories of theory. This would mean they could operate as observable and falsifiable "constructs", but simultaneously serve theoretical purposes. *Linked lives* should, in our point of view, also be used as a construct, as an observatory of theory, and as a set of empirical hypotheses. As such, a theoretical principle can, perhaps should, in our view, act as an empirical source of theory. This does not downgrade the purpose or the theoretical density of the concept. In fact, the life course theoretical principles' essence has never been to perform "top-down" authority on research topics. On the contrary, the life course perspective and its principles emerged in a quest to open way to new and necessary research, to broaden the thematic gates and dissolve disciplinary frontiers. This is the identity of life course research. And putting one of its theoretical principles to test is complying with this scientific identity.

Accordingly, one of the specific targets of this chapter is theoretical. This goal is to give analytical attention to the above-mentioned superiority of interpersonal relationships in the understanding of the life course, thus inverting the attention that is usually given to the *linked lives* principle. It has already been hinted and stated in the life course literature that there is a significant lack of equivalence between the *linked lives'* theoretical recognition and importance, on the one hand, and its empirical practice, on the other (Carr 2018; Settersten 2015, 2018). This lack of equivalence finds echoes in the decreased quantitative expression of this principle when compared to other life course principles (Cultural and Historical Location, Timing of Lives and Agency), mainly in terms of proportional presence in the literature, as we will confirm in the data presentation in this chapter. As argued, "the real action for life course research is not found in agency or structure, but instead in their interaction and, especially, in the deep and complicated level of interpersonal relationships" (Landes and Settersten 2019, 9). And yet, the idea of "superiority of individual records", advocated by Thomas and Znaniecki (1984 [1928]: 294–295), left its mark in the field. Although these interpersonal relationships, as opposed to individual self-contained trajectories, are currently acknowledged as preferable, we risk stating that the hegemonic approach is still based, to a certain degree, on social atomism. This chapter ultimately aims to restore *linked lives'* theoretical centrality in the life course perspective (Sect. 3 of this chapter).

The two other specific goals of this chapter are analytical: descriptive and summing up the family linked lives map, thus aiming to contribute to detailed, comprehensive and holistic knowledge on how the *linked lives* principle is tackled and operationalised in (published) research. This is done, first, through descriptive analysis mainly directed at portraying the detail and evolution of the field, aimed at closing the gap regarding its "nature, length, purposes, or consequences" (Settersten 2015, 217), as well as elucidating the levels, factors, outcomes, life course phases, spheres of life and types of impacts of the links tying family members' lives together. At a second stage, using a multivariate quantitative method highly suitable to handling multiple categorical variables, family linked lives literature profiles were analytically identified and discussed within the life course perspective.

The interpersonal feature of social relations can concern two individuals isolated on an island, the globalised society, and—this is the real issue for life course researchers—anything in between. Alongside Norbert Elias legacy, some authors would even (theoretically) argue that the interpersonal feature of life is necessarily embedded in each individual, meaning that individuals are themselves microcosms of their interpersonal relations. In this chapter, the *family* level is used as the most relevant observatory of *linked lives*. *Family linked lives* are, in this analysis, considered to be *a privileged intersectional observatory* of all the levels and principles involved in the life course dynamics identified in the life course *cube* by Bernardi, Huinink, and Settersten (2019b). The authors define the life course as a multidimensional individual behavioural process and a set of axes of interdependencies of times, domains, and levels, and aim to offer a more integrated approach than the life course principles. Its focus on interdependencies as a central aspect to life course pairs with our attempt to characterise the different linked impacts. The *cube* efficiently promotes the distinction of levels of analysis, likewise we also take into account the differentiation between individual and aggregate levels (the supra-individual level). But additionally, we argue that the "linked lives" principle is a (omitted) sublevel between the individual and the supra-individual levels. *Linked lives* may be understood indeed as a(nother) "societal subsystem" among the many possible. Therefore, it is our understanding that family linked lives operate at a "frontier" level between the two operationalised by Bernardi, Huinink, and Settersten (2019a), but that this frontier level may be, perhaps should be, empirically autonomous, while theoretically interdependent. Lives are inherently and inevitably social, and social relationships and their importance have been recognised since the very beginning of classical sociological production. But in the context of the life course, family interdependencies embody great importance and representativeness in the field (Billari 2009).

METHOD

Our bibliometric analysis on how *linked lives* within the family have been tackled in (published) research does not follow a single strategy or an isolated source of data. It gathers together different efforts and multiple strategies. Table 31.1 delineates and compiles the different strategies and data used in this chapter. We used two datasets, as explained in Table 31.1.

The goal of this literature review is not the traditional one. It has neither a "formal" objective (usually used to attest the researcher's affiliation to a certain field, providing evidence of knowledge in identifying the notable, important and/or polemic authors) nor an "instrumental" objective (with the references being selected to more directly contribute to an argument, or to justify the need to conduct certain research). Thus, this analysis serves the autonomous propose of providing understanding on the arena of published research on linked lives. It is not a means to an end, but an end in itself.

RESTORING *LINKED LIVES*| RELATIVE IMPORTANCE

The life course perspective has excelled at tying in conceptual frameworks to understand the development of human life and its social contexts, at different levels, and in recognising diverse intersections of people, spheres of life, or generations. The four guiding principles of the life course perspective recognised by Glen Elder Jr. are, conjointly, consolidated, consensual, and consistently mobilised in the life course literature.[1] Together, these principles—Historical and Cultural location, Timing of Lives, Agency and Linked

Table 31.1 Methodological Strategy: datasets and data analysis

	Privileged observatories' reference dataset	*Linked lives publications' dataset*
Purpose of the analysis	Mapping the existing published research on family linked lives, restoring the importance of this life course principle, identifying gaps and biases, for a better designed agenda for the future The context of linked lives compared with other life course principles (in privileged observatories)	The **details** of how lives are linked in the published research on family linked lives (in a comprehensive collection and selection of publications on family linked lives). Its **arena and configurations**
Data collection	Selection of two observatories: collection of all articles of the journal Advances in Life Course Research (N = 383) + collection of all abstract books of the Conferences of the Society for Longitudinal and Lifecourse Studies (N = 9 abstract books)	Systematic collection of (mainly English written, but also Portuguese and French) bibliographical references on family linked lives[a]: • Data collection carried out between January to May 2019 (Publications dates comprised between 1980 and May 2019) • Various sources: university libraries and repositories, bibliographical databases, publishers, journals and research centres • Two main search strategies were employed: (i) via keywords related to the life course and linked lives, as well as various synonyms; and/or (ii) via census, where all content (all titles, and when necessary, abstracts) of privileged sources were checked • After collecting all the references, the database was reduced to a more specific selection, ensuring that they complied with the defined criteria of inclusion and were related with a family linked lives effect (N = 507 publications)

	Privileged observatories' reference dataset	Linked lives publications' dataset
Data analysis	Descriptive Analysis: frequencies	Descriptive Analysis: frequencies and crosstabs
Multiple Correspondence Analysis (MCA) to identify and discuss profiles (privilege associations between categories)
Cluster analysis (hierarchical and non-hierarchical) to group publications (N = 507) according to their profile and calculate the weight of each group (cluster)
Data presentation	Line graphs with evolution of the use of life course principles and word clouds	Descriptive references and MCA analysis (Joint Category Plot + MCA table listing measures and contributions per active variable)
Software	MaxQda ® + Wordle ®	Mendeley for organization + Excel for coding + SPSS (Version 25.0) for data analysis
Data Coding	Lexical search and automatic coding of the four life course principles (and proxy denominations)
Word frequencies and exclusion of irrelevant words in titles in MaxQda + Word count and graphical representation in Wordle	The research team discussed the relevant variables to be identified in each publication and designed a coding scheme. Some codes were determined prior to data analysis, others arose from the empirical material, and some changed throughout the coding process. After concluding the coding, multiple answer situations and residual frequency codes were recoded

(continued)

Table 31.1 (continued)

	Privileged observatories' reference dataset	Linked lives publications' dataset
Variables	Observatories (Advances in Life Course Research—ALCR, and the Society for Longitudinal and life course Studies—SLLS) + Year of publication (before 2009, 2009 and after) + life course principles (agency, timing of lives, cultural and historical location, linked lives) and words in titles	Publication document variables: language used in documents; publication type and year; main and secondary disciplinary field of the publication; number of authors of the document; country of nationality of institution of the first author. These variables are the ones that characterize the life course field as a whole, as an interdisciplinary arena Methodological approaches' variables: methodological nature of the document (empirical, theoretical, methodological); if empirical, number of countries studied, what countries studied; main data collection; main data analysis methods; longitudinal design and/or data. These variables are the ones that characterize the life course research and "craft", as an analytical apparatus to study the individuals and groups over time Linked lives effect variables: type of impact concerned (according to our typology of impacts regarding the different family members, individual and household level indicators and time, explained further on); its implication (positive, negative or ambiguous); life course stages (childhood, youth, adulthood or old age); family ties (parents, children, brothers, etc.); spheres of life (education, work, etc.). These variables are the ones that characterize the specificity of the linked lives principle See Annex Table 7.3 for more information on the coding variables The variables used in MCA enabled the identification and discussion of "family linked lives" profiles in the life course publication. Moreover, the selection was also guided by a statistical criterion. Several binary variables were excluded because one of the two categories was residual, thus they had low variation, and, consequently, would not differentiate the profiles

[a] The Life course perspective is Anglo-Saxon in its origin, and its development has been internationalized mainly through English written publications. However, relevant debates, findings and empirical research have been carried out and published in other languages. Therefore, we also included the French and the Portuguese-written literature. None of these exceptions, and consequent inclusions, have biased the results as prior preliminary findings based only on English-written literature, have shown extremely similar results

lives—promote an "holistic understanding of life over time and in various changing social contexts" (Elder et al. 2003, 13).

The understanding of the *linked lives* principle, in particular, demands the examination of how life courses are intertwined with close relations and, specifically, how life events or transitions can impact trajectories, transitions, or adjustments in the life courses of those who are related to them. In fact, some authors argue that "human agency is profoundly affected by interpersonal relationships and other social factors. Because agency and linked lives are inseparable, agency cannot be conceptualised as an individual characteristic of 'independent' actors" (Landes and Settersten 2019, 1). As such, *linked lives* should be used transversally in life course research. Not only is that still not the case, but its autonomous use is also below its potential.

In comparison with other life course principles, the linked lives principle's *supporting* rather than *leading* role in life course research, theory, and craft, is clear. In this section of the chapter, we aim to identify and interpret the relevance, role, and presence of these four principles, comparatively, and to analyse whether linked lives has actually been an under-explored principle. We will present three lines of argument in that regard.

The first line of argument has to do with the unit of analysis. One of the identified downsides of linked lives studies is that most of the times they resort to data from a single informant who provides information on the other members of her/his network (Carr 2018), which inevitably results in incomplete and less accurate accounts of social relations and their effects. In our data of the linked lives publications dataset, we did indeed find that a very limited number of published studies on family linked lives actually had families or other groups as units of analysis (only 1.2% of the publications used families or groups as unit of analysis). Nonetheless, the analysis of the methodologies used for capturing the linked lives data shows a significant expression of quantitative methods that are capable of tackling dyadic or group data (for instance Multilevel, Multichannel, and Actor-Partner models, that have been gaining popularity in the analysis of linked lives effects, see, for example, the studies of Ehrlich et al. 2019 and Krutova et al. 2018), contrary to qualitative research, which is dominated by individual interview research designs.

This leads us to the second line of argument, related to the methodological advances of *linked lives*, which are still not keeping up with its conceptual depth (Carr 2018). Its theoretical recognition has not shown a suitable methodological reflection, namely in terms of the methods and techniques specifically created, used, or combined to tackle the specificity of the interdependencies of and in people's lives. The underdevelopment of linked lives' methodologies is important to understand the theoretical and empirical pace of the progress of knowledge in the field. In fact, the methodological development of the life course has also led to the development of "more ambitious theory", which can be explored by "refining well-established quantitative and qualitative methods and by incorporating multiple methods from different traditions and disciplines" (Bernardi et al. 2019a, 1). In this regard, we found in the family linked lives' literature a mirror of what happens in the life course perspective (and, to some extent, in social sciences, more generally). The hegemony of quantitative studies compared to qualitative studies (81% quantitative *vs.* 19% qualitative), a lack of cross-country comparative research (93.2% involving only one country *vs.* 6.7% involving more than one country), and the majority cross-sectorial longitudinal (*versus* a minority based on multilevel longitudinal data, which, on the one hand, reflects the potential for analysis of each one of the life course principles).[2] On the other hand, the analysis of the linked lives' literature also demonstrates other specific trends: (i) a recent increasing diversification of the methods used to address linked lives data (which is also associated with the type of data collected and used, as well as the creative use of methodology and the emergence of specific techniques and softwares able to tackle multilevel and/or longitudinal analysis for both descriptive and inferential purposes); (ii) a significant increase in multilevel, multi-actor, and multichannel analysis (and subsequent increase of holistic and multi-individual data); and (iii) a modest rise in the number of articles discussing the methodology and epistemology behind linked lives research.

Finally, a third line of argument concerns the actual empirical and analytical investment in the linked lives research (in comparison with the other life course principles). Our comparison and analysis of the proportion of the uses of the four life course principles was based on our "Privileged Observatories' Reference Dataset". The Advances in Life Course Research's (ALCR) articles reflect the journal's agenda to a certain extent, and the abstracts of the oral communications submitted to the Society of Longitudinal and Lifecourse Studies's (SLSS) Conferences, in contrast, reflect a more bottom-up process of agenda making. Figure 31.1 represents the uses of the different principles in the ALCR articles, and Fig. 31.2 in the SLLS conference (abstracts) books.

From the analysis of the journal articles solely, we can argue that the *linked lives* concept is, empirically, and in fact, the least used, and the most consistently so (Fig. 31.1). It is only joined by the "agency" principle in this relative lack of representation (which, however, has had exceptions over the years). One of the reasons for this lower frequency of use might be that both the agency, and the linked lives principles benefit relatively more from qualitative perspectives in a field dominated by quantitative approaches. As such, the lack of representation of linked lives and agency might be proxies of an interdisciplinary field that is still far from being an inter-methodological one (Nico 2015).

We can also observe an increase in the use of the *Historical and Cultural Location* principle, both in the articles and abstracts, which could be a sign of the field's openness to other sociological areas and likewise to other countries (which will also be reflected in the findings reported below), moreover, implying cross-countries comparisons. This is also evidence of how the field grew beyond the frontiers of psychology, truly taking into account the social

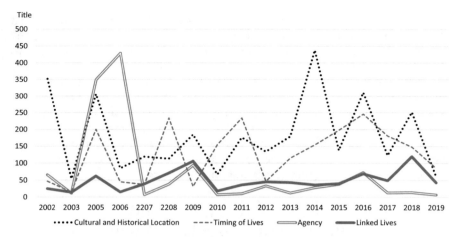

Fig. 31.1 Uses of the life course principles in ALCR articles (2000–2019) (*Source* The 383 articles of the Advances in Life Course Research [ALCR] Journal)

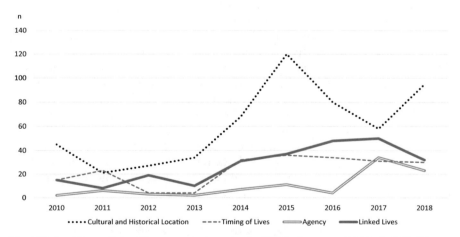

Fig. 31.2 Uses of the life course principles in SLLS abstracts (2010–2018) (*Source* The 9 abstract books of the Society for Longitudinal and Lifecourse Studies' Conferences)

(historical and cultural) context in which the timing, agency, and interdependency of the events occur. Additionally, we can also highlight that the use of the linked lives principle has been increasingly visible in conference papers (Fig. 31.2), indicating a potential future rising application of the principle both as an empirical and as a theoretical concept in life course research. It might indicate a peek into the future editorial trends of life course publications.

Departing from our argument of the high conceptual importance of the linked lives life course principle compared with others (a view that is shared with and based on other authors), with our data we were able to confirm that this principle is, in practice, in numeric inferiority. We associate this with the hegemony of quantitative life course studies, that in a way are associated to individual surveys, and thus, individual units of analysis. Looking towards the future, we optimistically realise that there have been recent methodological developments to address various different units of analysis, that have not yet been published, but already shown with presented research, more than ever, centred on linked lives. The *momentum* for the linked lives principle research appears to be drawing near, if methodology allows. The pandemic context and the methodological imagination demands from researchers, will also, in our opinion, perform an important role in this regard.

SCRATCHING THE SURFACE OF THE "LINKED FAMILY LIVES" MANTRA

Our strategies to systematically grasp the trends of linked lives' published research supported the goal of "scratching the surface" of the linked lives' research field. In this section of the chapter, we aim to identify several characteristics of what links people in the family: type of impact[3] (longitudinal, bi-linked, extra-linked, intra-linked, household); positive or negative impact; family relations involved (parent-child, siblings, couple, various direct, other links); the time lag between factor and outcome events (one or more time phases); life phase of the factor and outcome (birth to childhood, up to young adulthood, up to adulthood, up to old age, during the life course); and life sphere of the factor event and outcome event (education, work, residential, health, conjugality, parenthood, emotional, other spheres, financial, holistic).We are, again, using the two datasets and strategies (as identified in Table 31.1: Privileged observatories' reference dataset; and the linked lives publications' dataset) to render, as much as possible, an inclusive perspective of this issue.

From Life Course to Family Life

One of the strategies was to analyse the words used in the titles of an important journal of the life course field, to provide some transversal, albeit superficial, insight on the content of the central research themes of the articles. Comparing the most frequent words of the titles of all the publications in the Advances in Life Course Research before and after life course's "coming of age" as determined by Billari in 2009, we can observe that the field has grown in size and diversity (Figs. 31.3 and 31.4).[4]

Before 2009, the concepts employed were more limited to "life course", "transition", and "adulthood". The "period" of life studied, in this case, the transition to adulthood, was the most referred aspect, and also more mentioned than other type of valuable references such as methodological, national, or conceptual ones. After 2009, many more topics emerge, and

Fig. 31.3 Words in titles before the coming of age (2000–2009) in the Advances in Life Course Research Journal (*Source* The 383 articles of the Advances in Life Course Research [only the titles])

Fig. 31.4 Words in titles after the coming of age (2010–2019) in the Advances in Life Course Research Journal (*Source* The 383 articles of the Advances in Life Course Research [only the titles])

among them family (as well as fertility, trajectories, and social). This is an indication of how the field grew, conceptually and empirically, with an "explosion" of concepts and processes strongly related to family (such as fertility, parenthood); approaches (gender, generation, social, differences, comparison); longitudinal research features (trajectories, pathways, mobility); and also to "periods" of life that indirectly relate to family research (adulthood, childhood, retirement, etc.). Our data confirms the 2009 maturity turning point in the life course research pathway (Billari 2009). It also clearly shows how the expansion and maturation of the life course research field is associated with (although not exclusively) the inclusion of and interaction with family research.

A Panoramic View of How Family Lives Are Linked

To comprehensively understand how family lives are being approached in the published studies, here, we describe our analysis of the Linked Lives Publications' Dataset. The final sample (N = 507) was composed of publications between 1980 and May 2019.

Can family linked lives be tackled by an approach exclusively centred in the individual? Or are lives linked precisely because they bridge different levels (individual, inter-individual, household)? We observed that the intra-linked impact (which refers to the impact of household level indicators on the life of an individual household member) is the most studied type of impact (N = 174, 34.3% of all publications), followed by the household level effect on the household. These studies reflect the dominance of explaining social phenomena with more aggregate levels and in top-down processes. Less attention has been given to bottom-up explanations or more individually caused impacts. As such, the predominance of the intra-linked impact is observed in all decades (1980–1989; 1990–1999; 2000–2009; 2010–2019), however, the latest decades demonstrate more balanced proportions between the different types of impacts, highlighting a combination of different influences and hinting at new developments in the field.

What is specifically meant by "over" the life course in family linked lives studies? Regarding the distances of the life stages studied between predictors and outcomes events, the most frequent is only one lag (22.7%), that is, one step ahead in the life course in relation to the identified stages of the life course (childhood, youth, adulthood, and old age). These are studies that analyse the medium-term effects of events of the life course, and that are more suitable to contribute to the prevention of certain scarring effects in life. The same moment (immediate effects) or 2 lags (more long-term effects) have similar proportions (18.8 and 15.8%, respectively). Across time, the immediate, medium, or long-term effects of life events have become more balanced. The consolidation of evidence-based public policies and, related to that, the growth of impact studies, have likely contributed to fast science products and publications. At the same time, we have been observing a proliferation of long-term longitudinal research. However, studying families across time is a big endeavour, considering the volume and complexity of the generated data.

What are the types of kinship tying people together in family linked lives research? It is hardly surprising that the most studied family tie in the linked lives literature is the parent-child one, representing almost two-thirds of the studies (N = 202), and essentially regarding the effects of parents' lives, events, conditions on children's trajectories, thus disregarding bidirectional generational effects. On the one hand, this unidirectional focus on the approach to generational change reflects the enduring relevance of parent-child relations and parental effects, but at the same time makes it evident that there is ample room for improvement, innovation, and imagination in the linked lives field. It is also important to refer to the high proportion of studies that approach family in general terms, without specifying the links at stake (n = 160). This could illustrate the relative lack of focus of these studies, of course combined with an important and ambitious holistic view of the life course and inter-relations within the family. But it also represents a positive effort to frame dyadic relations in the larger multi-generational family context (Leopold 2012; Shapiro and Cooney 2007). Linked lives studies centred on couples were also revealed as being of some importance (n = 72), very often focusing on intimate lives and gender inequality issues, topics that, as we know, are also discussed outside the borders of the specific literature of life course research or sociology of family. Nonetheless, it is important to state that all the links gained relevance over time, and more recently, likewise the couple and generalised approach (family dynamics as a whole), which could reflect stronger attention to a holistic approach to life course and linked lives. Studies focusing on new forms of family arrangements, like living apart, together or same-sex couples, are still lacking in *linked lives* studies, generally speaking.

Regarding what types of events are linking these family lives together, we detected that in terms of factor variables, the holistic approach (considered when studies used three or more different spheres of life) is the most frequent, followed by the emotional, conjugal, and residential spheres, to a larger extent affecting the emotional spheres of life, as well as the holistic, health, and work spheres. Observing how these life sphere factors and outcomes connect, we see that the most frequent connection is between the holistic character as factor and the holistic character as outcome. An example of such study is Wickrama et al. (2008), which traces the impact of parental education and family life events on youth depressive trajectories and adult social status trajectories. This suggests the vagueness of the field and the lack of focus it demonstrates in disclosing exactly how lives may be linked. But it could also indicate an effort to avoid compartmenting life in boxes, as was done in the previous Life Cycle paradigm from which the life course spun off decades ago. Moreover, the other more frequent links are between the emotional/subjective, conjugality, or health spheres, involving the emotional sphere, reflecting a still prominent psychological approach in the life course field. With this, we can conclude that life course phenomenon is predominantly explained by holistic, emotional, or subjective related variables. Hence, despite the fact that quantitative methods are the most used in the study of linked lives within the family, they are used in a qualitative approach to life (using psychological and subjective models of explanation).

What are the spheres of lives per life stages studied as predictors and as outcomes tying family lives together? On the one hand, concerning the explaining factors, the studies encompassing childhood focus more on the residential and health related events. Until young adulthood, the emotional and holistic variables are more frequently used. Regarding the life stage up to adulthood, the proportions are more balanced, with many spheres covered: holistic, emotional, conjugality, residential, and work. This is clearly related with the demographically dense period of life that "adulthood" represents.

One of the main themes integrated in the residential sphere is related to migration. Regarding old age, holistic and health predictors are more common. On the other hand, taking the outcomes studied into account, we can see that the emotional sphere is common across all stages. Apart from the aforesaid events, regarding childhood, the dependent variables are more education related. For up to young adulthood, the educational sphere remains, but the residential aspects gain importance as explanatory phenomena. The explained variables concerning adulthood and old age are again distributed across many spheres, with the effect on the holistic sphere more frequent, as well as the impacts on aspects of parenthood, work, and health.

FAMILY LINKED LIVES PROFILES IN THE LIFE COURSE RESEARCH ARENA

To describe the associations between all the characteristics in the life course publications, in order to identify the privileged configurations—"family linked lives" profiles—a multiple correspondence analysis (MCA) was performed. All the characteristics of the publications were converted in categorical variables and MCA is the most appropriate multivariate quantitative method to simultaneously deal with the multidimensionality and the interrelations of the categorical variables (Greenacre 2007; Ramos and Carvalho 2011). Like in standard principal component analysis (PCA), a set of dimensions (factors in PCA) are defined. Each dimension is composed of all the input variables with different contributions. The dimensions that explain more variance are selected to identify the principal theoretical axes that explain the associations between all the multiple input variables, reducing the multidimensionality of the initial data matrix. Using these dimensions, MCA also enables the representation of the structure of the associations between all the categories in a subspace, usually in two-dimensional graphs (Carvalho 2008). As presented in Fig. 31.5, this graphical representation also helps to identify the privileged associations between the categories that have the highest contribution in one or both dimensions. Geometric proximity enables the identification of different configurations which represent, in this research, "family linked lives" profiles in the life course publications. Later, cluster analysis was performed on a group of publications (N = 507) according to their profile. A hierarchical cluster analysis was first performed to check the adjustment to the MCA solution. Then an optimal algorithm (k-means) (Hair et al. 2014) was used to quantify the weight of each group of publications.

Considering the variance accounted for by inertia, only the first two dimensions stand out and, therefore, only those were selected for analysis. The discrimination measures and the contributions of each input variable that compose dimensions 1 and 2 can be found in Table 31.2, based on the highest discrimination measures.

Dimension 1 represents *linked lives research*, as it is mainly defined by the lives linked (family links between its members), the life sphere factor (life

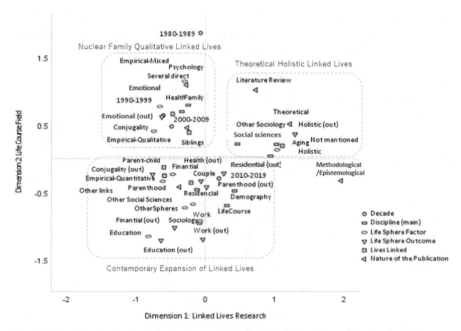

Fig. 31.5 Topological configuration of "family linked lives" profiles in the life course publication (*Source* N = 507 publications of authors' dataset on linked lives)

Table 31.2 Discrimination measures and contribution of the variables

Active Variables	*Dimension 1:* Linked lives Research		*Dimension 2:* Life Course Field	
	Discrimination	*Contribution %*	*Discrimination*	*Contribution %*
Discipline	0.154	6.7	**0.468**	24.2
Decade	0.089	3.9	*0.305*	15.8
Lives Linked	**0.569**	24.8	0.075	3.9
Nature of the Publication	*0.371*	16.2	0.259	13.4
Life Sphere Factor	**0.518**	22.6	**0.394**	20.4
Life Sphere Outcome	**0.594**	25.9	**0.430**	22.3
Total	2.295	100.0	1.931	100.0
Inertia	0.383		0.322	

Note The cut-off used to identify the most relevant variables was inertia: mean of the discrimination measures for each dimension. Values in bold are above inertia for each dimension. The discrimination measures in italic are close to the *cut-off* inertia sphere of the predictor event studied) and the life sphere outcome (life sphere of the consequence of the event studied). This dimension illustrates precisely how the two (or more) lives link, more specifically, the sphere of life of the first event/s or moment/s observed, and the sphere of life of the second event/s or moment/s observed, reinforcing the idea that the life course dynamics are multi-agent. It clearly shows that what happens in the family does not stay in the family. Although all these publications are related to families, family households, relations, dynamics, etc., the lives of their members are linked, in these researches and publications, by events related to other spheres of life. As such, the lives of family members are linked through different combinations of spheres of life, not only by family, housing, or household events (particularly visible in the third quadrant). Dimension 1 represents *Linked Lives Research* not only because of the importance of these above-mentioned variables that concern specifically the nature and the dynamic of the interdependency of lives, but because it illustrates the very amplitude of the analytical zooms that research can perform on these relationships. As such, we observe the shift in this specificity across the horizontal axe (Fig. 31.5). We observe very particular and family related linked lives (such as "conjugal", "parent child", "other direct kinship" relationships), studied from specified sectorial points of view, both as a factor and as an outcome of the relationships (such as "education", "health", "work", "emotional") (at the left, with negative coordinates); opposed to the "holistic" character of the family relationships, that operate among many members of the family and across one's complete life span (hence "aging") (at the right, with positive coordinates).

Dimension 2, in contrast, represents the *life course field*, since the most relevant variables were the discipline, followed by life sphere factor and life sphere outcome. The decade was also an important variable to define dimension 2, as it represents the wider context in which research on linked lives is produced. We can verify how the discipline of each publication is relevant to structure the space of the Family Linked Lives Literature. In this case, we observe more recent and specialised thematic or disciplinary life course arenas of study (with "demography", life course", "sociology", "2010–2019") with negative coordinates of the vertical axe, opposing to the more general disciplinary life course arenas related to the very emergence of this paradigm ("social sciences", "other sociology", "Psychology") (with positive coordinates of the vertical axe).

Figure 31.5 presents the topological configuration of *Linked Lives and Life Course*. Three profiles of publications/research were identified, providing important data on the diversity, and to a certain extent, the evolution of the family linked lives research field. The *theoretical holistic linked lives* profile (cluster with 27.2% of publications) associates theoretical literature with the holistic life sphere factor and life sphere outcome. This is the linked lives principle being used in a more conceptual and aggregate way, as a premise. No specific discipline is associated but the thematic interdisciplinary field of Ageing. This apparent lack of specificity of the section of the field may be understood in two, if not opposite, then complementary ways. On the one hand, this profile reveals the vague, undifferentiated, almost abstract, way the linked lives concept is used, without an empirical, specific, and/or explicit, operationalisation of how lives are linked. But it can also lead us (back) to a strong argument of the life course perspective itself: a multi-thematic field of studies, united by the theoretical framework rather than by any research topic, discipline, or subfield—namely by the life course theoretical principles and by this vigorous concern to look at all research subjects through a time-lens. This profile seems, here in a positive manner, to illustrate the "mantra" of the undeniable, but somewhat intangible, importance of linked lives in and over the life course. Some examples are found in Mills and Blossfeld (2013) on the theoretical development of family formation changes, as well as Settersten (2015) on relationships in the context of time and the life course.

Another profile is more clearly framed in specific decades, namely in 1990–1999 and 2000–2009. This profile (cluster with 31.6% of publications), which we have named *nuclear family qualitative linked lives,* associates these decades with the above-mentioned minority of empirical studies using qualitative and/or mixed research designs and techniques. Not surprisingly, in these publications we find a great predominance of the emotional and the psychological spheres of life, spheres that are relevant both to factor and to outcome events. As such, this profile includes disciplines such as Psychology and Family. Here, the study of linked lives is strongly determined by the analysis of dyadic links, such as those implied in conjugality or relations between siblings. This is not equivalent to saying this profile refers to the "nuclear family" in its traditional and functional Parsonian version. On the contrary, in these "direct" links we find same-sex couples, recomposed families, single parenthood, just to mention some examples of the mismatch with the traditional and time-static version of "family".

Comparing the *theoretical holistic linked lives* profile to the above-mentioned *nuclear family qualitative linked lives,* we can observe that what is gained in specificity (of disciplines, spheres of life, temporal location, etc.) is lost in the broadness, the transversality, and the cross-cutting feature found in *theoretical holistic linked lives* profile. There is a clear transition from the theoretical to the empirical arena of life course studies, and Psychology and Family had important roles in this regard. Family Studies contributed to this important and undeniable part of the DNA of the life course and linked lives research field. In this profile, lives are linked through the emotions and self-reported health status of the family members. Studies such as Swartz's article (2008) on family capital and intergenerational support, or Thomas and Kalucy's (2002) qualitative study on the impact of parents with mental illness on the family, illustrate this very well.

The last profile clearly represents the most recent and contemporary scenario, from the last decade to be more precise. In a way, it captures an *ante camera* of the future agenda, in that it is composed of an explosion of disciplines, methods, spheres of life, etc. With this MCA we captured the moment of the eruption, but it remains to be seen on which ground the sparks of all these variables fall, so as to speak. We have named this last profile (cluster with 41.2% of the publications) as *contemporary expansion of linked lives*. It is mainly composed of the numerically predominant quantitative studies. But in terms of discipline, the field has opened up to areas such as demography, life course, and other social sciences; and it has also expanded to other spheres of life beyond those traditionally associated with the family spheres, such as the educational, residential, financial, and work-related (both as factor and as outcome). It is possible to observe a refinement of the types of findings, arguments, and contributions, the gaining of focus when compared to the previous decades and aforesaid profiles. The *nuclear family qualitative linked lives* is distinct from the *theoretical holistic linked lives* also because of the higher contribution of the empirical studies in the latter. On the other side, the distinction between the *nuclear family qualitative linked lives* profile and the *contemporary expansion of linked lives* is more centred on a diversification and maturation of this empirical feature, with a much larger diversity of topics under study and of disciplinary frameworks (particularly visible in the third quadrant). These also represent the increase of cross-national and/or longitudinal studies, like, for example, the study comparing Britain and Germany regarding retirement and income inequalities (Fasang 2012) or the longitudinal study of the impact of parental worklessness on the "Not in Education, Employment, or Training" (NEET) experience of their young adult children (Schoon 2014).

To sum up, the *linked lives* theoretical (more transversal in time) "mantra" and the disciplinary and empirical-methodological "expansion" co-exist (of the publications of 2010–2019 about 30% are from the Theoretical cluster, and about 50% are from the Expansion cluster). And this is exactly what is expected from a creative and critical field that keeps its feet on the ground.

Conclusions

In this chapter, we portrayed a panoramic analysis of how family linked lives have actually been tackled and studied in (published) research. This allowed us to put an end to taking the importance of linked lives for granted, and start taking it more seriously, empirically, and, we hope, theoretically. The data we gathered, processed, and analysed, enabled putting linked lives into perspective, that is, in relation to other life course principles, and it also allowed us to see the over and under-representations of topics, generations, kinships, methods, factors, and outcomes in the study of family linked lives. This mapping—made evidently through a selection and not a census of publications—not only contributed to more comprehensive knowledge about the profiles and trends in family linked lives published research, but it also provided us with means to identify the blind spots in research and potential drivers for further developments in the field. Primarily, we found that linked lives is, in itself, compared with other life course principles, an under-represented theoretical principle. The strong consensus around the theoretical importance of this principle acts, in a way, as an antidote to its empirical demonstration. Secondly, we found that, as in other life course principles and in life course in general, there is a chronic underuse of qualitative research. This is, however, particularly important to the linked lives principle due to its multilevel, systemic, interactional, and configurational nature. Studies on linked lives would benefit, relatively more than other life course principles, from this qualitative approach. In our view, it is crucial to develop a qualitative agenda in this regard, especially when the "multi-actor" longitudinal data is, in the context of quantitative research, either taking its first steps, or in long term under-use by life course and family researchers. Related to these aspects is the shorter windows of observation of linked lives in operation (compared to life course research in general), and unidirectional generational studies that concentrate, disproportionally to all the other research possibilities, in parent-to-child studies. In sum, multilevel, longitudinal and/or qualitative research on families lives and relationships are lacking in the life course and family research patrimony, and therefore, in our convict view, should not be absent from future agendas.

Scratching the surface of the "mantra" meant gathering detailed information about the levels, factors, outcomes, life course phases, spheres of life, and type of impacts, of the links binding family lives together. Here, we found evidence to argue that the linked lives field is, at its own slower pace, expanding and evolving in a similar fashion to the life course field itself, in some of the features identified by Billari in 2009, namely in what concerns the disciplinary diversification, the methodological sophistication, and subject topic increasing combinations and complexifications. Considering 2009 as the tipping point of the development of the life course field, we were able to testify a significant growth of the linked lives' research. However, by placing our findings in the current context, we are also able to observe an explosion of linked lives research, specially within the family, linking family members through their health, work, education trajectories, both in short and long-term (very long, inter-generationally long).

But imagination also requires methods. Based on our analysis, we argue that an even greater interdependent relationship between family research and the life course should be on the agenda. Life course's exponential development of methods and algorithms can enlarge the horizons of family research (especially true for quantitative methods), by not being confined to one-plus-one individual accounts of family lives and relations when it comes to data collection, and particularly, data analysis. Our data has shown this mismatch may be due to the persistent underuse of alternative units of analysis other than the individual one, a factor that considerably impairs the study of family dynamics, links, effects, and processes. Additionally, our analysis also reflects an increasing diversification of the methods used to tackle linked lives data; a relevant increase in multilevel, multi-actor, and multichannel analysis, as well as an extension of articles discussing the methodology and epistemology behind linked lives research. In turn, family research has the ability to exemplarily operationalise concrete meanings and dynamics of how lives are linked, helping to restore the importance of this theoretical principal, but simultaneously taking it off the theoretical pedestal and immersing it into the empirical messy, complex, rich arena of real interpersonal relations.

Summing up, the linked lives principle has been proving its valuable potential to contribute to the understanding of family and intergenerational relations and interdependencies, and therefore represents a promising area within life course, family, and sociological fields. As pointed out by Shanahan and MacMillan (2008, 279), "the life course is not a systematic theory, it probably never will be, and that is probably okay. What is lost in the rigor of theory is gained in the flexibility of a paradigm". But we may aim to collectively design an agenda that is respectful of this *marriage* between "family" and "linked lives", while keeping the (methodological) spark alive.

Notes

1. Originally, the life course principles comprised Agency, Cultural and Historical Location, Timing of Lives and Linked lives. Other publications have considered a 5 principles typology, that also include Life Long Development.
2. Cross-sectorial longitudinal surveys are applied to a single unit of analysis, namely individuals with no interrelations among them; usually covering several topics/sectors of life. Multilevel Longitudinal Surveys are applied to individuals that are clustered in a larger unit of analysis, namely schools (take PISA as an example) or households (HILC-EU, for instance).
3. Longitudinal impact concerns the consequences of an individual event at a given point in time, in the life of that same individual at another point in time. Bi-linked impact includes the consequence of an individual event at a given point in time in the life of a member of the same household. Extra-linked impact refers to consequences of an individual event at a given point in time, in household level indicators. Intra-linked impact comprises the consequences of an indicator at the household level in the life of a household member. And household impact consists of the consequences of an indicator at the household level in another household level indicator at another point in time.
4. According to this Editorial article in 2009, the life course, as a scientific field, reached a state of maturity that can be attested by the exponential growth in the number of publications classified under the "life course".

Annex

See Table 31.3.

Table 31.3 Coding variables

Scope	Variables	Categories
Publication (Life course Field)	Year of publication	
	Publication type	Book
		Chapter
		Article
		Working paper
		Report
		Conference paper
		Thesis
		Other
	Language	English
		Portuguese
		French
	Main disciplinary area	Sociology
		Psychology (and development)
		Demography
		Life course
		History
		Aging
		Youth and childhood studies
		Family
		Social sciences in general
		Other sociology areas (methods, education, gender, migration, policy, social work and criminology)
		Other social sciences (economics, philosophy, geography, communication)
		Health and epidemiology
		Management and related (labor and industrial resources, managements and human resources)

(continued)

Table 31.3 (continued)

Scope	Variables	Categories
	Secondary disciplinary area	
	Number of authors	
	Institutional nationality of first author	Country
	Number of countries studied (if empirical)	
	What countries studied	
Methods (Life course Research Craft)	Methodological nature	Empirical quantitative
		Empirical qualitative
		Empirical mixed
		Literature review
		Theoretical
		Methodological and epistemological
	Data collection method 1 (methodological instrument of collection of information)	Thematic interviews (general qualitative interviews and semi structured interviews)
		In-depth biographical interviews and biographical and life stories)
		Cross time inquiries (longitudinal surveys, panel surveys and follow up inquires)
		Group unit of analysis (focus groups and family stories)
		Cross topic surveys
		Several methods
		Observation
		Secondary data (administrative data and bibliographic collection)

Scope	Variables	Categories
	Data collection method 2 (another methodological instrument of collection of information)	
	Data analysis method 1 (methodological instrument of treatment of information)	Thematic content analysis Holistic Analysis Holistic Content Analysis Discourse analysis Conversation analysis Sequence analysis Event history analysis and survival analysis Multilevel, multi-channel and actor-partner Regressions Structural equations Latent, path, growth Descriptive and bi-variate Multivariate
	Data analysis method 2 (another methodological instrument of treatment of information)	
	Use of longitudinal research design	Yes No
	Use of longitudinal data	Yes No
Linked impact (Linked lives Principle)	Type of impact	Longitudinal (individual level) Bi-linked Extra-linked Intra-linked Household Other

(continued)

Table 31.3 (continued)

Scope	Variables	Categories
	Implication of impact	Positive
		Negative
		Ambiguous or both
	Life course phase 1	Until childhood
	Life course phase 2	Until youth
		Until adulthood
		until old age
	Lag (duration between life course phase 1 and 2, longest considered)	Same moment
		1 lag
		2 lags
		3 lags
	Family tie 1 (place in the family)	Parent-child
	Family tie 2 (place in the family)	Couple
		Sibling
		Other links
		Several direct kinships
	Sphere of life 1	Education
	Sphere of life 2	Work/retirement
		Residential (and migration)
		Health (and death)
		Conjugality
		Parenthood
		Emotional/subjective (relational, developmental, conflict, caring, support)
		Other Financial

REFERENCES

Advances in Life Course Research. n.d. "Archives." Accessed 20 July 2019. https://www.sciencedirect.com/journal/advances-in-life-course-research/issues.

Bernardi, Laura, Johanes Huinink, and Richard Settersten Jr. 2019a. "Introduction to the Special Issue 'Theoretical and Methodological Frontiers in Life Course Research'." *Advances in Life Course Research* 41. https://doi.org/10.1016/j.alcr.2019.04.001.

Bernardi, Laura, Johanes Huinink, and Richard Settersten Jr. 2019b. "The Life Course Cube: A Tool for Studying Lives." *Advances in Life Course Research* 41. https://doi.org/10.1016/j.alcr.2018.11.004.

Billari, Francesco. 2009. "The Life Course Is Coming of Age." *Advances in Life Course Research* 14 (3): 83–86.

Carvalho, Helena. 2008. *Análise multivariada de dados qualitativos. Utilização da análise de correspondências múltiplas com o SPSS*. Lisboa: Edições Sílabo.

Carr, Deborah. 2018. "The Linked Lives Principle in Life Course Studies: Classic Approaches and Contemporary Advances." In *Social Networks and the Life Course*, edited by Duane F. Alwin, Diane Helen Felmlee, and Derek. A. Kreager, 41–63. Cham: Springer.

Ehrlich, Katherine B., Michelle R. vanDellen, Julia W. Felton, C. W. Lejuez, and Jude Cassidy. 2019. "Perceptions about Marital Conflict: Individual, Dyadic, and Family Level Effects." *Journal of Social and Personal Relationships* 36 (11–12) (November): 3537–3553. https://doi.org/10.1177/0265407519829846.

Elder, Glen H. 1974. *Children of the Great Depression*. Chicago: Chicago Press.

Elder, Glen H. 1994. "Time, Human Agency, and Social Change: Perspectives on the Life Course." *Social Psychology Quarterly* 57 (1): 4–15. https://doi.org/10.2307/2786971.

Elder, Glen H., and Janete Zollinger Giele. 2009. *The Craft of Life Course Research*. New York and London: The Guilford Press.

Elder, Glen H., Monica Kirkpatrick Johnson, and Robert Crosnoe. 2003. "The Emergence and Development of Life Course Theory." In *Handbook of the Life Course*, edited by Jeylan T. Mortimer, and Michael J. Shanahan, 3–19. New York: Kluwer Academic Publications.

Fasang, Anette Eva. 2012. "Retirement Patterns and Income Inequality." *Social Forces* 90 (3): 685–711. https://doi.org/10.1093/sf/sor015.

Greenacre, Michael. 2007. *Correspondence Analysis in Practice*. 2ª ed. London: Chapman & Hall / CRC.

Hair, Joseph, William C. Black, Barry J. Babin, and Rolphi E. Anderson. 2014. *Multivariate Data Analysis*. 7ª ed. Pearson New International Edition.

Krutova, Oxana, Pertti Koistinen, and Tapio Nummi. 2018. "The Effect of Partner Buffering on the Risk of Unemployment in Finland." *International Journal of Sociology and Social Policy* 38 (11/12): 982–1007.

Landes, Scott D., and Richard. A. Settersten Jr. 2019. "The Inseparability of Human Agency and Linked Lives." *Advances in Life Course Research* 42. https://doi.org/10.1016/j.alcr.2019.100306.

Leopold, Thomas. 2012. "Linked Lives Within Families and Across Generations." PhD diss., University of Bamberg.

Mills, Mellinda, and Hans-Peter Blossfeld. 2013. "The Second Demographic Transition Meets Globalization: A Comprehensive Theory to Understand Changes in

Family Formation in an Era of Rising Uncertainty." In *Negotiating the Life Course: Stability and Change in Life Pathways*, edited by Ann R. Evans, and Janeen Baxter, 9–33. Dordrecht: Springer.

Nico, Magda. 2015. "Bringing Life 'Back into Life Course Research': Using the Life Grid as a Research Instrument for Qualitative Data Collection and Analysis." *Quality & Quantity* 50: 2107–2120. https://doi.org/10.1007/s11135-015-0253-6.

Ramos, Madalena, and Helena Carvalho. 2011. "Perceptions of Quantitative Methods in Higher Education: Mapping Student Profile." *Higher Education* 61: 629–647. https://doi.org/10.1007/s10734-010-9353-3.

Society of Longitudinal and Life Course Studies. n.d. "Abstract Books 2010–2018." Accessed 20 July 2019. https://www.slls.org.uk/past-conferences.

Schoon, Ingrid. 2014. "Parental Worklessness and the Experience of NEET Among Their Offspring. Evidence from the Longitudinal Study of Young People in England (LSYPE)." *Longitudinal and Life Course Studies* 5 (2): 129–150. http://dx.doi.org/10.14301/llcs.v5i2.279.

Scott, Jacqueline, and Duane Alwin. 1998. "Retrospective Versus Prospective Measurement of Life Histories in Longitudinal Research." In *Methods of Life Course Research: Qualitative and Quantitative Approaches*, edited by Jacqueline Scott, and Duane Alwin, 98–127. https://dx.doi.org/10.4135/9781483348919.n5.

Settersten Jr, Richard. A. 2015. "Relationships in Time and the Life Course: The Significance of Linked Lives." *Research in Human Development* 12 (3–4): 217–223. https://doi.org/10.1080/15427609.2015.1071944.

Settersten Jr, Richard. A. 2018. "Nine Ways That Social Relationships Matter for the Life Course." In *Social Networks and the Life Course*, edited by Duane F. Alwin, Diane Helen Felmlee, and Derek A. Kreager, 27–40. Cham: Springer.

Shanahan, Michael J., and Ross Macmillan. 2008. *Biography and the Sociological Imagination: Contexts and Contingencies*. New York: W. W. Norton.

Shapiro, Adam, and Teresa Cooney. M. 2007. "Divorce and Intergenerational Relations Across the Life Course." *Advances in Life Course Research* 12: 191–219. https://dx.doi.org/10.1016/S1040-2608(07)12007-4.

Swartz, Teresa Toguchi. 2008. "Family Capital and the Invisible Transfer of Privilege: Intergenerational Support and Social Class in Early Adulthood." *New Directions for Child and Adolescent Development* 119: 11–24. https://doi.org/10.1002/cd.206.

Thomas, Lyndall. J., and Ross. S. Kalucy. 2002. "Parents with Mental Illness: A Qualitative Study of the Effects on Their Families." *Journal of Family Studies* 8 (1): 38–52. https://doi.org/10.5172/jfs.8.1.38.

Thomas, William I., and Florian Znaniecki. 1984 [1928]. *The Polish Peasant in Europe and America*. Chicago: University of Illinois Press.

Wickrama, Kandauda A. S., Rand D. Conger, and William T. Abraham. 2008. "Early Family Adversity, Youth Depressive Symptom Trajectories, and Young Adult Socioeconomic Attainment: A Latent Trajectory Class Analysis." *Advances in Life Course Research* 13: 161–192. https://doi.org/10.1016/S1040-2608(08)00007-5.

CHAPTER 32

Afterthoughts on an "Earthquake of Change"

Rita Gouveia, Jacques-Antoine Gauthier,
Almudena Moreno Mínguez, Anna-Maija Castrén,
Claude Martin, Vida Česnuitytė, Isabella Crespi,
and Katarzyna Suwada

"We live in extraordinary times" (Scott et al. 2014, xvi). This is the opening sentence of the Wiley Blackwell Companion to the Sociology of Families, referring to the transformations that affect family structures and practices at the turn of the twenty-first century and, in particular, to those transformations that were generated by the 2008 global economic crisis. In the context of 2020, this sentence could not be more appropriate. Moreover, it may not sufficiently characterise the present global pandemic that has seen individuals, families, and

---

Rita Gouveia was granted a post-doc scholarship funded by FCT- Grant SFRH/BPD/116958/2016, MCTE.

R. Gouveia (✉)
Institute of Social Sciences, University of Lisbon, Lisbon, Portugal
e-mail: rita.gouveia@ics.ul.pt

J.-A. Gauthier
University of Lausanne, Lausanne, Switzerland
e-mail: Jacques-Antoine.Gauthier@unil.ch

A. Moreno Mínguez
Campus María Zambrano, University of Valladolid, Segovia, Spain
e-mail: almudena@soc.uva.es

A.-M. Castrén
Department of Social Sciences, University of Eastern Finland, Kuopio, Finland
e-mail: anna-maija.castren@uef.fi

© The Author(s), under exclusive license to Springer Nature Switzerland AG 2021
A.-M. Castrén et al. (eds.), *The Palgrave Handbook of Family Sociology in Europe*, https://doi.org/10.1007/978-3-030-73306-3_32

communities struggling throughout the world. We can recall several moments in the history of humanity, from natural disasters to epidemics, wars, technological revolutions, and economic recessions that have prompted political, economic, cultural, and family change. Indeed, in the light of the COVID-19 pandemic, the same question that was posed by C. Wright Mills in his seminal work on the promise of the sociological imagination in the late 1950s could be asked today: "In what period have so many people been so totally exposed at so fast a pace to such earthquakes of change?" (Mills 1959, 4).

The COVID-19 pandemic is shaking our routines, rituals, relationships, and sociability because it is challenging our economic and social resilience. For us as social scientists and, in particular, as family sociologists, the pandemic and the turmoil it has caused in people's everyday lives is a challenge that tests the suitability of our theories, concepts, and research instruments. This volume is not immune to such a test and it would be pointless to write the final remarks without first sketching, even if in a more essayistic vein, how some of the topics covered in this handbook have been impacted by the pandemic. However, first and foremost, we want to reflect on how the contributions of this handbook may help us (re)frame some of the social impacts of the global crisis on the ways in which individuals live, think, and do family and intimacy in their specific social contexts.

This volume has been edited by eight committed scholars and board members of the European Sociological Association's Research Network on Families and Intimate Lives from eight European countries (Finland, France, Italy, Lithuania, Poland, Portugal, Spain, and Switzerland). During the final phase of the project, we shared our professional expertise and our personal experiences of eight different European countries that have been struck by the pandemic. It is evident that the COVID-19 pandemic cannot be limited to its epidemiological and economic dimensions but must be apprehended as a comprehensive social phenomenon that calls for multidimensional and multi-level frameworks. As social scientists, we need to both analyse and address the

---

C. Martin
EHESP, CNRS (National Centre of Scientific Research), Rennes Cedex, France
e-mail: claude.martin@ehesp.fr

V. Česnuitytė
Mykolas Romeris University, Vilnius, Lithuania
e-mail: v.cesnuityte@mruni.eu

I. Crespi
Department of Education and Tourism, University of Macerata, Macerata, Italy
e-mail: isabella.crespi@unimc.it

K. Suwada
Institute of Sociology, Nicolaus Copernicus University, Torun, Poland
e-mail: k.suwada@umk.pl

changing realities, "ones that are urgent for now, and others that are important for tomorrow" (Hanafi 2020, 1). Considering the threat of COVID-19 to health, income, social cohesion, and well-being, individuals and their families have been absorbed by a sense of uncertainty, insecurity, and anxiety together with collective displays of solidarity and altruistic action, as well as feelings of resentment and/or lack of trust in institutions and decision-makers. The pandemic has revealed pre-existing structural disparities but has also activated latent vulnerabilities and created new forms of social inequalities according to age, social class, gender, ethnicity, sexuality, and geographical location, for example (Braverman 2020).

Due to the various lockdowns, the "home" has become the fabric of life in which the spheres of intimacy, domesticity, education, work, and leisure are suddenly overlapping, creating a space for care and mutual support, as well as for stress, tension, and ambivalence. The need for negotiation between family members in order to balance the competing domains could not be more acute. On the one hand, this "return" to the importance of co-residence appears almost ironic because family sociology, although not neglecting the interdependencies taking place in the household, has been following an epistemological and methodological pathway of decentring the definitions of family that are solely based on co-residence and focusing instead on theorising families as relationships and practices based on affinity and closeness (cf. Part III). On the other hand, the anxiety and struggles faced by individuals, who, in accordance with the rules of physical distancing, are attempting to provide support across households, localities, and national borders, highlight the limitations of conceptualising the family exclusively on the basis of co-residence. Instead, it is more beneficial to understand families in terms of relationships, networks, meanings, and practices that cross the boundaries of domestic space and that can be diverse, transnational, and based on the various kinds of "glue" that bind individuals together.

The life-course perspective and particularly its core principles, *linked lives* and *trajectories* (Elder et al. 2003), can be mobilised in useful ways in order to assess how the pandemic reveals individuals' lives as being inherently interdependent: a change in one individual's life can have lasting effects on those with whom they are intimately engaged. During the pandemic, this interconnectedness has a dilemmatic nature since individuals, as human beings, are trapped between their basic need for social contact and physical proximity, their need to provide and/or receive emotional and practical support, and the risks of contamination and the obligation to respect the norms of social distancing.

We have witnessed multiple coping strategies and settings of confinement, each representing different challenges and vulnerabilities. Due to the heightened risk of older adults aged 65 years or more contracting the virus, multigenerational arrangements and interactions have been disrupted, with social contact between grandparents, their adult children, and grandchildren being discouraged. While some older adults have moved to their children's households in order to benefit from support, others have become socially isolated. For example, loneliness among older people in The Netherlands was found to have greatly increased after two months of the implementation of physical distancing measures (van Tilburg et al. 2020). COVID-19 outbreaks in nursing homes and restrictions on family visits also undermine intergenerational relationships and the well-being of the elderly. Post-separation families, as in the case of those families with children in shared custody arrangements, were challenged by the risks relating to disruption of the child-parent contact on the one hand and, on the other hand, by the risks relating to the continuous movement between parental households. As schools and day-care centres have been closing, dual-earner couples with underage children have been immersed in the challenges of family-work reconciliation. While in some cases gender inequalities have intensified with women taking on paid work, childcare, domestic tasks, and often caring for a dependent person (Collins et al. 2020), in other cases, the situation has revealed more gender-egalitarian practices between partners (Allon et al. 2020). In addition, recent reports indicate that there has been a drastic increase in domestic violence, which will cast a long shadow over familial relationships even after the pandemic is over (see, e.g., Ertan et al. 2020).

Young people have also been hit hard by the lockdowns. They have been overwhelmed by having to adapt to homeschooling and see their educational and professional projects put on hold, cope with the limited physical interaction with their peers, and face extended cohabitation with their parents and exceptionally complex negotiations of autonomy and independence (which has always characterised young adulthood but is now being exacerbated by the pandemic) (Magalhães et al. 2020). The role of non-human companions has increased, especially for people who live on their own. Dog owners in particular have benefited from regular walks and from the opportunity to interact with other people, despite the lockdowns (Oliva and Johnston 2020). We have observed friends living together during the lockdown, reminding us of the significance of friendship and of the "suffusion of boundaries" between family and friends (Pahl and Spencer 2004). We can also reflect on how the pandemic affects various conjugal arrangements, for example, Living Apart Together couples (LAT) with two households and Living Together Apart couples (LTA) who are obliged to stay together because of the financial impact of a separation (Martin et al. 2011), or individuals in in-and-out relationships facing complex negotiations regarding their intimacy and sexual practices.

Due to severe travel restrictions and measures such as mandatory quarantine after crossing national borders, transnational families are facing great demands and are being forced to renegotiate their long-distance care practices and adapt their individual and family migration projects. Again, persistent inequality shapes the experience of transnational lives, with "nationality, migrant status, financial resources, access to ICTs, age, health-status and life-course stage playing an important mediating role" in how people manage during the COVID-19 pandemic (Merla et al. 2020, 13). It is evident that the pandemic has exacerbated all social inequalities across societies (for France, for example, see Bajos et al. 2020; for a comparative perspective, see Reichelt et al. 2020).

We believe that this handbook can offer readers interested in families and intimate lives a rich starting point from which to assess the consequences of family change on individuals and groups, in the context of the current theoretical and methodological debates of family sociology in Europe. This project was started in a society that is very different from the one in which it is being concluded: a society struggling with COVID-19 and slowly coming to terms with its multiple consequences. Families continue to be the key axes of cohesion and of the social contract despite the diversity of practices, meanings, and relationships they entail. Family life keeps changing and we hope this volume can inspire the sociological imagination of the next generation of students, researchers, and scholars in general.

References

Alon, Titan M., Matthias Doepke, Jane Olmstead-Rumsey, and Michele Tertilt. 2020. "The Impact of COVID-19 on Gender Equality." *Covid Economics: Vetted and Real-Time Papers* 4: 62–85.

Bajos, Nathalie, Josiane Warszawski, Ariane Pailhé, Emilie Counil, Florence Jusot, Alexis Spire, Claude Martin, Laurence Meyer, Antoine Sireyjol, Jeanna-Eve Franck, and Nathalie Lydié. 2020. "Les inégalités sociales au temps du COVID-19." *Questions de Santé Publique* (40), Octobre 2020. Institut pour la Recherche en Santé Publique.

Braveman, Paula. April 2020. "COVID-19: Inequality Is Our Pre-existing Condition." *UNESCO Inclusive Policy Lab*.

Collins, Caitlyn, Liana Christin Landivar, Leah Ruppanner, and William J. Scarborough. 2020. "COVID-19 and the Gender Gap in WORK Hours." *Gender, Work & Organization*.

Elder, Glen H., Monica Kirkpatrick Johnson, and Robert Crosnoe. 2003. "The Emergence and Development of Life Course Theory." In *Handbook of the Life Course*, edited by Jeylan T. Mortimer, and Shanahan, Michael J., 3–19. Boston: Springer.

Ertan Deniz, Wissam El-Hage, Sarah Thierrée, Hervé Javelot, and Coraline Hingray. 2020. "COVID-19: Urgency for Distancing from Domestic Violence." *European Journal of Psychotraumatology* 11 (1): 1800245, https://doi.org/10.1080/20008198.2020.1800245.

Hanafi, Sari. April 2020. "Post-COVID-19 Sociology." *ISA Digital Platform*.

Magalhães, Pedro C., Rita Gouveia, Rui Costa-Lopes, and Pedro Adão E. Silva. 2020. "O Impacto Social da Pandemia. Estudo ICS/ISCTE Covid-19." *ICS/ISCTE Report*.

Martin, Claude, Andrew Cherlin, and Caitlin Cross-Barnet. 2011. "Living Together Apart in France and the United States." *Population-E* 66 (3–4): 561–558.

Merla, Laura, Majella Kilkey, and Loretta Baldassar. 2020. "Introduction to the Special Issue Transnational Care: Families Confronting Borders." *Journal of Family Research* 32(3), 393–414. https://doi.org/10.20377/jfr-420.

Mills, C. Wright. 1959. *The Sociological Imagination*. New York: Oxford University Press.

Oliva, Jessica Lee, and Kim Louise Johnston. 2020. "Puppy Love in the Time of Corona: Dog Ownership Protects Against Loneliness for Those Living Alone During the COVID-19 Lockdown." *International Journal of Social Psychiatry* 67 (3). https://doi.org/10.1177/0020764020944195.

Pahl, Ray, and Liz Spencer. 2004. "Personal Communities: Not Simply Families of 'Fate' or 'Choice'." *Current Sociology* 52 (2): 199–221.

Reichelt, Malte, Kinga Makovi, and Anahit Sargsyan. 2020. "The Impact of Covid-19 on Gender Inequality in the Labor Market and Gender-Role Attitudes." *European Societies* 23: S228–S245.

Scott, Jacqueline, Judith Treas, and Martin Richards, eds. 2014. *The Wiley Blackwell Companion to the Sociology of Families*. Hoboken: Wiley.

van Tilburg, Theo G., Stephanie Steinmetz, Elske Stolte, Henriëtte van der Roest, and Daniel H. de Vries. 2020. "Loneliness and Mental Health During the COVID-19 Pandemic: A Study Among Dutch Older Adults." *The Journals of Gerontology: Series B*.

Correction to: Migration and Families in European Society

Laura Zanfrini

Correction to:
Chapter 23 in: A.-M. Castrén et al. (eds.),
The Palgrave Handbook of Family Sociology in Europe,
https://doi.org/10.1007/978-3-030-73306-3_23

The original version of this chapter was inadvertently published with an incorrect affiliation of the author Laura Zanfrini in Chapter 23, which has now been updated from "Universita Cattolica, Milan, Italy" to "Fondazione ISMU, Milan, Italy". The chapter has been updated with the changes.

The updated version of this chapter can be found at
https://doi.org/10.1007/978-3-030-73306-3_23

© The Author(s), under exclusive license to Springer Nature
Switzerland AG 2021
A.-M. Castrén et al. (eds.), *The Palgrave Handbook of Family Sociology in Europe*, https://doi.org/10.1007/978-3-030-73306-3_33

Index

A

Adoption, 4, 7, 8, 73, 75–80, 88, 209, 415–417, 419–429, 436, 447, 460, 462

Adult, 19, 32, 53, 69, 73, 75, 77, 79, 81, 99, 113, 115, 142, 146, 172, 173, 212, 216, 223, 242, 243, 246, 265, 301, 302, 305, 308, 324, 330, 331, 352, 361, 369, 399, 400, 404, 406, 411, 412, 416, 420, 421, 437, 438, 442–444, 447, 462, 465, 499, 501, 504, 514, 527, 538–541, 564, 576, 580, 594, 595, 601, 625, 641

 adult children, 6, 115, 241, 243, 246, 265, 321–324, 328–336, 460, 481, 495, 497–499, 504, 505, 517, 518, 520–522, 526, 530, 531, 541, 559, 594, 600, 602, 630, 641

 adult, self-determining, 335

Affordability, 357, 364, 368, 369, 371

Ageing, 9, 109, 119, 173, 206, 248, 323, 459, 539–541, 545, 548, 549, 558, 592, 594, 597, 600, 628

 population ageing, 47, 160, 170, 224, 322, 591, 599

Agenda, 47, 71, 72, 75, 100, 225, 286, 291, 346, 348, 460, 469, 585, 612, 613, 620, 629, 631, 632

Ambivalence, 109, 110, 114, 115, 120, 122, 123, 125, 126, 181, 266, 323, 332, 497, 498, 505, 544, 592, 599–602, 641

Assisted reproduction, medically assisted procreation (MAP), 7, 76, 78, 79, 269, 415, 416, 419, 420, 423, 425, 428

Asylum, 537–539, 541–543, 545, 548

Attachment, 15–18, 25, 27, 30, 168, 228, 270, 439, 514

B

Benefit, 5, 18, 73, 88, 123, 149, 185, 186, 188, 190, 208, 211, 212, 214, 215, 217, 223, 225, 232–234, 244, 245, 247–249, 264, 268, 284, 323, 346, 357, 361, 362, 371, 381, 388, 390, 422, 457, 460, 515, 569, 579, 584, 620, 631, 641

 cash benefit, 206–209, 211, 213, 216–218, 243, 245, 247, 248, 349

 low flat rate benefit, 186, 228

Biographical approach, 327

Birth, 25, 28, 46, 47, 70, 73, 76–79, 81, 89, 91, 92, 94, 95, 99, 113, 159, 161–164, 186, 190, 208, 209, 211, 214, 233, 309, 322, 357, 366, 400, 401, 405–412, 417, 421, 426, 455, 458, 459, 467, 476, 481, 559, 561, 565, 577, 592, 595, 612, 622

 birth of a child, 484, 596

birth order, 309, 310
non-marital births, 163, 166
Bismarckian tradition, 186, 187
Blended family, 16, 19, 33, 286, 399, 401, 411
Bonds, 268, 269, 309, 321, 323, 399, 437, 447, 461, 514, 530, 602
  biological bonds, 307
  emotional bonds, 270, 311, 321, 330
Boundary(ies), 32, 101, 102, 107, 108, 110, 112, 114, 123, 139, 262, 264, 265, 268–270, 305, 410, 411, 444, 477, 548, 566, 567, 641

C

Capability, 392
Care
  care across borders, 497, 538, 546
  care across borders, 539
  cash for care, 211, 217, 349, 353, 354
  circulation of care, 498
  coordination and delegation of care, 500, 506
  dimensions of care, 546
  elder-care, 9, 21, 324, 545, 546
  global care chain, 545
  hands-on care, 9, 500–502, 505, 506, 539
  Ict-mediated transnational care, 546
  long-term care (LTC), 213, 214, 217, 230, 248
  organisation of care, 5, 205, 206, 209, 211, 213, 547
  professional care providers, 345, 349, 351, 353–355
Care arrangements
  care arrangements from a distance, 500
  care arrangements in the home country, 502
Care circulation, 9, 505, 542
Care gap, 226, 228, 233, 321, 322
Care institutions, 207, 209, 212
Care leaves, 205, 207, 208, 210, 214, 215, 217, 218
Care responsibilities, 9, 165, 166, 168, 233, 234, 363, 503, 545, 546

Care work, 89, 91, 95, 100, 168, 229, 233, 417, 545
Childbearing, 95, 162–167, 172, 173, 224, 227, 577
  childbearing postponement, 162
Childcare, 6, 9, 64, 91, 92, 95, 143, 148, 166, 168–170, 181, 182, 184, 186, 187, 200, 205, 208–213, 218, 225–228, 230, 231, 245, 248, 304, 345–349, 351–355, 357, 358, 361–371, 416, 423, 439, 442, 477, 481, 503, 504, 506, 539, 596, 602, 642
  non-parental childcare, 6, 345, 346, 350. *See also* Daycare
Child, children
  child best interest, 381–383, 385, 411, 420, 421
  child-rearing, 346, 378, 418, 436, 442, 445, 560, 596
  children's perspective, 409
  children's agency, 477, 481
  children's drawings, 137
  children's overall life satisfaction, 404, 406–408
  children's perspective, 6, 295, 304, 307
  children's satisfaction, 7
  children's subjective well-being, 400, 401, 404, 409, 412
  child well-being, 3, 6, 7, 187, 201, 305, 346, 366, 388, 389, 399, 400, 403, 422, 423, 427–429, 480
  UN Convention on the Rights of the Child, 420, 421
  welfare of the child, 421, 425
Childhood, 7, 24, 89, 92, 141, 143, 167, 230, 231, 243, 301, 302, 324, 346, 354, 362, 399, 400, 421, 444, 445, 476, 527, 576, 580, 592, 622–626
Childless, 96, 112, 166, 241, 246, 248, 270, 421, 559, 602, 603
Childlessness, 162, 558, 602
Choice, 4, 5, 30, 33, 75, 88, 92, 96, 98, 99, 112–114, 125, 164, 173, 207, 226, 241, 249, 261, 267, 322, 323, 331, 333–335, 347–349, 362, 364,

365, 367, 371, 378, 416, 462, 463, 470, 477, 483, 559, 569, 577, 578, 592, 593, 595–597, 603, 612
Circles, 18, 109, 124, 139, 142, 146–148, 265, 327, 391
  concentric circles, 139, 146–148, 327
Closeness, 5, 6, 260, 263, 268, 314, 322, 323, 641
Cohabitation, 16, 19, 22, 24, 91, 94, 95, 101, 163, 164, 166, 173, 307, 325, 399, 401, 403, 465, 467, 471, 475, 563, 577, 594, 601, 642
Cohort panel survey, 391
Commodity, 365, 371, 545
Commuting, 6, 311, 314, 401, 464
Companion animals, 269, 270
Comparative analysis, 3, 7, 207, 211, 385
Conciliation, 348, 349, 353
Configurational perspective, 566
Configuration, figuration, 4, 7, 9, 107–111, 113–126, 133, 149, 266, 267, 272, 301, 304, 306, 307, 309, 312, 314, 418, 424, 426, 436, 470, 497, 500, 558, 566–568, 626, 628
Confinement, 641
Conflict, 53, 71, 109, 112, 114–116, 118, 119, 121, 122, 138, 145, 146, 150, 208, 213, 225, 228, 229, 242, 259, 266, 272, 279, 283, 284, 287–289, 295, 305, 306, 312–314, 323, 324, 328, 332, 333, 346, 355, 383, 389, 391, 484, 497, 502, 505, 515, 543, 548, 568, 592, 599, 600, 602
Contact, 119, 144, 146, 165, 323, 332, 335, 378, 382, 383, 417, 479, 480, 486, 497, 500, 513–523, 525–527, 530, 531, 542, 543, 546, 548, 598, 641, 642
Control, 17, 19, 108, 119, 279, 281–288, 290–293, 334, 351, 438, 462, 483, 526, 530, 563
Coordination, 96, 98, 311, 498, 546
Couplehood, 286, 288, 290, 293, 294
  construction of couplehood, 289
Couple(s), 5, 6, 18–23, 25, 28–30, 33, 54, 71–76, 78, 79, 81, 89–92, 95, 96, 98, 113, 114, 120, 137, 139, 140, 142, 144, 146, 164, 166, 168, 189, 210, 214, 218, 224, 230, 241, 242, 246, 263, 264, 266, 267, 270, 279–296, 303, 323, 329, 352, 354, 381, 384, 402, 416, 420, 482–484, 486, 547, 559, 563, 567, 592, 594–598, 603, 604, 622, 625, 629, 642
  couple finances, 281, 289, 292–295
  dual-earner couples, 46, 54, 57, 642
  money in couples, 279–281, 283, 284, 288, 289, 291, 294, 295
COVID-19, 10, 65, 585, 604, 639–643
Crisis, 46, 64, 230, 324, 347, 438, 466, 483, 537, 584, 585, 639, 640
  pandemic crisis, 640
Cross-national, 3, 48, 100, 102, 288, 357, 575, 578, 583, 584, 630
Cultural
  cultural classification, 304, 309
  cultural ideal, 5, 70, 303, 322, 323, 328, 329, 334–336
  cultural inheritance, 26
  cultural intergenerational transfers, 502
  cultural pluralism, 460
  cultural transmission, 27, 504, 505
Custody, 143, 228, 305, 377–382, 388, 389, 391, 460, 541, 642
  join legal custody, 382
  joint legal custody, 377, 378

D

Daycare, 181–183, 186, 187, 197, 200, 201, 439
  day care centers, 213, 214. *See also* Childcare
Decision-making, 69, 76, 98, 113, 150, 279, 281–284, 293, 294, 366, 441, 476–478
Deep knowledge, 323, 329, 332
Defamilialisation/defamilialism/defamilialising policies, 180–184, 189, 206, 207, 217, 229, 231, 233, 506, 508. *See also* Familialisation/familialism/familialising policies

Degenderisation/degenderising, 180, 183–190, 196, 197, 200, 201. *See also* Genderisation/genderising

Demographic, 3, 4, 8, 85, 86, 89, 94, 95, 99, 159, 160, 162–166, 169, 170, 172, 240, 260, 322, 346, 366, 459, 470, 514, 577, 580, 581, 591, 593, 594, 599

  demographic changes, 95, 97, 99, 169, 170

  Demographic Transition, 89, 90, 94, 95, 162, 260

Denmark, 49, 53, 200, 225–229, 302, 303, 315, 324, 336, 337, 363, 369, 386, 436, 459, 462, 516–519, 579, 580, 600

Deprivation, 240, 247, 248, 583

  material deprivation, 241, 247, 248, 418, 424, 467, 583

  non-income deprivations, 241

Destandardisation, (de)-standardisation, 563, 564, 568, 576, 578. *See also* Standardisation

Digital technologies, 498, 504, 506

Dilemmas, 4, 107, 109–115, 118, 120–122, 125, 126, 181, 229, 594, 600

  dilemma-sensitive methods, 108

Distance, 6, 9, 73, 146, 147, 266, 268, 271, 304, 314, 322, 332, 333, 335, 364, 390, 440, 443, 467, 480, 483, 498, 499, 501–504, 516, 521, 522, 527, 530, 531, 539, 546–548, 562, 598, 624

Divorce, 7, 16, 18–20, 24, 27, 31, 72, 75, 76, 78, 88, 94, 95, 110, 112, 115, 123, 137, 138, 142, 147, 164, 166, 228, 283, 303, 305, 325, 328, 332, 377–382, 388–392, 399, 401–403, 410, 411, 439, 475, 476, 482, 483, 485, 486, 541, 558, 559, 561, 563, 592, 594, 595, 598, 603

Doing family, 96, 122, 124, 160, 164, 262, 478, 485, 547

Domestic work, 22, 232, 481, 496, 506, 545, 565

Double bind, 54, 109

Draw, 2, 5, 101, 133, 137, 139, 146, 148, 149, 151, 328, 334, 335, 362, 385, 436

  Draw and Write, 138

  Draw, Write and Tell, 138

  draw-your-day, 148

Dual earner family, 166, 231, 233

  couple, 46, 54, 57, 59, 279

  family, 166, 325

Durkheim, Émile, 3, 15–21, 23, 25, 26, 30, 31, 93

E

Early intervention, 446, 447

Economic, 1, 4–6, 8, 10, 26, 32, 45, 46, 49, 50, 59, 62–65, 86, 90–92, 95, 100, 108, 165–168, 171, 173, 180, 211, 225, 227, 229, 230, 240–243, 245, 247, 249, 250, 263, 271, 281–283, 285, 286, 291, 294, 322, 324, 325, 337, 364, 379, 387, 411, 418, 422–427, 436, 456, 458, 460, 462–466, 468, 470, 471, 476, 478, 480, 481, 487, 497, 501, 506, 507, 515, 518, 530, 542, 547, 559, 564, 575, 580, 582, 592, 593, 599, 601, 639, 640

  economic dimension, 640

  economic sustainability, 461

Education, 2, 8, 9, 21, 26, 45, 46, 52, 59, 65, 90, 92, 96, 99, 167, 172, 187, 200, 210, 211, 230, 240, 243, 245–247, 249, 265, 268, 282, 324, 325, 331, 335, 348, 349, 362, 366, 370, 371, 378, 379, 385, 416, 419, 422, 459, 463, 465, 470, 478, 483, 484, 486, 487, 505, 517, 523, 564, 565, 576, 578–585, 612, 622, 625, 626, 628, 631, 641

Educational gradient, 381, 382, 387, 390

Elderly, 5, 48, 65, 109, 115, 173, 188, 205, 206, 208, 212–215, 217, 218, 248, 263, 267, 322, 325, 466, 504, 526, 527, 547, 594, 600, 601, 642

Elias, Norbert, 15–17, 24, 27, 107–111, 115, 122, 124, 125, 266, 305, 308, 614

Embedded liberalism, 456, 464
Emotion, 5, 151, 242, 302, 328, 334, 547, 599, 629
　emotional closeness, 92, 265, 335, 479, 481, 497, 500, 513, 514, 540
　emotion map, 139, 144–146, 149
Employment, 2, 22, 28, 49, 50, 54, 57, 63, 65, 164, 166–168, 183, 210, 213, 214, 216, 224, 229, 230, 232, 234, 240, 243–245, 261, 283, 286, 294, 347, 349, 352, 354, 355, 364, 366, 368, 369, 419, 424, 426, 459, 465, 466, 481, 496, 505, 564–566, 579, 580, 582, 584, 592, 596, 598, 600
　employment rate, 46, 53, 65, 207, 212, 231, 383, 467
Entitlement, 210, 214, 215, 217, 241, 284, 285, 287, 349, 368–371, 503
Equalising, 362, 469
Equal opportunities, 47, 230, 366, 371, 470
Estonia, 7, 82, 250, 363, 368, 369, 400, 402–407, 409–411, 517, 518
Ethical, 76, 137, 150, 151, 325, 455
　ethical guidelines, 150
Ethnic penalties, 468
Europe, 1–5, 7, 8, 15, 22, 27, 49–51, 53, 57, 59, 63–65, 70, 71, 77, 80–82, 85, 86, 89–91, 94, 95, 99–101, 159, 160, 162–164, 166, 167, 170–172, 206, 207, 209, 211, 217, 232, 242, 246–249, 260, 266, 270, 280, 288, 324, 362, 363, 378, 379, 386, 390–392, 399, 436, 445, 455, 456, 458–460, 466, 470, 475, 476, 482–486, 495, 496, 500, 501, 506, 507, 515–521, 523, 527, 530, 531, 537–539, 543, 545, 564, 565, 577, 578, 581, 591, 598, 599, 602, 643
European Commission, 47, 57, 159, 172, 201, 208, 210, 213, 215, 230, 231, 362, 363, 369, 371, 436, 471, 531, 604
European Union's Survey on Income and Living Conditions (EU-SILC), 246, 350, 401–403

Eurostat, 200, 208, 219, 303, 346, 347, 351, 358, 368, 384, 392, 401–403, 518
Everyday life, 20, 25, 70, 134, 144, 260, 262–264, 269, 304, 305, 310, 311, 315, 484
Evolutionary perspective, 271, 272
Expectations, 6, 24, 47, 48, 85, 87, 88, 97, 98, 113, 115, 119, 160, 208, 262, 290, 293, 294, 301, 302, 310, 312, 321, 327–331, 334–337, 349, 364, 370, 401, 443, 446, 478, 480, 486, 497, 503, 505, 517, 604, 612
　expectations on relationships, 336
　normative expectations, 5, 96, 147, 259, 271, 279, 325, 328, 596
Extended leave, 186, 209

F
Fair treatment, 406–409
Familialisation/familialism/familialising policies, 181, 580
　explicit familialism, 207, 212, 218
　Implicit familialism, 207, 211, 212, 217, 218
　optional familialism, 207, 212, 218, 324, 508. *See also* Defamilialisation/defamilialism/defamilialising policies
Familialistic societies, 506
Family(ies)
　european families, 2, 4, 5, 15, 97, 108, 208, 307, 482, 516, 518, 523, 530
　Family biographies, 85, 94, 164
　family change, 3, 7, 137, 139–141, 148, 162, 165–167, 173, 379, 399–401, 403, 406, 409–412, 485, 639, 643
　family configuration, 9, 107–111, 113, 115–121, 123–126, 133, 267, 558, 566–568
　family de-institutionalisation, 167
　family destabilisation, 167
　family dynamics, 140, 144, 166, 172, 262, 482, 485, 486, 598, 625, 631

INDEX

family formation, 74, 160, 162, 166, 167, 169, 310, 402, 476, 481, 483, 559, 564, 580, 629
family generations, 495, 513, 515, 531
family instability, 387
family life cycle (FLC), 91, 96, 101, 548, 557
family meaning, 263, 267
family members, 8, 15, 17, 27, 32, 51, 58, 73, 92, 96, 98, 107, 109–116, 118, 119, 121, 122, 124–126, 140–142, 145–147, 164, 165, 173, 188, 206, 207, 211, 213, 214, 218, 223, 229, 247, 249, 270, 279, 284, 292, 303, 305, 307, 309, 311, 323, 327, 347, 386, 389, 400, 411, 439, 456, 457, 460, 461, 464, 466, 467, 476–481, 484, 485, 497–503, 506, 507, 515, 523, 526, 530, 537–539, 542–544, 547, 548, 559, 564, 567, 596, 598, 599, 603, 614, 628, 629, 631, 641
family migration, 460, 462, 463, 465, 475–479, 481, 486, 642
family policy, policies, 2, 4, 5, 7, 30, 31, 168, 170–172, 179, 180, 182, 184, 186, 188–190, 201, 207–209, 218, 224–228, 233, 234, 240, 295, 345–347, 349, 352, 357, 371, 381, 384, 386, 446, 565, 580, 584
family practices, 29, 97, 122, 123, 262, 264, 270, 271, 303, 355, 507
family relational aspects, 407–409, 412
family reunification, 456, 460, 461, 463, 464, 476, 537, 538, 541, 543
family reunion, 455, 460
Family Stress Model (FSM), 242, 243, 249
family systems, 577, 578
family terminology, 482
family trajectory, trajectories, 3, 9, 91, 101, 558, 559, 561–565, 567, 568

family values, 8, 165, 384, 440, 481, 483, 486, 602
migrant families, 8, 9, 136, 228, 455, 463, 464, 466, 467, 470, 476, 484–487, 503, 505, 515, 516, 527, 548
mixed families, 8, 139, 475, 476, 481, 482, 484–486
transnational families, 8, 143, 144, 475–477, 480, 481, 485, 495–499, 501, 503, 505, 507, 537, 539, 540, 542, 546–548, 642
Family life, 1, 2, 5–7, 10, 16, 18, 21, 27, 71–73, 76, 80, 81, 120, 136, 141, 148, 168, 171, 206, 218, 224, 225, 239, 242, 260, 261, 271, 302–307, 309, 311, 314, 316, 400, 401, 404, 405, 407–411, 435, 438, 441, 442, 445–447, 465, 481, 484, 537, 542, 561, 562, 567, 568, 591, 592, 594, 601, 602, 625, 643
organization of family life, 164, 207, 272, 315
Family networks, 149, 266, 295, 477, 530, 545, 549
Family Network Method (FNM), 111, 113, 115, 124
Family relations, 3, 8, 16, 27, 45, 48, 59, 69–74, 76, 78, 80, 81, 86, 88, 92, 94, 95, 97, 100, 101, 137, 165, 184, 242, 272, 301, 303–305, 307, 308, 310, 315, 436, 498, 515, 542, 593, 598–600, 602, 622
dehierarchisation of family relations, 95, 97
Family ties, 112, 113, 120, 211, 262, 324, 477, 485, 506, 577, 593
horizontal family ties, 165
vertical family ties, 322
Father(s), 16, 17, 24–26, 31, 34, 73, 74, 77, 78, 80, 111, 112, 115, 116, 123, 137, 143, 145, 146, 165, 166, 168, 170, 171, 181, 184–186, 190, 197, 209, 224–228, 230–234, 310, 312, 313, 332, 333, 335, 346, 348, 352, 354, 355, 378, 380–382, 384, 386, 389–391, 401, 410, 411, 420, 437, 439–441, 480, 486, 500–502, 504, 523, 538, 540, 542, 548

father involvement, 381, 384, 390, 391
father quota, 181, 185, 190, 196
Fertility, 4, 79, 89–91, 94–96, 99, 112, 159–162, 164, 166–172, 182, 183, 207, 225, 380, 401, 417, 419, 427, 459, 482, 591, 623
  fertility changes, 162, 164
  fertility recuperation, 162
  low fertility, 159, 160, 162, 165, 169, 170, 206, 207, 229
  sub-replacement fertility, 159, 160, 166, 171, 172, 379
Finland, 25, 49, 50, 82, 113, 114, 200, 225–229, 248, 250, 369, 386, 436, 446, 462, 518, 538, 539, 541–543, 547, 580, 640
Foster care, 7, 316, 415–417, 419–423, 425–429
Frame, 2, 87, 88, 93, 95, 310, 323, 436, 437, 440, 442, 445, 446, 463, 568, 625
  Frame Selection, 88
  historical frame, 335, 336
France, 7, 25, 30, 48, 50, 57, 62, 71, 77, 80, 163, 166, 168, 200, 263, 345–349, 351–355, 357, 363, 365, 370, 379, 381, 384, 386, 387, 435–437, 446, 459, 462, 467, 468, 480, 483, 500, 507, 517–519, 579–581, 593, 597, 640, 643
Friction, 292, 314
Friendship, 140, 147, 262, 265, 267, 323, 567, 602, 603, 642
Functional solidarity, 498, 514, 516, 530

G

Gender
  gender arrangements, 100, 101
  gender equality, 7, 22, 46–48, 53, 64, 72, 113, 114, 168–172, 181, 187, 201, 210, 225–228, 231, 233, 280, 346, 378–380, 384–387, 391, 392, 443, 461, 502
  gender equality index (GEI), 386, 387, 391, 392
  gender identity, 46, 72, 73, 81, 293, 565
  gender ideology, ideologies, 229, 230, 232, 282, 283, 286, 293, 294, 480
  gender inequality, 4, 21, 23, 25, 28, 46, 48, 59, 63, 168, 208–210, 218, 227, 282, 288–290, 294, 348, 349, 503, 565, 604, 625, 642
  gender perspective, 22, 53, 59, 64, 95, 167, 229, 477
  gender revolution, 168
  gender roles, 4, 5, 9, 58, 63, 86, 92, 93, 95, 114, 140, 144, 165–167, 169, 173, 181, 183, 184, 186, 187, 189, 197, 224, 227, 288, 303, 306, 441, 468, 496, 499, 501, 503–507, 558, 568, 592, 594, 596, 597, 599, 601
  gender theory, 21
Gendered
  gendered division of unpaid work, 64
  gendered housework, 51, 58, 64, 165
  gendered pay gap, 57, 59, 63
Genderisation/genderising, 180, 183, 184, 201, 218
  explicitly genderising, 186, 188–190, 196, 200, 201
  implicitly genderising, 186–190, 196, 201. *See also* Degenderisation/degenderising
Generalised norms, 321, 328
Generational independence, 322, 324, 336
Generations and Gender Programme (GGP), 172
Geographical, 45, 71, 171, 207, 260, 267, 311, 316, 325, 367, 476, 516, 527, 599, 641
  geographical distance, 477, 478, 485, 496–499, 501, 506, 513, 516, 520–523, 525, 527, 530, 531, 601
  geographical proximity, 496, 498, 516, 520, 598, 599
Germany, 48, 62, 64, 82, 123, 161, 162, 172, 190, 242, 248, 250, 324, 369, 379, 381, 382, 447, 459, 460,

462, 463, 467, 483, 498, 504, 505, 507, 517–519, 541, 566, 580, 581, 600, 630
Goldilocks principle, 322, 334–336
Grandparenting, grandparents, 112, 146, 211, 232, 269, 312, 322, 323, 328, 333, 335, 347–349, 351, 354, 355, 412, 439, 481, 486, 497, 499, 502–504, 506, 541, 602, 641
Greece, 51, 82, 163, 166, 229, 230, 232, 233, 250, 468, 503, 505, 517–519, 538, 539, 541, 580, 582
Guest worker, 455, 456, 483, 496, 504, 530
Guidelines, 7, 47, 210, 378, 415, 417, 419–425, 427, 428
  ethical guidelines, 150
  visual research guidelines, 150

H

Health Behaviour in School-aged Children (HBSC), 382, 385–387, 392
Household, 6, 16, 21, 23, 29, 48, 53, 54, 64, 73, 91–93, 98, 100, 107, 108, 110–112, 114–116, 124, 125, 137, 140, 141, 144, 148, 166, 180, 188, 241, 242, 246–248, 259, 263, 265, 270, 280–286, 291, 292, 294, 302, 305, 309–315, 324, 336, 346, 347, 350, 351, 354, 355, 357, 364, 368, 378, 382, 384, 385, 390, 391, 399–403, 405–412, 422, 458, 467, 470, 478, 500, 501, 503, 530, 546, 547, 557, 561, 563, 567, 579, 583, 584, 595, 597, 622, 624, 628, 641, 642
  familial household, 241, 246, 248, 249
  household composition, 9, 110, 111, 403, 409, 412, 558, 595
  household income, 7, 92, 246, 284, 348, 349, 354, 355, 583
  household structures, 110, 160, 248, 262, 400, 401, 403, 411, 558, 566
Human rights, 69–73, 75–78, 81, 82, 463, 464

European Convention on Human Rights (ECHR), 70–72, 75, 79–82
European Court of Human Rights (ECTHR), 3, 70–72, 75–81
Hybridity, 484

I

Iceland, 82, 190, 200, 225–229, 363, 368, 459, 507, 518
Identity formation, 485, 486, 565
Immigrant assimilation and integration, 483
Immigration history, 459
Income, 3, 7, 28, 51, 59, 64, 119, 166, 185, 186, 190, 211, 215–217, 226, 227, 240–245, 247, 248, 282, 285–287, 290–295, 346–348, 351, 354, 355, 357, 362, 363, 367, 368, 384, 385, 389, 390, 392, 418, 419, 426, 461, 464, 501, 517, 544, 545, 579, 582–584, 597, 630, 641
  income determinants, 45, 59, 63
  income replacement principle, 181, 185, 188, 196, 197
  source of income, 243, 427
Individualisation, 10, 16–19, 24, 25, 27–29, 32, 86, 95, 96, 99, 165, 261, 262, 264, 322, 335, 336, 563–565, 577, 578, 580, 604
Individualism, 16, 18, 19, 23, 25–27, 30, 31, 286, 593, 594, 598, 602
Inequalities, 2, 3, 7, 9, 21–23, 25–27, 29, 32, 33, 45, 48, 51, 64, 65, 98, 170, 171, 173, 260, 262, 267, 287, 288, 362–364, 368, 371, 379, 469, 486, 568, 580, 582, 583, 593, 594, 604, 641
  accumulation of inequalities, 59, 63
  gender inequality, 4, 21, 23, 25, 28, 46, 48, 59, 63, 168, 208–210, 218, 227, 282, 288–290, 294, 348, 349, 503, 565, 604, 625, 642
  structural inequality, 63
Institutional, 4, 30, 31, 46, 48–50, 91, 95, 100, 126, 165, 167–169, 171, 206, 207, 209, 210, 212, 217, 246,

282, 324, 337, 351, 352, 385, 439, 470, 475, 486, 496, 497, 545, 565, 566, 576, 578, 579, 581, 584, 599
institutional dimension, 46, 64
Institutionalisation, 325, 377, 378, 465, 546, 563, 564, 566, 568
Intact families, 380, 385, 390, 391, 475, 487
Integration, 8, 10, 47, 49, 59, 63, 149, 267, 457, 462–466, 470, 485, 486, 505, 566, 569
  integration agreement, 462
  paradox of integration, 469
Interaction, 5, 10, 23, 81, 88, 95, 102, 110, 113–115, 118, 121, 125, 141, 144, 147, 151, 246, 260, 263, 265, 289, 293, 307, 322, 323, 328, 329, 335, 336, 369, 390, 469, 496, 497, 499, 514, 527, 543, 547, 558, 560, 612, 614, 623, 631, 641, 642
  asymmetrical, 324, 329
  intergenerational, 115, 323, 324, 336
  micro-interaction, 328
Interdependence (interdependency), 9, 107, 109, 110, 115, 116, 119, 123, 126, 139, 266, 309, 311, 324, 560, 612, 621, 628
Intergenerational, 3, 8, 9, 18, 26, 30, 119, 122, 137, 187, 188, 201, 249, 321, 322, 324, 327, 328, 437, 476, 478, 484, 495–500, 505–507, 515, 516, 591, 599, 601, 612, 629
  intergenerational contact, 513–515, 517–519, 521, 523, 525–527, 530
  intergenerational solidarity, 10, 495–499, 506, 507, 513–516, 520, 531, 566, 592, 593, 595, 599
Intergenerational relations, relationships, 120, 188, 321, 322, 324, 495–497, 507, 568, 632, 642
  emotional quality of intergenerational relations, 323
Intermarriage rates, 483
International comparison, 10, 436
International Network on Leave Policies and Research, 208, 224

International Survey of Children's Well-being "Children's Worlds" (ISCWEB), 7, 400–402, 404
Interview, 23, 113, 114, 121, 124, 125, 135, 136, 139–142, 144, 147, 148, 151, 264, 290, 292, 293, 307, 311–313, 316, 325, 327, 328, 330–332, 351, 416, 429, 501, 507, 517, 538, 539, 543, 561, 562, 619
Intimacy, 5, 19, 97, 98, 111, 165, 259, 261, 262, 264–266, 268–271, 311, 314, 498, 546, 640–642
Italy, 82, 162, 163, 166, 190, 224, 229–233, 250, 324, 367, 387, 459, 460, 462, 464, 468, 479, 502, 503, 505, 517–519, 545, 580, 582, 602, 640

K
Kin-keeping, 323
Kinning, 269, 498, 545
Kinship
  networks, 165
  verticalization of kinship, 165

L
Law, 3, 18, 25, 30–32, 72, 75, 77–80, 114, 189, 214, 262, 465, 537
  family law, 69, 70, 74, 78, 80, 81, 240, 380, 381, 458
  human rights law, 69, 70, 75, 80
Left behind children, 461, 480, 481
Leitbilder, 112, 124
Life course, life-course, lifecourse, 3, 9, 10, 24, 46, 63, 86, 91, 95–97, 99, 120, 125, 162, 164, 166, 172, 173, 227, 261, 266, 267, 270, 295, 482, 484, 486, 496, 497, 505, 527, 542, 548, 558–561, 564–569, 576, 577, 593–596, 611–615, 619–622, 624–626, 628–632
  life course perspective, 9, 120, 335, 482, 558, 559, 561, 563, 565–569, 594, 611–615, 620, 629, 641
  life course regime, 565, 568

life course research, 325, 560, 563, 569, 612–614, 619, 621, 623, 625, 631
   standardisation of the life course, 10, 91, 564
Life stage, 45, 48, 51, 53, 54, 57, 59, 63, 65, 502, 561, 567, 569, 604, 624, 625
   late working life stage, 48
Linguistic turn, 134
Linked lives, 10, 120, 165, 266, 559, 568, 612–615, 619–622, 624–626, 628–632, 641
Litigation, 70, 71, 383, 385
   strategic litigation, 71
Living arrangements, 89, 91, 92, 101, 111, 173, 213, 263, 378, 379, 381–384, 388, 400, 401, 406, 409, 583
Lockdown, 65, 641, 642
Longitudinal, 28, 137, 295, 361, 362, 391, 412, 482, 485, 558, 561, 568, 569, 620, 622–624, 630–632
   longitudinal surveys, 172, 632
Love, 5, 6, 17–19, 21, 24, 29, 30, 34, 92, 97, 98, 109, 144, 266, 280, 288, 289, 291, 292, 294, 295, 304, 314, 331, 334, 335, 439, 440, 442, 476

M

Male breadwinner, 53, 54, 100, 165, 166, 168, 206, 229, 288, 355, 379, 380, 384, 391, 480, 506, 540, 565
Map
   emotion map, 139, 144–146, 149
   Four Field Map, 146
   My Family Map, 142–144
Marriage
   contracted marriage, 462
Master status, 10, 565
Materiality, 5, 144, 263, 312
Material well-being, 405
Maternity, 53, 75, 77, 81, 565
   maternity leave, 169, 186, 190, 196, 197, 208, 209, 223, 224, 226, 230, 231, 233, 346, 353, 354, 565
Maternity leave, 169, 186, 190, 196, 197, 208, 209, 223, 224, 226, 230, 231, 233, 346, 353, 354, 565
Matthew effect, 362
Meanings, 4, 5, 29, 74, 115, 121, 122, 136, 141, 148, 149, 240, 260, 264, 267, 269–271, 280, 283, 312, 440, 484, 632, 641, 643
Meta-analyses, 378, 388, 389, 422, 423
Method(s), 4, 108, 111, 113, 115, 116, 120, 121, 125, 133, 135–144, 148–151, 241, 249, 250, 260, 271, 316, 383, 419, 425, 558, 561, 614, 619, 620, 625, 626, 629–631
   Family Network Method (FNM), 111, 113, 115, 124
   mixed-methods research, 133, 148, 561
   visual methodologies, 133, 137, 149, 150
   visual research method, 135, 136
Migrancy, 544
Migrants, 8, 9, 224, 248, 455–458, 460–467, 469, 471, 475–479, 482, 483, 486, 496, 498–507, 515, 516, 518, 520–523, 525–527, 530, 531, 537, 539, 540, 545, 546
   migrants' offspring, 458, 467–470
Migration
   economics migration, 456
   emancipatory potential of migration, 506
   permanent migration, 456
Migratory trajectories, 476
Mixed partnerships, 482–485
Mobility, 9, 26, 149, 164, 173, 260, 325, 335, 418, 457, 469, 479, 481, 486, 496, 503, 504, 513, 531, 537, 597, 598, 603, 604, 623
Modernisation, 86, 89–91, 93, 96, 97, 229, 261, 513
Modernity, 16, 19, 25, 26, 34, 86, 95, 121, 124, 134, 261, 437, 602
Modern technology, 523
Money, 5, 6, 18, 25, 29, 108, 181, 187, 188, 279–296, 313, 329, 331, 333, 380, 405, 500–502, 513, 514, 539, 544, 547

independent money management, 285–287, 292
individualised money management, 286, 291
money in couples, 279–281, 283, 284, 288, 291, 294, 295
money in couples, 281, 288
social meaning of money, 283, 284
Mothering, 144, 439, 442, 443, 480, 486, 546
Mothers, 18, 24, 27, 28, 30, 33, 47, 53, 54, 74, 77, 78, 87, 111, 123, 166–170, 180, 181, 184–186, 190, 197, 208–210, 225, 227, 228, 230, 232–234, 245, 246, 269, 346–349, 353, 354, 357, 364, 380–384, 389–391, 420, 437–441, 444, 446, 458, 459, 478–481, 486, 500, 502–504, 523, 540, 541, 545–548, 566, 594, 600, 602
Multilevel, 9, 367, 518, 523, 584, 619, 620, 631, 640

N
National Board of Health and Welfare (NBHW), 419–422, 424–427, 429
Need for care, 214, 543–546, 549, 594
Negotiation, 20, 28, 98, 261, 263, 269, 295, 306, 313, 480, 484, 487, 499, 576, 593, 641
Netherlands, The, 5, 51, 53, 54, 64, 82, 161, 166, 200, 201, 205, 207, 209–217, 250, 363, 365, 367, 368, 386, 447, 459, 462, 463, 467, 483, 498, 507, 516–519, 580, 642
Network, 6, 8, 10, 116, 119–121, 125, 143, 146, 147, 214, 229, 234, 263, 266, 272, 306, 411, 426, 480, 498, 503, 515, 516, 543, 585, 602, 603, 619
Family Network Method (FNM), 111, 113, 115, 124
Neuroparenting, 445
New social risk (NSR), 582–584
New technologies, 479, 513, 604
Non-heteronormative, 266
Non-human, 269, 642

Nordic countries, 57, 163, 168, 169, 171, 172, 190, 225–230, 232–234, 436, 577–580, 583
Norms, 3, 5, 24, 28, 29, 32, 33, 46, 49, 70, 86, 87, 91, 96, 101, 112, 122, 124, 165, 171, 210, 260, 261, 284, 287, 290, 293, 295, 301, 304, 314, 324, 327, 337, 364, 380, 411, 416, 461, 479, 486, 496, 499, 501, 514–516, 530, 560, 565, 578, 594, 598–600, 641
cultural norms, 91, 96, 182, 183, 364, 390, 505, 546, 567, 568, 576
Norway, 7, 48, 82, 143, 166, 190, 200, 225–227, 229, 345–349, 352–355, 357, 369, 388, 471, 478, 479, 518, 600
Not in Education, Employment, or Training (NEET), 468, 630
Nuclear family, 17, 86, 91, 93, 101, 107, 110, 111, 122–126, 164, 260, 288, 302, 303, 306–308, 461, 477, 496, 507, 578, 629
deinstitutionalization (of the nuclear family), 96
de-standardisation (of the nuclear family), 95
nuclear family model, 125, 302, 303, 309

O
Obligations, 5, 119, 120, 124, 205–208, 210, 211, 218, 229, 245, 262, 293, 301, 306, 309, 311, 330, 334, 464, 478, 480, 487, 496–498, 502, 516, 530, 545, 593, 594, 598–602, 604

P
Pandemic, 10, 65, 585, 612, 622, 639–642
crisis, 640
Parental
assessment of parental potential, 7, 415
parental authority, 30, 336, 437–440, 443
parental behaviour, 418, 422, 427, 428, 436, 437, 443

parental determinism, 437, 445
parental leave, 5, 22, 47, 169, 170, 173, 181, 182, 184–187, 190, 196, 197, 208–212, 218, 223–228, 230–234, 248, 249, 346, 349, 352, 353, 355, 369, 384, 416, 423
parental licensing, 416, 421
parental vetting, 416, 421
Parental leave, 5, 22, 47, 169, 170, 173, 181, 182, 184–187, 190, 196, 197, 208–212, 218, 223–228, 230–234, 248, 249, 346, 349, 352, 353, 355, 369, 384, 416, 423
  eligibility for parental leave, 225, 227
Parenthood, 7, 10, 24, 25, 73, 90, 91, 96, 101, 110, 163, 164, 166, 208, 210, 218, 227, 228, 262, 295, 303, 322, 325, 361, 379, 415, 417–419, 421, 422, 439, 441, 496, 541, 559, 561, 563, 565, 567, 622, 623, 626, 629
  good parenthood, 418
Parenting
  parenting cultures, 411
  parenting deficit, 439, 440
  parenting expert, 438
  parenting programme, 438
  parenting style, 242, 249, 418, 443
  parenting support policies, 418
  positive parenting, 438
  requirements for parenting, 95, 97
Parents, 5–7, 18, 24–26, 28–30, 48–50, 69, 74, 76, 78–81, 96–99, 110–112, 115, 116, 123, 124, 137, 138, 143, 144, 164, 169, 170, 173, 181, 185, 190, 197, 208–212, 214, 218, 223, 224, 226–234, 240–244, 246–248, 259, 265, 266, 269, 289, 301, 305–308, 311–313, 321–324, 328–330, 332–336, 346–349, 351, 354, 355, 361, 363, 365–369, 377, 378, 382–385, 389, 390, 399, 400, 402, 403, 405–411, 416–418, 420, 422, 424–426, 428, 435–443, 445–447, 455, 458, 460, 461, 464, 465, 479, 480, 496–498, 501–503, 505, 514, 517–523, 525–527, 530, 531, 540–542, 545, 566, 583, 584, 591, 593, 594, 599–602, 624, 642
  over-involved parents, 332, 333
  under-involved parents, 332
  working parents, 169–171, 211, 223, 230
Participation profiles, 560, 561, 567, 568
Partner choice, 482, 483, 485
Part-time employment, 22, 47, 53, 207, 211, 218, 347, 566
Paternity, 53, 73, 75–77, 81, 231
Paternity leave, 169, 186, 190, 197, 209, 223, 231, 233, 346
Pavolini, Emmanuele, 363, 364, 369, 584
Personal life, 31, 32, 259–262, 264, 267–269, 271, 563, 567
Personal networks, 9, 96, 112, 120, 265, 266, 567–569
Personal recognition, 17, 19, 21
Pets, 33, 144, 259, 269, 270, 292. *See also* Companion animals
Pfau-Effinger, Birgit, 100, 101, 122, 182
Phillipson, Chris, 592, 595, 603
Photo, photography, 312
  family photography, 140, 141
  photo elicitation, 140, 148
  photographs, 4, 133, 135–137, 140, 141, 149, 151
Plantenga, Janneke, 365
Poland, 5, 7, 48, 50, 54, 59, 63, 163, 166, 170, 182, 183, 196, 201, 205, 207, 209–218, 250, 363, 400–407, 409–411, 459, 478, 479, 502, 504, 506, 517, 518, 640
Policy, 5, 32, 46–49, 54, 64, 86, 100, 101, 160, 168–173, 179–190, 197, 200, 205–210, 212, 215, 216, 223–225, 227–230, 233, 234, 240, 241, 245, 246, 249, 279, 283, 294, 336, 346, 353, 355, 357, 362, 368, 370, 371, 381, 383, 384, 416, 417, 419, 428, 436, 440, 441, 444–446, 456, 462–464, 468–470, 475, 478, 479, 486, 537, 541, 542, 548, 565, 569
  active labour market policies, 584

policy instruments, 239, 240, 244, 246–249
residual-liberal welfare policy, 182
Politicisation, 437
Pooling (of resources), 165, 285
partial pooling, 285–287
Population, 54, 89, 111, 120, 159, 171, 173, 233, 247, 267, 321, 347, 350, 352, 363, 364, 368, 370, 378, 380, 384, 385, 391, 401, 402, 458–460, 467, 470, 482, 485, 514, 516, 518, 520–523, 527, 530, 531, 564, 582, 584, 597
population ageing, 47, 160, 170, 224, 322, 591, 599
Portugal, 5, 48–54, 56–59, 62, 63, 65, 82, 170, 197, 201, 205, 207, 209–217, 229–233, 250, 364, 387, 517–519, 562, 567, 580, 640
Postdivorce family arrangements, 377
Poverty, 2, 5, 173, 211, 212, 224, 239–249, 357, 362, 364, 368, 369, 416, 418, 422, 424, 461, 467, 515, 583, 584
child poverty, 246–248, 384, 387
intergenerational poverty, 243, 249
poverty threshold, 241, 242, 250
Power, 4, 6, 9, 22, 23, 26, 29, 45, 48, 52, 62, 95, 97, 98, 108, 109, 113–115, 119, 120, 122, 124–126, 136–138, 180, 250, 270, 279, 281–284, 287–290, 292–295, 305, 312, 314, 364, 367, 385, 392, 444, 478, 481, 501, 565
Practicalities, 310, 365
Practices, 3, 5, 6, 9, 26, 28, 29, 32, 76, 79, 97, 107, 110, 112, 121, 122, 125, 133, 144, 148, 149, 151, 205, 242, 246, 260, 262–270, 272, 283, 289, 290, 293, 294, 302–307, 310, 314, 316, 325, 364, 383, 386, 401, 412, 417, 427, 428, 439, 445, 471, 478–481, 484, 487, 497–499, 505, 506, 538, 539, 541, 542, 544–548, 598, 639, 641–643
Pre-school, 182, 187, 200, 201, 346–349, 351, 352, 354, 355, 357, 358, 361
Pre-school services, 345, 353

Prevalence of JPC, 7, 379, 385, 386, 392
Priorities, 22, 214, 216, 217, 305, 367, 369, 426, 496, 565, 602
Private life, 33, 72, 73, 80, 189, 348, 442
Privilege, 21, 310, 312–314
Proximity, 146, 259, 311, 313, 314, 440, 497, 513, 521, 598, 599, 626, 641
Publications, 2, 23, 27, 89, 150, 422, 612, 619, 621, 622, 624, 626, 628–630, 632
Public policy, 32, 64, 80, 187, 206, 217, 219, 239, 345, 347, 348, 355, 357, 385, 435, 445, 446, 579, 624
Public service, 363, 459
Pure relationship, 17, 28, 29, 34, 97, 261

Q
Qualitative, 5, 121, 123, 125, 126, 135, 141, 263, 271, 283, 284, 290, 291, 302, 321, 379, 412, 446, 477, 482, 507, 531, 561, 563, 601, 619, 620, 625, 629, 631
qualitative interview, 121, 144, 264, 322, 538
Quantitative, 7, 113, 124–126, 241, 249, 263, 283, 378, 385, 412, 456, 467, 470, 482, 507, 561, 563, 569, 578, 614, 619, 620, 622, 625, 626, 630, 631

R
Rational choice, 88, 271, 272, 365
Refamilialisation, 217
Reflexivity, 113, 261, 577
Refugee(s), 140, 363, 368, 457, 460, 461, 463, 464, 466, 537–543, 548
Relatedness, 5, 6, 73, 148, 259, 268, 269, 303
Relationality, 264, 269, 544
Relational well-being, 400, 406, 407
Relationships
family relationships, 8, 9, 32, 114, 116, 120, 138, 139, 144, 181,

206, 241, 243, 250, 265, 267, 272, 304, 311, 388, 401, 404, 435, 484, 530, 541, 558, 561, 563, 566–569, 592, 594, 599, 628
  relationship diagram, 327
  relationship dynamics, 322
  relationship work, 322, 323, 331
Relatives, 7, 19, 22, 33, 91, 92, 112, 116, 125, 137, 143, 144, 146, 147, 149, 165, 212–215, 259, 263, 265, 266, 280, 294, 304, 337, 347, 351, 354, 357, 441, 458, 460, 465, 476, 496, 503–507, 515, 516, 561, 566, 582, 600, 620, 625
Remittances, 465, 478, 479, 499–501, 504, 541, 544, 546
  financial remittances, 500, 505, 506
  remittances circulation, 499
  remitting practices, 501
  reverse social remittances, 505
  social remittance, 479, 499, 502, 546
Research
  mixed-methods research, 133, 148, 561
  researching 'with', 136, 138
  visual research guidelines, 150
  visual research methods, 135, 136
Resources, 22, 24, 32, 45, 46, 49, 63, 107, 108, 115, 116, 118–121, 126, 172, 211, 239–241, 246, 263, 267, 279, 282, 290, 306, 312, 313, 323, 325, 336, 348, 349, 352, 354, 355, 364, 367, 369, 370, 390, 418, 424, 467, 468, 478, 481, 497, 498, 514, 539, 560, 579, 584, 595, 604
Rights, 19, 24, 30, 70–72, 76, 94, 168, 189, 201, 207, 214, 215, 217, 218, 228–230, 306, 312, 313, 392, 401, 406, 444, 456–458, 461, 462, 596, 597
  human rights, 69–73, 75–79, 81, 82, 456, 463, 464
  right to marry, 70, 72, 75, 81
  right to respect family life, 70–72
Risk factors, 416, 419, 421–423, 427
Romania, 7, 51, 163, 166, 363, 369, 400–406, 409–411, 459, 504, 506, 518

Routines, 20, 22, 25, 88, 116, 133, 144, 265, 270, 281, 302, 309–311, 313, 314, 351, 390, 498, 500, 547, 564, 600, 602, 640
Rules, 33, 74, 77, 79–81, 207, 216, 248, 269, 311, 313, 363, 381, 385, 437, 461–463, 515, 563, 641
Rush hour of life, 48, 53, 54, 57–59, 63–65

S
School-to-work transition, 566, 579–582, 584
Second Demographic Transition (SDT), 4, 7, 86, 90, 93–95, 166, 260, 325, 378, 379
  Second Demographic Transition theory, 378
Second generations, 458, 467, 468, 483, 486
Segregation, 52, 57, 354, 355, 463, 484
  vertical segregation, 52, 62, 64
Separation, 7, 16, 19, 20, 23, 24, 27, 29, 30, 92, 110, 112, 137, 139, 173, 228, 265, 303, 377–379, 381, 382, 387, 388, 390–392, 399, 401, 410, 411, 465, 476, 479–481, 486, 538, 540, 541, 543, 548, 559, 592, 594, 595, 598, 602, 642
Sequence analysis, 561, 562
Sex, 21, 22, 30, 32, 59, 74, 76, 81, 96, 108, 243, 347, 354, 355, 401, 569
  legal sex, 72, 73, 75, 79, 81
Sexual, 3, 19, 27, 29, 71, 73, 79, 95, 97, 167, 264, 266, 325, 642
  sexual orientation, 46, 72, 79
Sexuality, 29, 73, 136, 265, 267, 641
Sibling(s), 6, 26, 74, 91, 92, 108, 111–113, 115, 125, 138, 265, 301–303, 305–315, 322, 323, 328, 333, 335, 403, 523, 561, 567, 598, 600, 601, 603, 622, 629
Siblingship
  long and wide siblingship, 307–309, 311, 313
  real siblingship, 307
  short and narrow siblingship, 307, 308, 311, 315

Sibling studies, 306
Skills, 22, 50, 144, 149, 173, 240, 244, 268, 281, 390, 400, 406, 409–411, 442, 466, 468, 478, 504, 544, 580–582
Social
  social capital, 242, 267, 390, 468, 479, 499, 514, 603
  social dimension, 46, 64
  social distance, 459, 466
  social problem, 306, 422, 440
  social services, 206, 207, 240, 417, 421, 466
  social work, 245, 246, 304, 416, 417, 420, 426, 460
Social class(es), 9, 33, 45, 59, 62, 64, 96, 98, 122, 126, 141, 241, 260, 262, 265, 267, 336, 345, 349, 363, 439, 597, 598, 600, 604, 641
Social construction, 21, 93, 96, 97, 269
  social construction of reality, 88, 93
Social investment paradigm, 245
Social networking sites (SNS), 268
Social policy/policies, 5, 27, 48, 77, 179, 180, 183, 184, 188, 239, 240, 243, 245–247, 249, 347, 354, 436, 445, 506, 565, 581, 584
  active social policy (ASP), 245
  anti-poverty social policy, 244. *See also* Policy/policies
Societal transformations, 165, 171–173, 260
Socio-cultural perspective, 260, 271, 272
Socio-economic challenges, 421–423, 425
Southern European countries, 5, 54, 170, 207, 229, 230, 232, 527, 578, 599, 602
Spain, 7, 48, 50, 54, 57, 59, 162, 163, 170, 197, 200, 201, 229–233, 324, 345–349, 352–355, 357, 364, 367–369, 379, 381, 382, 387, 459, 460, 464, 468, 480, 500, 503, 517, 518, 579, 580, 600, 602, 640
Spencer, Liz, 33, 136, 147, 265, 267, 567, 603, 642
Spheres of life/lives, 89, 208, 272, 614, 615, 625, 628–631
Statistical correlations, 418, 423

Stratification, 8, 364, 390, 457, 582
  civic stratification, 457
Stratified reproduction, 416, 545
Structural, 3, 4, 28, 49, 50, 74, 85, 86, 90, 95, 100, 101, 110, 126, 167, 206, 260, 261, 265, 267, 268, 282, 346, 362, 364, 367, 369, 371, 390, 399, 402, 463, 470, 475, 477, 497, 523, 537, 538, 544, 548, 561, 576, 577, 641
  structural dimension, 46, 63
  structural living conditions, 45, 49
Substitution thesis, 346
Suffusion, 147, 265, 567
Supply-side funding, 365
Support, 4, 5, 9, 32, 47, 57–59, 64, 69, 71, 72, 91, 92, 102, 107, 108, 112, 113, 115, 116, 118, 119, 140, 147, 167, 169–173, 182–184, 186–189, 197, 201, 205–209, 211–214, 216–218, 224, 225, 227, 229, 231, 232, 234, 240, 241, 244, 246, 248, 262, 265, 266, 268, 282, 283, 292, 295, 303, 304, 307, 313, 314, 321–324, 337, 346, 347, 357, 366, 369, 384, 389, 416, 419, 422–424, 426–428, 439, 443, 444, 446, 463, 464, 468, 477, 481, 484, 496–504, 513–517, 523, 530, 531, 543, 544, 546, 559, 564, 566, 578–580, 584, 594, 599–603, 622, 641
  downward support, 502
Surrogacy, 76, 78, 80, 259, 268, 269
Survey of Health, Ageing and Retirement in Europe (SHARE), 517, 518, 531, 595
Sweden, 5, 48, 51, 53, 54, 57, 59, 166, 169, 181, 182, 190, 200, 205, 207, 209–218, 224–229, 363, 369, 370, 379, 381, 384–387, 391, 416, 417, 423, 425, 428, 436, 446, 462, 516–519, 543, 580
Switzerland, 116, 118, 123, 161, 162, 172, 517–519, 541, 547, 562, 564, 566, 567, 640
Synchronicity, 311

T

Transfers, 207, 209, 225, 233, 240, 245, 247, 280, 321, 354, 423, 427, 495–497, 499, 500, 505, 506, 513–516, 544, 547, 601
  downward transfers, 499, 502
  upward transfers, 498, 499
Transition to adulthood, 10, 49, 162, 163, 567, 575–577, 579, 580, 584, 622
Transnational, 3, 8, 424, 471, 475, 476, 479, 480, 485, 498, 500, 504, 641
  transnational care, 9, 496, 500, 504, 506, 537–539, 541–546, 548
  transnational families, 8, 143, 144, 475–477, 480, 481, 485, 495, 496, 546, 547, 642
  transnational links, 462
  transnational motherhood, 144, 479, 480, 496, 540
  transnational parenting, 479, 481, 486, 537–539
Tripartition, 10, 576

U

Uncertainty, 28, 99, 171, 173, 310, 314, 580, 641
Unemployment, 23, 49, 65, 215, 216, 232, 245, 270, 295, 347, 418, 422–424, 427, 466, 515, 565, 579, 582–584, 592, 593, 596, 601
Union, 23, 25, 28, 72–76, 81, 163, 164, 325, 475, 482, 483, 485, 559, 563, 581, 591, 596
  union dissolution, 165, 173
  union formation, 162, 163, 173
United Kingdom (UK), 48, 59, 182, 183, 201, 248, 324, 363, 369, 383, 386, 423, 436–439, 444, 446, 459, 462, 463, 477, 478, 480, 484, 504, 505, 518, 579–581, 593
Unpaid work, 3, 47–51, 54, 57, 59, 63, 65, 168, 170, 224

V

Value of Children, 86, 90, 100
Vignette(s), 139, 140, 148, 327
Visual, 4, 116, 133–137, 140, 141, 144, 148–151, 263, 480
visual images, 134–136
visual methodologies, 133, 137, 149, 150
visual research guidelines, 150
visual research methods, 135, 136
Voice(ing), 7, 136, 138, 140, 142, 150, 151, 169, 172, 291, 305, 543

W

We-I balance, 15, 16
Welfare regimes, 8, 100, 171, 172, 180, 229, 283, 345, 352, 355, 357, 469, 496, 578, 579, 583, 584
Welfare state, 2, 4, 22, 46, 168–171, 179, 205–212, 218, 223, 225, 229, 232, 240, 245, 249, 265, 321, 322, 324, 325, 337, 346, 347, 445, 499, 513, 515, 519, 560, 563, 565, 567, 582
  welfare state typology, 169
Well-being, 7, 94, 151, 171, 172, 208, 239, 240, 242, 243, 249, 283, 305, 323, 389–391, 399–401, 403–407, 409, 411, 412, 465, 466, 500, 503, 505, 506, 542, 547, 641, 642
  theory of homeostasis of the subjective well-being, 404
Weness, 110–114, 120, 121, 123, 125
Work-life balance (WLB), 47, 48, 53, 63, 64, 169, 223–225, 228–230, 232, 346, 355, 596

Y

Young people, 49, 50, 64, 138–140, 172, 173, 241, 312, 325, 422, 437, 575, 577–584, 642
Youth, 48, 49, 57, 59, 65, 324, 382, 418, 427, 575–578, 580, 584, 600, 624, 625
  youth poverty, 576, 582–585
  youth regulation, 581
  youth transition regimes, 579
  youth unemployment, 576, 580–582, 585
  youth welfare citizenship, 579, 580

Z

Zombie category, 31, 32, 261